Discover
Japan

Experience the best
of Japan

This edition written and researched by

Chris Rowthorn,
Ray Bartlett, Andrew Bender, Laura Crawford,
Craig McLachlan, Rebecca Milner, Simon Richmond,
Benedict Walker, Wendy Yanagihara

Central
Honshū

p145

p51 Tokyo

Kansai &
Western
Honshū

p259 p197

Kyoto

Contents

Contents

Discover Japan

In Focus

Survival Guide

This Is Japan

Japan is a world apart – a wonderful little planet floating off the coast of China. It is a kind of cultural Galápagos, a place where a unique civilisation has been allowed to grow and unfold on its own, unmolested by invading powers.

Japan's ancient culture is a bounty of riches.
From the retina-burning splendour of a Kyoto geisha dance to the spare beauty of a Zen rock garden, Japan has the power to enthral even the most jaded traveller.

Japan is a place to leave your comfort zone without being uncomfortable.
Whether it's staying in a ryokan (traditional Japanese inn), soaking in a bubbling onsen (hot spring) or gazing at the apparition of a geisha, Japan offers regular doses of 'Wow!' against a backdrop of ultramodern comfort.

Savouring the delights of Japanese cuisine is half the reason to come to Japan.
Indeed, many travellers come to Japan solely to sample the delights of Japanese food on its home turf. Eat just one meal in a top-flight Tokyo sushi restaurant and you'll see why: the Japanese attention to detail, genius for presentation and insistence on the finest ingredients result in food that can change your perception of what is possible in the culinary arena.

The wonders of Japan's natural world are a well-kept secret.
The hiking in the Japan Alps and Hokkaidō is world class, and with an extensive hut system you can do multiday hikes with just a day pack. Down south, the coral reefs of Okinawa will have you wondering if you've somehow been transported to Thailand. And you never have to travel far in Japan to get out in nature: in cities like Kyoto, a few minutes of travel will get you into forested mountains.

> ❝
>
> Japan has the power to enthral even the most jaded traveller
>
> ❞

Maiko (apprentice geisha) in Gion (p221)
FRANK CARTER/ GETTY IMAGES ©

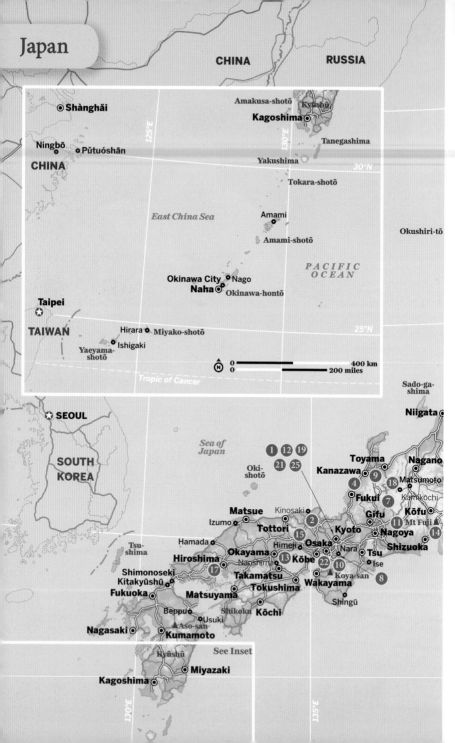

25
Top Highlights

Sea of Okhotsk

RUSSIA

Rebun-tō
Rishiri-tō

Shiretoko National Park

Daisetsuzan National Park
Abashiri
Takikawa Biei
Akan National Park
Otaru Hokkaidō Kushiro
Sapporo Obihiro
Niseko Shikotsu-tōya National Park

Hakodate

Aomori
Hachinohe
Towada-Hachimantai National Park
Akita Morioka
Kakunodate
Sakata Shinjō
Tsuruoka
Yamagata Sendai
Fukushima

Honshū
Nikkō
Utsunomiya
Maebashi Mito
Urawa
TOKYO ③ ⑤ ⑥ ⑯ ⑳ ㉔
Chiba
Yokohama

PACIFIC OCEAN

ELEVATION
	3000m
	2500m
	2000m
	1500m
	1000m
	750m
	500m
	250m
	0

45°N
40°N
35°N

1 Temples & Gardens, Kyoto
2 Onsen, Kinosaki
3 Japanese Cuisine, Tokyo
4 Staying in a Ryokan, Ishikawa Prefecture
5 Cherry-Blossom Viewing, Tokyo
6 Tokyo's Tsukiji Market
7 Hiking in the Japan Alps
8 Nara's Tōdai-ji & Daibutsu (Great Buddha)
9 Kenroku-en, Kanazawa
10 Kōya-san
11 Hiking, Magome to Tsumago
12 Geisha Dances, Kyoto
13 Naoshima
14 Mt Fuji
15 Castle, Himeji
16 Sumo, Tokyo
17 Hiroshima
18 Kamikōchi
19 Nishiki Market, Kyoto
20 Tokyo's Modern Architecture
21 Kabuki, Kyoto
22 Dōtombori, Osaka
23 Skiing, Niseko
24 Shopping in Tokyo
25 Arashiyama Bamboo Grove, Kyoto

0 ——— 500 km
0 ——— 250 miles

Ogasawara Archipelago (500km)

140°E 145°E

25 Japan's Top Highlights

Temples & Gardens, Kyoto

With over 1000 temples to choose from, you're spoiled for choice in Kyoto. Spend your time finding one that suits your taste. If you like things gaudy and grand, you'll love the retina-burning splendour of Kinkaku-ji (p227). If you prefer *wabi-sabi* to rococo, then you'll find the tranquility of Hōnen-in (p222) or Shōren-in (p216) more to your liking. And don't forget that temples are where you find the best gardens: you'll find some of the finest at Ginkaku-ji (p223), Ryōan-ji (p227) and Tōfuku-ji (p233). Below: Ginkaku-ji

ANTONY GIBLIN / GETTY IMAGES ©

② Onsen

There's nothing like lowering yourself into the tub at a Japanese onsen (natural hot spring bath). The 'ahhh' that you emit is just a simple way of saying 'Damn, I'm glad I came to Japan!'. If you're lucky, the tub is outside and there's a nice stream running nearby. The Japanese have turned the simple act of bathing into a folk religion and the country is dotted with temples and shrines to this most relaxing of faiths. For the classic onsen experience, head to Kinosaki (p301).

Japanese Cuisine

Japan is a food-lover's paradise and the cuisine (p366) is incredibly varied, running the gamut from impossibly fresh sushi around Tsukiji Market to grilled skewers of chicken under the train tracks in Yūrakuchō. In a city like Tokyo, you could eat a different Japanese specialty cuisine every night for a month without repeating yourself. There's no doubt that a food tour of Japan will be memorable, but there's just one problem: once you try the real thing in Japan, the restaurants back home will pale in comparison. The only solution is another trip to Japan!

Below: Sushi

The Best...
Onsen (Hot Springs)

KINOSAKI
Japan's classic onsen town is everything an onsen town ought to be: quaint, friendly and packed with good ryokan. (p301)

THE KAYŌTEI
The Kayōtei is a first-class onsen ryokan in Ishikawa Prefecture, an easy three-hour train ride from Kyoto. (p195)

SHIN-HOTAKA ONSEN
Shin-Hotaka Onsen is a superb onsen resort located at the base of the northern Japan Alps. (p166)

KURAMA ONSEN
Located less than an hour north of Kyoto by train, this quaint onsen feels worlds away. (p236)

The Best...
Ryokan (Traditional Inns)

TAWARAYA
Kyoto's Tawaraya is a secret world all of its own – once you enter, you may never want to leave. (p241)

HIIRAGIYA
Hiiragiya gives Tawaraya stiff competition for the title of 'Kyoto's best ryokan'. (p241)

BENIYA MUKAYŪ
Relax with morning yoga and a private outdoor cypress bath at this Central Honshū retreat. (p195)

NISHIMURAYA HONKAN
As soon as you enter the elegant courtyard of Nishimuraya Honkan, you'll know you're in for something special. (p303)

Top left: Tawaraya Ryokan (p241)

④ Staying in a Ryokan

Eat in your bedroom. Spend the day lounging in a robe. Soak in a bath while looking at a garden. Don't lift a finger except to eat. Sound relaxing? Then we recommend a night in a top-flight ryokan (traditional Japanese inn) such as those at the hot springs of Ishikawa Prefecture (p184). The Japanese had the spa thing figured out long before they even heard the word 'spa'. If your finances don't run to a first-class one, even the most humble ryokan will give you a taste of how the Japanese used to live.

⑤ Cherry-Blossom Viewing

If you think of the Japanese as a sober, staid and serious people, then you owe it to yourself to join them under a cherry tree in the springtime for a *hanami* (blossom viewing) party (p61) in a place such as Tokyo's Ueno-kōen. Bottom left: Meguro-gawa (p61)

Tokyo's Tsukiji Market

If it swims in the sea, it's probably on sale in Tokyo's Tsukiji Market (p66). The mother of all fish markets, Tsukiji is a sprawling monument to the Japanese love of seafood. It's a must for sushi fans and anyone who loves a good market tour. Even if you don't want to wake up early to see the tuna auction, if Tokyo is in your Japan itinerary, you've gotta make the pilgrimage to Tsukiji.

Hiking in the Japan Alps

Close your eyes and picture Japan. If all you see are geisha, Zen gardens, bullet trains and hyper-modern cities, then you might be in for a surprise when you get to the Japan Alps (p162). Hike right into the heart of the high peaks here and you might think you're in New Zealand or the Rockies. You can go hut to hut here among the peaks for a week with nothing but a solid day pack.

Nara's Tōdai-ji & Daibutsu (Great Buddha)

Here's the drill: go to the temple of Tōdai-ji (p292) in Nara and stop for a moment outside the main hall. Then, without looking up, step into the hall. Calm your thoughts. Now raise your eyes to behold the Great Buddha. This is probably the closest one can come to enlightenment without years of meditation. Perhaps no other sight in Japan has as much impact as this cosmic Buddha – you can almost feel the energy radiating out from its vast bulk. Below: Daibutsu

8

The Best...
Places to Eat

TOKYO
With more Michelin stars than any city on earth, Tokyo is the best eating city on earth. (p99)

KYOTO
Kyoto is *the* place to sample traditional Japanese cuisine, known as *kaiseki* (Japanese haute cuisine; (p243).

NAGASAKI
Nagasaki has always been Japan's gateway to the rest of Asia and its cuisine is redolent of mainland flavours. (p339)

OSAKA
The motto of this city is '*kuidaore*' (eat until you drop), so, naturally, it's a food-lover's paradise. (p277)

GREGORY FERGUSON / GETTY IMAGES ©

Kenroku-en, Kanazawa

This is one of the country's top three gardens. Developed over 200 years by the Maeda clan as part of Kanazawa-jō castle, Kenroku-en (p189) is said to incorporate the six attributes of a perfect landscape. Stroll the meandering paths along arching bridges, gurgling fountains and plum and pine groves, and savour the garden's highlights – the unique Kenroku-en Kikuzakura cherry tree, and the iconic Kotoji-tōrō stone lantern by Kasumiga-ike pond. A visit to Kenroku-en is best capped off with a cup of green powdered tea at the Shigure-tei Teahouse.

The Best...
Cities for Temples, Shrines and Gardens

KYOTO
You could spend a month in Kyoto and see a different garden, temple and shrine each day. (p197)

NARA
Nara is a compact wonder of a city that some consider the birthplace of Japanese culture. (p287)

KANAZAWA
Kanazawa is thick with traditional culture and home to one of Japan's finest gardens: Kenroku-en. (p185)

TOKYO
That's right: amid all that concrete and neon there are some wonderful hints of traditional Japan. (p51)

FRAEDDARIC SOREAU / GETTY IMAGES ©

Kōya-san

10

Riding the funicular up to the sacred Buddhist monastic complex of Kōya-san (p296), you almost feel like you're ascending to another world. The place is permeated with a kind of august spiritual grandeur and nowhere is this feeling stronger than in the vast Oku-no-in cemetery. Trails weave their way among towering cryptomeria trees and by the time you arrive at the main hall, a sudden appearance by a Buddha would seem like the most natural thing in the world. Left: Jizō statues at Oku-no-in, Kōya-san

Hiking, Magome to Tsumago

11

A beautifully preserved post town in southern Nagano-ken, Tsumago (p181) is home to traditional wooden inns. From Tsumago follow the old Nakasendō post road (p180) up through sleepy alpine hamlets, old-growth cedar forests and waterfalls to Magome-tōge pass before continuing to Magome. The 8km hike winds past farmhouses, waterwheels and rice paddies that time seems to have passed by. Right: Nakasendō post road

CHRISTIAN KOBER / GETTY IMAGES ©

12

Geisha Dances, Kyoto

We can't stress this enough: if you find yourself in Kyoto (p197) when the geisha dances are on (usually in the spring), then do everything in your power to see one (p251). It's hard to think of a more colourful, charming and absorbing stage spectacle. If you're like us, you might find that the whole thing takes on the appearance of a particularly vivid dream. When the curtain falls after the final burst of colour and song, the geisha might just continue to dance in your mind for hours afterward. Above: Kyō Odori performance (p252)

MITSUE NAGASE ©

13 # Naoshima

What would happen if you took a whole island and turned it into an art museum? Japan's Benesse Corporation decided to find out and the result is the Inland Sea art-lover's paradise of Naoshima (p311). The island is dotted with art museums and installations; even the local *sentō* (public bath) has been turned into an art project of sorts. You can stay here in a yurt, a quaint local inn, or in one of the art museums. It is, simply put, one of Japan's most interesting attractions.

Left: Yayoi Kusama "Pumpkin"

Mt Fuji

Even from a distance Mt Fuji (p126) will take your breath away. Close-up, the perfectly symmetrical cone of Japan's tallest peak is nothing short of awesome. Dawn from the summit? Pure magic. Fuji-san is Japan's most revered and timeless attraction. Hundreds of thousands of people climb it every year, continuing a centuries-old tradition of pilgrimages up this sacred volcano. Those who'd rather search for picture-perfect views from the less-daunting peaks nearby can follow in the steps of Japan's most famous painters and poets.

(14)

The Best...
Places to Hike

KAMIKŌCHI
Kamikōchi is a pristine alpine sanctuary in the heart of the Northern Japan Alps. (p163)

TSUMAGO & MAGOME
The mountainous Nakasendō used to be one of the main highways between Tokyo and Kyoto. (p180)

TATEYAMA
If you want to get high in the Japan Alps without hiking, take the Tateyama-Kurobe Alpine Route. (p182)

KYOTO
Surrounded by mountains on three sides, Kyoto happens to be one of the best places in Japan for hiking. (p202)

GRANT FAINT / GETTY IMAGES ©

The Best...
Only in Japan Experiences

KARAOKE
There's nothing like grabbing the mic to 'entertain' your friends in the land where they invented the pastime. (p174)

RIDING THE *SHINKANSEN* (BULLET TRAIN)
Train freaks will love Japan's famed *shinkansen*. (p402)

JOINING A *HANAMI* (CHERRY-BLOSSOM VIEWING) PARTY
When the *sakura* (cherry trees) burst into bloom, Japan goes wild. (p61)

SPOTTING A GEISHA IN KYOTO
The sight of a geisha shuffling to an appointment is a moment of pure magic. (p221)

CLIMBING MT FUJI
Whether it's from a speeding *shinkansen* or from one of the lakes at the base of the mountain, the sight of Mt Fuji is unforgettable. (p126)

Castles

Japan's castles have about as much in common with their European counterparts as kimono have in common with Western dinner dresses. Their graceful contours belie the grim military realities that lay behind their construction. Towering above the plains, they seem designed more to please the eye than to protect their lords. If you've got an interest in the world of samurai, shōguns and military history, you'll love Japan's castles. They come in all sizes, in original or reconstructed form, and are found throughout the country – the recently renovated Himeji-jō (p309) is a must-see. Left: Himeji-jō; Above: Corridor inside Himeji-jō

LEFT: KEVIN FRATES / GETTY IMAGES © ; ABOVE: DAVID CLAPP / GETTY IMAGES ©

Sumo

Sitting ringside at Ryōgoku Kokugikan (p113) when two *yokozuna* (sumo grand champions) clash is like watching two mountains get into a shoving match. You can just about feel the earth shake. Even if you're up in the nosebleed seats, catching a sumo match is a highlight of any Japan trip. It's just so different from any other sport we know of: the salt-throwing ritual, the other-worldly calls of the referee, the drawn-out staring matches before the bout, the whole thing just screams 'only in Japan!'

OLIVER GOUJON / GETTY IMAGES ©

R CREATION / GETTY IMAGES ©

Hiroshima

Seeing the city's leafy boulevards, it's hard to picture Hiroshima (p316) as a devastated victim of an atomic bomb. Monuments in the Peace Memorial Park hint at the story, but it's not until you walk through the Memorial Museum that the terrible reality becomes clear. But outside the quiet of the park, energetic Hiroshima rolls on. A visit here is a heartbreaking, important, history lesson, but the city and its people ensure that's not the only memory you leave with.

Left: Atomic Bomb Dome (p316)

Kamikōchi

One of the most stunning natural vistas in Japan, Kamikōchi (p163) is a highland valley surrounded by the eye-popping summits of the Northern Japan Alps. Trails start from the photogenic Kappa-bashi bridge and follow the pristine Azusa-gawa river through tranquil forests. The birthplace of Japanese alpinism, Kamikōchi can be the gateway for ascending Yariga-take (3180m) or for a simple 1-hour stroll along the river to the local hot spring baths. In winter, you can trek in through the access tunnel and have the entire valley to yourself for a snowshoe jaunt.

The Best...
Places to Learn About Japanese History

KYOTO
Capital of Japan for more than 1000 years, Kyoto is the stage where much of Japanese history played out. (p197)

NARA
Nara was the first permanent, long-term capital of Japan and it remains a storehouse of Japanese tradition. (p287)

TOKYO
In historical terms, Tokyo is a mere upstart compared to Kyoto or Nara, but it's still packed with interesting historical sites. (p51)

HIROSHIMA
Hiroshima, the scene of Japan's greatest tragedy, manages to leave the visitor with a feeling of hope for the future. (p316)

Nishiki Market, Kyoto

There's something strangely enjoyable about touring a food market where over half of the goods on display are utterly baffling (is it a food, a spice or some sort of Christmas tree decoration?). Even after years in Japan, we're not sure about some of the things on sale here, but we love wandering Kyoto's Nishiki Market (p210). The place positively oozes 'old Japan' atmosphere and you can imagine what it was like here before someone decided to attach the word 'super' to the word 'market'.

LONELY PLANET / GETTY IMAGES ©

The Best...
Places for Kids

TOKYO
If your kids are not fans of traditional Japanese culture, then Tokyo is the best city in Japan to keep them happy. (p77)

NARA
Nara is one of those rare Japanese cities where parents can indulge their interest in traditional culture without the kids going bonkers from boredom. (p287)

KYOTO
Sure, your kids might not appreciate the Zen gardens, but there are heaps of things they will enjoy in Kyoto. (p197)

OKINAWA
If your kids are the outdoors types, then a trip down to Okinawa is sure to please. (p343)

20 Tokyo's Modern Architecture

Japan may be known for its traditional temples, but Tokyo's cityscape is a veritable open-air museum of contemporary structures. The capital has come a long way from copying the Eiffel Tower – these days you'll find dozens of inspired and original works by a pantheon of the world's greatest designers. Fill up on such architectural eye-candy at the chic boutiques in Omote-sandō (p116), the quirky postmodern projects on Odaiba (p88), or even the new army of office towers in Marunouchi (p60). Left: Tokyo International Exhibition Center, Odaiba, by architectural firm AXS Satow Inc

TIM HUGHES / GETTY IMAGES ©

Kabuki

For sheer other-worldly bizarreness, few theatrical spectacles come close to kabuki. It doesn't really matter if you don't understand the words, as the colour and action of kabuki make it one of the most entertaining, if flummoxing, ways to lose yourself in Japan. Kyoto's venerable Minami-za Theatre (p253) or Tokyo's Kabuki-za (p112) are the most atmospheric places to catch a kabuki performance.

ARIYOSHI RITA / GETTY IMAGES ©

KARIN SLADE / GETTY IMAGES ©

Dōtombori, Osaka

Osaka's Dōtombori district (p279) is what Lady Gaga would look like if she was a city. It's an over-the-top neon madhouse where human peacocks prowl beneath giant plastic crabs and *fugu* the size of small airships (don't worry, we're not hallucinating – you'll see what we mean when you get there). Allow yourself to be carried along by the human tide that rushes through the endless arcades here and be sure to stop for some octopus balls or automatic sushi.

Skiing

Travellers the world over are finally savvy to one of Japan's greatest secrets: skiing. From the Japan Alps in Central Honshū (p145) to the Hokkaidō highlands (p328), this is one country where it pays to pack a few extra layers. Well-priced equipment rental shops will have you on the slopes in no time, while onsen are waiting to receive you for a unique après-ski experience. Indeed, there is nothing quite like a hot bath and a cold sake after a day of black diamonds. Below: Skiier, Niseko (p328)

The Best...
Pop Culture Paradises

SHIBUYA
Shibuya is the shopping paradise at the centre of Tokyo's youth universe. (p73)

AKIHABARA
Tokyo's Akihabara (or 'Akiba' to the locals) is electronics and geek heaven. (p79)

HARAJUKU
If you've ever seen a photo of a Tokyo Goth Girl, you can be pretty sure it was snapped in Tokyo's Harajuku district. (p75)

KYOTO INTERNATIONAL MANGA MUSEUM
If you're an anime *otaku* (comic freak), then you'll be in heaven at Kyoto's wonderful International Manga Museum. (p210)

Shopping in Tokyo

If you want to see some incredible shops, you've got to come to a country that's been running a multibillion-dollar trade surplus for the last several decades. If it's available to humanity, you can buy it in Japan. Whether it's US$100 melons or curios from ¥100 shops (where everything goes for about US$1), you'll be amazed at the sheer variety of the goods on offer in Tokyo. Head to the boutiques of Ginza (p115) to see the glitterati do their shopping or join the mere mortals in Shibuya (p116) and Shinjuku (p117). Below: Shibuya 109 (p116)

The Best...
Places to Shop

TOKYO
If it can't be found in a store somewhere in Tokyo, it probably doesn't exist. (p114)

KYOTO
Kyoto has everything from traditional shops and trendy boutiques to treasure-filled flea markets. (p253)

OSAKA
Osaka is a city of merchants and you better believe the shopping's good here. (p283)

NAOSHIMA
The island-turned-art museum of Naoshima, in Japan's Inland Sea, is a good place to find quirky souvenirs. (p311)

24

FRANK DELIY / GETTY IMAGES ©

(25)

Arashiyama Bamboo Grove, Kyoto

Western Kyoto is home to one of the most magical places in all Japan: the famed bamboo grove (p229) in Arashiyama. The visual effect of the seemingly infinite stalks of bamboo is quite different from any forest we've ever encountered – there's a palpable presence to the place that is utterly impossible to capture in pictures, but don't let that stop you from trying. If you've seen *Crouching Tiger, Hidden Dragon*, then you have some idea of what this place is about.

Japan's
Top Itineraries

Tokyo & Around
Capital Sights & Day Trips

5 DAYS

If your time in Japan is limited, consider spending the whole time in Tokyo and making a few day trips outside the city. Fly into Narita or Haneda airport (the latter is closer to the city).

PACIFIC OCEAN

① Tokyo (p51)

Base yourself in a convenient transport hub like Shinjuku, Shibuya, Ginza or the Tokyo Station area. Visit Tsukiji Market on your first morning (a good idea if you've got jet lag). Next, head up to Asakusa to visit the temple of Sensō-ji, then over to nearby Ueno for the Tokyo National Museum. The next day, take the loop line to Harajuku and walk to Meiji-jingū, the city's finest Shintō shrine, then take a stroll down chic Omote-sandō. From there, head up to Shibuya to soak up some of modern Tokyo. Make sure you spend an evening wandering east Shinjuku to experience Tokyo's neon madness.

TOKYO ➡ NIKKŌ

🚃 **One hour 45 minutes** Tōbu Nikkō line *tokkyū* (limited express) from Tokyo's Asakusa Station to Nikko.

② Nikkō (p131)

Nikkō, a World Heritage Site, is one of the most rewarding day trips out of Tokyo. It's a collection of spectacular and gaudy (at least by Japanese standards) temples and shrines surrounded by towering evergreens.

TOKYO ➡ KAMAKURA

🚃 **One hour** JR Yokosuka line from Tokyo Station or Shōnan Shinjuku line from Shinjuku, Shibuya or Ikebukuro.

③ Kamakura (p141)

While you can certainly see temples in Tokyo (for example, Asakusa's Sensō-ji), if you really want to soak up the ambience of Buddhist Japan, head south to the coastal town of Kamakura to see the Daibutsu (Great Buddha), as well as lots of small Buddhist temples.

TOKYO ➡ MT FUJI

🚃 **One hour 45 minutes** Direct bus from the Shinjuku Highway Bus Terminal in Tokyo to Kawaguchi-ko and Fuji-Yoshida (Mt Fuji Station), at the base of Mt Fuji.

④ Mt Fuji (p126)

The symbol of Japan, Mt Fuji is occasionally visible from skyscrapers in Tokyo on really clear days, but to maximise your chances of seeing the mountain, head to the towns at its base (but don't bother going on a cloudy day – the mountain will not be visible).

Tokyo's skyline as seen from Tokyo City View (p69)

5 DAYS

Tokyo to Kyoto
Something Old & Something New

If you've got a week to spend in Japan, you should see Tokyo and Kyoto. These two cities will give you a taste of the two faces of Japan: hypermodern and charmingly traditional. Spend two days in each city and add one day in Nara (very near Kyoto) to round things out.

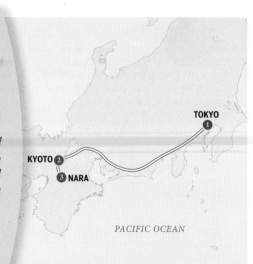

TOKYO ①

KYOTO ②
③ NARA

PACIFIC OCEAN

❶ Tokyo (p51)

You'll probably fly into either Narita or Haneda airport (if you have a choice, opt for the latter, since it's closer to the city). It's a good idea to choose a hotel or ryokan (traditional Japanese inn) in an area with plenty of nightlife, shopping, dining and transport options. Shinuku, Shibuya, Roppongi, Ginza and the Tokyo Station area all fit this bill. Wake early on your first day to check out Tsukiji Market. Then head to Shibuya or Shinjuku to soak up the modern side of Tokyo. On the following day, go to Asakusa to enter the spiritual hub of Tokyo: Sensō-ji, and, if time permits, cross town and visit Meiji-jingū (the city's most important shrine). From Meiji-jingū, it's a short walk to Harajuku and the ultra-fashionable arcade known as Omote-sandō, which is where many Japanese fashion trends first see the light of day. Other areas to check out include the electronics district of Akihabara, the high-end shopping district of Ginza and the nightlife zone of Roppongi.

TOKYO ➲ KYOTO

🚆 **Two hours and 45 minutes** *Shinkansen* (bullet train) between Tokyo Station and Kyoto Station (leaving Tokyo, sit on the north/right side of the train and keep your eyes peeled for Mt Fuji soon after passing Yokohama).

❷ Kyoto (p197)

Spend your first day in the Southern Higashiyama district checking out some of Japan's most amazing sights: Kiyomizu-dera, Maruyama-kōen, Chion-in and Shōren-in. The next day, visit the Northern Higashiyama district, walking from Nanzen-ji to Ginkaku-ji via the Tetsugaku-no-Michi (Path of Philosophy). Spend one day downtown exploring Nishiki Market and the nearby shopping streets. Spend at least one evening strolling the Gion entertainment area, and if you're lucky, you might catch sight of a geisha. Finally, if time allows, head to the west side of town to visit the Arashiyama & Sagano district, where you'll find some of the city's most impressive sights, including the famous bamboo grove and Tenryū-ji.

KYOTO ➲ NARA

🚆 **45 minutes** JR Nara line or Kintetsu *tokkyū*

❸ Nara (p287)

If you've got more than two days in Kansai, then consider making a day trip to Nara from Kyoto (there's little need to spend the night in Nara, since it's so close to Kyoto). First, relax for a while in the superb Isui-en, then check out the awe-inspiring Daibutsu (Great Buddha) at Tōdai-ji. If time permits, continue to explore Nara-kōen, making your way all the way up to Kasuga Taisha, an incredibly atmospheric shrine.

Kinkaku-ji (p227), Kyoto
KEITH LEVIT / DESIGN PICS / CORBIS ©

10 DAYS

Kansai in Depth
Japan's Cultural Heartland

Kansai contains the highest concentration of must-see sights in all of Japan. If you want to see a lot of traditional Japanese sights without spending a lot of time in transit, then spending your entire trip in Kansai is a great idea.

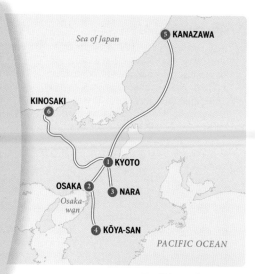

Sea of Japan

5 KANAZAWA

KINOSAKI
6

1 KYOTO

OSAKA 2
Osaka-wan **3 NARA**

4 KŌYA-SAN

PACIFIC OCEAN

❶ Kyoto (p197)

Kyoto is the obvious place to base your-self: it's central and it's got a wide range of excellent accommodation, not to mention the nation's finest temples, gardens and shrines. If possible, fly into Kansai International Airport (KIX). Spend a day in Kyoto exploring the Higashiyama area (both southern and northern), followed by another day strolling through the bamboo groves of Arashiyama & Sagano.

KYOTO ➔ OSAKA

🚃 **About 45 minutes** Take a limited express *shinkaisoku* on the JR line from Kyoto Station to Osaka Station (or, if you have a Japan Rail Pass, you can take the *shinkansen*, which takes 15 minutes). The private Hankyū and Keihan lines also connect Kyoto and Osaka.

❷ Osaka (p268)

Since you won't be going to Tokyo on this trip, you'll want to check out the urban Japan experience in Osaka, a very short train ride from Kyoto. The Minami district is the best place to explore for those with limited time.

KYOTO ➔ NARA

🚃 **About 45 minutes** Take the JR Nara line from Kyoto Station or Nara Station. If you want to go in more comfort, take a *tokkyū* on the Kintetsu line from Kintetsu Kyoto Station to Kintetsu Nara Station (it takes just over half an hour).

❸ Nara (p287)

Nara is the most rewarding day trip out of Kyoto. Spend your day exploring the attractions of Nara-kōen, the park that contains all the must-sees of the city.

KYOTO ➔ KŌYA-SAN

🚃 **About two and a half hours** Take a limited express *shinkaisoku* on the JR line from Kyoto Station to Osaka Station (about 45 minutes, or, if you have a Japan Rail Pass, you can take the *shinkansen*, which takes 15 minutes). Then, take the Midōsuji subway line to Nankai Namba Station and get on the Nankai-Dentetsu line *kyūkō* (express) to Kōya-san (one hour and 40 minutes).

❹ Kōya-san (p296)

Spend a night at a Buddhist monastery in the Buddhist centre of Kōya-san, high in the mountains of Wakayama, south of Kyoto.

KYOTO ➔ KANAZAWA

🚃 **About two hours and 15 minutes** Take the *tokkyū* Thunderbird from Kyoto Station to Kanazawa Station.

❺ Kanazawa (p185)

While not technically part of Kansai, Kanazawa is so close, both in spatial and spiritual terms, that it may as well be. Take the comfortable express train up here from Kyoto and enjoy one of Japan's best gardens – Kenroku-en – as well as a fantastic preserved district (not to mention great seafood and friendly people).

KYOTO ➔ KINOSAKI

🚃 **About two and a half hours** Take a *tokkyū* train from Kyoto Station to Kinosaki Station.

❻ Kinosaki (p301)

Kinosaki, a charming onsen (hot spring) resort on the Sea of Japan coast, is a great way to wind up your stay in Kansai. You can soak away in the baths and relax in a ryokan before heading home.

Deer in Nara-kōen (p289), Nara
SUNNYWINDS / GETTY IMAGES ©

10 DAYS

Tokyo to Kyoto via the Japan Alps
Japan's Classic Route

The classic Tokyo–Japan Alps–Kyoto route is the best way to get a quick taste of the country. You'll experience three faces of Japan: the modern wonders of Tokyo, the traditional culture of Kyoto and the natural beauty of the Japan Alps.

Sea of Japan

TAKAYAMA ② = ③ KAMIKŌCHI

TOKYO ①

KYOTO ④   NAGOYA

⑤ NARA

PACIFIC OCEAN

① Tokyo (p51)

Spend two or three days in the capital soaking up the modern side of Japan before heading west to discover a completely different Japan.

TOKYO ➡ TAKAYAMA

🚄 **Four hours** Take a *shinkansen* from Tokyo Station to Nagoya Station (one hour and 45 minutes), then take a *tokkyū* from Nagoya Station to Takayama Station (two hours and 15 minutes).

② Takayama (p154)

Takayama is the gateway to the Northern Japan Alps and a fine destination in its own right. Explore the Sanmachi-suji district and check out the thatched-roof houses in Hida-no-Sato.

TAKAYAMA ➡ KAMIKŌCHI

🚌 **One hour and 15 minutes** Take a bus from Takayama to Hirayu Onsen (one hour) and then another to Kamikōchi (15 minutes).

③ Kamikōchi (p163)

Kamikōchi offers the finest alpine panorama in the Northern Alps (at least the finest panorama accessible without having to hike). Stay at least a night to soak up the mountain air and scenery. If you're a hiker, hike up the Azusa-gawa, a beautiful stream that runs through the valley.

KAMIKŌCHI ➡ KYOTO

🚌 **One hour and 15 minutes** Take a bus from Kamikōchi to Hirayu Onsen (15 minutes) then another to Takayama (one hour). 🚄 **About three hours and 15 minutes** Take a *tokkyū* from Takayama Station to Nagoya Station (two hours and 15 minutes), followed by a *shinkansen* from Nagoya Station to Kyoto Station (about one hour).

④ Kyoto (p197)

Spend three or four days in the old capital enjoying some of Japan's finest temples, gardens and shrines. At the very least, check out both the Higashiyama area (north and south) and the Arashiyama & Sagano area.

KYOTO ➡ NARA

🚄 **About 45 minutes** Take the JR Nara line from Kyoto Station or Nara Station. If you want to go in more comfort, take a *tokkyū* on the Kintetsu line from Kintetsu Kyoto Station to Kintetsu Nara Station (it takes just over a half an hour).

⑤ Nara (p287)

With an enormous Buddha statue, herds of deer, plenty of greenery and lots for the kids to do, Nara is one of Japan's most rewarding destinations.

Arashiyama (p228), Kyoto
TOTORORO / GETTY IMAGES ©

2 WEEKS

Tokyo to Hiroshima via Kyoto
From the Capital to the Inland Sea

Start in the capital, then hop on the bullet train to sample the traditional delights of Kyoto. Then head west along the Inland Sea, stopping at the art island of Naoshima, then continue on to Hiroshima and Miyajima.

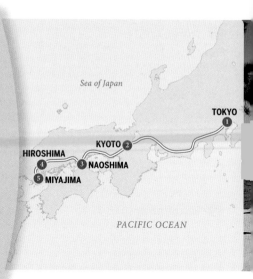

Sea of Japan

TOKYO ①

KYOTO ②

HIROSHIMA
④
③ NAOSHIMA

⑤ MIYAJIMA

PACIFIC OCEAN

---

① Tokyo (p51)

You'll want to spend about two or three days in Tokyo before heading west. Visit Tsukiji Market your first morning, for a truly sensory experience first up. Next, head to Asakusa to visit the temple of Sensō-ji, followed by a trip to Tokyo National Museum, in nearby Ueno. The next day, take the loop line to Harajuku and walk to Meiji-jingū, the city's finest Shintō shrine, then take a stroll down chic Omote-sandō. From there, head up to Shibuya to soak up some of modern Tokyo. Make sure you spend an evening wandering east Shinjuku, since this is where you'll get full experience of Tokyo's neon madness.

TOKYO ⮕ KYOTO

🚄 **Two hours and 45 minutes** Take a *shinkansen* between Tokyo Station and Kyoto Station. Keep your eyes peeled soon after leaving Tokyo and you just might catch a glimpse of Mt Fuji if the weather is really clear.

② Kyoto (p197)

Spend a day in Kyoto exploring the Higashi-yama area, followed by another day strolling through the bamboo groves of Arashiyama & Sagano. If possible, spend three or four days

in Kyoto and consider a day trip to Nara if time allows. Nara is an easy trip from Kyoto, but spending a night is also a good option if you really want to slow down.

KYOTO ⮕ NAOSHIMA

🚄 **One hour and 50 minutes** Take a *shinkansen* from Kyoto Station to Okayama Station (one hour), then a train to Uno Station (50 minutes). ⚓ **20 minutes** Take a ferry from Uno Port to Naoshima.

③ Naoshima (p311)

Naoshima is easily one of Japan's most interesting attractions; it's a small island in the Inland Sea that has been converted into one giant art museum (well, there are several museums, installations and galleries dotted all around the place). It's worth spending at least one night here to get the most out of the experience.

NAOSHIMA ⮕ HIROSHIMA

⚓ **20 minutes** Take a ferry from Naoshima to Uno Port. 🚄 **One hour and 35 minutes** Take a train from Uno Station to Okayama Station (50 minutes) and then a *shinkansen* from Okayama Station to Hiroshima Station (45 minutes).

⑤ **Miyajima** (p322)

You've probably seen pictures of the famous floating torii (shrine gate) at Miyajima (well, just offshore). In addition to this superb sight, there is plenty to do on this green and mountainous island.

MIYAJIMA ➡ TOKYO

⛴ **45 minutes** Take a ferry from Miyajima back to Hiroshima Station. 🚃 **About four hours** Take a *shinkansen* from Hiroshima Station to Tokyo Station.

⑥ **Tokyo** (p51)

After returning to Tokyo, you might want to pack in some last-minute souvenir shopping and dining in the capital before catching your flight home.

④ **Hiroshima** (p316)

A few hours west from Naoshima, Hiroshima is an essential stop for anyone with an interest in Japanese history. The displays at the Peace Park are both sobering and saddening, but the vitality of the modern city will give you faith in the ability of the human spirit to bounce back from tragedy. You can stay overnight in Hiroshima, or on the nearby island of Miyajima.

HIROSHIMA ➡ MIYAJIMA

⛴ **45 minutes** Take a ferry from Hiroshima Peace Park direct to Miyajima.

Japan Month by Month

Top Events

 Gion Matsuri, July

 Cherry-Blossom Viewing, April

 Takayama Matsuri, April

Tenjin Matsuri, July

Shōgatsu (New Year), 31 December to 3 January

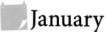 January

Japan comes to life after the lull of the New Year holiday. Winter grips the country in the mountains and in the north, but travel is still possible in most places.

Shōgatsu (New Year)

New Year (31 December to 3 January) is one of the most important celebrations in Japan and includes plenty of eating and drinking. The central ritual, *hatsu-mōde,* involves the first visit to the local shrine to pray for health, happiness and prosperity during the coming year. Keep in mind that a lot of businesses and attractions shut down during this period and transport can be busy as people head back to their hometowns.

Skiing

While many ski areas open in December, the ski season really gets rolling in January.

February

It's still cold in February in most of Japan (with the exception of Okinawa). Skiing is in full swing and this is a good time to soak in onsen (hot springs).

Setsubun Matsuri

On 2, 3 or 4 February, to celebrate the end of winter and drive out evil spirits, the Japanese engage in throwing roasted beans while chanting *'oni wa soto, fuku wa uchi'* (meaning 'out with the demons, in with good luck'). Check local shrines for events.

Yuki Matsuri

Drawing over two million annual visitors, Sapporo's famous snow festival really warms up winter in Hokkaidō in early February. Teams from around the world compete to

April Geisha at *hanami* (cherry-blossom viewing), Kyoto
CLAIRE TAKACS / GETTY IMAGES ©

create the most impressive ice and snow sculptures. After touring the sculptures, head to one of the city's friendly pubs and eateries to warm up with sake and great local food.

 # March

By March it's starting to warm up on the main islands of Japan. Plums start the annual procession of blossoms across the archipelago. This is a pleasant time to travel in Honshū, Kyūshū and Shikoku.

 ## Plum-Blossom Viewing

Not as famous as the cherries, but quite lovely in their own right, Japan's plum trees bloom from late February into early March. Strolling among the plum groves at places like Kyoto's Kitano Tenman-gū is a fine way to spend an early spring day in Japan.

 # April

Spring is in full swing by April. The cherry blossoms usually peak early in April in most of Honshū. Japan is beautiful at this time, but places like Kyoto can be crowded.

 ## Cherry-Blossom Viewing

When the cherry blossoms burst into bloom, the Japanese hold rollicking *hanami* (cherry-blossom viewing) parties. It's hard to time viewing the blossoms: to hit them at their peak in Tokyo or Kyoto, you have to be in the country from around 25 March to 5 April.

 ## Takayama Matsuri

The first part of this festival, the Sannō Matsuri, is held on 14 and 15 April. The festival floats here are truly spectacular. Book well in advance if you want to spend the night or come back in October for the second part, the Hachiman Matsuri.

 # May

May is one of the best months to visit Japan. It's warm and sunny in most of the country. Book accommodation well in advance during the April/May Golden Week holidays.

 ## Golden Week

Most Japanese are on holiday from 29 April to 5 May, when a series of national holidays coincide. This is one of the busiest times for domestic travel, so be prepared for crowded transport and accommodation.

 ## Sanja Matsuri

The grandest of all Tokyo festivals is held on the third weekend in May. It features hundreds of *mikoshi* (portable shrines) paraded through Asakusa, starting from Asakusa-jinja.

 # June

June is generally a lovely time to travel in Japan – it's warm but not sweltering. Keep in mind that the rainy season generally starts in Kyūshū and Honshū sometime in June. It doesn't rain every day but it can be humid.

 ## Japan Alps Hiking Season

Most of the snow has melted off the high peaks of the Japan Alps by June and hikers flock to the trails. You should check conditions before going, however, as big snow years can mean difficult conditions for hikers and skiers.

July

The rainy season ends in Honshū sometime in July and, once it does, the heat cranks up and it can be very hot and humid. Head to Hokkaidō or the Japan Alps to escape the heat.

 # August

August is hot and humid across most of Japan. Once again, Hokkaidō and the Japan Alps can provide some relief. Several of the year's best festivals and events happen in August.

Matsumoto Bonbon

Matsumoto's biggest event takes place on the first Saturday in August, when hoards people perform the 'bonbon' dance through the city streets.

O-Bon

This Buddhist observance, which honours the spirits of the dead, occurs in mid-August (it is one of the high-season travel periods). This is a time when ancestors return to earth to visit their descendants. Lanterns are lit and floated on rivers, lakes or the sea to help guide them on their journey. See also Daimon-ji Gozan Okuribi.

Daimon-ji Gozan Okuribi

Huge fires in the shape of Chinese characters and other symbols are set alight in Kyoto during this festival, which forms part of O-Bon (Festival of the Dead). It's one of Japan's most impressive spectacles.

Mt Fuji Climbing Season

Mt Fuji officially opens to climbing on 1 July, and the months of July and August are ideal for climbing the peak.

Gion Matsuri

Held on 17 and 24 July, this is the mother of all Japanese festivals. Dozens of huge floats are pulled through the streets of Kyoto by teams of chanting citizens. On the three evenings preceding the parade, people stroll through Shijō-dōri's street stalls dressed in beautiful *yukata* (light cotton kimonos).

Tenjin Matsuri

Held on 24 and 25 July, this is your chance to see the city of Osaka let its hair down. Try to make the second day of the festival, when huge crowds carry *mikoshi* through the city.

 # September

Sometime in early to mid-September, the heat breaks and temperatures become very pleasant in the main islands. Skies are generally clear at this time, making it a great time to travel.

Kishiwada Danjiri Matsuri

Huge *danjiri* (festival floats) are pulled through the narrow streets in the south of Osaka during this lively festival on 14 and 15 September. Much

alcohol is consumed and occasionally the *danjiri* go off course and crash into houses.

October

October is one of the best months to visit Japan: the weather can be warm or cool and it's usually sunny. The autumn foliage peaks in the Japan Alps at this time.

 Kurama-no-hi Matsuri

On 22 October, huge flaming torches are carried through the streets of the tiny hamlet of Kurama in the mountains north of Kyoto. This is one of Japan's more primeval festivals.

November

November is also beautiful for travel in most of Japan. Skies are reliably clear and temperatures are pleasantly cool. Snow starts to fall in the mountains and foliage peaks in places like Kyoto and Nara. Expect crowds.

 Shichi-Go-San (7-5-3 Festival)

This is a festival in honour of girls aged three and seven and boys aged five. On 15 November, children are dressed in their finest clothes and taken to shrines or temples, where prayers are offered for good fortune.

December

December is cool to cold across most of Japan. The Japanese are busy preparing for the New Year. Most things shut down from 29 or 30 December, making travel difficult (but transport runs and accommodation is open).

Far left: February Yuki Matsuri, Sapporo
Below: May Portable shrine, Sanja Matsuri festival

(FAR LEFT) TRAVEL PIX / GETTY IMAGES ©: (BELOW) GARY CONNER / GETTY IMAGES ©

What's New

For this new edition of Discover Japan, our authors hunted down the fresh, the transformed, the hot and the happening. Here are a few of our favourites. For up-to-the-minute recommendations, see lonelyplanet.com/japan.

1 EXTENDED SHINKANSEN LINES
The Hokuriku Shinkansen (bullet train) cuts travel time between Tokyo and Kanazawa to just over two hours. This new line makes it extremely easy and comfortable to do the Tokyo–Kyoto–Kanazawa loop, one of the top one-week Japan travel itineraries.

2 CHEAP YEN
The Japanese yen has plunged recently against most currencies, making Japan (at least areas outside of Tokyo) seem positively cheap in comparison to some destinations.

3 HANEDA AIRPORT EXPANSION
Tokyo's 'second' airport, Haneda International Airport, is now serving an increasing number of international flights. This is a huge boon to travellers, since Haneda is significantly closer to central Tokyo than Narita Airport.

4 DISCOUNT NARITA EXPRESS (N'EX) TICKETS
Tourists can purchase Narita Express tickets for a mere ¥1500, a huge savings over the normal fare of ¥3020. It's not clear how long this policy will stay in effect. Check online (www.jreast.co.jp/e/nex) for details.

5 MORE JAPAN RAIL PASSES
Japan Rail has released a raft of new pass options for tourists, including a three-day Kantō area (Tokyo and surrounds) pass covering Narita, Nikkō and Fuji-san; a four-day pass for travel in Hiroshima and Western Honshū; a four-day Hokuriku travel pass; and a five-day pass for travel in Kansai and to Hiroshima. See p404 for details.

6 TSUKIJI MARKET MOVING
Tsukiji's famous fish market is on course to move to a new home on Tokyo Bay in late 2016. Only a short time remains to see this classic Tokyo sight in its present form. (p66)

7 NEW TAX EXEMPTIONS
Until recently, only certain non-consumable items such as electronics were tax-exempt for tourists, but now many consumable items like food, cosmetics, beverages and medicine also qualify for tax-exempt status when making purchases over ¥5000. Look for signs indicating special tax-exempt stores.

8 BETTER WI-FI COVERAGE
While most hotels in Japan used to offer only in-room LAN cable internet access, wi-fi is becoming the new norm. Free wi-fi is also becoming increasingly available in restaurants, cafes, bars, airports and even some train stations. Some major cities even offer w-fi on the street.

9 OKADA MUSEUM OF ART
Showcasing the dazzling Japanese, Chinese and Korean art treasures of industrialist Okada Kazuo, this mammoth museum is a great addition to Hakone's showcases of world-class art. (p139)

Get Inspired

 ## Books

o **The Roads to Sata** (nonfiction; 1985; Alan Booth) An account of a four-month walk from Hokkaidō to Kyūshū.

o **Inventing Japan: 1853–1964** (nonfiction; 2004; Ian Buruma) A brilliant and concise history of Japan as it went from a closed country to a First World nation.

o **Dogs and Demons** (nonfiction; 2002; Alex Kerr) A clear-eyed look at the state of modern Japan by one of the ultimate Japan insiders.

Films

o **Tampopo** (1985) Itami Jūzō's film about *rāmen* (egg noodles) is told in the manner of a spaghetti Western.

o **Osōshiki** (The Funeral; 1984) A penetrating look at Japanese society through the lens of a funeral – a classic from Itami Jūzō.

o **My Neighbor Totoro** (1988) This touching children's story is the perfect introduction to the work of Miyazaki Hayao, the master of Japanese anime.

Music

o **The New Best of Shoukichi Kina & Champloose** (Shoukichi Kina & Champloose) A mix of mellow and upbeat Okinawan-style music.

o **Okinawa Jyoka** (Tokiko Kato) Mellow tunes with an Okinawan vibe.

o **World Order** (Sudo Genki) Check out the video of this song online (the one shot in Japan is best).

Websites

o **Hyperdia Japan** (www.hyperdia.com) Get Japan transport information (fares, times etc) in English.

o **Japan Ministry of Foreign Affairs** (MOFA; www.mofa.go.jp) Useful visa info and embassy/consulate locations.

o **Japan Rail** (www.japanrailpass.net) Information on rail travel in Japan, with details on the Japan Rail Pass.

Short on time?

This list will give you an instant insight into Japan.

Read *Memoirs of a Geisha*, by Arthur Golden, is the classic tale of a Kyoto geisha.

Watch The story of emotional near misses in Tokyo, *Lost in Translation* is a great pretrip look at Japan.

Listen Female vocalist Moto Chitose's album, *Hainumikaze*, is head and shoulders above the standard J-pop offerings.

Log on Japan National Tourism Organization (JNTO; www.jnto.go.jp) provides information on all aspects of travel in Japan.

Women practising calligraphy
MICHAEL HITOSHI / GETTY IMAGES ©

Need to Know

*For more information, see
Survival Guide (p385)*

Currency
Yen (¥)

Language
Japanese

Visas
Issued on arrival for most
nationalities for stays of up
to 90 days.

Money
ATMs are available in
post offices and some
convenience stores. Credit
cards are accepted in most
hotels and department
stores, but only some
restaurants and ryokan.

Mobile Phones
Only 3G phones work
in Japan. SIM cards for
phones are not available,
but data-only SIM cards are
available for smartphones
and tablets.

Wi-Fi
Wi-fi, particularly free wi-fi, is
less common in Japan than
in some other countries.
Available in some cafes,
restaurants, bars and hotels.

Internet Access
Internet cafes are common
in big cities. Many hotels have
LAN cable access and some
also have wi-fi.

Tipping
Tipping is not practiced in Japan.

When to Go

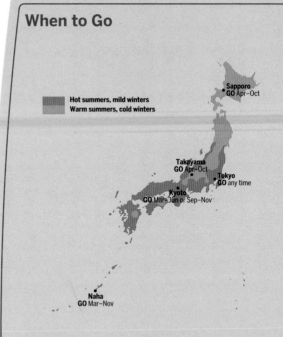

Hot summers, mild winters
Warm summers, cold winters

Sapporo
GO Apr–Oct

Takayama
GO Apr–Oct

Tokyo
GO any time

Kyoto
GO Mar–Jun or Sep–Nov

Naha
GO Mar–Nov

High Season
(Apr–early
May, mid-Aug,
New Year)
○ Kyoto, Nara and
other Honshū
tourist cities are
crowded during the
cherry-blossom
season (late March
into early April)
and autumn foliage
season.

Shoulder
(Jun–Jul,
Sep–mid-Dec)
○ June and July
is rainy season
in most of Japan
(Hokkaidō
excepted). While it
doesn't rain every
day, it can be pretty
humid.

Low Season
(Jan–Mar)
○ Winter is cool
or cold in most of
Honshū, but it's fine
for travel. Be ready
for snow in the
mountains.

Advance Planning

○ **Several months before** Make accommodation reservations
several months in advance if you are travelling in cherry-blossom
season (March and April) and the autumn foliage season in Honshū
(October and November).

○ **One month before** Buy a Japan Rail Pass. This pass, which is only
available for purchase outside of Japan, can save you a lot of money
if you are planning to travel extensively by rail within Japan.

Daily Costs

Budget Less than ¥8000
- Guest house accommodation: ¥2800
- Two simple restaurant meals: ¥2000
- Train/bus transport: ¥1500
- One temple/museum admission: ¥500
- Snacks, drinks, sundries: ¥1000

Midrange ¥8000–¥20,000
- Business hotel accommodation: ¥9000
- Two midrange restaurant meals: ¥4000
- Train/bus transport: ¥1500
- Two temple/museum admissions: ¥1000
- Snacks, drinks, sundries: ¥2000

Top End More than ¥20,000
- First-class hotel accommodation: ¥20,000
- Two good restaurant meals: ¥6000
- Two taxi rides: ¥3000
- Two temple/museum admissions: ¥1000
- Snacks, drinks, sundries: ¥2000

Exchange Rates

Australia	A$1	¥95
Canada	C$1	¥98
Europe	€1	¥133
New Zealand	NZ$1	¥88
UK	£1	¥188
US	US$1	¥121

For current exchange rates see www.xe.com

What to Bring

- **International licence** If you plan to rent a car in Japan, get an international licence from your country's automobile association.
- **Japan Rail Pass** You must purchase this pass before arriving in Japan.
- **Slip-on shoes** You'll be taking off your shoes a lot, especially in Kyoto.

Arriving in Japan

Narita International Airport (Tokyo; p118)

Trains Narita Express (N'EX) to Tokyo Station; 53 minutes; ¥3020

Limousine buses one hour and 45 minutes to most city destinations; ¥3500

Taxis 90 minutes; around ¥30,000 to the city

Haneda Airport (Tokyo; p119)

Monorail 15 minutes; ¥490

Limousine buses 30 to 90 minutes, depending upon destination in Tokyo; from ¥930

Taxis around ¥6000 to Tokyo

Kansai International Airport (Kyoto; p250)

Express trains 75 minutes to Kyoto; ¥2850

Limousine buses 90 minutes to Kyoto; ¥2550

Taxis 90 minutes to Kyoto; ¥3600

Getting Around

- **Air** Japan's domestic flight network is efficient, reasonably priced and comfortable.
- **Bus** Long-distance and local buses are comfortable and widely available.
- **Car** Driving in Japan is surprisingly easy, but you'll need an international licence. Avoid driving in big cities like Tokyo.
- **Taxi** These are found everywhere and can be cheap for groups, especially in Kyoto.
- **Train** Japan has one of the best train systems in the world, including the famous *shinkansen* (bullet trains).

Sleeping

- **Hotels** From cheap 'business' hotels to first-class international-standard ones.
- **Guest houses** Traveller-friendly and cheap.
- **Ryokan** Traditional Japanese inns.
- **Youth hostels** Plentiful and cheap.

Be Forewarned

- **Crowds** Kyoto and Nara can be very crowded in cherry-blossom season (late March to early April).
- **Heat** Most of Japan is very hot and humid in July and August.
- **New Year holiday** Most businesses and many sights shut down from 27 December to 3 January.

Tokyo

Tokyo is like 10 normal cities crammed into one megacity.

Chaotic yet organised, hypermodern yet utterly classic, garish yet demure, unique yet unquestionably Japanese, Tokyo is a paradox that – like a pop star – seems smug in its greatness yet obsessed with reinvention.

It's a city bent on collecting superlatives, and since the early days of Edo, Tokyo's done everything in its power to stay ahead of the pack, from reclaiming miles of swampland to transforming war-torn moonscapes into shimmering skyscraper districts.

Today, that constant hunger for improvement and change has created a tapestry of sensorial madness unlike anywhere else in the world. In sheer size and scope alone, Tokyo far outweighs other major global centres.

Simply put, Tokyo is a city that everyone should visit at least once in their lifetime.

Shibuya Crossing (p74)

51

Tokyo Sky Tree (p87)

Tokyo

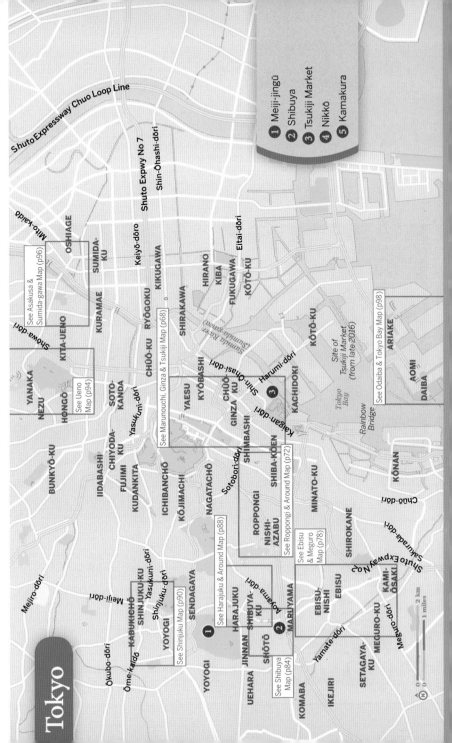

Shuto Expressway Chuo Loop Line

1 Meiji-jingū
2 Shibuya
3 Tsukiji Market
4 Nikkō
5 Kamakura

Mito-kaidō

Showa-dōri

OSHIAGE
SUMIDA-KU
KURAMAE
KITA-UENO
YANAKA
NEZU
HONGŌ
BUNKYŌ-KU

Keiyō-dōri

Shin-Ohashi-dōri

Shuto Expwy No 7

HIRANO
KIBA
FUKUGAWA
KŌTŌ-KU
KIKUGAWA
SHIRAKAWA
RYŌGOKU
CHŪŌ-KU

Eitai-dōri

See Asakusa & Sumida-gawa Map (p96)
See Ueno Map (p94)
See Marunouchi, Ginza & Tsukiji Map (p68)

Sumida River (Sumida-gawa)

Site of Tsukiji Market (from late 2016)

KŌTŌ-KU
ARIAKE
AOMI
DAIBA

See Odaiba & Tokyo Bay Map (p98)

SOTO-KANDA
CHIYODA-KU
FUJIMI
KUDANKITA
IIDABASHI
ICHIBANCHŌ
KŌJIMACHI
NAGATACHŌ

Yasukuni-dōri
Yasukuni-dōri

KYŌBASHI
YAESU
GINZA KU
CHŪŌ
SHIMBASHI

Shin-Ohashi-dōri
Harumi-dōri

KACHIDOKI
3
Kaigan-dōri

Tokyo Bay

Rainbow Bridge

KŌNAN

Chūō-dōri

Mejiro-dōri
Meiji-dōri
Shinjuku-dōri
Shinjuku-dōri

KABUKICHŌ
SHINJUKU-KU
YOYOGI
SENDAGAYA

See Shinjuku Map (p90)
See Harajuku & Around Map (p88)
See Roppongi & Around Map (p72)

Sotobori-dōri

SHIBA-KŌEN
ROPPONGI
NISHI-AZABU
MINATO-KU
SHIROKANE

See Ebisu & Meguro Map (p78)

EBISU
EBISU-NISHI

KAMI-ŌSAKI

Shuto Expwy No 2
Sakurada-dōri

Ōkubo-dōri
Ōme-kaidō

YOYOGI
UEHARA
JINNAN
SHŌTŌ
HARAJUKU
SHIBUYA-KU
MARUYAMA

Aoyama-dōri

1
2

See Shibuya Map (p84)

KOMABA
IKEJIRI
SETAGAYA-KU
MEGURO-KU

Yamate-dōri
Meguro-dōri

Shutō

N
0 — 2 km
0 — 1 miles

Tokyo Highlights

Meiji-jingū

For a break from Tokyo's seemingly endless concrete and neon, head to Meiji-jingū (p76). Sitting amid a rolling expanse of forest, this shrine serves as a retreat for harried Tokyoites. A walk down any of the tree-lined avenues is the perfect way to spend a few peaceful hours in the city. Buy an *omikuji* (paper fortune) at the shrine to check your luck and keep your eyes peeled for a traditional Japanese wedding.

STEVE GOLDEN / GETTY IMAGES ©

Shibuya

Shibuya (p73) is Tokyo at its most Tokyoesque: throngs of people, huge neon signs, busy overhead train lines and an almost infinite number of shops and restaurants. If you've seen *Lost in Translation*, you've seen Shibuya: many of the city scenes were shot here. The people-watching here is the best anywhere and the shopping is among the best in the city. Left: Shibuya Crossing (p74)

DAVID KOITER / GETTY IMAGES ©

Tsukiji Market

3

The mother of all fish markets, Tsukiji (p66) is far more than just the tuna auction for which it's famed. It's aisle upon aisle of weird and wonderful things pulled from the sea, at least half of which you might not even recognise as edible food products. Right: Red octopus

4

Nikkō

In a country where the default colour for temples is bare wood, Nikkō (p131) stands out like a peacock among pigeons. This shrine/temple complex three hours north of Tokyo is the closest Japan has ever gotten to the riotous exuberance of rococo. Nikkō vies with Kamakura as the Tokyo area's most rewarding day trip; an express train to Nikkō takes only 1¾ hours. If you're not going to Kyoto, this is highly recommended. Above left: Tōshō-gū (p132)

5

Kamakura

Only about an hour away from Tokyo by express train, Kamakura (p141) feels like a different world. This seaside collection of temples and shrines, and one giant bronze Buddha statue, makes a fine day trip out of the city, especially if you need a break from the big city. Like Nikkō, this is highly recommended if you're not heading to Kyoto. Above right: Daibutsu (p142)

Tokyo's Best…

Experiences

○ **Shibuya Crossing** When the lights turn green here, a human tide steps off the curb. (p74)

○ **Roppongi** A cosmopolitan interzone where the world comes to drink. (p65)

○ **Tokyo Metropolitan Government Offices** There's no finer view of the city. (p78)

○ **Tsukiji Market** Sensory overload at dawn. (p66)

Places to Stay

○ **Park Hyatt Tokyo** An oasis of calm and beauty in the sky above Tokyo. (p97)

○ **Sawanoya Ryokan** A quiet gem in Yanaka with wonderful hospitality and traditional baths. (p98)

○ **Hotel S** Boutique property steps from Roppongi's nightlife. (p93)

○ **Hōshi Onsen Chōjūkan** A brilliant choice for the classic onsen (hot springs) ryokan (traditional Japanese inn) experience. (p136)

Places to Shop

○ **Ginza** Head to Ginza to check out where the old money shops for international luxury items. (p115)

○ **Shinjuku** Start at Takashimaya Times Sq and go from there. (p117)

○ **Harajuku** The wide boulevard known as Omote-sandō here is the closest Japan will ever get to Paris. (p116)

○ **Shibuya** More department stores, boutiques and record stores than anywhere on earth. (p116)

Need to Know

Escapes

o **Nikkō** Phantasmagorical temples and shrines among towering trees. (p131)

o **Kamakura** A great Buddha and quiet temples by the sea. (p141)

o **Hakone** Onsen, Fuji views and a lovely lake in the mountains. (p137)

o **Minakami & Takaragawa Onsen** Classic riverside onsen within easy reach of Tokyo. (p135)

RESOURCES

o **JNTO Tourist Information Center** (www.jnto.go.jp) The best English-speaking Tourist Information Centre in the city.

o **Metropolis** (http:// metropolis.co.jp) This free English-language magazine is another good source of info. Available at big bookshops and foreigner-friendly businesses.

o **Go Tokyo** (www.gotokyo. org) Municipally run website detailing what to see, do and eat in greater Tokyo. Walking-tour ideas are also on offer.

o **Tokyo Art Beat** (www. tokyoartbeat.com) Bilingual art and design guide with a regularly updated list of events.

o **Grutt Pass** (www. rekibun.or.jp/grutto) If you're planning on sticking around Tokyo for a week or more, then consider investing in a Grutt Pass – a booklet of discount coupons to over 70 museums in greater Tokyo.

GETTING AROUND

o **Walk** Explore the urban hubs of Tokyo on foot.

o **Taxi** Only catch one if you miss the last train (Tokyo taxi prices are high).

o **Subway** Unless the loop line is more direct, the subway will get you around all parts of the city.

o **JR Yamanote loop line** From one Tokyo hub to the next (except places off the line, like Roppongi).

o **Private train lines** For day trips to places like Nikkō and Kamakura.

BE FOREWARNED

o **Rush hour** There are huge crowds on subways and trains in and around Tokyo from 7am–9am and 4.30pm–7pm. Travel outside these hours is much more comfortable.

o **Summer (July and August)** Can be very hot and humid in Tokyo. Be prepared to sweat if you come during these months. Winter can be chilly, but not too cold.

Left: Shopping in Harajuku (p116); **Above:** Stone statues in Nikkō (p131)

Strolling Yanaka

This walk takes you through the neighbourhood of Yanaka, one of the few areas of Tokyo that retains buildings from before WWII – quite a contrast to the urban hubs of the city. Don't start out too late as many temples close their doors by 5pm.

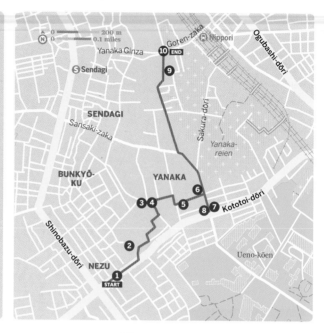

WALK FACTS

- **Start** Nezu Station
- **Finish** Yanaka Ginza
- **Distance** About 2km
- **Duration** About two hours

① Kototoi-dōri

From exit 1 of Nezu Station head up Kototoi-dōri. Here, a handful of traditional, wooden two-storey merchants' houses – with a shop on the ground floor and the living quarters above – remain alongside the mid-20th-century concrete buildings with colourful awnings. Don't miss the shops selling *sembei* (rice crackers) and *wagashi* (Japanese sweets).

② Gyokurin-ji

Pay a visit to the temple Gyokurin-ji. Just inside the grounds, on your right, a stone wall guards a narrow alley: follow it. This twisting path takes you deep into Yanaka's most atmospheric quarters.

③ Enju-ji

When you emerge from the back alleys, head left and you'll soon spot a pretty cluster of temples, including Enju-ji, which has some fantastic gnarled trees.

④ Himalayan Cedar Tree

Double back towards the fork in the road marked by an ancient, thick-trunked Himalayan cedar tree. On the left side of the tree is a classic, old-school corner shop.

⑤ Allan West Studio

Continue past the shop to the studio of painter Allan West.

6 SCAI the Bathhouse

The next landmark is SCAI the Bathhouse, a centuries-old public bathhouse that became a contemporary-art gallery in 1993.

7 Shitamachi Museum Annex

One block over, the Shitamachi Museum Annex preserves an old liquor shop built in 1910; it's free to enter.

8 Kayaba Coffee

If you're in need of a break, you can soak up more local atmosphere over coffee at Kayaba Coffee. From here, double back, taking a left at the fork and then heading down the narrow road to the left of the Yamazaki shop. You can safely put away the guidebook – it's a straight shot up to Yanaka Ginza – and enjoy the stroll past temples, tiny galleries and craft shops.

9 Asakura Chōso Museum

You'll soon come to the Asakura Chōso Museum; the entrance is on your right. Sculptor Asakura Fumio (artist name Chōso; 1883-1964) designed this atmospheric house himself, which includes a central water garden, a studio with vaulted ceilings and a 'sunrise room'; it's now a museum with a number of the artist's signature realist works, mostly of people and cats, on display. The museum is closed on Mondays and Fridays.

10 Yanaka Ginza

When you reach an intersection with lively vendors – that's Yanaka Ginza. Join the locals as they shop and snack their way up and down the lane. Walk west and you can pick up the subway at Sendagi Station; to the east is Nippori Station, where you can hop on the JR Yamanote line.

Tokyo in...

TWO DAYS

Start the day with a pilgrimage to **Meiji-jingū** (p76) in Harajuku, followed by a stroll through the pop-culture bazaar along **Takeshita-dōri** (p76). Have lunch at **Harajuku Gyōza Rō** (p103), then check out the architecture along Omote-sandō. Head to Shinjuku in the evening for a dose of neon and a drink in one of the watering holes of Golden Gai. The next day, visit the old side of town for some sightseeing in Asakusa and Ueno, then take our walking tour through Yanaka. Finish with dinner at **Hantei** (p105).

FOUR DAYS

On day three, take a taxi at dawn to the **Tsukiji Market** (p66), followed by sushi breakfast at **Daiwa Sushi** (p100). Walk to nearby **Hama-rikyū Onshi-teien** (p64), then scoot over to Ginza and its delectable *depachika* (basement food hall). Catch an exhibition at the **Mori Art Museum** (p69) in Roppongi, followed by a nightcap. On your last day, hit up urban onsen Oedo Onsen Monogatari then go explore anime-mad Akihabara. After dark, make a beeline for neon-lit Shibuya.

Girl on Takeshita-dōri (p76), Harajuku
LLUÍS VINAGRE · WORLD PHOTOGRAPHY / GETTY IMAGES ©

Discover Tokyo

At a Glance

○ **Ginza** (p64) The first 'modern' district in the city, this is still where the old money shops.

○ **Roppongi** (p65) The cosmopolitan dining and nightlife hub that's boomed in recent years.

○ **Shibuya** (p73) The centre of Tokyo's youth and fashion worlds.

○ **Shinjuku** (p77) The most Tokyoesque part of Tokyo – neon, skyscrapers and masses of people.

○ **Ueno** (p80) Home of the city's best park and many of its museums.

○ **Asakusa** (p85) Old-school Tokyo with the city's most popular Buddhist temple.

Kabukichō (p79) at night
LUCIANO MORTUL/SHUTTERSTOCK ©

◎ Sights & Activities

Tokyo is endless in size and scope and can feel more like a collection of cities than one cohesive one. In Edo times, the city was divided into Yamanote ('uptown' or 'high city') and Shitamachi ('downtown' or the 'low city'). On the elevated plain west of the castle (now the Imperial Palace), Yamanote was where the feudal elite built their estates. In the east, along the banks of the Sumida-gawa, Shitamachi was home to the working classes, merchants and artisans.

Even today, remnants of this distinction exist: the east side of the city is still a tangle of alleys and tightly packed quarters. Neighbourhoods such as Asakusa and Ueno retain a down-to-earth vibe, more traditional architecture and an artisan tradition – the closest approximation to old Edo that remains. This is one of the best places to put the guidebook away and just explore.

Yamanote developed into the moneyed commercial and business districts. Further west, newer neighbourhoods such as Shinjuku and Shibuya came to life after WWII – this is the hypermodern Tokyo of riotous neon and giant video screens.

MARUNOUCHI (TOKYO STATION AREA) 丸の内 (東京駅)

The Imperial Palace marks the centre of the city. Though the palace itself is closed to the public, much of the grounds are now parks open to all, including Kitanomaru-kōen, which has a handful of museums.

To the east of the palace you'll find the bustling business district of Marunouchi.

Cherry-Blossom Viewing

When it comes to cherry-blossom viewing, parks such as **Ueno-kōen** (p81), **Yoyogi-kōen** (p75) and **Shinjuku-gyoen** (p71) are obvious choices. Here are two spots known only by locals that blissfully fly under the radar in spring:

Meguro-gawa (目黒川; Map p78; S Hibiya line to Naka-Meguro) Naka-Meguro's canal is lined with *sakura* (cherry trees) that form an awesome pale pink canopy. Local restaurants set up food stalls and, rather than staking out a seat, visitors stroll under the blossoms, hot wine in hand.

Aoyama Rei-en (青山霊園; Map p72; 2-32-2 Minami-Aoyama, Minato-ku; R Chiyoda line to Nogizaka, exit 5 or Ginza line to Gaienmae, exit 1B) This sprawling cemetery, with many famous inhabitants, comes alive with cherry blossoms blanketing the tombs and statues. It's a pretty, if not unusual, *hanami* (blossom-viewing) spot. Why should the dead have all the fun?

In the past decade, several glossy towers have replaced the tired, almost Soviet-style structures that once characterised Marunouchi.

Naka-dōri, which runs parallel to the palace between Hibiya and Ōtemachi stations, is a pretty, tree-lined avenue with upscale boutiques and patio cafes. Once famous for being deserted at nights and on weekends, Marunouchi is now an increasingly popular place to hang out.

Imperial Palace
Palace

(皇居; Kōkyo; Map p68; ☏ 3213-1111; http://sankan.kunaicho.go.jp/english/index.html; 1 Chiyoda, Chiyoda-ku; S Chiyoda line to Ōtemachi, exits C13b & C10) FREE The Imperial Palace grounds occupy the site of the original Edo-jō, the Tokugawa shōgunate's castle when they ruled the land. As it's the home of Japan's emperor and some of the imperial family, the palace is off limits. You can take a free tour of some of the surrounding grounds. If you're not on the tour, two bridges – the iron Nijū-bashi and the stone Megane-bashi – comprise a famous landmark which can be viewed from the southwest corner of Imperial Palace Plaza.

National Museum of Modern Art (MOMAT)
Museum

(国立近代美術館; Kokuritsu Kindai Bijutsukan; Map p62; ☏ 5777-8600; www.momat.go.jp/ english; 3-1 Kitanomaru-kōen, Chiyoda-ku; adult/student ¥420/130, extra for special exhibitions; ◷ 10am-5pm Tue-Thu, Sat & Sun, to 8pm Fri; S Tōzai line to Takebashi, exit 1b) This collection of over 9000 works is one of the country's best. All pieces date from the Meiji period onwards and impart a sense of a more modern Japan through portraits, photography and contemporary sculptures and video works. There's a wonderful view from the museum towards the Imperial Palace East Garden.

Intermediatheque
Museum

(Map p68; ☏ 03-5777-8600; www.intermedia theque.jp; 2nd & 3rd fl, JP Tower, 2-7-2 Marunouchi, Chiyoda-ku; ◷ 11am-6pm Tue, Wed, Sat, Sun, to 8pm Thu, Fri; R JR Yamanote line to Tokyo, Marunouchi exit) FREE Dedicated to interdisciplinary experimentation, Intermediateque cherry picks from the vast collection of the University of Tokyo (Tōdai) to craft a fascinating and wholly contemporary museum experience. Go from viewing the best ornithological taxidermy collection in Japan to a giant pop-art print or the beautifully encased skeleton of a dinosaur. A handsome Tōdai lecture hall is reconstituted as a forum for events including the playing of 1920s jazz recordings on a gramophone or old movie screenings.

Greater Tokyo

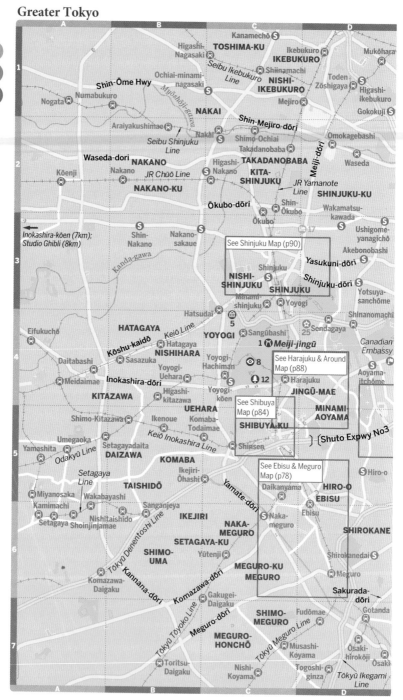

Kanamechō Ⓢ
Higashi-Nagasaki Ⓡ
TOSHIMA-KU
Ikebukuro Ⓡ
IKEBUKURO
Mukōhara Ⓡ
Seibu Ikebukuro Line
Shiinamachi Ⓡ
NISHI-IKEBUKURO
Toden Zōshigaya Ⓢ
Higashi-ikebukuro Ⓢ
Ochiai-minami-nagasaki Ⓢ
Shin-Ōme Hwy
Mejiro Ⓡ
Gokokuji Ⓢ
Nogata Ⓡ
Numabukuro Ⓡ
NAKAI
Myōshōji-gawa
Shin-Mejiro-dōri
Omokagebashi Ⓡ
Araiyakushimae Ⓡ
Nakai Ⓡ
Shimo-Ochiai
Takadanobaba Ⓢ
Waseda Ⓡ
Seibu Shinjuku Line
Waseda-dōri
NAKANO
Kōenji Ⓡ
Nakano Ⓡ
JR Chūō Line
Nakano Ⓢ
Higashi-Nakano Ⓢ
TAKADANOBABA
KITA-SHINJUKU
JR Yamanote Line
SHINJUKU-KU
Meiji-dōri
NAKANO-KU
Ōkubo-dōri
Shin-Ōkubo Ⓡ
Wakamatsu-kawada Ⓢ
Inokashira-kōen (7km); Studio Ghibli (8km)
Shin-Nakano Ⓢ
Nakano-sakaue Ⓢ
Ōkubo Ⓡ
Ushigome-yanagichō Ⓢ
17
Akebonobashi Ⓢ
Kanda-gawa
NISHI-SHINJUKU
See Shinjuku Map (p90)
Shinjuku Ⓡ
Yasukuni-dōri
SHINJUKU
Shinjuku-dōri
Yotsuya-sanchōme Ⓢ
Minami-shinjuku Ⓡ
Yoyogi Ⓡ
Hatsudai Ⓡ
5
Shinanomachi Ⓡ
HATAGAYA
Keiō Line
YOYOGI
Sangūbashi Ⓡ
1 Ⓜ Meiji-jingū
25 Sendagaya Ⓡ
Eifukuchō Ⓡ
Kōshū-kaidō
Hatagaya Ⓡ
NISHIHARA
8
See Harajuku & Around Map (p88)
Canadian Embassy
Daitabashi Ⓡ
Sasazuka Ⓡ
Yoyogi-Hachiman Ⓡ
12
Harajuku Ⓡ
Meidaimae Ⓡ
Inokashira-dōri
Yoyogi-Uehara Ⓡ
Higashi-kitazawa Ⓡ
Yoyogi-kōen Ⓢ
JINGŪ-MAE
Aoyama-itchōme Ⓢ
KITAZAWA
UEHARA
See Shibuya Map (p84)
MINAMI-AOYAMA
Shimo-Kitazawa Ⓡ
Ikenoue Ⓡ
Komaba-Todaimae Ⓡ
SHIBUYA-KU
Umegaoka Ⓡ
Setagayadaita Ⓡ
Keiō Inokashira Line
Shinsen Ⓡ
Shuto Expwy No3
Yamashita Ⓡ
Odakyū Line
DAIZAWA
KOMABA
Ikejiri-Ōhashi Ⓡ
Yamate-dōri
See Ebisu & Meguro Map (p78)
Hiro-o Ⓢ
Setagaya Line
Daikanyama Ⓡ
HIRO-O
Miyanosaka Ⓡ
Wakabayashi Ⓡ
TAISHIDŌ
Sanganjaya Ⓡ
IKEJIRI
Naka-meguro Ⓢ
EBISU
Kamimachi Ⓡ
Nishitaishido Ⓡ
Shoinjinjamae Ⓡ
Setagaya Ⓡ
Tōkyū Denentoshi Line
NAKA-MEGURO
Ebisu Ⓡ
SHIROKANE
SETAGAYA-KU
SHIMO-UMA
Yūtenji Ⓡ
MEGURO-KU
Shirokanedai Ⓢ
Komazawa-Daigaku Ⓡ
Kannana-dōri
MEGURO
Meguro Ⓡ
Tōkyū Tōyoko Line
Komazawa-dōri
Gakugei-Daigaku Ⓡ
Sakurada-dōri
Meguro-dōri
SHIMO-MEGURO
Fudōmae Ⓡ
Gotanda Ⓡ
MEGURO-HONCHŌ
Tōkyū Meguro Line
Musashi-Koyama Ⓡ
Ōsaki-hirokōji Ⓢ
Toritsu-Daigaku Ⓡ
Nishi-Koyama Ⓡ
Togoshi-ginza Ⓡ
Tōkyū Ikegami Line
Ōsaki Ⓡ

Map Scale
0 — 2 km
0 — 1 miles

Sugamo

Arakawa Streetcar Line

Sengoku

Shin-Ōtsuka

NISHI-NIPPORI

Nishi-Nippori

ARAKAWA-KU

Minowa

Nippori

BUNKYŌ-KU

Myōgadani

YANAKA

Sendagi

NEZU

Uguisudani

Iriya

Kokusai-dōri

TAITŌ-KU

Todai-mae

UENO

Nezu

Ueno

Keisei Ueno

HONGŌ

See Asakusa & Sumida-gawa Map (p96)

Inarichō

ASAKUSA

OSHIAGE

Asakusa

Tokyo Sky Tree Station

KOISHIKAWA

Edogawabashi

Kōrakuen

Kasuga

See Ueno Map (p94)

Shin-okachimachi

Kuramae

KAGURAZAKA

7 16

21

KURAMAE

Asakusabashi

Suidōbashi

Suehirochō

27

Iidabashi

JR Chūō Line

AKIHABARA

SUMIDA-KU

19

Ochanomizu

23

11

29

Asakusabashi

15

KUDANKITA

Kudanshita

2

28

Akihabara

4

13

Jimbōchō

Bakuroyokoyama

Ryōgoku

Keiyō-dōri

CHIYODA-KU

10

Kanda

24

Higashi-nihombashi

Shuto Expwy No 7

Narita (60km)

3

CHŪŌ-KU

RYŌGOKU

Kikukawa

Kōjimachi

Hanzōmon

20

Hamachō

Morishita

SHIRAKAWA

Yotsuya

Fushimi-yagura

MARUNOUCHI

Ningyōchō

14

Kiyosumi-shirakawa

Akasaka-mitsuke

Kokkai-gijidōmae

Tokyo

KYŌBASHI

Kayabachō

6

KIYOSUMI

KIBA

9

Sakuradamon

Yūrakuchō

Hatchōbori

KŌTŌ-KU

Kasumigaseki

Ginza

Monzen-nakachō

FUKAGAWA

ROPPONGI

Toranomon

GINZA

St Luke's International Hospital

Etchujima

Eitai-dōri

Roppongi

Shimbashi

Tsukiji

Kiba

SHIBA-KŌEN

Shiodome

Tsukijishijō

Tsukishima

Keiyō Line

See Roppongi & Around Map (p72)

See Marunouchi, Ginza & Tsukiji Map (p68)

TSUKIJI

Azabu-jūban

Daimon

Hamamatsuchō

KACHIDOKI

Akabanebashi

Shibakōen

Hinode Pier

Toyosu

Mita

Hinode

KŌTŌ-KU

Shin-Toyosu

Tokyo Disney Resort (6km)

Shibaura Futō

Shijo-mae

Tatsumi

Bayshore Line Expwy

Shirokane Takanawa

Tamachi

Site of Tsukiji Fish Market (from late 2016)

Ariake Tennis-no-mori

Sengakuji

Ariake Tennis-no-mori

Shinonome

Kokusai Tenjijō

Ariake

Takanawadai

See Odaiba & Tokyo Bay Map (p98)

ARIAKE

Shinagawa

Kita Shinagawa

Tennōzu-Isle

22

Odaiba

Daiba

Kaihin-kōen

Tokyo Teleport

Kokusai-tenjijō

Seimon

AOMI

Aomi

Tokyo Bay

SHINAGAWA-KU

Shin-Banba

Fune-no-Kagakukan

Haneda (10km)

Telecom Center

Chūō-dōri

Greater Tokyo

Tokyo Station Landmark

(東京駅; Map p68; www.tokyostationcity.com/en; 1-9 Marunouchi, Chiyoda-ku; ☒JR lines to Tokyo Station) Following a major renovation and expansion completed in time for its centenary in 2014, Tokyo Station is in grand form. Kingo Tatsuno's elegant brick building on the Marunouchi side has been expertly restored to include domes faithful to the original design, decorated inside with relief sculptures. Tokyo Station Hotel (p92) occupies the south end of the building; to the north is **Tokyo Station Gallery** (Map p68; www.ejrcf.or.jp/gallery; Tokyo Station, 1-9-1 Marunouchi, Chiyoda-ku; admission price differs for each exhibition; ☉10am-6pm Tue-Thu, Sat & Sun, to 8pm Fri; ☒JR lines to Tokyo, Marunouchi north exit), which hosts interesting exhibitions and the useful JR East Travel Service Center (p120).

GINZA & TSUKIJI 銀座 • 築地

Ginza is Tokyo's answer to New York's Fifth Ave or London's Oxford St. In the 1870s the area was the first neighbourhood in Tokyo to modernise, welcoming Western-style brick buildings, the city's first department stores, gas lamps and other harbingers of globalisation.

Today, other shopping districts rival it in opulence, vitality and popularity, but Ginza retains a distinct snob value. It's therefore a superb place to window-shop and people-watch. Ginza is also Tokyo's original gallery district, and there are still many in the neighbourhood.

The heart of Ginza is the 4-chōme crossing, where Chūō-dōri and Harumi-dōri intersect. Narrow Namiki-dōri is Tokyo's most exclusive nightlife strip, where elegant women in kimono wait on company execs and politicians in members-only bars and clubs. Stroll down here in the evening and you might catch a glimpse of this secretive world.

A short walk to the southeast is a luxury commercial centre of a different sort: Tsukiji Market (p66).

Hama-rikyū Onshi-teien Gardens

(浜離宮恩賜庭園; Detached Palace Garden; Map p68; www.tokyo-park.or.jp/park/format/index028.html; 1-1 Hama-rikyū-teien, Chūō-ku; adult/child ¥300/free; ☉9am-5pm; ⑤Ōedo line to Shiodome, exit A1) This beautiful garden, one of Tokyo's finest, is all that remains of a shōgunal palace that once extended into the area now occupied by Tsukiji Market. The main features are a large duck pond with an island that's home to a charming tea pavilion, **Nakajima no Ochaya** (中島の御茶屋; Map p68; www.tokyo-park.or.jp/park/format/restaurant028.html; 1-1 Hama-rikyū Onshi-teien, Chūō-ku; tea set ¥500; ⏰9am-4.30pm; 🚃Ōedo line to Shiodome, exit A1), as well as some wonderfully manicured trees (black pine, Japanese apricot, hydrangeas etc), some of which are hundreds of years old.

Shiseido Gallery
Art Gallery

(資生堂ギャラリー; Map p68; 📞3572-3901; www.shiseido.co.jp/e/gallery/html; Basement fl, 8-8-3 Ginza, Chūō-ku; ⏰11am-7pm Tue-Sat, to 6pm Sun; Ⓢ Ginza line to Shimbashi, exit 1 or 3) **FREE** The cosmetics company Shiseido runs its experimental art space out of the basement of its Shiseido Parlour complex of cafes and restaurants. An ever-changing selection, particularly of installation pieces, lends itself well to the gallery's high ceiling.

Ginza Graphic Gallery
Art Gallery

(ギンザ・グラフィック・ギャラリー; Map p68; 📞3571-5206; www.dnp.co.jp/gallery/ggg; 7-7-2 Ginza, Chūō-ku; ⏰11am-7pm Tue-Fri, to 6pm Sat; Ⓢ Ginza line to Ginza, exit A2) **FREE**

Monthly changing exhibits of graphic arts from mostly Japanese artists but with the occasional Western artist. Focuses on advertising and poster art. The annual Tokyo Art Directors Conference exhibition takes place here in July.

ROPPONGI & AROUND 六本木

Once primarily known for its debauched nightlife, Roppongi has reinvented itself over the last decade and now has an air of sophistication (at least during the day).

The transformation started with the opening in 2003 of **Roppongi Hills** (六本木ヒルズ; Map p72; www.roppongihills.com/en; 6-chōme Roppongi, Minato-ku; ⏰11am-11pm; Ⓢ Hibiya line to Roppongi, exit 1), an enormous complex with shops, offices, restaurants and an art museum. It took developer Mori Minoru no fewer than 17 years to acquire the land and construct his labyrinthine kingdom. He envisioned improving the quality of urban life by centralising home, work and leisure into a utopian microcity.

A grand vision realised? It's a matter of opinion, but similar structures, such as **Tokyo Midtown** (東京ミッドタウン;

Ginza

Don't Miss
Tsukiji Market

Tsukiji Market is the world's biggest seafood market, moving about 2000 tonnes of seafood a day. All manner of creatures pass through the market, but it's the *maguro* (bluefin tuna) that has emerged as the star. The tuna auction starts at 5am. The market is slated to move to Toyosu, an island on Tokyo Bay, in November 2016.

東京都中央卸売市場 Tokyo Metropolitan Central Wholesale Produce

Map p68

☏ 3261-8326

www.tsukiji-market.or.jp

5-2-1 Tsukiji, Chūō-ku

🕒 5am-1pm; closed Sun, most Wed & all public holidays

S Hibiya line to Tsukiji, exit 1

Working Market

Even if you don't arrive at dawn, you can still get a flavour of the frenetic atmosphere of the other parts of the market. Tsukiji is very much a working market, where handcarts and forklifts perform a perfect high-speed choreography not accounting for the odd tourist, and you'll have to exercise caution to avoid getting in the way. Don't come in large groups, with small children or in nice shoes, and don't touch anything you don't plan to buy.

Seafood Intermediate Wholesalers Area

Tsukiji isn't just the tuna auction, though. The **Seafood Intermediate Wholesalers Area** (水産仲卸業者売場; Map p68; ⏱9-11am), which opens to the public from 9am, is arguably more interesting – it is certainly more colourful. Here you can see a truly global haul of sea creatures, from gloriously magenta octopuses to gnarled turban shells. All are laid out for buyers in styrofoam crates – it's a photographer's paradise, though again you'll need to be careful. Get here as early as possible; by 11am the crowds have dwindled and the sprinkler trucks plough through to prep the empty market for tomorrow's sale.

Outer Market

The **Outer Market** (場外市場; Jōgai Shijō; Map p68; ⏱5am-2pm; [S] Hibiya line to Tsukiji, exit 1) is where rows of vendors hawk related goods, such as dried fish and seaweed, rubber boots and crockery – it's far more pedestrian friendly. Of particular note is Uogashi-yokochō, a cluster of tiny sushi restaurants inside the market, where you can feast on some ultrafresh fish. There's also the market's Shintō shrine, Namiyoke-jinja, whose deity protects seafarers.

There's a **Tourist Information Center** (Map p68; ☎03-6264-1925; www.tsukiji.or.jp; 4-16-2 Tsukiji, Chuo-ku; ⏱9.30am-1.30pm Mon-Sat, 10am-2pm Sun; [S] Hibiya line to Tsukiji, exit 1) in the Outer Market with maps and English-speaking staff.

Visiting the Tuna Auction

Seeing all the action of the tuna auction calls for dedication – some people start queuing for a spot before sunrise – but it's worth the effort. Here are some tips to help make your visit a success.

1 GET AN EARLY START

Tsukiji's famous tuna auction is without a doubt one of Tokyo's highlights, but it's only for the hardy. Up to 120 visitors a day are allowed to watch from a gallery between 5.25am and 6.15am. You must be at the **Fish Information Center** (おさかな普及センター; Osakana Fukyū Senta; Map p68; Kachidoki Gate, 6-20-5 Tsukiji, Chūō-ku), by the market's Kachidoki-mon, at 5am to register as a visitor, though the queue begins to form up to an hour earlier. It's first come, first served, so to ensure you make the cut, it's a good idea to arrive by 4am. Public transport doesn't start up early enough to get you here on time, so you'll have to take a taxi or hangout nearby all night.

2 ETIQUETTE

The market has banned visitors to the tuna auction in the past, so please be on your best behavior so as not to give the authorities any reason to do so again. Note that in addition to regular market holidays (Wednesday and Sunday), the tuna auction also closes to visitors during busy periods (like December and January). Check the calendar here: www.tsukiji-market.or.jp/tukiji_e.htm.

3 MARKET ON THE MOVE

The whole show will pack up in late 2016, when the market moves to Toyosu, an island of reclaimed land on Tokyo Bay; it's not clear yet whether visitors will be allowed in to the auction – or any part of the market – in its new digs.

Marunouchi, Ginza & Tsukiji

Map p72; www.tokyo-midtown.com/en; 9-7 Akasaka, Minato-ku; ⊙11am-11pm; S̄ Ōedo line to Roppongi, exit 8), which now anchors the other side of Roppongi, followed. The latest is **Toranomon Hills** (Map p72; http:// toranomonhills.com; 1-23 Toranomon, Minato-ku; S̄ Ginza line to Toranomon, exit 1), another development from Mori Building, which opened in 2014.

Mori Art Museum   Museum

(森美術館; Map p72; www.mori.art.museum; 52nd fl, Mori Tower, Roppongi Hills, 6-10-1 Roppongi, Minato-ku; adult/student/child ¥1500/1000/500; ⊙10am-10pm Mon-Wed, to 5pm Tue, Sky Deck 10am-10pm; S̄ Hibiya line to Roppongi, exit 1) Atop Mori Tower this gigantic gallery space sports high ceilings, broad views and thematic programs that continue to live up to all the hype associated with Roppongi Hills. Contemporary exhibits are beautifully presented and include superstars of the art world from both Japan and abroad.

Admission to the musem is shared with **Tokyo City View** (東京シティビュー; Map p72; ☎6406-6652; www.roppongihills.com/ tcv/en; 52nd fl, Mori Tower, Roppongi Hills, 6-10-1 Roppongi, Minato-ku; incl with admission to Mori Art Museum, observatory only adult/student/ child ¥1500/1000/500; ⊙10am-11pm Mon-Thu & Sun, to 1am Fri & Sat; S̄ Hibiya line to Roppongi, exit 1), which wraps itself around the 52nd floor. From this 250m-high vantage point you can see 360-degree views of the seemingly never-ending city. Weather permitting you can also pop out to the rooftop Sky Deck (additional ¥500; 11am to 8pm) for alfresco views.

Suntory Museum of Art   Museum

(サントリー美術館; Map p72; ☎3479-8600; www.suntory.com/sma; 4th fl, Tokyo Midtown, 9-7-4 Akasaka, Minato-ku; admission varies, free for children & junior-high-school students; ⊙10am-6pm Sun-Thu, to 8pm Fri & Sat; ⊞ Ōedo line to Roppongi, exit 8) Since its original 1961 opening, the Suntory Museum of Art has subscribed to an underlying philosophy of lifestyle art. Rotating exhibitions focus on the beauty of useful things: Japanese ceramics, lacquerware, glass, dyeing, weaving and such. Its current Midtown digs, designed by architect Kuma Kengō, are both understated and breathtaking.

21_21 Design Sight

Museum

(21_21デザインサイト; Map p72; ☎3475-2121; www.2121designsight.jp; Tokyo Midtown, 9-7-6 Akasaka, Minato-ku; adult/child ¥1000/free; ⏰11am-8pm Wed-Mon; Ⓢ Ōedo line to Roppongi, exit 8) An exhibition and discussion space dedicated to all forms of design, the 21_21 Design Sight acts as a beacon for local art enthusiasts, whether they be designers themselves or simply onlookers. The striking concrete and glass building, bursting out of the ground at sharp angles, was designed by Pritzker Prize–winning architect Andō Tadao.

National Art Center Tokyo

Museum

(国立新美術館; Map p72; ☎5777-8600; www. nact.jp; 7-22-1 Roppongi, Minato-ku; admission varies by exhibition; ⏰10am-6pm Wed, Thu & Sat-Mon, to 8pm Fri; Ⓢ Chiyoda line to Nogizaka, exit 6) Designed by Kurokawa Kishō, this architectural beauty has no permanent collection, but boasts the country's largest exhibition space for visiting shows, which have included Renoir, Modigliani and the Japan Media Arts Festival. Apart from exhibitions, a visit here is recommended to admire the building's awesome undulating glass facade, its cafes atop giant inverted cones and the great gift shop **Souvenir From Tokyo** (スーベニアフロムトーキョー; Map p72; www.souvenirfromtokyo.jp; basement fl, National Art Center Tokyo, 7-22-2 Roppongi, Minato-ku; ⏰10am-6pm Sat-Mon, Wed, Thu, to 8pm Fri; Ⓢ Chiyoda line to Nogizaka, exit 6).

Tokyo Tower

Tower

(東京タワー; Map p72; www.tokyotower.co.jp/ english; 4-2-8 Shiba-kōen, Minato-ku; adult/ child main deck ¥900/400, plus special deck ¥1600/800; ⏰observation deck 9am-10pm; 🚃Ōedo line to Akabanebashi, Akabanebashi exit) Something of a shameless tourist trap, this 1958-vintage tower remains a beloved symbol of the city's post-WWII rebirth. At 333m it's 13m taller than the Eiffel Tower, which was the inspiration for its design. It's also painted bright orange and white in order to comply with international aviation safety regulations.

The main observation deck is at 145m (there's another 'special' deck at 250m). There are loftier views at the more expensive Tokyo Sky Tree.

National Art Center Tokyo

Zōjō-ji
Buddhist Temple

(増上寺; Map p72; ☎03-3432-1431; www.zojoji.
or.jp/en/index.html; 4-7-35 Shiba-kōen, Minato-
ku; ◷dawn-dusk; ⑤Ōedo line to Daimon,
exit A3) FREE One of the most important
temples of the Jōdō (Pure Land) sect of
Buddhism, Zōjō-ji dates from 1393 and
was the funerary temple of the Tokugawa
regime. It's an impressive sight, particularly the main gate, **Sangedatsumon** (解
脱門; Map p72), constructed in 1605, with
its three sections designed to symbolise
the three stages one must pass through
to achieve nirvana. The **Daibonsho** (Big
Bell; 1673) is a 15-tonne whopper considered one of the great three bells of the
Edo period.

EBISU & MEGURO 恵比寿・目黒

Named for the prominent beer manu-
facturer that once provided a lifeline for
most of the neighbourhood's residents,
Ebisu has morphed into a hip neighbourhood with a generous smattering of
excellent restaurants and bars.

A short zip along the 'Skywalk' from
Ebisu Station takes you to **Yebisu Garden
Place** (恵比寿ガーデンプレイス; Map
p78; www.gardenplace.jp; 4-20 Ebisu, Shibuya-
ku; �Rℝ JR Yamanote line to Ebisu, east exit),
another one of Tokyo's 'microcities' with
a string of shops and restaurants, office
buildings and two museums.

Meguro is one stop south on the JR
Yamanote line.

Tokyo Metropolitan Museum of Photography
Museum

(東京都写真美術館; Map p78; ☎3280-0099;
www.syabi.com; 1-13-3 Mita, Meguro-ku; admission ¥600-1650; ◷10am-6pm Tue, Wed, Sat &
Sun, to 8pm Thu & Fri; ⓡ JR Yamanote line to Ebisu, east exit) Tokyo's principal photography
museum is closed through August 2016
for renovations. In addition to drawing on
its extensive collection, the museum also
hosts travelling shows (usually several
exhibitions happen simultaneously; ticket
prices depend on how many you see).
The museum is at the far end of Yebisu
Garden Place, on the right side if you're
coming from Ebisu Station.

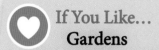

If You Like...
Gardens

If you like the greenery on offer in the
Hama-Rikyū Onshi-teien (p64), you might
like these gardens:

1 IMPERIAL PALACE EAST GARDEN
(東御苑; Kōkyo Higashi-gyoen; Map p68;
http://sankan.kunaicho.go.jp; 1 Chiyoda, Chiyoda-
ku; ◷9am-4pm Nov-Feb, to 4.30pm Mar–mid-Apr,
Sep & Oct, to 5pm mid-Apr–Aug, closed Mon & Fri
year-round; ⑤Chiyoda line to Ōtemachi, exit C13b
or C10) Crafted from part of the original castle
compound, these lovely free gardens allow you to
get close-up views of the massive stones used to
build the castle walls, and even climb the ruins of
one of the keeps, off the upper lawn. The number of
visitors at any one time is limited, so it never feels
crowded. Most people enter through Ōte-mon, the
closest gate to Tokyo Station, and once the principal
entrance to Edo Castle.

2 SHINJUKU-GYOEN
(新宿御苑; Map p90; ☎3350-0151; www.
env.go.jp/garden/shinjukugyoen; 11 Naito-chō,
Shinjuku-ku; adult/child ¥200/50; ◷9am-4.30pm
Tue-Sun; ⑤Marunouchi line to Shinjuku-gyoenmae,
exit 1) Though Shinjuku-gyoen was designed as an
imperial retreat (completed 1906), it's now a park
for everyone. The wide lawns make it a favourite for
urbanites in need of a quick escape from the hurly-
burly of city life. Don't miss the recently renovated
greenhouse, with its giant lily pads and perfectly
formed orchids, and the cherry blossoms in spring.

3 KIYOSUMI-TEIEN
(清澄庭園; Map p62; http://teien.tokyo-
park.or.jp/en/kiyosumi/index.html; 3-3-9 Kiyosumi,
Kōtō-ku; adult/child ¥150/free; ◷9am-5pm;
⑤Ōedo line to Kiyosumi-Shirakawa, exit A3)
Kiyosumi-teien started out in 1721 as the villa of
a *daimyō* (domain lord; regional lord under the
shōguns). After the villa was destroyed in the
1923 earthquake, Iwasaki Yatarō, founder of the
Mitsubishi Corporation, purchased the property.
He used company ships to transport prize
stones here from all over Japan, which are set
around a pond ringed with Japanese black pine,
hydrangeas and Taiwanese cherry trees.

Roppongi & Around

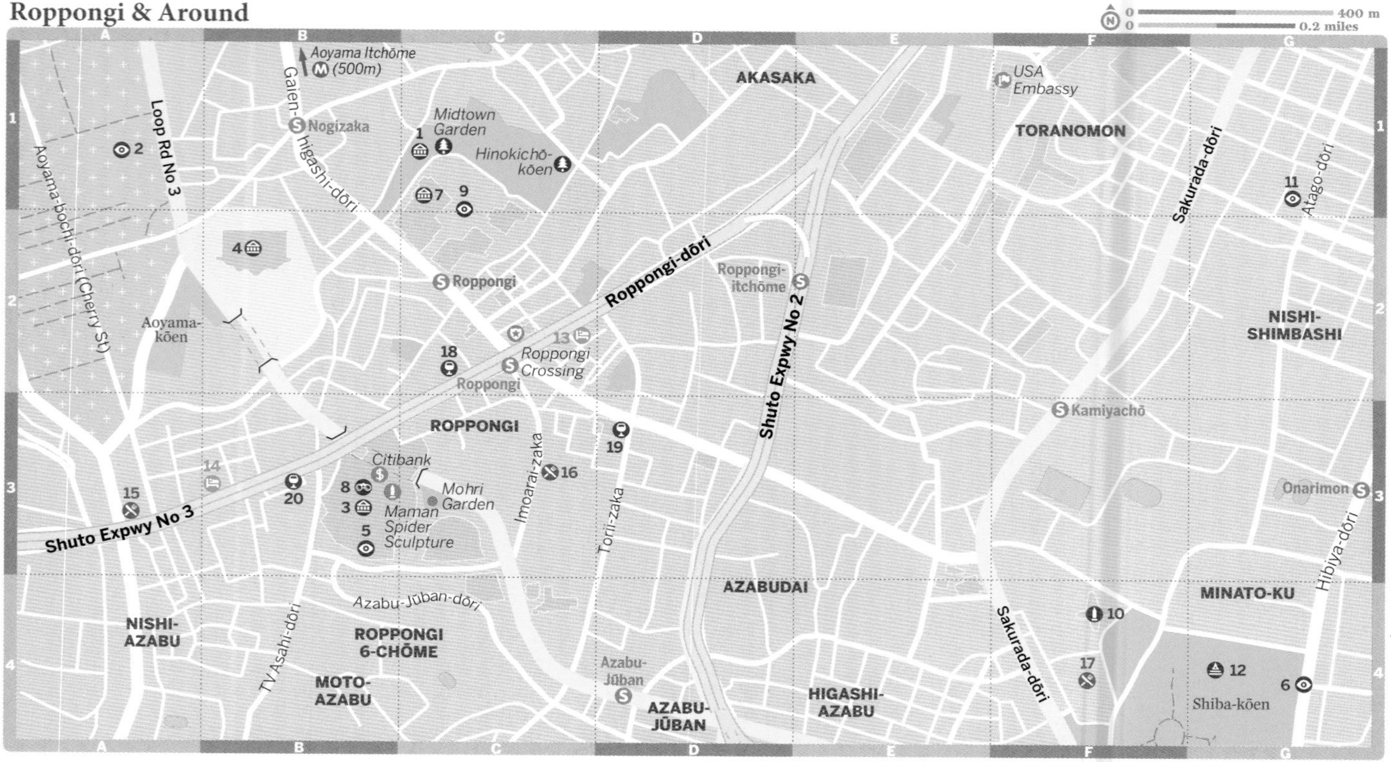

N

0   400 m
0   0.2 miles

Loop Rd No 3

2

Aoyama Itchōme
M (500m)

Nogizaka S
Gaien-higashi-dōri

Aoyama-bochi-dōri (Cherry St)

Aoyama-kōen

4

Midtown
Garden

1
7
9
Hinokichō
Kōen

Roppongi S

Roppongi-dōri

AKASAKA

TORANOMON

USA
Embassy

Sakurada-dōri

Atago-dōri

11

NISHI-
SHIMBASHI

Onarimon S
Hibiya-dōri

MINATO-KU

6

12

Shiba-kōen

10

17

Sakurada-dōri

Kamiyachō S

Roppongi-
itchōme S

Shuto Expwy No 2

HIGASHI-
AZABU

AZABUDAI

AZABU-
JŪBAN

Azabu-
Jūban S

19

16

Tori-zaka

Imoarai-zaka

13
18
Roppongi
Crossing
Roppongi S

ROPPONGI

Mohri
Garden
Maman
Spider
Sculpture

Citibank
8
3
5

20

14

15

Shuto Expwy No 3

NISHI-
AZABU

MOTO-
AZABU

ROPPONGI
6-CHŌME

Azabu-jūban-dōri

TV Asahi-dōri

Roppongi & Around

Beer Museum Yebisu   Museum

(エビスビール記念館; Map p78; ☎5423-7255; www.sapporoholdings.jp/english/guide/yebisu; 4-20-1 Ebisu, Shibuya-ku; ⊗11am-7pm Tue-Sun; ⚇JR Yamanote line to Ebisu, east exit) **FREE** Photos, vintage bottles and posters document the rise of Yebisu, and beer in general, in Japan at this small museum located where the actual Yebisu brewery stood until 1988. At the 'tasting salon' you can sample four kinds of Yebisu beer (¥400 each). It's behind the Mitsukoshi department store at Yebisu Garden Place.

Tokyo Metropolitan Teien Art Museum   Museum

(東京都庭園美術館; Map p78; www.teien-art-museum.ne.jp; 5-21-9 Shirokanedai, Minato-ku; admission varies; ⊗10am-6pm, closed 2nd & 4th Wed each month; ⚇JR Yamanote line to Meguro, east exit) Although the Teien museum hosts regular art exhibitions – usually of decorative arts – its appeal lies principally in the building itself: it's an art-deco structure, a former princely estate built in 1933, designed by French architect Henri Rapin.

The museum reopened in late 2014 after a lengthy renovation and now includes a modern annex designed by artist Sugimoto Hiroshi.

SHIBUYA 渋谷

Shibuya is the centre of the city's teen culture, and its brightly dressed, bleached-hair denizens aren't shy about living loud. If a local friend asks to meet

Shibuya 109 (p116)
KOKOROIMAGES.COM/GETTY IMAGES ©

you at Shibuya, you'll probably gather at **Hachikō** (ハチ公) plaza in front of the station. The always-buzzing **Shibuya Crossing** leads from the station to the pedestrian street **Centre-gai**, Shibuya's main artery.

On the east side of the station, the 34-floor **Shibuya Hikarie** building, which opened in 2012, is full of upmarket shops and restaurants that threaten to attract grown-up sophisticates to Shibuya.

Shibuya Crossing   Street

(渋谷スクランブル交差点; Shibuya Scramble; Map p84; ⊞JR Yamanote line to Shibuya, Hachikō exit) Rumoured to be the world's busiest, this intersection in front of Shibuya Station is famously known as 'The Scramble'. It's an awesome spectacle of giant video screens and neon, guaranteed to give you a 'Wow – I'm in Tokyo!' feeling. People – sometimes more than a thousand with every light change – come from all directions at once, yet still manage to dodge each other with a practiced, nonchalant agility.

Hachikō Statue   Statue

(ハチ公像; Map p84; Hachikō Plaza; ⊞JR Yamanote line to Shibuya, Hachikō exit) Come meet Tokyo's most famous pooch, Hachikō. This Akita dog came to Shibuya Station everyday to meet his master, a professor, returning from work. The professor died in 1925, but Hachikō kept coming to the station until his own death 10 years later. The story became legend and a small statue was erected in the dog's memory in front of Shibuya Station.

Shibuya Center-gai   Street

(渋谷センター街; Shibuya Sentā-gai; Map p84; ⊞JR Yamanote line to Shibuya, Hachikō exit) Shibuya's main drag is closed to cars and choc-a-block with fast-food joints and high-street fashion shops. At night, lit bright as day, with a dozen competing soundtracks (coming from who knows where), wares spilling onto the streets, shady touts in sunglasses, and strutting teens, it feels like a block party – or Tokyo's version of a classic Asian night market.

Shibuya Crossing

Detour:
Ghibli Museum

Master animator Miyazaki Hayao, whose Studio Ghibli (pronounced 'jiburi') produced *Princess Mononoke* and *Spirited Away*, designed this museum himself. Fans will enjoy the original sketches; kids, even if they're not familiar with the movies, will fall in love with the fairy-tale atmosphere and the climbable Cat Bus. Don't miss the original 20-minute animated short playing on the 1st floor.

Getting to the **Ghibli Museum** (ジブリ美術館; www.ghibli-museum.jp; 1-1-83 Shimo-Renjaku, Mitaka-shi; adult ¥1000, child ¥100-700; ⏱10am-6pm Wed-Mon; 🚃JR Chūō line to Mitaka, south exit) is all part of the adventure. Tickets must be purchased in advance, and you must also choose the exact time and date of your visit. You can do this online through a travel agent before you arrive in Japan (the easy option) or from a kiosk at any Lawson convenience store in Tokyo (the difficult option, as it will require some Japanese-language ability to navigate the ticket machine). Both options are explained in detail on the website, where you will also find a useful map.

A minibus (return trip/one way ¥300/200) leaves for the museum approximately every 20 minutes from the south exit of Mitaka Station (bus stop 9). Alternatively, you can walk there in about 15 minutes by following the canal and turning right when you reach a park. The museum is actually on the western edge of Inokashira-kōen and you can walk there through the park from Kichijōji Station in about 30 minutes.

Myth of Tomorrow   Public Art
(明日の神話; Asu no Shinwa; Map p84; 🚃JR Yamanote line to Shibuya, Hachikō exit) Okamoto Tarō's mural, *Myth of Tomorrow* (1967), was commissioned by a Mexican luxury hotel but went missing two years later. It finally turned up in 2003 and, in 2008, the haunting 30-metre-long work, which depicts the atomic bomb exploding over Hiroshima, was installed inside Shibuya Station. It's on the 2nd floor, on the way to the Inokashira line.

Shibuya Hikarie   Building
(渋谷ヒカリエ; Map p84; 📞5468-5892; www.hikarie.jp; 2-21-1 Shibuya, Shibuya-ku; 🚃JR Yamanote line to Shibuya, east exit) This glistening 34-storey tower, which opened in 2012, is just the first step in what promises to be a massive redesign of Shibuya. There are shops on the lower floors and a couple of worthwhile attractions on the 8th floor, including the design museum **d47 Museum** (www.hikarie8.com/d47museum; ⏱11am-8pm).

HARAJUKU & AROUND 原宿

Harajuku is Tokyo's catwalk, where the city's fashionistas come to shop and show-off. But not everything here is about frip and frivolity: there's also Tokyo's signature Shintō shrine, Meiji-jingū, plus excellent art museums and contemporary architecture.

Yoyogi-kōen   Park
(代々木公園; Map p62; 🚃JR Yamanote line to Harajuku, Omote-sandō exit) If it's a sunny and warm weekend afternoon you can count on there being a crowd lazing around the large grassy expanse that is Yoyogi-kōen. You can also usually find revellers and noisemakers of all stripes, from hula-hoopers to African drum circles to a group of retro greasers dancing around a boom box. It's an excellent place for a picnic and probably the only place in the city where you can reasonably toss a frisbee without fear of hitting someone.

RUDI VAN STARREX/GETTY IMAGES ©

Don't Miss
Meiji-jingū

Tokyo's grandest Shintō shrine is dedicated to the Emperor Meiji and Empress Shōken. Constructed in 1920, the shrine was destroyed in WWII air raids and rebuilt in 1958; however, unlike so many of Japan's postwar reconstructions, Meiji-jingū has an authentic feel. The towering 12m wooden *torii* gate that marks the entrance was created from a 1500-year-old Taiwanese cypress.

The shrine itself occupies only a small fraction of the sprawling forested grounds. **Meiji-jingū Gyoen** (明治神宮御苑; Inner Garden; Map p76; admission ¥500; ⌚9am-4.30pm, to 4pm Nov-Feb; 🚉JR Yamanote line to Harajuku, Omote-Sandō exit) was once imperial land; the Meiji emperor himself designed the iris garden here to please the empress. The garden is most impressive when the irises bloom in June.

NEED TO KNOW

明治神宮; Map p76; www.meijijingu.or.jp; 1-1 Yoyogi Kamizono-chō, Shibuya-ku; ⌚dawn-dusk; 🚉JR Yamanote line to Harajuku, Omote-sandō exit

Takeshita-dōri   Street
(竹下通り; Map p88; 🚉JR Yamanote line to Harajuku, Takeshita exit) This is Tokyo's famous teen-fashion bazaar, where trendy duds sit alongside the trappings of various fashion subcultures (colourful tutus for the *decora*; Victorian dresses for the Gothic Lolitas). Be warned: this pedestrian alley is a pilgrimage site for

teens from all over Japan, which means it can get packed.

Ukiyo-e Ōta Memorial Museum of Art   Museum
(浮世絵太田記念美術館; Map p88; 📞3403-0880; www.ukiyoe-ota-muse.jp; 1-10-10 Jingūmae, Shibuya-ku; adult ¥700-1000, child free; ⌚10.30am-5.30pm Tue-Sun, closed 27th to end of month; 🚉JR Yamanote line to Harajuku,

Tokyo for Children

In many ways, Tokyo is a parent's dream: hyperclean, safe and with every mod-con. The downside is that most of the top attractions aren't that appealing to little ones.

Older kids and teens, however, should get a kick out of Tokyo's pop culture and neon streetscapes. **Shibuya** and **Harajuku** in particular are packed with the shops, restaurants and arcades that local teens love.

Odaiba is a popular destination for local families. Here, kids can meet ASIMO the humanoid robot at the **National Museum of Emerging Science & Innovation** (p89) and go wild at virtual-reality arcade **Tokyo Joypolis** (p91).

Tokyo Disney Resort (p91) has all the classic rides and is another top draw. There's also the **Ghibli Museum** (p75), which honours Japan's own animation genius, Miyazaki Hayao *(Princess Mononoke, Spirited Away)*. If your kids have caught the Japanese character bug, reward good behaviour with a trip to toy emporium **KiddyLand** (p117).

Japanese kids are wild about **trains** – chances are yours will be, too. The southern terrace at Shinjuku Station overlooks the multiple tracks that feed the world's busiest train station. Another treat is a ride on the driverless Yurikamome Line that weaves in between skyscrapers.

Omote-sandō exit) This small, peaceful museum houses the excellent *ukiyo-e* (woodblock prints) collection of Ōta Seizo, the former head of the Toho Life Insurance Company. Seasonal, thematic exhibitions are easily digested in an hour and usually include a few works by masters such as Hokusai and Hiroshige.

Omote-sandō   Street
(表参道; Map p88; S Ginza line to Omote-sandō, exits A3 & B4, R JR Yamanote line to Harajuku, Omote-sandō exit) This regal boulevard was originally designed as the official approach to Meiji-jingū. Now it's a fashionable strip lined with high-end boutiques. Those designer shops come in designer buildings, which means Omote-sandō is also one of the best places in the city to see contemporary architecture.

Nezu Museum   Museum
(根津美術館; Map p88; ☎ 3400-2536; www. nezu-muse.or.jp; 6-5-1 Minami-Aoyama, Minato-ku; adult/student/child ¥1000/800/free, special exhibitions ¥200 extra; ⏰ 10am-5pm Tue-Sun; S Ginza line to Omote-sandō, exit A5) Nezu Museum offers a striking blend of old and new: a renowned collection of Japanese,

Chinese and Korean antiquities in a gallery space designed by contemporary architect Kuma Kengo. Select items from the extensive collection are displayed in seasonal exhibitions.

SHINJUKU 新宿

Here in Shinjuku, much of what makes Tokyo tick is crammed into one busy district: upscale department stores, anachronistic shanty bars, buttoned-up government offices, swarming crowds, streetside video screens, hostess clubs, hidden shrines and soaring skyscrapers.

At the heart of Shinjuku is the sprawling train station, which acts as a nexus for over three million commuters each day, making it one of the busiest in the world. The west side of the station (Nishi-Shinjuku) is a perfectly planned expanse of gridded streets and soaring corporate towers. Tokyo's municipal government moved here in 1991 from Yūrakuchō.

The east side of Shinjuku is one of Tokyo's largest – and liveliest – entertainment districts.

Ebisu & Meguro

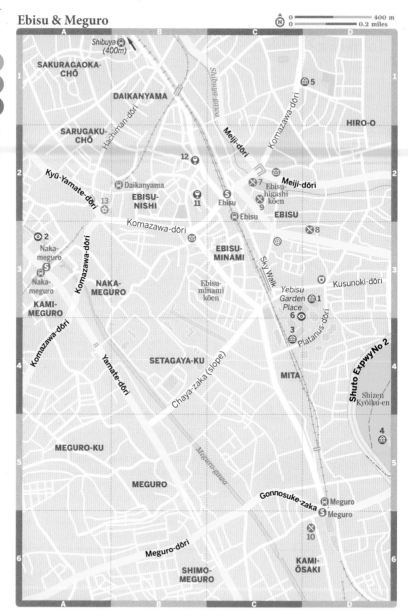

Tokyo Metropolitan Government Offices
Building

(東京都庁; Tokyo Tochō; Map p90; www.metro. tokyo.jp/ENGLISH/TMG/observat.htm; 2-8-1 Nishi-Shinjuku, Shinjuku-ku; ⏰observatories 9.30am-11pm; **S** Ōedo line to Tochōmae, exit A4) **FREE** Tokyo's seat of power, designed by Tange Kenzō, looms large and looks somewhat like a pixelated cathedral. Take an elevator from the ground floor of Building 1 to one of the twin 202m-high observatories for panoramic views over

Ebisu & Meguro

the never-ending cityscape (the views are virtually the same from either tower). On a clear day, look west for a glimpse of Mt Fuji.

Shinjuku I-Land   Public Art

(新宿アイランド; Map p90; 6-5-1 Nishi-Shinjuku, Shinjuku-ku; Ⓢ Marunouchi line to Nishi-Shinjuku) An otherwise ordinary office complex, Shinjuku I-Land (1995) is home to more than a dozen public artworks, including one of Robert Indiana's *Love* sculptures and two *Tokyo Brushstroke* sculptures by Roy Lichtenstein. The courtyard, with stonework by Giulio Paolini and a dozen restaurants, makes for an attractive lunch or coffee stop.

Kabukichō   Neighbourhood

(歌舞伎町; Map p90; ℞ JR Yamanote line to Shinjuku, east exit) Tokyo's most notorious red-light district, which covers several blocks north of Yasukuni-dōri, was famously named for a kabuki theatre that was never built. Instead you'll find an urban theatre of a different sort playing out in the neighbourhood's soaplands (bathhouses just shy of antiprostitution laws), peep shows, cabarets, love hotels and fetish bars. It's generally safe to walk through, though men and women both may attract unwanted attention – best not to go alone.

KŌRAKUEN & AROUND 後楽園

Kōrakuen and its surrounds formed part of the Edo-era Yamanote district of villas belonging to the governing elite. A short walk from Iidabashi Station is the neighbourhood of Kagurazaka, an atmospheric former geisha district.

Koishikawa Kōrakuen   Gardens

(小石川後楽園; Map p62; 1-6-6 Kōraku, Bunkyō-ku; adult/child ¥300/free; ⊙9am-5pm; ℞ JR Sōbu line to Iidabashi, exit C3) Established in the mid-17th century as the property of the Tokugawa clan, this formal strolling garden incorporates elements of Chinese and Japanese landscaping. It's among Tokyo's most attractive gardens, although nowadays the *shakkei* (borrowed scenery) also includes the other-worldly Tokyo Dome. Don't miss the Engetsu-kyō (Full-Moon Bridge), which dates from the early Edo period; the name will make sense when you see it.

Yasukuni-jinja   Shinto Shrine

(靖国神社; Map p62; ☎3261-8326; www.yasukuni.or.jp; 3-1-1 Kudan-kita, Chiyoda-ku; ⊙6am-5pm; Ⓢ Hanzōmon line to Kudanshita, exit 1) Literally 'For the Peace of the Country Shrine', Yasukuni is the memorial shrine to Japan's war dead, around 2.5 million souls. Completed in 1869, it has unusual *torii* gates made of steel and bronze. It is also incredibly controversial: in 1979 14 class-A war criminals, including WWII general Hideki Tōjō, were enshrined here.

Yūshū-kan   Museum

(遊就館; Map p62; ☎3261-8326; www.yasukuni.or.jp/english/yushukan; 3-1-1 Kudankita, Chiyoda-ku; adult/student ¥800/500; ⊙9am-4pm; Ⓢ Hanzōmon line to Kudanshita, exit 1) Most history museums in Japan skirt the issue of war or focus on the burden of the common people. Not so here: Yūshū-kan begins with Japan's samurai tradition and ends with its defeat in WWII. It is unapologetic and has been known to boil the blood of some visitors with its particular view of history.

AKIHABARA 秋葉原

'Akiba' is the cenure of Tokyo's *otaku* (geek) subculture. But you don't have to

obsess about manga or anime to enjoy this quirky neighbourhood. It's equal parts sensory overload and cultural mind-bender.

Pick up a map at **Tokyo Anime Center Akiba Info** (東京アニメセンターAkiba Info; Map p62; www.animecenter.jp; 2nd fl, Akihabara UDX Bldg, 4-14-1 Soto-Kanda, Chiyoda-ku; ⏰11am-7pm Tue-Sun; 🚃JR Yamanote line to Akihabara, Electric Town exit); the helpful staff here speak English.

Akihabara Electric Town
Neighbourhood

(秋葉原電気街; Akihabara Denki-Gai; Map p62; 🚃JR Yamanote line to Akihabara, Electric Town exit) Post WWII, Akihabara Station became synonymous with a black market for radio parts and other electronics. After the 1960s and '70s when the district was *the* place to hunt for bargains on new and used electronics, Akihabara saw its top shopping mantle increasingly usurped by discount stores elsewhere in the city. It has long since bounced back by reinventing itself as the centre of the *otaku* (geek)

universe, catching J-pop culture fans in its gravitational pull.

UENO 上野

Ueno is the cultural heart of Tokyo and has been the city's top draw for centuries. At the centre of the neighbourhood is a sprawling park, Ueno-kōen, with the city's greatest concentration of museums, including the Tokyo National Museum.

Tokyo National Museum
Museum

(東京国立博物館; Tokyo Kokuritsu Hakubutsukan; Map p94; 📞3822-1111; www.tnm.jp; 13-9 Ueno-kōen, Taitō-ku; adult/student/child & senior ¥620/¥410/free; ⏰9.30am-5pm Tue-Thu year round, to 8pm Fri, to 6pm Sat & Sun (Mar-Dec); 🚃JR Yamanote line to Ueno, Ueno-kōen exit) If you visit only one museum in Tokyo, make it this one. The Tokyo National Museum holds the world's largest collection of Japanese art, including ancient pottery, Buddhist sculptures, samurai swords, colourful *ukiyo-e* (woodblock prints), gorgeous kimonos and much, much more. Visitors with only a couple of hours to

spare should hone in on the Honkan (Main Gallery) and the enchanting Gallery of Hōryū-ji Treasures, which displays masks, scrolls and gilt Buddhas from Hōryū-ji (in Nara Prefecture, dating from 607).

Ueno-kōen   Park

(上野公園; Map p94; ⏰5am-11pm; 🚃JR Yamanote line to Ueno, Ueno-kōen & Shinobazu exits) Sprawling Ueno-kōen has wooded pathways that wind past centuries-old temples and shrines – even a zoo. At the southern tip is a large pond, Shinobazu-ike, choked with lily pads. Stroll down the causeway to Benten-dō, a temple dedicated to Benzaiten (the water goddess). From here you can get a good look at the birds and botany that thrive in the park; you can also rent row boats (per hour ¥600). Navigating the park is easy, thanks to large maps in English.

Ueno Tōshō-gū   Shinto Shrine

(上野東照宮; Map p94; www.uenotoshogu. com; 9-88 Ueno-kōen, Taitō-ku; admission ¥500; ⏰9.30am-4.30pm; 🚃JR Yamanote line to Ueno, Shinobazu exit) Like its counterpart in Nikkō (p132), this shrine inside Ueno-kōen was built in honour of Tokugawa Ieyasu, the warlord who unified Japan. Resplendent in gold leaf and ornate details, it dates from 1651 (though it recently underwent a touch-up). You can get a pretty good look from outside the gate, if you want to skip the admission fee.

Kiyōmizu
Kannon-dō   Buddhist Temple

(清水観音堂; Map p94; 1-29 Ueno-kōen, Taitō-ku; ⏰9am-4pm; 🚃JR Yamanote line to Ueno, Shinobazu exit) Ueno-kōen's Kiyōmizu Kannon-dō is one of Tokyo's oldest structures: established in 1631 and in its present position since 1698, it has sur-vived every disaster come its way. It's a miniature of the famous Kiyomizu-dera in Kyoto and is a pilgrimage site for women hoping to conceive.

Tokyo National Museum

HISTORIC HIGHLIGHTS

It would be a challenge to take in everything the sprawling Tokyo National Museum has to offer in a day. Fortunately, the Honkan (Main Gallery) is designed to give visitors a crash course in Japanese art history from the Jōmon era (13,000–300 BC) to the Edo era (AD 1603–1868). The works on display here are rotated regularly, to protect fragile ones and to create seasonal exhibitions – you're always guaranteed to see something new.

Buy your ticket from outside the main gate then head straight to the Honkan with its sloping tile roof. Stow your coat in a locker and take the central staircase up to the 2nd floor, where the exhibitions are arranged chronologically. Allow two hours for this tour of the highlights.

The first room on your right starts from the beginning with **ancient Japanese art ❶**. Be sure to pick up a copy of the brochure Highlights of Japanese Art at the entrance.

Continue to the **National Treasure Gallery ❷**. 'National Treasure' is the highest distinction awarded to a work of art in Japan. Keep an eye out for more National Treasures, labelled in red, on display in other rooms throughout the museum.

Moving on, stop to admire the **art of the Imperial court ❸**, the **samurai armour and swords ❹** and the **ukiyo-e and kimono ❺**.

Next, take the stairs down to the 1st floor, where each room is dedicated to a different craft, such as lacquerware or ceramics. Don't miss the excellent examples of **religious sculpture ❻** and **folk art ❼**.

Finish your visit with a look inside the enchanting **Gallery of Hōryū-ji Treasures ❽**.

Ukiyo-e & Kimono (Room 10)
Chic silken kimono and lushly coloured *ukiyo-e* (woodblock prints) are two icons of the Edo era (AD 1603–1868) *ukiyo* – the 'floating world', or world of fleeting beauty and pleasure.

Japanese Sculpture (Room 11)
Many of Japan's most famous sculptures, religious in nature, are locked away in temple reliquaries. This is a rare chance to see them up close.

MUSEUM GARDEN

Don't miss the garden if you visit during the few weeks it's open to the public in spring and autumn.

Heiseikan & Japanese Archaeology Gallery

Research & Information Centre

Hyōkeikan

Kuro-mon

Main Gate

Gallery of Hōryū-ji Treasures
Surround yourself with miniature gilt Buddhas from Hōryū-ji, said to be one of Japan's oldest Buddhist temples, founded in 607. Don't miss the graceful Pitcher with Dragon Head, a National Treasure.

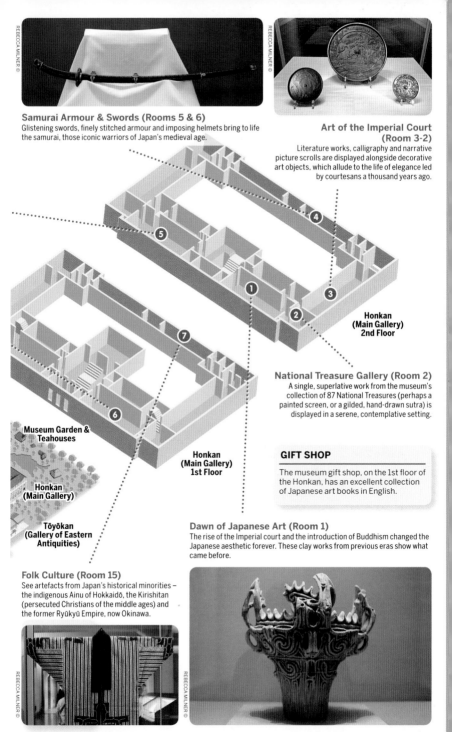

Samurai Armour & Swords (Rooms 5 & 6)
Glistening swords, finely stitched armour and imposing helmets bring to life the samurai, those iconic warriors of Japan's medieval age.

Art of the Imperial Court (Room 3-2)
Literature works, calligraphy and narrative picture scrolls are displayed alongside decorative art objects, which allude to the life of elegance led by courtesans a thousand years ago.

Honkan (Main Gallery) 2nd Floor

National Treasure Gallery (Room 2)
A single, superlative work from the museum's collection of 87 National Treasures (perhaps a painted screen, or a gilded, hand-drawn sutra) is displayed in a serene, contemplative setting.

Museum Garden & Teahouses

Honkan (Main Gallery) 1st Floor

Honkan (Main Gallery)

Tōyōkan (Gallery of Eastern Antiquities)

GIFT SHOP
The museum gift shop, on the 1st floor of the Honkan, has an excellent collection of Japanese art books in English.

Dawn of Japanese Art (Room 1)
The rise of the Imperial court and the introduction of Buddhism changed the Japanese aesthetic forever. These clay works from previous eras show what came before.

Folk Culture (Room 15)
See artefacts from Japan's historical minorities – the indigenous Ainu of Hokkaidō, the Kirishitan (persecuted Christians of the middle ages) and the former Ryūkyū Empire, now Okinawa.

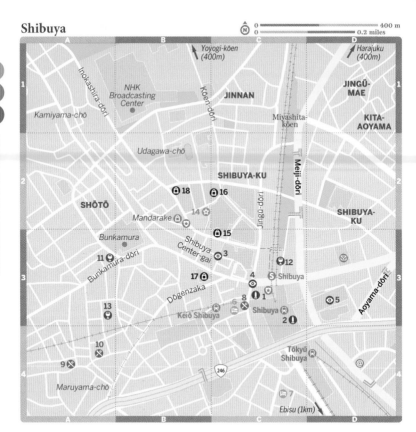

Shibuya

Ueno Zoo
Zoo

(上野動物園; Ueno Dōbutsu-en; Map p94; www.tokyo-zoo.net; 9-83 Ueno-kōen, Taitō-ku; adult/child ¥600/free; ⊙9.30am-5pm Tue-Sun; ⓡJR Yamanote line to Ueno, Ueno-kōen exit) Japan's oldest zoo is home to animals from around the globe, but the biggest attractions are two giant pandas that arrived from China in 2011 – Rī Rī and Shin Shin. There's also a whole area devoted to lemurs, which makes sense given Tokyoites' love of all things cute.

National Science Museum
Museum

(国立科学博物館; Kokuritsu Kagaku Hakubutsukan; Map p94; www.kahaku.go.jp; 7-20 Ueno-kōen, Taitō-ku; adult/child ¥600/free; ⊙9am-5pm Tue-Thu, Sat & Sun, to 8pm Fri; ⓡJR Yamanote line to Ueno, Ueno-kōen exit) The Japan Gallery here showcases the rich and varied wildlife of the Japanese archipelago, from the bears of Hokkaido to the giant beetles of Okinawa. Elsewhere in the museum: a rocket launcher, a giant squid, an Edo-era mummy, and a digital seismograph that charts earthquakes in real time. There's English signage throughout, plus an English-language audio guide (¥300).

National Museum of Western Art
Museum

(国立西洋美術館; Kokuritsu Seiyō Bijutsukan; Map p94; www.nmwa.go.jp; 7-7 Ueno-kōen, Taitō-ku; adult/student ¥420/130, 2nd & 4th Sat free; ⊙9.30am-5.30pm Tue-Thu, Sat & Sun, to 8pm Fri; ⓡJR Yamanote line to Ueno, Ueno-kōen exit) The permanent collection here runs from medieval Madonna and child images to 20th-century abstract expressionism, but is strongest in French impressionism, including a whole gallery of Monet.

Shibuya

The main building was designed by Le Corbusier in the late 1950s and is now on Unesco's World Heritage List.

Shitamachi Museum   Museum
(下町風俗資料館; Map p94; ☎3823-7451; www.taitocity.net/taito/shitamachi; 2-1 Ueno-kōen, Taitō-ku; adult/child ¥300/100; ⏰9.30am-4.30pm Tue-Sun; 🚉JR Yamanote line to Ueno, Shinobazu exit) This museum re-creates life in the plebeian quarters of Tokyo during the Meiji and Taishō periods (1868–1926), before the city was twice destroyed by the Great Kanto Earthquake and WWII. There are old tenement houses and shops that you can enter.

Ameya-yokochō   Market
(アメヤ横町; Map p94; 4 Ueno, Taitō-ku; 🚉JR Yamanote line to Ueno, Ueno-kōen exit) Step into this alley paralleling the JR Yamanote line tracks, and ritzy, glitzy Tokyo feels like a distant memory. This open-air market got its start as a black market, post WWII, when American goods were sold here. Today, it's filled with vendors selling everything from fresh seafood and exotic cooking spices to jeans and sneakers.

ASAKUSA & SUMIDA-GAWA
浅草・隅田川

Asakusa, with its ancient temple, Sensō-ji, retains a lot of that old Shitamachi spirit. At the turn of the last century, the neighbourhood was a pleasure district likened to Montmartre in Paris, though hardly any of that old bawdiness remains today.

The neighbourhoods across the Sumida-gawa, too, look much like they have for decades, having experienced little of the development seen elsewhere in the city – save for Tokyo Sky Tree. Given its location, among low-lying residential buildings and unburied electrical wires, Tokyo's newest landmark looks as though it were dropped here by aliens.

Ryōgoku, also east of the Sumida-gawa, is home to the national sumō stadium Kokugikan – you'll often see chubby wrestlers waddling around Ryōguku Station.

Super Dry Hall   Architecture
(フラムドール; Flamme d'Or; Map p96; 1-23-1 Azuma-bashi, Sumida-ku; 🅂Ginza line to Asakusa, exit 4) Designed by Philippe Starck and completed in 1989, the Asahi Beer headquarters, with its telltale golden plume, is a Tokyo landmark. The golden bit, which weighs more than 300 tonnes, is open to interpretation: Asahi likes to think it is the foam to the building's beer mug. Locals call it the 'golden turd'.

Mokuhankan   Printmaking
(木版館; Map p96; ☎070-5011-1418; http://mokuhankan.com/parties; 2nd fl, 1-41-8 Asakusa, Taitō-ku; ¥2000 per person; ⏰10am-5.30pm; 🚉Tsukuba Express to Asakusa, exit 5) Try your hand at making ukiyo-e (woodblock prints) at this studio run by expat David Bull. Hour-long 'print parties' take place daily; sign up online. There's a shop here too, where you can see Bull and Jed Henry's humorous Ukiyo-e Heroes series – prints featuring video-game characters in traditional settings.

TTSTUDIO/SHUTTERSTOCK ©

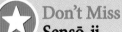 Don't Miss
Sensō-ji

Tokyo's most visited temple enshrines a golden image of Kannon (the Buddhist Goddess of Mercy), which, according to legend, was miraculously pulled out of the nearby Sumida-gawa by two fishermen in AD 628. The image has remained on the spot ever since; the present structure dates from 1958. Entrance to the temple complex is via the fantastic, red **Kaminari-mon** (雷門; Thunder Gate).

Through the gate, protected by Fūjin (the god of wind) and Raijin (the god of thunder), is **Nakamise-dōri**, the temple precinct's shopping street. Here everything from tourist trinkets to genuine Edo-style crafts is sold. At the end of Nakamise-dōri is the temple itself, and to your left you'll spot the 55m **Five-storey Pagoda** (五重塔). It's a 1973 reconstruction of a pagoda built by Tokugawa Iemitsu and is even more picturesque at night, all lit up.

It's a mystery as to whether or not the ancient image of Kannon actually exists, as it's not on public display. This doesn't stop a steady stream of worshippers from visiting. In front of the temple is a large incense cauldron: the smoke is said to bestow health and you'll see people rubbing it into their bodies through their clothes.

At the eastern edge of the temple complex is **Asakusa-jinja** (浅草神社), a shrine built in honour of the brothers who discovered the Kannon statue that inspired the construction of Sensō-ji. (Historically, Japan's two religions, Buddhism and Shintō were intertwined and it was not uncommon for temples to include shrines and vice versa). The current building, painted a deep shade of red, dates to 1649 and is a rare example of early-Edo architecture. It's also the epicentre of one of Tokyo's most important festivals, May's Sanja Matsuri.

NEED TO KNOW

浅草寺; Map p96; ☎03-3842-0181; www.senso-ji.jp; 2-3-1 Asakusa, Taitō-ku; ⏱24hr; Ⓢ Ginza line to Asakusa, exit 1

Tokyo Sky Tree   Tower

(東京スカイツリー; Map p96; www.tokyo-skytree.jp; 1-1-2 Oshiage, Sumida-ku; admission 350m/450m observation decks ¥2060/3090; ⏱8am-10pm; Ⓢ Hanzōmon line to Oshiage, Sky Tree exit) Tokyo Sky Tree opened in May 2012 as the world's tallest 'free-standing tower' at 634m. Its silvery exterior of steel mesh morphs from a triangle at the base to a circle at 300m. There are two observation decks, at 350m and 450m. You can see more stuff during daylight hours – at peak visibility you can see up to 100km away, all the way to Mt Fuji – but it is at night that Tokyo appears truly beautiful.

Edo-Tokyo Museum   Museum

(江戸東京博物館; Map p62; ☎3626-9974; www.edo-tokyo-museum.or.jp; 1-4-1 Yokoami, Sumida-ku; adult/child ¥600/free; ⏱9.30am-5.30pm Tue-Sun, to 7.30pm Sat; Ⓡ JR Sōbu line to Ryōgoku, west exit) This history museum does an excellent job laying out Tokyo's miraculous transformation from feudal city to modern capital, through city models, miniatures of real buildings, reproductions of old maps and ukiyo-e (woodblock prints). Don't miss the life-sized replica of the original Nihonbashi. There is English signage throughout and there's also a free audio guide available (¥1000 deposit).

Museum of Contemporary Art, Tokyo (MOT)   Museum

(東京都現代美術館; Map p62; www.mot-art-museum.jp; 4-1-1 Miyoshi, Kōtō-ku; adult/child ¥500/free; ⏱10am-6pm Tue-Sun; Ⓢ Ōedo line to Kiyosumi-Shirakawa, exit B2) For a primer in the major movements of post-WWII Japanese art, a visit to the permanent collection gallery here should do the trick. Temporary exhibitions, on changing subjects (including fashion, architecture, and design) cost extra. The building's stone, steel and wood architecture by Yanagisawa Takahiko is a work of art in its own right. The museum is on the edge of Kiba-kōen, a well-signposted 10-minute walk from the subway station.

If You Like...
Museums

If you enjoyed the artistic offerings at the Tokyo National Museum, you'll probably enjoy a visit to the following museums:

1 JAPANESE SWORD MUSEUM

(刀剣博物館; Map p62; www.touken.or.jp; 4-25-10 Yoyogi, Shibuya-ku; adult/student/child ¥600/300/free; ⏱9am-4.30pm Tue-Sun; Ⓡ Keiō New line to Hatsudai, east exit) In 1948, after American forces returned the katana (Japanese swords) they'd confiscated during the postwar occupation, the national Ministry of Education established a society, and this museum, to preserve the feudal art of Japanese sword-making. There are dozens of swords on display here, with English explanations throughout.

2 YAMATANE MUSEUM OF ART

(山種美術館; Map p78; ☎5777-8600; www.yamatane-museum.or.jp; 3-12-36 Hiroo, Shibuya-ku; adult/student/child ¥1000/800/free, special exhibits extra; ⏱10am-5pm Tue-Sun; Ⓡ JR Yamanote line to Ebisu, west exit) When Western ideas entered Japan following the Meiji Restoration (1868), many artists set out to master oil and canvas. Others poured new energy into nihonga – Japanese style painting, usually done with mineral pigments on silk or paper – and the masters are represented here. From the collection of 1800 works, a small number are displayed in thematic exhibitions.

3 CRAFTS GALLERY

(東京国立近代美術館 工芸館; Map p62; www.momat.go.jp/english; 1 Kitanomaru-kōen, Chiyoda-ku; adult/child ¥210/70, 1st Sun of month free; ⏱10am-5pm Tue-Sun; Ⓢ Tōzai line to Takebashi, exit 1b) Housed in a vintage red-brick building this annex of MOMAT stages excellent changing exhibitions of mingei (folk crafts): ceramics, lacquerware, bamboo, textiles, dolls and much more. Artists range from living national treasures to contemporary artisans. The building was once the headquarters of the imperial guards, and was rebuilt after its destruction in WWII.

Harajuku & Around

ODAIBA & TOKYO BAY
お台場・東京湾

Developed mostly in the '90s on reclaimed land, Odaiba is a bubble-era vision of urban planning, where the buildings are large and striking – **Tokyo Big**

Sight (Tokyo International Exhibition Center; Map p98) features four giant upside-down pyramids – the streets are wide and the waterfront is the main attraction. Love it or hate it, you'll definitely feel like you're in an alternate Tokyo.

TOKYO SIGHTS & ACTIVITIES

With its giant malls and entertainment centres, Odaiba is a popular with families and also as a teen date spot. Don't miss the 18m tall model of a **Gundam** (ガンダム; Map **p98**) robot in front of the Diver City mall.

Travelling to Odaiba is most fun on the driverless Yurikamome monorail, which departs from Shimbashi Station and snakes through skyscrapers before crossing the Rainbow Bridge.

Ōedo Onsen Monogatari   Onsen

(大江戸温泉物語; Map p98; www.ooedoonsen.jp; 2-6-3 Aomi, Kōtō-ku; adult/child from ¥1980/900, after 6pm from ¥1480/900; ⏰11am-9am, last entry 7am; ℞Yurikamome line to Telecom Centre, Rinkai line to Tokyo Teleport with free shuttle bus) Just to experience the truly Japanese phenomenon that is an amusement park centred on bathing is reason enough to visit. The baths, which include gender-divided indoor tubs and outdoor *rotemburo* (outdoor baths), are filled with real onsen (hot-spring) water, pumped from 1400m below Tokyo Bay. The *iwashioyoku* (hot-stone bath) and *tsunaburo* (hot-sand bath) cost extra, as do massages, and require reservations. Visitors with tattoos will be denied admission.

National Museum of Emerging Science & Innovation (Miraikan)   Museum

(未来館; Map p98; www.miraikan.jst.go.jp; 2-3-6 Aomi, Kōtō-ku; adult/child ¥620/210; ⏰10am-5pm Wed-Mon; ℞Yurikamome line to Telecom Centre) *Miraikan* means 'hall of the future', and the fascinating exhibits here present the science and technology that will shape the years to come. Lots of hands-on displays make this a great place for kids and curious adults. There are several demonstrations, too, including the humanoid robot ASIMO and the lifelike android Otonaroid. The Gaia dome theatre/planetarium has an English audio option and is popular; reserve your seats as soon as you arrive.

Odaiba Kaihin-kōen   Park

(お台場海浜公園; Odaiba Marine Park; Map p98; www.tptc.co.jp/en/park/tabid/846/Default.aspx; 1-4-1 Daiba, Minato-ku; ⏰24hr; ℞Yurikamome line to Odaiba Kaihin-kōen) One of the best views of Tokyo is from this park's promenades and elevated walkways – especially at night, when old-fashioned *yakatabune* (low-slung wooden boats) bedecked with lanterns traverse the bay. Also here you'll find an 800m-long man-made **beach** and

Shinjuku-gyoen (p71)

JOHN W BANAGAN/GETTY IMAGES ©

Shinjuku

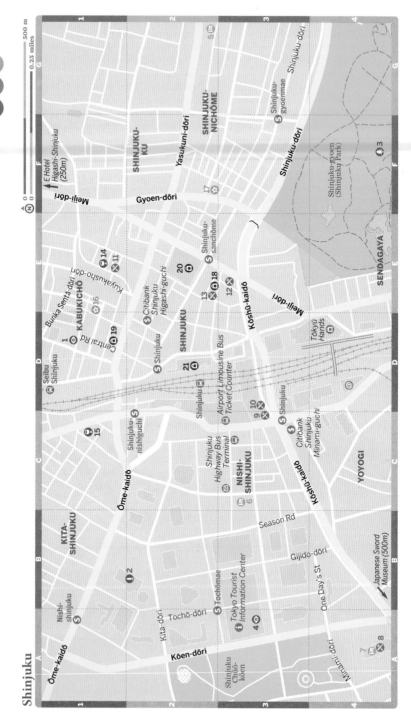

500 m
0.25 miles

E Hotel
Higashi-Shinjuku (250m)

KITA-SHINJUKU

NISHI-SHINJUKU

KABUKICHŌ

SHINJUKU-KU

SHINJUKU-NICHŌME

SHINJUKU

SENDAGAYA

YOYOGI

Shinjuku-gyoen (Shinjuku Park)

Meiji-dōri

Gyoen-dōri

Yasukuni-dōri

Shinjuku-dōri

Shinjuku-dōri

Kōshū-kaidō

Meiji-dōri

Ōme-kaidō

Ōme-kaidō

Kōshū-kaidō

Season Rd

Gijido-dōri

One Day's St

Minami-dōri

Tochō-dōri

Kita-dōri

Kōen-dōri

Kuyakusho-dōri

Bunka Senta-dōri

Central Rd

Shinjuku-nishiguchi

Shinjuku Higashi-guchi

Shinjuku Minami-guchi

Shinjuku-sanchōme

Nishi-shinjuku

Seibu Shinjuku

Shinjuku-gyoemmae

Citibank Shinjuku

Citibank Shinjuku

Tōkyū Hands

Shinjuku Highway Bus Terminal

Airport Limousine Bus Ticket Counter

Tochōmae

Tokyo Tourist Information Center

Shinjuku Chūō-kōen

Japanese Sword Museum (500m)

Shinjuku

an 11m replica of the Statue of Liberty – a very popular photo-op with the Rainbow Bridge in the background.

Tokyo Joypolis   Amusement Park

(東京ジョイポリス; Map p98; http://tokyo-joypolis.com; 3rd-5th fl Decks Tokyo Beach, 1-6-1 Daiba, Minato-ku; adult/child ¥800/300, all-rides passport ¥3900/2900, passport after 5pm ¥2900/1900; ⏰10am-10pm; 🚉Yurikamome line to Odaiba Kaihin-kōen) This indoor amusement park is stacked with virtual-reality attractions and adult thrill rides, such as the video-enhanced Halfpipe Canyon; there are rides for little ones, too. Separate admission and individual ride tickets (most ¥500) are available, but if you plan to go on more than a half-dozen attractions the unlimited 'passport' makes sense.

Tokyo Disney
Resort   Amusement Park

(東京ディズニーリゾート; www.tokyodisney resort.co.jp; 1-1 Maihama, Urayasu-shi; 1-day ticket for 1 park adult/child ¥6400/4200, after 6pm ¥3400; ⏰varies by season; 🚉JR Keiyō line to Maihama) At this very popular resort, you'll find not only Tokyo Disneyland, modelled after the California original, but also Tokyo DisneySea – a clever add-on that caters more to adults – and Disney-run hotels. Tickets can be booked online and it's worth packing a *bentō* (boxed meal), as on-site restaurants are almost always overrun with diners.

Sleeping

Tokyo is known for being an expensive place to sleep; however, more and more attractive budget and mid-range options are popping up every year. The best deals are on the east side of town, in Ueno and Asakusa. Wherever you decide to stay, advanced booking is highly recommended. You will almost always find cheaper hotel rates online (often from the hotel's own website). Note that some midrange and budget options do not accept credit cards, so come prepared with cash.

MARUNOUCHI (TOKYO STATION AREA) 丸の内 (東京駅)

Central and convenient for travel in and out of Tokyo, Marunouchi makes sense as a base, though rates here are among the highest in the city.

Yaesu Terminal
Hotel   Business Hotel ¥¥

(八重洲ターミナルホテル; Map p68; 📞3281-3771; www.yth.jp; 1-5-14 Yaesu, Chūō-ku; s/d ¥11,500/16,500; ❄@🛜; 🚉JR lines to Tokyo, Yaesu north exit) This sleek little business hotel on cherry-tree-lined Sakura-dōri has contemporary lines and a minimalist look. Though room sizes are generally tiny, they're decently priced for this neighbourhood and showcase modern, sporting, contemporary art by radiographic artist Steven Meyers.

Below: Tsukiji Market (p66); Right: Tokyo Station (p64)
(BELOW) CURIOSO/SHUTTERSTOCK ©: (RIGHT) KORKUSUNG/SHUTTERSTOCK ©

Tokyo Station Hotel
Luxury Hotel ¥¥¥

(東京ステーションホテル; Map p68; ☎5220-1112; www.tokyostationhotel.jp; 1-9-1 Marunouchi, Chiyoda-ku; r from ¥41,000; ⊖❄@☏; 🚃JR lines to Tokyo, Marunouchi south exit) Representing a return to the classics, the Tokyo Station Hotel has brushed up handsomely as part of the heritage building's restoration. Rooms are spacious and decorated in an opulent European fashion, with tall ceilings, marble counters and dripping chandeliers. Some rooms have views of the Imperial Palace.

GINZA & TSUKIJI 銀座 • 築地

In Ginza you'll have excellent shopping, cafes and restaurants at your doorstep, not to mention the Imperial Palace and Tsukiji Market. This, of course, comes with a price.

Mitsui Garden Hotel Ginza Premier
Hotel ¥¥

(三井ガーデンホテル銀座プレミア; Map p68; ☎03-3543-1131; www.gardenhotels. co.jp; 8-13-1 Ginza, Chūō-ku; r from ¥16,000; ⊖❄@☏; 🚇Ginza line to Shimbashi, exit 1) If you book ahead and online, this upmarket business hotel is a steal. It is reasonably priced and has a great location, pleasantly decorated rooms, and a high-rise lobby with killer Shiodome and Tokyo Tower views.

Imperial Hotel
Luxury Hotel ¥¥¥

(帝国ホテル; Map p68; ☎3504-1111; www. imperialhotel.co.jp; 1-1-1 Uchisaiwai-chō, Chiyoda-ku; s/d from ¥42,770/48,710; ⊖❄@☏☁; 🚇Hibiya line to Hibiya, exit A13) The present building is the successor to Frank Lloyd Wright's 1923 masterpiece, and small tributes to the architect's style can be found in the lobby and elsewhere. The rooms are not the most stylish in Tokyo, but are large, comfortable and generally have impressive views; the ones on the

Imperial floor are the most up-to-date. Service here is virtually peerless.

ROPPONGI & AROUND 六本木

If nightlife features prominently on your agenda, Roppongi is a good place to hang your hat.

Hotel S
Boutique Hotel ¥¥

(ホテル S; Map p72; ☑03-5771-2469; http://hr-roppongi.jp; 1-11-6 Nishi-Azabu, Minato-ku; r from ¥18,200; ❀@⌖; ⑤Hibiya line to Roppongi, exit 2) The eight styles of room at this boutique property capture the arty design spirit of Roppongi. Some of the more expensive duplex-type rooms have Japanese design elements such as tatami (in charcoal) and circular *hinoki* (cypress-wood) bathtubs. The entry-level rooms are also a cut above the usual.

B Roppongi
Business Hotel ¥¥

(ザ・ビー六本木; Map p72; ☑5412-0451; www.theb-hotels.com/the-b-roppongi/en/index.html; 3-9-8 Roppongi, Minato-ku; s/d incl breakfast from ¥13,600/14,100; ⊜@⌖; ⑤Hibiya line to Roppongi, exit 5) The slick, white-brown rooms here range in size from 10 to 31 sq metres, albeit with small, prefab bathrooms. Atmosphere is business-casual and the location is perfect for Roppongi's nocturnal attractions. If it's full there a couple of other B hotels nearby in Akasaka.

SHIBUYA & AROUND 渋谷

Staying in Shibuya puts you right in the thick of things, and the rail access is excellent. Though if you're not planning on taking advantage of the local nightlife, you might want to pick somewhere a little more peaceful.

Dormy Inn Premium Shibuya Jingūmae
Business Hotel ¥¥

(ドーミーインプレミアム渋谷神宮前; Map p88; ☑5774-5489; www.hotespa.net/hotels/shibuya; 6-24-4 Jingūmae, Shibuya-ku; s/d from ¥11,490/15,990; ⊜❀⌖; ⑬JR Yamanote line to Harajuku, Omote-sandō exit) This flashy new property from the Dormy Inn chain of business hotels has typically small rooms with double beds (140cm)

Ueno

N
0 — 400 m
0 — 0.2 miles

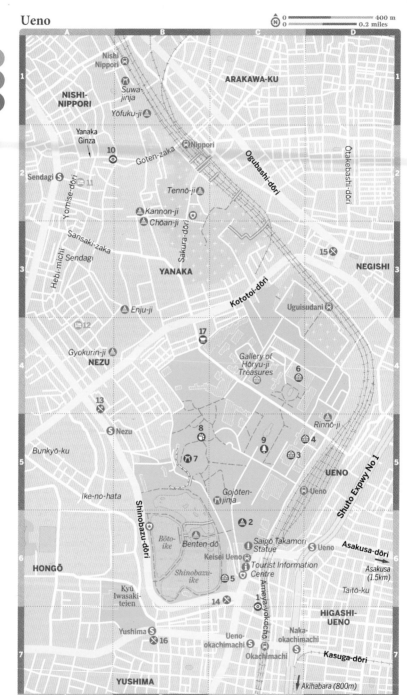

Nishi Nippori

Suwa-jinja

Yōfuku-ji

ARAKAWA-KU

NISHI-NIPPORI

Yanaka Ginza

10

Goten-zaka

Nippori

Ogubashi-dōri

Otakebashi-dōri

Sendagi

11

Yomise-dōri

Tennō-ji

Kannon-ji
Chōan-ji

Sakura-dōri

15

NEGISHI

Sansaki-zaka

Sendagi

Hebi-michi

YANAKA

Kototoi-dōri

Enju-ji

12

Gyokurin-ji

NEZU

Uguisudani

17

Gallery of Hōryū-ji Treasures

6

13

Nezu

Rinnō-ji

Bunkyō-ku

8

9

4

3

7

UENO

Ueno

Ike-no-hata

Shinobazu-dōri

Gojōten-jinja

Shuto Expwy No 1

2

HONGŌ

Bōto-ike

Benten-dō

Shinobazu-ike

Saigō Takamori Statue

Ueno

Asakusa-dōri

Keisei Ueno

Tourist Information Centre

Asakusa (1.5km)

5

Kyū Iwasaki-teien

14

Ameyayokochō

1

Taitō-ku

Yushima

16

Ueno-okachimachi

Naka-okachimachi

HIGASHI-UENO

YUSHIMA

Okachimachi

Kasuga-dōri

Akihabara (800m)

Ueno

but a host of perks: free breakfast and noodles in the evening, laundry facilities, a communal bath and shuttle service to Shibuya Station (7am to noon).

Shibuya Granbell Hotel
Boutique Hotel ¥¥¥

(渋谷グランベルホテル; Map p84; 5457-2681; www.granbellhotel.jp; 15-17 Sakuragaoka-chō, Shibuya-ku; s/d from ¥13,000/22,000; ❀✳@☎; ☒ JR Yamanote line to Shibuya, south exit) Though priced about the same as a business hotel, the Granbell is far more stylish. Some rooms have glass-enclosed bathrooms, Simmons beds and pop-art curtains. The hotel is on the quieter side of Shibuya, towards Daikanyama; still, it's just a few minutes' walk to the station.

Excel Hotel Tōkyū
Hotel ¥¥¥

(エクセルホテル東急; Map p84; 5457-0109; www.tokyuhotelsjapan.com/en/TE/TE_SHIBU/index.html; 1-12-2 Dōgenzaka, Shibuya-ku; s/d from ¥24,948/34,452; ❀✳@☎♨; ☒ JR Yamanote line to Shibuya, Hachikō exit) This hotel is right on top of Shibuya Station, a location you'll be grateful for after a long day. Rooms are spacious though ordinary. Prices rise along with the floor numbers, but you can get a pretty good view with a simple upgrade for ¥2000 per night to a 'city view' room. The hotel is part of the Mark City complex.

SHINJUKU 新宿

As a major transport hub on the west side of the city, Shinjuku makes for a convenient base, though it's mostly big-name hotels here.

National Museum of Western Art (p84)
SIRA ANAMWONG/SHUTTERSTOCK ©

95

TOKYO

Asakusa & Sumida-gawa

0   500 m
0   0.25 miles

TAITŌ-KU

MATSUGAYA

NISHI-ASAKUSA

ASAKUSA

HANAKAWADO

KAMINARI-MON

KOMAGATA

KOTOBUKI

SUMIDA-KU

OSHIAGE

Sumida-gawa (Sumida River)

Shuto Expwy No 6

Sumida-kōen

Hanakawado-kōen

Asakusa-kōen

Higashi-Mukōjima

Mukōjima

Narihira

Higashi-Komagata

Honjo-azumabashi

Oshiage

Tokyo Sky Tree Station

Sensō-ji

Niten-mon

Hōzō-mon

Five-Storey Pagoda

Hanayashiki Amusement Park

Awashima-dō

Higashi Hongan-ji

Tsukuba Express Asakusa

Tōbu Asakusa

Asakusa

Tokyo Cruise Asakusa Pier

Azuma-bashi

Kototoi-bashi

Azumabashi

Komagata-bashi

Ferries to Hama-rikyū Onshi-teien & Odaiba

Nui (600m)

Kokusai-dōri

Kototoi-dōri

Yoshino-dōri

Mitsume-dōri

Edo-dōri

Umamichi-dōri

Nakamise-dōri

Shin-Nakamise-dōri

Sushiya-dōri

Denbō-in-dōri

Hoppy-dōri

Hisago-dōri

Kappabashi Hon-dōri

Kappabashi-dōri

Chinyoko-dōri

Orange-dōri

Kaminari-mon-dōri

Asakusa-dōri

Asakusa

Metro-dōri

Dembōin-dōri

Tawaramachi

1
2
3
5
6
7
8
9
10
11
12
13
14

Asakusa & Sumida-gawa

Note that many budget hotels in Shinjuku that target foreign travellers are in the red light district, Kabukichō; while it's highly unlikely you'd encounter any real danger, some might find it unpleasant to walk past shady characters night after night.

E Hotel Higashi-Shinjuku   Business Hotel ¥¥

(イーホテル東新宿; Map p62; www.shinjuku hotel.co.jp/eng; 2-3-15 Kabukichō, Shinjuku-ku; s/d from ¥9000/11,000; ⊝ ✳ @ �ⓢ; ⓢ Ōedo line to Higashi-Shinjuku, exit A1) This traveller favourite has an excellent location – just in front of the Higashi-Shinjuku subway station – plus friendly staff and lots of city information. The rooms are typically small but have a clean, modern feel and comfortable double beds. Those on the main street might get some noise, but some have nice night views. There's a coffee shop on the ground floor.

Citadines   Apartments ¥¥

(シタディーン; Map p90; ☎ 5379-7208; www. citadines.com; 1-28-13 Shinjuku, Shinjuku-ku; r from ¥14,256; ⊝ ✳ @ ⓢ ♨; ⓢ Marunouchi line to Shinjuku-gyoenmae, exit 2) Bright and modern, Citadines has compact studios with queen-sized beds, kitchenettes and a sitting area. Rooms sleep up to three. It's a bit far from the Shinjuku action, though travellers staying for more than a few days will likely come to appreciate the relative quiet. There's a fitness room and laundrette too. English is spoken.

Kadoya Hotel   Hotel ¥¥

(かどやホテル; Map p90; ☎ 3346-2561; www. kadoya-hotel.co.jp; 1-23-1 Nishi-Shinjuku, Shinjuku-ku; s/d from ¥9000/14,000; ⊝ ✳ @ ⓢ; ⓡ JR Yamanote line to Shinjuku, west exit) Kadoya has been welcoming foreign tourists for decades and is above all friendly and accommodating. The standard rooms show their age, but are clean and comfortable, and a steal for Nishi-Shinjuku. The newer 'comfort' rooms (from ¥19,500) have more space, Simmons beds, Japanese-style bathtubs and the best decor. There's also a coin laundry.

Park Hyatt Tokyo   Luxury Hotel ¥¥¥

(パークハイアット東京; Map p90; ☎ 5322-1234; http://tokyo.park.hyatt.com; 3-7-1-2 Nishi-Shinjuku, Shinjuku-ku; d from ¥43,000; ⊝ ✳ @ ⓢ ♨ ♿; ⓢ Ōedo line to Tochōmae, exit A4) The Park Hyatt still looks as tasteful and elegant as it did when it opened 20 years ago. The hotel starts on the 41st floor of a Tange Kenzō–designed skyscraper in west Shinjuku, meaning even the entry-level rooms have otherworldly views. Perks for guests include complimentary mobile-phone rentals (you pay for outgoing calls only) and morning yoga classes.

UENO 上野

If you'd like to immerse yourself in historic Tokyo, then Ueno, with its welcoming, inexpensive ryokan (traditional inns), is an excellent choice. A direct train connects Ueno with Narita Airport.

Odaiba & Tokyo Bay

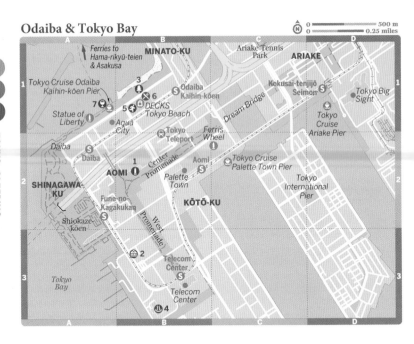

Odaiba & Tokyo Bay

Sawanoya Ryokan   Ryokan ¥¥

(旅館澤の屋; Map p94; ☏ 3822-2251; www.
sawanoya.com; 2-3-11 Yanaka, Taitō-ku; s/d from
¥5184/9720; ❄️ ❄️ @ 🛜 📶; S Chiyoda line
to Nezu, exit 1) Sawanoya is a gem in quiet
Yanaka, with very friendly staff and all the
traditional hospitality you would expect
of a ryokan. The shared cypress and
earthenware baths are the perfect balm
after a long day (some rooms have their
own bath, too). The lobby overflows with
information about travel options in Japan
and bicycles are available for rent.

Annex Katsutarō
Ryokan   Ryokan ¥¥

(アネックス勝太郎旅館; Map p94; ☏ 3828-
2500; www.katsutaro.com; 3-8-4 Yanaka, Taitō-
ku; s/d from ¥6500/10,800; ❄️ ❄️ @ 🛜 📶;
S Chiyoda line to Sendagi, exit 2) More like a
modern hotel than a traditional ryokan,
the family-run Annex Katsutarō has
spotless, thoughtfully arranged tatami
rooms with attached bathrooms. Though
a bit of a walk from the sights in Ueno, it's
ideal for exploring the old Yanaka district.
Breakfast and bicycles are available for a
small fee.

ASAKUSA & SUMIDA-GAWA
浅草 ● 隅田川

While not central, Asakusa has an attractive, unpretentious, traditional atmosphere and the city's best hostels.

Nui   Hostel ¥

(ヌイ; Map p62; ☏ 6240-9854; http://back
packersjapan.co.jp/nui_en; 2-14-13 Kuramae,
Taitō-ku; dm/d from ¥2700/6800; ❄️ ❄️ @ 🛜;

TOKYO SLEEPING

S Ōedo line to Kuramae, exit A7) In a former warehouse, this hostel has raised the bar for stylish budget digs in Tokyo. High ceilings mean bunks you can comfortably sit up in, and there is an enormous shared kitchen and workspace. Best of all is the ground floor bar and lounge, with furniture made from salvaged timber; it's a popular local hang-out.

Sukeroku No Yado Sadachiyo
Ryokan ¥¥

(助六の宿貞千代; Map p96; ☎3842-6431; www.sadachiyo.co.jp; 2-20-1 Asakusa, Taitō-ku; d with/without 2 meals from ¥33,600/19,600; ⊝ ❄ @ 🛜; **S** Ginza line to Asakusa, exit 1) This stunning ryokan virtually transports its guests to old Edo. Gorgeously maintained tatami rooms are spacious for two people, and all come with modern, Western-style bathrooms. Splurge on an exquisite meal here, and make time for the *o-furo* (traditional Japanese bath), one made of fragrant Japanese cypress and the other of black granite. Look for the rickshaw parked outside.

Eating

When it comes to Tokyo superlatives, the city's eating scene takes the cake. There are more restaurants in this pulsing megalopolis than in any other city in the world. And the quality is unparalleled, too – you're rarely more than 500m from a good, if not great, restaurant.

Best of all, you can eat well on any budget in pretty much every neighbourhood. Lunch is usually excellent value, with many pricier restaurants offering cheaper courses during the noontime hours. Reservations are necessary only at upmarket restaurants, though they're a good idea at midrange places (especially on Friday and Saturday evenings) if you have a party that's larger than two.

Older neighbourhoods like Ueno and Asakusa are known for their traditional, sometimes century-old, restaurants. Cosmopolitan Roppongi has the most variety in terms of international cuisine. For sushi, Ginza and Tsukiji are tops; Ginza is also known for its upscale restaurants. Westside neighbourhoods

Gyūdon, a Japanese dish of rice topped with beef

RACHEL LEWIS/GETTY IMAGES ©

like Ebisu, Shibuya and Harajuku have more trendy joints. Of course there are a numerous exceptions to all of this, too!

MARUNOUCHI (TOKYO STATION AREA) 丸の内（東京駅）

There are also plenty of places to eat within Tokyo Station.

Tokyo Rāmen Street   Rāmen ¥

(東京ラーメンストリート; Map p68; www.tokyoeki-1bangai.co.jp/ramenstreet; B1 First Avenue Tokyo Station, 1-9-1 Marunouchi, Chiyoda-ku; rāmen from ¥800; ⏰7.30am-10.30pm; 🚇JR lines to Tokyo Station, Yaesu south exit) Eight hand-picked *rāmen-ya* operate minibranches in this basement arcade on the Yaesu side of Tokyo Station. All the major styles are covered – from *shōyu* (soy-sauce base) to *tsukemen* (cold noodles served on the side). Long lines form outside the most popular, but they tend to move quickly.

Hōnen Manpuku   Japanese ¥¥

(豊年萬福; Map p62; 📞03-3277-3330; www.hounenmanpuku.jp; 1-8-16 Nihombashi-Muromachi, Chūō-ku; mains ¥1280-1850; ⏰11.30am-2.30pm, 5-11pm Mon-Sat, 5-10pm Sun; 📖; Ⓢ Ginza line to Mitsukoshimae, exit A1) Offering a riverside terrace in warmer months, Hōnen Manpuku's interior is dominated by giant *washi* (Japanese handmade paper) lanterns beneath which patrons tuck into bargain-priced beef or pork sukiyaki and other traditional dishes. Ingredients are sourced from gourmet retailers in Nihombashi. Lunchtime set menus are great value.

GINZA & TSUKIJI 銀座

Sushi breakfast at Tsukiji is a classic Tokyo experience.

Daiwa Sushi   Sushi ¥¥

(大和寿司; Map p68; 📞3547-6807; Bldg 6, 5-2-1 Tsukiji, Chūō-ku; sushi set ¥3500; ⏰5am-1.30pm Mon-Sat, closed occasional Wed; 😐; Ⓢ Ōedo line to Tsukijishijomae, exit A1) Waits of over one hour are commonplace at Tsukiji's most famous sushi bar, after which you'll be expected to eat and run. But it's all worth it once your first piece of delectable sushi hits the counter. Unless you're comfortable ordering in Japanese, the standard set (seven *nigiri*, plus *maki* and miso soup) is a good bet; there's a picture menu.

Trattoria Tsukiji Paradiso!   Italian ¥¥

(Map p68; 📞03-3545-5550; www.tsukiji-paradiso.com; 6-27-3 Tsukiji, Chūō-ku; mains ¥1500-3600; ⏰11am-2pm, 6-10pm; Ⓢ Hibiya line to Tsukiji, exit 2) Paradise for food lovers, indeed. This charming, aqua-painted trattoria plays on its proximity to Tsukiji with seafood pasta dishes that will make you want to lick the plate clean. Its signature linguine is packed with shellfish in a scrumptious tomato, chilli and garlic sauce. Lunch (from ¥980) is a bargain; book for dinner.

Kyūbey   Sushi ¥¥¥

(久兵衛; Map p68; 📞3571-6523; www.kyubey.jp; 8-7-6 Ginza, Chūō-ku; sushi sets lunch ¥5000-8400, dinner from ¥10,500; ⏰11.30am-2pm & 5-10pm Mon-Sat; 📖; Ⓢ Ginza line to Shimbashi, exit 3) Since 1936, Kyūbey's quality and presentation has won it a moneyed and celebrity clientele. Even so, this is a supremely foreigner-friendly and relaxed restaurant. Expect personal greetings in English by the owner Imada-san and his team of talented chefs who will make and serve your sushi, piece by piece.

Maru   Japanese ¥¥¥

(銀座圓; Map p68; 📞03-5537-7420; www.maru-mayfont.jp/ginza; 2nd fl, Ichigo Ginza 612 Bldg, 6-12-15 Ginza, Chūō-ku; lunch/dinner from ¥1100/6000; ⏰11.30am-2pm, 5.30-9pm Mon-Sat; 📖; Ⓢ Ginza line to Ginza, exit A3) Maru offers a modern take on *kaiseki* (Japanese haute cuisine). The chefs are young and inventive and the appealing space is dominated by a long, wooden, open kitchen counter across which you can watch them work. Its good-value lunches offer a choice of mainly fish dishes.

ROPPONGI & AROUND 六本木

The basement of Tokyo Midtown (p65) has dozens of reasonably priced options as well as takeaway counters – perfect for a picnic lunch in the garden out back.

Gonpachi
Izakaya ¥

(権八; Map p72; ☏5771-0170; www.gonpachi. jp/nishiazabu; 1-13-11 Nishi-Azabu, Minato-ku; skewers ¥180-1500, lunch sets weekday/weekend from ¥800/2050; ⏰11.30am-3.30am; 🚬📶; 🇸Hibiya line to Roppongi, exit 2) Over the last decade this cavernous old Edo-style space (which inspired a memorable set in Quentin Tarantino's *Kill Bill*) has cemented its rep as a Tokyo dining institution with other less-memorable branches scattered around the city. *Kushiyaki* (charcoal-grilled skewers) are served here alongside noodles, tempura and sushi.

Jōmon
Izakaya ¥¥

(ジョウモン; Map p72; ☏03-3405-2585; www. teyandei.com/jomon_rop; 5-9-17 Roppongi, Minato-ku; skewers ¥150-1600; ⏰6pm-5am; 🚬📶; 🇸Hibiya line to Roppongi, exit 3) This wonderfully cosy kitchen has bar seating, rows of ornate *shōchū* (liquor) jugs lining the wall and hundreds of freshly prepared skewers splayed in front of the patrons – don't miss the heavenly *zabuton* beef stick (¥400). It's almost directly across from the Family Mart – look for the name in Japanese on the door.

Tofuya-Ukai
Kaiseki ¥¥¥

(とうふ屋うかい; Map p72; ☏3436-1028; www.ukai.co.jp/english/shiba; 4-4-13 Shiba-kōen, Minato-ku; lunch/dinner set menu from ¥5500/8400; ⏰11.30am-10pm (last order 8pm); 🚬📶; 🇸Toei Ōedo line to Akabanebashi, exit 8) One of Tokyo's most gracious restaurants is located in a former sake brewery (moved from northern Japan), with an exquisite traditional garden, in the shadow of Tokyo Tower. Seasonal preparations of tofu and accompanying dishes are served in the refined *kaiseki* (Japanese haute cuisine) style. Make reservations well in advance.

EBISU & MEGURO 恵比寿・目黒

Tonki
Tonkatsu ¥

(とんき; Map p78; 1-2-1 Shimo-Meguro, Meguro-ku; meals ¥1900; ⏰4-10.45pm Wed-Mon, closed 3rd Mon of month; 🚬📶; 🚆JR Yamanote line to Meguro, west exit) One of Tokyo's best *tonkatsu* (crumbed pork cutlet) restaurants, Tonki has a loyal following. The seats at the counter – where you can watch the perfectly choreographed chefs – are the most coveted. From the station, walk down Meguro-dōri, take a left at the first alley and look for a white sign and *noren* (doorway curtains) across the sliding doors.

Afuri
Rāmen ¥

(あふり; Map p78; 1-1-7 Ebisu, Shibuya-ku; noodles from ¥750; ⏰11am-5am; 🚬📶; 🚆JR Yamanote line to Ebisu, east exit) Hardly your typical, surly *rāmen-ya*, Afuri has upbeat young cooks and a hip industrial interior. The unorthodox menu might draw eye-rolls from purists, but house specialities such as *yuzu-shio* (a light, salty broth flavoured with yuzu, a type of citrus) draw

A variety of Japanese dishes
OLEKSIY MAKSYMENKO/GETTY IMAGES ©

lines at lunchtime. Order from the vending machine.

Ippo
Izakaya ¥¥

(一歩; Map p78; ☎ 3445-8418; 2nd fl, 1-22-10 Ebisu, Shibuya-ku; dishes ¥500-1500; ⏱6pm-3am; 🚉JR Yamanote line to Ebisu, east exit) This mellow little *izakaya* (Japanese pubeatery) specialises in simple pleasures: fish and sake (there's an English sign out front that says just that). The friendly chefs speak some English and can help you decide what to have grilled, steamed, simmered or fried. The entrance is up the wooden stairs.

Ouca
Ice Cream ¥

(櫻花; Map p78; www.ice-ouca.com; 1-6-6 Ebisu, Shibuya-ku; ice cream from ¥390; ⏱11am-11.30pm Mar-Oct, noon-11pm Nov-Feb; 🚉JR Yamanote line to Ebisu, east exit) Green tea isn't the only flavour Japan has contributed to the ice-cream playbook; other delicious innovations available at Ouca include *kuro-goma* (black sesame) and *beni imo* (purple sweet potato).

SHIBUYA 渋谷

For more options, check out the restaurants on the 6th and 7th floors of Shibuya Hikarie (p75); the basement (level 3) food court has good takeaway options, too.

d47 Shokudō
Japanese ¥

(d47食堂; Map p84; www.hikarie8.com/d47shokudo/about.shtml; 8th fl, Shibuya Hikarie, 2-21-1 Shibuya, Shibuya-ku; meals ¥1100-1680; ⏱11am-2.30pm, 6-11pm; ☺📷; 🚉JR Yamanote line to Shibuya, east exit) There are 47 prefectures in Japan and d47 serves a changing line-up of *teishoku* (set meals) that evoke the specialities of each, from the fermented tofu of Okinawa to the stuffed squid of Hokkaido. A larger menu of small plates is available in the evening. Picture windows offer birds-eye views over the trains coming and going at Shibuya Station.

Food Show
Supermarket ¥

(フードショー; Map p84; basement fl, 2-24-1 Shibuya, Shibuya-ku; ⏱10am-9pm; 📷; 🚉JR Yamanote line to Shibuya, Hachikō exit) This takeaway paradise in the basement of Shibuya Station has steamers of dumplings, crisp *karaage* (Japanese-style fried chicken), heaps of salads and

TOKYO EATING

Grilled fish

cakes almost too pretty to eat. Look for discount stickers on *bentō* (boxed meals) and sushi sets after 5pm. A green sign pointing downstairs marks the entrance at Hachikō Plaza.

Kaikaya
Seafood ¥¥

(開花屋; Map p84; ☎ 3770-0878; www.kaikaya. com; 23-7 Maruyama-chō, Shibuya-ku; lunch from ¥780, dishes ¥680-2300; ⏱ 11.30am-2pm, 5.30-11.30pm Mon-Fri, 5.30-11.30pm Sat & Sun; ☺ 🖬; 🚃 JR Yamanote line to Shibuya, Hachikō exit) 🖉 Kaikaiya is one chef's attempt to bring the beach to Shibuya. Most everything on the menu is caught in nearby Sagami Bay and the superfresh seafood is served both Japanese and Western-style. One must try *maguro no kama* (tuna collar). Kaikaya is a boisterous, popular place; reservations are recommended.

Matsukiya
Sukiyaki ¥¥¥

(松木家; Map p84; ☎ 3461-2651; 6-8 Maruyama-chō, Shibuya-ku; sukiyaki from ¥5250; ⏱ 11.30am-1.30pm, 5-11pm Mon-Sat; 🖬; 🚃 JR Yamanote line to Shibuya, Hachikō exit) Matsukiya has been making *sukiyaki* (thinly sliced beef, simmered and then dipped in raw egg) since 1890 and they really, really know what they're doing. It's worth upgrading to the premium course (¥7350) for even meltier meat, cooked to perfection at your table. There's a white sign out front and the entrance is up some stairs. Reservations are recommended.

HARAJUKU & AROUND 原宿

Sticky sweet crepes are the official food of teeny-bopper Takeshita-dōri.

Harajuku Gyōza-rō
Gyōza ¥

(原宿餃子楼; Map p88; 6-4-2 Jingūmae, Shibuya-ku; 6 gyōza ¥290; ⏱ 11.30am-4.30am; 🖬; 🚃 JR Yamanote line to Harajuku, Omote-sandō exit) *Gyōza* (dumplings) are the only thing on the menu here, but you won't hear any complaints from the regulars who queue up to get their fix. Have them *sui* (boiled) or *yaki* (pan-fried), with or without *niniku* (garlic) or *nira* (chives) – they're all delicious. Expect to wait on weekends.

Maisen
Tonkatsu ¥

(まい泉; Map p88; http://mai-sen.com; 4-8-5 Jingūmae, Shibuya-ku; lunch/dinner from ¥995/1680; ⏱ 11am-10pm; ☺ 🖬; 🖪 Ginza line to Omote-sandō, exit A2) You could order something else (like fried shrimp), but everyone else will be ordering the famous *tonkatsu* (breaded, deep-fried pork cutlets). There are different grades of pork on the menu, including prized *kurobuta* (black pig), but even the cheapest is melt-in-your-mouth divine. The restaurant is housed in an old public bathhouse. A takeaway window serves delicious *tonkatsu sando* (sandwich).

Yanmo
Seafood ¥¥¥

(やんも; Map p88; www.yanmo.co.jp/aoyama/ index.html; basement fl, T Place bldg, 5-5-25 Minami-Aoyama, Minato-ku; lunch/dinner course from ¥1100/7560; ⏱ 11.30am-2pm, 6-10.30pm Mon-Sat; ☺; 🖪 Ginza line to Omote-sandō, exit A5) Fresh caught seafood from the nearby Izu Peninsula is the speciality at this upscale, yet unpretentious restaurant. If you're looking to splash out on a seafood dinner this is a great place to do so. The reasonably priced courses include sashimi, steamed and grilled fish. Lunch is a bargain, but you might have to queue. Reservations are essential for dinner.

SHINJUKU 新宿

Shinjuku has an overwhelming number of restaurants in all styles and budgets. If you want to narrow down your choices – or grab a quick bite without having to brave the crowds – head to one of the *resutoran-gai* (restaurant 'towns') found on the top floor of most department stores; both **Lumine** (ルミネ; Map p90; www. lumine.ne.jp/shinjuku; Shinjuku Station, Shinjuku-ku; ⏱ 11am-11pm; 🚃 JR Yamanote line to Shinjuku, south exit) and **Mylord** (ミロード; Map p90; www.shinjuku-mylord.com; Shinjuku Station, Shinjuku-ku; ⏱ 11am-11pm; 🚃 JR Yamanote line to Shinjuku, south exit), inside Shinjuku Station near the south exit, have reasonably priced options.

Nagi
Rāmen ¥

(凪; Map p90; www.n-nagi.com; 2nd fl, Golden Gai G2, 1-1-10 Kabukichō, Shinjuku-ku; rāmen from ¥820; ⏱24hr; 🛄; 🚇JR Yamanote line to Shinjuku, east exit) The house speciality at this atmospheric noodle joint, up a treacherous stairway in Golden Gai, is *niboshi rāmen* (egg noodles in a broth flavoured with dried sardines). There is almost always a wait; first purchase your order from the vending machine inside, then claim your spot at the end of the line. Look for the sign with a red circle.

Nakajima   Kaiseki ¥

(中嶋; Map p90; 📞3356-4534; www.shinjyuku-nakajima.com; basement fl, 3-32-5 Shinjuku, Shinjuku-ku; lunch/dinner from ¥800/8640; ⏱11.30am-2pm & 5.30-10pm Mon-Sat; 🛄; Ⓢ Marunouchi line to Shinjuku-sanchōme, exit A1) In the evening, this Michelin-starred restaurant serves exquisite *kaiseki* (Japanese haute cuisine) dinners. On weekdays, it also serves a set lunch of humble *iwashi* (sardines) for one-tenth the price; in the hands of Nakajima's chefs they're divine. The line for lunch starts to form shortly before the restaurant opens at 11.30am. Look for the white sign at the top of the stairs.

Tsunahachi   Tempura ¥¥

(つな八; Map p90; 📞3352-1012; www.tunahachi.co.jp; 3-31-8 Shinjuku, Shinjuku-ku; lunch/dinner from ¥1296-2268; ⏱11am-10.30pm; 🛄; 🚇JR Yamanote line to Shinjuku, east exit) Tsunahachi has been expertly frying prawns and seasonal vegetables for nearly 90 years. The sets are served in courses so each dish comes piping hot. Sit at the counter for the added pleasure of watching the chefs at work. Indigo *noren* (curtains) mark the entrance.

Kozue   Japanese ¥¥¥

(梢; Map p90; 📞5323-3460; http://tokyo.park.hyatt.jp/en/hotel/dining/Kozue.html; 40th fl, Park Hyatt, 3-7-1-2 Nishi-Shinjuku, Shinjuku-ku; lunch/dinner course from ¥2700/15,000; ⏱11.30am-2.30pm, 5.30-9.30pm; 🛄; Ⓢ Ōedo line to Tochōmae, exit A4) It's hard to beat Kozue's combination of exquisite, seasonal Japanese cuisine, artisan crockery and soaring views over Shinjuku from the floor to ceiling windows. Reservations are essential.

KŌRAKUEN & AROUND 後楽園

Tokyo Dome City has dozens of restaurants, mostly family-friendly chains.

Kado   Traditional ¥¥

(カド; Map p62; 📞3268-2410; http://kagurazaka-kado.com; 1-32 Akagi-Motomachi, Shinjuku-ku; lunch/dinner sets from ¥800/3150; ⏱11.30am-2.30pm & 5-11pm; 🛄; 🚇Tōzai line to Kagurazaka, exit 1) Set in an old wooden house, Kado specialises in *katei-ryōri* (home-cooking). Dinner is a set course of seasonal dishes (such as grilled quail or crab soup). At lunch there's no English menu, so your best bet is the カド定食 (*kado teishoku*), the daily house special. Bookings are required for dinner; the restaurant has a wooden facade and a white lantern out front.

Canal Cafe   Italian ¥¥

(カナルカフェ; Map p62; 📞3260-8068; www.canalcafe.jp; 1-9 Kagurazaka, Shinjuku-ku; lunch from ¥1600, dinner mains ¥1500-2800; ⏱11.30am-11pm Tue-Sat, to 9.30pm Sun; 🛄; 🚇JR Sōbu line to Iidabashi, west exit) Along the languid moat that forms the edge of Kitanomaru-kōen, this is one of Tokyo's best alfresco dining spots. The restaurant serves tasty wood-fired pizzas, seafood pastas and grilled meats, while over on the 'deck side' you can settle in with a sandwich, muffin or just a cup of coffee.

UENO 上野

In and around the open-air market Ameya-yokochō (p85) there are numerous casual restaurants that open up onto the street. It's a fun place to dine in the evenings. **Yanaka Ginza** (谷中銀座; Map p94; 🚇JR Yamanote line to Nippori, north exit) has snack vendors and takeaway counters.

Shinsuke   Izakaya ¥¥

(シンスケ; Map p94; 📞3832-0469; 3-31-5 Yushima, Bunkyō-ku; ⏱5-9.30pm Mon-Fri, to 9pm Sat; 🛄; Ⓢ Chiyoda line to Yushima, exit 3) In business since 1925, Shinsuke is pretty much the platonic ideal of an *izakaya*: long cedar counter, 'master' in *happi* (traditional short coat) and *hachimaki* (traditional headband) and smooth-as-silk *dai-ginjo* (premium grade sake). The only part that seems out of place is the friendly staff who go out of their way to explain the dishes in English.

Hantei
Traditional Japanese ¥¥

(はん亭; Map p94; ☎3828-1440; www.hantei.co.jp/nedu.html; 2-12-15 Nezu, Bunkyō-ku; lunch/dinner course from ¥3150/2835; ⏰noon-3pm & 5-10pm Tue-Sun; 🇮; Ⓢ Chiyoda line to Nezu, exit 2) Housed in a beautifully maintained, century-old traditional wooden building, Hantei is a local landmark. Delectable skewers of seasonal *kushiage* (fried meat, fish and vegetables) are served with small, refreshing side dishes. Lunch courses include eight sticks and dinner courses start with six, after which you'll continue to receive additional rounds (¥210 per skewer) until you say stop.

Izu-ei Honten
Unagi ¥¥

(伊豆栄本店; Map p94; www.izuei.co.jp; 2-12-22 Ueno, Taitō-ku; set meals ¥2160-4860; ⏰11am-9.30pm; 😐🇮; 🚃JR Yamanote line to Ueno, Hirokōji exit) Izu-ei's twin delights are its delicious *unagi* (eel) and its elegant, traditional atmosphere, with waitresses in kimonos and tatami seating (there are chairs, too).

Sasa-no-Yuki
Tofu ¥¥

(笹乃雪; Map p94; ☎3873-1145; 2-15-10 Negishi, Taitō-ku; dishes ¥400-700, lunch/dinner course from ¥2200/5000; ⏰11.30am-8pm Tue-Sun; 🌿🇮; 🚃JR Yamanote line to Uguisudani, north exit) 🍴 Sasa-no-Yuki opened its doors in the Edo period and continues to serve its signature dishes, with tofu made fresh every morning with water from the shop's own well. Some treats to expect: *ankake-dofu* (tofu in a thick, sweet sauce) and *goma-dofu* (sesame tofu). The best seats overlook a tiny garden with a koi pond.

ASAKUSA & SUMIDA-GAWA
浅草・隅田川

Don't miss the snack vendors on Nakamise-dōri, dishing out traditional treats such as *mochi* (sticky-rice cakes) stuffed with sweet bean paste.

Daikokuya
Tempura ¥

(大黒家; Map p96; www.tempura.co.jp/english/index.html; 1-38-10 Asakusa, Taitō-ku; meals ¥1550-2100; ⏰11am-8.30pm Mon-Fri, to 9pm Sat; 🇮; Ⓢ Ginza line to Asakusa, exit 1) Near Nakamise-dōri, this is the place to get old-fashioned tempura fried in pure sesame oil, an Asakusa speciality. It's in

Tempura

a white building with a tile roof. If there's a queue (and there often is), you can try your luck at the annexe one block over.

Rokurinsha
Rāmen ¥

(六厘舎; Map p96; www.rokurinsha.com; 6th fl, Solamachi, 1-1-2 Oshiage, Sumida-ku; rāmen from ¥850; ⏱10.30am-11pm; ⊖回; Ⓢ Hanzōmon line to Oshiage, exit B3) Rokurinsha's specialty is *tsukemen* – *rāmen* noodles served on the side with a bowl of concentrated soup for dipping. The noodles here are thick and perfectly al dente and the soup is a rich *tonkotsu* (pork bone) base. It's an addictive combination that draws lines to this outpost in Tokyo Sky Tree Town.

Komagata Dojō
Traditional Japanese ¥

(駒形どぜう; Map p96; ☎3842-4001; 1-7-12 Komagata, Taitō-ku; mains from ¥1550; ⏱11am-9pm; ⊖回; Ⓢ Ginza line to Asakusa, exits A2 & A4) Since 1801, Komagata Dojō has been simmering and stewing *dojō* (Japanese loach, which looks something like a miniature eel). *Dojō-nabe* (loach hotpot), served here on individual *hibachi*

(charcoal stove), was a common dish in the days of Edo, but few restaurants serve it today. The open seating around wide, wooden planks heightens the traditional flavour. There are lanterns out front.

Otafuku
Traditional Japanese ¥¥

(大多福; Map p96; ☎3871-2521; www.otafuku.ne.jp; 1-6-2 Senzoku, Taitō-ku; oden ¥110-550, course ¥5400; ⏱5-11pm Tue-Sat, to 10pm Sun; 回; 🚆 Tsukuba Express line to Asakusa, exit 1) Celebrating its centenary in 2015, Otafuku specialises in *oden,* classic Japanese stew. It's simmered at the counter and diners pick what they want from the pot, one or two items at a time. You can dine cheaply on radishes and kelp, or splash out on scallops and tuna – either way you get to soak up Otafuku's convivial, old-time atmosphere.

To find Otafuku, look for a shack-like entrance and lantern on the northern side of Kototoi-dōri.

ODAIBA & TOKYO BAY
お台場・東京湾

All of Odaiba's giant malls have restaurant floors with family-friendly options.

Bills
International ¥

(ビルズ; Map p98; www.bills-jp.net; 3rd fl Seaside Mall, DECKS Tokyo Beach, 1-6-1 Daiba, Minato-ku; mains from ¥1300; ⏱9am-10pm Mon-Fri, 8am-10pm Sat & Sun; ⊖🛜回♿; 🚆Yurikamome line to Odaiba Kaihin-kōen) Australian chef Bill Granger has had a big hit with his restaurant chain in Japan – which is unsurprising given how inviting and spacious a place this is. The menu includes his classics such as ricotta hotcakes, and lunch and dinner mains such as *wagyu* burgers. The terrace also has great bay views.

Sake bottles

TY Harbor Brewery American ¥¥
(Map p62; ☎5479-4555; www.tyharborbrewing.co.jp; 2-1-3 Higashi-Shinagawa, Shinagawa-ku; lunch set ¥1200-1700, dinner mains from ¥1700; ⏰11.30am-2pm, 5.30-10pm; 🚗📋; S Rinkai line to Tennōzu Isle, exit B) In a former warehouse on the waterfront, TY Harbor serves up excellent burgers, steaks and crab cakes with views of canals around Tennōzu Isle. It also brews its own beer on the premises. Call ahead to book a seat on the terrace.

🍷 Drinking & Nightlife

Tokyo's nightlife is undoubtedly one of the city's highlights. Whatever stereotypes you may have held about Japanese people being quiet and reserved will fall to pieces after dark. Tokyo is a 'work hard, play hard' kind of place and you'll find people out any night of the week.

Shinjuku is the city's largest nightlife district. Roppongi is known as the place where *gaijin* (foreigners) congregate – it can feel a bit like entering the world of *Bladerunner* or *Star Wars*, where throngs of the galaxy's most unscrupulous citizens gather under the sizzling neon lights. Ginza and Marunouchi are loaded with places for local office workers to unwind.

Night clubs are mostly clustered in Shibuya and Roppongi. Most of the big clubs have discount flyers that can be printed or downloaded from their websites. Everyone needs to show photo ID at the door.

It's not all about the booze: Tokyo has some fantastic cafes too, including some wacky themed ones.

MARUNOUCHI (TOKYO STATION AREA) 丸の内 (東京駅)
Cafe Salvador Cafe
(Map p68; www.cafecompany.co.jp/brands/salvador/marunouchi; 3-2-3 Marunouchi, Chiyoda-ku; ⏰7am-11pm Mon-Fri, 10am-11pm Sat, 10am-8pm Sun; @📶; R JR Yūrakuchō line to Yūrakuchō, Kokusai Forum exit) Comfy sofas, piles of glossy magazines, quirky art on the walls, free wi-fi and plenty of electricity outlets, make this affordable counter-service cafe one of the most convivial along ritzy Naka-dōri. Plenty of caffeinated drinks are supplemented by salads, sandwiches and fresh bakes.

So Tired Bar
(ソータイアード; Map p68; ☎5220-1358; www.heads-west.com/shop/so-tired.html; 7th fl, Shin-Marunouchi Bldg, 1-5-1 Marunouchi, Chiyoda-ku; ⏰11am-4am Mon-Sat, to 11pm Sun; R JR lines to Tokyo, Marunouchi north exit) The best thing about this bar on the lively 7th floor of the Shin-Maru Building is that you can buy a drink at the counter and take it out to the terrace. The views aren't sky-high, instead you feel curiously suspended among the office towers, hovering over Tokyo Station below.

GINZA & TSUKIJI 銀座 ・築地
Kagaya Izakaya
(加賀屋; Map p68; ☎03-3591-2347; www1.ocn.ne.jp/~kagayayy/index.html; B1 flr, Hanasada Bldg, 2-15-12 Shimbashi, Minato-ku; ⏰7pm-midnight Mon-Sat; R JR Yamanote line to Shimbashi, Shimbashi exit) It is safe to say that there is no other bar owner in Tokyo who can match Mark Kagaya for brilliant lunacy. His side-splitting antics are this humble *izakaya*'s star attraction, although his mum's nourishing home-cooking also hits the spot. Bookings are essential.

Cha Ginza Teahouse
(茶・銀座; Map p68; www.uogashi-meicha.co.jp/shop/ginza; 5-5-6 Ginza, Chūō-ku; tea set ¥500; ⏰11am-6pm, shop until 7pm Tue-Sun; S Ginza line to Ginza, exit B3) At this slick contemporary tearoom, it costs ¥600 for either a cup of perfectly prepared *matcha* (green tea), and a small cake or two, or for a choice of *sencha* (premium green tea). Buy your token for tea at the shop on the ground floor which sells top-quality teas from various growing regions in Japan.

ROPPONGI & AROUND 六本木
SuperDeluxe Lounge
(スーパー・デラックス; Map p72; ☎5412-0515; www.super-deluxe.com; B1 fl, 3-1-25 Nishi-Azabu, Minato-ku; admission varies; S Hibiya line to Roppongi, exit 1B) This groovy basement

performance space, also a cocktail lounge and club of sorts, stages everything from hula-hoop gatherings to literary evenings and creative presentations in the 20 x 20 PechaKucha (20 slides x 20 seconds) format. Check the website for event details. It's in an unmarked brown-brick building by a shoe-repair shop.

Pink Cow   Bar
(ピンクカウ; Map p72; www.thepinkcow. com; B1 fl, Roi Bldg, 5-5-1 Roppongi, Minato-ku; ⊙5pm-late Tue-Sun; ⑤Hibiya line to Roppongi, exit 3) With its animal-print decor, rotating display of local artwork and terrific all-you-can-eat buffet (¥2000) every Friday and Saturday, the Pink Cow is a funky, friendly place to hang out. Also host to stitch-and-bitch evenings, writers' salons and indie-film screenings, it's a good bet if you're in the mood to mix with a creative crowd.

Agave   Bar
(アガヴェ; Map p72; ☎03-3497-0229; www. agave.jp; B1 fl, 7-15-10 Roppongi, Minato-ku; ⊙6.30pm-2am Mon-Thu, to 4am Fri & Sat; ⑤Hibiya or Ōedo line to Roppongi, exit 2) Rawhide chairs, cruzas de rosas (crosses decorated with roses) and tequila shots for the willing make Agave a good place for a long night in search of the sacred worm. Luckily, this gem in the jungle that is Roppongi is more about savouring the subtleties of its 400-plus varieties of tequila than tossing back shots of Cuervo.

EBISU 恵比寿

Buri   Bar
(ぶり; Map p78; ☎3496-7744; 1-14-1 Ebisu-nishi, Shibuya-ku; ⊙5pm-3am; ⑤JR Yamanote line to Ebisu, west exit) Buri – the name means 'super' in Hiroshima dialect – is one of Ebisu's most popular tachinomi-ya (standing bars). On almost any night you can find a lively crowd packed in around the horseshoe-shaped counter here. Generous quantities of sake (over 50 varieties; ¥750) are served semifrozen, like slushies in colourful jars.

Enjoy House   Bar
(Map p78; http://enjoyhouse.jugem.jp; 2nd fl, 2-9-9 Ebisu-nishi, Shibuya-ku; drinks from ¥600; ⊙noon-late; ⑤JR Yamanote line to Ebisu, west exit) Decked out with velveteen booths, fairy lights and foliage, Enjoy House is a deeply funky place to spend the evening. DJs spin regularly, but there's still no cover charge. By day it's a burger shop. Look for the name painted in red letters in English on the 2nd-floor window.

SHIBUYA 渋谷

Good Beer Faucets   Bar
(グッドビアフォウセッツ; Map p84; http:// shibuya.goodbeerfaucets.jp; 2nd fl, 1-29-1 Shōtō, Shibuya-ku; beer from ¥800; ⊙5pm-midnight Mon-Thu, Sat, to 3am Fri, 4-11pm Sun; ⊜⊛; ⑤JR Yamanote line to Shibuya, Hachikō exit) With 40 shiny taps, Good Beer Faucets has one of the city's best selections of Japanese craft brews and regularly draws a full house of locals and expats. The interior is chrome and concrete (and not at all grungy). Come for happy hour (5pm to 8pm Monday to Thursday, 4pm to 7pm Sunday) and get ¥200 off any beer.

Womb   Club
(ウーム; Map p84; ☎5459-0039; www.womb. co.jp; 2-16 Maruyama-chō, Shibuya-ku; cover ¥2000-4000; ⊙11pm-late Fri & Sat, 4-10pm Sun; ⑤JR Yamanote line to Shibuya, Hachikō exit) A longtime (in club years, at least) fixture on the Tokyo scene, Womb gets a lot of big name international DJs playing mostly house and techno. Frenetic lasers and strobes splash across the heaving crowds, which usually jam all four floors. Warning: can get sweaty.

Tight   Bar
(タイト; Map p84; www.tight-tokyo.com; 2nd fl, 1-25-10 Shibuya, Shibuya-ku; drinks from ¥500; ⊙6pm-2am Mon-Sat, to midnight Sun; ⑤JR Yamanote line to Shibuya, Hachikō exit) This teeny-tiny bar is wedged among the wooden shanties of Nonbei-yokochō, a narrow nightlife strip along the JR tracks. Like the name suggests, it's a tight fit, but the lack of seats doesn't keep regulars away: on a busy night, they line the stairs. Look for the big picture window.

HARAJUKU 原宿

Two Rooms
Bar

(トゥールームス; Map p88; ☎ 3498-0002; www.tworooms.jp; 5th fl, AO bldg, 3-11-7 Kita-Aoyama, Minato-ku; ◷ 11.30am-2am Mon-Sat, to 10pm Sun; Ⓢ Ginza line to Omote-sandō, exit B2) Expect a crowd dressed like they don't care that wine by the glass starts at ¥1500. You can eat here too, but the real scene is at night by the bar. Call ahead (staff speak English) on Friday or Saturday night to reserve a table on the terrace, which has sweeping views towards the Shinjuku skyline.

Omotesando Koffee
Cafe

(Map p88; http://ooo-koffee.com; 4-15-3 Jingūmae, Shibuya-ku; espresso ¥250; ◷ 10am-7pm; Ⓢ Ginza line to Omote-sandō, exit A2) Tokyo's most *oshare* (stylish) coffee stand is a minimalist cube set up inside a half-century-old traditional house. Be prepared to circle the block trying to find it, but know that an immaculate macchiato and a seat in the garden await you.

SHINJUKU 新宿

The main drag on the east side of Shinjuku Station, Yasukuni-dōri, is wall-to-wall *izakaya*. The most ambient watering holes can be found further down in Golden Gai, a cluster of eccentric, closet-sized bars in what was originally a post-WWII black market. It's known to be a haunt for writers and artists. Though most establishments are likely to give tourists a cool reception, there are a few friendly places. Cover charges (of ¥500 and up) are standard at bars in Golden Gai.

Kabukichō is Tokyo's most notorious red-light district, full of cabarets, hostess (and host!) clubs, love hotels and fetish bars. If you're curious to take a peek, it's generally safe to stroll through, though it's wise not to go alone. Note that if you follow a tout to a bar or club here you will likely end up with a hefty bill.

Zoetrope
Bar

(ゾートロープ; Map p90; http://homepage2. nifty.com/zoetrope; 3rd fl, 7-10-14 Nishi-Shinjuku, Shinjuku-ku; ◷ 7pm-4am Mon-Sat; ⓡ JR Yamanote line to Shinjuku, west exit) A must visit for whisky fans, Zoetrope has no less than 300 varieties of Japanese whisky (from ¥700) behind its small counter – including some no longer commercially available. The owner speaks some English

Izakaya, Asakusa

and can help you pick from the daunting menu. He'll also let you choose the soundtrack to play alongside the silent films he screens on the wall.

Albatross G — Bar

(アルバトロスG; Map p90; www.alba-s.com/index.html; 1-1-7 Kabukichō, Shinjuku-ku; cover charge ¥500, drinks from ¥500; ⏰7pm-5am; 🚇JR Yamanote line to Shinjuku, east exit) With glittering chandeliers dripping from the ceiling and gilded frames on the walls, Albatross G has the decadent look down. If the counter is full there's more seating upstairs.

New York Bar — Bar

(ニューヨークバー; Map p90; 📞5323-3458; http://tokyo.park.hyatt.com; 52nd fl, Park Hyatt, 3-7-1-2 Nishi-Shinjuku, Shinjuku-ku; ⏰5pm-midnight Sun-Wed, to 1am Thu-Sat; 🚇Ōedo line to Tochōmae, exit A4) You may not be lodging at the Park Hyatt, but you can still ascend to the 52nd floor to swoon over the sweeping nightscape from the floor-to-ceiling windows at this bar (of *Lost in Translation* fame). There's a cover charge of ¥2200 after 8pm (7pm Sunday) and live music nightly; cocktails start at ¥1800. Note: dress code enforced.

Kabuki-za (p112)

AKIHABARA 秋葉原

@Home Cafe — Cafe

(@ほぉ〜むカフェ; Map p62; www.cafe-at home.com; 4th-7th fl, 1-11-4 Soto-Kanda, Chiyoda-ku; drinks from ¥500; ⏰11.30am-10pm Mon-Fri, 10.30am-10pm Sat & Sun; 🚇JR Yamanote line to Akihabara, Electric Town exit) *Kawaii* (cute) waitresses, dressed as French maids, play childrens' games with customers at this quintessential 'maid cafe'. You'll be welcomed as *go-shujinsama* (master) the minute you enter. It's a little titillating, perhaps, but this is no sex joint – just (more or less) innocent fun for Akiba's *otaku*. Dishes, such as curried rice, are topped with smiley faces.

UENO 上野

Torindō — Teahouse

(桃林堂; Map p94; 1-5-7 Ueno-Sakuragi, Taitō-ku; tea set ¥810; ⏰9am-5pm; 🚇Chiyoda line to Nezu, exit 1) Sample a cup of paint-thick *matcha* (powdered green tea) at this tiny teahouse on the edge of Ueno-kōen. Tradition dictates that the bitter tea be paired with something sweet, so choose from the artful desserts in the glass counter, then pull up a stool at the

communal table. It's a white building with persimmon-coloured door curtains.

ASAKUSA & SUMIDA-GAWA
浅草・隅田川

Popeye
Pub

(ポパイ; Map p62; www.40beersontap.com; 2-18-7 Ryōgoku, Sumida-ku; ⏰5-11pm Mon-Sat; 🚇; 🚃JR Sōbu line to Ryōgoku, west exit) Popeye boasts an astounding 70 beers on tap, including the world's largest selection of Japanese beers – from Echigo Weizen to Hitachino Nest Espresso Stout. The happy-hour deal (5pm to 8pm) offers select brews with free plates of pizza, sausages and other munchables. It's extremely popular and fills up fast; get here early to grab a seat.

Kamiya Bar
Bar

(神谷バー; Map p96; 📞3841-5400; www.kamiya-bar.com; 1-1-1 Asakusa, Taitō-ku; ⏰11.30am-10pm Wed-Mon; S Ginza line to Asakusa, exit 3) One of Tokyo's oldest Western-style bars, Kamiya opened in 1880 and is still hugely popular – though probably more so today for its enormous, cheap draft beer (¥1020 for a litre). It's special speciality, however, is Denki Bran, a herbal liquor that's been produced in-house for over a century. Order at the counter, then give your tickets to the server.

ODAIBA & TOKYO BAY
お台場・東京湾

Jicoo the
Floating Bar
Cocktail Bar

(ジークザフローティングバー; Map p98; 📞0120-049-490; www.jicoofloatingbar.com; admission ¥2600; ⏰8-10.30pm Thu-Sat; 🚃Yurikamome line to Hinode or Odaiba Kaihin-kōen) For a few nights a week, the futuristic cruise-boat Himiko, designed by manga and anime artist Leiji Matsumoto, morphs into this floating bar. Board on the hour at Hinode pier and the half-hour at Odaiba Kaihin-kōen. The evening-long 'floating pass' usually includes some sort of live music. Space is limited; make a reservation online in advance.

 # Entertainment

LIVE MUSIC

In Tokyo you can hear everything from classical to folk to electronica. A good number of 'live houses' – small venues where indie and up-and-coming bands perform – are clustered in Shibuya. **Tokyo Dross** (http://tokyodross.blogspot.jp) pulls together listings of the best upcoming shows.

WWW
Live Music

(Map p84; www-shibuya.jp/index.html; 13-17 Udagawa-chō, Shibuya-ku; tickets ¥2000-5000; 🚃JR Yamanote line to Shibuya, Hachikō exit) Tokyo's newest, big-hitting music venue used to be an art-house cinema. It still has the tiered floor (though the seats are gone) so everyone can see the stage. The line-up varies from indie pop to punk to electronica, but this is one of those rare venues where you could turn up just about any night and hear something good.

Unit
Live Music

(ユニット; Map p78; 📞5459-8630; www.unit-tokyo.com; 1-34-17 Ebisu-nishi, Shibuya-ku; ¥2500-5000; 🚃Tōkyū Tōyoko line to Daikanyama) On weekends, this subterranean club has two shows: live music in the evening and a DJ-hosted event after hours. Acts range from Japanese indie bands to overseas artists making their Japanese debut. Unit is less grungy than other Tokyo live houses; it draws a stylish young crowd and, thanks to its high ceilings, it doesn't get too smoky.

Shinjuku Pit Inn
Jazz

(新宿ピットイン; Map p90; 📞3354-2024; www.pit-inn.com; basement fl, 2-12-4 Shinjuku, Shinjuku-ku; admission from ¥3000; ⏰matinee 2.30pm, evening show 7.30pm; S Marunouchi line to Shinjuku-sanchōme, exit C5) This is not the kind of place you come to talk over the music. Aficionados have been coming here for more than 40 years to listen to Japan's best jazz performers. Weekday matinees feature new artists and cost only ¥1300.

THEATRE & DANCE

Kabuki is Tokyo's signature form of performing arts. You can also catch other forms of traditional theatre, such as *nō* (stylised dance-drama) and bunraku (classic puppet theatre), throughout the year, though performances are irregular.

Kabuki-za
Traditional Theatre

(歌舞伎座; Map p68; ☎ 3545-6800; www. kabuki-bito.jp/eng; 4-12-15 Ginza, Chūō-ku; tickets ¥4000-20,000, single-act tickets ¥800-2000; 🚇 Hibiya line to Higashi-Ginza, exit 3) The flamboyant facade of this venerable theatre, recently completely reconstructed to incorporate a tower block, makes a strong impression. It is a good indication of the extravagant dramatic flourishes that are integral to the traditional performing art of kabuki. Check the website for performance details and to book tickets; you'll also find an explanation about cheaper one-act, day seats.

A full kabuki performance comprises three or four acts (usually from different plays) over an afternoon or an evening (typically 11am to 3.30pm or 4.30pm to 9pm), with long intervals between the acts. Be sure to rent a headset for blow-by-blow explanations in English, and pick up a *bentō* to snack on during the intervals.

If four-plus hours sounds too long, 90 sitting and 60 standing tickets are sold on the day for each single act. They are at the back of the auditorium but still provide good views. Some acts tend to be more popular than others, so ask ahead as to which to catch and arrive at least 1½ hours before the start of the performance.

Robot Restaurant
Cabaret

(ロボットレストラン; Map p90; ☎ 3200-5500; www.robot-restaurant.com; 1-7-1 Kabukichō, Shinjuku-ku; tickets ¥7000; 🕐 shows at 4pm, 5.55pm, 7.50pm & 9.45pm; 🚇 JR Yamanote line to Shinjuku, east exit) This Kabukichō spectacle is wacky Japan at its finest, with giant robots manned by bikini-clad women and enough neon to light all of Shinjuku. Reservations aren't necessary but they're highly recommended. If you've booked ahead, be sure to arrive at least 30 minutes before the show. Look for discount tickets in English-language free mags around town.

National Theatre
Traditional Theatre

(国立劇場; Kokuritsu Gekijō; Map p62; ☎ 03-3265-7411; www.ntj.jac. go.jp/english; 4-1 Hayabusa-chō, Chiyoda-ku; tickets from ¥1500; 🚇 Hanzōmon line to Hanzōmon, exit 1) This is the capital's premier venue for traditional performing arts with a 1600-seat and a 590-seat auditorium. Performances include kabuki, *gagaku* (music of the imperial court) and bunraku (classic puppet theatre). Earphones with English translation are available for hire (¥650 plus ¥1000

Yomiuri Giants fans at Tokyo Dome

deposit). Check the website for performance schedules.

National Nō Theatre
Traditional Theatre

(国立能楽堂; Kokuritsu Nō-gakudō; Map p62; ☏3423-1331; www.ntj.jac.go.jp/english; 4-18-1 Sendagaya, Shibuya-ku; tickets from ¥2600; 🚉JR Sōbu line to Sendagaya) The traditional music, poetry and dances that *nō* (stylised Japanese dance-drama) is famous for unfold here on an elegant cypress stage. Each seat has a small screen that can display an English translation of the dialogue. Shows take place only a few times a month.

The theatre is 400m from Sendagaya Station; from the exit, walk right along the main road and turn left at the traffic light.

SPORT

Sumo is fascinating, highly ritualised and steeped in Shintō tradition. It's also the only traditional Japanese sport that still has enough clout to draw big crowds and dominate prime-time TV.

Tournaments take place in Tokyo at Ryōgoku Kokugikan in January, May and September. Other times of year you can drop in on an early-morning practice session at one of the stables, like Arashio Stable (p114).

Baseball is more of an obsession than a sport in Japan, and it's worth getting tickets to a game if only to see the fans go wild at each play and to witness the perfectly choreographed 7th-inning stretch. Within Tokyo, the Yomiuri Giants and Yakult Swallows are cross-town rivals.

Baseball season runs from April through October. Check the schedules on the stadium websites.

Ryōgoku Kokugikan
Sumo

(両国国技館; Ryōgoku Sumo Stadium; Map p62; ☏3623-5111; www.sumo.or.jp; 1-3-28 Yokoami, Sumida-ku; admission ¥2200-14,800; 🚉JR Sōbu line to Ryōgoku, west exit) If you're in town when a tournament is on – for 15 days each January, May and September – catch the big boys in action at Japan's largest sumo stadium. Doors open at 8am, but the action doesn't heat up until

---

Getting Tickets

Found a show or event that strikes your fancy? **Ticket Pia** (チケットぴあ; ☏0570-02-9111; http://t.pia.jp; ⏱10am-8pm) handles just about everything, including concerts and theatre performances major and minor. Tickets (when not sold out) can be purchased up to three days before the show. There are convenient branches on the 4th floor of **Shibuya Hikarie** (p75) and inside the **Asakusa Tourist Information Center** (p120).

---

the senior wrestlers hit the ring around 2pm. Tickets can be bought online one month before the start of the tournament.

A limited number of general-admission tickets are sold only on the day of the match from the box office in front of the stadium. You'll have to line up very early (say 6am) on the last couple of days of the tournament to snag one.

If you get there in the morning when the stadium is still pretty empty, you can usually sneak down to the box seats. You can rent a radio (¥100 fee, plus ¥2000 deposit) to listen to commentary in English. Stop by the basement restaurant to sample *chanko-nabe* (the protein-rich stew eaten by the wrestlers) for just ¥250 a bowl.

Tokyo Dome
Baseball

(東京ドーム; Map p62; www.tokyo-dome.co.jp/e; 1-3 Kōraku, Bunkyō-ku; tickets ¥2200-6100; 🚉JR Chūō line to Suidōbashi, west exit) Tokyo Dome (aka 'Big Egg') is home to the Yomiuri Giants. Love 'em or hate 'em, they're the most consistently successful team in Japanese baseball. If you're looking to see the Giants in action, the baseball season runs from the end of March to the end of October. Tickets sell out in advance; get them early at www.giants.jp/en.

Below: Window display, Ginza; **Right:** A shop in Marunouchi

Arashio Stable — Sumo

(荒汐部屋; Arashio-beya; Map p62; ☎3666-7646; www.arashio.net/tour_e.html; 2-47-2 Hama-chō, Nihombashi, Chūō-ku; Ⓢ Toei Shinjuku line to Hamachō, exit A2) **FREE** Catch morning sumo practice between 7.30am-10am – at this friendly stable. Call the day before to double check that practice is on; more info on the English website.

 ## 🔒 Shopping

Ginza is Tokyo's original shopping district, full of department stores and boutiques. For younger shoppers, however, the fashion scene has shifted westward, to trendy neighbourhoods like Shibuya and Harajuku. Tokyo still has a strong artisan tradition and you can find craft stores in older neighbourhoods such as Ueno and Asakusa.

Major hubs like Shibuya, Shinjuku, Ikebukuro and Ueno, which have department stores, electronic stores and popular chain stores, are all convenient shopping destinations. Akihabara has a particularly high concentration of electronics stores, and is the place to go for anime and manga.

More and more stores are offering dutyfree shopping so make sure to have your passport on you.

MARUNOUCHI (TOKYO STATION AREA) 丸の内 (東京駅)

Takashimaya — Department Store

(高島屋; Map p68; www.takashimaya.co.jp/tokyo/store_information; 2-4-1 Nihombashi, Chūō-ku; ⏱10am-8pm; Ⓢ Ginza line to Nihombashi, Takashimaya exit) The design of Takashimaya's flagship store (1933) tips its pillbox hat to New York's Gilded Age with marble columns, chandeliers and uniformed female elevator operators announcing each floor in high-pitched sing-song voices. Take your passport and you can get a free Shoppers Discount card giving you 5% off purchases over ¥3000.

Muji
Clothing, Homewares

(無印良品; Map p68; www.muji.com; 3-8-3 Marunouchi, Chiyoda-ku; ⏰10am-9pm; 🚆JR Yamanote line to Yūrakuchō, Kyōbashi exit) The flagship store of the famously understated brand sells elegant, simple clothing, accessories and homewares. There are scores of other outlets across Tokyo, including a good one in Tokyo Midtown, but the Yūrakuchō store also has bicycle rental and a great cafeteria.

Ōedo Antique Market
Antiques

(大江戸骨董市; Map p68; ☎6407-6011; www.antique-market.jp; 3-5-1 Marunouchi, Chiyoda-ku; ⏰9am-4pm 1st & 3rd Sun of month; 🚆JR Yamanote line to Yūrakuchō, Kokusai Forum exit) Held in the courtyard of Tokyo International Forum on the first and third Sunday of every month, this is a colourful event and a good chance to bargain for retro and antique Japanese goods, from old ceramics to kitsch plastic figurines.

GINZA 銀座

Akomeya
Food

(Map p68; ☎03-6758-0271; www.akomeya.jp; 2-2-6 Ginza, Chūō-ku; ⏰11am-9pm shop; 11.30am-10pm restaurant; Ⓢ Yūrakuchō line to Ginza-itchome, exit 4) Rice is at the core of Japanese cuisine and drink. This stylish store sells not only many types of the grain but also products made from it (such as sake), a vast range of quality cooking ingredients and a choice collection of kitchen, home and bath items.

Takumi
Crafts

(たくみ; Map p68; ☎3571-2017; www.ginza-takumi.co.jp; 8-4-2 Ginza, Chūō-ku; ⏰11am-7pm Mon-Sat; Ⓢ Ginza line to Shimbashi, exit 5) You'll be hard pressed to find a more elegant selection of traditional folk crafts, including toys, textiles and ceramics from around Japan. Ever thoughtful, the shop also encloses information detailing the origin and background of the pieces if you make a purchase.

Dover Street Market Ginza — Fashion

(DSM; Map p68; ☎6228-5080; http://ginza.doverstreetmarket.com; 6-9-5 Ginza, Chūō-ku; ⏰11am-8pm Sun-Thu, to 9pm Fri & Sat; Ⓢ Ginza line to Ginza, exit A2) A department store as envisioned by Kawakubo Rei (of Comme des Garcons), DSM has seven floors of avant-garde brands, including several Japanese labels and everything in the Comme des Garçons line-up. The quirky art installations alone make it worth the visit.

Uniqlo — Fashion

(ユニクロ; Map p68; www.uniqlo.com; 5-7-7 Ginza, Chūō-ku; ⏰11am-9pm; Ⓢ Ginza line to Ginza, exit A2) This now global brand has made its name by sticking to the basics and tweaking them with style. Offering inexpensive, quality clothing, this is the Tokyo flagship store with 11 floors and items you won't find elsewhere.

SHIBUYA 渋谷

Tōkyū Hands — Variety

(東急ハンズ; Map p84; http://shibuya.tokyu-hands.co.jp; 12-18 Udagawa-chō, Shibuya-ku; ⏰10am-8.30pm; Ⓡ JR Yamanote line to Shibuya, Hachikō exit) This DIY and zakka (miscellaneous goods) store has eight fascinating floors of everything you didn't know you needed. Like reflexology slippers, bee-venom face masks and cartoon-character-shaped rice-ball moulds. It's perfect for souvenir hunting, too.

Fake Tokyo — Fashion

(Map p84; ☎5456-9892; www.faketokyo.com; 18-4 Udagawa-chō, Shibuya-ku; ⏰noon-10pm; Ⓡ JR Yamanote line to Shibuya, Hachikō exit) This is one of the best places in the city to discover hot new Japanese designers. It's actually two shops in one: downstairs is Candy, full of brash, unisex streetwear; upstairs is Sister, which specialises in more ladylike items, both new and vintage. Look for the 'Fake Tokyo' banners out front.

Shibuya 109 — Fashion

(渋谷109; Ichimarukyū; Map p84; www.shibuya109.jp/en/top; 2-29-1 Dōgenzaka, Shibuya-ku; ⏰10am-9pm; Ⓡ JR Yamanote line to Shibuya, Hachikō exit) See all those dolled-up teens walking around Shibuya? This is where they shop. Nicknamed marukyū, this cylindrical tower houses dozens of small boutiques, each with its own carefully styled look. Even if you don't intend to buy anything, you can't understand Shibuya without making a stop here.

Parco — Department Store

(パルコ; Map p84; ☎3464-5111; www.parco-shibuya.com; 15-1 Udagawa-chō, Shibuya-ku; ⏰10am-9pm; Ⓡ JR Yamanote line to Shibuya, Hachikō exit) Not your typical fussy department store, Parco customers are more likely to be art-school students than ladies who lunch. Lots of Japanese fashion designers have shops here.

HARAJUKU & AROUND 原宿

Omote-sandō is lined with upscale boutiques. Narrow, meandering Cat St, which intersects it, offers a more chilled-out shopping experience. The web of alleys surrounding the two, known as Ura-Hara (literally 'behind Harajuku'), is where you'll find the small boutiques and vintage shops that keep the neighbourhood's indie spirit alive.

Sou-Sou — Fashion

(そうそう; Map p88; ☎3407-7877; http://sousounetshop.jp; 5-3-10 Minami-Aoyama, Minato-ku; ⏰11am-8pm; Ⓢ Ginza line to Omote-sandō, exit A5) Sou-Sou gives traditional Japanese clothing items – such as split-toed tabi socks and haori (coats with kimono-like sleeves) – a contemporary spin. It is best known for producing the steel-toed, rubber-soled tabi shoes worn by Japanese construction workers in fun, playful designs.

Laforet — Fashion

(ラフォーレ; Map p88; www.laforet.ne.jp; 1-11-6 Jingūmae, Shibuya-ku; ⏰11am-8pm; Ⓡ JR Yamanote line to Harajuku, Omote-sandō exit) Laforet has been a beacon of cutting-edge Harajuku style for decades. Don't let the Topshop on the ground floor fool you; lots of quirky, cult favourite brands still cut their teeth here.

Musubi
Speciality Shop

(むす美; Map p88; http://kyoto-musubi.com/; 2-31-8 Jingūmae, Shibuya-ku; ⏰11am-7pm Thu-Tue; 🚃JR Yamanote line to Harajuku, Takeshita exit) *Furoshiki* are versatile squares of cloth that can be folded and knotted to make shopping bags and gift wrap. This shop sells pretty ones in both traditional and contemporary patterns. There is usually an English-speaking clerk who can show you how to tie them, or pick up one of the English-language books sold here.

KiddyLand
Toys

(キデイランド; Map p88; www.kiddyland.co.jp/en/index.html; 6-1-9 Jingūmae, Shibuya-ku; ⏰10am-9pm; 🚃JR Yamanote line to Harajuku, Omote-sandō exit) This multistorey toy emporium is packed to the rafters with character goods. It's not just for kids either; you'll spot plenty of adults on a nostalgia trip down the Hello Kitty aisle.

Oriental Bazaar
Souvenirs

(オリエンタルバザー; Map p88; www.orientalbazaar.co.jp; 5-9-13 Jingūmae, Shibuya-ku; ⏰10am-6pm Mon-Wed & Fri, to 7pm Sat & Sun; 🚃JR Yamanote line to Harajuku, Omote-sandō exit) Oriental Bazaar stocks a wide selection of souvenirs at very reasonable prices. Items to be found here include fans, pottery, *yukata* (light summer kimonos) and T-shirts, some made in Japan, but others not (read the labels).

SHINJUKU 新宿

Isetan
Department Store

(伊勢丹; Map p90; www.isetan.co.jp; 3-14-1 Shinjuku, Shinjuku-ku; ⏰10am-8pm; Ⓢ Marunouchi line to Shinjuku-sanchōme, exits B3, B4 & B5) Most department stores play to conservative tastes, but this one doesn't. Women should head to the Re-Style section on the 2nd floor for an always changing line-up of up-and-coming Japanese designers. Men get a whole building of their own (connected by a passageway). Don't miss the basement food hall, featuring some of the country's top purveyors of sweet and savoury goodies.

Don Quijote
Variety

(ドン・キホーテ; Map p90; ☎5291-9211; www.donki.com; 1-16-5 Kabukichō, Shinjuku-ku; ⏰24hr; 🚃JR Yamanote line to Shinjuku, east exit) This fluorescent-lit bargain castle is filled to the brim with weird loot. Chaotic piles of knockoff electronics and designer

Omote-sandō

goods sit alongside sex toys, fetish costumes and packaged foods. Though it's now a national chain, it started as a rare (at the time) 24-hour store for the city's night workers.

RanKing RanQueen
Variety

(ランキンランキン; Map p90; basement fl, Shinjuku Station, Shinjuku-ku; ◷10am-11pm; ℝJR Yamanote line to Shinjuku, east exit) If it's trendy, it's here. This clever shop stocks only the top-selling products in any given category, from eyeliner and soft drinks to leg-slimming massage rollers. Look for it just outside the east-exit ticket gates of JR Shinjuku Station.

Disk Union
Music

(ディスクユニオン; Map p90; 3-31-4 Shinjuku, Shinjuku-ku; ◷11am-9pm; ℝJR Yamanote line to Shinjuku, east exit) Scruffy Disk Union is known by local audiophiles as Tokyo's best used CD and vinyl store. Eight storeys carry a variety of musical styles; if you still can't find what you're looking for there are several other branches in Shinjuku that stock more obscure genres (pick up a map here).

AKIHABARA & AROUND 秋葉原

Mandarake Complex
Manga, Anime

(まんだらけコンプレックス; Map p62; www.mandarake.co.jp; 3-11-2 Soto-Kanda, Chiyoda-ku; ◷noon-8pm; ℝJR Yamanote line to Akihabara, Electric Town exit) When *otaku* dream of heaven, it probably looks a lot like this giant go-to store for manga and anime. Eight storeys are piled high with comic books and DVDs, action figures and cell art just for starters. The 5th floor, in all its pink splendour, is devoted to women's comics, while the 4th floor is for men.

2k540 Aki-Oka Artisan
Crafts

(アキオカアルチザン; Map p62; www.jrtk.jp/2k540; 5-9-23 Ueno, Taitō-ku; ◷11am-7pm Thu-Tue; ℝGinza line to Suehirochō, exit 2) This ace arcade under the JR tracks (its name refers to the distance from Tokyo Station) offers an eclectic range of stores selling Japanese-made goods – everything from pottery to cute aliens, a nod to Akihabara from a mall that is more akin to Kyoto than Electric Town. The best for colourful crafts is **Nippon Hyakkuten** (日本百貨店; http://nippon-dept.jp).

Boat tour, Tokyo

Yodobashi Akiba
Electronics

(ヨドバシカメラ Akiba; Map p62; www.
yodobashi-akiba.com; 1-1 Kanda Hanaoka-chō,
Chiyoda-ku; ⏰9.30am-10pm; 🚉JR Yamanote
line to Akihabara, Shōwa-tōriguchi exit) This is
the monster branch of Shinjuku's Yodobashi Camera where many locals shop. It
has eight floors of electronics, cameras,
toys, appliances, CDs and DVDs at an in-
store branch of Tower Records, and even
restaurants. Ask about export models and
VAT-free purchases.

mAAch ecute
Mall

(Map p62; www.maach-ecute.jp; 1-25-4 Kanda-
Sudachō, Chiyoda-ku; ⏰11am-9pm Mon-Sat, to
8pm Sun; 🚉Chūō or Sōbu lines to Akihabara,
Electric Town exit) JR has another shopping and dining hit on its hands with this
complex crafted from the old station and
railway arches at Mansei-bashi. Crafts,
homegoods, fashions and food from
across Japan are sold here; look out for
Tatazumai which stocks more than 50
types of craft beer, cider and sakes, and
Obscura Coffee Roasters.

ASAKUSA & SUMIDA-GAWA
浅草 ● 隅田川

Tokyo Hotarudo
Vintage

(東京蛍堂; Map p96; http://tokyohotarudo.com;
1-41-8 Asakusa, Taitō-ku; ⏰11am-8pm Wed-Sun;
🚉Tsukuba Express to Asakusa, exit 5) This
curio shop is run by an eccentric young
man who prefers to dress as if the 20th
century hasn't come and gone already.
If you think that sounds marvellous, then
you'll want to check out his collection of
vintage dresses and bags, antique lamps,
watches, and decorative *objet*.

Bengara
Crafts

(べんがら; Map p96; www.bengara.com; 1-35-6
Asakusa, Taitō-ku; ⏰10am-6pm Mon-Fri, to 7pm
Sat & Sun, closed 3rd Thu of month; 🚉Ginza line
to Asakusa, exit 1) By now you're familiar with
noren, the curtains that hang in front of
shop doors. This store sells beautiful ones,
made of linen and coloured with natural
dyes (like indigo or persimmon) or decorated with ink-brush paintings. There are
smaller items too, such as pouches and
book covers, made of traditional textiles.

Riverboat Cruise

Riverboats were once a primary
means of transport in Tokyo, and
the Sumida-gawa was the main
'highway.' You can experience this
centuries-old tradition (and happily
combine sightseeing and transport)
by hopping on one of the water buses
run by **Tokyo Cruise** (水上バス; Suijō
Bus; 📞0120-977-311; http://suijobus.co.jp).

Of the four routes, the Sumida-
gawa line is the most popular,
which runs from Asakusa to Hama-
rikyū-teien (¥720, 35 minutes) and
terminates at **Hinode Pier** (日の出
桟橋; Map p62; 🚉Yurikamome Line to
Hinode, east exit) on Tokyo Bay.

The Asakusa–Odaiba Direct Line
connects Asakusa with Odaiba
Kaihin-kōen (¥1520, 50 minutes),
also via the Sumida-gawa. If you're
planning to take this route, try to
catch one of the two spaceshiplike
boats, *Himiko* and *Hotaluna*,
designed by famous manga artist
Leiji Matsumoto.

Fujiya
Crafts

(ふじ屋; Map p96; 2-2-15 Asakusa, Taitō-ku;
⏰10.30am-6.30pm Fri-Wed; 🚇Ginza line to
Asakusa, exit 1) Fujiya specialises in *tenugui*:
dyed cloths of thin cotton that can be
used as tea towels, kerchiefs, gift wrap
(the list goes on; they're surprisingly
versatile). Here they come in traditional
designs and humorous modern ones.

Solamachi
Mall

(ソラマチ; Map p96; 1-1-2 Oshiage, Sumida-ku;
⏰10am-9pm; 🚇Hanzōmon line to Oshiage, exit
B3) It's not all cheesy Sky Tree swag here
at this mall under the tower (though you
can get 634m-long rolls of Sky Tree toilet
paper). Shops on the 4th floor offer a
better-than-usual selection of Japanese-y
souvenirs, including pretty trinkets made
from kimono fabric and quirky fashion
items.

ℹ️ Information

Money

Getting cash is easier in Tokyo than elsewhere in Japan, and even though most places take credit cards, it's still a good idea to have some cash as back-up. 7-Eleven conveniences stores and post offices with international ATMs can be found in every neighbourhood. Major hubs like Shinjuku, Shibuya, Roppongi and Ginza also have 24hr **Citibank** (シティバンク; www.citibank.co.jp/en) ATMs that accept cards from every country.

Tourist Information

There are tourist information centres at both terminals at **Narita Airport** (1st fl, terminals 1 & 2; 🕒8am-10pm) and in the international terminal of **Haneda Airport** (2nd fl Arrival Lobby; 🕒5.30am-1am) with English-speaking staff who can help you get oriented. They cannot make bookings though.

Asakusa Culture Tourist Information Center (浅草文化観光センター; Map p96; 📞3842-5566; http://taitonavi.jp; 2-18-9 Kaminarimon, Taitō-ku; 🕒9am-8pm; 🅂Ginza line to Asakusa, exit 2) Run by Taitō-ku, this TIC has lots of info on Asakusa and Ueno, and a Pia ticket counter (for purchasing tickets to concerts and shows), near the entrance to Sensō-ji.

JNTO Tourist Information Center (Map p68; 📞3201-3331; www.jnto.go.jp; 1st fl, Shin-Tokyo Bldg, 3-3-1 Marunouchi, Chiyoda-ku; 🕒9am-5pm; 🅁JR Yamanote line to Yūrakuchō, Tokyo International Forum exit) Run by the Japan National Tourism Organisation (JNTO), this TIC has information on Tokyo and beyond.

JR East Travel Service Center (JR東日本訪日旅行センター; Map p68; www.jreast.co.jp/e/customer_support/service_center_tokyo.html; Tokyo Station, 1-9-1 Marunouchi, Chiyoda-ku; 🕒7.30am-8.30pm; 🅁JR Yamanote line to Tokyo, Marunouchi north exit) Tourist information, luggage storage, money exchange, and bookings for ski and onsen getaways. There are branches in the two airports, too.

Tokyo Tourist Information Center (東京観光情報センター; Map p90; 📞5321-3077; www.gotokyo.org; 1st fl, Tokyo Metropolitan Government bldg 1, 2-8-1 Nishi-Shinjuku, Shinjuku-ku; 🕒9.30am-6.30pm; 🅂Ōedo line to Tochōmae, exit A4) Combine a trip to the observatories at the Tokyo Metropolitan Government Offices with a stop at the city's official TIC. There's another branch located right outside the ticket gates of the Keisei Ueno line (which services Narita Airport).

Sumida-gawa

NICOLAS MCCOMBER/GETTY IMAGES ©

Suica & Pasmo Cards

Getting a prepaid train pass – either the Suica or Pasmo, which are interchangeable – is highly recommended, even for a short trip. With one of these cards, which are fitted with electromagnetic chips, you'll be able to breeze through the ticket gates of any train or subway station in the city without having to work out fares or transfer tickets. Fares for pass users are slightly less (a couple of yen per journey) than for paper ticket holders.

Both Suica and Pasmo cards can be purchased from ticket vending machines in most train and subway stations (Suica from JR line machines and Pasmo from subway and commuter line machines). A minimum charge of ¥1000 plus a deposit of ¥500, refundable if you return your card to a train station window, is required. You can charge the cards, in increments of ¥1000, at the same vending machines.

To use it, simply wave it over the card reader; you will need to do this to enter and exit the station.

ℹ Getting There & Away

Air

Tokyo has two major airports: **Narita Airport** (NRT; 成田空港; ☏ 0476-34-8000; www.narita-airport.jp) and **Haneda Airport** (HND; 羽田空港; ☏ international terminal 6428-0888; www.tokyo-airport-bldg.co.jp/en). Narita is 66km east of Tokyo, in neighbouring Chiba prefecture. Haneda Airport is more convenient, within the city limits and near Tokyo Bay. Most international flights operate through Narita while domestic travel is usually funnelled through Haneda. However, Haneda opened an international wing in October 2010 and is now handling an increasing number of international flights. Be warned that some flights into Haneda arrive in the middle of the night, when public transport isn't running – so you'll need to factor in the cost of a taxi.

Immigration and customs procedures are usually straightforward, but they can be time-consuming. Note that Japanese customs officials can be very scrupulous; backpackers arriving from anywhere even remotely exotic (the Philippines, Thailand etc) can expect some questions and perhaps a thorough search.

It is important to note that there are two distinct terminals at Narita, separated by a five-minute train ride. Be sure to check which terminal your flight departs from, and give yourself plenty of time to get out to Narita. Airport officials recommend leaving at least four hours before your flight.

ℹ Getting Around

To/From Narita Airport

With the exception of very early morning flights, public transport can usually meet all arrival and departure times.

Depending on where you're headed, it's generally cheaper and faster to travel into Tokyo by train than by limousine bus. However, rail users will probably need to change trains somewhere, and this can be frustrating on a jetlagged first visit.

Bus services provide a hassle-free direct route to many major hotels, and you don't have to be a hotel guest to use them; a short taxi ride (and there are always taxis waiting in front of big hotels) can take you the rest of the way.

We don't recommend taking a taxi from Narita – it'll set you back around ¥30,000. Figure one to two hours into your itinerary to get to/from Narita.

Bus

Friendly Airport Limousine (☏ 3665-7220; www.limousinebus.co.jp/en; 1-way fare ¥3150) Operates scheduled, direct, all-reserved buses between Narita Airport and major hotels and train stations in Tokyo. The journey takes 1½ to two hours depending on traffic. At the time of research, discount round-trip 'Welcome to Tokyo Limousine Bus Return Voucher' tickets (¥4500) were available for foreign tourists; ask at the ticket counter at the airport.

Access Narita (アクセス成田; Map p68; ☎0120-600-366; www.accessnarita.jp) Discount buses connect Narita Airport to Tokyo Station and Ginza (¥1000, one to 1¼ hours). There's no ticket counter at the airport, just go directly to bus stop 31 at Terminal 1 or stops 2 or 19 at Terminal 2. You can reserve tickets online (a safer bet for trips to the airport), but unfortunately only in Japanese.

Train

Keisei Skyliner (京成スカイライナー; www. keisei.co.jp/keisei/tetudou/skyliner/us) The quickest service into Tokyo runs nonstop to Nippori (¥2470, 36 minutes) and Ueno (¥2470, 41 minutes) stations, where you can connect to the JR Yamanote line or the subway (Ueno Station only). Trains run twice an hour, 8am to 10pm. Foreign nationals can purchase advanced tickets online for slightly less (¥2200).

The Skyliner & Tokyo Subway Ticket (www.keisei.co.jp/keisei/tetudou/skyliner/us/ value_ticket/subway.html; ¥2800-3500), which combines a one-way ticket on the Skyliner and a one-, two- or three-day subway pass, is a good deal.

Narita Express (N'EX; 成田エクスプレス; www.jreast.co.jp/e/nex) A swift and smooth option, especially if you're staying on the west side of the city, N'EX trains depart Narita approximately every half-hour between 7am and 10pm for Tokyo Station (¥3020, 53 minutes). They also run less frequently into Shinagawa (¥3110, 65 minutes), Shibuya (¥3110, 73 minutes), Shinjuku (¥3190, 80 minutes) and Ikebukuro (¥3190, 86 minutes).

At the time of research, Japan Rail was offering half-price N'EX tickets for foreign tourists travelling from the airport; ask at the JR East Travel Service centres inside either terminal at Narita Airport.

Long-haul JR passes are valid on N'EX trains, but you must obtain a seat reservation (no extra charge) from a JR ticket office.

To/From Haneda Airport

From downtown Tokyo, it takes far less time to reach Haneda Airport than Narita. Taxis to the city centre cost around ¥6000; this will be your only option if your flight gets in before dawn.

Friendly Airport Limousine (www.limousinebus. co.jp/en) Coaches connect Haneda with major hubs such as Shibuya (¥1030), Shinjuku (¥1230), Roppongi (¥1130) and Ginza (¥930); fares double after midnight. Travel times vary wildly, taking anywhere from 30 to 90 minutes depending on traffic. The last bus of the day departs for Shibuya Station at 12.30am; service resumes at 5.45am.

Keikyū (☎5789-8686; www.haneda-tokyo-access.com/en) Airport *kyūkō* (limited-express) trains depart several times an hour (5.30am to midnight) for Shinagawa (¥410, 12 minutes) on the JR Yamanote line. From Shinagawa, some trains continue along the Asakusa subway line, which serves Higashi-Ginza, Nihombashi and Asakusa stations.

Tokyo Monorail (東京モノレール; www.tokyo-monorail.co.jp/english) Leaving approximately every 10 minutes (5am to midnight)

Subway station

Train Tips

As far as public transport networks go, no city can touch Tokyo's awesome network of trains and subway lines. It's clean, quick, efficient and convenient, but it does have its quirks. Some tips:

○ Figure out the best route to your destination with the app Navitime for Japan Travel; you can download routes to be used offline, too.

○ Avoid rush hour (around 8am to 9.30am and 5pm to 8pm), when 'packed in like sardines' is an understatement.

○ Note your last train. The whole system shuts down from approximately midnight to 5am. The last train of the night can also be especially crowded (often with swaying drunks).

○ If you can't work out how much to pay, one easy trick is to buy a ticket at the cheapest fare (¥133 for JR; ¥165 for Tokyo Metro; ¥174 for Toei) and use one of the 'fare adjustment' machines, near the exit gates, to settle the difference at the end of your journey.

○ Most train stations have multiple exits – make sure you get the right one (which can save you a lot of time and confusion above ground). There are usually maps in the station that show which exits are closest to major area landmarks.

for Hamamatsuchō Station (¥490, 15 minutes), which is a stop on the JR Yamanote line.

Taxi

It rarely makes economic sense to take a taxi, unless you've got a group of four. The meter starts at a steep ¥730, which gives you 2km of travel. After that, the meter starts to clock an additional ¥100 for every 280m (and up to ¥90 for every two minutes you sit idly in traffic). Figure around ¥3000 for a ride from Roppongi to Ginza. It's best to have cash on you, as not all taxis take credit cards.

While it's possible to hail a cab from the street, your best bet is a taxi stand in front of a train station. Taxis with their indicator in red are free; green means taken.

Even in Tokyo, most cabbies don't speak English and have trouble finding all but the most well-known spots. Fortunately many have GPS systems, so have an address or a business card for your destination handy.

Train

Tokyo's train network includes JR lines, a subway system, and private commuter lines. It's so thorough, especially in the city centre, that you rarely have to walk more than 10 minutes from a station to your destination. Stations have English signage.

Tickets are sold from vending machines near the automated ticket gates. Look for the newer touch-screen ones that have an English option. Fares are determined by how far you ride; there should be a fare chart above the ticket machines. You'll need a valid train ticket to exit the station.

Day Passes

Day passes can save you money, though only if you plan to cover a lot of ground in one day. You'll need to get one that covers the rail lines you'll be using, and purchase it from one of the station windows on those lines.

Tokyo Metro 1-Day Open Ticket Costs ¥710 (child ¥360) and covers Tokyo Metro subway lines.

Common 1-Day Ticket Costs ¥1000 (child ¥500) and covers both Tokyo Metro and Toei subway lines.

Tokyo Combination Ticket Costs ¥1590 (child ¥800) and covers JR trains in Tokyo, all subway lines and Toei buses.

Subway Lines

There are a total of 13 colour-coded subway lines zigzagging through Tokyo. Four are operated by TOEI; nine belong to Tokyo Metro. Transfers between lines within the same group are seamless; if you plan to switch between TOEI trains and Tokyo Metro trains, you'll need to purchase a transfer ticket at the start of your journey.

AROUND TOKYO

Mt Fuji Area

Mt Fuji (富士山周辺; Fuji-san; 3776m), Japan's highest and most famous peak, is obviously this region's natural draw. In addition to climbing Fuji-san, visitors can hunt for precious views of the sacred volcano, and get outdoorsy around the Fuji Five Lakes (Fuji go-ko) with plenty of camping, hiking and lake activities.

 Tours

Discover Japan Tours Guided Tour
(www.discover-japan-tours.com/en; two-day tours per person ¥10,000) Reputable company offering guided tours from Tokyo for groups of two or more, and specialising in less-frequented routes.

 **Information**

All of the following have English-speaking staff and brochures on climbing and sights.

Fuji-Yoshida Tourist Information Center
(☎0555-22-7000; ⏰9am-5pm) Next to Fujisan (Mt Fuji) train station, the clued-up staff can provide info on climbing, and brochures and maps of the area.

Kawaguchi-ko Tourist Information Center
(☎0555-72-6700; ⏰8.30am-5.30pm Sun-Fri, to 7pm Sat) Next to Kawaguchi-ko Station. Has English speakers as well as maps and brochures.

Getting There & Away

The Mt Fuji area is most easily reached from Tokyo by bus or train. The two main towns on the north side of the mountain, Fuji-Yoshida and Kawaguchi-ko, are the principal gateways. It's also possible

Mt Fuji (p126)

TAKESHI.K/GETTY IMAGES ©

TOKYO MT FUJI AREA

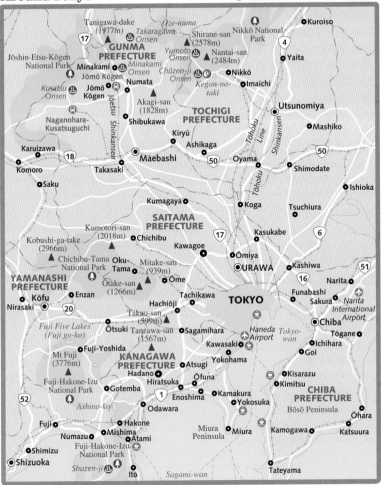

to bus in from Tokyo straight to the Kawaguchi-ko Fifth Station on the mountain during the official climbing season.

Coming from western Japan (Kyoto, Osaka), you can take an overnight bus to Kawaguchi-ko.

Bus

Frequent **Keiō Dentetsu** (📞 03-5376-2222; www.highwaybus.com) and **Fujikyū Express** (📞 0555-72-6877; http://transportation.fujikyu. co.jp) buses (¥1750, one hour and 50 minutes) operate directly to Kawaguchi-ko Station, and Fujisan Station in Fuji-Yoshida, from the **Shinjuku Highway Bus Terminal** (📞 03-5376-2222; http://

highway-buses.jp; 🚉 Yamanote Line to Shinjuku, West exit).

Coming from western Japan, the overnight bus departs from Osaka's Higashi-Umeda Subway Station (¥8700, 10.15pm) via Kyoto Station (¥8000, 11.18pm) to Kawaguchi-ko Station (arrives 8.32am).

Train

JR Chūō Line trains go from Shinjuku to Ōtsuki (*tokkyū* ¥2570, one hour; *futsū* ¥1320, 1½ hours), where you transfer to the Fuji Kyūkō Line for Fujisan (¥1020, 55 minutes) and Kawaguchi-ko (¥1140, 65 minutes).

Climbing Mt Fuji: Know Before You Go

Although children and grandparents regularly reach the summit of Mt Fuji, this is a serious mountain. It's high enough for altitude sickness, and on the summit it can go from sunny and warm to wet, windy and cold remarkably quickly. Even if conditions are fine, you can count on it being close to freezing in the morning, even in summer. Also be aware that visibility can rapidly disappear with a blanket of mist rolling in suddenly. At a minimum, bring clothing appropriate for cold and wet weather, including a hat and gloves. You should also bring water, a map and light snacks. If you're climbing at night, bring a torch (flashlight) or headlamp, and spare batteries.

Descending the mountain is much harder on the knees than ascending; hiking poles can help. To avoid altitude sickness, be sure to take it slowly and take regular breaks. If you're suffering severe symptoms, you'll need to make an immediate descent.

The *Shobunsha Yama-to-kōgen Mt Fuji Map* (山と高原地図・富士山; in Japanese), available at major bookshops, is the most comprehensive map of the area.

For summit weather conditions, see www.snow-forecast.com/resorts/Mount-Fuji/6day/top.

MT FUJI 富士山

♩ 555

Of all the iconic images of Japan, Mt Fuji is the real deal. Admiration for the mountain appears in Japan's earliest recorded literature, dating from the 8th century. Back then the now dormant volcano was prone to spewing smoke, making it all the more revered. Mt Fuji continues to captivate both Japanese and international visitors. In 2013, the year Fuji was granted World Heritage status, some 300,000 people climbed the peak.

At the summit, the crater has circumference of 4km. As expected, views are spectacular, but be prepared for it to be clouded over. The highest point (3776m) is on the opposite side of the crater, and there's a post office if you want to send a postcard back home.

Climbing Mt Fuji is an excellent online resource featuring info needed by climbers. The *Climbing Mt Fuji* brochure, available at the Fuji-Yoshida Tourist Information Center, is also worth picking up.

When to Go

The official climbing season is from 1 July to 31 August. It's a busy mountain during these two months, with occasional queues for the rush to see sunrise. To get around the crowds, consider heading up on a weekday or starting earlier during the day to avoid the afternoon rush, and spend a night in a mountain hut.

Authorities strongly caution against climbing outside the regular season, when the weather is highly unpredictable and first-aid stations on the mountain are closed. Despite this, many people do climb out of season, as it's the best time to avoid the crowds. During this time, climbers generally head off at dawn, and return early afternoon – however, mountain huts on the Kawaguchi-ko Trail stay open through mid-September when weather conditions may still be good; none open before July, when snow still blankets the upper stations.

Outside of the climbing season, check weather conditions carefully before setting out, bring appropriate equipment, do not climb alone, and be prepared to retreat at any time. A guide can be invaluable.

Once snow or ice is on the mountain, Fuji becomes a very serious and dangerous undertaking and should only be attempted by those with winter mountaineering equipment and plenty of experience. It's highly advised that off-season climbers register with the local police department for safety reasons; fill out the form at the Kawaguchi-ko or Fuji-Yoshida Tourist Information Center.

Trails

The mountain is divided into 10 'stations' from base (First Station) to summit (Tenth). From the base station is the original pilgrim trail, but these days most climbers start from the halfway point at one of the four Fifth Stations, which is accessed via bus. All the routes converge at the Eighth Station, so be sure you take the right path on the way down.

To time your arrival for dawn you can either start up in the afternoon, stay overnight in a mountain hut and continue early in the morning, or climb the whole way at night. You do not want to arrive on the top too long before dawn, as it's likely to be very cold and windy.

Fifth Station Routes

There are four Fifth Station trails for climbing Mt Fuji: Kawaguchi-ko, also known as Yoshida (2305m); Suba-shiri (1980m); Fujinomiya (2380m); and Gotemba (1440m). Allow five to six hours to reach the top (though some climb it in half the time) and about three hours to descend, plus 1½ hours for circling the crater at the top.

The **Kawaguchi-ko Trail** is by far and away the most popular route. It's accessed from Kawaguchi-ko Fifth Station (aka Mt Fuji Fifth Station), and has the most modern facilities and is easiest to reach from Kawaguchi-ko town.

 Sleeping

From the Fifth Stations and up, dozens of mountain huts offer hikers simple hot meals and a place to sleep (with/without meals from ¥7560/5400). Though much maligned for their spartan conditions (a blanket on the floor sandwiched between other climbers), these huts can fill up

Hikers on the Mt Fuji summit

PONGNATHEE KLUAYTHONG/SHUTTERSTOCK ©

Top Views of Mt Fuji

Mt Fuji has many different personalities depending on the season. Winter and spring months are your best bet for seeing it in all its clichéd glory; however, even during these times the snowcapped peak may be visible only in the morning before it retreats behind its cloud curtain. Its elusiveness, however, is part of the appeal, making sightings all the more special. Here are some of our top spots for viewing, both in the immediate and greater area:

- **Kawaguchi-ko:** On the north side of the lake, where Fuji looms large over its shimmering reflection.

- **Motosu-ko:** The famous view depicted on the ¥1000 bill can be seen from the northwest side of the lake.

- **Panorama-dai:** The end of this **hiking trail** (パノラマ台) rewards you with a magnificent front-on view of the mountain.

- **Kōyō-dai:** From this **lookout**, Mt Fuji is particularly stunning in the autumn colours.

---

fast – reservations are recommended and are essential on weekends. **Taishikan** (太子館; ☎ 22-1947; http://www.mfi.or.jp/w3/home0/taisikan; per person with two meals from ¥8500) and **Fujisan Hotel** (富士山ホテル; ☎ 0555-22-0237; www.fujisanhotel.com; per person with/without 2 meals from ¥8350/5950) at the Eighth Station (Kawaguchi-ko Trail) usually have an English speaker on hand. Most huts allow you to rest inside as long as you order something. Camping on the mountain is not permitted, other than at the designated campsite near the Kawaguchi-ko Fifth Station.

The Subashiri Fifth Station has the atmospheric **Higashi Fuji Lodge** (☎ 75-2113; r ¥5000), which is very convenient for the off-season trekkers, and cooks up steaming *soba* (buckwheat noodles) with mushrooms and Fuji herbs.

ⓘ Getting There & Around

For those wanting to start trekking as soon as they arrive from Tokyo, Keiō Dentetsu Bus (p125) runs direct buses (¥2700, 2½ hours; reservations necessary) from the Shinjuku Highway Bus Terminal to Kawaguchi-ko Fifth Station (does not operate in winter).

Buses run from both Kawaguchi-ko Station and Fujisan Station to the starting point at Kawaguchi-ko Fifth Station (one way/return ¥1540/2100, 50 minutes) roughly mid-April to early December. In the trekking season, buses depart hourly from around 7am until 8pm (ideal for climbers intending to make an overnight ascent). Returning from Fifth Station, buses head back to town from 8am to 9pm.

In the off season, the first bus inconveniently leaves Kawaguchi-ko and Fujisan Stations at 9.10am, and the last bus returns at 3.30pm, meaning most trekkers will need to get a taxi (around ¥12,000, plus ¥2100 tolls) in the morning to have enough time, before getting the bus back. The bus schedule is highly seasonal; call Fujikyū Yamanashi bus (p125) or your hotel for details.

In the low season you should be able to find other trekkers to share a taxi at K's House (p130). Car hire is another option (particularly if there's a group), costing around ¥6800 per day, plus fuel and tolls.

To get to the Subashiri Fifth Station trail, you can catch a train from Kawaguchi-ko to Gotemba (¥1470), from where regular buses head to the Subashiri access point. Check timetables carefully before heading off.

FUJI FIVE LAKES 富士五湖
☎ 555

The Fuji Five Lakes (Fuji go-ko) region is a postcardlike area around Fuji's northern foothills; its lakes act as natural reflecting pools for the mountain's perfect cone. Yamanaka-ko is the easternmost lake, followed by Kawaguchi-ko, Sai-ko, Shōji-ko and Motosu-ko. Particularly during the autumn *kōyō* (foliage) season, the lakes make a good overnight trip out of Tokyo, for leisurely strolling, lake activities and for hiking in the nearby mountains.

Fuji-Yoshida and Kawaguchi-ko are the most accessible and developed areas. Kawaguchi-ko is the most popular place to stay, with best range of accommodation, but both make good bases if you plan on climbing Mt Fuji and don't intend on overnighting in a mountain hut.

Fuji-Yoshida 富士吉田

Not actually a lake, Fuji-Yoshida is one of the main gateway towns for the Fuji Five Lakes area. The central district, **Gekkō-ji**, feels like the little town that time forgot, with original mid-20th-century facades. The Fujisan Station is in the centre of Fuji-Yoshida.

◉ Sights & Activities

Fuji Sengen-jinja   Shinto Shrine
(冨士浅間神社; ☎0555-22-0221; http://sengenjinja.jp/index.html; 5558 Kami-Yoshida, Fuji-Yoshida; ⊘grounds 24hr; staffed 9am-5pm)
FREE A necessary preliminary to the Mt Fuji ascent was a visit to this deeply wooded, atmospheric temple, which has been located here since the 8th century. Notable points include a 1000-year-old cedar; its main gate, which is rebuilt every 60 years (slightly larger each time); and its two one-tonne *mikoshi* (portable shrines) used in the annual Yoshida no Himatsuri (Yoshida Fire Festival). From Fujisan Station it's a 20-minute uphill

walk, or take a bus to Sengen-jinja-mae (¥150, five minutes).

Togawa-ke Oshi-no-ie Restored Pilgrim's Inn   Historic Building
(御師旧外川家住宅; 3-14-8 Kami-Yoshida; adult/child ¥100/50; ⊘9.30am-4.30pm, closed Tue) Fuji-Yoshida's *oshi-no-ie* (pilgrims' inns) have served visitors to the mountain since the days when climbing Mt Fuji was a pilgrimage rather than a tourist event. Very few still function as inns, but Togawa-ke Oshi-no-ie offers some insight into the fascinating Edo-era practice of Mt Fuji worship.

Kawaguchi-ko 河口湖

Easily the most popular place to stay in Fuji Five Lakes, Kawaguchi-ko is the closest town to four of the five lakes and departure points for climbing Mt Fuji. Even if you have no intention of climbing, this is a great spot to hang out and enjoy what the Fuji Five Lakes region has to offer, along with great Mt Fuji views.

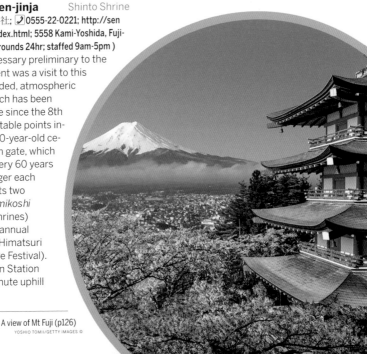

A view of Mt Fuji (p126)
YOSHIO TOMII/GETTY IMAGES ©

Fujisan Train Station

In 2011, Fuji-Yoshida Station changed its name to Fujisan Station. It's also commonly referred to as Mt Fuji Station in English. This is not to be confused with the Kawaguchi-ko Fifth Station which is also commonly referred to as Mt Fuji Fifth Station. It's not a train station but a climbing access point (and bus stop) on the mountain, the starting point for the Kawaguchi-ko Trail to the summit. Confused yet?

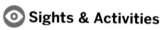 Sights & Activities

Kachi Kachi Yama Ropeway
Ropeway

(カチカチ山ロープウェイ; www.kachi kachiyama-ropeway.com; 1163-1 Azagawa; one way/return adult ¥410/720, child ¥210/360; ⊙9am-5pm) On the lower eastern edge of the lake, this ropeway runs to the **Fuji Viewing Platform** (1104m). If you have time, there is a 3½-hour hike from here to **Mitsutōge-yama** (三つ峠山; 1785m); it's an old trail with excellent Fuji views. Ask at Kawaguchi-ko Tourist Information Center for a map.

Fuji Visitor Center
Visitor Centre

(富士ビジターセンター; ☎72-0259; www. yamanashi-kankou.visitor/index.html; 6663-1 Funatsu; ⊙8.30am-5pm) **FREE** Get up to speed on Mt Fuji at this well-presented visitor centre. An English video (12 minutes) with a blockbuster movie soundtrack is a little cheesy, but it gives a good summary of the mountain and its geological history. There's also an observation deck and restaurant.

Sleeping

K's House Mt Fuji
Hostel ¥

(☎83-5556; http://kshouse.jp/fuji-e/index. html; 6713-108 Funatsu; dm from ¥2500, d with/ without bathroom ¥7800/6800; ⊜@🛜)

K's is expert at providing a welcoming atmosphere, spacious Japanese-style rooms and helpful English-speaking staff. There's a fully loaded kitchen, mountain bikes for hire and comfy common areas to meet fellow travellers/climbers and free pickup from Kawaguchi-ko Station. Its bar **Zero Station** (⊙6pm-midnight) is stumbling distance away. Rooms fill up fast during the climbing season.

Fuji Lake Hotel
Hotel ¥¥

(☎72-2209; www.fujilake.co.jp; 1 Funatsu; r per person with 2 meals from ¥15,552; ❄@🛜) On Kawaguchi-ko's south shore, this stylish 1935 vintage hotel offers either Mt Fuji or lake views from its Japanese-Western combo rooms. Some rooms have private *rotemburo*, otherwise there's a common onsen.

Sunnide Resort
Hotel ¥¥

(サニーデリゾート; ☎76-6004; www.sunnide. com; 2549-1 Ōishi; r per person with two meals from ¥13,000, cottages from ¥16,000; ❄@🛜) Offering views of Mt Fuji from the far side of Kawaguchi-ko, friendly Sunnide has hotel rooms and cottages with a delicious outdoor bath. You can splash out in the stylish suites or the discounted 'backpacker' rates (¥4400, no views), if same-day rooms are available. Breakfast/dinner costs from ¥2000/1800.

Kozantei Ubuya
Ryokan ¥¥¥

(湖山亭うぶや; ☎72-1145; www.ubuya.co.jp; 10 Asakawa; r per person with 2 meals from ¥20,100; ❄@🛜) Elegant and ultra stylish, Ubuya offers unobstructed panoramic views of Mt Fuji reflected in Kawaguchi-ko that are simply unbeatable. Splash out on the more expensive suites to enjoy the scene while soaking in an outdoor tub on your balcony decking. One for the honeymooners.

Eating

Kawaguchi-ko's local noodles are *hōtō*, hand-cut and served in a thick miso stew with pumpkin, sweet potato and other vegetables.

Hōtō Fudō
Noodles ¥¥

(ほうとう不動; ☎ 72-8511; www.houtou-fudou.
jp; 707 Kawaguchi; hōtō ¥1080; ⏱11am-7pm)
Hōtō is a hearty meal best sampled at this
chain, which has five branches around
town. This is the most architecturally
interesting one, an igloo-like building in
which you can also sample *basashi* –
horsemeat sashimi (¥1080).

Sanrokuen
Teppanyaki ¥¥

(山麓園; ☎ 0555-73-1000; 3370-1 Funatsu; set
meals ¥2100-4200; ⏱11am-7.30pm Fri-Wed;
📷) Here diners sit on the floor around
traditional *irori* charcoal pits grilling their
own meals – skewers of fish, meat, tofu
and veggies. From Kawaguchi-ko Station,
turn left, left again after the 7-Eleven and
after 600m you'll see the thatched roof
on the right.

Getting Around

From Fujisan Station it's an eight-minute bus ride
(¥240) or five-minute train (¥220) to Kawaguchi-
ko Station.

The **Retro-bus** (two-day passes adult/child
¥1200/600) has hop-on-hop-off service from
Kawaguchi-ko Station to all of the sightseeing
spots around the western lakes. One route follows

Kawaguchi-ko's northern shore, and the other
heads south and around Sai-ko and Aokigahara.

There is a Toyota Rent-a-Car (☎ 72-1100, in
English 0800-7000-815) a few minutes' walk from
Kawaguchi-ko Station; head right from the station,
turning right at the next intersection. Sazanami
(⏱7am-5pm summer, 9am-5pm winter), on
Kawaguchi-ko's southeast shore, rents regular
bicycles (¥400/1500 per hour/day), electric
pedal-assisting bicycles (¥600/2600 per hour/
day) and row boats (¥1000/2500 per hour/day).

Nikkō 日光

☎ 0288 / POP 98,000

Ancient moss clinging to a stone wall;
rows of perfectly aligned stone lanterns;
vermilion gates and towering cedars: this
is only a pathway in Nikkō, a sanctuary
that enshrines the glories of the Edo
period (1603–1868). Scattered among
hilly woodlands, Nikkō is one of Japan's
major attractions. The drawback is that
plenty of other people have discovered it
too; high season (summer and autumn)
and weekends can be extremely crowded
and the spirituality of the area can feel a
little lost.

Jizō statues, Nikkō

Under Restoration

A few of Nikkō's temples have been undergoing restoration work for the past few years and this is set to continue. The Sanbutsu-dō Hall at Rinnō-ji, the temple's main hall, is undergoing major renovation works and is due for completion in 2020. At Tōshō-gū, the Yōmei-mon Gate will be under scaffolding until 2018.

It's certainly possible to visit Nikkō as a day trip from Tokyo, though spending at least one night allows for an early start before the crowds arrive. And a couple of nights gives you time to explore the gorgeous natural scenery in the surrounding area.

◎ Sights

The World Heritage Sites around Tōshō-gū are Nikkō's centrepiece. Most sites are open from 8am to 4.30pm (until 3.30pm from November to March). To avoid the hordes, visit early on a weekday. Be sure to pick up a map from the tourist information office, as finding the English signposts to the shrines and temples can be tricky.

Tōshō-gū   Shinto Shrine
(東照宮; www.toshogu.jp; 2301 Sannai; adult/child ¥1300/450; ⏰8am-4.30pm Apr-Oct, 8am-3.30pm Nov-Mar) A World Heritage Site, Tōshō-gū is a brilliantly decorative shrine in a beautiful natural setting. Among its notable features is the dazzling 'Sunset Gate' Yōmei-mon.

As the shrine gears up for its 400th anniversary a major restoration programme is underway. Until at least 2018, the Yōmei-mon and Shimojinko (one of the Three Sacred Storehouses) will be obscured by scaffolding. Don't be put off visiting, as Tōshō-gū remains an impressive sight. A new museum building is also set to open during 2015.

The stone steps of **Omotesandō**, lead past the towering stone *torii* (entrance gate) **Ishi-dorii** (石鳥居), and the **Gōjūnotō** (五重塔; Five Storey Pagoda), a 1819 reconstruction of the mid 17th century original, to **Omote-mon** (表門), Tōshō-gū's main gateway, protected on either side by Deva kings.

In Tōshō-gū's initial courtyard are the **Sanjinko** (三神庫; Three Sacred Storehouses); on the upper storey of the Kamijinko (upper storehouse) are relief carvings of 'imaginary elephants' by an artist who had never seen the real thing. Nearby, the **Shinkyūsha** (神厩舎; Sacred Stable) is adorned with relief carvings of monkeys. The allegorical 'hear no evil, see no evil, speak no evil' simians demonstrate three principles of Tendai Buddhism.

Further into Tōshō-gū's precincts, to the left of the drum tower, is **Honji-dō** (本地堂), a hall known for the painting on its ceiling of the Nakiryū (Crying Dragon). Monks demonstrate the hall's acoustic properties by clapping two sticks together. The dragon 'roars' (a bit of a stretch) when the sticks are clapped beneath its mouth, but not when they are clapped elsewhere.

Once the scaffolding comes off in 2018, the **Yōmei-mon** (陽明門; Sunset Gate) will be grander than ever, its gold leaf and intricate, coloured carvings and paintings of flowers, dancing girls, mythical beasts and Chinese sages, all shiny and renewed. Worrying that the gate's perfection might arouse envy in the gods, those responsible for its construction had the final supporting pillar placed upside down as a deliberate error.

Gōhonsha (御本社), the main inner courtyard, includes the **Honden** (本殿; Main Hall) and **Haiden** (拝殿; Hall of Worship). Inside these halls are paintings of the 36 immortal poets of Kyoto, and a ceiling-painting pattern from the Momoyama period; note the 100 dragons, each different. *Fusuma* (sliding door) paintings depict a *kirin* (a mythical beast that's part giraffe and part dragon).

To the right of the Gōhonsha is **Sakashita-mon** (坂下門), into which is carved a tiny wooden sculpture of the **Nemuri-neko** (眠り猫; Sleeping Cat) that's famous for its lifelike appearance (though admittedly the attraction is lost on some visitors). From here it's an uphill path through towering cedars to the appropriately solemn **Okumiya** (奥宮), Ieyasu's tomb.

Bypassed by nearly everyone at Tōshō-gū is the marvellous **Nikkō Tōshō-gū Museum of Art** (日光東照宮美術館; ☎0288-54-0560; http://www.toshogu.jp/shisetsu/bijutsu.html; 2301 Yamanouchi; adult/child ¥800/400; ⏱9am-4.30pm Apr-Oct, 9am-3.30pm Nov-Mar) in the old shrine offices, showcasing fine paintings on its doors, sliding screens, frames and decorative scrolls, some by masters including Yokoyama Taikan and Nakamura Gakuryo. Follow the path to the right of Omote-mon to find it.

Rinnō-ji   Buddhist Temple
(輪王寺; ☎0288-54-0531; http://rinnoji.or.jp; 2300 Yamanouchi; adult/child ¥400/200; ⏱8am-4.30pm Apr-Oct, 8am-3.30pm Nov-Mar) This Tendai-sect temple was founded 1200 years ago by Shōdō Shōnin. The exterior of the **Sambutsu-dō** (三仏堂; **Three-Buddha Hall**) is under wraps for restoration until 2020. Inside sit a trio of 8m gilded wooden Buddha statues: Amida Nyorai (a primal deity in the Mahayana Buddhist canon), flanked by Senjū (deity of mercy and compassion) and Batō (a horse-headed Kannon).

Taiyūin-byō   Shinto Shrine
(大猷院廟; adult/child ¥550/250; ⏱8am-4.30pm Apr-Oct, 8am-3.30pm Nov-Mar) Ieyasu's grandson Iemitsu (1604–51) is buried here and although it houses many of the same elements as Tōshō-gū (storehouses, drum tower, Chinese-style gates etc), the more intimate scale and setting in a cryptomeria forest make it very appealing.

Look for dozens of lanterns donated by *daimyō* (domain lords), and the gate Niō-mon, whose guardian deities have a hand up (to welcome those with pure hearts) and a hand down (to suppress those with impure hearts).

Futarasan-jinja   Shinto Shrine
(二荒山神社; www.futarasan.jp; adult/child ¥200/100) Set among cypress trees, this very atmospheric shrine was also founded by Shōdō Shōnin; the current building dates from 1619, making it Nikkō's oldest. It's the protector shrine of Nikkō itself, dedicated to Nantai-san (2484m), the mountain's consort, Nyotai-san, and their mountainous progeny, Tarō. There are other branches of the shrine on Nantai-san and by Chūzenji-ko.

Shin-kyō bridge, Nikkō
DANIEL CHUI/GETTY IMAGES ©

Eating & Drinking

A local speciality is *yuba* (the skin that forms when making tofu) cut into strips; better than it sounds, it's a staple of *shōjin ryōri* (Buddhist vegetarian cuisine). You'll see it all over town, in everything from *yuba soba* (noodles) to *age yuba manju* (fried bean buns).

Nikkō Coffee Cafe

(日光珈琲; http://nikko-coffee.com; 3-13 Honchō; coffee ¥550, meals from ¥1000; ⏰10am-5pm Tue-Sun) A century-old rice shop has been sensitively reinvented as this retro-chic cafe with a garden, where expertly made hand-dripped coffee is served alongside cakes and snack meals such as bacon, cheese and egg galette (buckwheat pancake) or pork curry.

Nagomi-chaya Japanese ¥¥

(和み茶屋; 0288-54-3770; 1016 Kamihatsu-ishi; dishes/set-course meal from ¥450/1620; ⏰11.30am-4pm Thu-Tue) A faithful picture menu makes ordering simple at this sophisticated arts-and-crafts style cafe near the top of Nikkō's main drag. The beautifully prepared *kaiseki* style lunches are a great deal.

Gyōshintei Kaiseki ¥¥¥

(尭心亭; 53-3751; www.meiji-yakata.com/gyoushin; 2339-1 Sannai; set-courses lunch/dinner from ¥2138/4514; ⏰11am-7pm;) Splash out on deluxe spreads of vegetarian *shōjin-ryōri*, featuring local bean curd and vegetables served half a dozen delectable ways, or the *kaiseki* courses which include fish. The elegant tatami dining room overlooks a carefully tended garden which is part of the Meji-no-Yakata compound of chic restaurants close by the World Heritage Sites.

ℹ Information

Kyōdo Center Tourist Information Office (54-2496; www.nikko-jp.org; 591 Gokomachi; ⏰9am-5pm) This is the main tourist information office with English speakers (guaranteed between 10am and 2pm) and maps for sightseeing and hiking. There are several computers available for internet use.

Nikkō Post Office (日光郵便局; 54-0101; 896-1 Nakahatsuishi-machi) Three blocks northwest of the Kyōdo Center Tourist

Takaragawa Onsen

Information Office. There is another branch **(Rte 119; ☺8.45am-7pm Mon-Fri, 9am-5pm Sat & Sun)** across the street from Tōbu Nikkō Station on Rte 119; both have international ATMs.

Tōbu Nikkō Station Tourist Information Desk (☎54-0864; ☺8.30am-5pm) At the Nikkō train station, there's a small information desk where you can pick up a town map and get help in English to find buses, restaurants and hotels.

ⓘ Getting There & Away

Nikkō is best reached from Tokyo via the Tōbu Nikkō line from Asakusa Station. You can usually get last-minute seats on the hourly reserved *tokkyū* (limited-express) trains (¥2700, 1¾ hours). *Kaisoku* (rapid) trains (¥1360, 2½ hours, hourly from 6.20am to 5.30pm) require no reservation. For the *tokkyū*, you may have to change at Shimo-imaichi. Be sure to ride in the last two cars to reach Nikkō (some cars may separate at an intermediate stop).

JR Pass holders can take the Tohoku Shinkansen from Tokyo to Utsunomiya (¥4930, 54 minutes) and change there for an ordinary train to Nikkō (¥740, 45 minutes).

Both JR Nikkō Station (designed by Frank Lloyd Wright) and the nearby Tōbu Nikkō Station lie southeast of the shrine area within a block of Nikkō's main road (Rte 119, the old Nikkō-kaidō). From the station, follow this road uphill for 20 minutes to reach the shrine area, past restaurants, souvenir shops and the main tourist information centre, or take a bus to the Shin-kyō bus stop (¥200). Bus stops are announced in English. Buses leave from both JR and Tōbu Nikkō Station; buses bound for both Chūzen-ji Onsen and Yumoto Onsen stop at Shin-kyō and other stops around the World Heritage Sites.

Train/Bus Passes

Tōbu Railway (www.tobu.co.jp/foreign) Offers two passes covering rail transport from Asakusa to Nikkō (though not the *tokkyū* surcharge, from ¥1040) and unlimited hop-on-hop-off bus services around Nikkō. Purchase these passes at the **Tōbu Sightseeing Service Center (Map p96; ☎03-841-2871; www.tobu.co.jp/foreign; ☺ 7.45am-5pm)** in Asakusa Station.

All Nikkō Pass (adult/child ¥4520/2280) Valid for four days and includes buses to Chūzen-ji Onsen and Yumoto Onsen.

Detour:
Chūzen-ji Onsen

This highland area 11.5km west of Nikkō offers some natural seclusion and striking views of Nantai-san from Chūzen-ji's lake, Chuzenji-ko. The lake itself is 161m deep and a fabulous shade of deep blue in good weather with the usual flotilla of sightseeing boats.

Buses run from Tōbu Nikkō Station to Chūzen-ji Onsen (¥1150, 45 minutes) or use the economical Tōbu Nikkō Bus Free Pass, available at Tōbu Nikkō Station.

Two-Day Nikkō Pass (adult/child ¥2670/1340) Valid for two days and includes buses to the World Heritage Sites.

Tōbu Nikkō Bus Free Pass

If you've already got your rail ticket, two-day bus-only passes allow unlimited rides between Nikkō and Chūzen-ji Onsen (adult/child ¥2000/1000) or Yumoto Onsen (adult/child ¥3000/1500), including the World Heritage Site area. The **Sekai-isan-meguri** (World Heritage Bus Pass; adult/child ¥500/250) covers the area between the stations and the shrine precincts. Buy these at Tōbu Nikkō Station.

Minakami & Takaragawa Onsen
水上温泉・宝川温泉

☎0278 / POP 21,000

In the northern region of the Gunma Prefecture is the sprawling onsen town of Minakami. Surrounded by beautiful natural forests and mountains, and cut through by the gushing Tone-gawa (Tone River), it's a mecca for outdoor-adventure sports, hiking and skiing enthusiasts. The area is also home to Takaragawa Onsen (about 30 minutes away by road), a riverside spa ranked among the nation's best.

The train station is in the village of Minakami.

Activities

Takaragawa Onsen   Onsen

(宝川温泉; www.takaragawa.com; admission ¥1500; ⏰9am-5pm) This stunning outdoor onsen offers four large rock pools cascading beside Tone-gawa and shaded by a lush forest riddled with meandering paths, wooden huts, folk and religious statues. All the pools, bar one for women only, are mixed, but modesty towels are available (¥100). Buses run here hourly from Minakami Station (¥1150, 40 minutes).

Hōshi Onsen Chōjūkan   Onsen

(法師温泉長寿館; www.houshi-onsen.jp; 650 Nagai; admission for day trippers ¥1000; ⏰10.30am-1.30pm Thu-Tue) The main bathhouse at this ryokan is a handsome wooden structure from 1896, with rows of individual bathing pools and a unique style of water bubbling up from below. It's mixed bathing, with an additional modern bathhouse just for women and *rotemburo*.

Sleeping

Tenjin Lodge   Lodge ¥¥

(天神・ロッジ; ☎0278-25-3540; www.tenjinlodge.com; 220-4 Yubiso; r per person from ¥5000; 🛜) Ideally located at the foot of Tanigawa-dake, across from a lovely waterfall and nearby swimming holes, this lodge offers comfy, spacious Japanese- and Western-style rooms; ask for a riverside one. Welcoming hosts offer home-cooked meals (breakfast ¥800, dinner ¥1200) as well as plenty of local knowledge and adventure sports options.

Hōshi Onsen
Chōjūkan   Ryokan ¥¥¥

(法師温泉長寿館; ☎0278-66-0005; www.houshi-onsen.jp; 650 Nagai; r per person incl 2 meals from ¥13,800; Ⓟ) Perfectly rustic and supremely photogenic, this lodging is one of Japan's finest *onsen ryokan*, with a stunning 1896 wooden bathhouse.

From Gokan Station (two stops before Minakami) take a bus to Sarugakyō (¥730, 40 minutes) then change to another infrequent bus for Hōshi Onsen (¥590, 15 minutes), or take a taxi (¥3000).

Ōsenkaku   Ryokan ¥¥¥

(汪泉閣; ☎0278-75-2611; www.takaragawa.com; 1899 Fujiwara; s/d with 2 meals & shared bathroom from ¥13,400/20,600; ❄🛜) 🍃 They hardly come more traditional than this riverside inn split over three buildings, the oldest of which is the 1936 No 1 Annexe – so close to the rushing water it sounds as if you're in it! Slip off your choice of *yukata* (cotton robe) and you can be, as the ryokan has 24-hour use of adjacent Takaragawa Onsen.

Eating

La Biere   Pizza ¥

(ラ・ビエール; ☎0278-72-2959; www.3-sui.com/labiere.html; pizzas from ¥800; ⏰11am-2.30pm & 5-8.30pm Wed-Mon; 🖥) Simple and tasty wood-fired pizzas are served in this cute pizzeria with pot plants and umbrella-covered decking out the front. Take-away is also available. La Biere is in Minakami Village, a 15-minute walk from the train station.

Kadoya   Soba ¥¥

(そば処角弥; ☎0278-72-2477; www.kadoya-soba.com; 189-1 Yubiso; soba for 2 from ¥2700; ⏰11am-2.30pm) Expect to queue at this popular 'local' specialising in *hegi soba* (soba flavoured with seaweed and served on a special plate, a *hegi*). The noodles are hand-rolled fresh every day and the staff close up shop once they sell out. Kadoya is a five-minute walk from Alpine Cafe.

Information

Minakami Onsen Tourist Information Center (水上温泉旅館協同組合; ☎0278-72 2611; www.minakamionsen.com; ⏰8.30am-4.30pm Jun-Oct, 9am-4.30pm Nov-May) Across from Minakami Station, this office has very helpful English-speaking staff, brochures and bus schedules. Also see www.enjoy-minakami.jp.

ⓘ Getting There & Away

From Ueno, take the Joetsu Shinkansen (¥4200, 50 minutes) or JR Takasaki line (¥1940, two hours) to Takasaki and transfer to the Jōetsu line (¥970, one hour). You can also catch the Joetsu Shinkansen to Jōmō Kōgen from Tokyo/Ueno (¥5390/5180, 1¼ hours), from where buses run to Minakami (¥620, 25 minutes).

....

Hakone　箱根

🎵0460 / POP 13,500

If you only have a day or two outside Tokyo, Hakone can give you almost everything you could desire from the Japanese countryside – spectacular mountain scenery crowned by Mt Fuji, onsen and traditional inns. It's also home to world-class art museums. Ashino-ko is in the centre of it all and provides the foreground for the iconic image of Mt Fuji with the *torii* gate of the Hakone-jinja rising from the lake.

During holidays, Hakone can be quite busy and feel highly packaged. To beat the crowds, plan your trip during the week. For more information, try www.hakone.or.jp/english.

ⓘ Getting There & Away

The private Odakyū line from Shinjuku Station goes directly into Hakone-Yumoto, the region's transit hub. Use either the convenient Romance Car (¥2080, 90 minutes) or *kyūkō* (regular-express) service (¥1190, two hours); the latter may require a transfer at Odawara. The last trains from Hakone-Yumoto to Shinjuku run at 7.45pm weekdays and 8.50pm Saturday and Sunday for the Romance Car, and 10.30pm weekdays and 11pm Saturday and Sunday for the Odakyū line.

JR Pass holders can take the Kodama Shinkansen (¥3880, 50 minutes) or the JR Tōkaidō line (*futsū* ¥1790, one hour; *tokkyū* ¥2390, one hour) from Tokyo Station or the Shōnan-Shinjuku line from Shinjuku (¥1450, 80 minutes) to Odawara and change there for trains or buses for Hakone-Yumoto.

The narrow-gauge, switchback Hakone-Tōzan line runs from Odawara via Hakone-Yumoto to Gōra (¥670, one hour).

Odakyū's **Hakone Freepass** (箱根フリーパス), available at Odakyū stations and Odakyū Travel branches, is an excellent deal, covering the return fare to Hakone and unlimited use of most modes of transport within the region, plus other discounts. It's available as a two-day pass (adult/child from Shinjuku ¥5140/1500, from Odawara if you're not planning on returning to Shinjuku

Torii (shrine gate), Hakone

¥4000/1000) or a three-day pass (adult/child from Shinjuku ¥5640/1750, from Odawara ¥4500/1250). Freepass holders need to pay an additional limited-express surcharge (¥890 each way) to ride the Romance Car.

For those wanting to combine Hakone with Mt Fuji on their itinerary, there is the **Fuji Hakone Pass** (¥7400), a three-day pass offering discount round-trip travel from Shinjuku as well as unlimited use of most transport in the Hakone and Fuji areas.

ℹ Getting Around

Part of Hakone's popularity comes from the chance to ride assorted *norimono* (modes of transport): switchback train (from Hakone-Yumoto to Gōra), cable car (funicular), ropeway (gondola), ship and bus. Check out www.odakyu.jp, which describes this circuit.

Boat

From Tōgendai, sightseeing boats criss-cross Ashino-ko to Hakone-machi and Moto-Hakone (adult/child ¥1000/500, 30 minutes).

Bus

The Hakone-Tōzan and Izu Hakone bus companies service the Hakone area, linking most of the sights. Hakone-Tōzan buses, included in the Hakone Freepass, run between Hakone-machi and Odawara (¥1180, 55 minutes) and between Moto-Hakone and Hakone-Yumoto (¥960, 35 minutes).

Cable Car & Ropeway

Gōra is the terminus of the Hakone-Tōzan railway and the beginning of the cable car to Sōun-zan, from where you can catch the Hakone Ropeway line to Ōwakudani and Tōgendai.

Luggage Forwarding

At Hakone-Yumoto Station, deposit your luggage with **Hakone Baggage Service** (箱根キャリーサービス; ☎86-4140; per piece from ¥800; ⏰8.30am-7pm) by noon, and it will be delivered to your inn within Hakone from 3pm. Hakone Freepass holders get a discount of ¥100 per bag.

HAKONE-YUMOTO ONSEN
箱根湯元温泉

Hakone-Yumoto is the starting point for most visits to Hakone. Though heavily visited, it's an ambient riverside resort town with a high concentration of onsen, the main attraction here.

🏃 Activities

Hakone Yuryō   Onsen
(箱根湯寮; ☎0460-85-8411; www.hakoneyuryo.jp; 4 Tonosawa; adult/child ¥1400/700, private baths from ¥3900; ⏰10am-8pm Mon-Fri, to 9pm Sat & Sun) A free shuttle bus will whisk you in three minutes from Hakone-Yumoto station to this idyllic onsen complex ensconsed in the forest. The *rotemburo* are spacious, and leaf shaded. There's also private ones you can book in advance. No tattoos allowed.

Yunessun
JOHN S LANDER / GETTY IMAGES ©

Tenzan Tōji-kyō · Onsen

(天山湯治郷; www.tenzan.jp; 208 Yumoto-chaya; adult/child ¥1300/650; ⏰9am-10pm) Soak in *rotemburo* of varying temperatures and designs (one is constructed to resemble a natural cave) at this large, popular bath 2km southwest of town. To get here, take the 'B' Course shuttle bus from the bridge outside the Hakone-Yumoto Station (¥100). Tattoos are allowed.

😴 Sleeping

Omiya Ryokan · Ryokan ¥¥

(📞85-7345; www.o-miya.com; 116 Yumoto-chaya; r with breakfast from ¥9300, weekends with two meals ¥13,400; ❄️ 📶) Lower weekday prices make this simple ryokan an attractive proposition for its tatami rooms, some with mountain views. There's a small indoor onsen. To get here, take the 'B' course bus from Hakone-Yumoto Station.

Fukuzumirō · Ryokan ¥¥¥

(福住楼; 📞85-5301; www.fukuzumi-ro.com; 74 Tōnozawa; s/d per person incl 2 meals from ¥22,150/38,000; ❄️ 📶) This exquisite 125-year-old inn sports detailed woodwork, public onsen baths and rooms with sun terraces with views of the Haya-kawa; the small, quiet room overlooking the garden was a favourite of author Kawabata Yasunori. It's about 10 minutes' walk down from Tōnozawa Station on the Hakone-Tōzan railway, or a short taxi ride from Hakone-Yumoto.

KAI Hakone · Ryokan ¥¥¥

(界箱根; 📞050-3786-0099; http://global.hoshinoresort.com/kai_hakone/; 230 Yumoto-chaya; s/d with two meals from ¥31,000/62,000; ❄️ @ 📶) Less than a 10-minute bus ride from Hakone-Yumoto, this sleek resort is nestled amid soaring stands of bamboo, and overlooks the river. Spacious rooms mix traditional and contemporary styles. Highlights include infinity-style onsen pools, English-speaking staff and delicious *kaiseki* meals.

ℹ️ Information

Hakone-Yumoto Tourist Information Center
(📞85-8911; www.hakone.or.jp; ⏰9am-5.45pm) Make your first stop at the most clued-up of several tourist information centres scattered around Hakone. This is the best place for maps and information about hiking trails and all the attractions. Staffed by helpful English speakers, it's across the main road from the train station.

MIYANOSHITA & KOWAKIDANI
宮ノ下・小涌谷

The first worthwhile stop on the Hakone-Tōzan railway towards Gōra, this village has antique shops along the main road, some splendid ryokan, and a pleasant **hiking** trail skirting up 800m Sengen-yama (浅間山). The trailhead is just below Fujiya Hotel, marked by a shrine.

Next stop along is Kowakidani, home to a giant onsen complex and the highly impressive collection of the Okada Museum of Art.

◎ Sights & Activities

Okada Museum of Art · Museum

(岡田美術館; 📞0460-87-3931; www.okada-museum.com; 483-1 Kowakidani; adult/student ¥2800/1800; ⏰9am-4.30pm) Showcasing the dazzling Japanese, Chinese and Korean art treasures of industrialist Okada Kazuo, this mammoth museum should not be missed. You could spend hours marvelling at the beauty of so many pieces, including detailed screen paintings and exquisite pottery. The museum is opposite the Kowakien stop.

Yunessun · Onsen

(箱根小涌園ユネッサン; www.yunessun.com; 1297 Ninotaira; Yunessun adult/child ¥2900/1600, Mori-no-Yu adult/child ¥1900/1200, both ¥4100/2100; ⏰9am-7pm Mar-Oct, to 6pm Nov-Feb) Best described as an onsen amusement park with a whole variety of baths and outdoor water slides, Yunessun is mixed bathing so you'll need to bring a swimsuit; the connected Mori-no-Yu complex (11am-9pm) is traditional single-sex bathing. Take a bus from

Hakone-machi, Gōra or Hakone-Yumoto to the Kowakien stop.

Sleeping

Fujiya Hotel Hotel ¥¥¥
(富士屋ホテル; ☏82-2211; www.fujiya hotel.jp; 359 Miyanoshita; d from ¥21,670; ⊕✳@🛜🖲) One of Japan's finest Western-heritage hotels. the beautifully detailed Fujiya opened in 1878 and played host to Charlie Chaplin back in the day (Room 45). Now sprawled across several wings, it remains dreamily elegant. It's worth a visit to soak up the retro atmosphere, stroll through the hillside gardens and greenhouse, and to have tea in the lounge.

CHŌKOKU-NO-MORI & GŌRA 彫刻の森・強羅

Gōra, one stop after Chōkoku-no-mori, is the terminus of the Hakone-Tōzan line and the starting point for the funicular and cable-car trip to Tōgendai on Ashi-no-ko.

Sights

Hakone Open-Air Museum Museum
(彫刻の森美術館; www.hakone-oam.or.jp; 1121 Ninotaira; adult/child ¥1600/800; ⊙9am-4.30pm) On a rolling, leafy hillside setting, this safari for art lovers, includes an impressive selection of 19th- and 20th-century Japanese and Western sculptures (including works by Henry Moore, Rodin and Miró) as well as an excellent Picasso Pavilion with more than 300 works ranging from paintings and glass art to tapestry.

Hakone Museum of Art Museum
(箱根美術館; www.moaart.or.jp; 1300 Gōra; adult/child ¥900/free; ⊙9.30am-4.30pm, closed Thu) Sharing grounds with a lovely velvety moss garden and teahouse (¥700 matcha green tea and sweet), this museum has a collection of Japanese pottery dating from as far back as the Jōmon period (some 5000 years ago). The gardens are spectacular in autumn.

Eating

Gyōza Center Japanese ¥
(餃子センター; ☏0460-82-3457; www.gyozacenter.com; 1300 Gōra; mains from ¥800; ⊙11.30am-3pm & 5-8pm, closed Sat; 🗐) The humble gyōza (dumpling) stars at this cosy, long-running restaurant in a dozen different varieties. No vegetarian options though, unfortunately. It's between Gōra and Chōkoku-no-mori Stations on a corner, with an English sign.

Itoh Dining by Nobu Japanese ¥¥¥
(☏0460-83-8209; http://www.itoh-dining.co.jp/; 1300-64 Gōra; lunch/dinner from ¥3000/7000; ⊙11.30am-3pm & 5-9pm; 🖊🗐) Savour some premium Japanese beef, cooked teppanyaki-style in front of you by the chef at this elegant restaurant, a branch of the celeb chef Nobu's dining empire. It's just uphill from Koenshimo Station on the funicular, one stop from Gōra.

SŌUN-ZAN & ŌWAKUDANI 早雲山・大桶谷

From Gōra, continue to near the 1153m-high summit of Sōun-zan by cable car (¥410, 10 minutes).

From Sōun-zan, there are several **hiking trails** including one to Kami-yama (1¾ hours) and another up to Ōwakudani (1¼ hours). The latter is sometimes closed due to the mountain's toxic gases. Check at the tourist information office.

Sōun-zan is the starting point for the **Hakone Ropeway**, a 30-minute, 4km gondola ride to Tōgendai (one way/return ¥1330/2340), stopping at Ōwakudani en route. In fine weather Mt Fuji looks fabulous from here.

Ōwakudani is a volcanic cauldron of steam, bubbling mud and mysterious smells where you can buy onsen tamago, eggs boiled and blackened in the sulphurous waters. Don't linger, as the gases are poisonous. From here you can take the **Ōwakudani-Togendai Nature Trail**, a one hour hike.

ASHI-NO-KO 芦ノ湖

Between Tōgendai, Hakone-machi and Moto-Hakone, this lake is touted as the primary attraction of the Hakone region; but it's Mt Fuji, with its snow-clad slopes glimmering in reflection on the water, that lends the lake its poetry.

HAKONE-MACHI & MOTO-HAKONE 箱根町・元箱根

The sightseeing boats across Ashi-no-ko deposit you at either of these two towns, both with sights of historical interest.

Sights

Hakone Sekisho — Museum

(箱根関所, Hakone Checkpoint Museum; www. hakonesekisyo.jp; 1 Hakone-machi; adult/child ¥500/250; ◷9am-4.30pm Mar-Nov, to 4pm Dec-Feb) You're free to walk through this 2007 reconstruction of the feudal-era checkpoint on the Old Tōkaidō Hwy, but to enter any of the buildings you'll need to buy a ticket. One displays Darth Vader–like armour and grisly implements used on lawbreakers. There's basic English explanations on only some displays.

Narukawa Art Museum — Museum

(成川美術館; ☎0460-83-6828; www.narukawamuseum.co.jp; 570 Moto-Hakone; adult/child ¥1200/800; ◷9am-5pm) Art comes in two forms here – in the exquisite Japanese-style paintings, *nihonga*, on display, and in the stunning Mt Fuji views from the panarama lounge looking out across the lake. Don't miss the cool kaleidoscope displays.

Hakone-jinja — Shinto Shrine

(箱根神社; ◷9am-4pm) A pleasant stroll around Ashi-no-ko follows a cedar line path to this shrine set in a wooded grove, in Moto-Hakone. Its signature red *torii* (gate) rises from the lake; get your camera ready for that picture-postcard shot.

....

Kamakura 鎌倉

☎0467 / POP 173,500

An hour from Tokyo, Kamakura was Japan's first feudal capital, between 1185 and 1333, and its glory days coincided with the spread of populist Buddhism in Japan. This legacy is reflected in the area's high concentration of stunning temples. The town has a laid-back, earthy

Ashi-no-ko

vibe complete with organic restaurants and summer beach shacks – which can be added to sunrise meditation and hillside hikes as reasons to visit. Kamakura does tend to get packed on weekends and in holiday periods, so plan accordingly.

Sights & Activities

Kenchō-ji — Buddhist Temple

(建長寺; www.kenchoji.com; 8 Yamanouchi; adult/child ¥300/100; 8.30am-4.30pm) Established in 1253, Japan's oldest Zen monastery is still active today. The central Butsuden (Buddha Hall) was brought piece by piece from Tokyo in 1647. Its Jizō Bosatsu statue, unusual for a Zen temple, reflects the valley's ancient function as an execution ground – Jizō consoles lost souls. Other highlights include a bell cast in 1253 and the juniper grove, believed to have sprouted from seeds brought from China by Kenchō-ji's founder some seven centuries ago.

Engaku-ji — Buddhist Temple

(円覚寺; www.engakuji.or.jp; 409 Yamanouchi; adult/child ¥300/100; 8am-4.30pm Mar-Nov, to 4pm Dec-Feb) One of Kamakura's five major Rinzai Zen temples Engaku-ji was founded in 1282 as a place where Zen monks might pray for soldiers who lost their lives defending Japan against Kublai Khan. All of the temple structures have been rebuilt over the centuries; the Shariden, a Song-style reliquary, is the oldest, last rebuilt in the 16th century. At the top of the long flight of stairs is the Engaku-ji bell, the largest bell in Kamakura, cast in 1301.

Tsurugaoka Hachiman-gū — Shinto Shrine

(鶴岡八幡宮; http://hachimangu.or.jp; 2-1-31 Yukinoshita; 9am-4pm) FREE Kamakura's most important shrine is, naturally, dedicated to Hachiman, the god of war. Minamoto Yoritomo himself ordered its construction in 1191 and designed the pine-flanked central promenade that leads to the coast. The sprawling grounds are ripe with historical symbolism: the Gempei Pond, bisected by bridges, is said to depict the rift between the Minamoto (Genji) and Taira (Heike) clans.

Daibutsu — Monument

(大仏; www.kotoku-in.jp; Kōtoku-in, 4-2-28 Hase; adult/child ¥200/150; 8am-5.30pm Apr-Sep,

Engaku-ji

GEMMA FERRANDO/GETTY IMAGES ©

to 5pm Oct-Nov) Kamakura's most iconic sight, an 11.4m-high bronze statue of Amida Buddha (*amitābha* in Sanskrit), is in Kōtoku-in, a Jōdo sect temple. Completed in 1252, it's said to have been inspired by Yoritomo's visit to Nara (where Japan's biggest Daibutsu holds court) after the Minamoto clan's victory over the Taira clan. Once housed in a huge hall, today the statue sits in the open, the hall having been washed away by a tsunami in 1495.

Hase-dera   Buddhist Temple
(長谷寺, Hase Kannon; www.hasedera.jp; 3-11-2 Hase; adult/child ¥300/100; ⏰8am-4.30pm) The focal point of this Jōdo sect temple, one of the most popular in the Kantō region, is a 9m-high carved wooden *jūichimen* (11-faced) Kannon statue. Kannon (*avalokiteshvara* in Sanskrit) is the bodhisattva of infinite compassion and, along with *Jizō*, is one of Japan's most popular Buddhist deities. The temple is about 10 minutes' walk from the Daibutsu and dates back to AD 736, when the statue is said to have washed up on the shore near Kamakura.

Eating

Vegetarians can eat well in Kamakura; pick up the free, bilingual *Vegetarian Culture Map* at the Tourist Information Center.

Bowls Donburi Café   Japanese ¥
(鎌倉どんぶりカフェbowls; http://bowls-cafe.jp; 2-14-7 Komachi; meals ¥880-1680; ⏰11am-3pm & 5-10pm; ✋@🛜🖊📱) The humble *donburi* (rice bowl) gets a hip, healthy remake here at this modern bright cafe, with toppings such as roasted tuna, soy sauce and sesame oil. You get a discount if you discover the word *atari* at the bottom of the bowl. Also serves excellent coffee and has free wi-fi and computer terminals with internet.

Matsubara-an   Noodles ¥¥
(松原庵; 📞0467-61-2299; http://matsubara-an.com/kamakura/shop.php; 4-10-3 Yuiga-hama; mains ¥860-1720; ⏰11am-9pm; 📱) Dinner reservations are recommended for this upscale *soba* restaurant in a lovely old house. Try the tempura *goma seiro soba* (al dente noodles served cold with sesame dipping sauce). Dine alfresco or indoors where you can watch noodles being handmade. From Yuiga-hama Station (Enoden line) head towards the beach and then take the first right. Look for the blue sign.

Information

For information about Kamakura, see www.city.kamakura.kana gawa.jp/english.

Kamakura Post Office (郵便局; 📞22-1200; 1-10-3 Komachi; ⏰9am-7pm Mon-Fri, to-3pm Sat) Has ATMs inside.

Tourist Information Center (鎌倉市観光協会観光総合案内所; 📞22-3350; ⏰9am-5pm) Just outside the east exit of Kamakura Station, the English speaking staff are helpful and can book accommodation. Pick up a guide to Kamakura's temples (¥1700), as well as free brochures and maps for the area.

Getting There & Away

JR Yokosuka-line trains run to Kamakura from Tokyo (¥920, 56 minutes) and Shinagawa (¥720, 46 minutes), via Yokohama (¥340, 27 minutes). Alternatively, the Shōnan Shinjuku line runs from the west side of Tokyo (Shibuya, Shinjuku and Ikebukuro, all ¥920) in about one hour, though some trains require a transfer at Ōfuna, one stop before Kita-Kamakura. The last train from Kamakura back to Tokyo Station is 11.20pm and Shinjuku 9.16pm.

Odakyū Enoshima/Kamakura Free Pass (from Shinjuku ¥1470) Valid for one day; includes transport to Fujisawa Station (where it meets the Enoden Enoshima line), plus use of the Enoden.

Getting Around

You can walk to most temples and shrines from Kamakura or Kita-Kamakura Stations. Sites in the west, like the Daibutsu, can be reached via the Enoden line from Kamakura Station to Hase (¥200) or by bus from Kamakura Station stops 1 and 6.

Kamakura Rent-a-Cycle (レンタサイクル; per hr/day ¥800/1800; ⏰8.30am-5pm) is outside the east exit of Kamakura Station, and right up the incline.

Central Honshū

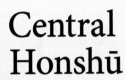

Central Honshū is the place for hot springs, hiking and history. The main island of Japan is neatly bisected by the Japan Alps, which form the rocky spine of the country. The northern end of the Alps, between Kamikōchi and Tateyama, is the most popular area in Japan for hiking and mountain climbing in the summer months. The cities of Matsumoto and Takayama serve as gateways to the Japan Alps and each is a worthy destination in its own right: Takayama has a wonderfully preserved historical district and Matsumoto is home to a spectacular castle.

To the west, on the Japan Sea coast, you'll find Kanazawa. Historically at the forefront of culture and the arts in Japan, it's brimming with temples, museums and traditional houses.

Cental Honshū can easily be visited en route from Tokyo to Kyoto, or vice versa, and a stop at one of the area's fine onsen (hot springs) is the perfect way to recover from travel fatigue.

Hiking in the Japan Alps
MEGUMI TANAKA / GETTY IMAGES ©

Tateyama Ropeway (p182)

Central Honshū

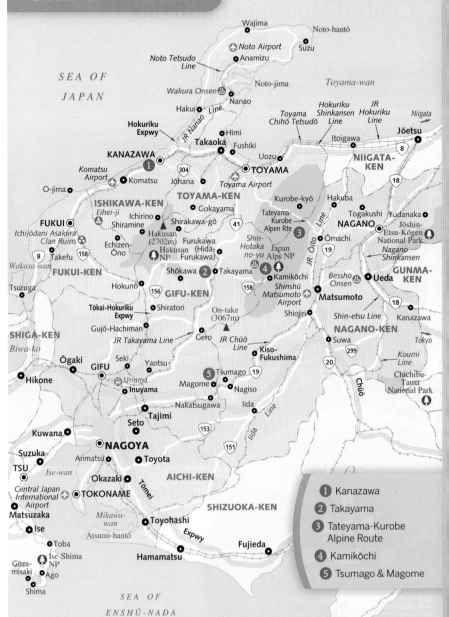

0 ——————— 50 km
0 ——————— 25 miles

SEA OF
JAPAN

Wajima
Noto-hantō
Noto Airport
Anamizu
Suzu
Noto Tetsudō
Line
Wakura Onsen
Nanao
Noto-jima
Toyama-wan
Hakui
Line
JR Nanao Line
Himi
Fushiki
Takaoka
Uozu
Hokuriku
Expwy
Toyama
Chihō Tetsudō
Hokuriku
Shinkansen
Line
JR
Hokuriku
Line
Itoigawa
Niigata
Jōetsu
KANAZAWA
TOYAMA
NIIGATA-
KEN
Komatsu
Airport
Komatsu
Jōhana
Toyama Airport
O-jima
ISHIKAWA-KEN
Gokayama
Kurobe-kyō
Hakuba
TOYAMA-KEN
Eihei-ji
Ichirino
Shiramine
Shirakawa-gō
Tateyama-
Kurobe
Alpen Rte
Togakushi
Yudanaka
NAGANO
Jōshin-
Etsu-Kōgen
National Park
FUKUI
Ichijōdani Asakura
Clan Ruins
Echizen-
Ōno
Hakusan
(2702m)
Hakusan (Hida-
NP Furukawa)
Furukawa
Ōmachi
Shin-
Hotaka
no-yu
Japan
Alps NP
JR Ōito Line
Nagano
Shinkansen
Takefu
Shōkawa
Takayama
Kamikōchi
Bessho
Onsen
Ueda
GUNMA-
KEN
FUKUI-KEN
Hokunō
Shinshū
Matsumoto
Airport
Matsumoto
Wakasa-wan
Tsuruga
GIFU-KEN
On-take
(3067m)
Shiojiri
Shin-etsu Line
Karuizawa
Tōkai-Hokuriku
Expwy
Shiratori
Gujō-Hachiman
Gero
JR Chūō
Line
Suwa
NAGANO-KEN
Tokyo
SHIGA-KEN
JR Takayama Line
Kiso-
Fukushima
Koumi
Line
Biwa-ko
Ōgaki
Seki
Yaotsu
Tsumago
Magome
Nagiso
Chūō
Chichibu-
Tama
National Park
Hikone
GIFU
Unuma
Nakatsugawa
Iida
Iida
Line
Inuyama
Kuwana
Tajimi
Seto
Suzuka
NAGOYA
Toyota
TSU
Arimatsu
AICHI-KEN
Ise-wan
Okazaki
Tōmei
Central Japan
International
Airport
TOKONAME
SHIZUOKA-KEN
Matsuzaka
Ise
Mikawa-
wan
Toyohashi
Expwy
Gōza-
misaki
Toba
Ise-Shima
NP
Ago
Fujieda
Hamamatsu
Shima
SEA OF
ENSHŪ-NADA

1 Kanazawa
2 Takayama
3 Tateyama-Kurobe
   Alpine Route
4 Kamikōchi
5 Tsumago & Magome

Central Honshū Highlights

Kanazawa

Kanazawa (p185) is a small but sprawling city packed with worthwhile attractions including one of Japan's finest gardens, well-preserved traditional enclaves and intriguing temples and museums. With express train connections to Kyoto and new *shinkansen* (bullet train) services to Tokyo, Kanazawa is the 'buzz' destination on any Tokyo–Kyoto itinerary. It can also be easily paired with excursions to Noto-hantō, the Japan Alps and Takayama. Below: Geisha houses

1

DAVID HILL / GETTY IMAGES ©

2 Takayama

In view of the Japan Alps and rich in history, Takayama (p154) makes the perfect side trip between Tokyo and Kyoto. It's a bit over two hours north of Nagoya by direct express, but it feels worlds away. The wonderfully preserved Sanmachi-suji (p155) district has some incredible old merchants' houses and nearby Hida-no-Sato (p158) has a collection of thatched-roof houses brought from across the region. Left: Traditional house, Hida-no-Sato

TAKASHI TSUJINAKA / GETTY IMAGES ©

CHRISTOPHER GROENHOUT / GETTY IMAGES ©

Tateyama-Kurobe Alpine Route ③

A testament to Japanese engineering, this route (p182) is a series of lifts, buses and trolleys that goes up, over and through the Northern Japan Alps. For those who want to get among the peaks without sweating, this is the way to go. The eastern and western gateways to the route are Matsumoto and Toyama, now directly connected to Tokyo by *shinkansen*, respectively. Right: Mount Tateyama

④

Kamikōchi

A pristine sanctuary surrounded by high mountains walls, Kamikōchi (p163) is arguably the most scenic spot in the entire Japan Alps. With several lodges and hotels scattered along the banks of the crystal-clear Azusa-gawa, it makes a great base for hiking. You can choose from gentle day hikes along the mostly flat river valley, or set off for multiday treks among the high peaks. Above left: Footbridge over the Azusa-gawa

⑤

Tsumago & Magome

If you crave a taste of old Japan and some excellent natural scenery, the walk from Magome (p180) to Tsumago (p181) is sure to please. These two preserved towns on the old Nakasendō route, which connected Tokyo (then known as Edo) and Kyoto, via the Japan Alps, are about as picturesque as Japan gets. This is a great way to enjoy some traditional scenery while giving the legs a good workout. Above right: Tsumago

Central Honshū's Best...

Hiking Areas

○ **Kamikōchi** An alpine sanctuary with comfortable lodges and fantastic hiking. (p163)

○ **Shin-hotaka Onsen** Take the ropeway (tramway) to the ridge and keep on climbing. (p166)

○ **Tateyama-Murodō Plateau** Take the Alpine Route to this plateau high in the Alps and set out on an adventure. (p182)

○ **Hakuba** In summer this skiing hub draws hikers to some of the region's highest peaks. (p171)

Onsen (Hot Springs)

○ **Shin-hotaka-no-yu** This riverside *rotemburo* is one of Japan's most scenic. (p167)

○ **Shirahone Onsen** Make a day-trip to Kōkyō Notemburo or pick a ryokan (traditional Japanese inn) straddling the gorge to soak in these famed, milky white waters. (p171)

○ **Nozawa Onsen** Picturesque onsen town and ski resort with multiple free bathing spots. (p169)

○ **Kaga Onsen** One area with three hot-spring villages, including lovely Yamanaka Onsen. (p194)

Traditional Accommodation

○ **Sumiyoshi Ryokan** Friendly, but not fancy, this delightful antique inn oozes atmosphere at the right price. (p159)

○ **Beniya Mukayu** A sumptuous fusion of modernity and tradition, Mukayu has mastered the Japanese art of hospitality. (p195)

○ **The Kayōtei** Simply put: one of the best onsen ryokan in Japan. (p195)

○ **Yarimikan** An easy journey from Takayama brings you to this magical riverside onsen ryokan. (p166)

Need to Know

Experiences

○ **Kenroku-en** Considered one of Japan's finest gardens. (p189)

○ **Asama Onsen Taimatsu Matsuri** A spectacular fire festival in Matsumoto. (p177)

○ **Azusa-gawa** The crystal-clear waters of this stream in Kamikōchi might remind you of New Zealand. (p163)

○ **Takayama Matsuri** Central Honshū's best festival features awesome parade floats. (p155)

○ **Tsumago & Magome** Overnight in one and hike to the other of these delightful Nakasendo towns (p180).

Left: Kenroku-en (p189);
Above: Tateyama-Kurobe Alpine Route (p182)
(LEFT) IPPEI NAOI / GETTY IMAGES ©;
(ABOVE) TATEYAMA / GETTY IMAGES ©

○ **Three months before** Get in shape if you plan to do serious hiking or climbing in the Japan Alps.

○ **Three months before** Make accommodation bookings early if you plan to stay in or near the Japan Alps during foliage season (October in most of the Japan Alps).

○ **One month before** Get an international driver's licence if you plan to explore Central Honshū by car (which is a good way to cover a lot of ground in this area).

○ **One week before** Check snow conditions if you are hiking early or late in the Japan Alps hiking season (this means any time before early June or after 1 October).

○ **Walk or cycle** Around Takayama, Kanazawa and the Japan Alps.

○ **Tateyama-Kurobe Alpine Route** Across the Japan Alps.

○ **Train or bus** Between cities and towns.

○ **Rent a car** Around Central Honshū if you want more freedom than trains or buses allow.

○ **Winter (December to March)** Can be very cold in Central Honshū, particularly in the mountains. Hiking is not possible at higher elevations between late October and late May (unless you are an experienced winter mountaineer).

○ **Conditions** Can change quickly in the Japan Alps, even during the normal hiking months of July and August.

○ **Japan Alps** Can be very crowded on summer weekends, particularly in the mid-August O-Bon holiday period.

Central Honshū Itineraries

By adding the traditional attractions of Takayama or Kanazawa and the scenic wonders of the Japan Alps to your standard Tokyo–Kyoto itinerary, your Japan trip is set to gain a lot of depth and variety.

3 DAYS

TOKYO TO KYOTO VIA THE JAPAN ALPS
Takayama & The Japan Alps

If you've only got limited time in Japan but would like to see a little bit more than just Tokyo and Kyoto, this jaunt is the perfect add-on. A bit over two hours north of Nagoya, which is on the Tōkaidō *shinkansen* (bullet train) line that runs between Tokyo and Kyoto, Takayama is the ideal place to base yourself for this itinerary. Takayama is a historical city with a well-preserved traditional district and a variety of foreigner-friendly ryokan and restaurants. It also serves as the gateway to the Northern Japan Alps.

Take a *shinkansen* from Kyoto or Tokyo to ❶ **Nagoya** and switch to an express train north to ❷ **Takayama** (p154). Spend your first day exploring Takayama. Check out the traditional wooden houses in the Sanmachi-suji area, walk over to the Takayama Yatai Kaikan, which houses the festival floats used in the Takayama Matsuri, and take a bus, taxi or bicycle over to Hida-no-Sato, a collection of thatched-roof houses from the region. Then, take the bus (actually, two buses) to ❸ **Kamikōchi** (p163), do some hiking, spend the night and then make your way back to Kyoto or Tokyo via Takayama (or Matsumoto). Note that it's also possible to get to Kanazawa by bus or train from Takayama, and then continue south to Kyoto by train, or onwards to Tokyo by *shinkansen*.

KYOTO TO TOKYO VIA TATEYAMA
Kanazawa & the Alpine Route

5 DAYS

If you start in Tokyo and travel to Kyoto by *shinkansen*, this itinerary allows you to return to Tokyo without retracing your steps. This is a good trip for hikers and you should budget a night or two up in the mountains (in a mountain lodge or tent) to enjoy the brilliant hiking of the Northern Japan Alps. Note that this route is only possible from mid-April to mid-November (and sometimes the route opens later and closes earlier due to snowfall).

Start in ❶ **Kyoto** (p197), where you can catch a direct express train to ❷ **Kanazawa** (p185). Spend a day in Kanazawa enjoying Kenroku-en and the city's temples. Then,

take an express train to Toyama and switch to local trains for the journey to the western terminus of the ❸ **Tateyama-Kurobe Alpine Route** (p182), which will bring you by a funicular and bus to the Murodō-daira. Consider spending a night here in one of the hiking lodges, which will allow you to do some hiking – maybe you can bag the 3015m peak of Tateyama. Then, continue east along the Alpine Route to the JR Oito line, which will bring you to the city of ❹ **Matsumoto** (p174), where you can catch an express train to Tokyo.

Matsumoto-jō (p175), Matsumoto
NORBERTO CUENCA / GETTY IMAGES ©

Central Honshū

HIDA DISTRICT
飛驒地域

Takayama　高山

☑ 0577 / POP 92,750

A working city that has retained its traditional charm, Takayama boasts one of Japan's most atmospheric townscapes and best-loved festivals. Its present layout dates from the late 17th century and includes a wealth of museums, galleries and temples for a city of this size.

Takayama should be considered a high priority on any visit to Central Honshū. Meiji-era inns, hillside shrines and temples and a pretty riverside setting beckon you. Excellent infrastructure and friendly, welcoming locals, seal the deal. Give yourself two or three days to enjoy it all, if you can. Takayama is easily explored on foot or by bicycle and is the perfect start or end point for trips into Hida and the Northern Japan Alps.

Almost all of the main sights are clearly signposted in English and within walking distance of the station, which sits between the main streets of Kokubunji-dōri and Hirokōji-dōri. Both run east and cross the Miya-gawa (river) where they become Yasugawa-dōri and Sanmachi-dōri, respectively. Once across the river (about 10 minutes' walk), you're in the middle of the infinitely photogenic Sanmachi-suji (district) of sake breweries, cafes, retailers and immaculately preserved old private houses (古い町並み; *furui machinami*).

A Takayama Matsuri *yatai* (float)
KORKUSUNG/SHUTTERSTOCK ®

Sights & Activities

SANMACHI-SUJI

This original district of three main streets of merchants (Ichino-machi, Nino-machi and Sanno-machi) has been immaculately preserved. Sake breweries are designated by spheres of cedar fronds hanging above their doors; some are open to the public in January and early February, but most sell their brews year round. You'll find artisans, antiques, clothiers and cafes. Day and night, photographic opportunities abound.

Takayama Shōwa-kan   Museum

(高山昭和館; ☎0577-33-7836; 6 Shimoichino-machi; adult/child ¥500/300; ⏰9am-5pm) This nostalgia bonanza from the Shōwa period (1926–1989) concentrates on the years between 1955 and 1965, a time of great optimism between Japan's postwar malaise and pre-Titan boom. Lose yourself among the delightful mishmash of endless objects, from movie posters to cars and everything between, lovingly presented in a series of themed rooms.

Yoshijima Heritage House   Historic Building

(吉島家, Yoshijima-ke; ☎0577-32-0038; 1-51 Ōjin-machi; adult/child ¥500/300; ⏰9am-5pm Mar-Nov, to 4.30pm Wed-Sun Dec-Feb) Design buffs shouldn't miss Yoshijima-ke, which is well covered in architectural publications. Its lack of ornamentation allows you to focus on the spare lines, soaring roof and skylight. Admission includes a cup of delicious shiitake tea, which you can also purchase for ¥600 per can.

Kusakabe Folk Crafts Museum   Museum

(日下部民藝館, Kusakabe Mingeikan; ☎0577-32-0072; 1-52 Ōjin-machi; adult/child ¥500/300; ⏰9am-4.30pm Mar-Nov, to 4pm Wed-Mon Dec-Feb) This building dating from the 1890s showcases the striking craftsmanship of traditional Takayama carpenters. Inside is a collection of folk art.

Takayama Matsuri

One of Japan's great festivals, the **Takayama Matsuri** is in two parts. On 14 and 15 April is the Sannō Matsuri; a dozen *yatai* (floats), decorated with carvings, dolls, colourful curtains and blinds, are paraded through the town. In the evening the floats are decked out with lanterns and the procession is accompanied by sacred music. Hachiman Matsuri, on 9 and 10 October, is a slightly smaller version. Book accommodation months in advance.

Takayama Museum of History & Art   Museum

(飛騨高山まちの博物館, Hida-Takayama Machi no Hakubutsukan; ☎0577-32-1205; 75 Kamiichino-machi; ⏰museum 9am-7pm, garden 7am-9pm) **FREE** Not to be confused with the Hida Takayama Museum of Art, this free museum is situated around pretty gardens and features 14 themed exhibition rooms relating to local history, culture, literature and the arts.

Hida Folk Archaeological Museum   Museum

(飛騨民族考古館, Hida Minzoku Kōkō-kan; ☎0577-32-1980; 82 Kamisanno-machi; adult/child ¥500/200; ⏰7am-5pm Mar-Nov, 9.30am-4pm Nov-Feb) A former samurai house boasting interesting secret passageways and an old well in the courtyard.

SAKURAYAMA HACHIMAN-GŪ SHRINE & AROUND

Takayama Festival Floats Exhibition Hall   Museum

(高山屋台会館, Takayama Yatai-kaikan; 178 Sakura-machi; adult/child ¥820/410; ⏰8.30am-5pm Mar-Nov, 9am-4.30pm Dec-Feb) A rotating selection of four of the 23 multi-tiered *yatai* (floats) used in the Takayama Matsuri can be appreciated here. These spectacular creations, some dating from

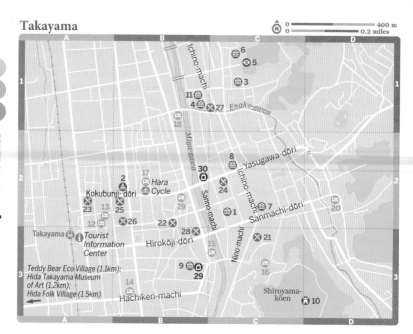

Takayama

Takayama

⊙ Sights
1	Hida Folk Archaeological Museum	C2
2	Hida Kokubun-ji	B2
3	Karakuri Museum	C1
4	Kusakabe Folk Crafts Museum	B1
5	Sakurayama Hachiman-gū	C1
6	Takayama Festival Floats Exhibition Hall	C1
7	Takayama Museum of History & Art	C2
8	Takayama Shōwa-kan	C2
9	Takayama-jinya	B3
10	Takayama-jō	D3
11	Yoshijima Heritage House	B1

⊜ Sleeping
12	Best Western Hotel	A2
13	Guesthouse Tomaru	A2
14	Hida Takayama Temple Inn Zenkō-ji	B3
15	Honjin Hiranoya	C3
16	Hōshōkaku	C3
17	Rickshaw Inn	B2
18	Sumiyoshi Ryokan	B1
19	Tanabe Ryokan	B2
20	Yamakyū	D2

⊗ Eating
21	Center4 Hamburgers	C3
22	Chapala	B2
23	Chitose	A2
24	Ebisu-Honten	C2
25	Heianraku	B2
26	Kotarō	B2
27	Kyōya	C1
28	Restaurant Le Midi	B3

⊟ Shopping
29	Jinya-mae Asa-ichi	B3
30	Miya-gawa Asa-ichi	B2

the 17th century, are prized for their flamboyant carvings, metalwork and lacquerwork. Some floats feature *karakuri ningyō* (marionettes) that perform amazing feats courtesy of eight accomplished puppeteers manipulating 36 strings.

The museum is on the grounds of the stately **Sakurayama Hachiman-gū** (桜山

八幡宮; ☏0577-32-0240; www.hidahachimangu. jp/english; 178 Sakura-yama) **FREE** shrine, which presides over the festival and is dedicated to the protection of Takayama.

Karakuri Museum   Museum
((飛騨高山獅子会館)からくりミュージアム; ☏0577-32-0881; 53-1 Sakura-machi; adult/child

¥600/400; ⏰9am-4.30pm) On display are over 800 *shishi* (lion) masks, instruments and drums related to festival dances. The main draw is the twice-hourly puppet show where you can see the mechanical *karakuri ningyō*, in action.

TERAMACHI, SHIROYAMA-KOEN & AROUND

These lovely, hilly districts to the east are linked by a well-signposted walking path. Teramachi has over a dozen temples and shrines you can wander around before taking in the greenery of Shiroyama-kōen. Various trails lead through the park and up the mountainside to the ruins of the castle, **Takayama-jō** (高山城跡; Shiroyama-kōen).

Takayama-jinya Historic Building
(高山陣屋; ☎0577-32-0643; 1-5 Hachiken-machi; adult/child ¥430/free; ⏰8.45am-4.30pm Sep-Jul, to 6pm Aug) These sprawling grounds south of Sanmachi-suji house the only remaining prefectural office building of the Tokugawa shōgunate, originally the administrative centre for the Kanamori clan. The present main building dates back to 1816 and was used as local government offices until 1969. There's also a rice granary, garden and a torture chamber with explanatory detail. Free guided tours in English are available (reservations advised).

Hida Kokubun-ji
Buddhist Temple
(飛騨国分寺; ☎0577-32-1395; 1-83 Sōwa-chō; treasure hall adult/child ¥300/250; ⏰9am-4pm) The original buildings of Takayama's oldest temple were constructed in the 8th century, but later destroyed by fire. The oldest of the present buildings dates from the 16th century. The

temple's treasure hall houses some Important Cultural Properties, and the courtyard boasts a three-storey pagoda and an impressively gnarled gingko tree believed to be 1200 years old.

AROUND TAKAYAMA

Hida Takayama Museum of Art Museum
(飛騨高山美術館, Hida Takayama Bijutsukan; ☎0577-35-3535; www.htm-museum.co.jp; 1-124-1 Kamiokamoto-chō; adult/child ¥1300/800; ⏰9am-5pm) Set back from town, lovers of art-nouveau and art-deco glassware and furniture will appreciate this large private gallery with a ritzy cafe, its own London Bus shuttle (ask at the Tourist Information Center) and a spectacular glass fountain by Ren Lalique.

Teddy Bear Eco Village Gallery
(飛騨高山テディベアエコビレッジ; ☎0577-37-3525; www.teddyeco.jp/english; 3-829-4 Nishinoishiki-machi; adult/child ¥600/400; ⏰10am-4pm) You'll know if you're one of *those* people who *have* to see this collection of over 1000 little fluffy

Takayama-jinya
CHEN WS/SHUTTERSTOCK ©

CHIARA SALVADORI/GETTY IMAGES ©

Don't Miss
Hida Folk Village

The sprawling, open-air Hida-no-Sato is a highly recommended half-day trip. It features dozens of traditional houses and buildings, which were dismantled at their original sites throughout the region and rebuilt here. Well-presented displays offer the opportunity to envision rural life in previous centuries. During clear weather, there are good views of the Japan Alps. To get here, hire a bicycle or catch a bus from Takayama bus station (¥200, 10 minutes); be sure to check return bus times.

NEED TO KNOW

飛騨の里, Hida-no-sato; ☏0577-34-4711; www.hidanosato-tpo.jp/english12; 1-590 Kamiokamoto-chō; adult/child ¥700/200; ⊗8.30am-5pm

guys from around the world, some over 140 years old, housed in a building just a little bit older. The annexed cafe is a lovely spot to enjoy a healthy something in the outdoors. Ask for directions at the Tourist Information Center.

Sleeping

One of Takayama's pleasures is its variety of high-quality accommodation, both Japanese and Western, for all budgets. If visiting during festival times, book accommodation months in advance and ex-pect to pay a 20% premium. The Ryokan Hotel Association can further assist with lodging enquiries: www.takayamaryokan.jp/english.

Rickshaw Inn   Hotel ¥

(力車イン; ☏0577-32-2890; www.rickshawinn.com; 54 Suehiro-chō; s without bathroom from ¥4200, tw with/without bathroom from ¥11,900/10,200; ⊙@) Well positioned on the fringe of Takayama's entertainment district, this travellers' favourite is great value. There's a range of room types, a small kitchen, laundry facilities and a cosy lounge. Friendly English-speaking owners are founts of information about Takayama.

Guesthouse Tomaru Guesthouse ¥
(飛騨高山ゲストハウスとまる; ☏0577-62-9260; www.hidatakayama-guesthouse.com; 6-5 Hanasato-machi; dm ¥2800, s & d ¥6500-7500, tr ¥9000; @ 🛜) Visitors love the friendly homestay vibe of this small, centrally located guesthouse. Pleasant rooms with homely touches are kept spotlessly clean. There's free wi-fi and a shared kitchen.

Hida Takayama Temple Inn Zenkō-ji Hostel ¥
(飛騨高山善光寺宿坊; ☏0577-32-8470; www.takayamahostelzenkoji.com; 4-3 Tenman-machi; dm ¥2500, s ¥3000; P ➔ 🛜) Good karma washes over this branch of Nagano's famous Zenkō-ji temple, where donations are accepted in return for accommodation. Private rooms are generously proportioned around a courtyard garden. Even the dorms have temple charm. There's a shared kitchen and no curfew for respectful guests.

Sumiyoshi Ryokan Ryokan ¥¥
(寿美吉旅館; ☏0577-32-0228; www.sumiyoshi-ryokan.com; 4-21 Hon-machi; r per person with/without 2 meals from ¥11,000/7000; P @) The kind owners of this delightfully antiquey inn, set in a Meiji-era merchant's house, have been welcoming guests from abroad for years. Some rooms have river views through panes of antique glass, and the common baths are made of wood and slate tiles. One room has a private bath.

Yamakyū Ryokan ¥¥
(山久; ☏0577-32-3756; www.takayama-yamakyu.com; 58 Tenshōji-machi; r with/without meals from ¥8100/5940; P @ 🛜) Occupying a lovely hillside spot opposite Hokke-ji temple, Yamakyū is a 20-minute walk from the train station. Inside, antique-filled curio cabinets, clocks and lamps line the red-carpeted corridors. All 20 tatami rooms have a sink and toilet, and the common baths are of a high standard. Some English is spoken. This is an excellent choice for a ryokan experience without the expense.

Gasshō-zukuri Architecture

Hida winters are unforgiving. Inhabitants braved the elements long before the advent of propane heaters and 4WD vehicles. The most visible symbol of their adaptability is *gasshō-zukuri* architecture; steeply slanted straw-roofed homes that dot the regional landscape.

Sharply angled roofs prevent snow accumulation, a serious concern in an area where most mountain roads close from December to April. The name *gasshō* comes from the Japanese word for prayer, because the shape of the roofs was thought to resemble hands clasped together. *Gasshō* buildings often featured pillars crafted from stout cedars to lend extra support. The attic areas were ideal for silk cultivation. Larger *gasshō-zukuri* buildings were inhabited by wealthy families, with up to 30 people under one roof. Peasant families lived in huts so small that today they'd only be considered fit for tool sheds.

The art of *gasshō-zukuri* construction is dying out. Most remaining examples have been relocated to folk villages, including Hida-no-Sato, Ogimachi, Suganuma and Ainokura. Homes that are now neighbours may once have been separated by several days of travel on foot or sled. These cultural preservation efforts have made it possible to imagine a bygone life in the Hida hills.

If You Like…
Takayama

If you like Takayama we think you'll like these other less-visited but wonderful Central Honshū destinations:

1 HIDA-FURUKAWA
Just 15 minutes north of Takayama by train (JR line, ¥230, 15 minutes) this town has some a fine carp-filled canals lined by old *kura* (storehouses).

2 INUYAMA
About 30 minutes northwest of Nagoya by train (Meitetsu Inuyama line, ¥540, 30 minutes), Inuyama is home to National Treasure castle Inuyama-jō, some quaint streets and nearby rivers.

3 ECHIZEN ŌNO
It takes some commitment to get to this small, all-but-forgotten Fukui Prefecture town, with its rows of temples and aging population, but its little *yamashiro* (mountain castle) is a delight.

Best Western Hotel   Hotel ¥¥
(ベストウェスタンホテル高山; ☎0577-37-2000; www.bestwestern.co.jp; 6-6 Hanasato-machi; s/d/tw from ¥6900/12,700/13,700; 🌐📶) Popular with overseas guests, this tourist hotel's refurbished rooms have a splash of colour. Good-value rates can be found online and sometimes include a breakfast buffet. It's a hop, skip and a jump from the station.

Honjin Hiranoya   Ryokan ¥¥¥
(本陣平野屋; ☎0577-34-1234; www.honjinhi ranoya.co.jp/english; 1-5 Hon-machi; r per person with 2 meals from ¥12,600; 🅿) For something a little different, choose the contemporary elegance of the executive rooms in the more expensive Kachoan wing. Otherwise opt for a classical river-view room in the Bekkan (Annexe) wing. There's a free shuttle bus from the train station, or it's a 10-minute walk. Expect the highest service levels, English-speaking staff and exquisite cuisine. Highly recommended.

Hōshōkaku   Ryokan ¥¥¥
(宝生閣; ☎0577-34-0700; www.hoshokaku. co.jp/english; 1-88 Baba-machi; r per person with 2 meals from ¥9720; 🅿) Surrounded by the greenery of Shiroyama-kōen, this upscale hillside ryokan on the edge of town has wonderful outdoor rooftop hot springs with city views and sumptuous *kaiseki* cuisine. If arriving by train, it's easiest to grab a taxi out here.

Tanabe Ryokan   Ryokan ¥¥¥
(旅館田邊; ☎0577-32-0529; www.tanabe-ryokan.jp; 58 Aioi-chō; r per person with 2 meals from ¥12,960; 🌐@) This elegant, atmospheric inn has a premium, central location and friendly, welcoming staff who speak some English. All tatami rooms have an en-suite bath, although the lovely common baths with their beamed ceilings are worth enjoying. A sumptuous dinner of *kaiseki*-style Hida cuisine completes the experience.

🍴 Eating

Takayama's specialities include *soba*, *hoba-miso*, *sansai* (mountain vegetables) and Hida-*gyū*. Street foods include *mitarashi-dango* (skewers of grilled riceballs seasoned with soy sauce) and *shio-sembei* (salty rice crackers). *Hida-gyū* turns up on *kushiyaki* (skewers), in *korokke* (croquettes) and *niku-man* (steamed buns). If you're on a budget, keep an eye out for the numerous bakeries around town where you can stock up on delicious, inexpensive fresh breads and sandwiches.

Heianraku   Chinese ¥
(平安楽; ☎0577-32-3078; 6-7-2 Tenman-machi; dishes from ¥700; 🕚11.30am-1.30pm & 5-10pm Wed-Mon; 🍴) Atmospheric, inexpensive, welcoming and delicious are all words that spring to mind when describing this wonderful second-generation eatery serving up Chinese delights in a traditional Japanese shopfront on Kokubunji-dōri. It's a few steps before Hida Kokubun-ji on the

opposite side of the street. The *gyōza* and meatballs are spot on. English is spoken.

Chitose   Noodles ¥

(ちとせ; 📞0577-32-1056; 6-19 Hanasato-machi; noodles from ¥500; 🕐11am-3pm & 5-7.30pm Wed-Mon) Delicious, chunky *yaki-soba* (fried noodles) and *chūka-soba* noodle soups are the speciality at this cheap-as-chips local fave that will fill your belly and satisfy your wallet. Top your *yaki-soba* with a deliciously drippy fried egg to complete the experience. Highly recommended.

Chapala   Mexican ¥

(チャパラ; 📞0577-34-9800; 1 Hanakawa-chō; mains ¥500-980; 🕐6pm-10.30pm Mon-Sat, closed 1st Mon of each month; 📖) The enthusiastic, local owner of this friendly restaurant does a great job bringing the flavours of Mexico to a quiet Japanese street. The taste and dainty portions of tacos, quesadillas and guac' and chips won't match California or Guadalajara, but the place is adorable and patrons love it. Where else can you eat tacos with chopsticks while swilling Coronas and sake?

Ebisu-Honten   Noodles ¥

(恵比寿本店; 📞0577-32-0209; www.takayama-ebisu.jp/emenu; 46 Kamini-no-machi; noodle bowls from ¥880; 🕐10am-5pm Thu-Tue; 🖊📖) These folks have been making *teuchi* (handmade) *soba* since 1898. Try their cold *zaru soba* (¥880) to strip it bare and taste the flavour of the noodles. The *tororo nameko soba* (¥1220) is also very good: noodles in a hot soup with boiled mushroom and grated mountain potato. The building has an interesting red-glass sign with white characters and a little roof on it.

Center4 Hamburgers   Burgers ¥¥

(📞0577-36-4527; www.tiger-center4.com; 94 Kamiichino-machi; burgers from ¥760; 🕐11am-9.30pm; 📖) Word has spread that this young Japanese couple are living their dream, welcoming visitors from around the world – so you might have to wait for a table to enjoy their delicious comfort food, prepared with love. On the menu: juicy home-style burgers (including veggie), club sandwiches, and chilli and clam chowder, served up in a funky din-ing room that feels like the extension of someone's home. Top it off with a world beer, a decent red or a milkshake and you'll be too floaty to waste time feeling guilty about taking a break from *soba*.

Kotarō   Tonkatsu ¥¥

(小太郎; 📞0577-32-7353; 6-1 Tenman-machi; meals ¥1050-2100; 🕐11.30am-2pm & 5-9pm Thu-Tue; 📖) Expect satisfaction from this compact workman-like eatery whose chef has spent over 25 years mastering the art of *tonkatsu* and other fried goodies. Generous *teishoku* (from ¥1050) feature crispy, crunchy *katsu*, cooked to perfection, accompanied by perfectly balanced sides: fluffy rice, rich miso soup, fruit, salad and pickles. Try the cheese *katsu* (¥1350) for something different.

Kyōya   Shokudō ¥¥

(京や; 📞0577-34-7660; 1-77 Ōjin-machi; mains ¥700-5000; 🕐11am-10pm Wed-Mon; 📖) This traditional eatery specialises in regional dishes such as *hoba-miso* and Hida-*gyû soba*. Seating is on tatami mats around long charcoal grills, under a cathedral ceiling supported by dark timbers. It's on a corner, by a bridge over the canal. Look for the sacks of rice over the door.

Restaurant Le Midi   French ¥¥¥

(📞0577-36-6386; www.le-midi.jp/english; 2-85 Hon-machi; appetisers ¥650-3400; Hida-*gyû* dishes ¥2400-7500; 🕐11.30am-2pm & 6-9pm Fri-Wed; 📖) One street back from the river,

Morning Markets

Daily *asa-ichi* (morning markets) are a wonderful way to wake up and meet people. The **Jinya-mae Asa-ichi** (1-5 Hachiken-machi) is in front of Takayama-jinya; the larger **Miya-gawa Asa-ichi** (宮川朝市) runs along the east bank of the Miya-gawa, between Kaji-bashi and Yayoi-bashi. Stalls range from farm-fresh produce to local arts and crafts. Autumnal apples are out of this world!

Detour:
Shirakawa-gō

Ogimachi, the Shirakawa-gō region's central settlement, has some 600 residents and the largest concentration of *gasshō-zukuri* buildings – over 110. It's also the most accessible. Pick up a free English-language map at the **Tourist Information Office** (観光案内所; ☎0576-96-1013; 2495-3 Ogimachi; ☺9am-5pm), by the main bus stop outside the Folk Village. Be sure to bring enough cash – there are no ATMs and credit cards are not accepted.

this upscale restaurant serves traditional French cuisine with a Japanese twist. Mouth-watering appetisers include Hida-beef carpaccio and onion gratin soup. Lunch set meals range from ¥1800 to ¥4800 and set-course dinners including hors d'oeuvres, mains, soup, salad and coffee start at ¥4800. For dessert, the local *sukune kabocha* (pumpkin) pudding is a must. If you're feeling French and fancy, you're unlikely to be disappointed.

ℹ Information

Tourist Information Center (飛騨高山観光案内所; ☎0577-32-5328; www.hida.jp/english; ☺8.30am-5pm Nov-Mar, to 6.30pm Apr-Oct) Directly in front of JR Takayama Station, knowledgeable English-speaking staff dispense English and other language maps and a wealth of pamphlets on sights, accommodation, special events and regional transport. Staff are unable to assist with accommodation reservations.

ℹ Getting There & Away

From Tokyo or Kansai, the most efficient way to reach Takayama is via Nagoya on the JR Takayama line (Hida *tokkyū*, ¥5510, 2¼ hours); the mountainous train ride along the Hida-gawa

is *gorge*-ous. Some trains continue on to Toyama (¥2840, 90 minutes), where you can connect to Kanazawa (¥2150, 40 minutes).

Nōhi Bus (濃飛バス; ☎0577-32-1688; www.nouhibus.co.jp/english) Operates highway bus services between Takayama and Tokyo's Shinjuku Station (¥6690, 5½ hours, several daily, reservations required), Matsumoto (¥3190, 2½ hours) and Kanazawa (¥3390, 2¼ hours). Takayama's bus station is adjacent to the train station. Schedules vary seasonally and some routes don't run at all during winter, when many roads are closed.

ℹ Getting Around

Most sights in Takayama can be covered easily on foot. You can amble from the train station to Teramachi in about 20 minutes. Takayama is bicycle friendly. Some lodgings lend bikes, or you can hire one from **Hara Cycle** (ハラサイクル; ☎0577-32-1657; 61 Suehiro-chō; 1st hr ¥300, additional hr ¥200, day ¥1300; ☺9am-8pm Wed-Mon).

NORTHERN JAPAN ALPS 北日本アルプス

Boasting some of Japan's most dramatic scenery, the Northern Japan Alps of Gifu, Toyama and Nagano Prefectures contain stunning peaks above 3000m, accessible even to amateur hikers. Also called the Hida Ranges, the most spectacular scenery is protected within the 174,323-hectare Chūbu-Sangaku National Park (中部山岳国立公園). Highlights include hiking the valleys and peaks of Kamikōchi, doing it easy on the Shin-Hotaka Ropeway and soaking up the splendour of Hida's many mountain *rotemburo*. The northern part of the park extends to the Tateyama-Kurobe Alpine Route.

ℹ Getting There & Around

Matsumoto and Takayama are the gateway cities into the peaks, while the main transit hubs when you're up there are Hirayu Onsen and Kamikōchi. Buses make the journey from Takayama. From Matsumoto, it's a ride on the private Matsumoto Dentetsu train to Shin-Shimashima, then a bus. Either way, the journey is breathtaking.

Hiring a car is a good option if windy roads don't bother you, and you're not overnighting in Kamikōchi – the road between Naka-no-yu and Kamikōchi is open only to buses and taxis.

Kamikōchi 上高地

0260

Some of Japan's most spectacular scenery is found here – majestic snowcapped peaks, bubbling crystal brooks, wild monkeys, wildflowers and ancient forests. That said, it wouldn't be Japan without the crowds. Timing is everything.

Kamikōchi is closed from 15 November to 22 April, and in peak times (late July to late August, and during the foliage season in October) it can seem busier than Shinjuku Station – plan to arrive early in the day. June to July is rainy season. It's perfectly feasible to visit as a day trip but you'll miss out on the pleasures of staying in the mountains and taking uncrowded early-morning or late-afternoon walks.

Visitors arrive at Kamikōchi's sprawling bus station, surrounded by visitor facilities. A 10-minute walk along the Azusa-gawa takes you to Kappa-bashi, a bridge named after a legendary water sprite. Hiking trails begin here.

Activities

Bokuden-no-yu Onsen
(卜伝の湯; ☑0260-95-2407; admission ¥700; ☺noon-5pm) Not for the claustrophobic, the area's most unusual onsen – a tiny cave bath dripping with minerals – is found near the Nakano-yu bus stop, to the left of the bus-only tunnel into Kamikōchi. Pay at the small shop for the key to the little mountain hut housing the onsen. It's yours privately for up to 30 minutes.

Sleeping & Eating

Accommodation in Kamikōchi is expensive and advance reservations are essential. Except for camping, rates quoted here include two meals. Some lodgings shut down power in the middle of the night (emergency lighting stays on).

Dotted along the trails and around the mountains are dozens of spartan *yamagoya* (mountain huts), which provide two meals and a futon from around ¥8000 per person; some also serve simple lunches. Enquire before setting out to make sure there's one on your intended route.

The bus station has a very limited range of eateries and retailers. Depending on your length of stay, bring essential munchies and take your rubbish with you.

Tokusawa-en Campground ¥
(徳澤園; ☑0260-95-2508; www.tokusawaen. com/english.html; per person incl 2 meals campsite/dm ¥500/10,000, d & tw ¥14,900; ☺May-Oct) A marvellously secluded place

Kappa-bashi Bridge over Azusa-gawa, Kamikōchi
IMAGEWERKS/GETTY IMAGES ©

Hiking & Climbing in Kamikōchi

The river valley offers mostly level, short-distance, signposted walks.

A four-hour round trip starts east of Kappa-bashi past Myōjin-bashi (one hour) to Tokusawa (another hour) before returning. By Myōjin-bashi, the idyllic Myōjin-ike (pond) marks the innermost shrine of Hotaka-jinja (admission ¥300). West of Kappa-bashi, you can amble alongside the river to Weston Relief (monument to Walter Weston; 15 minutes) or to Taishō-ike (40 minutes).

Other popular hikes include the mountain hut at Dakesawa (2½ hours up) and fiery Yakedake (four hours up, starting about 20 minutes west of the Weston Relief, at Hotaka-bashi). From the peaks, it's possible to see all the way to Mt Fuji in clear weather – it's a breathtaking view.

Numerous long-distance hikes vary in duration from a few days to a week. Japanese-language maps of the area show routes and average hiking times between huts, major peaks and landmarks. Favourite hikes and climbs (which can mean human traffic jams during peak seasons) include Yariga-take (3180m) and Hotaka-dake (3190m).

A steep but worthwhile hike connects Kamikōchi and Shin-Hotaka. From Kappa-bashi, the trail crosses the ridge below Nishi-Hotaka-dake (2909m) at Nishi-Hotaka San-sō (cottage; three hours) and continues to Nishi-Hotaka-guchi, the top station of the Shin-Hotaka Ropeway. The hike takes nearly four hours in this direction but is far easier in reverse. To reach the ropeway, take a bus from Takayama or Hirayu Onsen.

in a wooded dell about 7km northeast of Kappa-bashi. It's both a camping ground and a lodge, and has Japanese-style rooms (shared facilities) and hearty meals served in a busy dining hall. Access is by walking only, and takes about two hours.

Forest Resort Konashi
Campground ¥

(森のリゾート小梨 Mori no rizōto Konashi; ☑0260-95-2321; www.nihonalpskankou.com; per person incl 2 meals campsite from ¥800, tw from ¥11,000; ☺office 7am-7pm) About 200m past the Kamikōchi Visitor Centre, this camping ground can get crowded. Rental tents are available from ¥7000 (July and August) and there's a small shop and restaurant.

Kamikōchi Gosenjaku Hotel & Lodge
Hotel ¥¥

(上高地五千尺ホテル・ロッヂ; ☑hotel 0260-95-2111, lodge 0260-95-2221; www.gosen

jaku.co.jp/english; 4468 Kamikōchi; per person incl 2 meals lodge skier's bed from ¥10,000, s/tw ¥24,000/12,000, hotel d from ¥17,500) By Kappa-bashi this compact lodge recently expanded to include a small hotel. The lodge has 34 Japanese-style rooms and some 'skier's beds'; basically curtained-off bunks. Rooms all have sink and toilet, but baths are shared. The hotel is more upscale with a combination of comfortable Western and Japanese rooms, some with balconies.

Kamikōchi Nishi-itoya Sansō
Inn ¥¥

(上高地西糸屋山荘; ☑0260-95-2206; www.nishiitoya.com; 4469-1 Kamikōchi; per person incl 2 meals dm from ¥8500, d from ¥9720; ☺@☎) This friendly lodge, west of Kappa-bashi, has a cosy lounge and dates from the early 20th century. Rooms are a mix of Japanese and Western styles, all with toilet. The shared bath is a large onsen facing the Hotaka mountains.

Kamikochi Imperial Hotel
Hotel ¥¥¥

(上高地帝国ホテル; ☎0260-95-2001; www. imperialhotel.co.jp/j/kamikochi; Azumino Kamikōchi; s & tw from ¥29,400; @) Expect exceptional service and rustic European Alps–styled rooms in this historic red-gabled lodge completed in 1933. Prices are elevated, but a wide range of stay plans are available and the hotel occasionally offers excellent packages including French haute cuisine. You may have to book a year in advance!

Kamonji-goya
Shokudō ¥

(☎0260-95-2418; dishes from ¥700; ⊙8.30am-4pm; 🖵) Kamikōchi's signature dish is *iwana* (river trout) grilled whole over an *irori*. This is *the* place to try it. The *iwana* set is ¥1500, or there's *oden* (fish-cake stew), *soba* and *kotsu-sake* (dried *iwana* in sake) served in a lovely ceramic bowl. It's just outside the entrance to Myōjin-ike.

ℹ Information

Kamikōchi is entirely closed from 16 November to 22 April. Serious hikers should consider insurance (保険; *hoken*; from ¥1000 per day), available at Kamikōchi bus station.

Kamikōchi Tourist Information Center (上高地インフォメーションセンター; ☎0260-95-2433; ⊙8am-5pm) This invaluable resource at the bus station complex provides info on hiking and weather conditions and offers the English-language *Kamikōchi Pocket Guide* with a map of the main walking tracks.

Kamikōchi Visitor Centre (上高地ビジターセンター; ☎0260-95-2606; ⊙8am-5pm) Ten minutes' walk from Kamikōchi bus station along the main trail, this is the place for information on Kamikōchi's flora, fauna, geology and history. You can also book guided walks to destinations including Taishō-ike and Myōjin-ike (per person from ¥500). English-speaking nature guides (from ¥2000 per hour) and climbing guides (around ¥30,000 a day) may be available.

ℹ Getting Around

Private vehicles are prohibited between Naka-no-yu and Kamikōchi; access is only by bus or taxi as far as the Kamikōchi bus station. Those with private cars can use car parks en route to Naka-no-yu in the hamlet of Sawando for ¥500 per day; shuttle buses (¥1800 return) run a few times per hour.

Buses run via Naka-no-yu and Taishō-ike to the bus station. Hiking trails commence at Kappabashi, which is a short walk from the bus station.

Sample Bus Routes & Fares: Northern Japan Alps

Within the Alps, schedules change seasonally. Alpico's 'Alps-wide Free Passport' (¥10,290) gives you four days unlimited rides between Matsumoto and Takayama, within the Chūbu-Sangaku National Park and includes Shirakawa-gō.

Tourist Information Centers can direct you to the latest schedules and fares.

FROM	TO	FARE (¥; ONE WAY)	DURATION (MIN; ONE WAY)
Takayama	Hirayu Onsen	1570	55
	Kamikōchi	2720	80
	Shin-Hotaka	2160	90
Matsumoto	Shin-Shimashima	700 (train)	30
	Kamikōchi	2650	95
Shin-Shimashima	Naka-no-yu	1700	50
	Kamikōchi	1950	70
	Shirahone Onsen	1450	75
Kamikōchi	Naka-no-yu	770	15
	Hirayu Onsen	1160	25
	Shirahone Onsen	1350	35
Hirayu Onsen	Naka-no-yu	580	10
	Shin-Hotaka	920	30

Shin-Hotaka Onsen
新穂高温泉

☎0578

The main reason people visit Shin-Hotaka Onsen, an otherwise sleepy hollow north of Fukuchi Onsen, is the Shin-Hotaka Ropeway, Japan's longest.

👁 Sights & Activities

Shin-Hotaka Ropeway — Ropeway
(新穂高ロープウェイ; ☎0578-89-2252; www.okuhi.jp/Rop/english.pdf; Shin-Hotaka; one-way/return ¥1600/2900; ⊙8.30am-4.30pm) From a starting elevation of 1308m, two cable cars whisk you to 2156m towards the peak of Nishi Hotaka-dake (2909m). Views from the top are spectacular, both from observation decks and walking trails. In winter, snows can be shoulder deep. In season, properly equipped hikers with ample time can choose from a number of hikes beginning from the top cable-car station (Nishi Hotaka-guchi) including hiking over to Kamikōchi (three hours), which is much easier than going the other way.

Nakazaki Sansou Okuhida-no-yu — Onsen
(中崎山荘奥飛騨の湯; ☎0578-89-2021; 710 Okuhida Onsengo Kansaka; adult/child ¥800/400; ⊙8am-8pm) Over 50 years old but completely rebuilt in 2010, this facility commands a spectacular vista of the mountains. The milky waters of its large indoor baths and *rotemburo* do wonders for dry skin.

🛌 Sleeping & Eating

Yarimikan — Ryokan ¥¥¥
(槍見舘; ☎0578-89-2808; www.yarimikan.com; Okuhida Onsen-gun Kansaka; r per person with meals from ¥16,350; P) Yarimikan is a wonderfully traditional *onsen ryokan* on the Kamata-gawa, with two indoor baths, eight riverside *rotemburo* (some available for private use) and 15 rooms. Guests can bathe 24 hours a day (it's stunning by moonlight) and day visitors are accepted between 10am and 2pm for ¥500. Cuisine features local Hida beef and grilled freshwater fish. It's just off Route 475, a few kilometres before the Shin-Hotaka Ropeway.

Shin-Hotaka Ropeway

JOHN S LANDER/GETTY IMAGES ©

 ## Don't Miss
Shin-Hotaka-no-yu

Exhibitionists will love this bare-bones *konyoku* (mixed bathing) *rotemburo* by the Kamata-gawa, visible from the bridge that passes over it. Entry is free (or by donation). Enter through segregated change rooms, and emerge into a single large pool. Be sure to mind your manners. When in Rome...

NEED TO KNOW

新穂高の湯; ☏0578-89-2458; Okuhida Onsengo Kansaka; ⊙8am-9pm May-Oct, closed Nov-Apr

---

Nonohana Sansō Inn ¥¥¥
(野の花山荘; ☏0578-89-0030; www.nono87. jp; r per person with 2 meals from ¥13,000; day guests adult/child ¥800/500; ⊙day guests 10am-5pm; P) Along a road that ascends from Route 475, Nonohana Sansō opened its doors in 2010. All tatami guestrooms are traditionally styled and have private facilities, although the lobby and lounge are refreshingly contemporary. There's an open kitchen preparing local specialities and the large *rotembu700* have a fantastic outlook – they're open to day visitors.

NAGANO PREFECTURE
長野県

Formerly known as Shinshū and often referred to as the 'Roof of Japan', Nagano Prefecture is a wonderful place to visit for its regal mountains, rich cultural history, fine architecture and cuisine.

In addition to a hefty chunk of the Japan Alps National Park, Nagano boasts several quasi-national parks that attract skiers, mountaineers and onsen aficionados.

Nagano, the prefectural capital and past host of the Olympic Games, is home to Zenkō-ji, a spectacular temple

of national significance. Ever-lovable Matsumoto, Nagano Prefecture's other main city, makes the most of its wonderful geography, vibrant city centre and photogenic original castle.

Shiga Kōgen 志賀高原

📞0269

The site of several events during the 1998 Nagano Olympics and the 2005 Special Olympics World Winter Games, Shiga Kōgen is Japan's largest ski resort and one of the largest in the world: there are 21 linked areas covering 80 runs.

Outside winter the mountain's lakes, ponds and overlooks make it an excellent destination for hikers. If you're not here to hike or ski, there's no compelling reason to visit.

 Activities

Shiga Kōgen Ski Area   Skiing
(志賀高原スキー場; 📞0269-34-2404; www.shigakogen.gr.jp; 1-day lift ticket ¥5000;

⏰8.30am-4.30pm Dec-Apr) This conglomeration of 21 ski areas is covered by one lift ticket, which gives access to all areas as well as the shuttle bus between various base lodges. Check out www.snowjapan.com for info on each individual area.

There is a huge variety of terrain for all skill levels. In the Hasuike area, in front of the Shiga Kōgen ropeway station, the office has English speakers who can help you navigate the slopes and book accommodation. **Hasuike** ski area is central and is good for learners and families; **Nishitate-yama** has long courses and great views; **Yakebitai-yama** is one of the biggest areas with a huge variety of terrain and panoramic views.

🛏 Sleeping & Eating

Villa Ichinose   Inn ¥¥
(ヴィラ・一の瀬; 📞0269-34-2704; www.villa101.biz/english; 7149 Hirao; r per person from ¥5000; P🛜) With a great location in front of the Ichinose bus stop, English-speaking staff and a friendly atmosphere,

this inn is popular with overseas guests. Japanese-style rooms have toilet only and Western-style rooms have their own bathroom. There's wi-fi in the lobby and a 24-hour public bath on the second floor.

Hotel Sunroute Shiga Kōgen   Hotel ¥¥¥

(ホテルサンルート志賀高原; ☑0269-34-2020; www.sunroute.jp/english; r per person incl 2 meals from ¥11,500; P) Popular with a Western crowd, this hotel is a three-minute walk from the Ichinose Diamond ski lift, with great access to other ski areas. The Western-style rooms have en-suite baths; some have mountain views. Staff communicate well in English.

Chalet Shiga   Inn ¥¥¥

(シャレー志賀; ☑0269-34-2235; www.shigakogen.jp/chalet/en; r per person with 2 meals from ¥10,200; P) Chalet Shiga is both convenient to the slopes and has a popular sports bar on site. Both Western- and Japanese-style rooms are available.

🛈 Getting There & Away

Direct buses run between Nagano Station and Shiga Kōgen, with frequent departures in ski season (¥1700, 70 minutes). You can also take a train from Nagano to Yudanaka and continue to Shiga Kōgen by bus – take a Hase-ike-bound bus and get off at the last stop (¥780, approximately 40 minutes).

Nozawa Onsen 野沢温泉

☑0269 / POP 3800

This wonderful working village tucked in a picturesque corner of the eastern Japan Alps is both a humming ski resort winter-long and a year-round onsen town – worth visiting any time of year.

Settled as early as the 8th century, it's compact and quaint, though the maze of narrow streets will challenge even the best of drivers.

169

Onsen water is still wisely used by many villagers for laundry, cooking and heating. There are 13 free onsen (for bathing) dotted about the town, each with a history. The waters here are hot and full of minerals – if you have silver jewellery, leave it in your room unless you don't mind it temporarily turning black.

Outside the busy ski-season, it's possible to briefly escape modernity and get a sense of life in an ancient mountain village.

Activities

Nozawa Onsen Snow Resort
Snow Sports

(野沢温泉スキー場; www.nozawaski.com/winter/en; 1-day lift ticket ¥4800; ☺8.30am-4.30pm Dec-Apr) Nozawa Onsen Snow Resort, one of Honshū's best, dominates the 'upper' village. The relatively compact resort with 21 lifts is easy to navigate and enjoy with a variety of terrain at all levels. The main base is around the Higake gondola station, where there are beginner and kid-friendly runs.

Snowboarders should try the Karasawa terrain park or the half-pipe at Uenotaira; advanced skiers will enjoy the steep and often mogulled Schneider Course. The lively village is great for after-ski action.

Sleeping

Lodge Nagano
Inn ¥

(ロッジながの; ☎0269-67-0259; www.lodgenagano.com; 6846-1 Toyosato; r per person incl breakfast from ¥4500, r in summer from ¥4000; ❀❀) This popular foreign-run guesthouse attracts lots of Aussie skiers (there's Vegemite in the dining room). It's a friendly, fun place with bunk dorms and tatami rooms, some with private bath.

Address Nozawa
Apartment ¥¥

(アドレス野沢; ☎0269-67-0360; www.addressnozawa.com; 9535 Nozawa Onsen; studios from ¥9000; ❀@❀♿) This innovative, boutique property was formerly a traditional inn. New owners sought to recreate a space that combined Japanese and European design elements and have done just that. Large Western-style rooms with tatami floors feature fresh colours, soft downy beds, bright bathrooms and a full kitchen stocked with breakfast provisions. There's an on-site onsen bath, kids' room, ski storage and plenty of high technology.

Mura-no-hoteru Sumiyoshi-ya
Ryokan ¥¥¥

(村のホテル住吉屋; ☎0269-85-2005; www.sumiyosiya.com; 8713 Toyosato; r per person with 2 meals from ¥17,820; ❀@) This wonderful ryokan, the oldest in town, has a wide range of inviting traditional room types, many with private bathrooms and great views. The communal onsen baths with stained glass windows are dreamy. Limited English is spoken

Skiing, Hakuba
JOHN BORTHWICK/GETTY IMAGES ©

but the friendly staff are committed to excellent service.

Kiriya Ryokan
Ryokan ¥¥¥

(桐屋旅館; ☎0269-85-2020; www.kiriya.jp; 8714-2 Nozawa Onsen; r per person with 2 meals from ¥13,500;) This friendly ryokan has been in the family for generations. The owner's attentive service and excellent English ensure its abiding popularity with overseas guests. All rooms have private toilets. Some have their own baths in addition to the large communal onsen baths. There's a guest laundry and a wonderful garden.

Eating & Drinking

Pasta di Pasta
Restaurant ¥

(パスタディパスタ; ☎0269-85-5055; www. pastadipasta.net; 8376-145 Toyosato; dishes ¥500-1200; ⏰lunch & dinner, hrs vary seasonally) Freshly cooked pasta, pizza and appetisers are the order of the day in this cosy upstairs eatery. The not-too-creamy *wafū sanshū no kinoko* pasta (three kinds of mushroom) is delicious.

Stay
Bar

(ステイ; www.seisenso.com) Stay is a cosy basement bar that's open late and is run by a music-loving Japanese man who has lived abroad.

Information

Nozawa Onsen Visitor Centre (野沢温泉ビジターセンター; ☎0269-85-3155; www. nozawakanko.jp/english; 9780-4 Toyosato; ⏰8.30am-6pm) In the centre of the village. Has English-speaking staff who can assist with accommodation and tour bookings.

Getting There & Away

There are direct buses between Nagano Station's east exit and Nozawa Onsen (¥1500, 90 minutes, seven buses per day in winter, three buses per day in summer). Alternatively, take a JR Iiyama-line train between Nagano and Togari Nozawa Onsen Station (¥760, 55 minutes). Regular buses connect Togari Nozawa Onsen Station and Nozawa Onsen (¥310, 20 minutes, nine per day). The bus station/ ticket office is about 200m from the main bus stop, which is in the middle of town. This can be a little

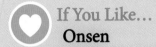

If You Like...
Onsen

If you like Shin-Hotaka Onsen (p166), we think you'll enjoy a soak in these other nearby onsen:

1 HIRAYU ONSEN
Hirayu is a transport hub just south of Kamikōchi. It's also home to a few nice onsen that make for a good soak after hiking in the Northern Japan Alps. To get here, take the bus from Takayama (¥1570, 55 minutes).

2 FUKUCHI ONSEN
This quiet onsen village is located near the more popular resort of Hirayu. Take the bus from Hirayu Onsen to get here.

3 SHIRAHONE ONSEN
This wonderful onsen village, in a gorge near the entrance to Kamikōchi, is a must for onsen lovers. It's a bus ride from Hirayu Onsen.

confusing, but there are staff around to help get people where they need to be.

Hakuba 白馬
☎0261

At the base of one of the highest sections of the Northern Japan Alps, Hakuba is one of Japan's main skiing and hiking centres. In winter skiers from across Japan and increasingly overseas flock to Hakuba's seven ski resorts. In summer the region draws hikers attracted by easy access to the high peaks. There are many onsen in and around Hakuba-mura, the main village, and a long soak after a day of action is the perfect way to ease your muscles.

Activities

Happō-One Ski Resort
Skiing

(八方尾根スキー所; ☎0261-72-3066; www. happo-one.jp/english; 1-day lift ticket ¥5000; ⏰Dec-Apr) Host of the downhill races at the 1998 Winter Olympics, Happō-One is one of Japan's best ski areas, with superb mountain views and beginner, intermediate and advanced runs catering to skiers and snowboarders. For the lowdown, check the excellent English-language homepage.

Hakuba 47 Winter Sports Park & Hakuba Goryū Ski Resort   Skiing

(Hakuba47ウインタースポーツパーク・白馬五竜スキー場; www.hakuba47.co.jp; 1-day lift ticket ¥5000; ⏱Dec-Apr) The interlinked areas of Hakuba 47 Winter Sports Park and Hakuba Goryū Ski Resort form the second major ski resort in the Hakuba area. There's a good variety of terrain at both areas, with about an equal number of skiers and boarders. Like Happō-One, this area boasts fantastic mountain views. A free shuttle bus from Hakuba-mura and Hakuba-eki provides the easiest access.

Mimizuku-no-yu   Onsen

(みみずくの湯; 5480 Ō-aza Hokujō; adult/child ¥500/250; ⏱10am-9.30pm, enter by 9pm) One

of Hakuba's many onsen. Many say this has the best mountain views from the tub.

Evergreen Outdoor   Adventure Sports

(www.evergreen-hakuba.com) This gang of friendly, outdoorsy folk offer an array of adventures with English-speaking guides year-round from about ¥5000. On offer are canyoning and mountain biking, as well as snowshoeing and backcountry treks in the winter.

HIKING

In summer you can take the gondola and the two upper chairlifts, then hike along a trail for an hour or so to Happō-ike (pond) on a ridge below Karamatsu-dake (唐松岳; 2695m). From here, follow a trail another hour up to Maru-yama, continue for 1½ hours to the Karamatsu-dake San-sō (mountain hut) and then climb to the peak of Karamatsu-dake in about 30 minutes. For gondola schedules and fares, visit the Hakuba Tourist Information Center (p174).

🛏 Sleeping & Eating

Snowbeds Backpackers   Hostel ¥

(スノーベッズバックパッカーズ; ☎0261-72-5242; www.snowbedsjapan.com; dm per person from ¥3900; P@🛜) This foreign-run backpackers has cheap but cramped bunk rooms and a nice communal area with a wood stove. It's close to the nightlife. Private rooms are also available.

Hakuba Panorama Hotel   Inn ¥¥

(白馬パノラマホテル; ☎0261-85-4031; www.hakuba-panorama.com; 3322-1 Hokujō; d per person incl breakfast from ¥7600; P🛜) About 300m from one of the lifts at Happō-One, this Australian-run outfit has bilingual

Happō-ike
MASAYUKI/SHUTTERSTOCK ©

Japanese staff, an on-site travel agency and a variety of room types with ensuite bathrooms. There's a guest laundry and a wonderful onsen.

Ridge Hotel & Apartments
Hotel ¥¥¥

(📞0261-85-4301; www.theridgehakuba. com; 4608 Hakuba; d from ¥10,400, apt from ¥36,000; 🅿❄@📶) Sophisticated, sexy and stylish, this stunning property has it all, year round: location, amenities, views. A variety of room types range from the sublime (Western-style rooms with Japanese elements) to the ridiculous (a gorgeous loft balcony suite in the shadow of the slopes). Obliging, attentive staff speak English well. Splurge if you can.

Hakuba Tokyu Hotel
Hotel ¥¥¥

(白馬東急ホテル; 📞0261-72-3001; www. tokyuhotelsjapan.com/en/; Happō-wadanomori; s/d incl breakfast from ¥19,200/27,200; 🅿📶) This elegant year-round hotel has large rooms with great views and a wonderful garden, popular for weddings. The Grand Spa boasts the highest alkaline content in the area, and there's both French and Japanese restaurants.

Bamboo Coffee Bar
Cafe ¥

(📞0261-85-0901; www.bamboohakuba.com; 🕐8am-6pm; 📶📱) On the left as you exit JR Hakuba Station, this wonderful modern cafe serves delicious specialty coffees, sweet treats and panini sandwiches. The mellow tunes, friendly staff and free wi-fi (with purchases) make it a great place to log on and get your bearings.

🍷 Drinking & Entertainment

Tanuki's
Sports Bar

(タヌキズ; 📞090-7202-9809; 6350-3 Hokujo; 🕐noon-late Thu-Tue) This neat little bar to your right as you exit JR Habuka Station serves juicy original burgers and your favourite fast foods in a welcoming environment with free pool, darts and foozball on the 2nd floor.

Northern Japan Alps

BY NAKANISHI NORIO, PROFESSIONAL MOUNTAIN GUIDE

1 TSURUGI-DAKE CLIMB
The 2999m peak of Tsurugi-dake is one of Japan's most impressive sights: the jagged ridges leading to the summit will tempt any serious hiker or mountain climber. The standard route is from Murodō-daira via Tsurugi-sawa-goya hut and back to Murodō. You can also start at Murodō, cross the summit and descend right into the Tsurugi-sawa valley or do this in reverse. Keep in mind this climb is fairly serious and is only for experienced climbers comfortable with heights and exposed routes.

2 MURODŌ TO TARŌBEI DAIRA TRAVERSE
This is the classic North Alps traverse. Start by taking the Tateyama-Kurobe Alpine Route from Toyama up to the Murodō-daira and spend the night there – don't miss the onsen. Then, climb off the plateau and traverse the long mountain ridge to the south, stopping for the night en route at the huts at Goshiki-ga-hara and Tarōbei-daira, before exiting at Oritate or continuing south in the direction of Shin-Hotaka Onsen or even Kamikōchi.

3 ABOVE KAMIKŌCHI: YARIGA-TAKE & THE HODAKAS
Kamikōchi is an alpine sanctuary surrounded by high mountains on all sides. Unlike Murodō-daira, Kamikōchi sits at the base of the mountains. You can enjoy gentle hikes along the Azusa-gawa in the valley or climb the peaks that loom over the valley. The route over the Hodaka Range to the Matterhorn-like spire of 3180m Yariga-take is a classic.

The Pub
Pub

(📞0261-72-4453; www.thepubhakuba.com; 🕐4.30pm-late; @📶) The only English pub in the village is found in a Swiss-style chalet on the grounds of the Momonoki hotel. By Japanese standards, it's huge and happening. There's a daily happy hour, free internet and wi-fi.

Hakuba Bike Bar
Bar

(白馬バイクバー; www.bikebar-hakuba.com) This fun, disco-lit basement bar in Hakuba Goryū has a refreshingly hippie vibe – these guys think they're pretty cool, and by many standards, they are. It's about 10 minutes' walk from the Sky 4 Gondola and has billiards, early-evening film nights for families (Ninja juice is served) and karaoke.

Information

Hakuba Accomodation Information Centre (白馬宿泊情報センター, Hakuba Shukuhaku Jōhō Sentā; ☎0261-72-6900; www.hakuba1.com/english; ☉7am-6pm) For information, maps and lodging assistance. Located to the right of Hakuba Station.

Hakuba Tourist Information Center (白馬村観光案内所; ☎0261-72-3232; www.vill.hakuba.nagano.jp/english; ☉8.30am-5.30pm) Provides maps and leaflets relating to tourism in the area. In addition to all things winter, the website has detailed information on summer gondola operating schedules and fares. It's just outside Hakuba Station.

Getting There & Away

Hakuba is connected with Matsumoto by the JR Ōito line (*tokkyū* ¥2320, one hour; *futsū* ¥1140, 1½ hours). Continuing north, change trains at Minami Otari to meet the JR Hokuriku line at Itoigawa: it's a pretty journey on a little two-carriage train, taking an hour from Minami Otari to Itoigawa with connections to Niigata, Toyama and Kanazawa.

There is one direct service per day (Super Azusa #3) from Shinjuku to Hakuba, via Matsumoto (*tokkyū* ¥7780, four hours). It departs Shinjuku at 7.30am and returns from Hakuba at 2.38pm.

Alpico group operates buses from Nagano Station (¥1600, approximately 70 minutes) and Shinjuku Nishi-guchi in Tokyo (¥4850, 4½ hours), as well as a 'Ninja' bus service direct from Narita airport (from ¥9000). See www.alpico.co.jp/traffic/express/narita_hakuba/en for details.

Matsumoto　松本
☎0263 / POP 243,000

Embraced by seven great peaks to the west (including Yariga-take, Hotaka-dake and Norikura-dake, each above 3000m) and three smaller sentinels to the east (including beautiful Utsukushi-ga-hara-kōgen), Matsumoto occupies a protected position in a fertile valley no more than 20km across at its widest. Views of the regal Alps are never far away and sunsets are breathtaking.

Formerly known as Fukashi, Nagano prefecture's second-largest city has been here since the 8th century. In the 14th and 15th centuries, it was the castle town of the Ogasawara clan

Nawate-dōri
KORKUSUNG/SHUTTERSTOCK ©

and continued to prosper through the Edo period, to the present.

Today, Matsumoto is one of Japan's finest cities – an attractive, cosmopolitan place loved by its residents. Admirers from around the world come to enjoy its superb castle, pretty streets, galleries, cafes and endearing vistas. With plenty of well-priced, quality accommodation and excellent access to/from and around the town, Matsumoto is the perfect base for exploring the Japan Alps and the Kiso and Azumino Valleys.

⊙ Sights & Activities

Matsumoto-jō   Castle
(松本城; ☎ 0263-32-9202; 4-1 Marunōchi; adult/child ¥610/310; ⌚ 8.30am-5pm early Sep–mid-Jul, to 6pm mid-Jul–Aug) Must-see Matsumoto-jō is Japan's oldest wooden castle and one of four castles designated National Treasures – the others are Hikone, Himeji and Inuyama. The striking black and white three-turreted *donjon* was completed around 1595, earning the nickname Karasu-jō (Crow Castle). You can climb steep steps all the way to the top, with impressive views and historical displays on each level. Don't miss the recently restored *tsukimi yagura* (moon-viewing pavilion). The **Goodwill Guide Group** (☎ 0263-32-7140) offers free one-hour tours by reservation.

Admission includes entry to the Matsumoto City Museum.

Former Kaichi School   Museum
(旧開智学校, Kyū Kaichi Gakkō; ☎ 0263-32-5275; 2-4-12 Kaichi; adult/child ¥300; ⌚ 8.30am-4.30pm daily Mar-Nov, Tue-Sun Dec-Feb) A few blocks north of the castle, the former Kaichi School is both an Important Cultural Property and the oldest elementary school in Japan, founded in 1873. It opened its doors as an education museum in 1965. The building is an excellent example of Meiji-era architecture.

Matsumoto City Museum of Art   Museum
(松本市美術館, Matsumoto-shi Bijutsukan; ☎ 0263-39-7400; 4-2-22 Chūō; adult/child ¥410/200; ⌚ 9am-5pm Tue-Sun) This sleek museum has a good collection of Japanese artists, many of whom hail from Matsumoto or whose works depict scenes of the surrounding countryside. Highlights include the striking avant-garde works of local-born, internationally renowned Kusama Yayoi.

NAKAMACHI

The charming former merchant district of Nakamachi (中町) by the Metoba-gawa, with its *namako-kabe kura* (lattice-walled storehouses) and Edo-period streetscapes, makes for a wonderful stroll. Many buildings have been preserved and transformed into cafes, galleries and craft shops specialising in wood, glass, fabric, ceramics and antiques.

Nawate-dōri   Street
(縄手道り) Nawate-dori, a few blocks from the castle, is a popular place for a stroll. Vendors along this riverside walk sell antiques, souvenirs and delicious *taiyaki* (filled waffle in the shape of a carp) of varying flavours. Look for the big frog statue by the bridge.

Matsumoto Timepiece Museum   Museum
(松本市時計博物館, Matsumoto-shi Tokei Hakubutsukan; ☎ 0263-36-0969; 4-21-15 Chūō; adult/student ¥300/150; ⌚ 9am-5pm Tue-Sun) Home to Japan's largest pendulum clock (on the building's exterior) and over 300 other timepieces including fascinating medieval Japanese creations, this museum shows Japan's love of *monozukuri*, the art of creating things.

FURTHER AFIELD

Northeast of downtown, **Utsukushi-ga-hara Onsen** (美ヶ原温泉; not to be confused with Utsukushi-ga-hara-kōgen) is a pretty spa village, with a quaint main street and views across the valley. **Asama Onsen**'s (浅間温泉) history is said to date back to the 10th century and includes writers and poets, though it looks quite generic now. Both areas are easily reached by bus from Matsumoto's bus terminal.

Below: Details from a *ukiyo-e* (woodblock print);
Right: Matsumoto-jō (p175)
(BELOW) TEVE VIDLER/GETTY IMAGES ©; (RIGHT) SKYEARTH/SHUTTERSTOCK ©

To the east of Matsumoto, the stunning alpine plateau of **Utsukushi-ga-hara-kōgen** (美ヶ原高原; 2000m) boasts over 200 varieties of flora that come alive in the summer. It's a great day trip from Matsumoto, reached via an ooh-and-ahh drive along twisty mountain roads called Azalea Line and Venus Line (open late April to early November). A car will give you the freedom to explore the beauty, but there's also a bus in season (¥1500 one-way, 1½ hours).

Utsukushi-ga-hara Open Air Museum   Museum

(美ヶ原美術館, Utsukushi-ga-hara Bijutsukan; ☏0263-86-2331; www.utsukushi-oam.jp; adult/child/student ¥1000/700/800; ◷9am-5pm late Apr-early Nov) Atop Utsukushi-ga-hara-kōgen plateau you'll find this seemingly random sculpture garden with some 350 pieces, mostly by Japanese sculptors. The surrounding countryside provides an inspiring backdrop. Nearby are pleasant walks and the opportunity to see cows in pasture (a constant source of fascination in Japan). Buses (¥1500, 1½ hours) run several times daily during the warmer months, athough a rental car is good option if windy roads don't faze you.

Japan Ukiyo-e Museum   Museum

(日本浮世絵美術館; www.japan-ukiyoe-museum.com; 2206-1 Koshiba; adult/child ¥1200/600; ◷10am-5pm Tue-Sun) Housing more than 100,000 wood-block prints, paintings, screens and old books, this renowned museum exhibits but a fraction of its collection. The museum is approximately 3km from JR Matsumoto Station, 15 minutes' walk from Ōniwa Station on the Matsumoto Dentetsu line (¥180, six minutes), or about ¥2000 by taxi.

Matsumoto Open-Air Architectural Museum   Museum

(松本市歴史の里, Matsumoto-shi Rekishi-no-sato; ☏0263-47-4515; 2196-1 Shimadachi; adult/child ¥400/300; ◷9am-4.30pm Tue-Sun)

Adjacent to the better known Japan Ukiyo-e Museum, amid fields and rice paddies beneath the gaze of the Alps, stand these five examples of striking late Edo- and early Showa-era architecture for you to explore. The museum is approximately 3km from JR Matsumoto Station, 15 minutes' walk from Ōniwa Station on the Matsumoto Dentetsu line (¥180, six minutes), or about ¥2000 by taxi.

Festivals & Events

Locals love to celebrate – you're never far from a festival here.

Matsumoto-jō
Taiko Matsuri   Music
The castle grounds and beyond ring out with the sound and energy of Taiko drumming during this awesome festival, held the balmy last weekend of July.

Matsumoto Bonbon   Parade
Matsumoto's biggest event takes place on the first Saturday in August, when over 25,000 people of all ages perform the 'bonbon' dance through the streets, well into the hot summer's night. Be prepared to be drawn into the action.

Asama Onsen
Taimatsu Matsuri   Parade
Around the start of October, Asama Onsen celebrates the spectacular and slightly manic fire festival, wherein groups of men, women and children, shouting 'wa-sshoi!', like a mantra, parade burning bales of hay through narrow streets to an enormous bonfire at Misha-jinja.

Sleeping

Matsumoto is compact enough that you can stay anywhere downtown and get around easily. Most business hotels are by the station, but there are some great traditional options in picturesque Nakamachi.

Matsumoto BackPackers
Hostel ¥

(☏0263-31-5848; www.matsumotobp.com/en; Shiraita 1-1-6; dm per person ¥3000; ❄ 🛜) By the river, just a few minutes' walk from JR Matsumoto Station, you'll find this clean, friendly addition to the Matsumoto traveller's scene. These are the cheapest, most central dorm beds in town.

Marunouchi Hotel
Hotel ¥¥

(丸の内ホテル; ☏0263-35-4500; matsumoto-marunouchi.com/eng; 3-5-15 Ōte; s/d from ¥6600/9000; ❄ 🛜) It's hard to fault this new hotel, occupying a prime spot near the castle. Right-priced rooms are refreshingly stylish and comfortable; deluxe rooms approach Western standard sizes at 27 sq m. Standard rooms are more compact, but cheaper. Suites are a nice option for those wanting something special. Some rooms have views of the castle.

Nunoya
Inn ¥¥

(ぬのや旅館; ☏0263-32-0545; www.mcci.or.jp/www/nunoya/en; 3-5-7 Chūō; r per person from ¥4500) Few inns have more heart than this simple, traditional charmer, meticulously kept by its friendly owner. The spotless inn has shiny dark-wood floors and atmospheric tatami rooms. No meals are served, but you're right in the heart of the best part of town. If you don't mind sharing a bathroom, the rate is a bargain for this much character.

Seifūsō
Ryokan ¥¥

(静風荘; ☏0263-46-0639; www.ryokanseifuso.jp/english; 634-5 Minami-asama; s/d from ¥3990/8280; 🅿 @) Free pick-up (arrange in advance) and free bicycles make up for the fact that this inn is closer to Asama-onsen than Matsumoto. It's run by a friendly family who love to welcome overseas guests. Japanese-style rooms are clean and bright, have a nice outlook and shared baths. Once you're there, take bus 2 to get back into town.

Marumo
Ryokan ¥¥

(まるも; ☏0263-32-0115; www.avis.ne.jp/~marumo/index.html; 3-3-10 Chūō; r per person ¥5250; 🛜) Between Nakamachi and the river, this creaky wooden ryokan dates from 1868 and has lots of tradition-al charm, including a bamboo garden and coffee shop. Although the rooms aren't huge and don't have private facilities, it's quite popular, so book ahead.

Ohgatou Hotel
Hotel ¥¥¥

(王ヶ頭ホテル; ☏0263-31-2751; www.ougatou.jp; Utsukushi-ga-hara-kōgen; d per person with 2 meals from ¥15,000) A night at the isolated Ogato Hotel atop the beautiful Utsukushi-ga-hara-kōgen plateau is something to remember. Rooms are plush, comfy and reasonably priced. Oversized suites have decadent baths overlooking the plateau and the cloud line: you'll think you're on Cloud Nine as you wake.

Sugimoto
Ryokan ¥¥¥

(旅館すぎもと; ☏0263-32-3379; www.ryokan-sugimoto.com; 451-7 Satoyamabe; r per person from ¥15,000; ❄ 🛜; 🚌Utsukushigahara Onsen Line, Town Sneaker North Course) A lack of English-speaking staff at this upscale ryokan in Utsukushi-ga-hara Onsen may be its only downfall for non-Japanese speakers. With some fascinating elements, such as the art collection, underground passageway and bar full of single malts, this is a unique property. Rooms range in size and decor, but all are ineffably stylish and the cuisine is top-notch.

Eating & Drinking

For a coffee and cake, cafes line the banks of the Metoba-gawa and Nawate-dōri.

Delhi
Curry ¥

(デリー; ☏0263-35-2408; 2-4-13 Chūō; curries with rice ¥650-850; ⏱11.30am-6pm Thu-Tue; 🗒) One of our favourites, this little 'ma and pa' outfit has been serving delicious curry rice (Japanese style) in an adorable former storehouse by the river since 1970. If you like *tonkatsu*, you must try the *katsu karē* (¥850). Cheap and cheerful.

Kane
Taiwanese ¥

(香根; ☏0263-36-1303; 2-8-5 Ōte; dishes ¥700-900; ⏱5.30pm-2am; 🖊🗒) This simple Taiwanese eatery near the castle serves amazing spicy soups, noodles and veggies, as well as the standard array of Chinese fare at very reasonable prices. There's a picture menu.

Nomugi
Noodles ¥¥

(野麦; ☎0263-36-3753; 2-9-11 Chūō; soba ¥1100; ⏰11.30am-5pm Thu-Mon; ✈) In Nakamachi, this is one of central Japan's finest *soba* shops. Its owner used to run a French restaurant in Tokyo before returning to his home town. Keeping things Zen, there are two dishes: *zaru-soba* and *kake-soba*. Oh, and beer.

Shizuka
Izakaya ¥¥

(しづか; ☎0263-32-0547; 4-10-8 Ōte; plates from ¥480; ⏰noon-11pm Mon-Sat; 📖) This wonderfully traditional *izakaya* serves favourites such as *oden* and *yakitori* as well as some more challenging specialities.

Old Rock
Pub

(オールドロック; ☎0263-38-0069; 2-30-20 Chūō; mains from ¥750; ⏰11.30am-2.30pm & 6pm-midnight) In the perfect spot a block south of the river, across from Nakamachi, is this popular pub with good lunch specials and a wide range of beers.

Sorpresa
Bar

(ソルプレーサ; ☎0263-37-0510; 1-2-1 Honjō, Hotel Buena Vista 14F; ⏰5.30pm-midnight) Come for the unbeatable views from this swanky top-floor bar at the Buena Vista Hotel. It's also a high-end French restaurant, if you fancy, but it's possible to come just to imbibe.

ⓘ Information

Although small streets radiate somewhat confusingly from the train station, soon you're on a grid. Most local sights are within 20 minutes' walk of the train station.

Online, visit: www.city. matsumoto.nagano.jp.

Tourist Information Center (松本市観光案内所; ☎0263-32-2814; 1-1-1 Fukashi; ⏰9.30am-5.45pm) This excellent Tourist Information Center inside JR Matsumoto Station has friendly English-speaking staff and a wide range of well-produced English language materials on the area.

ⓘ Getting There & Away

Air
Shinshū Matsumoto airport has flights to Fukuoka, Osaka and Sapporo.

Bus
Alpico runs buses between Matsumoto and Shinjuku in Tokyo (¥3400, 3¼ hours, 24 daily), Osaka (¥5850, 5¾ hours, two daily; one longer overnight service) and Nagoya (from ¥3600, 3½ hours, 10 daily). **Nōhi Bus** services Takayama (¥3900, 2½ hours, at least six daily). Reservations are advised. The Matsumoto Bus Terminal is in the basement of the ESPA building opposite JR Matsumoto Station.

Car
Renting a car is a great way to explore the beauty outside town, but expect narrow, windy roads. There are several agencies around the station. Rates are generally around ¥6500 per day.

Yakitori (skewers of grilled chicken & vegetables)
MIXA/GETTY IMAGES ©

Train

Matsumoto is connected with Tokyo's Shinjuku Station (*tokkyû* ¥6380, 2¾ hours, hourly), Nagoya (*tokkyû* ¥5510, two hours) and Nagano (Shinano *tokkyû* ¥2320, 50 minutes; *Chūō futsû* ¥1140, 1¼ hours). There's also infrequent direct services to Osaka (*tokkyû* ¥8850, 4½ hours).

 Getting Around

Matsumoto-jō and the city centre are easily covered on foot and free bicycles are available for loan – enquire at the Tourist Information Center. Three 'town sneaker' loop bus routes operate between 9am and 5.30pm for ¥200 per ride (¥500 per day); the blue and orange routes cover the castle and Nakamachi.

An airport shuttle bus connects Shinshū Matsumoto airport with downtown (¥600, 25 minutes); a taxi costs around ¥5000.

Kiso Valley Nakasendō 木曽谷中仙道

🎵 0264

The Nakasendō was one of the five highways of the Edo period connecting Edo (now Tokyo) with Kyoto. Much of the route is now followed by National Roads,

however, in this thickly forested section of the Kiso Valley, there are several sections of the twisty, craggy post road which have been carefully restored, the most impressive being the 7.8km stretch between Magome and Tsumago, two of the most attractive Nakasendō towns. Walking this route is one of Japan's most rewarding tourist experiences.

It's worth a stay in any or all of these special towns to have them to yourself once the day trippers clear out. For street foods, look for *gohei-mochi* (skewered rice dumplings coated with sesame-walnut sauce) and in autumn you can't miss *kuri-kinton* (chestnut dumplings).

MAGOME 馬籠

In Gifu-ken, pretty Magome is the furthest south of the Kiso Valley post towns. Its buildings line a steep, cobblestone pedestrian road that's unfriendly to heavy wheelie suitcases, but its rustic shopfronts and mountain views will keep your finger on the camera shutter.

From Magome, the 7.8km hike to Tsumago follows a steep, largely paved road until it reaches its peak at the top of Magome-tōge (pass); elevation 801m.

Tsumago

After the pass, the trail meanders past waterfalls, forest and farmland. The route is easiest in this direction, from Magome (elevation 600m) to Tsumago (elevation 420m). The route is clearly signposted in English; allow about three to six hours to enjoy it.

If fitness or a disability might prevent you from appreciating this amazing walk, there is an easier way. The Magome–Tsumago bus (¥600, 30 minutes, two to three daily in each direction) also stops at Magome-tōge. If you alight and begin the walk here, it's a picturesque 5.2km downhill run through to Tsumago.

If you do the hike, both towns offer a handy baggage forwarding service from either Tourist Information Office to the other. Deposit your bags between 8.30am and 11.30am, for delivery by 1pm.

 Sleeping & Eating

Minshuku Tajimaya   Minshuku ¥¥
(民宿但馬屋; ☎0264-69-2048; www.kiso-tajimaya.com; 4266 Magome; s/d with 2 meals ¥9720/17,280; ❄✿🖥) This pleasant historical inn has compact rooms and friendly staff, although the location of the bathrooms can be inconvenient. The array of local specialities served in the common dining area is impressive, as are the *hinoki* (cypress baths).

Magome-Chaya   Minshuku ¥¥
(馬籠茶屋; ☎0264-59-2038; en.magomechaya.com; 4296 Magome; r per person with 2 meals from ¥7980) This popular *minshuku* is almost halfway up the hill, near the water wheel. Room-only plans are available.

ℹ Information

Tourist Information Center (観光案内館; ☎0264-59-2336; ❄9am-5pm) Located somewhat inconveniently halfway up the hill, to the right. A baggage forwarding service to Tsumago is available.

TSUMAGO 妻籠

Tsumago feels like an open-air museum, about 15 minutes' walk from end to end. It was designated by the government as a protected area for the preservation of traditional buildings, where modern developments such as telephone poles aren't allowed to mar the scene. The dark-wood glory of its lattice-fronted buildings is particularly beautiful at dawn and dusk. Film and TV crews are often spotted here.

On 23 November, the **Fūzoku Emaki** parade is held along the Nakasendō in Tsumago, featuring townsfolk in Edo-period costume.

◉ Sights & Activities

Waki-honjin (Okuya) & Local History Museum   Museum
(脇本陣 (奥谷) ・歴史資料館, Rekishi Shiryōkan; adult/child ¥600/300; ❄9am-5pm) The former rest stop for the *daimyō's* retainers, this *waki-honjin* was reconstructed in 1877 by a former castle builder under special dispensation from Emperor Meiji. It contains a lovely moss garden and a special toilet built in case Meiji happened to show up; he never did. The adjacent Local History Museum houses elegant exhibitions about Kiso and the Nakasendō, with some English signage.

Tsumagojuku-honjin   Historic Building
(妻籠宿本陣; adult/child ¥300/150; ❄9am-5pm) It was in this building that the *daimyō* themselves would spend the night, although the building's architecture is more noteworthy than its exhibits. A combined ticket (adult/child ¥700/350) includes admission to Waki-honjin and the Local History Museum, opposite.

Kisoji Resort   Onsen
(木曽路館, Kisoji-kan; ☎0264-58-2046; 2278 Azuma; baths ¥700; ❄9am-7pm) A few kilometres above Tsumago, you'll find this *rotemburo* with panoramic mountain vistas, a sprawling dining room and a souvenir shop.

🛏 Sleeping & Eating

Oyado Daikichi   Minshuku ¥¥
(御宿大吉; ☎0264-57-2595; r per person with 2 meals from ¥8600; ❄✿@) Popular with foreign visitors, this traditional-looking inn benefits from modern construction

Tateyama-Kurobe Alpine Route

From mid-April to mid-November, the popular seasonal 90km Tateyama-Kurobe Alpine Route (立山黒部アルペンルート) connects Tateyama (Toyama Prefecture) with Shinano-ōmachi (Nagano Prefecture).

Travel is possible in either direction; we'd suggest using the route to travel between Kanazawa/Toyama and Matsumoto. Full details can be found online at www.alpen-route.com/english.

The fare for the entire route is ¥10,850 one way or ¥18,260 return; tickets for individual sections are available. It takes at least six hours, one way. If you're starting in Toyama and are not heading to Matsumoto, you may find a return trip to Murodō (¥6710), the route's highest point (2450m), sufficient.

Start the journey before 9am at Dentetsu Toyama station on the chug-a-lug regional Toyama Chiho line bound for **Tateyama** (¥1200, one hour). The first stage of the route is the cable car up to **Bijodaira** (美女平; seven minutes).

Next is a bus journey up to **Murodō** (室堂; 50 minutes) via the spectacular alpine plateau of **Midagahara Kōgen**. Ten minutes' walk from Murodō is **Mikuri-ga-ike** (みくりが池) pond, where you'll find Japan's highest *onsen ryokan* (www.mikuri.com/english). Twenty minutes further on is **Jigokudani Onsen** (Hell Valley Hot Springs) – no bathing here, the waters are boiling! To the east, you can make the steep two-hour hike to the peak of **O-yama** (推山; 3003m) for an astounding panorama.

When you're ready, board the trolley bus that tunnels through Mount Tateyama for 3.7km to **Daikanbō** (10 minutes). From here, the Tateyama Ropeway whisks you 488m down to **Kurobe-daira** (seven minutes) with breathtaking views of the valley below. The next step is the underground Kurobe cable car to **Kurobeko** (¥840, five minutes). You'll emerge to see the massive **Kurobe Dam**.

Trolley buses (16 minutes) whisk you through a 5.8km tunnel to the end of your journey at **Ogizawa**. From here there's one last bus to **Shinano-ōmachi Station** (40 minutes, elevation 712m) – you made it !

and has a prime location on the top of the hill – all rooms have a lovely outlook. It's at the very edge of town.

Fujioto
Ryokan ¥¥

(藤乙; ☏0264-57-3009; www.tsumago-fujioto.jp; r per person with 2 meals from ¥10,800; 😊❄🛜) The owner of this unpretentious, welcoming inn speaks some English, French, Italian and Spanish. It's a great place to have your first ryokan experience as most staff are able to communicate with travellers well, especially over the wonderful *kaiseki* dinner, served in the dining room. Corner upstairs rooms have lovely views. You can also stop by for lunch – try the Kiso Valley trout (¥1350).

Yoshimura-ya
Noodles ¥

(吉村屋; ☏0264-57-3265; dishes ¥700-1500; 🕙10am-5pm; 🍜📶) If you're hungry after a long walk, the handmade *soba* here will fill you up.

ℹ️ Information

Tourist Information Center (観光案内館; ☏0264-57-3123; www.tumago.jp/english; 2159-2 Azuma; 🕙8.30am-5pm) Tsumago's Tourist Information Center is in the centre of town, by the antique phone booth. Some English is spoken and there's English-language literature. Ask here for any directions.

Getting There & Away

Nagiso Station on the JR Chūō line serves Tsumago, though it is some distance from the town. A few *tokkyū* daily stop in Nagiso (from Nagoya ¥2840, one hour); otherwise change at Magome's Nakatsugawa Station (*futsū* ¥320, 20 minutes).

There's an infrequent bus service between Magome and Tsumago (¥600, 25 minutes), via Magome-tōge.

Buses run between Tsumago and Nagiso Station (¥270, 10 minutes, eight per day).

KISO-FUKUSHIMA 木曽福島

North of Tsumago and Magome, Kiso-Fukushima is larger and considerably more developed, but its historical significance as an important checkpoint on the Nakasendō and its riverside position make it a pleasant lunch stop en route to (or from) Matsumoto.

From Kiso-Fukushima Station, turn right and head downhill towards the town centre and the Kiso-gawa. Sights are well signposted. Look for **Ue-no-dan** (上の段), the historic district of atmospheric houses, many of which are now retailers.

Sights

Fukushima Checkpoint Site Museum

(福島関所跡, Fukushima Sekisho-ato; adult/child ¥300/150; ⏰8am-5pm Apr-Oct, 8.30am-4pm Nov-Mar) This is a reconstruction of one of the most significant checkpoints on the Edo-period trunk roads. From its perch above the river valley, it's easy to see the barrier's strategic importance. Displays inside show the implements used to maintain order, including weaponry and *tegata* (wooden travel passes), as well as the special treatment women travellers received.

Eating

Kurumaya Honten Noodles ¥

(くるまや本店; ☎0264-22-2200; 5367-2 Kiso-machi, Fukushima; mains ¥630-1575; ⏰10am-5pm Thu-Tue; 🖐📖) One of Japan's most renowned *soba* shops, the classic presentation here is cold *mori* (plain) or *zaru* (with strips of nori seaweed) with a sweetish dipping sauce. It's near the first bridge at the bottom of the hill; look for the gears above the doorway.

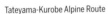
Tateyama-Kurobe Alpine Route

JTB PHOTO/UIG/GETTY IMAGES ©

Information

Tourist Information Center (木曽町観光協会, Kiso-machi Kankō Kyōkai; ☎0264-22-4000; 2012-10 Kiso-machi, Fukushima; ⏱9am-4.45pm) Across from the train station, these friendly ladies have some English maps, but appreciate some Japanese-language ability.

Getting There & Away

Kiso-Fukushima is on the JR Chūō line (*Shinano tokkyū*), easily reached from Matsumoto (¥2150, 38 minutes), Nakatsugawa (¥2150, 34 minutes) and Nagoya (¥4100, 1½ hours).

NARAI 奈良井

A less known, but equally important example of a Nakasendō post town, Narai is one of our favourites, tucked away in the folds of a narrow valley. Once called 'Narai of a thousand houses', it flourished in the Edo period when its proximity to the highest pass on the Nakasendō made it a popular resting place for travellers. Today, it's a conservation area with a preserved main street showcasing some wonderful examples of Edo-period architecture.

Narai is famed for *shikki* (lacquerware). Plenty of quality souvenir shops line the street, many with reasonable prices.

Sights

Nakamura House   Historic Building
(中村邸; ☎0264-34-2655; adult/child ¥300/free; ⏱9am-4pm) This wonderfully preserved former merchant's house and garden looks as if it has stood still while time passed by.

Sleeping & Eating

Echigo-ya   Ryokan ¥¥
(ゑちごや旅館; ☎0264-34-3011; www.narai jyuku-echigoya.jp; 493 Narai; r per person incl 2 meals from ¥15,660) In business for over 220 years, this charming family-run ryokan is one of a kind. With only two guestrooms, Echigo-ya provides a unique opportunity to experience the Japanese art of hospitality in its most undiluted form. Expect to feel like you've stepped back in time. Some Japanese-language ability will help

make the most of the experience. Book well in advance. Cash only.

Oyado Iseya   Minshuku ¥¥
(御宿伊勢屋; ☎0264-34-3051; www.oyado-iseya.jp; 388 Narai; r per person incl 2 meals from ¥9500) The streetfront of this former merchant house built in 1818 has been beautifully preserved. Now a pleasant 10-room inn, guestrooms are in the main house and a newer building out back.

Matsunami   Shokudo ¥
(松波; ☎0264-34-3750; 397-1 Narai; set menus from ¥850; ⏱11.30am-8pm Wed-Mon) This delightful little eatery on a corner serves simple favourites such as special-sauce *tonkatsu-don* (deep-fried pork cutlet on rice).

Information

Tourist Information Center (奈良井宿観光協会; ☎0264-54-2001; www.naraijuku.com) Inside Narai station, they have some English-language leaflets and a map. Little English is spoken.

Getting There & Away

Only *futsû* (local) trains stop at Narai, which is on the JR Chūō line. It takes no more than an hour or three to see the sights, making it a neat day trip from Matsumoto (¥580, 50 minutes), but you could easily pass a peaceful evening here. From Nagoya, change trains at Nakatsugawa (¥1320, 1½ hours) or Kiso-Fukushima (¥410, 20 minutes).

ISHIKAWA PREFECTURE

Ishikawa Prefecture (石川県; Ishikawa-ken), made up of the former Kaga and Noto fiefs, offers a blend of cultural and historical sights and natural beauty. Kanazawa, the Kaga capital and power base of the feudal Maeda clan, boasts traditional architecture and one of Japan's most famous gardens. To the north, the peninsula, Noto-hantō, has sweeping seascapes and quiet fishing villages. Hakusan National Park, near the southern tip of the prefecture, offers great hiking. You can find good overviews at www.hot-ishikawa.jp.

Kanazawa 金沢

♪076 / POP 462,360

Kanazawa's array of cultural attractions makes it the drawcard of the Hokuriku region. Best known for Kenroku-en, a castle garden dating from the 17th century, it also boasts beautifully preserved samurai and geisha districts, attractive temples and a wealth of museums. We recommend a two- or three-day stay to take it all in.

Sights & Activities

Kanazawa is a sprawling city with two almost parallel rivers traversing its core. Most areas of interest are located a good distance from the impressive JR Kanazawa Station area, into which most visitors arrive. With the recent arrival of the Hokuriku Shinkansen speeding into town, this area is abuzz with activity. The terminus of the city's substantial bus network, which can at first seem a little confusing, is also here.

Heading south of the station along Hyakumangoku-dōri, you'll reach Kōrinbō (the shopping and business district) before arriving in Katamachi, by the banks of the Sai-gawa; this is the place to eat, drink and be merry. If you're staying near the station, note that buses stop early in the evening and taxis back from the action cost at least ¥1300.

Teramachi and Nishi-chaya-gai are just over the bridge from Katamachi, but the mainstay of sights are to its east. To their north, across the Asano-gawa, lies pretty Higashi-chaya-gai in the shadow of hilly Utatsuyama's many temples. Heading west will loop you back to the station, passing Ōmi-chō Market, a must see.

D.T. Suzuki Museum Museum
(鈴木大拙館; ♪076-221-8011; www.kanazawa-museum.jp/daisetz/english; 3-4-20 Honda-machi; adult/senior/child ¥300/200/free; ⊙9.30am-4.30pm Tue-Sun) This spiritual museum is a tribute to Daisetsu Teitaro Suzuki, one of the foremost Buddhist philosophers of our time. Published in Japanese and English, Suzuki is largely credited with introducing Zen to the west. This stunning concrete complex embodies the heart of Zen. Come to learn about the man and practise mindfulness by the water mirror garden.

Kanazawa Castle Park Landmark
(金沢城公園, Kanazawa-jō Kōen; ♪076-34-3800; www.pref.ishikawa.jp/siro-niwa/kanazawajou/e/; 1-1 Marunouchi; buildings/grounds ¥310/free; ⊙grounds 5am-6pm Mar-15 Oct, 6am-4.30pm 16 Oct-Feb, castle 9am-4.30pm) Originally built in 1580 this massive structure was called the 'castle of 1000 tatami' and housed the Maeda clan for 14 generations until it was ultimately destroyed by fire in 1881. The elegant surviving gate **Ishikawa-mon**

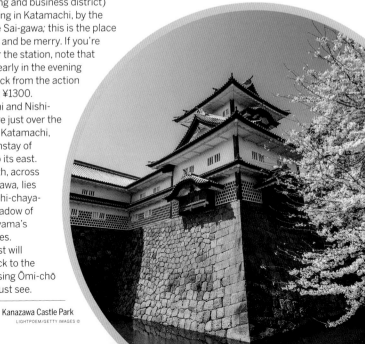

Kanazawa Castle Park
LIGHTPOEM/GETTY IMAGES ©

Kanazawa

Moroe Ōdōri

19 ✕

11 🏨

Shōwa Ōdōri

Kanazawa Tourist
ℹ Information Center

Kanazawa ✕ 20

24 🚲
25 🚲

18 ✕

12 🏨

14 🏨

10 🏨

8 ◎

Hyakumangoku-dōri

13 🏨

Tamagawa-
kōen

Hyakumangoku-dōri

Ohori Ōdōri

NAGAMACHI

Chūō-dōri

6 ◎
4 🏛

16 ✕
17 ✕ **KŌRINBŌ**

1 ◎
Kenroku-en

21 ✕ Hirosaka

2 🏛

22 ✕

KATAMACHI

Honda Ōdōri

Nishi-inter Ōdōri

Suzuki

Myōryū-ji (250m);
Kutani Kosen
Gama Kiln (750m)

TERAMACHI

3 🏛

(built in 1788) provides a dramatic entry from Kenroku-en; holes in its turret were designed for hurling rocks at invaders. Two additional buildings, the **Hishi-yagura** (diamond-shaped turret) and **Gojikken-nagaya** (armoury), were reconstructed by traditional means in 2001. Restoration and archaeological work is ongoing.

Ōmi-chō Market
Market

(近江町市場; 35 Ōmi-chō; ⏰9am-5pm) Between Kanazawa station and Kata-machi, you'll find this market, reminiscent of Tokyo's Tsukiji. A bustling warren of fishmongers, buyers and restaurants, it's a great place to watch everyday people in action or indulge in the freshest sashimi and local produce. The nearest bus stop is Musashi-ga-tsuji.

21st Century Museum of Contemporary Art
Museum

(金沢21世紀美術館; ☎076-220-2800; www.kanazawa21.jp; 1-2-1 Hirosaka; ⏰10am-6pm Tue-Thu & Sun, to 8pm Fri & Sat) FREE A low-slung glass cylinder, 113m in diameter, forms the perimeter of this contemporary gallery, which celebrated its 10th birthday in 2014. Entry to the museum is free, but admission fees are charged for exhibitions by contemporary artists from Japan and abroad. Inside, galleries are arranged like boxes on a tray. Check the English-language website for event info and exhibition admission fees.

Kanazawa Phonograph Museum
Museum

(金沢蓄音器館; ☎076-232-3066; 2-11-21 Owari-chō; admission ¥300; ⏰10am-5pm) Audio buffs will dig this museum of old-time phonographs and SP records, with daily demonstrations at 11am, 2pm and 4pm.

HIGASHI-CHAYA-GAI

Just north of Asano-gawa, Higashi-chaya-gai (Higashi Geisha District) is an enclave of narrow streets established early in the 19th century for geisha to entertain wealthy patrons. The slatted wooden facades of the geisha houses are romantically preserved.

Kanazawa

Shima — Museum

(志摩; ☎076-252-5675; www.ochaya-shima.
com/english; 1-13-21 Higashiyama; adult/child
¥400/300; ⊙9am-6pm) An Important Cultural Asset, this well-known, traditional-style former geisha house dates from 1820 and has an impressive collection of elaborate combs and *shamisen* picks.

Kaikarō — Museum

(懐華樓; ☎076-253-0591; www.kenrokuen.jp/
en/kaikaro; 1-14-8 Higashiyama; admission ¥700;
⊙9am-5pm) In Higashi-chaya-gai, Kaikarō is an early-19th-century geisha house refinished with contemporary fittings and art including a red lacquered staircase.

TERAMACHI DISTRICT

This hilly neighbourhood south of Sai-gawa, southwest of the centre, was established as a first line of defence and contains dozens of temples.

Myōryū-ji — Buddhist Temple

(妙立寺; ☎076-241-0888; 1-2-12 Nomachi; admission ¥800; ⊙9am-4.30pm Mar-Nov, to 4pm Dec-Feb, reservations required) In Teramachi, fascinating Myōryū-ji (aka Ninja-dera), completed in 1643, was designed to protect its Lord in case of attack. It contains hidden stairways, escape routes, secret chambers, concealed tunnels and trick doors. Contrary to popular belief, this ancient temple has nothing to do with ninja.

Admission is by tour only (in Japanese with an English guidebook). You must phone for reservations (in English).

Sleeping

Pongyi — Guesthouse ¥

(ポンギー; ☎076-225-7369; www.pongyi.
com; 2-22 Rokumai-machi; dm ¥2700, s/d
¥4500/6000; @) Run by a friendly Japanese man who did a stint in Southeast Asia as a monk, Pongyi is a charmingly renovated old shop alongside a canal. Cosy dorms are located in an annexed vintage *kura* (mud-walled storehouse).

Holiday Inn ANA Kanazawa Sky — Hotel ¥¥

(☎076-233-2233; www.holidayinn.com; 15-1
Musashi-machi; s/d from ¥6500/8800; ❇🛜)
Centrally located between JR Kanazawa Station and the sights, across the road from Ōmi-chō Market, this recently renovated hotel is an excellent mid-range choice with comfortable bedding and great views. It's on top of the M'Za department store, whose basement-level food court is all too convenient.

Yōgetsu — Minshuku ¥¥

(陽月; ☎076-252-0497; 1-13-22 Higashiyama; r per person with/without breakfast from ¥5000/
4500) In the heart of the picturesque Higashi-chaya district, this beautifully renovated 200-year-old geisha teahouse

DIANE COOK AND LEN JENSHEL/GETTY IMAGES ©

⭐ Don't Miss
Kenroku-en

Ranked as one of the top three gardens in Japan, this Edo-period garden draws its name (*kenroku* 'combined six') from a renowned Song-dynasty garden in China that dictated six attributes for perfection: seclusion, spaciousness, artificiality, antiquity, abundant water and broad views. Kenroku-en has them all. Arrive before the crowds to increase your chances of silent contemplation.

It is believed that the garden, originally belonging to an outer villa of Kanazawa-jō, was developed from the 1620s to the 1840s and was so named in 1822. It was first opened to the public in 1871.

NEED TO KNOW

兼六園; ☑ 076-234-3800; www.pref.ishikawa.jp/siro-niwa/kenrokuen/e/; 1-1 Marunouchi; adult/child ¥310/100; ⏰ 7am-6pm Mar-15 Oct, 8am-4.30pm 16 Oct-Feb

has only three rooms and features a circular *goemonburo* bath. No English is spoken, there's no wi-fi and it's tucked away, but it's perfect if tranquility, history and authenticity are what you're after.

Hotel Resol Trinity   Hotel ¥¥

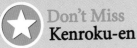

(ホテルレソルトリニティ; ☑ 076-221-9629; www.resol-hotel.jp/resol/en/hotels/trinity-kanazawa; 1-18 Musashi-machi; s/d from ¥6300/8000; @) This lovely niche hotel is a breath of fresh air. Rooms have a splash

of colour and have been designed to make you feel comfortable in a compact space. Its location is central to everything; you can walk to JR Kanazawa Station, Katamachi and Kenroku-en in about 15 minutes.

Hotel Dormy Inn
Kanazawa   Hotel ¥¥

(ドーミーイン金沢; ☑ 076-263-9888; www.hotespa.net/hotels/kanazawa; 2-25 Horikawa-shinmachi; s/d from ¥5990/7990; 🍴 @)

Detour:
Noto Peninsula

Rugged seascapes, rural life, seafood and a light diet of cultural sights make Noto Peninsula (Noto-hantō) a pleasant escape from Hokuriku's urban sprawl. The lacquer-making town of Wajima is the hub of the rugged north, known as Oku-Noto, and the best place to stay overnight. Famous products include *Wajima-nuri* lacquerware, *Suzu*-style pottery, locally harvested sea salt and *iwanori* seaweed.

Self driving from Kanazawa is easily the best way to see the peninsula. The 83km Noto Yūryo (能登有料; Noto Toll Rd) speeds you as far as Anamizu (toll ¥1180). Noto's mostly flat west coast appeals to cyclists, but cycling is not recommended on the Noto-kongō and east coasts because of steep, blind curves. In the centre of Oku-Noto, **Noto Satoyama Airport** connects the peninsula with Tokyo (Haneda). Hokutetsu runs buses between Kanazawa and Wajima (¥2200, two hours, 10 daily) and, less frequently, Monzen (¥740, 35 minutes).

Most sights can be reached by road only: hiring a car from Kanazawa is recommended. Otherwise, for the west Noto coast, take the JR Nanao line from Kanazawa to Hakui (*tokkyû* ¥1410, 45 minutes; *futsû* ¥760, one hour) and connect to buses. For Oku-Noto, trains continue to Wakura Onsen, connecting to less frequent buses.

Around the corner from JR Kanazawa Station, this popular, modern tourist hotel has well designed, functional rooms, a calcium-rich onsen *rotemburo* on the top floor, and a coin laundry.

Hotel Nikkō Kanazawa   Hotel ¥¥¥
(ホテル日航金沢; ☎076-234-1111; www. hnkanazawa.jp; 2-15-1 Honmachi; r from ¥12,800; ✳🛜) Kanazawa's most luxurious hotel, near JR Kanazawa Station, has a wide range of room types from singles to lavish suites, and an impressive selection of on-site restaurants and bars. Most rooms have exceptional views. The hotel turned 20 in 2014, but all rooms have been recently refurbished. The 'Luxe Style' and 'Stylish' rooms are worth the extra coin.

Eating

Seafood is the staple of Kanazawa's *Kaga ryōri* (Kaga cuisine); even the most humble train-station *bentō* (boxed meal) usually features some type of fish. *Oshi-zushi*, a thin layer of fish pressed atop vinegared rice, is said to be the precursor to modern sushi. Another favourite is *jibuni,* which is flour-coated duck or chicken stewed with shiitake and green vegetables.

The JR Kanazawa Station building has plenty of food outlets in its **Fureai-kan** (ふれあい館), otherwise, the neighbouring **Forus department store** has the 'Kuugo Dining Resort' on its 6th floor, with over 15 restaurants. Otherwise, head to Katamachi. Closer by, Ōmi-chō Market (p187) has fresh-from-the-boat eateries; both are great for browsing.

Sentō   Chinese ¥
(仙桃; ☎076-234-0669; 88 Aokusa-machi, 2F Ōmichō Ichiba; dishes from ¥600, set menus from ¥900; ⏱11am-3pm & 5-10.30pm Wed-Mon) Upstairs in Ōmi-chō Market, talented chefs from Hong Kong prepare authentic Szechuan- and Hong Kong–style dishes (including dim sum) from scratch. Healthy (yellow bean oil is used) and delicious lunch and dinner set menus are excellent value. The spicy, salted squid is exquisite, but we just had to come back for a second bowl of *tantanmen* (sesame and chilli *râmen*). Sluuuurp!

Full of Beans
Cafe ¥

(☎076-222-3315; www.fullofbeans.jp; 41-1 Satomi-chō; meals from ¥800; ⏰11.30am-3.30pm & 5-10pm Thu-Tue) A variety of Japanese and *yōshoku* (Western-style meals) are served in this stylish cafe in the quieter back streets of Katamachi – the website homepage will give you a sense of the vibe. It's a good place to try the Kanazawa speciality, *hanton raisu* (¥900), a bowl of rice topped with an omelette, fried seafood, ketchup and tartare sauce. YUM.

Aashirwad
Nepalese ¥

(アシルワード; ☎076-262-2170; 2-12-15 Kōrinbō; starters from ¥300, curries from ¥900; ⏰11am-10pm; 📖) Aashirwad offers authentic and flavoursome Nepali and Indian cooking served in funky, atmospheric surroundings on a quaint Kōrinbō back street. The staff are friendly, and the ambience and quality of this recent appearance on the Kanazawa restaurant scene are impressive. An extensive menu has all your favourites, but you just have to try the *momo* (Nepalese dumplings) for ¥650.

Cottage
International ¥

(コテージ; ☎076-262-3277; 2-8-16 Seseragi-dōri, rear of Kōrinbō 109; dishes from ¥780; ⏰noon-2.30pm & 6-9.30pm Thu-Tue) This popular home-style restaurant run by a friendly Irish and Japanese husband-and-wife team has moved to a new location. The food and welcoming vibe are still top notch, while thin-crust pizza, flavourful pastas, and hearty Irish stews feature on the eclectic, rotating menu.

Daiba Kanazawa Ekimae
Izakaya ¥

(台場金沢駅前店; ☎076-263-9191; 6-10 Konohana-machi, Kanazawa Miyako Hotel 1F; items from ¥420; ⏰11am-3pm & 5pm-midnight; 📖) This trendy spot in the Kanazawa Miyako Hotel building has a comprehensive Japanese menu and a limited English one with all the Western favourites and some local specialities. It's a great place for your first *izakaya* experience: try lots of small plates and don't forget the beer. Highly recommended.

Osteria del Campagne
Italian ¥¥

(オステリアデルカンパーニュ; ☎076-261-2156; 2-31-33 Katamachi; mains from ¥950, set menus from ¥3900; ⏰5pm-midnight Mon-Sat; 📖) This cosy, quietly fashionable Italian bistro serves lovely set-course menus, while à-la-carte offerings include housemade focaccia, salads, pastas, desserts and hors d'oeuvres you can eat with chopsticks! There's an English menu and friendly, professional staff.

Ōmi-chō Market (p187)
COWARDLION/SHUTTERSTOCK ©

Below: Sashimi; **Right:** JR Kanazawa Station
(BELOW) DIGIPUB/GETTY IMAGES ©: (RIGHT) COWARDLIONA/SHUTTERSTOCK©

Janome-sushi Honten
Sushi ¥¥

(蛇之目寿司本店; ☏076-231-0093; 1-1-12 Kōrinbō; set menu ¥1000-3400, Kaga ryōri sets from ¥4000; ⊙11am-2pm & 5-11pm Thu-Tue; 📖) Regarded for sashimi and Kaga cuisine since 1931, one of our Japanese friends says that when he eats here, he knows he's really in Kanazawa. You can't go wrong with the *saabisu ranchi* (lunch specials, from ¥1000).

Tamura
Izakaya ¥¥

(田村; ☏076-222-0517; 2-18 Namiki-machi; courses from ¥2000; ⊙5pm-11.30pm Thu-Tue; 📖) Favoured by Japanese celebrities, this riverside joint is as affable as its owner (who speaks some English). If you're going to do it, you're best to let him run the show – courses start at ¥2000, with the deluxe *omakase* at ¥8800.

❶ Information

Kanazawa Tourist Information Center (石川県金沢観光情報センター; ☏076-232-6200, KGGN 076-232-3933; www.kggn.sakura.ne.jp; 1 Hirooka-machi; ⊙9am-7pm) This excellent office inside JR Kanazawa Station has incredibly helpful staff and a plethora of well-made English-language maps, pamphlets and magazines, including *Eye on Kanazawa*. The friendly folk from the Goodwill Guide Network (KGGN) are also here to assist with hotel recommendations and free guiding in English – two weeks' notice is requested.

❶ Getting There & Away

Air
Nearby Komatsu airport (KMQ; www.komatsuairport.jp) has air connections with major Japanese cities, as well as Seoul, Shanghai and Taipei.

Bus
JR Highway Bus operates express buses from in front of JR Kanazawa Station's East exit, to

Tokyo's Shinjuku station (¥8000, 7½ hours) and Kyoto (¥4100, 4¼ hours). Hokutetsu Buses serve Nagoya (¥4100, four hours). Nōhi Bus Company services Takayama, via Shirakawa-go (¥3390, 2¼ hours).

Train

The JR Hokuriku line links Kanazawa with Fukui (*tokkyû* ¥2500, 45 minutes; *futsû* ¥1320, 1½ hours), Kyoto (*tokkyû* ¥6380, 2¼ hours), Osaka (*tokkyû* ¥7130, 2¾ hours) and Toyama (*futsû* ¥980, one hour).

Fares and travel times for the brand-new, blink-of-an-eye journey between Kanazawa and Toyama on the long-anticipated Hokuriku Shinkansen can be found online at http://english.jr-central.co.jp/info/. The direct journey between Kanazawa and Tokyo (¥14,120) is now just 2½ hours.

For the latest scheduled services of the Thunderbird Limited Express service between Osaka/Kyoto and Kanazawa, check www.hyperdia.com.

ⓘ Getting Around

JR Kanazawa Station is the hub for transit to/from and around Kanazawa.

Full-size bikes can be rented from JR Kanazawa Station Rent-a-Cycle (駅レンタサイクル; ☎076-261-1721; per hr/day ¥200/1200; ⏱8am-8.30pm) and Hokutetsu Rent-a-Cycle (北鉄レンタサイクル; ☎076-263-0919; per 4hr/day ¥630/1050; ⏱8am-5.30pm), in the offices of Nippon Rent-a-Car, both by the West exit.

There's also a pay-as-you-go bicycle rental system called 'Machi-nori'. The bikes are a bit dinky, but with a bit of planning, the system functions well. For the low down in English, go to www.machi-nori.jp/pdf/machinoriEnglishmap.pdf.

Buses depart from the circular terminus in front of the station's East exit. Any bus from station stop 7, 8 or 9 will take you to the city centre (¥200, day pass ¥900). The Kanazawa Loop Bus (single ride/day pass ¥200/500, every 15 minutes from 8.30am to 6pm) circles the major tourist attractions in 45 minutes. On Saturday, Sunday and holidays, the Machi-bus goes to Kōrinbō for ¥100.

Airport buses (¥1130, 45 minutes) depart from station stop 6. Some services are via Katamachi and Kōrinbō 109, but take one hour to reach the airport.

Detour:
Ichijōdani Asakura Clan Ruins

The truly unique experience that is the **Ichijōdani Asakura Clan Ruins** (一乗谷朝倉氏遺跡, Ichijōdani Asakura-shi Iseki; ☎0776-41-2330; www. info.pref. fukui.lg.jp/bunka/asakura_museum/080_ english/ruin.php; 4-10 Abaka; admission ¥210; ◷9am-4.30pm) is just a short drive through pretty countryside from Fukui city, in Fukui Prefecture, Ishikawa's smaller neighbour. Designated a National Historic Site, this unexpected find boasts one of the largest town ruins in Japan. Perched in a narrow valley between modest mountains, it's easy to see why the Asakura clan would have built their small fortified city here: it's very beautiful. You're free to wander along the restored street of merchants' houses and stroll through the lush grasses, following the remnants of the buildings up the hillside. It's a wonderful spot to sit, picnic and contemplate.

Numerous car-rental agencies are dotted around the station's west exit.

Kaga Onsen 加賀温泉
☎0761

This broad area consisting of three hot-spring villages, **Katayamazu Onsen**, **Yamashiro Onsen** and **Yamanaka Onsen**, is centred on Kaga Onsen and Daishōji Stations along the JR Hokuriku line and is famed for its onsen-ryokan, lacquerware and porcelain. Of the three villages, Yamanaka Onsen is the most scenic.

Sights & Activities

Kutaniyaki Art Museum   Museum
(石川県九谷焼美術館; ☎0761-72-7466; www. kutani-mus.jp/en; 1-10-13 Daishōji Jikata-machi; adult/child ¥500/free; ◷9am-5pm Tue-Sun) Stunning examples of bright and colourful local porcelain are on display here, an eight-minute walk from Daishōji Station.

Zenshō-ji   Buddhist Temple
(全昌寺; ☎0761-72-1164; 1 Daishōji Shinmei-chō; admission ¥500; ◷9am-5pm) The Daishōji Station area is crammed with temples including Zenshō-ji, which houses over 500 amusingly carved Buddhist arhat sculptures.

Yamanaka Onsen   Onsen
In lovely Yamanaka Onsen, the 17th-century haiku poet Basho rhapsodised on the chrysanthemum fragrance of the local mineral springs. It's still an ideal spot for chilling at the **Kiku no Yu** (菊の湯; admission ¥420; ◷6.45am-10.30pm) bathhouse, and for river walks by the Kokusenkei Gorge, spanned by the elegant **Korogi-bashi** (Cricket Bridge) and the whimsical, modern-art **Ayatori-hashi** (Cat's Cradle Bridge). Yamanaka Onsen is accessible by bus (¥410, 30 minutes) from Kaga Onsen Station.

Kosōyu   Onsen
(古総湯; admission ¥500, Sōyu combined ticket ¥700; ◷6am-10pm) Close to Kaga Onsen Station, Yamashiro Onsen is a sleepy town centred on a magnificent wooden bath-house that was recently rebuilt. Kosōyu has beautiful stained-glass windows and a rest area on the top floor; neighbouring Sōyu is a larger, more modern bathhouse.

Sleeping

The friendly folk at the **Yamanaka Onsen Tourism Association** (山中温泉観光協会; ☎0761-78-0330; www.yamanaka-spa.or.jp/eng-lish; 5-1 Yamanaka Onsen) can help with the difficult task of picking the right ryokan for your budget and tastes – there are many in this region. Our two favourites are below.

MIXA/GETTY IMAGES ©

Beniya Mukayū Ryokan ¥¥¥

(べにや無何有; ☑0761-77-1340; www.mukayu. com; 55-1-3 Yamashiro Onsen; per person with 2 meals from ¥34,000; P @) The friendly staff at this award-winning ryokan are committed to upholding the Japanese art of hospitality. Gorgeously minimalist, there's a sense of Zen pervading every aspect of the guest experience, from the welcoming private tea ceremony, to the gentle morning yoga classes. Rooms are a beautiful fusion of old and new – most feature private outdoor cypress baths.

Mukayū's cuisine showcases only the best and freshest local seasonal ingredients, exquisitely prepared and presented. Spa treatments leave you gently breathless.

The Kayōtei Ryokan ¥¥¥

(かよう亭; ☑0761-78-1410; www.kayotei.jp; 1-20 Higashi-machi, Yamanaka Onsen; per person with 2 meals from ¥40,110; P @) This delightful, opulent ryokan along the scenic Kokusenkei Gorge has only 10 rooms, giving it an intimate feel. Some rooms have private outdoor baths, with views over the gorge and a beautiful hidden waterfall.

🛈 Getting There & Away

The JR Hokuriku line links Kaga Onsen with Kanazawa (*tokkyû* ¥1510, 25 minutes; *futsû* ¥760, 44 minutes) and Fukui (*tokkyû* ¥1330, 21 minutes; *futsû* ¥580, 33 minutes). Willer Express (☑from outside Japan 050-5805-0383; http:// willerexpress.com) operates bus services from Tokyo to Kaga Onsen from ¥5000.

Ride the 'O-sanpo' shuttle bus (two-day pass ¥500) around Yamanaka Onsen, and enquire at the Tourist Association or your accomodation about the irregular tour bus to Daihonzan Eihei-ji (大本山永平寺; ☑0776-63-3640; www. global. sotozen-net.or.jp/eng/temples/foreigner/Eihei-ji. html; 5-15 Shihi, Eiheiji; adult/child ¥500/200; ◷9am-5pm).

In Yamashiro Onsen 'Can bus' (two-day pass ¥1200) operates a similar service around the various sights and onsen in the area.

Kyoto

For much of its history, Kyoto _was_ Japan. Even today, Kyoto is _the_ place to go to see what Japan is all about. Here is where you'll find all those things you associate with Japan: ancient temples, colourful shrines and sublime gardens. Indeed, Kyoto is the storehouse of Japan's traditional culture, and it's the place where even Japanese go to learn about their own culture.

With 17 Unesco World Heritage Sites, more than 1600 Buddhist temples and over 400 Shintō shrines, Kyoto is one of the world's most culturally rich cities. It is fair to say that Kyoto ranks with Paris, London and Rome as one of those cities that everyone should see at least once in their lives. And, needless to say, it should rank at the top of any Japan itinerary.

Geisha at Yasaka-jinja (p220)

Kiyomizu-dera (p217)

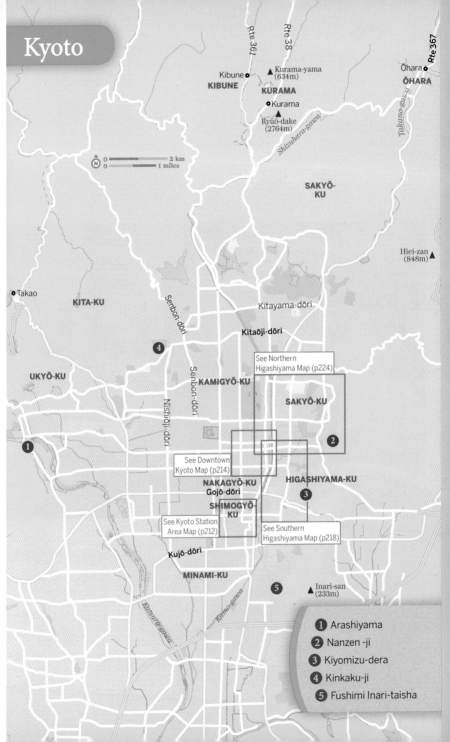

Kyoto

Kibune●
KIBUNE

Rte 361
Rte 38

▲ Kurama-yama
(634m)
KURAMA
●Kurama

Ryūō-dake
(2764m)

Shizuhara-gawa

Ōhara ●
Rte 367

ŌHARA

Takano-gawa

**SAKYŌ-
KU**

Hiei-zan
(848m) ▲

●Takao

KITA-KU

Kitayama-dōri

Kitaōji-dōri

Senbon-dōri

❹

See Northern
Higashiyama Map (p224)

UKYŌ-KU

Senbon-dōri

KAMIGYŌ-KU

Nishiōji-dōri

SAKYŌ-KU

❶

❷

See Downtown
Kyoto Map (p214)

NAKAGYŌ-KU
Gojō-dōri

HIGASHIYAMA-KU

❸

**SHIMOGYŌ-
KU**

See Kyoto Station
Area Map (p212)

See Southern
Higashiyama Map (p218)

Kujō-dōri

MINAMI-KU

❺

▲ Inari-san
(233m)

Katsura-gawa

Kamo-gawa

❶ Arashiyama
❷ Nanzen -ji
❸ Kiyomizu-dera
❹ Kinkaku-ji
❺ Fushimi Inari-taisha

Ⓝ
0 ——————— 2 km
0 ——————— 1 miles

Kyoto Highlights

Arashiyama

Located 8km west of the city centre, Arashiyama (p228) is the romantic side of Kyoto. Here you can enjoy cool breezes by the river against a backdrop of mountains, with colours that change with the seasons. The area was originally developed as a detached villa for the imperial family to escape the heat of summer.

FRANK CARTER / GETTY IMAGES ©

② Nanzen-ji

This stately Zen temple (p223) in the Higashiyama area is the perfect introduction to the world of Japanese temples. It's got everything from the classic dry landscape garden (sometimes called a 'Zen garden') to a soaring *san-mon* gate and several intimate subtemples scattered around its spacious grounds. Most of the precinct can be entered free of charge and an evening stroll here is nothing short of magical.

FRANK CARTER / GETTY IMAGES ©

Kiyomizu-dera

3

If you only see one temple in Kyoto, make it Kiyomizu-dera (p217). This flamboyant complex overlooking Kyoto is everything a temple shouldn't be: noisy, crowded and overtly mercantile. But we're willing to forgive these failings because it's an awful lot of fun, it's gorgeous in the spring and autumn, and it's got a holy spring that bestows longevity and health.

Kinkaku-ji

Talk about eye candy: the gold-plated main hall of this immensely popular temple (p227) in northwest Kyoto is probably the most impressive sight in all Kyoto – especially if your tastes run to the grand and gaudy. If you are lucky enough to be there on a bright, sunny day, you almost need sunglasses to look at it. Go early on a weekday morning to avoid the crush of people that descend on the temple each day.

Fushimi Inari-taisha

There are thousands of vermillion torii (Shintō shrine gates) spread all across the mountain here at this shrine (p230) in southeast Kyoto. Visit the main hall and then head up the hill through the hypnotic arcades of torii. Be prepared to be utterly mesmerized – it's quite unlike anything else on earth. If you have time, climb all the way to the summit and enjoy the views.

Kyoto's Best...

Places to Contemplate

○ **Nanzen-ji** A world of Zen temples and subtemples scattered amid the trees. (p223)

○ **Chion-in** A vast Pure Land Buddhist temple – the Vatican of Japanese Buddhism. (p220)

○ **Ginkaku-ji** The famed 'Silver Pavilion' boasts one of Kyoto's finest gardens. (p223)

○ **Hōnen-in** A secluded retreat only a short walk from perpetually crowded Ginkaku-ji. (p222)

Places to Stay

○ **Tawaraya** Some rank this sublime Kyoto ryokan (traditional Japanese inn) among the world's best accommodation. (p241)

○ **Hyatt Regency Kyoto** The slick, smooth and efficient Hyatt is Kyoto's best hotel. (p242)

○ **Ritz-Carlton Kyoto** Amazing views of the Higashiyama mountains complement well-designed rooms at this luxurious hotel. (p241)

○ **Westin Miyako Kyoto** This sprawling hotel claims one of Kyoto's best locations for sightseeing. (p243)

Places for a Walk

○ **Path of Philosophy (Tetsugaku-no-Michi)** Running along a canal in the Higashiyama district, this path is picturesque in any season. (p222)

○ **Kyoto Imperial Palace Park** Kyoto's central park, surrounding the palace, is a vast expanse of paths, fields and trees. (p213)

○ **Maruyama-kōen** Mobbed in the cherry-blossom season, this pleasant tree-studded park is usually peaceful. (p220)

○ **Gion** Stroll through the floating world and keep your eyes peeled for geisha. (p221)

Need to Know

Festivals

- **Daimon-ji Gozan Okuribi** Five giant characters are set alight on mountains around Kyoto during this awesome summer ritual. (p238)

- **Gion Matsuri** Considered the most important festival in Japan; the real fun is wandering downtown Kyoto in the nights leading up to the main event. (p237)

- **Aoi Matsuri** Watch fabulously costumed participants process from the Gosho to Shimogamo-jinja. (p237)

- **Kurama-no-hi Matsuri** Make your way into the mountains to witness this primeval event. (p238)

- **Kyoto Tourist Information Center** (p255) Conveniently located in Kyoto Station, this should be your first stop in Kyoto. Note that it's known as 'Kyo Navi' in Japanese. It's not far from either the *shinkansen* (bullet train) or the regular train entrance/exit.

- **Kyoto Visitor's Guide** Pick up a copy of this useful magazine at any major hotel in Kyoto; it's the best source of information on what's on while you're in town.

- **Walk or cycle** These are the best ways of seeing Kyoto.

- **Taxi** Catch one from Kyoto Station to your hotel or ryokan.

- **Subway** This is helpful if you have to move quickly across the city: if travelling between north and south, catch the Karasuma Subway line, which stops at Kyoto Station; between east and west, the Tōzai Subway line runs from Higashiyama and the west side of Kyoto.

- **Shinkansen** For rapid travel to/from Nagoya, Tokyo and Hiroshima.

- **Seasonal festivals** Cherry-blossom season and autumn foliage season draw huge crowds to Kyoto: escape them by going to lesser-known temples and shrines.

- **Summer (July and August)** These months are very hot and humid in Kyoto. You might consider doing your sightseeing in the early morning or late afternoon.

- **Slip-on shoes** These are very useful for exploring the temples of Kyoto (you have to slip off your shoes to enter most temple buildings). You'll also find them useful if you stay in a ryokan.

Left: *Maiko* (geisha in training) at a teahouse in Gion; **bove:** Path of Philosophy (Tetsugaku-no-Michi, p222)

(LEFT) IMRE CIKAJLO / GETTY IMAGES ©: (ABOVE) AJ1008 / GETTY IMAGES ©

Southern Higashiyama Walking Tour

The Southern Higashiyama area contains Kyoto's thickest concentration of first-class sights. A walk through this area is the perfect way to spend your first full day in the city. Note that this is also a pleasant route for an evening stroll.

WALK FACTS

- **Start** Gojō-zaka bus stop, Higashiōji-dōri
- **Finish** Jingū-michi bus stop, Sanjō-dōri; Higashiyama Station
- **Distance** 5km
- **Duration** Four hours

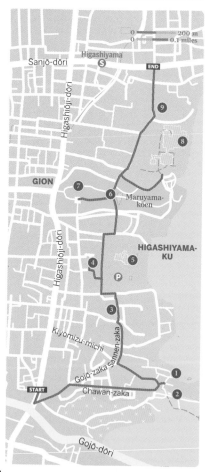

1 Tainai-meguri

Just to the left of the ticket window of Kiyomizu-dera, this small subterranean walk through the darkness easily qualifies as Kyoto's most unusual attraction. We won't say too much about it— just try it.

2 Kiyomizu-dera

At the top of Chawan-zaka, this grande dame of Kyoto temples commands an impressive view over the city. While you're visiting Kiyomizu-dera (p217), be sure to check out Jishu-jinga, home of the famous 'Love Stone', and take a sip of the holy water from the spring below the main hall.

3 Kasagi-ya

On the left just after you start down Sannen-zaka, Kasagi-ya (p248) is a charming little teahouse and the ideal place to stop for a cup of hot *matcha* (powdered green tea) in winter or an *uji kintoki* (shaved ice with sweetened green tea) in summer. Be prepared to ask a local shop owner to point it out.

4 Ishibei-kōji

After you descend Sannen-zaka and Ninen-zaka and start along Nene-no-Michi (just past the public toilet), you will find the entrance to this atmospheric pedestrian-only lane on your left. There is no English sign, so be prepared to ask someone. This is Kyoto's single-most attractive street.

5 Kōdai-ji

At the top of a flight of steps on the right of Nene-no-Michi, you will find Kōdai-ji (p219), a temple famous for interesting evening illuminations of its gardens. At night the bamboo forest here is surreal.

6 Maruyama-kōen

This fine park (p220) is wonderful for an alfresco lunch along this route, or just a quick can of coffee or tea (yes, a can). If you are at Maruyama-kōen during cherry-blossom season, be prepared for a rollicking scene.

7 Yasaka-jinja

Below (west) of Maruyama-kōen, you will find this attractive open-plan shrine (p220). Yasaka-jinja is usually busy with passing worshippers. If you are here on New Year's Eve or the first three days of the New Year, be ready for throngs of people.

8 Chion-in

An immense Pure Land Buddhist Temple, Chion-in (p220) is one of the great centres of Japanese Buddhism and it's grand in every way. Take off your shoes, enter the main hall and spend some time soaking up the atmosphere. It's free.

9 Shōren-in

A nice counterpoint to Chion-in, Shōren-in (p216) is a fine little Tendai sect temple with a wonderful garden and a lovely bamboo forest. You can sip a cup of *matcha* while gazing over the garden. Look for the giant camphor trees out front.

Kyoto in...

THREE DAYS

Spend your first day in the **Southern Higashiyama** (p216) district checking out some of Japan's most amazing sights: Kiyomizu-dera, Maruyama-kōen, Chion-in and Shōren-in. If time allows, continue to the **Northern Higashiyama** (p222) district to visit Nanzen-ji and the Tetsugaku-no-Michi. On the second day, head west to visit **Arashiyama and Sagano** (p228) and visit iconic sights such as the famous bamboo grove and Tenryū-ji. On your last day in town, check out Fushimi Inari-taisha and then visit the sights downtown, like Nishiki Market and the department stores' food floors. Don't forget to do an evening walk in Gion or Ponto-chō while you're in Kyoto.

ONE WEEK

On your first three or four days, follow the preceding itinerary. Then, on the following days, head north to **Kurama and Kibune** (p235); check out **Kinkaku-ji** (p227), the Zen garden at **Ryōan-ji** (p227), stroll the many subtemples of **Daitoku-ji** (p213), drop into **Tōfuku-ji** (p233) and consider a day trip to **Nara** (p287).

Above: Nishiki Market (p210)

AWL IMAGES / GETTY IMAGES ©

Kyoto

🎵 075 / POP 1.47 MILLION

At a Glance

- **Downtown Kyoto** (p210) Here's where you'll do a lot of your eating, dining, partying and maybe sleeping.

- **Southern Higashiyama** (p216) Kyoto's premier sightseeing district.

- **Northern Higashiyama** (p222) Another major sightseeing district, but with a bit more breathing room.

- **Arashiyama & Sagano** (p228) A seething tourist circus that quickly gives way to soothing bamboo groves and temples.

- **Kitayama Area** (p232) Rustic villages scattered among the mountains north of the city.

ℹ️ Orientation

Kyoto is laid out in a grid pattern and is extremely easy to navigate. Kyoto Station, the city's main station, is located at the southern end of the city, and the JR and Kintetsu lines operate from here. The real centre of Kyoto is located around Shijō-dōri, about 2km north of Kyoto Station via Karasuma-dōri. The commercial and nightlife centres are between Shijō-dōri to the south and Sanjō-dōri to the north, and between Kawaramachi-dōri to the east and Karasuma-dōri to the west.

◎ Sights

Although some of Kyoto's major sights are in the city centre, Kyoto's best sightseeing is on the outskirts of the city, along the base of the eastern and western mountains (known as Higashiyama and Arashiyama, respectively). Sights on the east side are best reached by bus, bicycle or the Tōzai subway line. Sights on the west side (Arashiyama etc) are best reached by bus or train (or by bicycle if you're very keen). Outside the city itself, the mountain villages of Ōhara, Kurama and Takao make wonderful day trips and are easily accessible by public transport.

The Kyoto Tourist Information Centre (TIC; p255) stocks several useful maps and bus guides.

KYOTO STATION AREA

Although most of Kyoto's attractions are further north, there are a few attractions within walking distance of the station. The most impressive sight in this area is the vast Higashi Hongan-ji, but don't forget the station building itself (京都駅; **Map p212; Karasuma-dōri, Higashishiokōji-chō, Shiokōji-saguru, Shimogyō-ku;** 🚉**Kyoto Station**) – it's an attraction in its own right.

Tō-ji

UNIVERSALIMAGESGROUP / GETTY IMAGES ©

206

Kyoto Tips

Common sense varies from place to place. In Kyoto, even if you dispense with common sense, you don't run the risk of serious trouble, but there are a few things to keep in mind to make everything easier and perhaps a little safer:

○ Look both ways when exiting a shop or hotel onto a footpath, especially if you have young ones in tow: Kyoto is a city of cyclists and there is almost always someone on a bicycle tearing in your direction.

○ Bring a pair of slip-on shoes to save you from tying and untying your shoes each time you visit a temple.

○ Don't take a taxi in the main Higashiyama sightseeing district during cherry-blossom season – the streets will be so crowded that it will be faster to walk or cycle.

○ Head for the hills to find the most beautiful sights. Yes, the middle of the city has some great sights, but as a general rule, the closer you get to the mountains, the more attractive the city gets.

Higashi Hongan-ji   Buddhist Temple
(東本願寺; Map p212; Karasuma-dōri, Shichijō-agaru, Shimogyō-ku; ⏰5.50am-5.30pm Mar-Oct, 6.20am-4.30pm Nov-Feb; 🚉Kyoto Station) **FREE** A short walk north of Kyoto Station, Higashi Hongan-ji (Eastern Temple of the True Vow) is the last word in all things grand and gaudy. Considering its proximity to the station, the free admission, the awesome structures and the dazzling interiors, this temple is the obvious spot to visit when near the station. The temple is dominated by the vast **Goei-dō** hall, said to be the second-largest wooden structure in Japan, standing 38m high, 76m long and 58m wide.

Nishi Hongan-ji   Buddhist Temple
(西本願寺; Map p212; Horikawa-dōri, Hanayachō-sagaru, Shimogyō-ku; ⏰6am-5pm Nov-Feb, 5.30am-5.30pm Mar, Apr, Sep & Oct, to 6pm May-Aug; 🚉Kyoto Station) **FREE** A vast temple complex located about 15 minutes' walk northwest of Kyoto Station, Nishi Hongan-ji comprises five buildings that feature some of the finest examples of architecture and artistic achievement from the Azuchi-Momoyama period (1568–1600). The **Goei-dō** (main hall) is a marvellous sight. Another must-see

building is the **Daisho-in** hall, which has sumptuous paintings, carvings and metal ornamentation. A small garden and two *nō* (stylised Japanese dance-drama) stages are connected with the hall. The dazzling **Kara-mon** has intricate ornamental carvings.

Tō-ji   Buddhist Temple
(東寺; Map p208; 1 Kujō-chō, Minami-ku; admission to grounds free, Kondō, Kōdō & Treasure Hall ¥500 each, pagoda, Kondō & Kōdō ¥800; ⏰8.30am-5.30pm, to 4.30pm Sep-Mar; 🚇Karasuma line to Kyoto, 🚉Kintetsu Kyoto line to Toji) One of the main sights south of Kyoto Station, Tō-ji is an appealing complex of halls and a fantastic pagoda that makes a fine backdrop for the monthly flea market held on the grounds. The temple was established in 794 by imperial decree to protect the city. In 823 the emperor handed it over to Kūkai (known posthumously as Kōbō Daishi), the founder of the Shingon school of Buddhism.

Umekōji Steam Locomotive Museum   Museum
(梅小路蒸気機関車館; Map p208; Kankiji-chō, Shimogyō-ku; adult/child ¥400/100, train ride ¥200/100; ⏰10am-5pm, closed Mon, except

Greater Kyoto

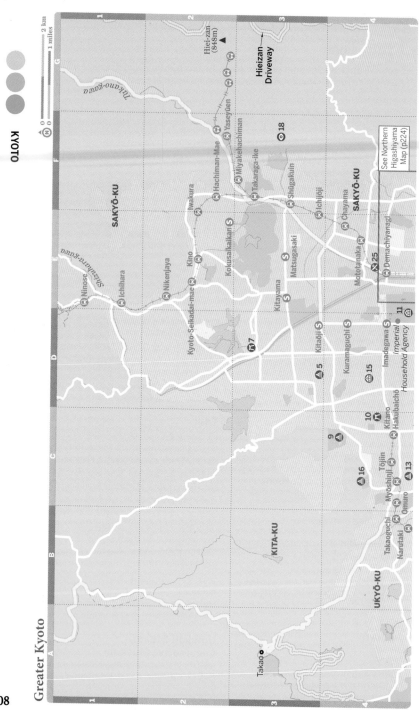

0 ─── 2 km
0 ─── 1 miles

KITA-KU

SAKYŌ-KU

SAKYŌ-KU

UKYŌ-KU

Hiei-zan
(848m)

Hieizan Driveway

Takano-gawa

Shizuhara-gawa

Takao

Ninose

Ichihara

Nikenjaya

Kino

Kyoto-Seikadai-mae

Iwakura

Hachiman-Mae

Yaseyūen

Miyakehachiman

Takaraga-ike

Kokusaikaikan S

Shūgakuin

Ichijōji

Chayama

Kitayama

Matsugasaki

Mototanaka

Demachiyanagi

Kitaōji S

Kuramaguchi S

Imadegawa S

Imperial Household Agency

Kitano Hakubaichō

Tōjin

Myōshinji

Omuro

Takaoguchi

Narutaki

See Northern Higashiyama Map (p224)

⊙ 18

▲ 5

🏛 15

🏛 11

🛏 10

▲ 9

▲ 16

▲ 13

🏯 7

✕ 25

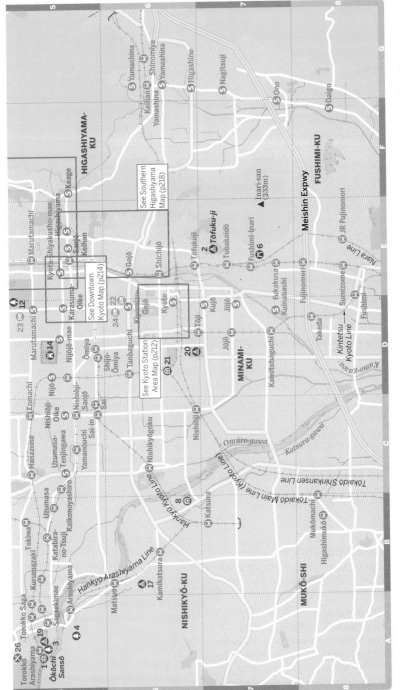

HIGASHIYAMA-KU

FUSHIMI-KU

MINAMI-KU

NISHIKYŌ-KU

MUKŌ-SHI

See Southern Higashiyama Map (p218)

See Downtown Kyoto Map (p214)

See Kyoto Station Area Map (p212)

▲ Inari-san (2233m)

Meishin Expwy

Kamo-gawa

Katsura-gawa

Omuro-gawa

Tōkaidō Shinkansen Line

Tōkaidō Main Line (Kyoto Line)

Hankyū Kyoto Line (Kyoto Line)

Hankyū Arashiyama Line

Nara Line

Kintetsu Kyoto Line

Ⓢ Yamashina
Ⓚ Keihan Yamashina
Ⓢ Higashiyama
Ⓢ Nagitsuji
Ⓢ Ono
Ⓢ Daigo
Ⓢ Shinomiya

Ⓢ Keage
Ⓢ Higashiyama
Ⓚ Sanjō Keihan
Ⓢ Kyoto-Shiyakusho-mae
Ⓢ Marutamachi
Ⓢ Karasumi-Oike
Ⓢ Gojō
Ⓚ Shichijō

Ⓚ Tōfukuji
2 ⚑ Tōfuku-ji
Ⓚ Tobakaidō
Ⓜ 6 Fushimi-Inari

Ⓢ Marutamachi
23 🍴 12 🍴
Ⓢ Marutamachi
🏛14
Ⓚ Nijōjō-mae
Ⓚ Ōmiya
Ⓚ Shijō-Ōmiya
Ⓚ Tanbaguchi
Ⓚ Kyōmachi
Ⓢ Gojō
Ⓢ Kyoto
Ⓢ Kujō
Ⓢ Jūjō

24 🍴 22
Ⓢ Tōji
Ⓢ Kujō
Ⓢ Jūjō

🏛 21
20
🏨

Ⓚ Fukakusa
Ⓚ Fujinomori
Ⓚ Sumizome
Ⓚ Fushimi
Ⓚ JR Fujinomori

Ⓚ Inaba
Ⓚ Kuinabashi
Ⓚ Takeda
Ⓚ Kamitobaguchi

Ⓚ Nishiōji

Ⓢ Nijō
Ⓢ Nishiōji-Oike
Ⓢ Nishiōji-Sanjō
Ⓚ Sai-in
Ⓚ Sai
Ⓢ Tenjingawa
Ⓢ Uzumasa-Tenjingawa
Ⓚ Yamanouchi

Ⓚ Hanazono
Ⓚ Ennamachi
Ⓚ Uzumasa
Ⓚ Katabira-no-Tsuji
Ⓚ Kaikonoyashiro

8 🏛
Ⓚ Katsura

🏨 17
Ⓚ Kamikatsura
Ⓚ Matsuo

Ⓚ Higashimukō
Mukōmachi

Ⓚ Tokiwa
Ⓚ Kurumazaki
Ⓚ Arashiyama
Ⓚ Sagaekimae
Ⓚ Kamikatsura

✕ 26 Torokko Saga
Torokko Arashiyama
1 🏛 19 🏨
🏛 3
Ōkōchi Sansō
🏛 4

209

Greater Kyoto

during spring break 25 Mar-7 Apr & summer break 21 Jul-7 Aug; 🚌 Kyoto City bus 33, 205 or 208 from Kyoto Station to Umekō-ji Kōen-mae) A hit with steam-train buffs and kids, this excellent museum features 18 vintage steam locomotives (dating from 1914 to 1948) and related displays. It is in the former JR Nijō Station building, which was recently relocated here and thoughtfully reconstructed. You can take a 10-minute ride on one of the smoke-spewing choo-choos (departures at 11am, 1.30pm and 3.30pm).

DOWNTOWN KYOTO

Downtown Kyoto looks much like any other Japanese city, but there are some excellent attractions to be found here, including Nishiki Market, the Museum of Kyoto, the Kyoto International Manga Museum and Ponto-chō. If you'd like a break from temples and shrines, then downtown Kyoto can be a welcome change. It's also good on a rainy day, because of the number of covered arcades and indoor attractions.

Nishiki Market   Market
(錦市場; Map p214; Nishikikōji-dōri, btwn Teramachi & Takakura, Nakagyō-ku; ⏰9am-5pm; S Karasuma line to Shijō, 🚊Hankyū line to Karasuma or Kawaramachi) If you're interested in seeing all the really weird and wonderful

foods that go into Kyoto cuisine, wander through Nishiki Market. It's in the centre of town, one block north of (and parallel to) Shijō-dōri, running west off Teramachi shopping arcade. This market is a great place to visit on a rainy day or if you need a break from temple-hopping. The variety of foods on display is staggering, and the frequent cries of *Irasshaimase!* (Welcome!) are heart-warming.

Kyoto International
Manga Museum   Museum
(京都国際マンガミュージアム; Map p214; www.kyotomm.jp/english; Karasuma-dōri, Oike-agaru, Nakagyō-ku; adult/child ¥800/300; ⏰10am-6pm, closed Wed; S Karasuma or Tōzai lines to Karasuma-Oike) This fine museum has a collection of some 300,000 manga (Japanese comic books). Located in an old elementary school building, the museum is the perfect introduction to the art of manga. While most of the manga and displays are in Japanese, the collection of translated works is growing. In addition to the galleries that show both the historical development of manga and original artwork done in manga style, there are beginners' workshops and portrait drawings on weekends.

Ponto-chō   Neighbourhood
(先斗町; Map p214; Ponto-chō, Nakagyō-ku; S Tōzai line to Sanjo-Keihan or Kyoto-

Shiyakusho-mae, 🚇Keihan line to Sanjo, Hankyū line to Kawaramachi) There are few streets in Asia that rival this narrow pedestrian-only walkway for atmosphere. Not much to look at by day, the street comes alive by night, with wonderful lanterns, traditional wooden exteriors, and elegant Kyotoites disappearing into the doorways of elite old restaurants and bars.

CENTRAL KYOTO

The area we refer to as Central Kyoto includes the Kyoto Imperial Palace Park, Nijō-jō, a couple of important shrines and the Nishijin weaving district, among other sights. It's flat and easy to explore by bicycle or on foot.

Kyoto
Imperial Palace   Historic Building
(京都御所, Kyoto Gosho; Map p208; Kyoto Gosho, Nakagyō-ku; 🚇Karasuma line to Marutamachi or Imadegawa) The Kyoto Imperial Palace, known as the Gosho in Japanese, is a walled complex that sits in the middle of the Kyoto Imperial Palace Park. While no longer the official residence of the Japanese emperor, it's still a grand edifice.

The original imperial palace was built in 794 and was replaced numerous times after destruction by fire. The present building, on a different site and smaller than the original, was constructed in 1855. Enthronement of a new emperor and other state ceremonies are still held here.

The Gosho does not rate highly in comparison with other attractions in Kyoto and you must apply for permission to visit. However, the surrounding Kyoto Imperial Palace Park is open to the public from dawn to dusk and can be visited freely without any application procedure. It's Kyoto's premier green space.

Imperial Household
Agency   Booking Office
(宮内庁京都事務所; Map p208; 🕿211-1215; ⏱8.45am-noon & 1-5pm Mon-Fri; 🚇Karasuma line to Imadegawa) Permission to visit the Gosho is granted by the Kunaichō, the Imperial Household Agency, which is inside the walled park surrounding the palace, a short walk from Imadegawa Station on the Karasuma line. You have to fill out an application form and show your passport. Children can visit if accompanied by

Nishiki Market

Kyoto Station Area

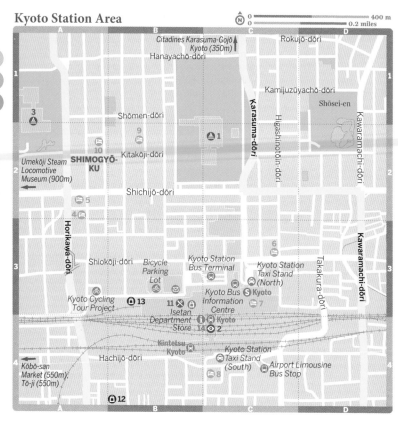

Kyoto Station Area

adults over 20 years of age (but are forbidden entry to the other three imperial properties of Katsura Rikyū, Sentō Gosho and Shūgaku-in Rikyū).

Permission to tour the palace is usually granted the same day (try to arrive at the office at least 30 minutes before the start of the tour you'd like to join). Guided tours, sometimes in English, are given at 10am and 2pm from Monday to Friday. The tour lasts about 50 minutes.

The Gosho can be visited without reservation during two periods each year, once in spring and once in autumn. The dates vary each year, but as a general guide, the spring opening is around the last week of April and the autumn opening is in the middle of November. Check with the Kyoto Tourist Information Centre (TIC; p255) for exact dates.

The Imperial Household Agency is also the place to make advance reservations to see the Sentō Gosho, Katsura Rikyū and Shūgaku-in Rikyū.

Sentō Gosho Palace

Historic Building

(仙洞御所; Map p224; ☎ 211-1215; Kyoto Gyōen, Nakagyō-ku; Ⓢ Karasuma line to Marutamachi or Imadegawa) The Sentō Gosho is the second imperial property located with the Kyoto Imperial Palace Park (the other one is the Gosho, which is located about 100m northwest). The structures within this walled compound are not particularly grand, but the magnificent gardens, laid out in 1630 by renowned landscape designer Kobori Enshū, are excellent.

It was originally constructed in 1630 during the reign of Emperor Go-Mizunō as a residence for retired emperors. The palace was repeatedly destroyed by fire and reconstructed; it continued to serve its purpose until a final blaze in 1854, after which it was never rebuilt. Today only two structures, the **Seika-tei** and **Yūshin-tei** teahouses, remain.

Visitors must obtain advance permission from the Imperial Household Agency and be more than 20 years old. One-hour tours (in Japanese) start daily at 11am and 1.30pm. The route takes you past lovely ponds and pathways and, in many ways, a visit here is more enjoyable than a visit to the Gosho, especially if you are a fan of Japanese gardens.

Kyoto Imperial Palace Park

Park

(京都御苑; Map p208; Kyoto Gyōen, Nakagyō-ku; ⏱ dawn-dusk; Ⓢ Karasuma line to Marutamachi or Imadegawa) FREE The Kyoto Imperial Palace (Kyoto Gosho) and Sentō Gosho are surrounded by the spacious Kyoto Imperial Palace Park, which is planted with a huge variety of flowering trees and open fields. It's perfect for picnics, strolls and just about any sport you can think of. Take some time to visit the pond at the park's southern end, which contains gorgeous carp. The park is most beautiful in the plum- and cherry-blossom seasons (late February and late March, respectively).

Daitoku-ji

Buddhist Temple

(大徳寺; Map p208; 53 Daitokuji-chō, Murasakino, Kita-ku; ⏱ dawn-dusk; Ⓢ Karasuma line to Kitaōji) FREE Daitoku-ji is a separate world within Kyoto – a world of Zen temples, perfectly raked gardens and wandering lanes. It's one of the most rewarding destinations in this part of the city, particularly for those with an interest in Japanese gardens. The temple serves as the headquarters of the Rinzai Daitoku-ji

Kyoto Imperial Palace Park

Downtown Kyoto

Downtown Kyoto

school of Zen Buddhism. The highlights among the 24 subtemples include **Daisen-in**, **Kōtō-in**, **Ōbai-in**, **Ryōgen-in** and **Zuihō-in**.

Nijō-jō
Castle
(二条城; Map p208; 541 Nijōjō-chō, Nijō-dōri, Horikawa nishi-iru, Nakagyō-ku; admission ¥600; ⏰8.45am-5pm, closed Tue in Dec, Jan, Jul & Aug; **S**Tōzai line to Nijō-jō-mae) The military might of Japan's great warlord generals, the Tokugawa shōguns, is amply demonstrated by the imposing stone walls and ramparts of their great castle, Nijō-jō, which dominates a large part of northwest Kyoto. Hidden behind these you will find a superb palace surrounded by beautiful gardens. As you might expect, a sight of this grandeur attracts a lot of crowds, so it's best to visit just after opening or shortly before closing.

This castle was built in 1603 as the official Kyoto residence of the first Tokugawa shōgun, Ieyasu. The ostentatious style of its construction was intended as a demonstration of Ieyasu's prestige and also to signal the demise of the emperor's power. As a safeguard against treachery, Ieyasu had the interior fitted with 'nightingale' floors (which squeak at every move, alerting people to intruders), as well as concealed chambers where bodyguards could keep watch.

After passing through the grand **Karamon gate**, you enter **Ninomaru** palace, which is divided into five buildings with numerous chambers. The **Ōhiroma Yonno-Ma** (Fourth Chamber) has spectacular screen paintings. Don't miss the excellent **Ninomaru Palace Garden**, which was designed by the tea master and landscape architect Kobori Enshū.

Nishijin
Neighbourhood
(西陣; Nishijin, Kamigyō-ku; 🚌Kyoto City bus 9 to Horikawa-Imadegawa) Nishijin is Kyoto's traditional textile centre, the source of all those dazzling kimono fabrics and obi (kimono sashes) that you see being paraded about town. The area is famous for Nishijin-ori (Nishijin weaving). There are quite a few *machiya* (traditional Japanese town houses) in this district, so it's a good place simply to wander.

Orinasu-kan
Museum
(織成館; Map p208; 693 Daikoku-chō, Kamigyō-ku; adult/child ¥500/350; ⏰10am-4pm Tue-Sun; 🚌Kyoto City bus No 9 to Horikawa-Imadegawa)

Nijō-jō

This atmospheric, and usually quiet, museum, housed in a Nishijin weaving factory, has impressive exhibits of Nishijin textiles. The **Susamei-sha** building across the street is also open to the public and worth a look.

SOUTHERN HIGASHIYAMA

The Higashiyama district, which runs along the base of the Higashiyama mountains (Eastern Mountains), is the main sightseeing district in Kyoto and it should be at the top of your Kyoto itinerary. It is thick with impressive sights: fine temples, shrines, gardens, museums, traditional neighbourhoods and parks.

Shōren-in   Buddhist Temple
(青蓮院; Map p218; 69-1 Sanjōbō-chō, Awataguchi, Higashiyama-ku; admission ¥500; ⊘9am-5pm; [S]Tōzai line to Higashiyama) This temple is hard to miss, with its giant camphor trees growing just outside the walls. Fortunately, most tourists march right on past, heading to the area's more famous temples. That is their loss, because this intimate little sanctuary contains a superb landscape garden, that you can enjoy while drinking a cup of green tea (ask at the reception office).

Sanjūsangen-dō
Temple   Buddhist Temple
(三十三間堂; Map p218; 657 Sanjūsangendōma wari-chō, Higashiyama-ku; admission ¥600; ⊘8am-4.30pm Apr-Oct, 9am-3.30pm Nov-Mar; 🚌Kyoto City bus 206 or 208 to Sanjūsangen-dō-mae, [S]Keihan line to Shichijō) This superb temple's name refers to the 33 *sanjūsan* (bays) between the pillars of this long, narrow building. The building houses 1001 wooden statues of Kannon (the Buddhist goddess of mercy); the chief image, the 1000-armed Senjū-Kannon, was carved by the celebrated sculptor Tankei in 1254. It is flanked by 500 smaller Kannon images, neatly lined in rows. The visual effect is stunning, making this a must-see in Southern Higashiyama and a good starting point for exploration of the area.

Left: Kiyomizu-dera; **Below:** Statues in Sanjūsangen-dō Temple
(LEFT) FRANK DEIM/GETTY IMAGES © ; (BELOW) PHOTO BY ILARIA LESCHIUTTA/GETTY IMAGES ©

Kyoto National Museum Museum

(京都国立博物館; Map p218; www.kyohaku.go.jp; 527 Chaya-machi, Higashiyama-ku; adult/student ¥500/250; ⊙9.30am-6pm, to 8pm Fri, closed Mon; 🚌Kyoto City bus 206 or 208 to Sanjūsangen-dō-mae, 🚆Keihan line to Shichijō) The Kyoto National Museum is Kyoto's premier art museum and plays host to the highest level exhibitions in the city. It was founded in 1895 as an imperial repository for art and treasures from local temples and shrines. In the original **main hall** there are 17 rooms with displays of over 1000 artworks, historical artefacts and handicrafts. The new **Heisei Chishinkan**, designed by Taniguchi Yoshio, opened in 2014, is a brilliant modern counterpoint to the original building.

Kiyomizu-dera Buddhist Temple

(清水寺; Map p218; 1-294 Kiyomizu, Higashi-yama-ku; admission ¥300; ⊙6am-6pm; 🚌Kyoto City bus 206 to Kiyomizu-michi or Gojō-zaka, 🚆Keihan line to Kiyomizu-Gojō) A buzzing hive of activity perched on a hill overlooking the basin of Kyoto, Kiyomizu-dera is one of Kyoto's most popular and most enjoyable temples. It may not be the tranquil refuge that many associate with Buddhist temples, but it represents the popular expression of faith in Japan. For those with children in tow, it is sure to delight as there are plenty of things to do here.

This ancient temple was first built in 798, but the present buildings are reconstructions dating from 1633. As an affiliate of the Hossō school of Buddhism, which originated in Nara, it has successfully survived the many intrigues of local Kyoto schools of Buddhism through the centuries and is now one of the most famous landmarks of the city (for which reason it can get very crowded during spring and autumn).

The **Hondō** (Main Hall) has a huge veranda that is supported by pillars and

217

0 — 400 m
0 — 0.2 miles

Oike-dōri
Oike-Ōhashi
Kyoto-Shiyakusho-mae

Sanjō
Sanjō Keihan

Higashiyama

Sanjō-dōri
Sanjō-Ōhashi
22

Hanami-kōji

Higashiōji-dōri

10

Furumonzen-dōri

Shinmonzen-dōri

1

Ponto-chō
Kiyamachi-dōri

23

Nawate-dōri

Shimbashi-dōri

SHINBASHI

25

Kawaramachi
Shijō-Ōhashi

29

Gion-Shijō

24

Shijō-dōri

18

Kiri-dōshi

11
7

Maruyama-kōen

GION

HIGASHIYAMA-KU
Higashi-Ōtani

27

28

Higashiōji-dōri

Kawaramachi-dōri

Kamo-gawa

Takase-gawa

Kawabata-dōri

Miyagawachō-dōri

3

Ebisu-jinja

26

Yasui
Konpira-gū

17

14

5
2

P

Yasaka-dōri

16

Kiyomizu-michi

21

19

8

Sannen-zaka

12

Kiyomizu Gojō

Gojō-Ōhashi

Gojō-dōri

15

Kawabata-dōri
Toiyamachi-dōri
Sayamachi-dōri

Gojō-zaka
Chawan-zaka

4

Gojō-zaka
Bus Stop

Yamatoōji-dōri

Higashiōji-dōri

Shibutani-dōri

Gojō-dōri

6

Shichijō-dōri

13

Shichijō

9

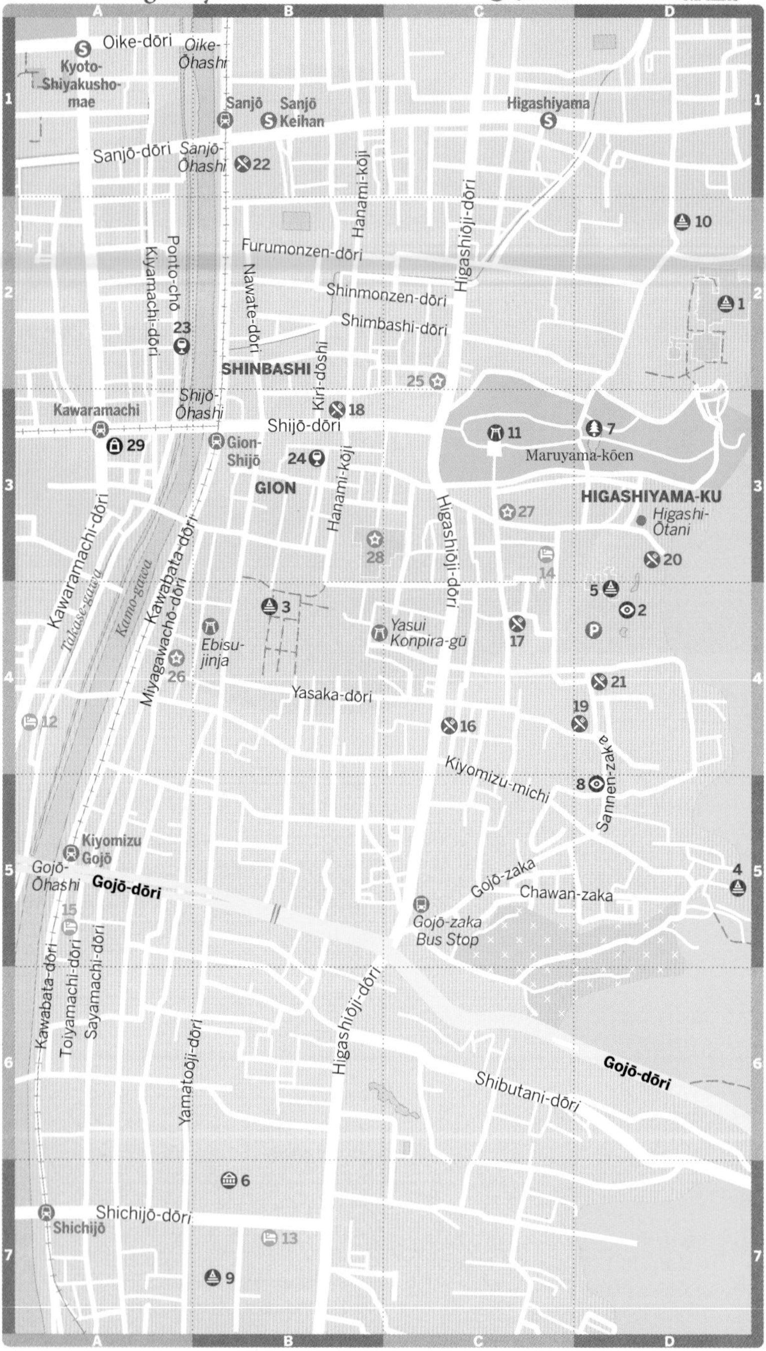

Southern Higashiyama

juts out over the hillside. Just below this hall is the waterfall **Otowa-no-taki**, where visitors drink sacred waters believed to bestow health and longevity. Dotted around the precincts are other halls and shrines. At **Jishu-jinja**, the shrine up the steps above the main hall, visitors try to ensure success in love by closing their eyes and walking about 18m between a pair of stones – if you miss the stone, your desire for love won't be fulfilled! Note that you can ask someone to guide you, but if you do, you'll need someone's assistance to find your true love.

Before you enter the actual temple precincts, check out the **Tainai-meguri**, the entrance to which is just to the left (north) of the pagoda that is located in front of the main entrance to the temple (there is no English sign). We won't tell you too much about it as it will ruin the experience. Suffice to say that by entering the Tainai-meguri, you are symbolically entering the womb of a female bodhi-sattva. When you get to the rock in the darkness, spin it in either direction to make a wish.

The steep approach to the temple is known as **Chawan-zaka** (Teapot Lane) and is lined with shops selling Kyoto handicrafts, local snacks and souvenirs.

Check at the Tourist Information Center (TIC) for the scheduling of special night-time illuminations of the temple held in the spring and autumn.

Ninen-zaka & Sannen-zaka
Neighbourhood

(二年坂・三年坂; Map p218; Higashiyama-ku; 🚌 Kyoto City bus 206 to Kiyomizu-michi or Gojō-zaka, 🚃 Keihan line to Kiyomizu-Gojō) Just downhill from and slightly to the north of Kiyomizu-dera, you will find one of Kyoto's loveliest restored neighbourhoods, the Ninen-zaka–Sannen-zaka area. It's a lovely place for a stroll. The name refers to the two main streets of the area: Ninen-zaka and Sannen-zaka, literally 'Two-Year Hill' and 'Three-Year Hill' (the years refer to the ancient imperial years when they were first laid out). These two charming streets are lined with old wooden houses, traditional shops and restaurants. If you fancy a break from sightseeing, there also are many teahouses and cafes along these lanes.

Kōdai-ji
Buddhist Temple

(高台寺; Map p218; 526 Shimokawara-chō, Kōdai-ji, Higashiyama-ku; admission ¥600; ⏰9am-5pm; 🚌 Kyoto City bus 206 to Yasui, 🅂 Tōzai line to Higashiyama) This exquisite temple was founded in 1605 by Kita-no-Mandokoro in memory of her late husband, Toyotomi Hideyoshi. The extensive grounds include gardens designed by

the famed landscape architect Kobori Enshū, and tea houses designed by the renowned master of the tea ceremony, Sen no Rikyū.

The temple holds three annual special night-time illuminations, when the gardens are lit by multicoloured spotlights. The illuminations are held from mid-March to early May, 1 to 18 August and late October to early December.

Maruyama-kōen   Park
(円山公園; Map p218; Maruyama-chō, Higashiyama-ku; **S** Tōzai line to Higashiyama) Maruyama-kōen is a favourite of locals and visitors alike. This park is the place to come to escape the bustle of the city centre and amble around gardens, ponds, souvenir shops and restaurants. Peaceful paths meander through the trees and carp glide through the waters of a small pond in the park's centre.

Yasaka-jinja   Shinto Shrine
(八坂神社; Map p218; 625 Gion-machi, Kita-gawa, Higashiyama-ku; ◷24hr; **S** Tōzai line to

Higashiyama) **FREE** This colourful and spacious shrine is considered the guardian shrine of the Gion entertainment district. It's a bustling, colourful place that is well worth a visit while exploring Southern Higashiyama; it can easily be paired with Maruyama-kōen, the park just up the hill.

Chion-in   Buddhist Temple
(知恩院; Map p218; 400 Rinka-chō, Higashiyama-ku; admission inner buildings & garden ¥500, grounds free; ◷9am-4.30pm; **S** Tōzai line to Higashiyama) A collection of soaring buildings and spacious courtyards, Chion-in serves as the headquarters of the Jōdo sect, the largest sect of Buddhism in Japan. It's the most popular pilgrimage temple in Kyoto and it's always a hive of activity. For visitors with a taste for the grand, this temple is sure to satisfy.

Chion-in was established in 1234 on the site where Hōnen, one of the most famous figures in Japanese Buddhism, taught his brand of Buddhism (Jōdo, or Pure Land, Buddhism) and eventually fasted to death.

Left: An outdoor restaurant in Maruyama-kōen; **Below:** Wooden plaques at Yasaka-jinja

(LEFT) EYEON/UIG VIA/GETTY IMAGES ©; (BELOW) LUCAS SCHIFRES/GETTY IMAGES ©

The oldest of the present buildings date to the 17th century. The two-storey **San-mon**, a Buddhist temple gate at the main entrance, is the largest temple gate in Japan and prepares you for the massive scale of the temple. The immense main hall contains an image of Hōnen. It's connected to another hall, the **Dai Hōjō**, by a 'nightingale' floor (that sings and squeaks at every move, making it difficult for intruders to move about quietly).

Up a flight of steps southeast of the main hall is the temple's **giant bell**, which was cast in 1633 and weighs 70 tonnes. It is the largest bell in Japan. The bell is rung by the temple's monks 108 times on New Year's Eve each year.

Gion
Neighbourhood

(祇園周辺; Map p218; Higashiyama-ku; **S** Tōzai line to Sanjō, **R** Keihan line to Gion-Shijō) Gion is the famous entertainment and geisha quarter on the eastern bank of the Kamogawa. While Gion's true origins were in teahouses catering to weary visitors to

Yasaka-jinja (a neighbourhood shrine), by the mid-18th century the area was Kyoto's largest pleasure district. Despite the looming modern architecture, congested traffic and contemporary nightlife establishments that have compromised its historical beauty, there are still some places left in Gion for an enjoyable walk.

Hanami-kōji runs north–south and bisects Shijō-dōri. The southern section is lined with 17th-century traditional restaurants and teahouses, many of which are exclusive establishments for geisha entertainment. At the south end you reach **Gion Corner** and **Gion Kōbu Kaburen-jō Theatre** (祇園甲部歌舞練場).

If you walk from Shijō-dōri along the northern section of Hanami-kōji and take your third left, you will find yourself on **Shimbashi** (sometimes called Shirakawa Minami-dōri), which is one of Kyoto's most beautiful streets and, arguably, the most beautiful street in all of Asia, especially in the evening and during cherry-blossom season. A bit further north lie **Shinmonzen-dōri** and **Furumonzen-dōri**, running east–west. Wander in either direction along these streets, which are packed with old houses, art galleries and shops specialising in antiques – but don't expect flea-market prices.

NORTHERN HIGASHIYAMA

The Northern Higashiyama area at the base of the Higashiyama mountains is one of the city's richest areas for sightseeing. It includes such first-rate attractions as Nanzen-ji, Ginkaku-ji, Hōnen-in and Shūgaku-in Rikyū. You can spend a wonderful day walking from Keage Station on the Tōzai subway line all the way north to Ginkaku-ji via the Tetsugaku-no-Michi (the Path of Philosophy), stopping in the countless temples and shrines en route.

Path of Philosophy (Tetsugaku-no-Michi)
Neighbourhood

(哲学の道; Map p224; Sakyō-ku; 🚌Kyoto City bus 5 to Eikandō-michi or Ginkakuji-michi, S Tōzai line to Keage) The Tetsugaku-no-

Michi is one of the most pleasant walks in all of Kyoto. Lined with a great variety of flowering plants, bushes and trees, it is a corridor of colour throughout most of the year. Follow the traffic-free route along a canal lined with cherry trees that come into spectacular bloom in early April. It only takes 30 minutes to do the walk, which starts at Nyakuōji-bashi, above Eikan-dō, and leads to Ginkaku-ji.

Hōnen-in
Buddhist Temple

(法然院; Map p224; 30 Goshonodan-chō, Shishigatani, Sakyō-ku; ⏰6am-4pm; 🚌Kyoto City bus 5 to Ginkakuji-michi) **FREE** One of Kyoto's hidden pleasures, this temple was founded in 1680 to honour the priest Hōnen. It's a lovely, secluded temple with carefully raked gardens set back in the woods. The temple buildings include a small gallery where frequent exhibitions featuring local and international artists are held. If you need to escape the crowds that positively plague nearby Ginkaku-ji, come to this serene refuge.

Hōnen-in is a 12-minute walk from Ginkaku-ji, on a side street above the Tetsugaku-no-Michi; you may have to ask for directions.

Path of Philosophy (Tetsugaku-no-Michi)

MICHAEL RUNKEL/GETTY IMAGES ©

MICHAEL RUNKEL/GETTY IMAGES ©

Don't Miss
Nanzen-ji

This is one of the most rewarding temples in Kyoto, with its expansive grounds and numerous subtemples. At its entrance stands the massive **San-mon**. Steps lead up to the 2nd storey, which has a fine view over the city. Beyond the gate is the main hall of the temple, above which you will find the **Hōjō**, where the Leaping Tiger Garden is a classic Zen garden well worth a look.

Nanzen-ji began as a retirement villa for Emperor Kameyama but was dedicated as a Zen temple on his death in 1291. Civil war in the 15th century destroyed most of the temple; the present buildings date from the 17th century. It operates now as headquarters for the Rinzai school of Zen.

While you're in the Hōjō, you can enjoy a cup of tea while gazing at a small waterfall (¥500; ask at the reception desk of the Hōjō).

NEED TO KNOW

南禅寺; Map p224; 86 Fukuchi-chō, Nanzen-ji, Sakyō-ku; admission Hōjō garden ¥500, San-mon gate ¥400, grounds free; ⏰8.40am-5pm Mar-Nov, to 4.30pm Dec-Feb; 🚌Kyoto City bus 5 to Eikandō-michi, Ⓢ Tōzai line to Keage

---

Ginkaku-ji   Buddhist Temple
(銀閣寺; Map p224; 2 Ginkaku-ji-chō, Sakyō-ku; admission ¥500; ⏰8.30am-5pm Mar-Nov, 9am-4.30pm Dec-Feb; 🚌Kyoto City bus 5 to Ginkakuji-michi stop) Home to a sumptuous garden and elegant structures, Ginkaku-ji is one of Kyoto's premier sites. The temple started its life in 1482 as a retirement villa for Shōgun Ashikaga Yoshimasa, who desired a place to retreat from the turmoil of a civil war. While the name Ginkaku-ji literally translates as 'Silver Pavilion', the shōgun's ambition to cover the building with silver was never realised. After Yoshimasa's death, the villa was converted into a temple.

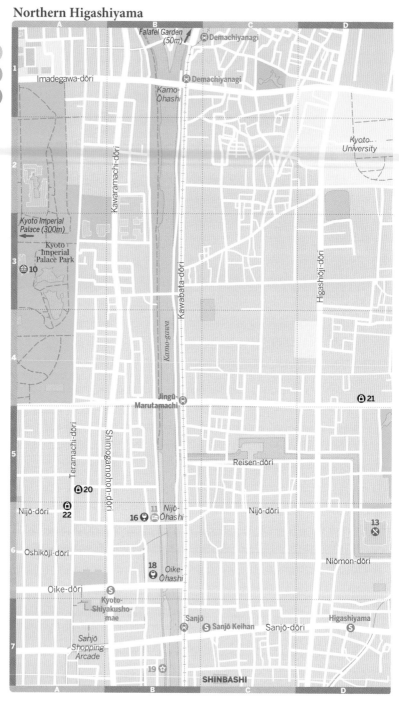

KYOTO

Falafel Garden (50m)

🚇 Demachiyanagi

🚇 Demachiyanagi

Imadegawa-dōri

Kamo-Ōhashi

Kawaramachi-dōri

Kyoto University

Kyoto Imperial Palace (300m)

Kyoto Imperial Palace Park
🏛 10

Kawabata-dōri

Higashiōji-dōri

Kamo-gawa

Jingū-Marutamachi

🔒 21

Teramachi-dōri

Shimogamohon-dōri

Reisen-dōri

🔒 20

Nijō-dōri
🔒 22

16 🚉 Nijō-Ōhashi

11 Nijō-Ōhashi

Nijō-dōri

13 ⊗

Oshikōji-dōri

Niōmon-dōri

18 🚉 Oike-Ōhashi

Oike-dōri
Ⓢ
Kyoto-Shiyakusho-mae

Sanjō
Ⓢ Sanjō Keihan

Sanjō-dōri

Higashiyama Ⓢ

Sanjō Shopping Arcade

19 ☆

SHINBASHI

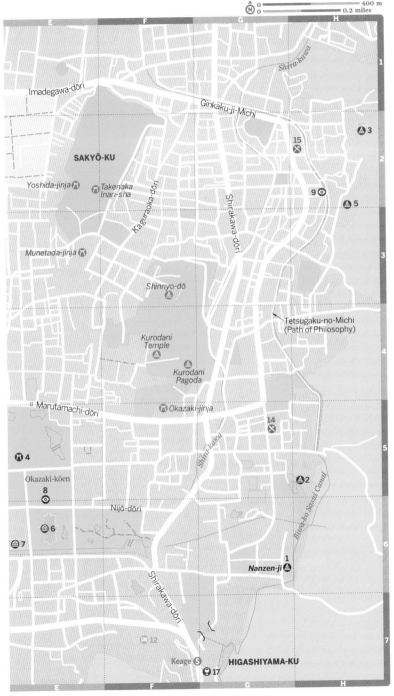

0
0

400 m
0.2 miles

N

Shira-kawa

Imadegawa-dōri

Ginkaku-ji-Michi

3

15

SAKYŌ-KU

9

Yoshida-jinja

Takenaka
Inari-sha

5

Kaguraoka-dōri

Munetada-jinja

Shirakawa-dōri

Shinnyo-dō

Tetsugaku-no-Michi
(Path of Philosophy)

Kurodani
Temple

Kurodani
Pagoda

Marutamachi-dōri

Okazaki-jinja

14

4

Shira-kawa

Okazaki-kōen

8

2

Nijō-dōri

6

Biwa-ko Sosui Canal

7

1

Nanzen-ji

Shirakawa-dōri

12

Keage

17

HIGASHIYAMA-KU

Northern Higashiyama

Okazaki-kōen Area　　Neighbourhood
(岡崎公園; Map p224; Okazaki, Sakyo-ku;
[S] Tōzai line to Higashiyama) Okazaki-kōen is
an expanse of parks and canals that lies
between Niōmon-dōri and Heian-jingū.
Two of Kyoto's significant museums can
be found here, as well as two smaller
museums. If you find yourself in Kyoto on
a rainy day and need to do some indoor
sightseeing, this area has enough to keep
you sheltered for most of the day.

**Kyoto Municipal
Museum of Art**　　Museum
(京都市美術館; Map p224; 124 Enshōji-chō,
Okazaki, Sakyō-ku; admission varies; ⊙9am-
5pm, closed Mon; [S] Tōzai line to Higashiyama)
This fine museum holds several major
exhibitions a year, as well as a variety of
free shows. It's always worth stopping by
to see if something is on while you are in
town. The pond behind the museum is a
great place for a picnic.

**National Museum of
Modern Art**　　Museum
(京都国立近代美術館; Map p224; www.momak.
go.jp; Enshōji-chō, Okazaki, Sakyō-ku; admission
¥430; ⊙9.30am-5pm, closed Mon; [S] Tōzai line
to Higashiyama) This museum is renowned
for its Japanese ceramics and paintings.
There is an excellent permanent collection, which includes many pottery pieces
by Kawai Kanjirō. The coffee shop here
overlooks a picturesque canal.

Heian-jingū　　Shinto Shrine
(平安神宮; Map p224; Nishitennō-chō, Okazaki,
Sakyō-ku; admission garden ¥600; ⊙6am-
5pm Nov-Feb, to 6pm Mar-Oct; [S] Tōzai line to
Higashiyama) One of Kyoto's more popular
sights, this shrine was built in 1895 to
commemorate the 1100th anniversary of
the founding of Kyoto. The shrine buildings are colourful replicas, reduced to a
two-thirds scale, of the Imperial Court
Palace of the Heian period (794–1185).
About 500m in front of the shrine is a
massive steel **torii** (shrine gate). Although
it appears to be entirely separate, this is
actually considered the main entrance to
the shrine itself.

**Shūgaku-in Rikyū
Imperial Villa**　　Notable Building
(修学院離宮; Map p208; ☏211-1215; Shūgaku-
in, Yabusoe, Sakyō-ku; 🚌Kyoto City bus 5 from
Kyoto Station to Shūgakuinrikyū-michi) **FREE**
Lying at the foot of Hiei-zan, this superb
imperial villa is one of the highlights of
northeast Kyoto. It was designed as a
lavish summer retreat for the imperial
family. The gardens here, with their views
down over the city of Kyoto, are worth the
trouble it takes to visit.

Construction of the villa was begun
in the 1650s by Emperor Go-Mizunō,
following his abdication. Work was
continued by his daughter Akeno-miya
after his death in 1680.

The villa grounds are divided into three enormous garden areas on a hillside – lower, middle and upper. Each has superb tea-ceremony houses: the upper, **Kami-no-chaya**, and lower, **Shimo-no-chaya**, were completed in 1659, and the middle teahouse, **Naka-no-chaya**, was completed in 1682. The gardens' reputation rests on their ponds, pathways and impressive use of *shakkei* (borrowed scenery) in the form of the surrounding hills. The view from Kami-no-chaya is particularly impressive.

One-hour tours (in Japanese) start at 9am, 10am, 11am, 1.30pm and 3pm; try to arrive early. A basic leaflet in English is provided and more detailed literature is for sale in the tour waiting room.

You must make reservations through the Imperial Household Agency (p211) – usually several weeks in advance.

NORTHWEST KYOTO

Northwest Kyoto has many excellent sights spread over a large area. Highlights include Kinkaku-ji (the famed Golden Pavilion) and Ryōan-ji, with its mysterious stone garden. Note that three of the area's main sights – Kinkaku-ji, Ryōan-ji

and Ninna-ji – can easily be linked together to form a great half-day tour out of the city centre.

Kinkaku-ji   Buddhist Temple
(金閣寺; Map p208; 1 Kinkakuji-chō, Kita-ku; admission ¥400; ⏰9am-5pm; 🚌Kyoto City bus 205 from Kyoto Station to Kinkakuji-michi, Kyoto City bus 59 from Sanjo-Keihan to Kinkakuji-mae) Kyoto's famed 'Golden Pavilion', Kinkaku-ji is one of Japan's best-known sights. The main hall, covered in brilliant gold leaf, shining above its reflecting pond is truly spectacular. Needless to say, due to its beauty, the temple can be packed any day of the year. Thus, we recommend going early in the day or just before closing, ideally on a weekday.

Ryōan-ji   Buddhist Temple
(龍安寺; Map p208; 13 Goryōnoshitamachi, Ryōan-ji, Ukyō-ku; admission ¥500; ⏰8am-5pm Mar-Nov, 8.30am-4.30pm Dec-Feb; 🚌Kyoto City bus No 59 from Sanjō-Keihan to Ryoanji-mae) You've probably seen a picture of the rock garden here – it's one of the symbols of Kyoto and one of Japan's better-known sights. Ryōan-ji belongs to the Rinzai school and was founded in 1450. The garden, an oblong of sand

National Museum of Modern Art

with an austere collection of 15 carefully placed rocks, apparently adrift in a sea of sand, is enclosed by an earthen wall. The designer, who remains unknown to this day, provided no explanation.

ARASHIYAMA & SAGANO AREA

Arashiyama and Sagano, at the base of Kyoto's western mountains (known as the Arashiyama), is Kyoto's second-most important sightseeing district after Higashiyama. On first sight, you may wonder what all the fuss is about: the main street and the area around the famous Tōgetsu-kyō bridge have all the makings of a classic Japanese tourist trap. But once you head up the hills to the temples hidden among the greenery, you will understand the appeal.

Bus 28 links Kyoto Station with Arashiyama. Bus 11 connects Keihan Sanjō Station with Arashiyama. The most convenient rail connection is the JR Sagano/San-in line from Kyoto Station or Nijō Station to Saga-Arashiyama Station (be careful to take only local trains, as expresses do not stop at Saga-Arashiyama). You can also take the Hankyū line from downtown Kyoto to Arashiyama Station, but this involves changing trains at Katsura. Finally, a fast way to get there from the middle of Kyoto (downtown and central Kyoto) is to take the Tōzai subway line to the western-most stop (Uzumasa-Tenjin-gawa) and take a taxi from there to Arashiyama (the taxi ride will take about 15 minutes and cost around ¥1600.

The sites in this section are all within walking distance of Arashiyama Station. We suggest walking from this station to Tenryū-ji, exiting the north gate, checking out the bamboo grove, visiting Ōkōchi Sansō, then walking north to Giō-jior Adashino Nembutsu-ji. If you have time for only one temple in the area, we recommend Tenryū-ji. If you have time for two, we suggest adding Giō-ji.

Tenryū-ji   Buddhist Temple
(天龍寺; Map p208; 68 Susukinobaba-chō, Saga-Tenryū-ji, Ukyō-ku; admission ¥600; ⏱8.30am-5.30pm, to 5pm 21 Oct-20 Mar; 🚌Kyoto City bus 28 from Kyoto Station to Arashiyama-Tenryuji-mae, 🚆JR Sagano/San-in line to Saga-Arashiyama or Hankyū line to Arashiyama, change at Katsura) This fine temple has one

Arashiyama Bamboo Grove

of the most attractive stroll gardens in all of Kyoto, particularly during the spring cherry-blossom and autumn-foliage seasons. The main 14th-century Zen garden, with its backdrop of the Arashiyama mountains, is a good example of *shakkei* (borrowed scenery). Unfortunately, it's no secret that the garden here is world class, so it pays to visit early in the morning or on a weekday.

Arashiyama Bamboo Grove Park

(嵐山竹林; Map p208; Ogurayama, Saga, Ukyō-ku; ⊙dawn-dusk; 🚌Kyoto City bus 28 from Kyoto Station to Arashiyama-Tenryuji-mae, 🚉JR Sagano/San-in line to Saga-Arashiyama or Hankyū line to Arashiyama, change at Katsura) **FREE** Walking into this extensive bamboo grove is like entering another world – the thick green bamboo stalks seem to continue endlessly in every direction and there's a strange quality to the light. You'll be unable to resist trying to take a few photos, but you might be disappointed with the results: photos just can't capture the magic of this place. The grove runs from just outside the north gate of Tenryū-ji to just below Ōkōchi Sansō villa.

Arashiyama Monkey Park Iwatayama Park

(嵐山モンキーパークいわたやま; Map p208; 8 Genrokuzan-chō, Arashiyama, Ukyō-ku; adult/child ¥550/250; ⊙9am-5pm 15 Mar-Oct, to 4pm Nov-14 Mar; 🚌Kyoto City bus 28 from Kyoto Station to Arashiyama-Tenryuji-mae, 🚉JR Sagano/San-in line to Saga-Arashiyama or Hankyū line to Arashiyama, change at Katsura) Though it is common to spot wild monkeys in the nearby mountains, here you can encounter them at a close distance and enjoy watching the playful creatures frolic about. It makes for an excellent photo opportunity, not only of the monkeys but also of the panoramic view over Kyoto. Refreshingly, it is the animals who are free to roam while the humans who feed them are caged in a box!

You enter the park near the south side of Tōgetsu-kyō, through the orange *torii* (shrine gate) of Ichitani-jinja. Buy your tickets from the machine to the left of the shrine at the top of the steps. Just be

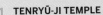
1 TENRYŪ-JI TEMPLE

One of my favourite gardens in Kyoto is inside this temple. When you stroll around the main hall to the far side, your breath will be taken away by the sight waiting for you. Stop to savour the view from many vantage points, as the pond garden is designed to have a perfect view from any point. This artificial landscape matches the natural landscape of mountains in the distance as if they are also part of the garden. This is *shakkei* or 'borrowed landscape'.

2 BAMBOO GROVE

Going out from the north garden exit of Tenryū-ji, suddenly you will find yourself in a lane surrounded by towering bamboo trees. You'll probably feel the temperature is several degrees cooler here. Early in the morning, on weekdays or in the low season, you may have the place all to yourself.

3 ŌKŌCHI-SANSŌ

This magnificent villa and garden was the lifetime work of Ōkōchi Denjirō, a famous samurai movie actor. Ōkōchi's villa is now open to the public to enjoy the garden and the views over Kyoto. The garden gives you ideas as to what you can do with your own even if it is a small one, as each part is designed in a small scale.

4 GIŌ-JI

Out of the 1600 temples in Kyoto, this is one of my all-time favourites. It hardly looks like a temple at all, but more like a small three-room hut with an intimate garden. If you go expecting a grand temple, you'll be disappointed, but if you slow down and soak up the calm stillness of the garden, you will emerge refreshed and alive.

LONELY PLANET/GETTY IMAGES ©

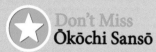

Don't Miss
Ōkōchi Sansō

This is the lavish estate of Ōkōchi Denjirō, an actor famous for his samurai films. The sprawling stroll gardens may well be the most lovely in all of Kyoto, particularly when you consider the brilliant views eastwards across the city. The house and teahouse are also sublime. Be sure to follow all the trails around the gardens. Hold onto the tea ticket you were given upon entry to claim the tea and cake that comes with admission.

NEED TO KNOW

大河内山荘; Map p208; 8 Tabuchiyama-chō, Sagaogurayama, Ukyō-ku; admission ¥1000; 🕙9am-5pm; 🚌Kyoto City bus 28 from Kyoto Station to Arashiyama-Tenryuji-mae, 🚆JR Sagano/ San-in line to Saga-Arashiyama or Hankyū line to Arashiyama, change at Katsura

warned: it's a steep climb up the hill to get to the monkeys. If it's a hot day, you're going to be drenched by the time you get to the spot where they gather.

SOUTHEAST KYOTO

Southeast Kyoto contains some of Kyoto's most impressive sights, including Tōfuku-ji, with its lovely garden, and Fushi-Inari Taisha, with its hypnotically beautiful arcades of Shintō shrine gates.

Fushimi Inari-Taisha Shinto Shrine
(伏見稲荷大社; Map p208; 68 Yabunouchi-chō, Fukakusa, Fushimi-ku; 🕙dawn-dusk; 🚆JR Nara line to Inari, Keihan line to Fushimi-Inari) **FREE**
With seemingly endless arcades of vermilion *torii* (shrine gates) spread across a thickly wooded mountain, this vast shrine complex is a world unto its own. It is, quite simply, one of the most impressive and memorable sights in all of Kyoto.

The entire complex, consisting of five shrines, sprawls across the wooded slopes of Inari-san. A pathway wanders 4km up the mountain and is lined with dozens of atmospheric sub-shrines.

Fushimi Inari was dedicated to the gods of rice and sake by the Hata family in the 8th century. As the role of agriculture diminished, deities were enrolled to ensure prosperity in business. Nowadays, the shrine is one of Japan's most popular, and is the head shrine for some 40,000 Inari shrines scattered the length and breadth of the country.

As you explore the shrine, you will come across hundreds of stone foxes. The fox is considered the messenger of Inari, the god of cereals, and the stone foxes, too, are often referred to as Inari. The key often seen in the fox's mouth is for the rice granary. On an incidental note, the Japanese traditionally see the fox as a sacred, somewhat mysterious figure capable of 'possessing' humans – the favoured point of entry is under the fingernails.

The walk around the upper precincts of the shrine is a pleasant day hike. It also makes for a very eerie stroll in the late afternoon and early evening, when the various graveyards and miniature shrines along the path take on a mysterious air. It's best to go with a friend at this time.

On 8 April there's a Sangyō-sai festival with offerings and dances to ensure prosperity for national industry. During the first few days in January, thousands of believers visit this shrine as their *hatsu-mōde* (first shrine visit of the New Year) to pray for good fortune.

SOUTHWEST KYOTO

Southwest Kyoto is home to two notable sights, including the famous 'Moss Temple' (Saihō-ji) and Katsura-Rikyū.

Saihō-ji   Buddhist Temple
(西芳寺; Map p208; 56 Jingatani-chō, Matsuo, Nishikyō-ku; admission ¥3000; ⏰Kyoto City bus 28 from Kyoto Station to Matsuo-taisha-mae, Kyoto bus 63 from Sanjō-Keihan to Koke-dera) Saihō-ji, one of Kyoto's best-known gardens, is famed for its superb moss garden, hence the temple's nickname: Koke-dera

If You Like...
Shintō shrines

If you like Fushimi Inari-Taisha, you'll like these two other Shintō shrines in Kyoto:

1 KAMIGAMO-JINJA
(上賀茂神社; Map p208; 339 Motoyama, Kamigamo, Kita-ku; ⏰6am-5pm; ⏰Kyoto City bus 9 to Kamigamo-misonobashi) Kamigamo-jinja is one of Japan's oldest shrines and predates the founding of Kyoto. Established in 679, it is dedicated to Raijin, the god of thunder, and is one of Kyoto's 17 Unesco World Heritage Sites. The present buildings (more than 40 in all), including the impressive **Haiden** hall, are exact reproductions of the originals, dating from the 17th to 19th centuries.

2 KITANO TENMAN-GŪ
(北野天満宮; Map p208; Bakuro-chō, Kamigyō-ku; ⏰5am-6pm Apr-Sep, 5.30am-5.30pm Oct-Mar; ⏰Kyoto City bus 50 from Kyoto Station to Kitano-Tenmangū-mae) The most atmospheric Shintō shrine in northwest Kyoto, Kitano Tenman-gū is also the site of Tenjin-San Market, one of Kyoto's most popular flea markets. It's a pleasant spot for a lazy stroll and the shrine buildings themselves are beautiful. The present buildings were built in 1607 by Toyotomi Hideyori; the grounds contain an extensive grove of plum trees, which burst into bloom in early March.

(Moss Temple). The heart-shaped garden, laid out in 1339 by Musō Kokushi, surrounds a tranquil pond. In order to limit the number of visitors, one must apply to visit and then copy a sutra with ink and brush before exploring the garden.

While copying a sutra might seem daunting, it's actually fairly self-explanatory and if you're lost, just glance at what the Japanese visitors are doing. It's not necessary to finish the entire sutra, just do the best you can. Once in the garden, you are free to explore on your own and at your own pace.

To visit Saihō-ji you must make a reservation. Send a postcard at least one week before the date you wish to visit and

Detour:
Miho Museum

Secluded amid hills and valleys near the village of Shigaraki, this knockout **museum** (ミホミュージアム; ☎0748-82-3411; www.miho.or.jp; 300, Tashiro Momodani; admission ¥1100; ☉10am-5pm Jan & Feb, mid-Jun–mid-Jul, mid-end Aug, mid-end Dec, closed some Mon & Tue, check website) houses the Koyama family collection of Japanese, Middle Eastern, Chinese and South Asian art, and beautifully displayed special exhibits. The facility is at least as impressive as the collection. The IM Pei–designed main building, reached from the ticket centre via a footpath and long pedestrian tunnel opening onto a gorge, feels like a secret hideout in a futuristic farmhouse.

The construction was quite an engineering feat: the top of the mountain was removed, the glass and marble building constructed, and the ground replaced as before around and above it, down to the massive red pine (a video explains it).

Take the JR Tōkaidō line from Kyoto or Osaka to Ishiyama Station, and change to a Teisan Bus bound for the museum (¥820, approximately 50 minutes). Double-check the website for opening times before setting out.

include your name, number of visitors, address in Japan, occupation, age (you must be over 18) and desired date (choice of alternative dates preferred). The address: Saihō-ji, 56 Kamigaya-chō, Matsuo, Nishikyō-ku, Kyoto-shi 615-8286, JAPAN.

Enclose a stamped self-addressed postcard for a reply to your Japanese address. You might find it convenient to buy an Ōfuku-hagaki (send and return postcard set) at a Japanese post office.

Katsura Rikyū · Historic Building
(桂離宮; Map p208; Katsura Detached Palace; Katsura Misono, Nishikyō-ku; 🚌Kyoto City bus 33 to Katsura Rikyū-mae, 🚉Hankyū line to Katsura) FREE Katsura Rikyū, one of Kyoto's imperial properties, is widely considered to be the pinnacle of Japanese traditional architecture and garden design. Set amid an otherwise drab neighbourhood, it is (very literally) an island of incredible beauty. The villa was built in 1624 for the emperor's brother, Prince Toshihito. Every conceivable detail of the villa – the teahouses, the large pond with islets and the surrounding garden – has been given meticulous attention.

Tours (in Japanese) start at 10am, 11am, 2pm and 3pm, and last 40 minutes. Try to be there 20 minutes before the

start time. An explanatory video is shown in the waiting room and a leaflet is provided in English.

You must make reservations, usually several weeks in advance, through the Imperial Household Agency (p211). There are those, however, who feel that the troublesome application process, the distance of the villa from downtown and the need to join a regimented tour detracts from the experience.

The villa is a 15-minute walk from Katsura Station, on the Hankyū line. A taxi from the station to the villa will cost around ¥700. Alternatively, Kyoto bus 33 stops at Katsura Rikyū-mae stop, which is a five-minute walk from the villa.

KITAYAMA AREA

Starting on the north side of Kyoto city and stretching almost all the way to the Sea of Japan, the Kitayama (Northern Mountains) are a natural escape prized by Kyoto city dwellers. Attractions here include the village of Ōhara, with its pastoral beauty, the fine mountain temple at Kurama, and the river dining platforms at Kibune.

ŌHARA

Since ancient times Ōhara (大原), a quiet farming town about 10km north of

JON BOWER AT APEXPHOTOS/GETTY IMAGES ©

Don't Miss
Tōfuku-ji

Home to a spectacular garden, several superb structures and beautiful precincts, Tōfuku-ji is one of the finest temples in Kyoto. It's well worth a special visit and can easily be paired with a trip to Fushimi Inari-Taisha (the two are linked by the Keihan train line).

Founded in 1236 by the priest Enni, Tōfuku-ji belongs to the Rinzai sect of Zen Buddhism. As this temple was intended to compare with Tōdai-ji and Kōfuku-ji in Nara, it was given a name combining characters from the names of each of these temples.

The present temple complex includes 24 subtemples; at one time there were 53. The huge **San-mon** is the oldest Zen main gate in Japan. The **Hōjō** (Abbot's Hall) was reconstructed in 1890; the Zen garden outside the Hōjō is pictured above. The gardens, laid out in 1938, are well worth a visit. The northern garden has stones and moss neatly arranged in a chequerboard pattern. From a viewing platform at the back of the gardens, you can observe the **Tsūten-kyō** (Bridge to Heaven), which spans a valley filled with maples.

Tōfuku-ji offers regular Zen meditation sessions for beginners, but don't expect coddling or English-language explanations: this is the real deal. Get a Japanese speaker to inquire at the temple about the next session (it holds about four a month for beginners).

Note that Tōfuku-ji is one of Kyoto's most famous autumn foliage spots, and it is invariably packed during the peak of colours in November. Otherwise, it's often very quiet.

NEED TO KNOW

東福寺; Map p208; 15-778 Honmahi, Higashiyama-ku; admission garden ¥400, Tsūten-kyō bridge ¥400, grounds free; 🕑9am-4pm Apr-Oct, 8.30am-4pm Nov-early Dec, 9am-3.30pm early Dec-Mar; 🚉Keihan line to Tōfukuji, JR Nara line to Tōfukuji

If You Like...
Temples

If you like Nanzen-ji, you'll like these other beautiful but slightly less visited temples:

1 EIKAN-DŌ

(永観堂; Map p224; 48 Eikandō-chō, Sakyō-ku; admission ¥600; ⏰9am-5pm; 🚌Kyoto City bus 5 to Eikandō-michi, Ⓢ Tōzai line to Keage) Perhaps Kyoto's most famous (and most crowded) autumn-foliage destination, Eikan-dō is a superb temple just a short walk south of the famous Path of Philosophy. Eikan-dō is made interesting by its varied architecture, its gardens and its works of art. It was founded as Zenrin-ji in 855 by the priest Shinshō, but the name was changed to Eikan-dō in the 11th century to honour the philanthropic priest Eikan.

2 KENNIN-JI

(建仁寺; Map p218; 584 Komatsu-chō, Yamatoōji-dōri, Shijo-sagaru, Higashiyama-ku; admission ¥500; ⏰10am-4pm; 🚌Keihan line to Gion-Shijō) Founded in 1202 by the monk Eisai, Kennin-ji is the oldest Zen temple in Kyoto. It is an island of peace and calm on the border of the boisterous Gion nightlife district and it makes a fine counterpoint to the worldly pleasures of that area. The highlight at Kennin-ji is the fine and expansive *karesansui* (dry-landscape rock garden). The painting of the twin dragons on the roof of the **Hōdō** hall is also fantastic.

3 MYŌSHIN-JI

(妙心寺; Map p208; 1 Myōshin-ji-chō, Hanazono, Ukyō-ku; admission to main temple free, other areas of complex ¥500; ⏰9.10-11.50am & 1-3.40pm; 🚌Kyoto City bus 10 from Sanjo-Keihan to Myōshin-ji Kita-mon-mae) Myōshin-ji is a separate world within Kyoto, a walled-off complex of temples and subtemples that invites lazy strolling. The subtemple of **Taizō-in** here contains one of the city's more interesting gardens. Myōshin-ji dates from 1342 and belongs to the Rinzai school. There are 47 subtemples, but only a few are open to the public.

Kyoto, has been regarded as a holy site by followers of the Jōdo school of Buddhism. The region provides a charming glimpse of rural Japan, along with the picturesque Sanzen-in, Jakkō-in and several other fine temples. It is most popular in autumn, when the maple leaves change colour and the mountain views are spectacular. During the peak foliage season of November, this area can get very crowded, especially on weekends. Kyoto bus 17 or 18 from Kyoto Station will drop you to the Ōhara stop (¥600, one hour).

Sanzen-in   Buddhist Temple

(三千院; 540 Raikōin-chō, Ōhara, Sakyō-ku; admission ¥700; ⏰9am-5pm Mar-Nov, to 4.30pm Dec-Feb; 🚌Kyoto bus 17 or 18 from Kyoto Station to Ōhara) Famed for its autumn foliage, hydrangea garden and stunning Buddha images, this temple is deservedly popular with foreign and domestic tourists alike. The temple's garden, **Yūsei-en**, is one of the most photographed sights in Japan, and rightly so.

Take some time to sit on the steps of the **Shin-den** hall and admire the beauty of the Yūsei-en. Then head off to see **Ōjō-gokuraku-in** (Temple of Rebirth in Paradise), the hall in which stands the impressive Amitabha trinity, a large Amida image flanked by attendants Kannon and Seishi (god of wisdom). After this, walk up to the garden at the back of the temple where, in late spring and summer, you can walk among hectares of blooming hydrangeas.

Sanzen-in was founded in 784 by the priest Saichō and belongs to the Tendai school. Saichō, considered one of the great patriarchs of Buddhism in Japan, also founded Enryaku-ji.

If you're keen for a short hike after leaving the temple, continue up the hill to see the rather oddly named **Soundless Waterfall** (Oto-nashi-no-taki; 音無の滝). Though in fact it sounds like any other waterfall, its resonance is believed to have inspired Shōmyō Buddhist chanting.

The approach to Sanzen-in is opposite the bus stop; there is no English sign but you can usually just follow the Japanese tourists. The temple is located about

600m up this walk on your left as you crest the hill.

Jakkō-in
Buddhist Temple

(寂光院; 676 Kusao-chō, Ōhara, Sakyō-ku; admission ¥600; ⏰9am-5pm Mar-Nov, to 4.30pm Dec-Feb; 🚌Kyoto bus 17 or 18 from Kyoto Station to Ōhara) Jakkō-in sits on the opposite side of Ōhara from the famous Sanzen-in. It's reached by a very pleasant walk through a quaint 'old Japan' village. It's a relatively small temple and makes an interesting end point to a fine walk in the country.

KURAMA & KIBUNE

Only 30 minutes north of Kyoto on the Eiden Eizan main line, Kurama (鞍馬) and Kibune (貴船) are a pair of tranquil valleys long favoured by Kyotoites as places to escape the crowds and stresses of the city below. Kurama's main attractions are its mountain temple and its onsen (hot springs). Kibune, over the ridge, is a cluster of ryokan (traditional inns) overlooking a mountain stream. It is best enjoyed in the summer, when the ryokan serve dinner on platforms built over the rushing waters of the Kibune-gawa, providing welcome relief from the summer heat.

The two valleys lend themselves to being explored together. In the winter one can start from Kibune, walk for an hour or so over the ridge, visit Kurama-dera and then soak in the onsen before heading back to Kyoto. In the summer the reverse is best; start from Kurama, walk up to the temple, then down the other side to Kibune to enjoy a meal suspended above the cool river.

If you happen to be in Kyoto on the night of 22 October, be sure not to miss the **Kurama-no-hi Matsuri** (Kurama Fire Festival), one of the most exciting festivals in the Kyoto area.

To get to Kurama and Kibune, take the Eiden Eizan line from Kyoto's Demachiyanagi Station. For Kibune, get off at the second-to-last stop, Kibune Guchi, take a right out of the station and walk about 20 minutes up the hill. For Kurama, go to the last stop, Kurama, and walk straight out of the station. Both destinations are ¥410 and take about 30 minutes to reach.

Kurama-dera
Buddhist Temple

(鞍馬寺; 1074 Kurama Honmachi, Sakyō-ku; admission ¥200; ⏰9am-4.30pm; 🚌Eiden Eizan line from Demachiyanagi to Kurama) Located high on a thickly wooded mountain, Kurama-dera is one of the few temples in modern Japan that still manages to retain an air of real spirituality. This is a magical place that gains a lot of its power from its brilliant natural setting.

The temple also has a fascinating history: in 770 the monk Gantei left Nara's Toshōdai-ji in search of a wilderness sanctuary in which to meditate. Wandering in the hills north of Kyoto, he came across a white horse

Sanzen-in

Below: Detail of a Gion Matsuri parade float; **Right:** Costumed women taking part in Aoi Matsuri

(BELOW) FRANK CARTER/GETTY IMAGES ©; (RIGHT) FRANK CARTER/GETTY IMAGES ©

that led him to the valley known today as Kurama. After seeing a vision of the deity Bishamon-ten, guardian of the northern quarter of the Buddhist heaven, Gantei established Kurama-dera just below the peak of Kurama-yama. Originally belonging to the Tendai school of Buddhism, Kurama has been independent since 1949, describing its own brand of Buddhism as Kurama-kyō.

The entrance to the temple is just up the hill from Kurama Station. A tram goes to the top for ¥100 or you can hike up in about 30 minutes (follow the main path past the tram station). The trail is worth taking (if it's not too hot), since it winds through a forest of towering old-growth cryptomeria trees, passing by **Yuki-jinja**, a small Shintō shrine, on the way. Near the peak, there is a courtyard dominated by the **Honden** (Main Hall); behind this a trail leads off to the mountain's peak.

At the top, you can take a brief detour across the ridge to **Ōsugi-gongen**, a quiet shrine in a grove of trees. Those who want to continue to Kibune can take the trail down the other side. It's a 1.2km, 30-minute hike from the Honden to the valley floor of Kibune. On the way down are two mountain shrines, **Sōjō-ga-dani Fudō-dō** and **Okuno-in Maō-den**, which make pleasant rest stops.

Kurama Onsen
Onsen

(鞍馬温泉; 520 Kurama Honmachi, Sakyō-ku; admission outdoor bath only ¥1000, outdoor & indoor bath ¥2500; ☉10am-9pm; ⊠Eiden Eizan line from Demachiyanagi to Kurama) One of the few onsen within easy reach of Kyoto, Kurama Onsen is a great place to relax after a hike. The outdoor bath has fine views of Kurama-yama, while the indoor bath area includes some relaxation areas in addition to the tubs. For both baths, buy a ticket from the machine outside the door of the main building.

236

To get to Kurama Onsen, walk straight out of Kurama Station and continue up the main street, passing the entrance to Kurama-dera on your left. The onsen is about 10 minutes' walk on the right. There's also a free shuttle bus between the station and the onsen, which meets incoming trains.

Festivals & Events

There are hundreds of festivals happening in Kyoto throughout the year. Listings of these can be found in the *Kyoto Visitor's Guide* or *Kansai Scene*. The following are some of the major and most spectacular festivals. These attract hordes of spectators from out of town, so you will need to book accommodation well in advance.

Setsubun Matsuri at Yoshida-jinja   Religious

This festival is held on the day of *setsubun* (2, 3 or 4 February; check with the TIC), which marks the last day of winter in the Japanese lunar calendar. In this festival, people climb up to Yoshida-jinja in the Northern Higashiyama area to watch a huge bonfire (in which old good luck charms are burned). It's one of Kyoto's more dramatic festivals. The action starts at dusk.

Aoi Matsuri   Parade

The Hollyhock Festival dates back to the 6th century and commemorates the successful prayers of the people for the gods to stop calamitous weather. These days the procession involves imperial messengers carried in ox carts and a retinue of 600 people dressed in traditional costume. The procession leaves at around 10am on 15 May from the Kyoto Gosho and heads for Shimogamo-jinja.

Gion Matsuri   Parade

Kyoto's most important festival, Gion Matsuri reaches a climax on 17 July with a parade of over 30 floats and a smaller parade on 24 July. On the three evenings

Detour:
Takao

Takao (高雄) is a secluded mountain village tucked far away in the northwestern part of Kyoto. It is famed for autumn foliage and the temples of Jingo-ji, Saimyō-ji and Kōzan-ji.

There are two options for buses to Takao: an hourly JR bus that leaves from Kyoto Station, which takes about an hour to reach the Takao stop (get off at the Yamashiro-Takao stop); and Kyoto city bus 8 from Shijō-Karasuma (get off at the Takao stop). To get to Jingo-ji from these bus stops, walk down to the river, then look for the steps on the other side.

preceding the 17th, people gather on Shijō-dōri dressed in beautiful *yukata* (light summer kimonos), to look at the floats and carouse from one street stall to the next.

Daimon-ji Gozan Okuribi   Cultural
This festival is celebrated on 16 August as a means of bidding farewell to the souls of ancestors. Enormous fires, in the form of Chinese characters or other shapes, are lit on five mountains. The largest fire is burned on Daimon-ji-yama, just above Ginkaku-ji, in Northern Higashiyama. The fires start at 8pm and the best perspective is from the banks of the Kamo-gawa.

Jidai Matsuri   Parade
The Festival of the Ages is of comparatively recent origin, only dating back to 1895. More than 2000 people, dressed in costumes ranging from the 8th century to the 19th century, parade from Kyoto Gosho to Heian-jingū on 22 October.

Kurama-no-hi Matsuri   Cultural
In perhaps Kyoto's most dramatic festival, the Kurama Fire Festival, huge flaming torches are carried through the streets of Kurama by men in loincloths on 22 October (the same day as the Jidai Matsuri). Note that trains to and from Kurama will be completely packed with passengers on the evening of the festival (we suggest going early and returning late).

Sleeping

The most convenient areas in which to be based, in terms of easy access to shopping, dining and sightseeing attractions, are downtown Kyoto and the Higashiyama area. The Kyoto Station area is also a good location, with excellent access to transport and plenty of shops and restaurants about. Transport information in the following listings is from Kyoto Station unless otherwise noted.

KYOTO STATION AREA

Capsule Ryokan Kyoto   Capsule Hotel ¥
(カプセル旅館京都; Map p212; ☎344-1510; www.capsule-ryokan-kyoto.com; 204 Tsuchihashi-chō, Shimogyō-ku; capsule ¥3500, tw per person from ¥3990; @ 🛜; 🚉 Kyoto Station) This unique new accommodation offers ryokan-style capsules (meaning tatami mats inside the capsules), as well as comfortable, cleverly designed private rooms. Each capsule also has its own TV and cable internet access point, while the private rooms have all the amenities you might need. Free internet, wi-fi and other amenities are available in the comfortable lounge.

It's near the southeast corner of the Horikawa–Shichijō intersection.

Tour Club   Guesthouse ¥
(ツアークラブ; Map p212; ☎075-353-6968; www.kyotojp.com; 362 Momiji-chō, Higashi-nakasuji, Shōmen-sagaru, Shimogyō-ku; d/tw/tr per person ¥3490/3885/2960; 🌐 @ 🛜; 🚉 Kyoto Station) This well-maintained guesthouse remains a favourite of foreign visitors to Kyoto. Facilities include internet access, a small Zen garden, laundry,

wi-fi, and free tea and coffee. Most private rooms have a private bathroom and toilet, and there is a spacious quad room for families. This is probably the best choice in this price bracket.

From Kyoto Station turn north off Shichijō-dōri two blocks before Horikawa (at the faux-Greco building) and keep an eye out for the English sign.

Budget Inn   Guesthouse ¥
(バジェットイン; Map p212; 📞075-344-1510; www.budgetinnjp.com; 295 Aburanokōji-chō, Aburanokōji, Shichijō-sagaru, Shimogyō-ku; tr/q/5-person r per person ¥3660/3245/2996; ➡@🛜; 🚉Kyoto Station) This well-run guesthouse is an excellent choice in this price bracket. It has eight Japanese-style private rooms, all of which are clean and well maintained. All rooms have a private bathroom and toilet, and can accommodate up to five people, making it good for families. The staff is very helpful and friendly, and internet access, laundry and wi-fi are available

Ryokan Shimizu   Ryokan ¥
(京の宿しみず; Map p212; 📞371-5538; www. kyoto-shimizu.net; 644 Kagiya-chō, Shichijō-dōri, Wakamiya-agaru, Shimogyō-ku; r per person from ¥5250, Sat & nights before holidays plus ¥1080; ➡@; 🚉Kyoto Station) A short walk north of Kyoto Station's Karasuma central gate, this friendly ryokan has a loyal following of foreign guests, and for good reason: it's clean, well run and fun. Rooms are standard ryokan style with one difference: all have private bathrooms and toilets. Bicycle rental is available.

Ibis Styles Kyoto Station   Hotel ¥¥
(イビススタイルズ 京都ステーション; Map p212; 📞693-8444; www.ibis.com; 47 Higashikujō-Kamitonoda-chō, Minami-ku; r from ¥6500-10,000; 🚉Kyoto Station) This great new business hotel just outside the south entrance to Kyoto Station offers excellent value. The rooms are small but packed with features you need. The staff and management are extremely efficient. All in all, this is a great option for the price.

Dormy Inn Premium
Kyoto Ekimae   Hotel ¥¥
(ドーミーインPREMIUM京都駅前; Map p212; 📞371-5489; www.hotespa.net/hotels/kyoto; Higashishiokōji-chō 558-8, Shimogyō-ku; tw/d from ¥12,500/11,890; @; 🚉Kyoto Station) Located almost directly across the street from Kyoto Station, this efficient new

Daimon-ji-yama bearing the character *dai* ('great') as part of Daimon-ji Gozan Okuribi

hotel is a great choice. Rooms are clean and well maintained and the on-site spa bath is a nice plus.

Hotel Granvia Kyoto   Hotel ¥¥¥
(ホテルグランヴィア京都; Map p212; ☎344-8888; www.granviakyoto.com; Karasuma-dōri, Shiokōji-sagaru, Shimogyō-ku; tw/d from ¥16,000/21,000; ❄️@♨️; 🚉Kyoto Station) Imagine being able to step out of bed and straight into the *shinkansen* (bullet train). This is almost possible when you stay at the Hotel Granvia, which is located directly above Kyoto Station. The rooms are clean, spacious and elegant, with deep bathtubs. This is a very professional operation with good on-site restaurants, some of which have views over the city.

DOWNTOWN KYOTO

Hotel Sunroute Kyoto   Hotel ¥¥
(ホテルサンルート京都; Map p218; ☎371-3711; www.sunroute.jp; 406 Nanba-chō, Kawaramachi-dōri, Matsubara-sagaru, Shimogyō-ku; r ¥6300-10,000; @🛜; 🚉Hankyū line to Kawaramachi) Located within easy walking distance of downtown, this brand-new hotel is a superb choice in this price bracket. As you'd expect, rooms aren't large, but

they have everything you need. It's well run and comfortable with foreign travellers. In-room internet is LAN cable only, but there's free wi-fi in the 2nd-floor lobby.

Hotel Unizo   Hotel ¥¥
(ホテルユニゾ京都; Map p214; ☎241-3351; www.hotelunizo.com/eng/kyoto; Kawaramachi-dōri, Sanjō-sagaru, Nakagyō-ku; s/d/tw from ¥10,000/17,000/19,000; ❄️@🛜; 🚌Kyoto City bus 5 to Kawaramachi-Sanjō, 🅂Tōzai line to Kyoto-Shiyakusho-mae) They don't get more convenient than this business hotel: it's smack in the middle of Kyoto's nightlife, shopping and dining district – you can walk to hundreds of restaurants and shops within five minutes. It's a standard-issue business hotel, with tiny but adequate rooms and unit bathrooms. Nothing special, but it's clean, well run and used to foreign guests

Mitsui Garden Hotel Kyoto Sanjō   Hotel ¥¥
(三井ガーデンホテル 京都三条; Map p214; ☎256-3331; www.gardenhotels.co.jp/eng/kyoto-sanjo; 80 Mikura-chō, Sanjō-dōri, Karasuma nishi-iru, Nakagyō-ku; s/d/tw from ¥6000/8700/9600; @; 🅂Tōzai or Karasuma lines to Karasuma-Oike) Just west of the

Hiiragiya Ryokan

downtown dining and shopping district, this is a clean and efficient hotel that offers good value for the price and reasonably comfortable rooms.

Royal Park Hotel The Kyoto
Hotel ¥¥

(ロイヤルパークホテル ザ 京都; Map p214; ☎ 241-1111; www.rph-the.co.jp; Sanjō-dōri, Kawaramachi higashi-iru, Nakagyō-ku; s/d from ¥10,000/12,500; 🛜; Ⓢ Tōzai line to Kyoto-Shiyakusho-mae, Ⓡ Keihan line to Sanjō) Located on Sanjō-dōri, a stone's throw from the river, this hotel commands a super-convenient location, with tons of shops and restaurants within easy walking distance. The hotel has a modern, chic feel, and rooms are slightly larger than at standard business hotels. The French bakery downstairs makes breakfast a breeze.

Tawaraya
Ryokan ¥¥¥

(俵屋; Map p214; ☎ 211-5566; 278 Nakahakusan-chō, Fuyachō, Oike-sagaru, Nakagyō-ku; r per person incl 2 meals ¥55,900-74,500; 🍽 @; Ⓢ Tōzai line to Kyoto-Shiyakusho-mae, exit 8) Tawaraya has been operating for more than three centuries and is one of the finest places to stay in the world. From the decorations to the service to the food, everything is simply the best available. It's a very intimate, warm and personal place that has many loyal guests.

It's centrally located within easy walk of two subway stations and plenty of good restaurants.

Kyoto Hotel Ōkura
Hotel ¥¥¥

(京都ホテルオークラ; Map p214; ☎ 211-5111; http://okura.kyotohotel.co.jp; 537-4 Ichinofunairi-chō, Kawaramachi-dōri, Oike, Nakagyō-ku; s/d/tw from ¥13,600/23,000/18,400; 🍽 @; Ⓢ Tōzai line to Kyoto-Shiyakusho-mae, exit 3) This towering hotel in the centre of town commands an impressive view of the Higashiyama mountains. Rooms are clean and spacious and many have great views, especially the excellent corner suites – we just wish we could open a window to enjoy the breeze.

You can access the Kyoto subway system directly from the hotel, which is convenient on rainy days or if you have luggage. You can often find great online

rates for the Ōkura and it's one of the better value places in this price bracket.

Hiiragiya Ryokan
Ryokan ¥¥¥

(柊屋; Map p214; ☎ 221-1136; www.hiiragiya.co.jp; Nakahakusan-chō, Fuyachō, Aneyakōji-agaru, Nakagyō-ku; r per person incl 2 meals ¥34,560-86,400; 🍽 @; Ⓢ Tōzai line to Kyoto-Shiyakusho-mae, exit 8) This elegant ryokan has long been favoured by celebrities from around the world. Facilities and services are excellent and the location is hard to beat. Ask for one of the newly redecorated rooms if you prefer a polished sheen; alternatively, request an older room if you fancy some 'Old Japan' *wabi-sabi* (imperfect beauty).

Ritz-Carlton Kyoto
Hotel ¥¥¥

(ザ・リッツ・カールトン京都; Map p224; ☎ 746-5555; www.ritzcarlton.com; 543 Hokoden-chō, Nijō-Ōhashi-hotori, Nakagyō-ku; r ¥65,000-200,000; @ 🛜; Ⓢ Tōzai line to Kyoto-Shiyakusho-mae, Ⓡ Keihan line to Sanjō or Jingū-Marutamachi) The brand-new Ritz-Carlton is an oasis of luxury that commands perhaps the finest views of any hotel in the city – it's located on the banks for the Kamo-gawa and huge windows in the east-facing rooms take in the whole expanse of the Higashiyama mountains. The rooms are superbly designed and supremely comfortable, with plenty of Japanese touches.

Common areas are elegant and the on-site restaurants and bars are excellent. Finally, there are fine spa, gym and pool facilities.

CENTRAL KYOTO

Palace Side Hotel
Hotel ¥¥

(ザ・パレスサイドホテル; Map p208; ☎ 415-8887; www.palacesidehotel.co.jp; Okakuen-chō, Karasuma-dōri, Shimotachiuri-agaru, Kamigyō-ku; s/tw/d from ¥6300/10,200/10,200; 🍽 @; Ⓢ Karasuma line to Marutamachi) Overlooking the Kyoto Imperial Palace Park, this excellent-value hotel has a lot going for it, starting with a friendly English-speaking staff, great service, washing machines, an on-site restaurant, well-maintained rooms and free internet terminals. The rooms are small but serviceable.

Tōyoko Inn Kyoto Gojō Karasuma — Hotel ¥¥

(東横INN京都五条烏丸; Map p208; ☎ 344-1045; www.toyoko-inn.com; Gojō Karasuma-chō 393, Karasuma-dōri, Matsubara-sagaru, Shimogyō-ku; s/tw incl breakfast from ¥6804/10,044; @; S Karasuama line to Gojō) Those familiar with the Tōyoko Inn chain know that this hotel brand specialises in simple, clean, fully equipped but small rooms at the lowest price possible. There are all kinds of interesting extras: free breakfast, free telephone calls inside Japan, and reduced rates on rental cars. Staff will even lend you a laptop if you need to check your email.

It's a little south of the city centre, but easily accessed by subway from Kyoto Station.

Citadines Karasuma-Gojō Kyoto — Hotel ¥¥¥

(シタディーン京都 烏丸五条; Map p208; ☎ 352-8900; www.citadines.jp; Matsuya-chō 432, Gojō-dōri, Karasuma higashi-iru, Shimogyō-ku; tw/d from ¥28,600/28,600; @; S Karasuma line to Gojō) On Gojō-dōri, a bit south of the main downtown district, but within easy walking distance of the Karasuma subway line (as well as the Keihan line), this serviced apartment–hotel is a welcome addition to the Kyoto accommodation scene. The kitchens allow you to do your own cooking and other touches make you feel right at home.

SOUTHERN HIGASHIYAMA

Hyatt Regency Kyoto — Hotel ¥¥¥

(ハイアットリージェンシー京都; Map p218; ☎ 541-1234; www.kyoto.regency.hyatt.com; 644-2 Sanjūsangendō-mawari, Higashiyama-ku; r from ¥28,500; ☺@☎; R Keihan line to Shichijō) The Hyatt Regency is an excellent, stylish and foreigner-friendly hotel at the southern end of Kyoto's Southern Higashiyama sightseeing district. Many travellers consider this the best hotel in Kyoto. The staff are extremely efficient and helpful (there are even foreign staff members – something of a rarity in Japan). The on-site restaurants and bar are excellent.

The stylish rooms and bathrooms have lots of neat touches. The concierges are knowledgeable about the city and they'll even lend you a laptop to check your email if you don't have your own.

Seikōrō — Ryokan ¥¥¥

(晴鴨楼; Map p218; ☎ 561-0771; www.ryokan.asia; 467 Nishi Tachibana-chō, 3 chō-me, Toiyamachi-dori, Gojō-sagaru, Higashiyama-ku; r per person incl 2 meals from ¥21,600; ☺@☎; R Keihan line to Kiyomizu-Gojō) The Seikōrō is a classic ryokan with a grandly decorated lobby. It's fairly spacious, with excellent, comfortable rooms, attentive service and a fairly convenient midtown location. Several of the rooms look over gardens and all have private bathrooms.

Women in traditional dress
COWARDLION/SHUTTERSTOCK ©

Motonago
Ryokan ¥¥¥

(旅館元奈古; Map p218; ☎561-2087; www.
motonago.com; 511 Washio-chō, Kōdaiji-michi,
Higashiyama-ku; r per person incl 2 meals from
¥18,350; 🚭@🛜; 🚌Kyoto City bus 206 to
Gion) This ryokan may have the best
location of any in the city, and it hits
all the right notes for one in this class:
classic Japanese decor, friendly service,
nice bathtubs and a few small Japanese
gardens.

NORTHERN HIGASHIYAMA

Westin Miyako Kyoto
Hotel ¥¥¥

(ウェスティン都ホテル京都; Map p224;
☎771-7111; www.miyakohotels.ne.jp/westin
kyoto; Keage, Sanjō-dōri, Higashiyama-ku; d/
tw from ¥16,200/16,200, Japanese-style r from
¥18,360; 🚭@🛜⛴; 🚇Tōzai line to Keage, exit
2) This grande dame of Kyoto hotels occupies a commanding position overlooking the Higashiyama sightseeing district
(meaning it's one of the best locations for
sightseeing in Kyoto). Rooms are clean
and well maintained, and staff are at
home with foreign guests. Rooms on the
north side have great views over the city
to the Kitayama mountains.

There is a fitness centre, as well as
a private garden and walking trail. The
hotel even has its own ryokan section for
those who want to try staying in a ryokan
without giving up the convenience of a
hotel.

ARASHIYAMA & SAGANO

Hoshinoya Kyoto
Ryokan ¥¥¥

(星のや京都; Map p208; ☎871-0001;
http://kyoto.hoshinoya.com/en; Arashiyama
Genrokuzan-chō 11-2, Nishikyō-ku; r per person
incl meals from ¥70,296; 🚌Kyoto City bus 28
from Kyoto Station to Arashiyama-Tenryuji-mae,
🚉JR Sagano/San-in line to Saga-Arashiyama or
Hankyū line to Arashiyama, change at Katsura)
Sitting in a secluded area on the south
bank of the Hozu-gawa in Arashiyama
(upstream from the main sightseeing
district), this modern take on the classic Japanese inn is quickly becoming a
favourite of well-heeled visitors to Kyoto
in search of privacy and a unique experience. Rooms feature incredible views of
the river and the surrounding mountains.

The best part is the approach: you'll be
chauffeured by a private boat from a dock
near Togetsu-kyō bridge to the inn (note
that on days following heavy rains, you'll
have to go by car instead). This is easily
one of the most unique places to stay in
Kyoto.

KANSAI AIRPORT

Hotel Nikkō
Kansai Airport
Hotel ¥¥

(ホテル日航関西空港; ☎072-455-1111; www.
nikkokix.com; Senshū Kūkō Kita 1, Izumisano-shi,
Osaka-fu; s/tw/d from ¥9500/11,000/14,500 ;
@🛜⛴; 🚉JR Haruka Airport Express to Kansai
Airport) The only hotel at the airport is the
excellent Hotel Nikkō Kansai Airport, connected to the main terminal building by
a pedestrian bridge (you can even bring
your luggage trolleys right to your room).
The rooms here are in good condition,
spacious and comfortable enough for
brief stays.

 # Eating

Kyoto is a great place to explore Japanese
cuisine and you'll find good restaurants
regardless of your budget. If you tire of
Japanese food, there are plenty of excellent international restaurants to choose
from. You'll find the thickest concentration of eateries in downtown Kyoto, but
also great choices in Southern Higashiy-
ama/Gion and in and around Kyoto
Station.

Because Kyoto gets a lot of foreign
travellers, you'll find a surprising number
of English menus and most places are
quite comfortable with foreign guests.

KYOTO STATION AREA

Kyoto Station building is chock-a-block
with restaurants, and if you find yourself anywhere near the station around
mealtime, this is probably your best bet in
terms of variety and price.

There are several food courts scattered
about the station building. The best of
these can be found on the 11th floor on the
west side of the building: the **Cube**
(ザ キューブ; Map p212; ☎371-2134; 11F Kyoto
Station Bldg, Karasuma-dōri, Shiokōji-sagaru,

Below: Udon noodles; **Right:** Nishiki Market (p210)

(BELOW) TENGNKOH@PHOTOGRAPHY/GETTY IMAGES ©; (RIGHT) LEWIS TSE PUI LUNG/GETTY IMAGES ©

Shimogyō-ku; 11am-10pm; Kyoto Station) food court and Isetan department store's **Eat Paradise** (イートパラダイス; Map p212; 352-1111; 11F Kyoto Station Bldg, Karasuma-dōri, Shiokōji-sagaru, Shimogyō-ku; 11am-10pm; Kyoto Station) food court. In Eat Paradise, we like Tonkatsu Wako for *tonkatsu* (deep-fried breaded pork cutlet), Tenichi for sublime tempura, and Wakuden for approachable *kaiseki* fare. To get to these food courts, take the west escalators from the main concourse all the way up to the 11th floor and look for the Cube on your left and Eat Paradise straight in front of you.

Other options in the station include **Kyoto Rāmen Koji** (京都拉麺小路; Map p212; 361-4401; 10F Kyoto Station Bldg, Karasuma-dōri, Shiokōji-sagaru, Shimogyō-ku; rāmen ¥700-1000; 11am-10pm; Kyoto Station), a collection of seven *rāmen* restaurants on the 10th floor (underneath the Cube). Buy tickets from the machines, which don't have English but have pictures on the buttons. In addition to *rāmen*, you can get green-tea ice cream and other Japanese desserts at Chasen, and *tako-yaki* (battered octopus pieces) at Miyako.

DOWNTOWN KYOTO

Downtown Kyoto has the best variety of approachable Japanese and international restaurants.

Ippūdō   Rāmen ¥

(一風堂; Map p214; 213-8800; Higashinotō-in, Nishikikōji higashi-iru, Nakagyō-ku; rāmen ¥750-950; 11am-2am; ; S Karasuma line to Shijō) There's a reason that there's usually a line outside this *rāmen* joint at lunchtime: the *rāmen* is awesome and the bite-sized *gyōza* (Chinese dumplings) are to die for. We recommend the *gyōza* set meal (¥750 or ¥850 depending on your choice of *rāmen*). It's on Nishiki-dōri, next to a post office and diagonally across from a Starbucks.

Kerala · Indian ¥

(ケララ; Map p214; ☎251-0141; 2nd fl, KUS Bldg, Kawaramachi-dōri, Sanjō-agaru, Nakagyō-ku; lunch/dinner from ¥850/2600; ⏲11.30am-2pm & 5-9pm; ✍️🏠; ⓢTōzai line to Kyoto-Shiyakusho-mae) This narrow restaurant upstairs on Kawaramachi-dōri is Kyoto's best Indian restaurant. The ¥850 lunch set menu is an excellent deal, as is the vegetarian lunch, and the English menu is a bonus. Dinners run closer to ¥2500 per head and are of very high quality. Finish off the meal with the incredibly rich and creamy coconut ice cream.

Nishiki Warai · Okonomiyaki ¥

(錦わらい; Map p214; ☎257-5966; 1st fl, Mizukōto Bldg, 597 Nishiuoya-chō, Nishikikōji-dōri, Takakura nishi-iru, Nakagyō-ku; okonomiyaki from ¥680; ⏲11.30am-midnight; 🏠; ⓢKarasuma line to Shijō, ⓡHankyū line to Karasuma) This Nishiki-dōri restaurant is a great place to try okonomiyaki (Japanese pancakes) in casual surroundings. It can get a little smoky, but it's a fun spot to eat. It serves sets from as little as ¥680

at lunch. It's about 20m west of the west end of Nishiki Market; look for the English sign in the window.

Saryo Zen Cafe · Cafe ¥

(茶寮「然」カフェ; Map p214; Zenkashoin Kyoto Muromachi Store, 271-1 Takoyakushi-chō, Muromachi-dōri, Nijō-sagaru, Nakagyō-ku; drinks from ¥1000; ⏲10am-7pm, closed 2nd & 4th Mon of month; 🏠; ⓢKarasuma or Tōzai line to Karasuma-Oike) This brilliant modern tea room is a great place for a break – a break from sightseeing and a break from the ubiquitous international coffee chains that are taking over the city. You can enjoy a nice cup of matcha tea here served with a delicious Kyoto sweet, all in extremely comfortable surroundings.

Café Bibliotec Hello! · Cafe ¥

(カフェビブリオティックハロー！; Map p214; ☎231-8625; 650 Seimei-chō, Nijō-dōri, Yanaginobanba higashi-iru, Nakagyō-ku; meals from ¥1000, coffee ¥450; ⏲11.30am-midnight; 🏠; ⓢTōzai line to Kyoto-Shiyakusho-mae) As the name suggests, books line the walls

245

Department Store Dining

Yes, we know: the idea of dining in a department store sounds as appetising as dining in a gas station. However, Japanese department stores, especially those in large cities such as Tokyo and Kyoto, are loaded with good dining options. And, unlike many street-level shops, they're usually fairly comfortable with foreign diners (if there's any communication trouble, they can always call down to the bilingual staff at the information counter).

On their basement floors, you'll find *depachika* (from the English word 'department' and the Japanese word *chika,* which means 'underground'). A good *depachika* is like an Aladdin's cave of gustatory delights that rivals the best gourmet shops in any Western city. Meanwhile, on their upper floors, you'll usually find a *resutoran-gai* ('restaurant city') that includes restaurants serving all the Japanese standards – sushi, noodles, *tonkatsu,* tempura – along with a few international restaurants, usually French, Italian and Chinese.

If you find yourself feeling peckish in downtown Kyoto, here are some good department dining options:

Takashimaya (p253), at the corner of Shijō and Kawaramachi streets, is an elegant department store with an incredible food floor (on the B1 level) and the best department store *resutoran-gai* in the city (on the 7th floor).

Daimaru (p253) is on the north side of Shijō, between Kawaramachi and Karasuma streets. It has a food floor that rivals the one at Takashimaya (note the awesome Japanese sweet section) and a solid *resutoran-gai* on the 8th floor.

of this cool cafe located in a converted *machiya* (traditional Japanese town house). You can get the usual range of coffee and tea drinks here, as well as light cafe lunches. It's popular with young ladies who work nearby and it's a great place to relax with a book or magazine. Look for the plants out the front.

Honke Tagoto   Noodles ¥
(本家田每; Map p214; ☎ 221-3030; 12 Ishibashi-chō, Sanjō-dōri, Kawaramachi Nishi iru, Nakagyō-ku; noodle dishes from ¥840; ⏰11am-9pm; 🖪; Ⓢ Tōzai Line to Kyoto Shiyakusho-mae) One of Kyoto's oldest *soba* restaurants makes a good break for those who have overdosed on *rāmen*. It's in the Sanjō covered arcade and you can see inside to the tables.

Musashi Sushi   Sushi ¥
(寿しのむさし; Map p214; ☎ 222-0634; Kawaramachi-dōri, Sanjō-agaru, Nakagyō-ku; all plates ¥140; ⏰11am-10pm; 🖪; Ⓢ Tōzai line to Kyoto-Shiyakusho-mae, 🚃 Keihan line to Sanjō) If you've never tried *kaiten-zushi* (conveyor-

belt sushi restaurant), don't miss this place – all the dishes are a mere ¥140. It's not the best sushi in the world, but it's cheap, reliable and fun. Needless to say, it's easy to eat here: you just grab what you want off the conveyor belt.

Kyōgoku Kane-yo   Unagi ¥¥
(京極かねよ; Map p214; ☎ 221-0669; 456 Matsugaechō, Rokkaku, Shinkyōgoku higashi-iru, Nakagyō-ku; unagi over rice from ¥1200; ⏰11.30am-9pm; 🖪; Ⓢ Tōzai line to Kyoto-Shiyakusho-mae) This is a good place to try *unagi* (eel), that most sublime of Japanese dishes. You can choose to either sit downstairs with a nice view of the waterfall, or upstairs on the tatami. The *kane-yo donburi* (eel over rice; ¥1200) set is excellent value. Look for the barrels of live eels outside and the wooden facade.

Ganko   Sushi ¥¥
(がんこ; Map p214; ☎ 255-1128; 101 Nakajima-chō, Sanjō-dōri, Kawaramachi higashi-iru, Nakagyō-ku; lunch ¥1000-2500, dinner around

¥5000; ⏰11am-11pm; 📷; S Tōzai line to Kyoto-Shiyakusho-mae or Sanjō Keihan, R Keihan line to Sanjō) This giant four-storey dining hall is part of Kansai's biggest sushi chain. The ground floor is the sushi area (you can order non-sushi dishes here as well); it has a long sushi counter and plenty of tables (and room for a stroller if you have tots in tow). It's very popular with both tourists and locals.

Tsukiji Sushisei Sushi ¥¥
(築地寿司清; Map p214; 📞252-1537; 581 Obiya-chō, Takakura-dōri, Nishikikōji-sagaru, Nakagyō-ku; sushi sets ¥1296-3150; ⏰11.30am-3pm & 5-10pm Mon-Fri, 11.30am-10pm Sat, Sun & holidays; 📷; S Karasuma line to Shijō) On the basement floor, next to Daimaru department store, this simple sushi restaurant serves excellent sushi. You can order a set or just point at what looks good. You can see inside the restaurant from street level, so it should be easy to spot.

mumokuteki cafe Vegetarian ¥¥
(ムモクテキカフェ; Map p214; www.mumo kuteki.com; 2nd fl, Human Forum Bldg, 351 Iseya-chō, Gokomachi-dōri, Rokkaku-sagaru, Nakagyō-ku; meals from ¥1500; ⏰11.30am-10pm; 🍴📷; R Hankyū line to Kawaramachi) This vegetarian cafe hidden above a shop in the Teramachi shopping arcade is a lifesaver for many Kyoto vegetarians. The food is tasty, varied and served in casual surroundings. Most of it is vegan, but non-vegan options are clearly marked on the menu. It's hidden up a flight of steps above a clothing shop called Spinns.

The steps up to the restaurant are located inside the shop.

Kiyamachi Sakuragawa
Kaiseki ¥¥¥
(木屋町　櫻川; Map p214; 📞255-4477; Kiyamachi-dōri, Nijō-sagaru, Nakagyō-

ku; lunch/dinner sets from ¥5000/10,000; ⏰11.30am-2pm & 5-9pm, closed Sun; S Tōzai line to Kyoto-Shiyakusho-mae) This elegant restaurant on a scenic stretch of Kiyamachi-dōri is an excellent place to try *kaiseki*. The modest but fully satisfying food is beautifully presented and it's a joy to watch the chef in action. The warmth of the reception adds to the quality of the food. Reservations are recommended and smart casual is the way to go here.

Yoshikawa Tempura ¥¥¥
(吉川; Map p214; 📞221-5544; www.kyoto-yoshi kawa.co.jp; Tominokōji, Oike-sagaru, Nakagyō-ku; lunch ¥3000-25,000, dinner ¥6000-25,000; ⏰11am-2pm & 5-8.30pm; 📷; S Tōzai line to Karasuma-Oike or Kyoto-Shiyakusho-mae) This is the place to go for delectable tempura. It offers table seating, but it's much more interesting to sit and eat around the small counter and observe the chefs at work. It's near Oike-dōri in a fine traditional Japanese-style building. Reservation required for tatami room; counter and table seating unavailable on Sunday.

Tsukemono (Japanese pickles)
COL/SHUTTERSTOCK ©

Roan Kikunoi
Kaiseki ¥¥¥

(露庵菊乃井; Map p214; ☎361-5580; www.
kikunoi.jp; 118 Saito-chō, Kiyamachi-dōri,
Shijō-sagaru, Shimogyō-ku; lunch/dinner from
¥4000/10,000; ⏰11.30am-1.30pm & 5-8.30pm;
🚃 📶; 🚊Hankyū line to Kawaramachi, Keihan
line to Gion-Shijō) Roan Kikunoi is a fantastic
place to experience the wonders of
kaiseki cuisine. It's a clean, intimate space
located right downtown. The chef takes
an experimental and creative approach
to *kaiseki* and the results are a wonder for
the eyes and palate. It's highly recommended. Reserve through your hotel or
ryokan concierge.

SOUTHERN HIGASHIYAMA

Kasagi-ya
Teahouse ¥

(かさぎ屋; Map p218; ☎561-9562; 349 Masuya
chō, Kōdai-ji, Higashiyama-ku; tea & sweets from
¥600; ⏰11am-6pm, closed Tue; 📶; 🚌Kyoto
City bus 206 to Higashiyama-Yasui) At Kasagi-
ya, on Sannen-zaka near Kiyomizu-dera,
you can enjoy a nice cup of *matcha*
(powdered green tea) and a variety of
sweets. This funky old wooden shop has
atmosphere to boot and friendly staff –
which makes it worth the wait if there's a

queue. It's hard to spot – you may have to
ask one of the local shop owners.

Kagizen Yoshifusa
Teahouse ¥

(鍵善良房; Map p218; ☎561-1818; www.kagizen.
co.jp; 264 Gion machi, Kita-gawa, Higashiyama-
ku; kuzukiri ¥900; ⏰9.30am-6pm, closed Mon;
📶; 🚊Hankyū line to Kawaramachi, Keihan line
to Gion-Shijō) This Gion institution is one of
Kyoto's oldest and best-known *okashi-ya*
(sweet shops). It sells a variety of traditional sweets and has a lovely tea room
out the back where you can sample cold
kuzukiri (transparent arrowroot noodles)
served with a *kuro-mitsu* (sweet black
sugar) dipping sauce, or just a nice cup of
matcha and a sweet.

Rāmen Santōka
Rāmen ¥

(らーめん山頭火; Map p218; ☎532-1335; www.
santouka.co.jp; Yamatoōji-dōri, Sanjō-sagaru
Higashi gawa, Higashiyama-ku; rāmen from ¥770;
⏰11am-2am Mon-Sat, to midnight Sun & national
holidays; 📶; 🚇Tōzai line to Sanjō-Keihan,
🚊Keihan line to Sanjō) The young chefs
at this sleek restaurant dish out some
seriously good Hokkaidō-style *rāmen*
(noodles in a meat broth with meat and
vegetables). You will be given a choice of
three kinds of soup when you order: *shio*

A dish of vegetables at Omen (p250)

(salt), *shōyu* (soy sauce) or miso – we highly recommend you go for the miso soup.

Hisago
Noodles ¥

(ひさご; Map p218; ☎561-2109; 484 Shimokawara-chō, Higashiyama-ku; meals from ¥900; ⏰11.30am-7.30pm, closed Mon; 📖; 🚌Kyoto City bus 206 to Higashiyama-Yasui) If you need a quick meal while in the main Southern Higashiyama sightseeing district, this simple noodle and rice restaurant is a good bet. It's within easy walking distance of Kiyomizu-dera and Maruyama-kōen. *Oyako-donburi* (chicken and egg over rice; ¥980) is the speciality of the house.

There is no English sign; look for the traditional front and the small collection of food models on display. In the busy seasons, there's almost always a queue outside.

Café 3032
Cafe ¥

(カフェ サンゼロサンニ; Map p218; ☎531-8869; 102 Tatsumi-chō, Higashiōji-dōri, Matsubara-agaru, Higashiyama-ku; light meals from ¥600; ⏰8am-10pm, closed irregularly; 📖; 🚌Kyoto City bus 206 to Higashiyama-Yasui) This super-casual cafe on Higashiōji, just down the hill from the main Southern Higashiyama sightseeing district, is a great place for a light lunch or cuppa while exploring the area. There's an English menu and foreign visitors are welcomed. The fare includes sandwiches, curry, beer and coffee.

Omen Kodai-ji
Noodles ¥¥

(おめん 高台寺店; Map p218; ☎541-5007; 358 Masuya-chō, Kodaiji-dōri, Shimokawara higashi-iru, Higashiyama-ku; noodles from ¥1150, set menu ¥1800; ⏰11am-9pm, closed irregularly; 🚌Kyoto City bus 206 to Higashiyama-Yasui) This branch of Kyoto's famed Omen noodle chain is the best place to stop while exploring the Southern Higashiyama district. It's in a remodelled Japanese building with a light, airy feeling. The signature udon (thick white wheat noodles) noodles are delicious and there are many other à la carte offerings.

Kikunoi
Kaiseki ¥¥¥

(菊乃井; Map p218; ☎561-0015; www.kikunoi. jp; 459 Shimokawara-chō, Yasakatoriimae-sagaru, Shimokawara-dōri, Higashiyama-ku; lunch/dinner from ¥4000/15,000; ⏰noon-1pm & 5-8pm; 🍴📖; 🚃Keihan line to Gion-Shijō) This is one of Kyoto's true culinary temples, serving some of the finest *kaiseki* (Japanese haute cuisine) in the city. Located in a hidden nook near Maruyama-kōen, this restaurant has everything necessary for the full over-the-top *kaiseki* experience, from setting, to service, to exquisitely executed cuisine, often with a creative twist. Reserve through your hotel or ryokan concierge.

NORTHERN HIGASHIYAMA

Goya
Okinawan ¥

(ゴーヤ; Map p224; ☎752-1158; 114-6 Nishida-chō, Jōdo-ji, Sakyō-ku; meals from ¥700; ⏰noon-5pm & 6pm-midnight, closed Wed; 📖; 🚌Kyoto City bus 5 to Ginkakuji-michi) We love this Okinawan-style restaurant for its tasty food, stylish interior and comfortable upstairs seating. It's perfect for lunch while exploring Northern Higashiyama and it's just a short walk from Ginkaku-ji. At lunch it serves simple dishes like taco rice (¥880) and *gōya champurū* (bitter melon stir-fry; ¥730), while dinners comprise a wide range of *izakaya* (Japanese pub) fare.

Falafel Garden
Israeli ¥

(ファラフェルガーデン; Map p208; ☎712-1856; www.falafelgarden.com; 15-2 Kamiyanagi-chō, Tanaka, Sakyō-ku; falafel from ¥410; ⏰11am-9.30pm; 🍴📖; 🚃Keihan line to Demachiyanagi) This funky place near Demachiyanagi Station serves excellent falafel and a range of other dishes, as well as offering a set menu (from ¥1000). We like its open, relaxed feeling, but the main draw is those tasty falafels!

Hinode Udon
Noodles ¥

(日の出うどん; Map p224; ☎751-9251; 36 Kitanobō-chō, Nanzenji, Sakyō-ku; noodles from ¥450; ⏰11am-3.30pm, closed Sun, 1st & 3rd Mon, except for Apr & Nov; 📖; 🚌Kyoto City bus 5 to Eikandō-michi) Filling noodle and rice dishes are served at this pleasant shop with an English menu. Plain udon (thick white wheat noodles) are only ¥500, but we recommend you spring for the *nabeyaki udon* (pot-baked udon in broth) for ¥950. This is a good lunch spot when you're temple-hopping in the Northern Higashiyama area.

Omen   Noodles ¥¥
(おめん; Map p224; ☎771-8994; 74 Jōdo-ji Ishibashi-chō, Sakyō-ku; noodles from ¥1150; ☎11am-9pm, closed Thu & 1 other day a month; ☎; ☎Kyoto City bus 5 to Ginkakuji-michi) This elegant noodle shop is named after the thick white noodles that are served in broth with a selection of seven fresh vegetables. Just say *omen* and you'll be given your choice of hot or cold noodles, a bowl of soup to dip them in and a plate of vegetables (put these into the soup along with sesame seeds).

There's also an extensive à la carte menu. You can get a fine salad here, brilliant *tori sansho yaki* (chicken cooked with Japanese mountain spice), good tempura and occasionally a nice plate of sashimi. Best of all, there's an English menu. It's about five minutes' walk from Ginkaku-ji in a traditional Japanese house with a lantern outside. Highly recommended.

ARASHIYAMA & SAGANO
Komichi   Cafe ¥
(こみち; Map p208; ☎872-5313; 23 Ōjōin-chō, Nison-in Monzen, Saga, Ukyō-ku; matcha ¥650; ☎10am-5pm, closed Wed; ☎Kyoto City bus 28 from Kyoto Station to Arashiyama-Tenryuji-mae, ☎JR Sagano/San-in line to Saga-Arashiyama or Hankyū line to Arashiyama, change at Katsura) This friendly little teahouse is perfectly located along the Arashiyama tourist trail. In addition to hot and cold tea and coffee, it serves *uji kintoki* (shaved ice with sweetened green tea) in summer and a variety of light noodle dishes year-round. The picture menu helps with ordering. The sign is green and black on a white background.

☕ Drinking

Kyoto has a great variety of bars, clubs and *izakayas*, all of which are good places to meet Japanese folks. And if you happen to be in Kyoto in the summer, many hotels and department stores operate rooftop beer gardens with all-you-can-eat-and-drink deals and good views of the city.

In addition to the places listed here, all the top-end hotels listed in the Sleeping section have at least one good bar on their premises. We particularly like the Hyatt's bar, **Tōzan** (Map p218; Sanjūsangendō-mawari, Hyatt Regency Kyoto; ☎Keihan line to Shichijō).

Atlantis   Bar
(アトランティス; Map p218; ☎241-1621; 161 Matsumoto-chō, Ponto-chō-Shijō-agaru, Nakagyō-ku; ☎6pm-2am, to 1am Sun; ☎Hankyū line to Kawaramachi) This is one of the few bars on Ponto-chō that foreigners can walk into without a Japanese friend. It's a slick, trendy place that draws a fair smattering of Kyoto's beautiful people, and wannabe beautiful people. In summer you can sit outside on a platform looking over the Kamo-gawa. It's often crowded so you may have to wait a bit to get in, especially if you want to sit outside.

Gion Finlandia Bar   Bar
(ぎおん フィンランディアバー; Map p218; ☎541-3482; www.finlandiabar.com; 570-123 Gion-machi minamigawa, Higashiyama-ku; admission ¥500, drinks around ¥900 ; ☎6pm-3am; ☎Keihan line to Gion-Shijō) This stylish Gion bar in an old geisha house is a great place for a civilised drink. The 1st floor is decorated with Finnish touches while the upstairs retains a Japanese feeling, with sunken floors and tatami mats. Admission is ¥500 and you can expect to pay around ¥3000 for a few drinks.

Tadg's Gastro Pub   Pub
(ダイグ ガストロ パブ; Map p224; ☎213-0214; http://tadgs.com; 1st fl, 498 Kamikoriki-chō, Nakagyō-ku; drinks from around ¥500; ☎lunch & dinner until late, closed Wed; ☎Tōzai line to Kyoto-Shiyakusho-mae) Looking out on a particularly scenic stretch of

Kiyamachi-dōri, Tadg's is a great place for a drink or two in the evening and you can choose from an extensive selection of craft beers, along with a variety of wines, sake and spirits. Seating is available, including an enclosed garden out the back for smokers.

Kick Up   Bar
(キックアップ; Map p224; ✆761-5604; Higashikomonoza-chō 331, Higashiyama-ku; drinks/food from ¥600/500; ◷7pm-midnight, closed Wed; Ⓢ Tōzai line to Keage) Located just across the street from the Westin Miyako Kyoto, this wonderful bar attracts a regular crowd of Kyoto expats, local Japanese and guests from the Westin. It's subdued, relaxing and friendly.

Bar K6   Bar
(バーK6; Map p224; ✆255-5009; 2nd fl, Le Valls Bldg, Nijō-dōri, Kiyamachi higashi-iru, Nakagyō-ku; drinks from ¥600; ◷6pm-3am, until 5am Fri & Sat; Ⓢ Tōzai line to Kyoto-Shiyakusho-mae, Ⓡ Keihan line to Jingu-Marutamachi) Overlooking one of the prettiest stretches of Kiyamachi-dōri, this upscale modern Japanese bar has a great selection of single malts and some of the best cocktails in town. There's even a local craft brew on

offer. It's popular with well-heeled locals and travellers staying at some of the top-flight hotels nearby.

Entertainment

Most of Kyoto's cultural entertainment is of an occasional nature, and you'll need to check with the TIC or *Kansai Scene* to find out whether anything interesting coincides with your visit.

GEISHA DANCES

In the spring and autumn, Kyoto's geisha (or, properly speaking, *geiko* and *maiko*) perform fantastic dances, usually on seasonal themes. For a small additional fee, you can participate in a brief tea ceremony before the show. We *highly* recommend seeing one of these dances if you are in town when they are being held. Ask at the tourist information centre or at your lodgings for help with ticket purchase. Tour companies can also help with tickets.

Miyako Odori   Dance
(都をどり; Map p218; ✆541-3391; www.miyako-odori.jp; Gionkobu Kaburenjo, 570-2

Miyako Odori

Gionmachi-minamigawa, Higashiyama-ku; seat reserved/nonreserved/reserved incl tea ¥4200/2500/4800; ⊙ shows 12.30pm, 2pm, 3.30pm & 4.50pm; 🚌 Kyoto City bus 206 to Gion, 🚉 Keihan line to Gion-Shijō) Presented by the Gion Kōbu geisha district, this is our favourite geisha dance in Kyoto. It's a real stunner and the colourful images will remain with you long after the curtain falls. It's held throughout April at the Gion Kōbu Kaburen-jō Theatre, on Hanami-kōji, just south of Shijō-dōri.

Gion Odori
Dance

(祇園をどり; Map p218; 📞 561-0224; Gion, Higashiyama-ku; admission/incl tea ¥3500/4000; ⊙ shows 1.30pm & 4pm; 🚌 Kyoto City bus 206 to Gion) This is a quaint and charming geisha dance put on by the geisha of the Gion Higashi geisha district. It's held from 1 to 10 November at the **Gion Kaikan Theatre** (祇園会館), near Yasaka-jinja.

Kamogawa Odori
Dance

(鴨川をどり; Map p224; 📞 221-2025; Ponto-chō, Sanjō-sagaru, Nakagyō-ku; normal/special seat/special seat incl tea ¥2000/4000/4500; ⊙ shows 12.30pm, 2.20pm & 4.10pm; Ⓢ Tōzai line to Kyoto-Shiyakusho-mae) Geisha dances from 1 to 24 May at Ponto-chō Kaburen-jō Theatre in Ponto-chō.

Kitano Odori
Dance

(北野をどり; 📞 461-0148; Imadegawa-dōri, Nishihonmatsu nishi iru, Kamigyō-ku; admission/with tea ¥4000/4500; ⊙ shows 1.30pm & 4pm) At Kamishichiken Kaburen-jō Theatre (上七軒歌舞練場), east of Kitano-Tenman-gū; 15 to 25 April.

Kyō Odori
Dance

(京おどり; Map p218; 📞 561-1151; Miyagawachō Kaburenjo, 4-306 Miyagawasuji, Higashiyama-ku; seat reserved/nonreserved ¥4000/2000, plus ¥500 incl tea; ⊙ shows 12.30pm, 2.30pm & 4.30pm; 🚉 Keihan line to Gion-Shijō) Put on by the Miyagawa-chō geisha district, this wonderful geisha dance is among the most picturesque performances of the Kyoto year. It's held from the first to the third Sunday in April at the **Miyagawa-chō Kaburen-jō Theatre** (宮川町歌舞練場), east of the Kamo-gawa between Shijō-dōri and Gojō-dōri.

GEISHA ENTERTAINMENT

If you want to see geisha perform and actually speak with them, one of the best ways is at **Gion Hatanaka** (祇園畑中; Map p218; 📞 541-5315; www.thehatanaka.co.jp; Yasaka-jinja Minami-mon mae, Higashiyama-ku; r per person incl 2 meals from ¥25,000; 🚌 Kyoto City bus 206 to Higashiyama-Yasui), a Gion ryokan that offers the **Kyoto Cuisine & Maiko Evening** (ぎおん畑中; Map p218; 📞 541-5315; www.kyoto-maiko.jp; Hatanaka Ryokan, 505 Minamigawa, Gion-machi, Yasaka-jinja Minamimon-mae, Higashiyama-ku; per person ¥18,000; ⊙ 6-8pm, every Mon, Wed, Fri & Sat; 🚌 Kyoto City bus 206 to Gion or Chionin-mae, 🚉 Keihan line to Gion-Shijō). Here, you can

Teramachi shopping arcade

enjoy elegant Kyoto *kaiseki* food while being entertained by real *geiko* and *maiko*.

KABUKI

Minami-za   Theatre

(南座; Map p214; 🎵 561-0160; www.kabuki-bito.jp; Shijō-Ōhashi, Higashiyama-ku; performances ¥4000-27,000; 🚉 Keihan line to Gion-Shijō)
The oldest kabuki theatre in Japan is the Minami-za theatre in Gion. The major event of the year is the **Kaomise festival** (1 to 26 December), which features Japan's finest kabuki actors. Other performances take place on an irregular basis – check with the TIC. The most likely months for performances are May, June and September.

Shopping

The heart of Kyoto's shopping district is around the intersection of Shijō-dōri and Kawaramachi-dōri. The blocks to the north and west of here are packed with stores selling both traditional and modern goods. Kyoto's largest department stores can be found in this area, such as:

Marui (マルイ (OIOI); Map p218; 🎵 075-257-0101; 68 Shin-chō, Shijō-dōri Kawaramachi Higashi-iru, Shimogyō-ku; 🕙 10.30am-8.30pm, restaurants 11am-10pm, supermarket 8am-10pm)

Takashimaya (高島屋; Map p214; 🎵 221-8811; Shijō-Kawaramachi Kado, Shimogyō-ku; 🕙 10am-8pm, restaurants to 9.30pm; 🚉 Hankyū line to Kawaramachi)

Daimaru (大丸; Map p214; 🎵 211-8111; Tachiuri Nishi-machi 79, Shijō-dōri, Takakura nishi-iru, Shimogyō-ku; 🕙 10am-8pm, restaurants 11am-9pm; Ⓢ Karasuma line to Shijō, 🚉 Hankyū line to Karasuma)

Fujii Daimaru (フジイダイマル; Map p214; 🎵 221-8181; Shijō-dōri, Teramachi nishi-iru; 🕙 10.30am-8pm; Ⓢ Hankyū line to Kawaramachi)

Some of the best shopping and people-watching can be had along Kyoto's three downtown shopping arcades: **Shinkyōgoku shopping arcade**, **Teramachi shopping arcade** and Nishiki Market (p210). Teramachi and Shinkyōgoku run parallel to each other in the heart of downtown. The former has a mix of tasteful and tacky shops; the latter specialises in tacky stuff for the hoards of schoolkids who visit Kyoto every year. Nishiki branches off Teramachi to the west, about 100m north of Shijō-dōri.

The place to look for antiques in Kyoto is Shinmonzen-dōri, in Gion. The street is lined with great old shops, many of them specialising in one thing or another (furniture, pottery, scrolls, prints etc). You can easily spend an afternoon strolling from shop to shop, but be warned: prices here are steep!

Teramachi-dōri, between Oike-dōri and Marutamachi-dōri, has a number of classic old Kyoto arts, crafts, antiques and tea shops. This is probably the best place for shopping if you're after 'old Kyoto' items.

Aritsugu   Knives

(有次; Map p214; 🎵 221-1091; 219 Kajiya-chō, Nishikikōji-dōri, Gokomachi nishi-iru, Nakagyō-ku; 🕙 9am-5.30pm; 🚉 Hankyū line to Kawaramachi) While you're in the Nishiki Market, have a look at this store – it's where you can find some of the best kitchen knives in the world. It also carries a selection of excellent and unique Japanese kitchenware.

Wagami no Mise   Handicrafts

(倭紙の店; Map p214; 🎵 341-1419; 1st fl, Kajinoha Bldg, 298 Ōgisakaya-chō, Higashinotōin-dōri, Bukkōji-agaru, Shimogyō-ku; 🕙 9.30am-5.30pm Mon-Fri, to 4.30pm Sat; Ⓢ Karasuma line to Shijō) A short walk from the Shijō-Karasuma crossing, this place sells a fabulous variety of handmade *washi* (Japanese handmade paper) for reasonable prices. It's one of our favourite shops in Kyoto for souvenirs.

Zōhiko   Lacquerware

(象彦; Map p224; 🎵 229-6625; www.zohiko.co.jp; 719-1 Yohojimae-chō, Teramachi-dōri, Nijō-agaru, Nakagyō-ku; 🕙 10am-6pm; Ⓢ Tōzai line to Kyoto-Shiyakusho-mae) Zōhiko is the best place in Kyoto to buy one of Japan's most beguiling art/craft forms: lacquerware. If you aren't familiar with just how beautiful these products can be, you owe it to yourself to make the pilgrimage to Zōhiko.

Markets

Markets are the best places to find antiques and bric-a-brac at reasonable prices and are the only places in Japan where you can actually bargain for a better price.

On the 21st of each month, **Kōbō-san Market** (弘法さん（東寺露天市）; Map p208; ☎691-3325; 1 Kujō-chō, Tō-ji, Minami-ku; ⏰dawn to dusk; ☒Kintetsu line to Tōji) is held at Tō-ji to commemorate the death of Kōbō Daishi (Kūkai), who in 823 was appointed abbot of the temple.

Another major market, **Tenjin-san Market** (天神さん, 北野天満宮露天市; Map p208; ☎461-0005; Kitano Tenman-gū, Bakuro-chō, Kamigyō-ku; ⏰dawn-dusk; ☒Kyoto City bus 50 or 101 to Kitano Tenmangū-mae), is held on the 25th of each month at Kitano Tenman-gū, marking the day of the birth (and, coincidentally, the death) of the Heian-era statesman Sugawara Michizane (845–903).

You'll find a great selection of cups, bowls, trays and various kinds of boxes.

If you want a gift or souvenir that really makes an impression, this is a great choice!

Bic Camera
Electronics

(ビックカメラ; Map p212; ☎353-1111; 927 Higashi Shiokōji-chō, Shimogyō-ku; ⏰10am-9pm; ☒Kyoto Station) This vast new shop is directly connected to Kyoto Station via the Nishinotō-in gate; otherwise, it's accessed by leaving the north (Karasuma) gate and walking west. You will be amazed by the sheer amount of goods this store has on display.

Æon Mall Kyoto
Shopping Centre

(イオンモール; Map p212; 1 Nishikujō Toriiguchi-chō, Minami-ku; ⏰10am-9pm, food floor until 10pm; ☒Kyoto Station) A five-minute walk southwest of Kyoto Station (exit Hachijō-guchi), this huge shopping mall is a good place to kill some time, grab a meal and do some shopping before getting on a train.

You'll find branches of most of the big Japanese retailers here, including Muji, Uniqlo, Monbell, Daiso and Sofmap (computers etc). The 4th floor is the food floor and is home to the usual Japanese and international chains.

Kyoto Handicraft Center
Crafts

(京都ハンディクラフトセンター; Map p224; ☎761-7000; www.kyotohandicraftcenter.com; 21 Entomi-chō, Shōgoin, Sakyō-ku; ⏰10am-7pm; ☒Kyoto City bus 206 to Kumano-jinja-mae) The Kyoto Handicraft Center sells a good range of Japanese arts and crafts. You can find such things as wood-block prints, Japanese dolls, damascene crafts, pearls, clothing and books. English-speaking staff are on hand and currency exchange is available. It's within walking distance of the main Higashiyama sightseeing route.

Ippōdō Tea
Tea

(一保堂茶舗; Map p224; ☎211-3421; www.ippodo-tea.co.jp; Teramachi-dōri, Nijō-agaru, Nakagyō-ku; ⏰9am-7pm Mon-Sat, to 6pm Sun & holidays; ☒Tōzai line to Kyoto-Shiyakusho-mae) This old-style tea shop sells the best Japanese tea in Kyoto. Its *matcha* makes an excellent and lightweight souvenir. Try a 40g container of *wa-no-mukashi* (meaning 'old-time Japan') for ¥1600, which makes 25 cups of excellent green tea. Ippo-dō is north of the city hall, on Teramachi-dōri. It has an adjoining tea-house (open 11am to 5.30pm).

ℹ Information

Money

Most of the major banks are near the Shijō-Karasuma intersection, two stops north of Kyoto Station on the Karasuma line subway.

International transactions (such as wire transfers) can be made at Citibank (シティバンク; Map p214; ☎212-5387; ⏰office 9am-3pm Mon-Fri, ATM 24hr; ☒Karasuma line to Shijō), just west of this intersection.

You can change travellers cheques at most post offices around town, including the Kyoto Central Post Office, next to Kyoto Station. Post offices also have ATMs that accept most foreign-issued cards. If your card doesn't work at postal ATMs, try the ATMs in 7-Eleven convenience stores. Failing that, try Citibank, which has a 24-hour ATM that accepts most foreign-issued cards.

Post

Kyoto Central Post Office (京都中央郵便局; Map p212; 365-2471; 843-12 Higashishiokōji-chō, Shimogyō-ku; 9am-9pm Mon-Fri, to 7pm Sat & Sun, ATMs 12.05am-11.55pm Mon-Sat, to 9pm Sun & holidays ; S Karasuma line to Kyoto) Conveniently located next to Kyoto Station (take the Karasuma exit; the post office is on the northwestern side of the station). There's an after-hours service counter on the southern side of the post office, open 24 hours a day, 365 days a year. The ATMs here are open *almost* 24 hours a day.

Tourist Information

Kyoto Tourist Information Center (京都総合観光案内所; TIC; Map p212; 343-0548; 2F Kyoto Station Bldg, Shimogyō-ku; 8.30am-7pm; S Karasuma line to Kyoto) Located in the main concourse on the 2nd floor of the Kyoto Station building that runs between the *shinkansen* (bullet train) station and the front of the station (near Isetan department store), this is the main tourist information centre in

Kyoto. English speakers are always on hand and, occasionally, speakers of other European and Asian languages are available.

Getting There & Away

Travel between Kyoto and other parts of Japan is a breeze. Kansai is served by the Tōkaidō and San-yō Shinkansen lines, several JR main lines and a few private rail lines. It is also possible to travel to/from Kyoto and other parts of Honshū, Shikoku and Kyūshū by long-distance highway buses. Finally, Kyoto is served by two airports (Kansai International Airport and Osaka Itami Airport). Kyoto is also relatively close to Nagoya, in case you can only get a flight to Centrair airport.

Air

Kyoto is served by Osaka Itami Airport (ITM), which principally handles domestic traffic, and the Kansai International Airport (KIX), which principally handles international flights. There are frequent flights between Tokyo and Itami (around ¥25,000, 80 minutes), but unless you're very lucky with airport connections you'll probably find it as quick and more convenient to take the *shinkansen*. There are ample connections to/from both airports, though the trip to/from Kansai International Airport takes longer and costs more.

Plates for sale at Kōbō-san Market

LAITR KEIOWS/SHUTTERSTOCK ©

Train

Shinkansen

Kyoto is on the Tōkaidō-San-yō Shinkansen line, which runs between Tokyo and Kyūshū, with stops at places such as Nagoya, Osaka, Kōbe, Himeji and Hiroshima en route. The *shinkansen* operates to/from Kyoto Station (Kyoto's main train station). On the Tokyo end, it operates from Tokyo, Shinagawa and Shin-Yokohama stations. Fares and times for Hikari (the second-fastest type of *shinkansen*) between Kyoto and the following cities are as follows.

Tokyo (¥13,080; 2¾ hours)

Nagoya (¥5070; 40 minutes)

Shin-Osaka (¥1420; 13 minutes)

Hiroshima (¥10,570; two hours)

Hakata (¥15,120; two hours, 45 minutes)

Regular Trains

Nara The private Kintetsu line (sometimes written in English as the Kinki Nippon railway) links Kyoto (Kintetsu Kyoto Station, south side of the main Kyoto Station building) and Nara (Kintetsu Nara Station). There are fast direct tokkyū (¥1110, 33 minutes) and ordinary express trains (¥610, 40 minutes), which may require a change at Saidai-ji.

The JR Nara line also connects Kyoto Station with JR Nara Station (express, ¥710, 41 minutes), and this is a great option for Japan Rail Pass holders.

Osaka The fastest train other than the *shinkansen* between Kyoto Station and Osaka is the JR *shinkaisoku* (special rapid train), which takes 29 minutes (¥560). In Osaka, the train stops at both Shin-Osaka and Osaka Stations.

There is also the cheaper private Hankyū line, which runs between Hankyū Kawaramachi, Karasuma and Ōmiya Stations in Kyoto and Hankyū Umeda Station in Osaka (*tokkyū* or limited express Umeda–Kawaramachi, ¥400, 40 minutes). These trains are usually more comfortable than the JR trains, and if you board at Kawaramachi or Umeda, you can usually get a seat.

Alternatively, you can take the Keihan main line between Demachiyanagi, Sanjō, Shijō or Shichijō Stations in Kyoto and Keihan Yodoyabashi Station in Osaka (*tokkyū* to/from Sanjō ¥410, 51 minutes). Yodoyabashi is on the Midō-suji subway line. Again, these are more comfortable than JR trains and you can usually get a seat if you board in Demachiyanagi or Yodoyabashi.

ℹ Getting Around
To/From the Airport

Osaka Itami Airport 大阪伊丹空港

There are frequent limousine buses between Osaka Itami airport and Kyoto Station (the Kyoto Station airport bus stop is opposite the south side of the station, in front of Avanti department store). Buses also run between the airport and various hotels around town, but on a less regular basis (check with your hotel). The journey should take around 55 minutes and the cost is ¥1280. Be sure to allow extra time in case of traffic.

At Itami, the stand for these buses is outside the arrivals hall; buy your tickets from the machines and ask one of the attendants which stand is for Kyoto (hint: you've got a better chance of getting a seat if you board at the South Terminal).

MK Taxi (☏778-4141; www.mktaxi-japan.com) offers limousine van service to/from the airport for ¥2400. Call at least two days in advance to reserve, or ask at the information counter in the arrivals hall on arrival in Osaka.

Kansai International Airport (KIX)
関西国際空港

The fastest, most convenient way to travel between KIX and Kyoto is on the special Haruka airport express, which makes the trip in about 75 minutes. Most seats are reserved (¥3370) but there are usually two cars on each train with unreserved seats (¥2850). Open seats are almost always available, so you don't have to purchase tickets in advance. First and last departures from Kyoto to KIX are 5.46am and 8.15pm; first and last departures from KIX to Kyoto are 6.30am Monday to Friday, 6.40am Saturday, Sunday and holidays and 10.16pm. Note that the Haruka is one of the few trains in Japan that is frequently late (although not usually by more than a few minutes). We suggest leaving a little extra time when heading from Kyoto to the airport to catch a flight.

It's also possible to travel by limousine bus between Kyoto and KIX (¥2550, about 90 minutes). In Kyoto, the bus departs from the same place as the Itami-bound bus.

A final option is the MK Taxi Sky Gate Shuttle limousine van service (☏778-5489; www.mktaxi-japan.com), which will pick you up anywhere in Kyoto city and deliver you to KIX for ¥3600. Call at least two days in advance to reserve. The advantage of this method is that you are delivered from door to door and you don't have to lug your baggage through the train station. MK has a counter in the arrivals hall of KIX, and if there's room they'll put you on the next van to Kyoto. A similar service is offered by Yasaka Taxi (☏803-4800).

Bicycle

Kyoto is a great city to explore on a bicycle; with the exception of outlying areas it's mostly flat and there is a bike path running the length of the Kamo-gawa.

There are two bicycle-parking lots in town that are convenient for tourists: one in front of Kyoto Station and another off Kiyamachi-dōri, between Sanjō-dōri and Shijō-dōri. It costs ¥150 per day to park your bicycle here. Be sure to hang onto the ticket you pick up as you enter.

Kyoto Cycling Tour Project (京都サイクリングツアープロジェクト; KCTP; Map p212; ☏354-3636; www.kctp.net/en; 552-13 Higashi-Aburanokoji-chō, Aburanokōji-dōri, Shiokōji-sagaru, Shimogyō-ku; ◷9am-7pm; Ⓢ Karasuma line to Kyoto, Ⓡ JR line to Kyoto) A great place to rent a bike. These folk rent bikes (¥1000 per day) that are perfect for getting around the city. KCTP also conducts a variety of excellent bicycle tours of Kyoto with English-speaking guides. These are a great way to see the city (check the website for details).

Public Transport

Bus

Kyoto has an extensive network of bus routes providing an efficient way of getting around at moderate cost. Many of the routes used by visitors have announcements in English. The core timetable for buses is between 7am and 9pm, though a few run earlier or later.

The TIC stocks the Bus Navi: Kyoto City Bus Sightseeing Map, which is a good map of the city's main bus lines. This map is not exhaustive. If you can read a little Japanese, pick up a copy of the regular (and more detailed) Japanese bus map available at major bus terminals throughout the city.

Entry to the bus is usually through the back door and exit is via the front door. Inner-city buses charge a flat fare (¥230), which you drop into the clear plastic receptacle on top of the machine next to the

driver on your way out. A separate machine gives change for ¥100 and ¥500 coins or ¥1000 notes.

On buses serving the outer areas, you take a numbered ticket (seiri-ken) when entering. When you leave, an electronic board above the driver displays the fare corresponding to your ticket number (drop the seiri-ken into the ticket box with your fare).

The main Kyoto Bus Information Centre (京都バス案内所; Map p212) is located in front of Kyoto Station. Here you can pick up bus maps, purchase bus tickets and passes (on all lines, including highway buses), and get additional information. Nearby, there's a convenient English/Japanese bus-information computer terminal; just enter your intended destination and it will tell you the correct bus and bus stop.

When heading for locations outside the city centre, be careful which bus you board. Kyoto city buses are green, Kyoto buses are tan and Keihan buses are red and white.

Subway

Kyoto has two efficient subway lines, which operate from around 5.30am to around 11.30pm. The minimum fare is ¥210 (children ¥110).

The quickest way to travel between the north and south of the city is the Karasuma subway line. The line has 15 stops and runs from Takeda in the far south, via Kyoto Station, to the Kyoto International Conference Hall (Kokusaikaikan Station) in the north.

The east-west Tōzai subway line crosses Kyoto from Uzumasa-Tenjingawa in the west, meeting the Karasuma line at Karasuma-Oike Station, and continuing east to Sanjō Keihan, Yamashina and Rokujizō, in the east and southeast.

Taxi

Kyoto taxi fares start at ¥640 for the first 2km. The exception is MK Taxi (p256), for which the fares of which start at ¥600.

MK Taxi also provides tours of the city with English-speaking drivers. For a group of up to four, prices start at ¥22,300 for a three-hour tour.

Most Kyoto taxis are equipped with satellite navigation systems. If you are going somewhere unusual, it will help the driver if you have the address or phone number of your destination, as both of these can be programmed into the system.

Kansai & Western Honshū

Kansai and western Honshū make the perfect add-ons to Kyoto. Kyoto, which is actually part of Kansai, can serve as the base or jumping-off point for exploring the incredible wonders of these two regions.

Kansai is Japan's cultural heartland and it's the place where Japanese culture really came into its own. Less than an hour from Kyoto you'll find Nara, the first permanent capital of Japan. It's a compact and rich storehouse of cultural treasures, including some of its finest temples and Buddhist images. Even closer is the city of Osaka, which duplicates the urban experience of Tokyo but on a more manageable scale, and has some memorable local foods. Next along is Kōbe, one of Japan's more cosmopolitan cities.

Continuing west along the Inland Sea brings you to the fascinating region of western Honshū, where you'll find the island-turned-art museum of Naoshima, the city of Hiroshima and the island of Miyajima, home to an iconic Shintō shrine.

Itsukushima-jinja (p323), Miyajima

Kansai & Western Honshū

SEA OF JAPAN

Oki-shotō

Daisen-Oki National Park

Shimane-hantō

MATSUE

Yonago

Daisen (1729m)

Izumo Taisha

Izumo

9

180

181

Ōda

Sanbe-san (1126m)

Nima

54

314

Gōtsu

HONSHŪ

Niimi

Hanada

SHIMANE-KEN

Shōbara

Tōjō

Miyoshi

54

Masuda

HIROSHIMA-KEN

Kurashiki

9

Tsuwano

Higashi-Hiroshima

Fukuyama

Washūzan

HIROSHIMA

2

Onomichi

❸

Kure

Marugame

❺

Miyajima (Itsuku-shima)

Inland Sea

Kanonji

9

YAMAGUCHI-KEN

Yosan Line

Iwakuni

Sea of Aki

Imabari

Kawanoe

◉**YAMAGUCHI**

San-yo Shinkansen

Iyomishima

Hōfu

Tokuyama

Yanai

11

Saijo

Niihama

32

Sea of Suo

SHIKOKU

MATSUYAMA

KŌCHI-KEN

Iyo

Ishizuchi Quasi National Park

194

KŌCHI

Yosan Line

380

EHIME-KEN

Tosa

❶ Nara-kōen

378

Ōzu

❷ Kinosaki Onsen

197

Yawatahama

Susaki

❸ Hiroshima

56

197

❹ Naoshima

Yodo Line

Dosan Line

❺ Miyajima

Uwajima

381

439

56

Tosa-Kuroshio Line

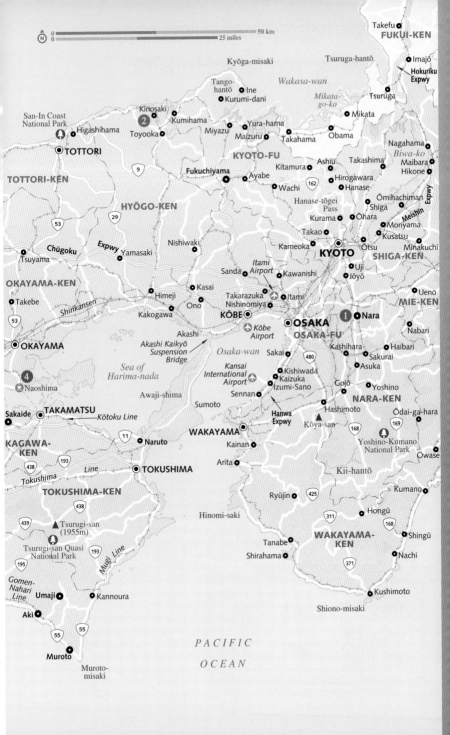

Kansai & Western Honshū Highlights

Nara-kōen

A fine park within easy strolling distance of Kintetsu Nara Station, Nara-kōen (p289) contains some of Japan's most important cultural and historical treasures. It also contains some virgin forest, said to be the world's only such example inside a city, and some 1200 deer who roam freely. This park is lovely in any season.

Kinosaki Onsen

On the Sea of Japan coast in northern Kansai, the picturesque town of Kinosaki (p301) is the place for the classic Japanese onsen (hot springs) experience. Put on your *yukata* (light cotton kimono) and a pair of sandals and spend the evening hopping from one fine hot spring to the next, then head back to your ryokan (traditional Japanese inn) and feast on locally caught king crabs.

Left: Guests entering an onsen in Kinosaki

Hiroshima

Reborn from the ashes of the 1945 atomic blast, Hiroshima (p316) is not a highlight in the traditional sense of the word. Rather it is a chance to learn about the horrors of nuclear war and the power of the human spirit to overcome adversity. While the displays relating to the blast are sobering in the extreme, they are also enlightening and the vibrant modern city of Hiroshima inspires hope for the future.

Right: Atomic Bomb Dome

Naoshima

Naoshima (p311) represents the perfect interplay of art, architecture and nature, showcasing world-class contemporary art museums, installations, and outdoor sculpture. Among the many works of prolific architect Andō Tadao here is Chichū Art Museum, an underground gallery where the art is illuminated only by natural light. Above: "*Le Banc*" by Niki de Saint Phalle

Miyajima

About an hour away from Hiroshima, the island of Miyajima (p322) is home to one of Japan's most iconic sights: the floating torii (Shintō shrine gate) of Itsukushima-jinja. After snapping the obligatory shot of the gate, head up nearby Misen, a 530m peak that offers sweeping views of the area. Miyajima is a great place to stay after visiting Hiroshima and these two destinations make an ideal overnight trip from Kansai.

Kansai & Western Honshū's Best...

Experiences

○ **Seeing the Daibutsu (Great Buddha)** This cosmic Buddha is truly awesome. (p292)

○ **Eating Hiroshima-style okonomiyaki** The city's signature dish (savoury pancakes with cabbage and noodles cooked on a griddle) is a delight. (p320)

○ **Friday night in Osaka's Dōtombori area** Osakans know how to party and this is where they do it. (p279)

○ **Seeing the floating torii at Miyajima** This is the mother of all Shintō shrine gates. (p323)

Places for a Walk

○ **Nara-kōen** Spend a day with the deer at this temple-strewn park. (p289)

○ **Kōya-san's Oku-no-in cemetery** Towering trees and moss-covered monuments make this both spooky and spiritual. (p297)

○ **Miyajima's Mt Misen** Climb to the peak for beautiful Inland Sea views. (p324)

○ **Kinosaki** A stroll along the canal in the evening is magic in the moonlight. (p301)

Places to Stay

○ **Nishimuraya Honkan** One of the finest ryokan in Japan. (p303)

○ **Shukubō at Kōya-san** *Shukubō* (temple lodgings) are the only way to go here. (p299)

○ **Iwasō Ryokan** The perfect place for a night on the island of Miyajima. (p325)

○ **Benesse House** Where else can you spend the night in an art museum? (p313)

Temples & Shrines

○ **Tōdai-ji** One of Japan's most impressive temples. (p292)

○ **Kōfuku-ji** A towering pagoda with fine Buddhist images. (p290)

○ **Kasuga Taisha** An ancient Shintō shrine surrounded by lanterns and forest. (p291)

○ **Kōya-san's Garan** Home to a fantastic 'Great Pagoda'. (p298)

○ **Itsukushima-jinja** Japan's famous 'floating torii'. (p323)

ADVANCE PLANNING

○ **Three months before** Reserve accommodation well in advance, especially important if you plan to stay at Benesse House on Naoshima, or in the *shukubō* (temple lodgings) at Kōya-san.

○ **One month before** Consider getting an international driver's licence. This is recommended if you want to go off the beaten track and explore western Honshū or Kansai by car.

○ **One month before** Get a Japan Rail Pass. Good value if you plan to do extensive train travel around Kansai and western Honshū. Note that you must purchase an 'exchange order' outside Japan and then convert it into an actual pass once you arrive.

GETTING AROUND

○ **Walk or cycle** The best ways to get around Nara, Kōya-san, Osaka, Kōbe, Hiroshima, Naoshima and Nagasaki.

○ **Ferry** This is only way to access the islands of Naoshima and Miyajima (both in western Honshū).

○ **Train** Best for short trips between cities in Kansai and western Honshū.

○ **Shinkansen (bullet train)** Go high-speed for longer journeys between Kyoto and Hiroshima.

BE FOREWARNED

○ **Summer (July and August)** These months can be very hot and humid in Kansai and western Honshū. You can escape the heat by going up to a place like Kōya-san.

○ **Seasonal festivals** Cherry-blossom season and autumn foliage season can bring huge crowds to Nara; escape them by going to lesser-known temples and shrines.

○ **Winter (November to March)** This season can be very cold up on Kōya-san.

Left: Hiroshima- style *okonomiyaki*;
Above: Kasuga Taisha (p291), Nara

Kansai & Western Honshū Itineraries

Using Kyoto as a base, it's possible to explore most of Kansai in a series of day trips. Once you've explored Kyoto and Kansai, consider heading west to Naoshima, Hiroshima and Miyajima.

KŌYA-SAN TO MIYAJIMA
Hiroshima & Miyajima

3 DAYS

This itinerary assumes that you've already explored Kyoto and Kansai; it's particularly good for holders of a Japan Rail Pass.

First, in order to experience Japan's rich Buddhist traditions, head south to the **❶ Kōya-san** (p296) temple complex deep in the mountains of southern Kansai.

Return to Kyoto (or Osaka) and then grab a *shinkansen* (bullet train) and head west along the Inland Sea. If you are a real fan of Japanese castles, consider stopping at **❷ Himeji** (p309) to see the castle there; Japan's most famous castle is fresh from a five-year renovation.

Otherwise, head straight to **❸ Hiroshima** (p316). Visit the Peace Memorial Park to learn about the city's tragic history, then spend the evening sampling Hiroshima's famous oysters and *okonomiyaki*.

The next day, make the short journey to **❹ Miyajima** (p322), where you can see one of Japan's most famous sights, the 'floating torii'. If you have time, climb up Misen to savour the views over the Inland Sea. Consider spending a night on Miyajima, as the island is lovely after the crowds depart.

Finally, return to Hiroshima and catch a *shinkansen* east to Kyoto or Tokyo.

5 DAYS

KYOTO TO MIYAJIMA VIA NAOSHIMA

Along the Inland Sea

Start in ❶ **Kyoto** and catch a *shinkansen* west to Okayama, where you can switch to a local train and then ferry to the wonderful island-turned-art museum of ❷ **Naoshima** (p311). We recommend spending one or two nights on Naoshima to get the most out of all the museums and galleries there.

Then return to the mainland and continue west to ❸ **Hiroshima** (p316). Allot at least half a day for the Peace Memorial Park to learn about the city's tragic history. Then, in the evening, gorge on Hiroshima's famous cuisine or catch a baseball game at the colourfully named Mazda Zoom-Zoom Stadium Hiroshima (p319), home of the Hiroshima Toyo Carp baseball team.

The following day, head to nearby ❹ **Miyajima** (p322) to check out the famous 'floating torii' and climb up Mt Misen. Again, if you can afford the time, it's a good idea to spend one night on Miyajima, especially if you intend to trek all the way back to Tokyo the following day.

Finally, return to Hiroshima and catch a *shinkansen* east to Kyoto or Tokyo.

Itsukushima-jinja (p323), Miyajima
JUDY BELLAH / GETTY IMAGES ©

Discover Kansai & Western Honshū

At a Glance

o **Osaka** All the urban madness of Tokyo in a more manageable package.

o **Nara** (p287) One of Japan's most rewarding destinations (especially for kids).

o **Kōya-san** (p296) An Esoteric Buddhist complex high in the mountains of southern Kansai.

o **Himeji** (p309) Home to Japan's finest castle.

o **Naoshima** (p311) An entire island turned into one giant art museum/project.

o **Hiroshima** (p316) A city with a tragic past and an uplifting present.

OSAKA

06 / POP 2,667,830

Japan's third-largest city, ultra-urban, hard-working Osaka (大阪) is an unabashed antidote to the fashion-forward frenzy of Tokyo and the prim propriety of Kyoto. This longtime capital of commerce is filled with down-to-earth citizens speaking colourful *Kansai-ben* (Kansai dialect) and neon-clad streetscapes bursting with over-the-top 3D signage.

Most of all, Osaka is famous for good food. The phrase *kuidaore* ('eat 'til you drop') is heard so frequently here that it's practically the city motto. Osaka is also a good place to experience a modern Japanese city. It's surpassed only by Tokyo as a showcase of the Japanese urban phenomenon.

This isn't to say that Osaka is particularly attractive; it can feel like an endless expanse of concrete boxes, *pachinko* (pinball) parlours and elevated highways. But the city somehow manages to rise above this and exert a peculiar charm, and bustling street life and a few architectural gems keep it interesting. At night, Osaka really comes into its own – this is when the streets come alive with flashing neon and beckoning residents with promises of tasty food and good times.

◎ Sights & Activities

UMEDA & OSAKA STATION AREA 梅田・大阪駅周辺

By day, Osaka's centre of gravity is this district, also known as Kita (north). There are few great attractions, but it does have the

Osaka Aquarium Kaiyūkan (p272)
ANTONY GIBLIN/GETTY IMAGES ©

eye-catching Umeda Sky building, department stores, lots of eateries, transit hubs and big-city bustle.

Umeda Sky Building
Notable Building

(梅田スカイビル; www.kuchu-teien.com; 1-1-88 Ōyodonaka, Kita-ku; admission ¥700; ⊙ observation decks 10am-10.30pm, last entry 10pm; 🚃 JR line to Osaka) Opened in 1993 and named one of the world's top 20 buildings, the Sky Building resembles a 40-storey, space-age Arc de Triomphe. Twin towers are connected at the top by a 'floating garden' (really a garden-free observation deck) with breathtaking 360-degree city views day or night. Getting there is half the fun – an escalator in a see-through tube takes you up the last five storeys, between the towers (not for vertigo sufferers). The architect, Hara Hiroshi, also designed **Kyoto Station** (p206).

Ohatsu Tenjin Shrine
Shinto Shrine

(お初天神, Tsuyu no Tenjinja; Map p270; 📞 06-6311-0895; www.tuyutenjin.com/en/; 2-5-4 Sonezaki; ⊙ 6am-midnight; **S** Midō-suji line to Umeda, 🚃 JR line to Osaka) **FREE** Hiding in plain sight amid the skyscrapers of Umeda, this 1300-year-old shrine owes its fame to one of Japan's best known tragic plays (based on true events). Star-crossed lovers Ohatsu, a prostitute, and Tokubei, a merchant's apprentice. Rather than live apart, they committed double suicide here in 1703, to remain together forever in the afterlife. History aside, the shrine looks pretty modern and well-scrubbed, festooned throughout with mementos to the lovers, including *ema* (votive plaques) inscribed by visitors.

There's a flea market the first Friday of each month.

Osaka Museum of Housing & Living
Museum

(大阪くらしの今昔館, Osaka Kurashi no Konjaku-kan; http://konjyakukan.com; 6-4-20 Tenjinbashi, 8th floor; admission ¥600; ⊙ 10am-5pm, closed Tue, day after national holiday & 3rd Mon; **S** Tanimachi line to Tenjinbashisuji-rokuchōme, exit 3) Two subway stops from Umeda, this museum contains a life-sized reproduction of an 1830s Osaka neighbourhood: shophouses, drug stores, an old-style *sentō* (public bath) and more. Enhancing the Edo Period mood, lighting

Osaka-jō (p270)

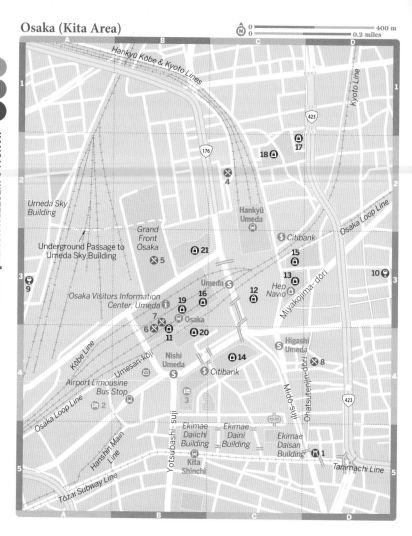

shifts between day and night, shops sell traditional toys and unique souvenirs, and for ¥200 visitors can rent kimono for photo-opps. Invest ¥100 in the English audio guide, since English signage is limited. The building is right behind as you exit the station.

Just outside is lively **Tenjinbashi-suji** shopping street, which claims to be Japan's longest shopping street at 3km. Pick up an English-language guide at the museum or along the route.

CENTRAL OSAKA

Osaka-jō   Castle

(大阪城, Osaka Castle; www.osakacastle.net; 1-1 Osaka-jō; grounds/castle keep free/¥600, ¥900 combined with Osaka Museum of History; ⏰9am-5pm, to 7pm Aug; **S** Chūo or Tanimachi line to Tanimachi 4-chōme, exit 9, **R** JR Osaka Loop line to Osaka-jō-kōen) After unifying Japan in the late 16th century, General Toyotomi Hideyoshi built this castle (1583) as a display of power, using, it's said, the labour of 100,000 workers. Although the present structure is a 1931 concrete reconstruction (refurbished 1997), it's nonetheless quite a sight, looming dramatically over the surrounding park and moat. Inside is an excellent collection of art, armour, and day-to-day implements related to the castle, Hideyoshi and Osaka. An 8th-floor observation deck has 360-degree views.

Osaka Museum of History   Museum

(大阪歴史博物館, Osaka Rekishi Hakubutsukan; www.mus-his.city.osaka.jp; 4-1-32 Ōtemae; admission ¥600, ¥900 combined with Osaka Castle; ⏰9.30am-5pm, to 8pm Fri, closed Tue; ⓢ Tanimachi or Chūō line to Tanimachi-yonchōme, exit 9) Built above the ruins of Naniwa Palace (c 650), visible through the basement floor, this museum houses dramatically illuminated recreations of the old city and life-sized figures in the former palace court. There are also interesting early-20th-century displays, and great views of Osaka-jō. English explanations are pretty sparse, so rent an English-language audio guide (¥200).

TENNŌ-JI & AROUND
天王寺周辺

Shin-Sekai   Area

(新世界; ⓢ Sakai-suji line to Ebisu-chō, exit 3 or Midō-suji line to Dōbutsuen-mae, exit 5) A century ago, Shin-Sekai ('new world') was home to an amusement park that defined cutting edge. Now this entertainment district mixes down-on-its-heels with retro

cool. It's centred around the 103m-high steel-frame tower **Tsūten-kaku** (通天閣; admission ¥700; ⓢ Midō-suji or Sakai-suji lines to Dōbutsu-en-mae Station, exit 5, ⓡ JR or Nankai lines to Shin-Imamiya Station) – built 1912, rebuilt 1956 – and surrounded by ancient *pachinko* parlours, rundown theatres and a few homeless folks and suspicious-looking characters. Shin-Sekai still attracts plenty of visitors for nostalgia and cheap eateries behind over-the-top signage, especially for *kushikatsu* (p280; deep-fried meat and vegetables on skewers).

Abeno Harukas   Notable Building

(あべのハルカス; www.abenoharukas-300.jp/en; 1-1-43 Abeno-suji; observation deck ¥1500; ⏰observation deck 10am-10pm; ⓢ Midō-suji or Tanimachi lines to Tennōji, ⓡ JR lines to Tennōji, Kintetsu line to Abeno-bashi) **FREE** Japan's tallest building (300m, 60 storeys), this César Pelli–designed tower opened in March 2014 and dominates Osaka's southern skyline, offering sweeping city views. It houses Japan's largest department store (Kintetsu, floors B2-14), other shops, a hotel, offices, restaurants (p278) and observation decks. Admission is free except for the tippy-top level **Harukas 300 observation deck** and the **Abeno Harukas Art Museum** (あべのハルカス美術館; 📞06-4399-9050; www.aham.jp; 16th fl, Abeno Harukas, 1-1-43 Abenosuji; varies by exhibition; ⏰10am-8pm Tue-Fri, to 6pm Sat & Sun), where temporary shows so far have

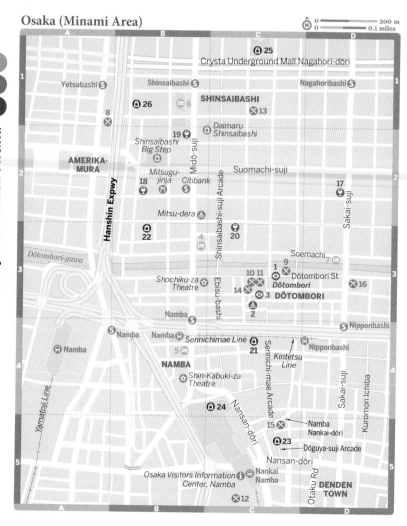

encompassed Renaissance painting to tantric Buddhist artifacts.

Although Abeno Harukas is Japan's tallest building, the tallest *structure* is Tokyo Sky Tree (p87), at 634m.

TEMPŌZAN 天保山

Trudging through Osaka's urban morass, you could easily forget that Osaka is actually a port city. Remind yourself with a trip Tempōzan, a bayside development with attractions especially appealing for those with children. Take the Chūō subway line

to Osakakō Station, come down the stairs of exit 1 and walk towards the big wheel.

Osaka Aquarium Kaiyūkan   Aquarium

(海遊館; www.kaiyukan.com; 1-1-10 Kaigan-dōri; adult/child ¥2300/1200; ⏱10am-8pm; S Chūō line to Osakakō, exit 1) Kaiyūkan is easily one of the world's best aquariums. An 800m-plus walkway winds past displays of sea life from around the Pacific 'ring of fire': Antarctic penguins, coral-reef butterflyfish, unreasonably cute Arctic otters, Monterey Bay seals and unearthly jellyfish. Most impressive is the ginormous central tank, housing a whale shark, manta and thousands of other fish and rays. There are good English descriptions, but the audioguide (¥500) gives more detail. Expect lots of families and school groups.

 ## Festivals & Events

Kishiwada Danjiri Matsuri Cultural
Osaka's wildest festival, on 14 and 15 September, is a kind of running of the bulls except with *danjiri* (festival floats), many weighing over 3000kg. The *danjiri* are hauled through the streets by hundreds of people using ropes – take care and stand back. Most of the action takes place on the second day and the best place to see it is west of Kishiwada Station on the Nankai *honsen* line (main rail line, from Nankai Station).

Tenjin Matsuri Cultural
Held on 24 and 25 July, this is one of Japan's three biggest festivals. Try to make the second day, when processions of *mikoshi* (portable shrines) and people in traditional attire start at Osaka Temmangū and end up in hundreds of boats on the O-kawa. As night falls, there is a huge fireworks display.

 ## Sleeping

Osaka has plenty of accommodation in all budgets - always check websites for discounted rates. Base yourself in Minami for access to a bigger selection of restaurants and shops, or in Kita for fast access to long-distance transport.

If exploring Osaka from a base in Kyoto, keep in mind that trains stop running before midnight (party-goers take note).

UMEDA, OSAKA STATION AREA & NAKA-NO-SHIMA

Hearton Hotel Nishi-Umeda Business Hotel ¥¥
(ハートンホテル西梅田; Map p270; ☑06-6342-1122; www.hearton.co.jp; 3-3-55 Umeda; s/tw/tr from ¥8100/11,400/15,000; ⊜☀ ☎; ⑤ Yotsubashi line to Nishi-Umeda, ⓡ JR lines to Osaka Station, west exit) At 18 storeys and 430 rooms, this large business hotel doesn't set any new style standards, but it boasts cheery staff, clean, comfy rooms, Japanese-Western breakfast buffet (¥1080 extra) and laundry machines, all a quick walk from JR Osaka Station and subway stops. Request a south-facing room unless you're OK with train noise.

Mitsui Garden Hotel Osaka Premier Hotel ¥¥¥

(三井ガーデンホテル大阪プレミア; 06-6444-1131; www.gardenhotels.co.jp/eng/osaka-premier/; 3-4-15 Naka-no-shima; s/d/tw from ¥22,700/26,000/26,000; ; S Yotsubashi line to Higobashi Station, exit 2) On Naka-no-shima, this handsome new hotel exudes contemporary cool from its granite lobby and fabric wall coverings to the city's best river views (request an east-facing room). Rooms offer wooden floors, clean, spare lines, lots of power outlets and large bathrooms with separate WC and bathing areas, and there are guest laundry machines and attractive common baths.

Check the website for significant discounts (some via the MGH Members club, which has free registration). It's about a five-minute walk from the subway station, along the river, or a hotel shuttle bus serves JR Osaka Station.

Hilton Osaka Hotel ¥¥¥

(ヒルトン大阪; Map p270; 6347-7111; www.osaka.hilton.com; 1-8-8 Umeda; s/d or tw from ¥21,622/25,780; ; JR line to Osaka) Across from JR Osaka Station's south exit, this large, excellent hotel is at home with foreign guests. Newly renovated rooms have wood finishes, *shoji* (paper screens) and *fusuma*-style (sliding doors) windows, blackout panels and plenty of power outlets. Facilities include a well-equipped fitness centre with 15m pool and the 35th-floor Windows on the World (p282) bar. There are seemingly infinite restaurant choices steps away.

CENTRAL OSAKA, SHINSAIBASHI & NAMBA AREAS

First Cabin Midosuji Namba Hotel ¥

(ファーストキャビン御堂筋難波; Map p272; 6631-8090; www.first-cabin.jp; 4th fl, Namba Midōsuji Bldg, 4-2-1 Namba; per person ¥5900; ; S Midō-suji line to Namba, exit 13) Imagine spending the night in a first-class suite of an Airbus A380 – inside an office building. Cabins, closed off by sliding

Left: A view from Hilton Osaka; **Below:** *Tako-yaki* (octopus balls), Dōtombori (p279)

(LEFT) HASAN DOGANTURK / ALAMY ©; (BELOW) BRENT WINEBRENNER/GETTY IMAGES ©

screens, contain private TV, locker and power outlets. They're segregated by gender, as are large common baths and showers. It's a top location with friendly service, but noise can travel; pack earplugs (like on that plane).

A lounge serves simple, inexpensive meals for breakfast and dinner.

Arietta Hotel
Hotel ¥¥

(アリエッタホテル大阪; ☎6267-2787; www.thehotel.co.jp/en/arietta_osaka; 3-2-6 Azuchi-machi; s/tw incl breakfast from ¥7776/10,800; ➲❄@☎; **S** Midō-suji line to Honmachi, exit 3) About 10 minutes' walk north of the Minami district, the Arietta has a warm, boutique-hotel feel, minimalist decor in good-sized rooms, with wood floors and tiled bathrooms, welcoming staff and a simple breakfast of breads, coffee and juice, all competitively priced. From the station, turn right at the first corner, and it's two and a half blocks ahead on the right.

Kaneyoshi Ryokan
Ryokan ¥¥

(かねよし旅館; Map p272; ☎6211-6337; www.kaneyosi.jp; 3-12 Soemonchō; per person from ¥6480; ❄@☎♨; **S** Sennichimae line to Nipponbashi, exit 2 or Midō-suji line to Namba, exit 14) In business for nearly a century right by Dōtombori – try for a room at the back, for river views – Kaneyoshi's current (1980s) building feels a bit dated, but there's eager-to-please staff, clean, comfy tatami (tightly woven floor matting) rooms with private bathrooms, and a simple common bath on the top (6th) floor. Though it's in the nightlife district, doors close at midnight.

No non-smoking rooms (though rooms are well aired).

Cross Hotel Osaka
Hotel ¥¥¥

(クロスホテル大阪; Map p272; ☎6213-8281; www.crosshotel.com/osaka; 2-5-15 Shinsai-bashisuji; s/d/tw from ¥16,170/24,255/27,720; ➲❄@☎; **S** Midō-suji line to Namba, exit

14) The Cross Hotel rocks a trendy, urban look with black, white and dark red motif, stylish restaurants, cafe and seasonal outdoor terrace for enjoying a generous breakfast buffet. Rooms are average size, but spacious Japanese-style bathrooms are a rare treat. Service is excellent and you'd have to sleep under Ebisu-bashi bridge for a more central location. Look for online specials.

Hotel Nikkō Osaka   Hotel ¥¥¥

(ホテル日航大阪; Map p272; ☏6244-1281; www.hno.co.jp; 1-3-3 Nishi-Shinsaibashi; s/d ¥30,000/36,000; ⊖❄@🗢; Ⓢ Midō-suji line to Shinsaibashi, exit 8) Along tree-lined Midō-suji, this luxe choice has pampering service, a sleek, newly updated look, comfortable, spacious rooms with fine mattresses, great eastern or western views from upper floors, 10 (count 'em) restaurants and lounges and its own subway exit. Discounted rates are often available online.

OTHER AREAS

Hostel 64 Osaka   Hostel ¥

(☏6556-6586; www.hostel64.com; 3-11-20 Shinmachi; dm/s/d from ¥3500/6000/8100; ⊖❄@🗢; Ⓢ Chūō line to Awaza, exit 2) This non-traditional hostel in a quiet neighbourhood northwest of Shinsaibashi is a little out of the way but worth the trip. There are Japanese- and Western-style private rooms, a small dorm with beds separated by screens, and a cosy lounge that doubles as a cafe-bar and simple breakfast room. Expect welcoming, knowledgeable staff and retro interiors befitting the 1960s building.

Bathrooms are shared and there's no elevator. From the station, exit right, turn right at the third stoplight and make the first left.

Shin-Osaka Youth Hostel   Hostel ¥

(新大阪ユースホステル; ☏6370-5427; http://osaka-yha.or.jp/shin-osaka-eng; 1-13-13 Higashinakajima, Koko Plaza; dm/tw ¥3400/9200; ⊖❄@🗢👬; 🚉 JR line to Shin-Osaka, east exit) Five minutes southeast of Shin-Osaka Station, this efficiently run hostel sits on the top floors of a contemporary, 10-storey tower with great views across the city. Rooms and common areas are big, well equipped and spotless; private rooms are great value. There's a daytime

A side dish of hijiki (sea green)

lockout (you can still use the lounge), midnight curfew and breakfast for ¥500.

Eating

UMEDA & OSAKA STATION AREA

Robatayaki Isaribi
Izakaya, Yakitori ¥¥

(炉ばた焼き漁火; Map p270; ☑6373-2969; www.rikimaru-group.com/shop/isaribi.html; 1-5-12 Shibata; dishes ¥324; ☺5-11.15pm; 🍴; 🚇JR line to Osaka) Head downstairs to this spirited, friendly *izakaya* for standards such as skewered meats, seafood, veggies fresh off the grill and giant pieces of *tori no karaage* (fried chicken). The best seats are at half-round counters, where your chef will serve you using a *loooong* paddle. Most dishes are ¥324.

Ganko Umeda Honten
Japanese ¥¥

(がんこ梅田本店; Map p270; ☑6376-2001; www.gankofood.co.jp; 1-5-11 Shibata; meals ¥780-5000; ☺11.30am-4am, to midnight Sun; 🍴; 🚇JR line to Osaka) At the main branch of this Osaka institution, a large dining hall serves a wide variety of set-course meals and sushi (à la carte or in sets), offering traditional, quality ingredients at a reasonable price. It's on the street along the west side of Hankyū Umeda Station. Look for the logo of the guy wearing a headband.

Yukari
Okonomiyaki ¥¥

(ゆかり; Map p270; ☑6311-0214; www.yukarichan.co.jp; Ohatsutenjin-dōri; okonomiyaki ¥800-1460; ☺11am-1am; 🍴🍴; 🚇JR line to Osaka) This popular restaurant in the Ohatsutenjin-dōri arcade serves up that great Osaka favourite, *okonomiyaki* (savoury pancakes), cooked on a griddle before you. There are lots to choose from the picture menu, including veg options, but the *tokusen mikkusu yaki* (mixed *okonomiyaki* with fried pork, shrimp and squid; ¥1080) is a classic. Look for red and white signage out front.

SHINSAIBASHI & AMERIKA-MURA

Café Absinthe
Mediterranean ¥¥

(カフェアブサン; Map p272; ☑6534-6635; www.absinthe-jp.com; 1-2-27 Kitahorie; mains lunch ¥800-1000, dinner ¥800-1600; ☺3pm-3am, to 5am Sat & Sun, closed Tue; 🍴; 🚇Midō-suji line to Shinsaibashi, exit 7) Friendly and trendy, near the western edge of Ame-Mura, Absinthe serves fantastic cocktails, non-alcoholic drinks and juices and a rare (for Japan) Mediterranean menu (falafel, hummus and babaganoush, plus pastas and pizzas). It's a tad pricey, but you're paying for quality ingredients, stylish surrounds and laid-back atmosphere; sliding doors create a sidewalk cafe vibe, weather permitting. And, yes, it does serve absinthe.

Le Coccole
Vegan ¥¥

(レ コッコレ; ☑6245-5556; www.le-coccole.jp; 3-4-1 Kita-kyuhoji-machi; small plates ¥400-900, mains ¥900-1400; ☺11:30am-10pm, until 6pm Sun, closed Mon & Tue; 🍴🍴; 🚇Midō-suji or Chūō Line to Honmachi, exit 11) At this adorable, all-vegan, mostly organic restaurant, lunch might be Indian curry or brown rice risotto, while dinner gets more Japanese-fusion with dishes like *hijiki* (sea green) samosas, shiitake mushroom cutlets, and pasta with dried tofu, shiitake, onion, *oba* (beefsteak plant) leaves and walnut and garlic sauce. From the cafe menu, try smoothies, coffees and tofu cheesecake.

Nishiya
Noodles ¥¥

(にし家; Map p272; ☑6241-9221; 1-18-18 Higashi Shinsaibashi; mains ¥650-1300, dinner courses ¥3000-5000; ☺11am-11pm Mon-Sat, to 9.30pm Sun; 🍴; 🚇Midō-suji line to Shinsaibashi, exit 5 or 6) A peaceful retreat from the busy streets of Shinsaibashi, this welcoming Osaka landmark serves udon noodles, hearty *nabe* (cast-iron pot) dishes, and *shabu-shabu* (thin slices of meat and vegetables cooked in a broth and dipped in sauce) for reasonable prices. Look for the traditional three-storey wooden building with sliding-door entrance, just north of the corner.

Restaurant Halls

From upper floors to shopping malls to underground shopping arcades, Osaka positively bursts with restaurant collections, with options for all price ranges. Not all have English menus, but many do have picture menus or food displays and prices in the windows, making it easy to browse. Here's a selection from north to south.

Grand Front Osaka (グランフロント大阪; Map p270; 🚉 JR Osaka Station, north exit) At the fancy new shopping mall north of JR Osaka Station, **Umekita Dining** on the 7th through 9th floors of the south building has 36 restaurants, most pretty splashy. For a different experience, **Umekita Cellar** is a food hall with, unusually, both eat-in and takeout options.

JR Osaka Station (JR大阪駅) The 70-plus eateries across multiple buildings here are almost overwhelming. To target your browsing, **Eki Marché** on the southwest side has dozens of small, reasonably priced spots such as **Kani Chahan-no-Mise** (かにチャーハンの店; Map p270; 🕿 06-6341-3103; 3-1-1 Umeda, Eki-Marché; mains from ¥680; 🕙 10am-10.30pm) for delectable crab fried rice, and a branch of **Kaiten Sushi Ganko** (回転寿司がんこ; Map p270; 🕿 06-4799-6811; 3-1-1 Umeda, Eki Marché; sushi plates ¥130-627; 🕙 11am-11pm) does *kaiten-sushi* (conveyor-belt sushi).

Namba Parks Mall (Map p272) On the 6th floor alone are 26 restaurants from *kushikatsu* to sushi, Chinese to Italian. At the far end, mostly organic **Sai-ji-ki** (菜蒔季; Map p272; 🕿 6636-8123; 6th fl, Namba Parks, 2-10-70 Namba-naka; lunch/dinner from ¥1510/1940; 🕙 11am-9pm; 🚭🍴👶; Ⓢ Midō-suji, Sennichimae, or Yotsubashi line to Namba) is an all-you-can-eat buffet.

Abeno Harukas (あべのハルカス; 1-1-43 Abeno-suji; 🚉 JR Lines to Tennō-ji, Kintetsu lines to Abenobashi) The main restaurant floors (12 through 14) of Japan's tallest skyscraper have some 44 restaurants among them, with specialities from *fugu* (puffer fish) to pizza. Try for a window seat for sweeping views.

DŌTOMBORI & AROUND

Dōtombori is crammed with eateries, most serving heaped portions of tasty food in a very casual atmosphere. It can be a lot of fun, and because it sees a lot of tourists, most of the big restaurants here have English menus.

Daiki Suisan   Sushi ¥
(大起水産; Map p272; 🕿 06-6214-1055; 1-7-24 Dōtombori; dishes ¥100-500; 🕙 11am-11pm; 🗾) There's a cheery bustle inside this hard-working *kaiten-sushi* restaurant in a prime Dōtombori location. Over 50 seats zigzag around counters where plates rotate, colour-coded by price and thoughtfully labelled in multiple languages. Non-sushi-eaters can get cooked foods including *tori no karaage* (fried chicken) and fried tuna. English-speaking staff help make sense of it all.

Chibō   Okonomiyaki ¥¥
(千房; Map p272; 🕿 6212-2211; www.chibo.com; 1-5-5 Dōtombori; mains ¥1004-1652; 🕙 11am-1am Mon-Sat, to midnight Sun; 🗾; Ⓢ Midō-suji line to Namba) A popular place to sample Osaka's signature dish. Try the house special *Dōtombori yaki,* a toothsome treat with pork, beef, squid, shrimp and cheese. Another unique specialty: *tonpei-yaki,* an omelette wrapped around fried pork. Some tables look out over the Dōtombori canal.

FRANK DEIM/GETTY IMAGES ©

Don't Miss
Dōtombori

Highly photogenic Dōtombori is the city's liveliest night spot and centre of the Minami (south) part of town. Its name comes from the 400-year-old Dōtombori-gawa canal, now lined with pedestrian walkways and a riot of illuminated billboards glittering off its waters (the running man advertising Glico candy is a landmark). Best views are from the bridge Ebisu-bashi at night.

Just south and parallel to the canal is the pedestrianised **Dōtombori Street** (道頓堀; Map p272; Ⓢ Midō-suji line to Namba), where dozens of restaurants and theatres vie for attention with the flashiest of singage: giant 3-D crab, puffer fish, dragon and more. There are plenty of tourists here, but hey, sometimes you're a tourist too, right?

Just south of Dōtombori Street is **Hōzen-ji** (法善寺; Map p272), a tiny temple hidden down a narrow paved alley off Senichi-mae arcade. The temple is built around a moss-covered **Fudō-myōō statue**. In place of standard offerings, people show their respects at the temple by splashing water over the statue, hence its bushy appearance. Running parallel to this alley is atmospheric **Hōzen-ji Yokochō** (法善寺横丁; Hōzen-ji Alley; Map p272; Ⓢ Midō-suji line to Namba), dotted with traditional restaurants and bars.

Further south, toward Nankai Namba Station, is a maze of arcades with more restaurants, *pachinko* parlours, strip clubs and who knows what else.

The nearest stations to Dōtombori are Namba, on the Midō-suji line, or Nipponbashi, on the Sakai-suji and Sennichimae lines.

Imai Honten   Noodles ¥¥
(今井本店; Map p272; ☑ 6211-0319; http://d-imai.com; 1-7-22 Dōtombori; dishes from ¥752;

🕐11am-10pm, closed Wed; ▣; Ⓢ Midō-suji line to Namba) Step into an oasis of calm amid Dōtombori's chaos to be welcomed by kimono-clad staff at one of the area's

Five Essential Osaka Foods

Okonomiyaki Thick, savoury pancakes filled with shredded cabbage and your choice of meat, seafood, vegetables and more (the name means 'cook as you like'). Often prepared on a *teppan* (steel plate) set into your table, the cooked pie is brushed with a savoury Worcestershire-style sauce, decoratively striped with mayonnaise and topped with dried bonito flakes which seem to dance in the rising steam. Slice off a wedge using tiny trowels called *kote*, and – warning – allow it to cool a bit before taking that first bite. Try it at **Chibō** (p278) in Dōtombori or **Yukari** (p277) in Umeda.

Tako-yaki The octopus dumpling counterpart to *okonomiyaki*: balls made of batter with a dollop of octopus (*tako* in Japanese) in the middle, served with picked ginger, topped with savoury sauce, powdered *aonori* (seaweed), mayonnaise and bonito flakes, and typically eaten with toothpicks. Any good street fair will have a booth selling them, or **Wanaka** (わなか; Map p272; 06-6631-0127; 11-19 Sennichi-mae; tako-yaki from ¥450 per 8; 10am-11pm Mon-Fri, from 8.30am Sat & Sun) is a classic *tako-yaki* stand just north of the **Dōguya-suji arcade** (p285).

Kushikatsu *Yakitori* is grilled meat, seafood and/or vegetables on a stick, and *kushikatsu* is the same ingredients breaded, deep fried and served with a savoury dipping sauce (double-dipping is a serious no-no). Goes very well with beer. The Shin-Sekai neighbourhood is famed for *kushikatsu* restaurants in the lanes south of Tsūten-kaku tower, including **Yokozuna** (横綱; 06-6630-8440; 3-6-1 Ebisu-higashi; dishes ¥100-550; 10am-11pm; S Midōsuji Line to Dōbutsu-en-mae, exit 5).

Kaiten-sushi Whether you call it conveyor-belt sushi, sushi-go-round or sushi train, sit at the counter and the plates of sushi come to you. This Osaka invention (in the 1950s) was long considered downmarket, but as Japan has gravitated toward cheap eats in the Great Recession, *kaiten-sushi* bars have been raising their quality. It'll never be a sushi master experience, but it's hard to beat for cheap and quick. Try it at **Daiki Suisan** (p278).

Kappō-ryōri Osaka-style *kaiseki*, a sophisticated, multicourse meal of seasonal dishes served with style on refined dishes to match the high-quality cuisine. It can be frightfully expensive, but **Shoubentango-tei** does a reasonably priced version in soothing surrounds.

oldest and most revered udon specialists. Try *kitsune udon* – noodles topped with soup-soaked slices of fried tofu. Look for the traditional front, and the willow tree outside.

Zauo
Seafood ¥¥

(ざうお難波本店; Map p272; 6212-5882; www.zauo.com; Washington Hotel Plaza B1 fl, Nipponbashi 1-1-13; meals ¥680-6000; 5pm-midnight Mon-Fri, 11.30am-midnight Sat & Sun; ; S Sakai-suji line to Nipponbashi, exit 6, or Midō-suji line to Namba) In this country where seafood is sometimes eaten so fresh it's still moving, Zauo has tables on long 'fishing boats' over tanks where patrons fish for their own dinner. If you're lucky enough to hook something, there's celebratory drumming and your fish is whisked away to be prepared how you like (priced according to the type of fish).

Shoubentango-tei

Kappō-Ryōri, Kaiseki ¥¥¥

(正弁丹吾亭; Map p272; ☎06-6211-3208; 1-7-12 Dōtonbori; dinner courses from ¥6000, mini kappō-kaiseki from ¥4000; ⏱5pm-10pm; 🍴; ⓢMidō-suji line to Namba) On Hōzen-ji Yokochō, the minimalist atmosphere of this graceful shop lets you feast your eyes on *kappō-ryōri*: a multicourse chef-driven extravaganza artfully presented in gorgeous pottery that might come topped with a colourful leaf or water-misted for just the right sheen. Since peak seasonal ingredients change virtually daily, you may never have the same dish twice here.

 Drinking & Nightlife

Osakans work hard, but when quitting time rolls around they know how to party. Stroll through Minami on a Friday night and you might think there's one bar for every resident, from *izakaya* to Irish pubs and cocktail bars with stunning views.

There's also a growing craft beer scene – look for the *Osaka Craft Beer Map* for dozens of places to sample it. Also great are summertime rooftop **beer gardens** offering all you can drink and eat in lively, casual surrounds – the one atop **Hanshin Department Store** (阪神梅田; Map p270; www.hanshin-dept.jp/hshonten; ⏱10am-8pm) is particularly good.

For club and entertainment events, pick up a copy of the English-language *Kansai Scene* (www.kansaiscene.com) or visit online.

UMEDA & OSAKA STATION AREA

Minami might be Osaka's real nightlife district, but there are bars, clubs and *izakaya* in the neighbourhoods to the south and east of Osaka Station, and around Hankyū Umeda Station.

Craft Beer Base
Bar

(クラフトビアベース; Map p270; 1-2-11 Ōyodo-minami; ⏱11am-11pm, from 3pm Tue; ⓢMidōsuji line to Umeda, ⓡJR lines to Osaka) In the shadow of the Umeda Sky Building, this bar/bottle shop specialises in local and worldwide craft beers. Order and enjoy around the counter, or climb the narrow stairs to a simple white-walled room. From Osaka or Umeda stations' north exits, take the underground passage toward Umeda Sky Building, and turn left.

Nightlife in Osaka

VINCENT ST. THOMAS/SHUTTERSTOCK ©

G Physique Gay Bar
(Map p270; www.physiqueosaka.com; 8-23 Dōyama-chō, 1F Sanyo-Kaikan Bldg; ⊙from 7pm, closing time varies; Ⓢ Midōsuji line to Umeda, Ⓡ JR lines to Osaka) In the warren of tiny bars of the Dōyama-chō, east of Osaka Station, gay men have been coming to this subtly stylish spot since 1993. There's no cover, reasonably priced drinks, and a warm welcome to locals and visitors alike.

Windows on the World Bar
(ウィンドーズオンザワールド; Map p270; 1-8-8 Umeda, Hilton Osaka, 35th fl; ⊙5.30pm-12.30am Mon-Thu & Sun, to 1am Fri & Sat; Ⓢ Yotsubashi-suji line to Nishi-Umeda, Ⓡ JR line to Osaka) An unbeatable spot for sophisticated drinks with a view, on the Hilton Osaka's 35th floor. There's a ¥1750 per person table charge (¥1200 for hotel guests) and drinks average ¥2000. Popular food menu items include a gourmet plate (¥3300) of smoked salmon, ham, cheese, salami, shrimp and more.

SHINSAIBASHI & AMERIKA-MURA

This is the place for a big night out in Osaka, with numerous bars, clubs and restaurants packed into streets and alleys.

Zerro Bar
(ゼロ; Map p272; 2-3-2 Shinsaibashi-suji; ⊙7pm-5am; Ⓢ Midō-suji line to Namba or Shinsaibashi) Zerro has a good range of drinks and food, energetic bilingual bartenders, and a street-level location ideal for a spot of people-watching. Come early for relaxed drinks and conversation; come late on the weekend for DJs, dancing and a lively crowd.

Cinquecento Bar
(チンクエチェント; Map p272; 2-1-10 Higashi-Shinsaibashi; ⊙7.30pm-5am Mon-Sat, 8pm-3am Sun; Ⓢ Midō-suji line to Namba or Shinsaibashi) The name is Italian for '500', appropriate since everything at this cosy bar costs ¥500. There's a hearty selection of food and the impressively extensive martini

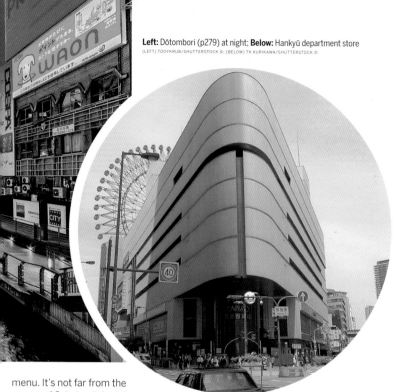

Left: Dōtombori (p279) at night; Below: Hankyū department store
(LEFT) TOOYKRUB/SHUTTERSTOCK ©; (BELOW) TK KURIKAWA/SHUTTERSTOCK ©

menu. It's not far from the corner of Sakai-suji; look for the 5 in a red circle.

Onzieme (11)   Club

(オンジェム; Map p272; www.onzi-eme.com; 11th fl, Midō-suji Bldg, 1-4-5 Nishi-Shinsaibashi; cover charge average ¥2500; S Midō-suji line to Shinsaibashi, exit 7) Osaka's largest and liveliest spot for nightlife at its craziest. An assortment of local and internationally acclaimed house, hip-hop and techno DJs showcase their talents nightly, with the posh interior reminiscent of some of the more famous London establishments.

Grand Café   Club

(グランドカフェ; Map p272; http://grandcafe osaka.com; B1 fl, Spazio Bldg, 2-10-21 Nishi-Shinsaibashi; S Midō-suji to Shinsaibashi) This hip underground club in Ame-Mura hosts a variety of electronica-DJ and hip-hop events. There's a comfy seating area and several dance floors. Look for the English sign at street level.

Shopping

Osaka has almost as many shops as restaurants: major department stores, international fashion, independent boutiques, electronic goods and secondhand stores. For overseas visitors, major department stores and many other large retailers can waive the sales tax on purchases over ¥10,000. Look for signage in the window or inquire; passport required.

UMEDA & OSAKA STATION AREA

Kita is a magnet for department stores clustered around its stations, such as:

Daimaru (大丸梅田店; Map p270; ☎06-6343-1231; www.daimaru.co.jp/umedamise; 3-1-1 Umeda; ⏰10am-8pm)

Hankyū (阪急梅田本店; Map p270; www.hankyu-dept.co.jp/honten; ⏰10am-8pm Sun-Thu, to 9pm Fri & Sat)

Denden Town & Otaku Road

From the Japanese word for electricity (*denki*), **Denden Town** – Osaka's version of Tokyo's Akihabara electronics district – is looking a bit tired these days, no doubt due to competition from megastores like Bic Camera and Yodobashi. Still, there's huge variety and some bargains (though make sure your gadget will work in your home country or with your operating system). Most stores are closed on Wednesdays.

One block west is **Otaku Road**, several blocks of shops for manga (Japanese comics), anime (Japanese animation) and their inspired merchandise, plus secondhand video games, and *cosplay* outlets.

Denden Town runs along Sakai-suji, starting southeast of Nankai Namba Station and continuing down to Ebisu-chō Station on the Sakai-suji subway line (exit 1a, 1b or 2).

Hanshin (p281)

Hep Five (Map p270; www.hepfive.jp; ⏰shops 10am-8pm, entertainment 10am-11pm) This complex is more youth-oriented and has a Ferris wheel on top.

Other shopping complexes include:

Grand Front Osaka (p278)

Hankyū Men's (阪急メンズ; Map p270; www.hankyu-dept.co.jp/mens/; ⏰11am-9pm Mon-Fri, 10am-9pm Sat, to 8pm Sun), in the ship-shaped Hep Navio building, will appeal to fashion-savvy guys.

Lucua (ルクア; Map p270; www.lucua.jp; ⏰shops 10am-9pm, dining 11am-11pm) in JR Osaka Station.

NU Chayamachi (NU茶屋町; Map p270; http://nu-chayamachi.com; ⏰fashion shops 11am-9pm, Tower Records 11am-11pm, restaurants 11am-midnight)

Yodobashi Umeda (Map p270; ⏰shops 9am-10pm, restaurants 11am-11pm) Features tech and fashion stores, plus dining options.

Also in the Osaka Station complex are branches of well-loved Japanese retailers **Tokyū Hands** (東急ハンズ; Map p270; www.tokyu-hands.co.jp; 10th-12th fl, Daimaru, 3-1-1 Umeda; ⏰10am-9pm, to 8.30pm Sun; 🚉JR line to Osaka) and **Uniqlo**, and the **Pokemon Centre** (ポケットモンスター; Map p270; 3-1-1 Umeda, Daimaru Department Store, 13th fl) for branded goods.

Maruzen & Junkudō Umeda Books
(丸善&ジュンク堂書店梅田店; Map p270; www.junkudo.co.jp/MJumeda.html; 7-20 Chaya-machi; ⏰10am-10pm; 🚉JR line to Osaka) This new behemoth bookshop, the largest in Osaka, is the result of two book specialists joining forces. There's a big range of English-language books on the 6th floor, with travel guides on the 3rd floor. It's in the new Andō Tadao–designed Chaska Chayamachi building.

SHINSAIBASHI, AMERIKA-MURA & NAMBA

Minami has a huge range of shops. International high-end brands fill Midō-suji, the main boulevard, between Shinsaibashi and Namba subway stations. Head east to the jam-packed Shinsaibashi-suji arcade for popular local and international chains, and Ame-Mura for out-there and vintage clothes, accessories for everything from your person to your car – at outrageously blinged-out **D.A.D** (D.A.D大阪アメリカ村店; Map p272; 2-8-29 Nishi-Shinsaibashi; ⏰11am-9pm; 🚇Midō-suji line to Shinsaibashi, exit 7) – and music. Massive shopping complexes dominate Namba, including **Osaka Takashimaya** (大阪タカ

シマヤ; Map p272; http://www.takashimaya. co.jp/osaka/store_information/index.html; 5-1-5 Namba; **S** Namba) department store and **Namba Parks Mall** (なんばパークス; Map p272; www.nambaparks.com; 2-10-70 Namba-naka; ⊙11am-9pm; **S** Midō-suji, Sennichimae, Yotsubashi line to Namba).

Dōguya-suji Arcade   Market
(道具屋筋; Map p272; www.doguyasuji.or.jp/ map_eng.html; **S** Midō-suji line to Namba) This blocks-long foodie's paradise sells just about anything related to the preparation, consumption and selling of food: all manner of pots, pans, knives, kitchen gadgets, tableware, even shopfront lanterns, bar signs and plastic food models. Start thinking about how to make room in the suitcase for that stuff you never realised you needed.

Village Vanguard   Books, Homewares
(ヴィレッジヴァンガード; Map p272; www. village-v.co.jp; 1-10-28 Nishi-Shinsaibashi; ⊙11am-11pm; **S** Midō-suji line to Shinsai-bashi, exit 7) A great starting point for fun, non-traditional, pop- and street-insiped mementos of your time in Japan. Village

Vanguard bills itself as an 'exciting' bookstore, but there's much more to the story: between the cluttered book and magazine racks are offbeat gifts, from animal-shaped coat hooks to design-led T-shirts, mobile-phone cases, kitchen devices, hip-hop hats, shoulder bags, homewares and more.

Tokyu Hands   Department Store
(東急ハンズ; Map p272; www.tokyu-hands. co.jp; 3-4-12 Minamisenba; ⊙10.30am-8.30pm; **S** Midō-suji line to Shinsaibashi) Nominally a DIY and houseware chain, Tokyū Hands is Japan's favourite place to browse for items you probably didn't need but will end up loving. It's stacked floor upon floor with obscure tools to design-forward lighting, clocks, curios and craft supplies, just for starters. There's a smaller branch in Umeda.

Bic Camera   Electronics
(ビックカメラ; Map p272; www.biccamera. co.jp/shoplist/nanba.html; 2-10-1 Sennichimae; ⊙10am-9pm; **S** Midō-suji or Sennichimae line to Namba) This vast store sells everything related to cameras, electronics and computers at competitive prices.

Shinsaibashi-Suji arcade

SURASSAWADEE/SHUTTERSTOCK ©

ℹ️ Information

Money

ATMs at Citibank, large post offices, and 7-Eleven stores take international cards. Major banks and post offices have currency-exchange services.

Citibank (シティバンク; Map p270; http://citibank.co.jp; 2nd fl, Dai-ichi Semei Bldg, 1-8-17 Umeda; ⏰9am-8pm Mon-Fri, 10am-5pm Sat & Sun, ATM 24hr; 🚆JR line to Osaka) Other branches at Shinsaibashi (Map p272; Midō-suji Diamond Bldg, 2-1-2 Nishi Shinsaibashi; ⏰9am-3pm Mon-Fri, ATM 24hr; Ⓢ Midō-suji line to Shinsaibashi) and Umeda (Map p270; 7th fl, ABC-MART Umeda Bldg, 1-27 Chaya-machi, across from Hankyū Station; ⏰9am-3pm & 5-7pm Mon-Fri, 10am-4pm Sat, ATM 8am-10pm; 🚆Hankyū line to Umeda or JR line to Osaka); there's also a 24-hour ATM at Kansai International Airport.

Post

Osaka Central Post Office (大阪中央郵便局; Map p270; 3-2-4 Umeda; postal services 9am-9pm, ATM 7am-11.30pm Mon-Fri, 8am-11.30pm Sat, 9am-9pm Sun; Ⓢ Midōsuji line to Umeda or Yotsubashi-suji line to Nishi-Umeda, 🚆JR line to Osaka)

Tourist Information

Tourist offices can help book accommodation if you visit in person. There are offices in the main stations, and information counters at the airports. To get the low-down on upcoming events, pick up a copy of *Kansai Scene* magazine, available for free at major bookshops.

Osaka Visitors Information Center, Umeda (大阪市ビジターズインフォメーションセンター・梅田; Map p270; 📞6345-2189; www.osaka-info.jp; 1st fl, North Central Gate, JR Osaka Station; ⏰8am-8pm; 🚆JR lines to Osaka Station) The main tourist office is inside JR Osaka Station. There is another office on the 1st floor of Nankai Namba Station (大阪市ビジターズインフォメーションセンター・なんば; Map p272; 📞6631-9100; ⏰9am-8pm; Ⓢ Namba, 🚆Nankai line to Namba Station).

ℹ️ Getting There & Away

Air

Two airports serve Osaka: **Kansai International Airport** (KIX; 関西空港; www.kansai-airport.or.jp/en) for all international and some domestic flights; and the domestic **Itami Airport** (ITM; 伊丹空港; http://osaka-airport.co.jp/), also confusingly called Osaka International Airport. KIX is about

Deer at Nara-Kōen (p289)

50km southwest of the city, on an artificial island in the bay. Itami is located in Osaka itself.

Train

Shin-Osaka Station is on the Tōkaidō-Sanyō Shinkansen (between Tokyo and Hakata in Fukuoka) and the eastern terminus of the Kyūshū Shinkansen to Kagoshima. There are direct trains to Tokyo (¥13,620, three hours), Hiroshima (¥9710, 1½ hours), Hakata (¥14,480, three hours), Kagoshima (¥21,380, 4¾ hours) and points in between.

Kyoto

While *shinkansen* is fastest between Kyoto and Shin-Osaka (from ¥1420, 14 minutes), JR *shinkaisoku* (special rapid train) between Kyoto Station and JR Osaka Station (¥560, 28 minutes) is more convenient to the city centre.

The Hankyū line runs between Hankyū Umeda Station in Osaka and Kawaramachi, Karasuma and Ōmiya stations in Kyoto (*tokkyū* limited express train to Kawaramachi ¥400, 44 minutes). The Keihan line runs between Sanjō, Shijō or Shichijō stations in Kyoto and Yodoyabashi Station in Osaka (*tokkyū* to Sanjō ¥410, 54 minutes), on the Midō-suji subway line.

Kōbe

The *shinkansen* runs between Shin-Kōbe Station and Shin-Osaka Station (from ¥1500, 13 minutes). There is also a JR *shinkaisoku* train between JR Osaka Station and Kōbe's Sannomiya and Kōbe stations (¥410, 22 minutes).

The Hankyū line is a little cheaper and usually less crowded. It runs from Osaka's Hankyū Umeda Station to Kōbe's Sannomiya Station (*tokkyū*, ¥320, 30 minutes).

Nara

The JR Kansai line links Osaka's Namba and Tennō-ji stations to JR Nara Station via Hōryū-ji (*yamatoji kaisoku*, ¥540, 50 minutes). The Kintetsu Nara line runs from Namba (Kintetsu Namba Station) to Kintetsu Nara Station (¥540, 40 minutes).

ℹ Getting Around

To/From the Airport

Kansai International Airport (KIX)

KIX is well connected to the city with direct train lines and buses.

The all-reserved Nankai Express Rapid runs to/from Nankai Namba Station (¥1430, 35 minutes); Nankai Airport Express trains take about 10 minutes longer and cost ¥920. JR's Haruka limited airport express runs between KIX and Tennō-ji Station (unreserved seat ¥1710, 33 minutes) and Shin-Osaka Station (¥2330, 49 minutes). Regular JR express trains called *kankū kaisoku* also run between KIX, Osaka Station (¥1190, 68 minutes) and Tennō-ji (¥1060, 50 minutes). All these stations connect to the Midō-suji subway line.

Airport limousine buses run to/from Osaka Station/Umeda area, Osaka City Air Terminal (OCAT), Namba, Uehonmachi and the Tempōzan area. The fare is ¥1550 for most routes (¥1050 to OCAT) and it takes an average of 50 minutes, depending on traffic (it can take up to 90 minutes to Umeda). See www.kate.co.jp for timetables.

Trains stop running from the airport at 11.30pm, and the last bus leaves just after midnight. If your flight arrives after this, your other option into Osaka is taxi. It takes about 50 minutes and there are standard fares to Osaka Umeda (¥14,500) and Namba (¥14,000). The late-night fare is an additional ¥2500. It's about ¥18,000 to Shin-Osaka.

Osaka Itami Airport

Frequent limousine buses connect the airport and various parts of Osaka. Buses run to/from Shin-Osaka Station (¥500, 25 minutes), Osaka and Namba stations (¥640, 25 minutes) every 20 minutes from about 8am to 9pm. At Itami, buy your tickets from the machine outside the arrivals hall. See www.okkbus.co.jp for timetables.

Train

Osaka has a good subway network and, like Tokyo, a JR loop line (known as the Kanjō-sen) that circles the city area, intersecting with the subways and other train lines. You're not likely to need any other form of transport unless you stay out late and miss the last train.

There are eight subway lines, but the one that short-term visitors will find most useful is the Midō-suji (red) line, running north-south, stopping at Shin-Osaka, Umeda (next to Osaka Station), Shinsaibashi, Namba and Tennō-ji stations. Most rides cost between ¥200 and ¥300, and day passes are available (per day Monday to Friday/Saturday and Sunday ¥800/600).

NARA

📞 0742 / POP 364,969

Japan's first permanent capital, Nara (奈良) is one of the country's most rewarding destinations. With eight Unesco World

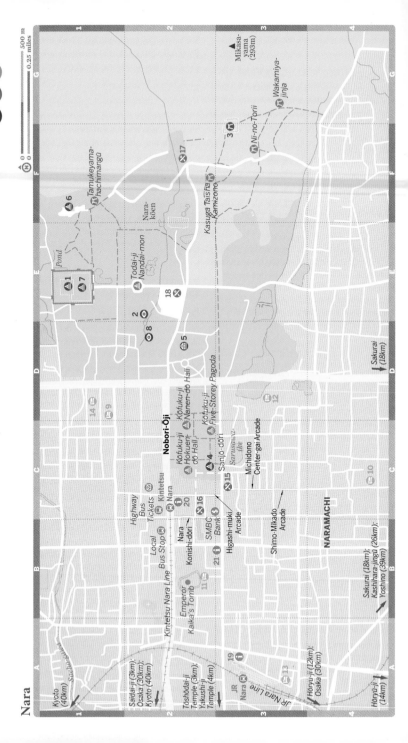

Nara

0 0 — 500 m
0 0 — 0.25 miles

Mikasa-
yama
(293m)

Wakamiya-
jinja

Ni-no-Torii

Tamukeyama-
hachimangū

Kasuga Taisha
Kamizono

Nara-
kōen

Pond

Todai-ji
Nandai-mon

Kōfuku-ji
Namen-do Hall

Kōfuku-ji
Hokuen-
do Hall

Kōfuku-ji
Five-Storey Pagoda

Nobori-Ōji

Sanjō-dōri

Sarusawa-
ike

Michidono
Center-gai Arcade

Highway
Bus
Tickets

Kintetsu
Nara

Local
Bus Stop

Nara
Konishi-dōri

SMBC
Bank

Higashi-muki
Arcade

Shimo-Mikado
Arcade

NARAMACHI

Emperor
Kaika's Tomb

Kintetsu Nara Line

JR
Nara

JR Nara Line

Kyoto
(40km)

Saidai-ji (3km);
Osaka (30km);
Kyoto (40km)

Tōshōdai-ji
Temple (3km);
Yakushi-ji
Temple (4km)

Sakurai (18km);
Kashihara-jingū (26km);
Yoshino (39km)

Hōryū-ji (12km);
Osaka (30km)

Hōryū-ji
(14km)

Sakurai
(18km)

Nara

Heritage Sites, it's second only to Kyoto as a repository of Japan's cultural legacy.

The centrepiece is the Daibutsu (Great Buddha), which rivals Mt Fuji and Kyoto's Golden Pavilion (Kinkaku-ji) as Japan's single most impressive sight. The Great Buddha is housed in Tōdai-ji, a soaring temple that presides over Nara-kōen, a park filled with other fascinating sights that lends itself to relaxed strolling amid greenery and tame deer.

Nara is also compact: it's quite possible to pack the highlights into one full day. Many people visit Nara as a side trip from Kyoto, by comfortable express trains in about half an hour, but with an overnight stay (there's high quality accommodation for all budgets) you might spend one day around the city centre and the other seeing the landmark temples west and southwest of Nara city.

◎ Sights

Nara retains its 8th century Chinese-style grid pattern of streets. There are two main train stations: JR Nara and Kintetsu Nara. JR Nara Station is a little west of the city centre (but still within walking distance of the sights), while Kintetsu Nara is right in the centre of town. Nara-kōen, which contains most of the important sights, is on the eastern side, against the bare flank of the mountain Wakakusa-yama. It's easy to cover the city centre and major attractions in nearby Nara-kōen on foot, although buses and taxis do ply the city.

NARA-KŌEN AREA 奈良公園

Many of Nara's most important sites are located around Nara-kōen, a fine park that occupies much of the east side of the city. The park is home to about 1200 deer, which in pre-Buddhist times were considered messengers of the gods and today enjoy the status of National Treasures. They roam the park and surrounding areas in search of handouts from tourists, often descending on petrified children who have the misfortune to be carrying food. You can buy *shika-sembei* (deer biscuits) from vendors for ¥150 to feed to the deer, and *shika-no-fun* (deer poo) chocolates to feed yourself.

Nara National Museum   Museum
(奈良国立博物館, Nara Kokuritsu Hakubutsu-kan; ☎ 050-5542-8600; www.narahaku.go.jp; 50 Noboriōji-chō; admission ¥520; ⏰ 9.30am-5pm, closed Mon) This museum is devoted to Buddhist art and is divided into two sections. Built in 1894, the **Nara Buddhist Sculpture Hall & Ritual Bronzes Gallery** contains a fine collection of *butsu-zō* (statues of Buddhas and Bodhisattvas). Buddhist images here are divided into categories, each with detailed English explanations for an excellent introduction to Mahayana Buddhist iconography. The newer **East and West wings**, a short walk away, contain the permanent collections (sculptures, paintings and calligraphy) and special exhibitions.

Kōfuku-ji
Buddhist Temple

(興福寺; www.kohfukuji.com) This temple was transferred here from Kyoto in 710. Although the original temple complex had 175 buildings, fires and destruction as a result of power struggles have left only a dozen standing. There are two pagodas – three storeys and five storeys – dating from 1143 and 1426, respectively. The taller of the two is the second-tallest in Japan, outclassed by the one at Kyoto's Tō-ji by a few centimetres.

Isui-en & Neiraku Art Museum
Gardens

(依水園・寧楽美術館; 74 Suimon-chō; admission museum & garden ¥650; ⊙9.30am-4.30pm, closed Tue except for Apr, May, Oct & Nov) This exquisite, contemplative Meiji-era garden features abundant greenery, ponds and walkways with stepping stones designed for you to observe each one as you walk, to appreciate their individual beauty. For ¥850 you can enjoy a cup of tea on tatami mats overlooking the garden. Admission covers the adjoining Neiraku Art Museum, displaying Chinese and Korean ceramics and bronzes in a quiet setting.

Yoshiki-en
Gardens

(吉城園; 68 Noboriōji-chō; free for foreign visitors, ¥250 for Japanese; ⊙9am-5pm, closed Jan-Feb) FREE This garden, located next door to Isui-en (to the right as you enter), is a stunner. Originally a residence of the high priest of Tōdai-ji, the present garden was laid out in 1918 and contains a lovely thatch-roof cottage, a pond and several walking paths. It's particularly lovely in November and early December, when the maples turn a blazing crimson. Look for the small English sign.

Tōdai-ji
Buddhist Temple

(東大寺) Nara's star attraction is the famous Daibutsu (Great Buddha), housed in the Daibutsu-den Hall of this grand temple. Though Tōdai-ji is often packed with tour groups and schoolchildren from across the country, it's big enough to absorb huge crowds and it belongs at the top of any Nara itinerary. Except for the Daibutsu-den Hall, most of Tōdai-ji's grounds can be visited free of charge. For more information about Tōdai-ji, see p292.

Kasuga Taisha

TOOYKRUB/SHUTTERSTOCK ©

Daibutsu-den Hall   Buddhist Temple

(大仏殿; Hall of the Great Buddha; 406-1 Zōshi-chō; admission ¥500, joint ticket with Tōdai-ji Museum ¥800; ⏱8am-4.30pm Nov-Feb, to 5pm Mar, 7.30am-5.30pm Apr-Sep, to 5pm Oct) Tōdai-ji's Daibutsu-den is the largest wooden building in the world. Incredibly, the present structure, rebuilt in 1709, is a mere two-thirds of the size of the original. The Daibutsu (Great Buddha) inside is one of the largest bronze figures in the world and was originally cast in 746. The present statue, recast in the Edo period, stands just over 16m high and consists of 437 tonnes of bronze and 130kg of gold.

Nigatsu-dō & Sangatsu-dō   Buddhist Temple

(二月堂、三月堂; Nigatsu-do free, Sangatsu-do ¥500; ⏱Nigatsu-do 7.30am-6pm Jun-Aug, 8am-5.45pm Apr-May & Sep-Oct, 8am-5.15pm Nov-Mar; Sangatsu-do 8am-4.30pm Nov-Feb, to 5pm Mar & Oct, 7.30am-5.30pm Apr-Sep) These sub-temples of Tōdai-ji are uphill from the Daibutsu-den and far less clamorous. Climb a lantern-lined staircase to Nigatsu-dō, a National Treasure from 1669 (originally built circa 750). Its verandah with sweeping views across the town (especially at dusk) may remind you of Kiyomizu-dera (p217) in Kyoto. This is where Nara's **Omizutori Matsuri** is held.

A short walk south of Nigatsu-dō is Sangatsu-dō, the oldest building in the Tōdai-ji complex and home to a small collection of fine Nara-period statues.

Kasuga Taisha   Shinto Shrine

(春日大社; 160 Kasugano-chō; ⏱dawn-dusk) FREE This sprawling shrine lies at the foot of a hill in a deeply wooded setting with herds of sacred deer awaiting handouts. Its pathways are lined with hundreds of lanterns, with many hundreds more in the shrine itself. They're illuminated in the twice-yearly **Mantōrō** lantern festivals.

Kasuga Taisha was founded in the 8th century by the Fujiwara family and was completely rebuilt every 20 years, according to Shintō tradition, until the end of the 19th century.

♥ If You Like...
Temples

If you like Tōdai-ji, we think you'll like these other beautiful temples in Nara Prefecture:

1 HŌRYŪ-JI

(法隆寺; www.horyuji.or.jp; admission ¥1000; ⏱8am-5pm Feb-Oct, to 4.30pm Nov-Mar) Hōryū-ji was founded in 607 by Prince Shōtoku, considered by many to be the patron saint of Japanese Buddhism. Hōryū-ji is a veritable shrine to Shōtoku and is renowned not only as the oldest temple in Japan, but also as a repository for some of the country's rarest treasures. Several of the temple's wooden buildings have survived earthquakes and fires to become the oldest of their kind in the world.

2 YAKUSHI-JI TEMPLE

(薬師寺; admission ¥500; ⏱8.30am-5pm) This temple houses some of the most beautiful Buddhist statues in all Japan. It was established by Emperor Temmu in 680 as a prayer for the healing of his wife. With the exception of the East Pagoda, which dates to 730 (and is due to be under renovation until 2018), the present buildings either date from the 13th century or are very recent reconstructions.

3 TŌSHŌDAI-JI TEMPLE

(唐招提寺; www.toshodaiji.jp; admission ¥600; ⏱8.30am-5pm, last entry by 4.30pm) This temple was established in 759 by the Chinese priest Ganjin (Jian Zhen), who had been recruited by Emperor Shōmu to reform Buddhism in Japan. The temple grounds are pleasantly wooded and mossy, making a good contrast to nearby Yakushi-ji, which is largely devoid of greenery.

🛏 Sleeping

Although Nara can be visited as a day trip from Kyoto or Osaka, it is pleasant to spend the night here, allowing for a more relaxing pace.

Guesthouse Nara Backpackers   Guesthouse ¥

(ゲストハウス 奈良バックパッカーズ; ☎22-4557; www.nara-backpackers.com; 31 Yurugichō; dm ¥2400, r without bathroom up to

Tōdai-ji

The Daibutsu (Great Buddha) at Nara's Tōdai-ji is one of the most arresting sights in Japan. The awe-inspiring physical presence of the vast image is striking. It's one of the largest bronze Buddha images in the world and it's contained in an equally huge building, the Daibutsu-den Hall, which is among the largest wooden buildings on earth.

Tōdai-ji was built by order of Emperor Shōmu during the Nara period (710–784) and the complex was finally completed in 798, after the capital had been moved from Nara to Kyoto. Most historians agree that the temple was built to consolidate the country and serve as its spiritual focus. Legend has it that over two million labourers worked on the temple, but this is probably apocryphal. What's certain is that its construction brought the country to the brink of bankruptcy.

The original Daibutsu was cast in bronze in eight castings over a period of three years. The Daibutsu, or certain parts of it, has been recast several times over the centuries. The original Daibutsu was covered in gold leaf and one can only imagine its impact on Japanese visitors during the eighth century AD.

The temple belongs to the Kegon school of Buddhism, one of the six schools of Buddhism popular in Japan during the Nara period. Kegon Buddhism, which comes from the Chinese Huayan Buddhist sect, is based on the Flower Garland Sutra. This sutra expresses the idea of worlds within worlds, all manifested by the Cosmic Buddha (Vairocana or Dainichi Nyorai). The Great Buddha and the figures that surround him in the Daibutsu-den Hall are the perfect physical symbol of this cosmological map.

FACT FILE

THE DAIBUTSU

» **Height**: 14.98m
» **Weight**: 500 tonnes
» **Nostril width**: 50cm

THE DAIBUTSU-DEN HALL

» **Height**: 48.74m
» **Length**: 57m
» **Number of roof tiles**: 112,589

Kokuzo Bosatsu
Seated to the left of the Daibutsu is Kokuzo Bosatsu, the bodhisattva of memory and wisdom, to whom students pray for help in their studies and the faithful pray for help on the path to enlightenment.

The Daibutsu (Great Buddha)
Known in Sanskrit as 'Vairocana' and in Japanese as the 'Daibutsu', this is the Cosmic Buddha that gives rise to all other Buddhas, according to Kegon doctrine. The Buddha's hands send the messages 'fear not' and 'welcome'.

JEFFREY FRIEDL ©

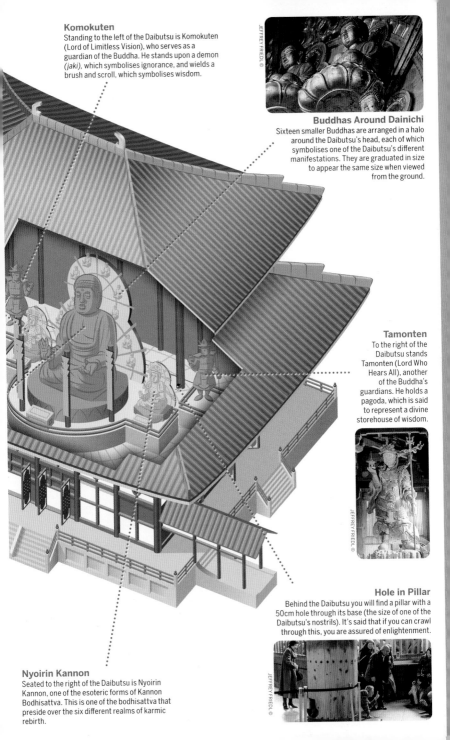

Komokuten
Standing to the left of the Daibutsu is Komokuten (Lord of Limitless Vision), who serves as a guardian of the Buddha. He stands upon a demon *(jaki)*, which symbolises ignorance, and wields a brush and scroll, which symbolises wisdom.

Buddhas Around Dainichi
Sixteen smaller Buddhas are arranged in a halo around the Daibutsu's head, each of which symbolises one of the Daibutsu's different manifestations. They are graduated in size to appear the same size when viewed from the ground.

Tamonten
To the right of the Daibutsu stands Tamonten (Lord Who Hears All), another of the Buddha's guardians. He holds a pagoda, which is said to represent a divine storehouse of wisdom.

Hole in Pillar
Behind the Daibutsu you will find a pillar with a 50cm hole through its base (the size of one of the Daibutsu's nostrils). It's said that if you can crawl through this, you are assured of enlightenment.

Nyoirin Kannon
Seated to the right of the Daibutsu is Nyoirin Kannon, one of the esoteric forms of Kannon Bodhisattva. This is one of the bodhisattva that preside over the six different realms of karmic rebirth.

JEFFREY FRIEDL ©

JEFFREY FRIEDL ©

JEFFREY FRIEDL ©

¥3800 per person; ✽ 🛜) An utterly charming stay in a traditional 1920s building, once a tea master's home. Choose from dorm rooms or three different-sized private tatami-mat rooms, some with garden views. Bathing facilities are shared (bring your own toiletries and towel, or buy or rent them here); shared kitchen for self-caterers. Per-night rates fall the longer you stay.

Guesthouse Sakuraya
Guesthouse ¥¥

(桜舎; www.guesthouse-sakuraya.com; 1 Narukawa-chō; s/d incl breakfast ¥6200/10,400; ✽ 🛜) This atmospheric stunner in Naramachi, just three quiet guest rooms in a former dyer's workshop, integrates both tradtional and contemporary touches around a lovely courtyard garden and common room and baths. One room has an ensuite toilet. The owner offers a 'Discovery of Japanese Culture' course (¥3000). If you're looking for a party, head elsewhere.

Hotel Fujita Nara
Hotel ¥¥

(ホテルフジタ奈良; 🕿 23-8111; http:// en.fujita-nara.com; 47-1 Shimosanjō-chō; s/d/tw from ¥8200/11,300/14,000; ✽ @ 🛜) In the heart of downtown Nara, about five minutes' walk from either main train station, this efficient hotel offers clean rooms, reasonable prices, some English-speaking staff and Japanese or Western breakfasts (¥1555).

Super Hotel Lohas JR Nara-eki
Business Hotel ¥¥

(スーパーホテルLohas・JR奈良駅; 🕿 27-9000; www.superhoteljapan.com/en/s-hotels/ nara-lohas.html; 1-2 Sanjō-honmachi; s/d/tw incl breakfast ¥7180/12,320/15,220; ✽ @ 🛜) Connected to JR Nara Station by an elevated walkway, this hotel has stylish, contemporary design, compact rooms with ensuite bathrooms, cheerful, efficient staff (some English-speaking), large communal onsen bath and coin-op laundry. Note: no in-room phones, but there are phones in the lobby.

Nara Hotel
Hotel ¥¥¥

(奈良ホテル; 🕿 26-3300; www.narahotel. co.jp/en; 1096 Takabatake-chō; s/tw from ¥19,008/34,452; ✽ @ 🛜) Founded in 1909, the grande dame of Nara hotels has hosted dignitaries from Edward VIII and Albert Einstein to the Dalai Lama. It retains a Meiji-era style in its traditional

Nara Hotel

exterior, high ceilings, gorgeous wood-work, refined Japanese and Western restaurants, bar and beautifully land-scaped grounds. Rooms are spacious and comfortable with big beds, though some have cramped unit bathrooms.

For historic atmosphere, we recommend the Honkan (main building) over the Shinkan (new building).

Wakasa Bettei   Ryokan ¥¥¥

(和鹿彩別邸; ☏0742-23-5858; www.n-wakasa. com/english; 1 Kita-handahigashi-machi; per person with no meals/two meals ¥22,727/34,546; ❄️🛜) This friendly, contemporary ryokan aims hard to please. The 11 stylish, large Japanese- and Western-style rooms have private facilities including stone or wooden bathtub, and the top-floor common bath has views of Tōdai-ji and Wakakusa-yama. We recommend the newer Bettei over the original (and still friendly) Hotel New Wakasa next door.

 # Eating

Nara is chock-a-block with good restaurants, mostly near the train stations and in Naramachi. For restaurant browsing, the covered arcade Higashi-muki Shōtengai, between Kintetsu Nara Station and Sanjō-dōri, has about a dozen restaurants: udon, sushi and Italian to fast food and coffee-and-sandwich chains.

Kameya   Okonomiyaki ¥

(かめや; ☏0742-22-2434; 9 Tarui-chō; mains ¥680-1140; 🕙11am-10pm; 📖) A giant red lantern marks the entrance to this casual, spirited okonomiyaki joint, going strong since the 1960s. There's a seemingly infinite number of combinations for the savoury pancakes; the 'mix okonomiyaki' contains squid, shrimp, pork and scallops. The yaki-soba roll has fried noodles inside. No English spoken, but staff make it work.

Mellow Café   Pizza, Desserts ¥

(メロー カフェ; ☏27-9099; 1-8 Konishi-chō; mains ¥710-1120, lunch specials ¥1200; 🕙11am-11.30pm; 🛜📖) Not far from Kintetsu Nara Station and down a narrow alley (look for the arbour and stone water barrel), this pleasant cafe centres on pasta and brick-oven pizzas, and desserts like the hojicha parfait (made with roasted-tea ice cream) or the Nara-inspired Bambi roll cake. Drinks include wine, cocktails and coffees.

Mizutani-chaya   Teahouse ¥

(水谷茶屋; ☏22-0627; 30 Kasugano-chō; mains ¥590-790; 🕙10am-4pm, closed Wed; 📖) In a small wooded clearing between Nigatsu-dō and Kasuga Taisha, this quaint thatched-roof teahouse is one of Nara's most atmospheric spots. Stop for a cup of matcha (powdered green tea, ¥700 including a sweet) or bowl of noodles for a quick pick-me up.

Yumekaze Plaza   Restaurant Mall ¥¥

(夢風ひろば; ☏0742-25-0870; www.yume-kaze.com; 16 Kasuganochō; 🕙vary by shop, mostly lunch and dinner) Adjacent to Nara-kōen and across from the Nara National Museum, this convenient collection of a dozen restaurants offers everything from handmade soba (at **Warabe Yorokobi An**, dishes ¥700-2000) to Italian (**Cafe I-lunga**, dishes ¥1100-1900) and wagashi (Japanese sweets) at **Tenpyō-an Cafe**, in attractively updated old-style buildings.

 # Information

The main JR Nara Station information centre (☏22-9821; www.narashikanko.or.jp/en; 🕙9am-9pm), in the old Nara Station building just outside the east exit of JR Nara Station, is the city's main tourist information centre and English speakers are usually on hand. If arriving at Kintetsu Nara Station, try the helpful Kintetsu Nara Station information office (☏24-4858; 🕙9am-9pm), near the top of the stairs above exit 3 from the station. Other information offices include the Nara City Tourist Information Centre (奈良市観光センター; ☏22-3900; 23-4 Kami-Sanjō-chō; 🕙9am-9pm).

All of the information offices stock useful maps and can assist with same-day hotel reservations.

Information centres can put you in touch with volunteer guides who speak English and other foreign languages, but you must book at least one day in advance. Try YMCA Goodwill Guides (☏45-5920; http://eggnara.tripod.com/home. htm) and Nara Student Guides (☏26-4753; www.narastudentguide.org).

❶ Getting There & Away

Bus

There is an overnight bus service between Tokyo's Shinjuku neighborhood and Nara (one way ¥5980 to ¥9500; rates vary by day). In Nara, call **Nara Kōtsū Bus** (☏22-5110; www.narakotsu.co.jp/kousoku, in Japanese) or check with the Nara City Tourist Information Centre for more details. In Nara, overnight buses leave from stop 4 in front of JR Nara Station east exit and from stop 20 outside Kintetsu Nara Station. In Tokyo, call **Kantō Bus** (☏03-3371-1225; www.kanto-bus.co.jp) or visit the Shinjuku highway bus terminal.

Buses to sights west (Yakushi-ji and Tōshōdai-ji) and southwest (Hōryū-ji) leave from stop 10, diagonally across from JR Nara Station, and stop 8 outside Kintetsu Nara Station.

Train

Kyoto

The Kintetsu line is the fastest and most convenient connection between Kyoto (Kintetsu Kyoto Station, in Kyoto Station) and central Nara (Kintetsu Nara Station). Comfortable, all-reserved *tokkyū* trains (¥1130, 35 minutes) run directly; *kyūkō* trains (¥620, 45 minutes) usually require a change at Yamato-Saidai-ji.

For Japan Rail Pass holders, the JR Nara line connects JR Kyoto Station with JR Nara Station (*kaisoku*; ¥710, 45 minutes) with several departures an hour.

Osaka

The Kintetsu Nara line connects Osaka (Namba Station) with Nara (Kintetsu Nara Station). *Kaisoku* and *futsū* services take about 40 minutes and cost ¥560. All-reserved-seat *tokkyū* trains take five minutes less but cost almost double.

For Japan Rail Pass holders, the JR Kansai line links JR Nara Station with Osaka (Namba and Tennō-ji stations), via *kaisoku* trains; (¥540, 45 minutes and ¥450, 30 minutes, respectively).

❶ Getting Around

To/From the Airport

Nara Kōtsū operates a limousine bus service (Nara Kōtsū; www.narakotsu.co.jp/kousoku/limousine/nara_kanku.html) between Nara and Kansai International (KIX; ¥2050, 90 mins, 6am-9pm) and Osaka Itami (ITM; ¥1480, 60 mins, 5am-5pm) airports, with departures roughly every hour. Buses depart from stop 4 in front of JR Nara Station east exit and stop 20 (Kansai International Airport) and 12 (Itami Airport) outside Kintetsu Nara Station. Purchase tickets at the ticket offices at the respective stations or the airports.

KŌYA-SAN 高野山

☏0736 / POP 3797

Kōya-san is a raised tableland in northern Wakayama-ken covered with thick forests and surrounded by eight peaks. The major attraction here is the Kōya-san monastic complex, which is the headquarters of the Shingon school of Esoteric Buddhism. Though not quite the Shangri-la it's occasionally described as, Kōya-san is one of Japan's most rewarding destinations, not just for the natural setting of the area but also as an opportunity to stay in temples and get a glimpse of some of the long-held traditions of Japanese religious life.

Although it is technically possible to visit Kōya-san as a day trip from Nara, Kyoto or Osaka, take it slow and stay overnight in one of the town's excellent *shukubō* (temple lodgings).

Kōya-san tends to be around 5°C colder than down on the plains, so bring warm clothes if you're visiting in winter, spring or autumn.

History

The founder of the Shingon sect of Esoteric Buddhism, Kūkai (known after his death as Kōbō Daishi), established a religious community here in 816. Kōbō Daishi travelled as a young priest to China and returned after two years to found the school. He is one of Japan's most famous religious figures and is revered as a Bodhisattva, calligrapher, scholar and inventor of the Japanese *kana* syllabary.

Followers of Shingon believe that Kōbō Daishi is not dead, but rather that he is meditating in his tomb in Kōya-san's Oku-no-in Cemetery, awaiting the arrival of Miroku (Maitreya, the future Buddha). Food is ritually offered in front of the tomb daily to sustain him during this meditation. When Miroku returns, it is thought that only Kōbō Daishi will be able to interpret

PAL TERAVAGIMOV/SHUTTERSTOCK©

Don't Miss
Oku-no-in

One of Japan's most intensely spiritual places, Oku-no-in is a memorial hall to Kōbō Daishi surrounded by a vast, forested Buddhist cemetery. The tall cedars and thousands of peaked stone stupas along the cobblestoned path can be utterly enchanting, especially in swirling mist. Any Japanese Buddhist who's anybody has had their remains, or at least a lock of hair, interred here to ensure pole position when the Buddha of the Future (Miroku Buddha) comes to earth.

At the northern end of the graveyard is the complex's the main building, **Tōrō-dō**. It houses hundreds of lamps, including two believed to have been burning for more than 900 years. Behind the hall you can see the closed doors of the Kōbō Daishi (Kūkai) mausoleum.

Along the way you'll pass the bridge Mimyo-no-hashi. Worshippers ladle water from the river and pour it over the nearby Jizō statues as an offering for the dead. The inscribed wooden plaques in the river are in memory of aborted babies and those who died by drowning.

Between the bridge and the Tōrō-dō is a wooden building the size of a large phone booth, which contains the Miroku-ishi. Pilgrims reach through the holes in the wall to try to lift a large, smooth boulder onto a shelf. The weight of the stone is supposed to change according to your weight of sin. We can only report that the thing was damn heavy!

Oku-no-in is easily reached on foot from the town centre, or you can take the bus east to Ichi-no-hashi-mae bus stop. From here cross the bridge, Ichi-no-hashi, and into the cemetery. Buses return to the centre of town from the Oku-no-mae bus stop (or walk it in about 30 minutes).

NEED TO KNOW
奥の院; ⊙Tōrō-dō 6am-5.30pm

Kōya-san

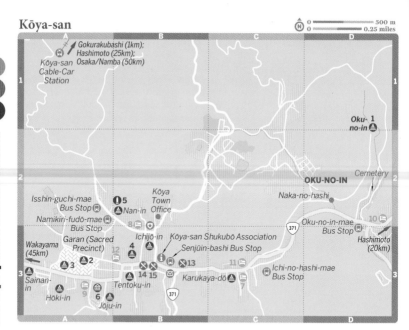

KANSAI & WESTERN HONSHŪ KŌYA-SAN

his heavenly message for humanity. Thus, the vast cemetery here is like an amphitheatre crowded with souls gathered in expectation of this heavenly sermon.

Over the centuries, the temple complex grew in size and attracted many followers of the Jōdo (Pure Land) school of Buddhism. During the 11th century, it became popular with both nobles and commoners to leave hair or ashes from deceased relatives close to Kōbō Daishi's tomb.

Kōya-san is now a thriving centre for Japanese Buddhism, with more than 110 temples. It is the headquarters of the Shingon sect, which numbers 10 million members and presides over nearly 4000 temples all over Japan.

⊙ Sights

The precincts of Kōya-san are divided into two main areas: the Garan (Sacred Precinct) in the west, where you will find interesting temples and pagodas, and the Oku-no-in, with its vast cemetery, in the east.

A joint ticket (shodōkyōtsu-naihaiken; ¥1500) that covers entry to Kongōbu-ji, the Kondō, Dai-tō, Treasure Museum and Tokugawa Mausoleum can be purchased at the Kōya-san Tourist Association office (p300).

Kongōbu-ji — Buddhist Temple
(金剛峯寺; admission ¥500; ⊙8.30am-5pm) This is the headquarters of the Shingon sect and the residence of Kōya-san's abbot. The present structure dates from the 19th century. The main hall's Ohiro-ma room has ornate screens painted by Kanō Tanyu in the 16th century. The rock garden is interesting for the sheer number of rocks used in its composition, giving the effect of a throng of petrified worshippers eagerly listening to a monk's sermon.

Admission includes tea and rice cakes served beside the stone garden.

Garan — Buddhist Temple
(伽藍; admission to each bldg ¥200; ⊙8.30am-5pm) In this temple complex of several halls and pagodas, the **Dai-tō** (大塔; Great Pagoda) pagoda, rebuilt in 1934 after a fire,

Kōya-san

Sleeping

More than 50 temples in Kōya-san offer temple lodgings (*shukubō*) that serve *shōjin-ryōri* (Buddhist vegetarian cuisine; no meat, fish, onions or garlic) meals and typically hold morning prayer sessions, which guests are welcome to join or observe.

Most lodgings *start* at ¥9500 per person including two meals, with a surcharge for solo guests. Prices can vary widely, both between temples and within them, depending upon room (most without ensuite bath and toilet), meals and season; generally, the more you pay, the better the room and the meals. Most *shukubō* ask that you check in by 5pm.

Reserve at least seven days in advance through the Kōya-san Shukubō Association (p300); you can fill out a request form online, in English.

Koyasan Guest House Kokuu
Guesthouse ¥

(高野山ゲストハウスKokuu; ☎26-7216; http://www.koyasanguesthouse.com; 49-43 Itogun Kōyachō Kōyasan; capsules from ¥3500, s/d/tr from ¥6000/9000/12,000; @ 🛜) This convivial place puts the Kōya-san experience within range of even the most budget-conscious backpackers. It's intimate, clean, woodsy, light and airy with capsule-style and nice private rooms, and shower cabinets down the hall. Knowledgeable, English-speaking staff can help arrange morning prayers and night tours, and prepare inexpensive breakfasts and light meals, like Indian curry, for dinner.

Reserve directly, not through the Shukubō Association.

Shōjōshin-in
Temple Lodge ¥¥

(清浄心院; ☎56-2006; r per person with meals from ¥9,720, with private bath from ¥16,200; 🛜) Friendly spot with in-room wi-fi and no extra charge for solo travellers. There's an atmospheric old kitchen under a tall wooden ceiling and gold-leaf *fusuma* doors. It's the closest *shukubō* to the entry to Oku-no-in.

is said to be the centre of the lotus-flower mandala formed by the eight mountains around Kōya-san. The main object of worship is the **Dainichi-nyōrai** (Cosmic Buddha) and his four attendant Buddhas, painted on pillars (originally, it's said, by Kōbō Daishi himself). It's since been repainted and is an awesome sight.

Treasure Museum
Museum

(霊宝館; Reihōkan; admission ¥600; ⏱8.30am-5.30pm May-Oct, to 5pm Nov-Apr) The Treasure Museum has a compact display of Buddhist works of art, all collected in Kōya-san. There are some very fine statues, painted scrolls and mandalas.

Tokugawa Mausoleum
Monument

(徳川家霊台; Tokugawa-ke Reidai; admission ¥200; ⏱8.30am-5pm) Built in 1643, the Tokugawa Mausoleum is actually two adjoining mausoleums in a clearing, of Tokugawa Ieyasu (on the right) and Tokugawa Hidetada (on the left), the first and second Tokugawa shoguns, respectively. They are ornately decorated, as with most structures associated with the Tokugawa regime. The mausoleum is near the Namikiri-fudō-mae bus stop (波切不動前バス亭).

Ekō-in
Temple Lodge ¥¥

(恵光院; 📞56-2514; www.ekoin@mbox.co.jp; r per person with meals from ¥10,800; @🛜) This lovely hillside temple is run by a friendly bunch of young monks, and rooms look onto beautiful gardens. Ekō-in is known for nighttime tours of Oku-no-in, in English and as one of the two temples in town (the other is Kongōbu-ji) where you can study seated meditation; call ahead. There's no solo traveller surcharge.

Fukuchi-in
Temple Lodge ¥¥

(福智院; 📞56-2021; r per person with meals from ¥12,960, single travellers ¥16,200; ❄@🛜) This fine temple has outdoor baths with onsen water and a lovely garden designed by the famous designer Shigemori Mirei. Wi-fi is available for limited durations near the temple office. Some staff speak English, though sometimes it's busy with Japanese bus tours.

Henjōson-in
Temple Lodge ¥¥

(遍照尊院; 📞56-2434; r per person with meals from ¥12,960, with bathroom ¥16,200) Nice rooms and communal baths make this a good choice, with an updated feel.

Sōji-in
Temple Lodge ¥¥¥

(総持院; 📞56-2111; r per person with meals from ¥18,360, single travellers ¥29,376) At home with foreign guests, this pleasantly modern temple lodge has a lovely garden, some rooms with ensuite baths and a wheelchair-accessible room with Western-style beds. The top rooms here are among the best in Kōya-san, and the high-quality meals also account for the price differential.

Eating

The culinary speciality of Kōya-san is *shōjin-ryōri,* elaborate and very tasty Buddhist vegan meals served at temple lodgings. If you're not staying over, reserve a *shōjin-ryōri* lunch at a temple, ahead of time through the Kōya-san Shukubō Association. Prices are fixed at ¥2700, ¥3800 and ¥5400, depending on the number of courses. Otherwise, most eateries around town close by late afternoon.

Bononsha
Vegetarian, Cafe ¥

(梵恩舍; 📞0736-56-5535; 730 Kōyasan; lunch set ¥1200; 🕙9am-5pm, closed Mon, Tue and irregularly; 🍴) Run by a delightful French-Japanese couple, this charming cafe with great old wooden beams is a relaxing spot for coffees and cakes like chocolate cake and tofu cheesecake. Daily lunch set menus are served until they run out (arrive early). It's also a gallery of local pottery.

Maruman
Shokudō ¥

(丸万; 📞56-2049; 778 Kōyasan; mains ¥850-1150, set menus ¥850-1880; 🕙9am-5pm, closed irregularly, usually Tue or Wed) This convenient *shokudō* serves standards like *katsu-don* (fried pork cutlet over rice, ¥820) represented by plastic food models in the window. It's diagonally across from the Shukubō Association office on the main street. **Nankai Shokudō** (南海食堂; 📞0736-56-2128; 777 Kōyasan; mains ¥550-900, teishoku ¥1200-1750) next door is similar.

ℹ️ Information

Kōya-san Shukubō Association (高野山宿坊協会; 📞56-2616; http://eng.shukubo.net/; 🕙8.30am-4.30pm Dec-Feb, to 5pm Mar-Jun & Sep-Nov, to 5.45pm Jul & Aug) In the centre of town in front of the Senjūin-bashi bus stop (千手院橋バス停), Kōya-san's well-equipped tourist information centre stocks maps and brochures, and English speakers are usually on hand. It also makes *shukubō* and dining reservations (in advance) and rents an English-language audio guide (¥500) to important sights around town, as well as bicycles.

Kōyasan Interpreter Guide Club (📞090-1486-2588, 090-3263-5184; www.geocities.jp/koyasan_i_g_c) This club offers four-hour private tours of Kōya-san for ¥5000 per group with a volunteer guide. Professional guides cost from ¥10,000 per four-hour tour. It also offers regularly scheduled tours (Wednesday, April to September) for ¥1000 per person.

Getting There & Away

Without a rental car, access to Kōya-san is via the Nankai Railway from Osaka. Trains from Namba Station (*kyūkō/tokkyū* ¥1260/2040, one hour and 40 minutes/43 minutes) terminate at Gokurakubashi, at the base of the mountain, where you board a cable car (gondola, five minutes, price included in train tickets) up to Kōya-san itself. From the cable-car station, take a bus into central Kōya-san; walking is prohibited on the connecting road.

Nankai's **Kōya-san World Heritage Ticket** (¥3400, www.nankaikoya.jp/en/stations/ticket.html) covers return train fare (including one-way *tokkyū* fare from Osaka), buses on Kōya-san and discounted admission to some sites.

From Kyoto, if you've got a Japan Rail Pass, take the JR line to Hashimoto, changing at Nara, Sakurai and Takada en route. At Hashimoto, connect to the Nankai line to Kōya-san (¥830, 50 minutes). Without a Japan Rail Pass, it's easier and quicker to connect to the Nankai line at Namba.

Getting Around

Buses run on three routes from the top cable-car station via the town centre to Ichi-no-hashi and Oku-no-in (¥410) via the tourist office at Senjūin-bashi (¥290). The bus office by the top cable-car station sells an all-day bus pass (*ichi-nichi furee kippu*; ¥830), but once up the hill, the sights are easily walkable in about 30 minutes. Take note of bus schedules before setting out, as buses run infrequently.

Bicycles can be rented (per hour/day ¥400/1200) at the Kōya-san Shukubō Association office.

KINOSAKI

♪ 0796 / POP 4134

In northern Hyōgo Prefecture, Kinosaki is one of Japan's best places to sample the classic onsen experience. A willow-lined canal runs through the town centre, and many of the houses, shops and restaurants retain their traditional charm. Add to this the delights of crab fresh from the Sea of Japan in winter, and you'll understand why this is one of our favourite overnight trips from the cities of Kansai.

◉ Sights & Activities

Kinosaki's biggest attraction is its seven onsen. Overnight guests *clip-clop* around the canal from bath to bath wearing *yukata* (light cotton kimono) and *geta*

Kinosaki

(wooden sandals). Most ryokan and hotels in town have their own *uchi-yu* (private baths), but also provide their guests with free tickets to the public baths (*soto-yu*).

Visitors might want to peek at the **Kinosaki Mugiwarazaikudenshokan** (城崎麦わら細工伝承館; 376-1 Yushima; admission ¥300; ⏱9am-5pm, closed Wed), which displays *mugiwarazaiku*, a local craft that employs barley straw cut into tiny pieces and applied to wood to form incredibly beautiful patterns. It's located off the canal, a short walk from Ichi-no-yu onsen.

The following is the full list of Kinosaki's *onsen*, in order of preference (get a map from the information office or your lodging):

Gosho-no-yu   Onsen
(御所の湯; admission ¥800; ⏱7am-11pm, enter by 10.30pm, closed 1st & 3rd Thu) Lovely log construction, a nice two-level *rotemburo* and fine maple colours in autumn. The entry area is decorated like the Kyoto Gosho (Imperial Palace).

Sato-no-yu   Onsen
(さとの湯; admission ¥800; ⏱1-9pm, enter by 8.40pm, closed Mon) Fantastic variety of

baths, including Arab-themed saunas, rooftop *rotemburo* and a 'Penguin Sauna' (basically a walk-in freezer – good after a hot bath). Women's and men's baths shift floors daily, so you'll have to go two days in a row to sample all of the offerings.

Kou-no-yu   Onsen
(鴻の湯; admission ¥600; ⏱7am-11pm, enter by 10.30pm, closed Tue) 🏊 The main feature here is the *teien-buro* (garden bath) that feels like a formal Japanese garden.

Ichi-no-yu   Onsen
(一の湯; admission ¥600; ⏱7am-11pm, enter by 10.30pm, closed Wed) While its main bath is showing its age, the 'cave' bath here is wonderful.

Yanagi-yu   Onsen
(柳湯; admission ¥600; ⏱3-11pm, enter by 10.40pm, closed Thu) Worth a quick soak as you make your way around town. Nice wooden construction.

Mandara-yu   Onsen
(まんだら湯; admission ¥600; ⏱3-11pm, enter by 10.40pm, closed Wed) Small wooden *rotemburo*.

Nunobiki Falls (p305)

AKIRAT2011 /GETTY IMAGES ©

Jizo-yu
Onsen

(地蔵湯; admission ¥600; ⏰7am-11pm, enter by 10.40pm, closed Fri) It feels like an old-school *sentō* (public bath) with a spacious main indoor tub but no *rotemburo*. Good if others are crowded.

Sleeping

Tsuruya
Ryokan ¥¥

(つるや; 📞32-2924; www.kinosaki-tsuruya. com/english.html; 606 Yushima; r per person with/without meals from ¥11,550/6830) A few metres before Kou-no-yu onsen (as you approach from the station), this simple ryokan is comfortable with foreign guests. The rooms are plain but sufficient (most don't have private bath or toilet) and the helpful manager speaks some English.

Suishōen
Ryokan ¥¥

(水翔苑; 📞32-4571; www.suisyou.com/en; 1256 Momoshima; r per person without meals ¥6480-15,876, with meals from ¥18,360; @ 📶) This excellent, modern, 34-room ryokan boasts a great onsen with indoor and outdoor baths, sauna and Japanese rooms with ensuite bath, around a fabulous garden where *nō* plays are projected on a stage. It's a short drive from the town centre, but they'll whisk you to and from the onsen of your choice in their own London taxi.

Ryokan Yamamotoya
Ryokan ¥¥

(旅館山本屋; 📞32-2114; www.kinosaki.com; 835 Yushima, Kinosakichō; r per person incl meals from ¥13,650; 📶) This fine ryokan is comfortable with foreign guests, with lovely rooms, cosy indoor-outdoor baths and excellent food. It's roughly in the middle of town, near Ichi-no-yu onsen. Rooms have river or mountain views but no private bath (sink and toilet only). Solo travellers are accepted in the spring and autumn only and must pay a single supplement.

Mikuniya
Ryokan ¥¥

(三国屋; 📞32-2414; www.kinosaki3928.com/english/index.htm; 221 Yushima; r per person with/without meals from ¥16,200/9720; @ 📶) With 12 rooms in a main building and annexe, this charming ryokan offers clean, freshly redecorated Japanese rooms with toilet and sink, soothing onsen baths and friendly, English-speaking owners. Wi-fi in main building only. It's about 150m on the right, on the street heading into town from the station.

Nishimuraya Honkan
Ryokan ¥¥¥

(西村屋本館; 📞32-2211; www.nishimuraya. ne.jp/honkan/english; 469 Yushima; r per person incl 2 meals from ¥30,390, solo travellers from ¥45,510; @ 📶) Now in its seventh generation, this luxurious hot spring inn is the real deal. Its maze-like layout lends a sense of privacy, the two onsen baths are exquisite, most rooms look out over private gardens, and there's a private gallery of art and historical artifacts. Seasonal *kaiseki* (Japanese haute cuisine) meals are the final touch.

Eating

Crab from the Sea of Japan is a speciality in Kinosaki during the winter months. It's called *kani* and the way to enjoy it is in *kani-suki,* cooked right at your table in a broth with vegetables. Note that most restaurants in Kinosaki shut down very early. This is because most people opt for the two-meal option at their accommodation. You should consider doing the same, at least during *kani* season.

Caffe Sorella
Cafe

(カフェ ソレッラ; 📞32-2059; 84 Yushima; coffee from ¥340; ⏰9.30am-5.30pm, closed irregularly; 📶) This simple coffee shop, about 75m north of Kinosaki Station on the main street, is a good place for a cuppa, nice brownies and an internet fix (there's free wi-fi if you order a drink). Order from the picture menu.

Gubigabu
Pub ¥¥

(グビガブ; 79 Yushima; mains ¥650-2700; ⏰11am-6pm, closed Wed; 🍴) This new craft-beer pub near the town centre serves a diverse menu from pastas, *jidori* (local chicken) and curry rice to beer snacks to accompany the house brews.

Daikō Shōten
Seafood ¥¥

(大幸商店; 📞32-3684; 130 Yushima; dishes ¥350-2500; ⏰10am-9pm, to 11pm mid-Apr–Oct;

📖) This seafood shop/*izakaya* serves up freshly caught local seafood fried, grilled, sauteed or raw in a casual atmosphere. The specialty *kaisen-don* (seafood over rice) is priced ¥1480 to ¥2500, or you'll never go wrong asking for the master's *osusume* (recommendations). It's diagonally across from Mikuniya; look for the blue awning and fish photos.

Orizuru
Sushi ¥¥

(をり鶴; ☎ 32-2203; 396 Yushima; meals ¥1250-5700; ☙ 11am-2pm & 5-9.30pm, closed Tue; 📖) For decent sushi and crab dishes, try this popular local restaurant on the main street. You can get a *jō-nigiri* (superior sushi set; ¥3700) or try the crab dishes in winter. It's between Ichi-no-yu and Gosho-no-yu, on the opposite side of the street.

ℹ️ Information

Opposite the station is an accommodation information office (お宿案内所; ☎ 32-4141; ☙ 9am-6pm), where the staff will gladly help you find a place to stay and make bookings, as well as provide maps of the town. The same office has rental bicycles available for ¥400/800 per two hours/day (return by 5pm).

ℹ️ Getting There & Away

Kinosaki is on the JR San-in line and there are a few daily *tokkyū* from Kyoto (¥4320, two hours and 25 minutes), Osaka (¥5080, two hours and 40 minutes) and Himeji (¥3340, one hour and 45 minutes).

KŌBE

☎ 078 / POP 1,553,789

Perched on a hillside sloping down to the sea, Kōbe (神戸) is one of Japan's most attractive and cosmopolitan cities. It was a maritime gateway from the earliest days of trade with China and home to one of the first foreign communities after Japan reopened to the world in the mid-19th century.

One of Kōbe's best features is its relatively small size – most sights can be reached on foot from the main train stations, making it a pleasure for casual wandering and stopping in its high quality restaurants and cafes. The most pleasant neighbourhoods to explore are Kitano-chō, Nankinmachi Chinatown and, after dark, the bustling area around Sannomiya Station.

◉ Sights

Kōbe's two main gateways are Sannomiya and Shin-Kōbe stations, with easy access to sights, lodging and dining on foot or short train ride. Sannomiya marks the city centre, while the *shinkansen* stops at Shin-Kōbe Station, uphill in the northeast corner of town. The two are connected by quick subway ride or about a 20-minute walk. Pick up a city map at one of the station tourist information offices.

Kōbe City Museum
Museum

(神戸市立博物館; Kōbe Shiritsu Hakubutsukan; http://www.city.kobe.lg.jp/culture/culture/institution/museum/main.html; 24 Kyōmachi; admission ¥200, up to ¥1000 during special exhibitions; ☙ 10am-5pm, additional hours during special exhibitions, closed Mon; 🚇 JR, Hankyū or Hanshin lines to Sannomiya Station) Ground yourself in Kōbe's history as a trading port and east-west meeting place, via art and artifacts with decent English signage. Items show foreign influence from clocks and oil lamps to hairstyles. It's pricey during special exhibits but worth it, especially when they include the museum's collection of *namban* (literally 'southern barbarian') art, a school of painting that developed when early Jesuit missionaries taught Western painting techniques to Japanese students.

Kitano-chō
Area

(北野町; ijinkan ¥350-750, combination tickets available; ☙ most ijinkan open 9am-6pm (until 5pm Oct-Mar); 🚇 JR San-yō Shinkansen to Shin-Kōbe or JR, Hankyū or Hanshin lines to Sannomiya) For generations of Japanese tourists, this pleasant, hilly neighbourhood *is* Kōbe, thanks to the dozen or so well-preserved homes of (mostly) Western trading families and diplomats who settled here during the Meiji period. Its winding streets, nostalgic brick- and weatherboard-built *ijinkan* (literally 'foreigners' houses'), cafes, restaurants and, yes, souvenir shops are great for strolling. All lend a European–American atmosphere, though admittedly it's probably less intriguing for Western visitors than for Japanese.

Kōbe Maritime Museum & Kawasaki Good Times World
Museum

(神戸海洋博物館 & カワサキワールド Kōbe Kaiyō Hakubutsukan & Kawasaki Wārudo; www.khi.co.jp/kawasakiworld/; 2-2 Hatoba-chō, Chūō-ku; admission ¥600; ⏰10am-5pm; Ⓢ Kaigan Subway Line to Minato Motomachi Station, ⓡ JR Kōbe line to Kōbe or Motomachi) This building is in two parts: an extensive collection of high-quality model ships and displays in the old-school **Maritime Museum**, and the fun, hands-on experience of modern technology in **Kawasaki Good Times World**. You've probably heard of Kawasaki's motorcycles, but this Kōbe-born company has also influenced tech from trains to robotics and aerospace. Clamber aboard a section of the original *shinkansen*, early aeroplanes and some very cool bikes. Yes, it's corporate promo, but it's also pretty impressive.

Nankinmachi (Chinatown)
Area

(南京町; ⓡ JR or Hanshin lines to Motomachi Station) This gaudy, bustling, unabashedly touristy collection of Chinese restaurants and trinket and medicinal herb stores should be familiar to anyone who's visited Chinatowns elsewhere. It's fun for a stroll, particularly in the evening when lights illuminate the elaborately painted shop facades. Restaurants tend toward the overpriced and may disappoint sophisticated palates (set meals from about ¥850), although it's one of the few places in Japan where street snacking is condoned (snacks from about ¥200).

Nunobiki Falls
Waterfall

(布引の滝, Nunobikinotaki; Ⓢ Shin-Kōbe, ⓡ Shin-Kōbe) FREE You'd never guess that such a beautiful natural sanctuary could sit so close to the city. This revered waterfall in four sections (the longest is 43m tall) has been the subject of art, poetry and worship for centuries – some of the poems are reproduced on stone tablets at the site. It's accessible by a steep, 400m path, from Shin-Kōbe Station. Take the ground-floor exit, turn left and walk under the station building to the path.

🛏 Sleeping

B Kōbe
Hotel ¥¥

(ザ・ビー神戸; ☎333-4880; www.theb-hotels.com/the-b-kobe/en; 2-11-5 Shimoyamate St, Chūō-ku; s/d/tw from ¥7200/8800/9800; ❄@🛜; Ⓢ Seishin-Yamate subway line to Sannomiya, ⓡ JR, Hankyū or Hanshin lines to Sannomiya) Steps from restaurants and nightlife and downhill from Kitano-chō,

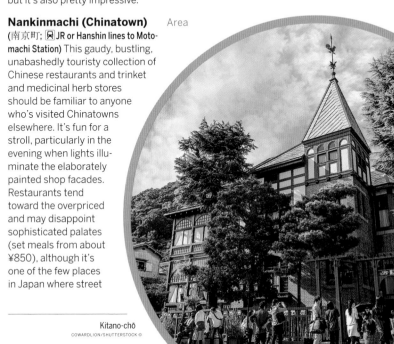

Kitano-chō

Below: Kōbe beef (p308); **Right:** Kōbe at night
(BELOW) JOESAYHELLO/SHUTTERSTOCK ©; (RIGHT) JOESAYHELLO/SHUTTERSTOCK ©

the B Kōbe is a good, utilitarian choice. Mood-lit hallways lined with earth-tone carpets and wall coverings lead to small-ish rooms (if you're only sleeping here the size shouldn't matter too much). There are laundry machines for guest use and free coffee in the lobby.

Hotel Trusty
Boutique Hotel ¥¥

(ホテルトラスティ神戸; ☎330-9111; www.trusty.jp/kobe; 63 Naniwamachi, Chūō-ku; s/d/tw from ¥9800/15,400/18,900; ❄@; ᖰJR, Hankyū or Hanshin lines to Sannomiya) The name screams 'standard-issue business hotel', but this intimate little hotel south of Sannomiya Station and behind city hall is actually a super-stylish boutique hotel. Rooms are on the small side, but they are immaculate and have design touches such as metal bathroom cups and soap dispensers.

Oriental Hotel
Hotel ¥¥¥

(神戸旧居留地オリエンタルホテル; ☎326-1500; www.orientalhotel.jp/en; 25 Kyōmachi, Chūō-ku; d/tw from ¥30,900/34,500; ❄@; ᖰJR Kōbe line, Hanshin or Hankyū to Sannomiya or Motomachi) One of Japan's most historic hotels (circa 1880), in the old foreigners' settlement, the Oriental was rebuilt after the 1995 earthquake and is now a sleek, elegant tower with a design sense deftly melding old Japan and new. Expect indulgent, English-speaking service and great views of the bay and mountains from the 17th-storey lobby and restaurant.

ANA Crowne Plaza Hotel Kōbe
Hotel ¥¥¥

(ANAクラウンプラザ神戸; ☎291-1121; www.anacrowneplaza-kobe.jp/en; 1-chome, Kitano-chō, Chūō-ku; s/d/tw from ¥9500/15,500/15,500; ❄@☏; ⓢSeishin-Yamate subway line, ᖰJR Shinkansen to Shin-Kōbe) Survey the bright lights of Kōbe from this 37-storey tower perched atop the city. Adjacent

to JR Shin-Kōbe Station, the Crowne Plaza offers clean, spacious rooms (even if bathroom fixtures feel a bit dated), English-speaking staff, multiple bars and restaurants, and a pool and fitness centre (surcharge ¥1080). More restaurants are downstairs in the **Oriental Avenue shopping centre** (アベニュー).

Eating

R Valentino
Italian ¥¥

(アール ヴァレンティーノ; ☎332-1268; www.r-valentino.com/english; 3rd fl, 4-5-13 Kanō-chō, Chūō-ku; mains ¥950-3200, lunch/ dinner set menus from ¥1800/4000; ⏰11.30am-2pm & 5.30pm-9pm; ⚒🍴; 🚉JR, Hanshin or Hankyū lines to Sannomiya) Run by Italians and popular with Japanese and foreign visitors alike, this easygoing eatery on a Sannomiya sidestreet is casual, comfortable and cosy with stone walls and rustic furniture. Look for dozens of pasta and brick-oven pizza options, plus meat and fish mains. Eager staff help explain the specials and make recommendations.

Grill Jūjiya
Yoshoku ¥¥

(グリル十字屋; ☎078-331-5455; 96 Edomachi; mains ¥750-2300; ⏰11am-8pm Mon-Sat; 🚉JR, Hanshin, Hankyū lines to Sannomiya Station) In this city thick with east–west heritage, this old-fashioned charmer specialises in *yōshoku*, Japanese takes on Western cooking: beef stew, grilled chicken, fried seafood, *hayashi* rice (rice with hashed beef, onions and savoury sauce). Wash them down with Japanese craft beers. It's been in business since the 1930s, though the building is newer. Head downstairs, next to a 7-Eleven.

Wanto Burger
Burgers ¥¥

(ワントバーガー; ☎078-392-5177; www.wantoburger.com; 3-10-6 Shimo-Yamate-dōri; burgers ¥970-4210; ⏰noon-10pm Mon-Sat, noon-5pm Sun; 🚉JR, Hanshin, Hankyū lines to Sannomiya Station) Run by a cool young crew, this spot looks like a vintage US diner, with long counter, groovy tunes and a few tables, but that's where the resemblance ends; it's utterly different in both taste and price because the burgers

307

The Skinny on Kōbe Beef

For foodies worldwide, the name Kōbe is synonymous with great beef. The delicate marbling of Kōbe beef lends a supple texture and, many say, sweetness that other varieties of beef lack. It accounts for a mere 0.06% of beef consumption nationwide, which helps explain its sky-high price.

Kōbe beef is just one of many types of *wagyu* (Japanese beef). The name 'Kōbe beef' is a trademark referring to the Tajima breed of Japanese black cows born, raised and slaughtered in Kōbe's home prefecture, Hyōgo. There's a widespread belief that the cows are massaged, fed beer and played soothing music, though the Kōbe Beef Marketing & Distribution Promotion Association (www.kobe-beef.jp) disavows it.

are made with Kōbe beef (you can also order somewhat less expensive varieties of *wagyū*).

Kōbe Plaisir
Steak ¥¥¥

(神戸プレジール; ☏078-571-0141; http://www.kobe-plaisir.jp/e-index.html; 2-11-5 Shimo-yamate-dōri, The B Hotel; lunch/dinner set menus from ¥3240/6480; ⏰11:30am-3pm, 5pm-10:30pm; Ⓢ Seishin-Yamate subway line to Sannomiya, Ⓡ JR, Hankyū or Hanshin lines to Sannomiya) You can't get any more loca-vore; ingredients come directly from the local branch of the Japan Agricultural Cooperative. You and your party can choose your preparation of Kōbe or other steak – *seiro-mushi* (steamed), *teppan-yaki* (grilled on a steel plate) or *shabu-shabu* – and sit back as a multicourse meat-and-veg feast unfolds before you.

ⓘ Information

Citibank (シティバンク; ⏰9am-3pm Mon-Fri, ATM 24hr; Ⓡ JR, Hankyū or Hanshin lines to Sannomiya) South of Sogo Department Store; the ATM accepts international cards.

Kōbe Information (インフォメーション神戸; ☏322-0220; ⏰9am-7pm; Ⓡ JR, Hankyū or Hanshin lines to Sannomiya) The city's main tourist information office is on the ground floor outside of JR Sannomiya Station's east gate. There's a smaller information counter on the 2nd floor of Shin-Kōbe Station, outside the main *shinkansen* gate. Both carry reasonably good free maps of the city, pamphlets and the

Kōbe Welcome Coupon booklet, with discounts to sights.

ⓘ Getting There & Away

Train

Sannomiya Station is the hub for rail travel to/from Osaka on the private Hankyū and Hanshin lines and most JR trains. On the JR Tōkaidō line, *shinkaisoku* (special rapid train) are the fastest between Sannomiya and Osaka Station (¥410, 22 minutes). Of the private lines, Hankyū is more convenient, connecting Kōbe Sannomiya Station and Hankyū Umeda Station (*tokkyū*, ¥320, 27 minutes), near Osaka Station.

Shin-Kōbe Station is on the Tōkaidō/San-yō and Kyūshū *shinkansen* lines. Destinations include Fukuoka (Hakata Station; ¥14,160, 2 hours 20 minutes), Tokyo (¥14,160, 3¼ hours), and other major stops including Osaka, Kyoto, Nagoya, Hiroshima and Kagoshima.

ⓘ Getting Around

To/From the Airport

Itami Osaka Airport

There are direct limousine buses to/from Osaka's Itami Airport (¥1050, 40 minutes). In Kōbe, the buses stop on the southwestern side of Sannomiya Station.

Kansai International Airport (KIX)

The most fun connection between Kōbe and KIX is by Bay Shuttle high-speed boat (¥1850, 31 minutes, approximately hourly), which drops you off by Kōbe's port; take the Portliner the rest of the way. By train, the fastest way is the JR *shinkaisoku* to/from Osaka Station, and the JR *kanku kaisoku* between Osaka Station and the airport (total cost ¥1660, total time 1¾ hours with good connections). There is also a direct limousine bus to/from the airport (¥2000, 1¼ hours), which is more convenient if you have a lot of luggage. The Kōbe airport bus stop is on the southwestern side of Sannomiya Station.

Public Transport

Kōbe is small enough to travel around on foot, but JR, Hankyū and Hanshin railway lines run east–west through town. The Seishin-Yamate Subway Line connects Shin-Kōbe and Sannomiya Stations (¥210, two minutes), or you can walk it in about 20 minutes. A **city-loop bus service** (per ride/all-day pass ¥260/660) makes a grand-circle tour of most of the city's sightseeing spots and main stations; look for the retro-style green buses.

HIMEJI

♪ 079 / POP 543,991

A visit to Himeji (姫路) is a must for any lover of Japanese history, especially castles. The recently renovated Himeji Castle, the finest in all of Japan, towers over this quiet city. Nearby, Kōkō-en is a rambling collection of nine meticulously reconstructed samurai houses and their gardens.

You can visit Himeji, on the *shinkansen* route, as a day trip from Kyoto, Nara, Osaka or Kōbe, or as a stopover en route to Okayama or Hiroshima.

◉ Sights

Himeji-jō   Castle
(姫路城; Himeji Castle; 68 Honmachi; adult/child ¥1000/300, combination ticket with Kōkō-en ¥1040/360; ⊙9am-5pm Sep-May, to 6pm Jun-Aug) Japan's most magnificent castle, Himeji-jō is one of only a handful

of original castles remaining (most are modern concrete reconstructions). Its nickname Shirasagi-jō ('White Egret Castle') comes from its lustrous white plaster exterior and stately form on a hill above the plain. There's a five-storey main keep (*tenshū*) and three smaller keeps, and the entire structure is surrounded by moats and defensive walls punctuated with rectangular, circular and triangular openings for firing guns and shooting arrows.

The main keep's walls also feature *ishiotoshi* – narrow openings that allowed defenders to pour boiling water or oil onto anyone trying to scale the walls after making it past the other defences. On balance, we recommend visitors to pay the admission charge and enter the castle by legitimate means.

Although there have been fortifications in Himeji since 1333, today's castle was built in 1580 by Toyotomi Hideyoshi and enlarged some 30 years later by Ikeda Terumasa. Ikeda was awarded the castle by Tokugawa Ieyasu when the latter's forces defeated the Toyotomi armies. In

Himeji-jō
LKUNL/SHUTTERSTOCK ©

Himeji

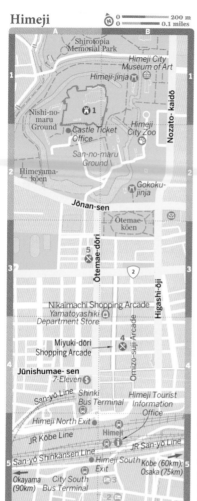

🛏 Sleeping

Himeji is easily visited as a day trip, but there are high quality station-area hotels for an overnight stay.

Dormy Inn Himeji　　　Hotel ¥¥
(ドーミーイン姫路; 160-2 Toyozawa-chō; s/d/tw ¥9200/14,300/16,900; ⊜❄@🛜) Although rooms are pretty compact, this new, 12-storey hotel has lots going for it: rooftop onsen baths (though only showers in rooms), sauna and laundry machines, crisp, modern-meets-rustic style, Chinese-style PJs instead of the usual *yukata* (bathrobe), all non-smoking rooms and free *rāmen* service nightly. It's a block south of the station.

Hotel Nikkō Himeji　　　Hotel ¥¥¥
(ホテル日航姫路; 🗎222-2231; 100 Minami-ekimae-chō; s/d or tw ¥13,000/23,000; ❄@🛜) Across from the station's south exit, Himeji's top hotel offers stylish (if somewhat dated) and fairly spacious rooms with Western-style bathtubs, several restaurants (Japanese, Chinese, Western), a relaxation spa, and a bar on the top floor. Significant discounts may be available online.

✖ Eating

Many restaurants in Himeji are located in the shopping arcades north of the station (en route to the castle).

Menme　　　Noodles ¥
(めんめ; 🗎225-0118; 68 Honmachi; noodles ¥550-950; ⏰11.30am-6pm, closed Wed; 🗎) They make their own noodles at this homey, cheerful little joint a few minutes'

the following centuries it was home to 48 successive lords.

Now is the prime time to visit because much of the castle was recently closed for a five-year renovation, so it's looking great.

It takes around 1½ hours to follow the arrow-marked route around the castle. Last entry is an hour before closing.

walk from the castle. It's not fancy, but it serves an honest, tasty bowl of udon to power you through the day. Look for the white *noren* (doorway curtain) showing noodles being rolled out.

Fukutei
Japanese ¥¥

(福亭; ☎222-8150; 75 Kamei-chō; dishes ¥480-980, lunch/dinner set menus ¥1350-2500/3200-4000; ☺11.30am-2.30pm & 5-10pm Mon-Fri, 11.30am-2.30pm & 5-9pm Sat & Sun; 🅿) This approachable, contemporary restaurant is a great choice for a civilised experience. The specialty is set menus: a little sashimi, some tempura and the usual nibbles on the side. At lunch try the daily special *omakase-zen* (tasting set; ¥1500).

ℹ Information

Himeji Tourist Information Office (姫路市観光案内所[姫路観光なびポート]; ☎287-0003; ☺9am-7pm) is on the ground floor of Himeji Station. Pick up the *Places of Interest Downtown Himeji* map or *Himeji Tourist Guide & Map*.

ℹ Getting There & Away

If you've got a Japan Rail Pass or are in a hurry, take the *shinkansen* from Kyoto (from ¥4770, 55 minutes), Hiroshima (¥7790, one hour), Shin-Osaka (¥3240, 35 minutes) and Shin-Kōbe (¥2600, 16 minutes). Otherwise, slower *shinkaisoku* trains on the JR Tōkaidō line run from Kyoto (¥2270, 94 minutes), Osaka (¥1490, one hour) and Kōbe's Sannomiya Station (¥970, 40 minutes).

NAOSHIMA

🎵087 / POP 3300

Until not too long ago, the arty isle of Naoshima was no different from many others in the Inland Sea: home to a dwindling population subsisting on the joint proceeds of a dying fishing industry and the old-age pension. Today, as the location of the Benesse Art Site Naoshima, Naoshima is one of the area's biggest tourist attractions, offering a unique opportunity to see some of Japan's best contemporary art in gorgeous natural settings.

The project started in the early '90s, when the Benesse Corporation chose Naoshima as the setting for its growing collection of modern art. Naoshima now has a number of world-class art galleries and installations, and has attracted

Benesse House (p313)

BENESSE HOUSE PARK. PHOTO: OSAMU WATANABE ©

creative types from all over the country to set up home here.

In addition to the main sites, numerous works of outdoor art are situated around the coast, including the *Yellow Pumpkin* sculpture by Kusama Yayoi that has become a symbol of the island.

Sights & Activities

During holiday seasons the museums can become quite crowded and you may find you have to queue.

Art House Project   Art Installation

(家プロジェクト; www.benesse-artsite.jp/art house; combined ticket ¥1030; ⊘10am-4.30pm Tue-Sun) In Honmura, half a dozen traditional buildings have been turned over to contemporary artists to use as the setting for creative installations. Highlights include Ōtake Shinrō's shacklike **Haisha** (は いしゃ), its Statue of Liberty sculpture rising up through the levels; James Turrell's experiment with light in **Minami-dera** (南寺), where you enter in total darkness... and wait; and Sugimoto Hiroshi's play on the traditional **Go'o Shrine** (護王神社), with a glass staircase, and narrow underground 'Stone Chamber'.

The sites are within walking distance of each other. Take the Naoshima bus to the Nōkyō-mae stop to start exploring. Buy a ticket at the tourist counter in the Miyanoura ferry terminal, at Honmura Lounge, or at the tobacco shop near the bus stop.

Benesse House Museum   Gallery

(ベネッセハウス; www.benesse-artsite.jp/ benessehouse-museum; admission ¥1030; ⊘8am-9pm) Award-winning architect Andō Tadao designed this stunning museum and hotel on the south coast of the island. Among the works here are pieces by Andy Warhol, David Hockney, Jasper Johns, and Japanese artists such as Ōtake Shinrō.

Chichū Art Museum   Gallery

(地中美術館; www.benesse-artsite.jp/chichu; admission ¥2060; ⊘10am-6pm Tue-Sun, to 5pm Oct-Feb) A short walk from Benesse House is this Andō Tadao creation. A work of art

itself, the museum consists of a series of cool concrete-walled spaces sitting snugly underground. Lit by natural light, it provides a remarkable setting for several Monet water-lily paintings, some monumental sculptures by Walter De Maria and installations by James Turrell. Outside is the Chichū garden, created in the spirit of Monet's garden in Giverny.

At peak times a 'timed ticket' system may be in place, designating the time you are able to purchase a ticket and enter.

Lee Ufan Museum   Gallery

(李禹煥美術館; www.benesse-artsite.jp/lee-ufan; admission ¥1030; ⊘10am-6pm Tue-Sun, to 5pm Oct-Feb) Adding to Benesse's suite of museums is yet another design from the irrepressible Andō. It houses works by the renowned Korean-born artist (and philosopher) Lee Ufan, who was a leading figure in the Mono-ha movement of the 1960s and '70s.

Naoshima Bath – I Heart Yū   Sento

(直島銭湯; www.benesse-artsite.jp/en/naoshimasento; admission ¥510; ⊘2-9pm Tue-Fri, 10am-9pm Sat & Sun) For a unique bathing experience, take a soak at this colourful fusion of Japanese bathing tradition and contemporary art, designed by Ōtake Shinrō, where there really is an elephant in the room. It's a couple of minutes' walk inland from Miyanoura port. Look for the building with the palm trees out front.

Sleeping

The accommodation scene is dominated by privately run *minshuku* (guesthouses). Not a lot of English is spoken, but locals are becoming increasingly used to foreign guests. If you prefer hotel-style facilities, Benesse House hotel is your only real option. Alternatively, stay in Okayama or Uno port on the mainland, or Takamatsu in Shikoku, and visit as a day trip. Rates increase during high season.

Tsutsuji-sō   Campground ¥

(つつじ荘; ☏087-892-2838; www.tsutsujiso. com; tents per person from ¥3780; ⊜) Perfectly placed on the beachfront not far from the Benesse Art Site area is this encampment of Mongolian-style *pao* tents. The cosy tents sleep up to four, have a small fridge and heater (but no air-con), and shared bathroom facilities. The tent-averse can opt instead for one of the caravans or cottages. Meals are available if reserved in advance. Cash only.

Minshuku Oyaji-no-Umi
Minshuku ¥

(民宿おやじの海; ☎ 090-5261-7670; http://ameblo.jp/naosima-oyajinoumi; per person from ¥4200;) This is a good option for friendly, family-style lodgings, with tatami rooms (separated by sliding doors) and shared bathroom, in an old house close to the Art House Project in Honmura. Owners don't speak English; it's best to book via email or the website if you don't speak Japanese. The entrance is next to the Cat Cafe.

Benesse House
Boutique Hotel ¥¥¥

(☎ 087-892-3223; www.benesse-artsite.jp/en/benessehouse; tw/ste from ¥32,000/59,000; ❄) A stay at this unique Andō-designed hotel-museum is a treat for art and architecture enthusiasts. Accommodation is in four different wings – Museum, Oval, Park and Beach – each with a clean, modern, clutter- and TV-free design, and decor featuring artworks from the Benesse collection.

A monorail takes guests up to the hilltop Oval wing (the most expensive of the options), where rooms are arranged around a pool of water open to the sky, and there are stunning views from the grassed rooftop. Rooms in Oval are spacious (though the bathrooms are standard-issue) and large windows make the most of the views; you may not want to come back down once you're up here. The Beach wing is a newer building by the sea, from where you can see the *Yellow Pumpkin* sculpture. Or stick close to the art with a stay in the Museum lodgings.

Children under seven years old aren't permitted in the Oval and Museum wings. Reserve well in advance.

🍴 Eating & Drinking

There are a few cafes in the Art House Project area and near the port at Miyanoura. Not many places open in the evenings and hours can be irregular.

Okayama (p322)

Below: Miyanoura port; **Right:** *Kaiseki* (Japanese haute cuisine)

(BELOW) JTB PHOTO/UIG/GETTY IMAGES ©; (RIGHT) KPG_PAYLESS/SHUTTERSTOCK ©

with rice) at lunchtime, and small dishes with drinks in the evening.

Shioya Diner
Cafe ¥

(シオヤダイナー; dishes ¥400-1000; ⊙11am-9pm Tue-Sun; 📶📱) With rock 'n' roll music, retro furniture and kitsch knick-knacks, Shioya is an odd mix of American diner and grandma's kitchen. The menu features tacos and chilli dogs, and they sometimes charcoal-grill Cajun chicken on the barbecue out front. It's a great place to relax over a coffee or a meal near Miyanoura port.

Cafe Salon Naka-Oku
Cafe ¥

(カフェサロン中奥; ☎087-892-3887; www.na-ka-oku.com; lunch from ¥650, dinner ¥380-750; ⊙11.30am-9pm Wed-Mon; 📱) Up on a small hill at the rear of a farming plot, Naka-Oku is a good option in the Honmura area, and one of only a couple of places open in the evenings here. It's all wood-beamed warmth and cosiness, with homey specialities like *omuraisu* (omelette filled

Genmai-Shinshoku Aisunao
Cafe ¥

(玄米心食あいすなお; http://aisunao.jp; meals ¥600-900; ⊙11am-5.30pm; 😊📶✏️📱) 🌱 A tranquil rest stop within the Art House Project area, Aisunao has seating on raised tatami flooring and a decidedly health-conscious menu – try the tasty Aisunao lunch set, with local brown rice, soup and veggies. Desserts (such as soy-milk ice cream), juices and fair-trade coffees are also on offer.

Cin.na.mon
Curry ¥

(シナモン; www.cin-na-mon.jp; meals ¥650-1000; ⊙11am-3pm & 5-10pm Tue-Sun; 📱) The laid-back team here serve curries, cakes and smoothies by day, and open up the bar (with some light meals and snacks) at night. It's a short walk from the Miyan-oura port.

Museum Restaurant
Issen
Kaiseki ¥¥¥

(日本料理一扇;  087-892-3223; www.benesse-artsite.jp/en/benessehouse/restaurant_cafe.html; breakfast ¥2100, lunch from ¥2000, dinner courses from ¥6500; ⊙7.30-9.30am, 11.30am-2.30pm & 6-9.45pm; 🖥 📵)
The artfully displayed *kaiseki* dinners at this Benesse House basement restaurant are almost too pretty to eat. Courses feature seafood, but there is a veg-dominated option (request a couple of days ahead), and the menu changes with the seasons. Breakfast and lunch are also served. Advance reservations are recommended.

🛈 Information

The ATMs at the post offices in Miyanoura and Honmura take international cards. Ask at the tourist office for directions.

Marine Station Tourist Information Centre (☑087-892-2299; www.naoshima.net; ⊙8.30am-6pm) At the Miyanoura ferry port. Has a comprehensive bilingual map of the island (also downloadable from the website), a walking map and a full list of accommodation options. Note that staff don't make accommodation reservations. Tickets for Art House Project can also be purchased here.

Honmura Lounge & Archive (☑087-840-8273; ⊙10am-4.30pm Tue-Sun) Tourist information in Honmura, with a rest area and left luggage service. Tickets for Art House Project can be purchased.

🛈 Getting There & Away

Naoshima can be visited as a day trip from Okayama or Takamatsu, and it makes a good stopover if you're travelling between Honshū and Shikoku.

From Okayama, take the JR Uno line to Uno (¥580, about an hour); this usually involves a quick change of trains at Chayamachi. Ferries go to Naoshima's main port of Miyanoura from the port near Uno Station (¥290, 15 to 20 minutes, 13 daily). There are also ferries from Uno to the port of Honmura (¥290, 20 minutes, five daily).

Takamatsu is connected to the port of Miyanoura by standard ferry (¥520, 50 minutes,

315

five daily) and high-speed boat (¥1220, 25 minutes, four daily on Fridays, weekends and holidays between March and November; one daily at other times).

Ferry timetables can be found on the Benesse Art Site website (www.benesse-artsite.jp) or at the tourist offices in Okayama and Takamatsu.

❶ Getting Around

Bicycle or the town bus are the best options for getting around Naoshima, though it's possible on foot if you have time – for example, it's just over 2km from Miyanoura port to Honmura and the Art House Project area. There is one **taxi** (☑ 087-892-3036) on Naoshima, taking up to nine passengers – this has to be reserved in advance of coming to the island.

Bicycle

Naoshima is great for cycling and there are a few rental places around Miyanoura ferry port. **Cafe Ougiya Rent-a-Cycle** (☑ 090-3189-0471; per day ¥300-500; ☺ 9am-7pm, to 6pm Dec-Feb) is inside the Marine Station at the port. A few electric bikes (¥1000 per day) and scooters (¥1500 per day) are also available.

Bus

Minibuses run between Miyanoura, Honmura and Tsutsuji-sō once or twice an hour. It costs ¥100 per ride. From Tsutsuji-sō, there's a free Benesse shuttle, stopping at all the Benesse Art Site museums. In busy seasons buses can fill up quickly, especially towards the end of the day when people are returning to the port to catch ferries. Be sure to check the timetables and allow yourself enough time.

HIROSHIMA 広島

☑ 082 / POP 1,174,200

To most people, Hiroshima means just one thing. The city's name will forever evoke thoughts of 6 August 1945, when Hiroshima became the target of the world's first atomic-bomb attack. Hiroshima's Peace Memorial Park is a constant reminder of that day, and it attracts visitors from all over the world. But leafy Hiroshima, with its wide boulevards and laid-back friendliness, is a far from depressing place. Present-day Hiroshima is home to a thriving and internationally minded community, and it's worth spending a couple of nights here to experience the city at its vibrant best.

Sights

Most sights can be reached either on foot or with a short tram ride. To catch a tram to the Atomic Bomb Dome and Peace Memorial Park area, hop on tram 2 or 6 at the terminal in front of the station (south exit) and get off at the Genbaku-dōmu-mae stop.

Atomic Bomb Dome Historic Site
(原爆ドーム, Genbaku Dome; 🚃 Genbaku-dōmu-mae) Perhaps the starkest reminder of the destruction visited upon Hiroshima in WWII is the Atomic Bomb Dome. Built by a Czech architect in 1915, it was the Industrial Promotion Hall until the bomb exploded almost directly above it. Everyone inside was killed, but the building was one of very few left standing near the epicentre. A decision was taken after the war to preserve the shell as a memorial.

Peace Memorial Park Park
(平和記念公園; Heiwa-kinen-kōen; 🚃 Genbaku-dōmu-mae) Hugged by rivers on both sides, Peace Memorial Park is a large, leafy space criss-crossed by walkways and dotted with memorials. Its central feature is the long tree-lined Pond of Peace leading to the **cenotaph** (原爆死没者慰霊碑). This curved concrete monument holds the names of all the known victims of the bomb. Also at the pond is the **Flame of Peace** (平和の灯), set to burn on until all the world's nuclear weapons are destroyed.

Look through the cenotaph down the pond and you'll see it frames the Flame of Peace and the Atomic Bomb Dome across the river – the park was planned so that these features form a straight line, with the Peace Memorial Museum at its southern end.

Just north of the road through the park is the **Children's Peace Monument**, inspired by Sadako Sasaki, who was two years old at the time of the atomic bomb. When Sadako developed leukaemia at 11 years of age, she decided to fold 1000 paper cranes. In Japan, the crane is the symbol of longevity and happiness, and she believed if she achieved that target she would recover. She died before reaching her goal, but her classmates folded the rest. A monument was built in 1958. Sadako's story inspired a nationwide spate of paper-crane folding that continues to this day. Surrounding the monument are strings of thousands of colourful paper cranes sent here from school children around the country and all over the world.

Nearby is the **Korean Atomic Bomb Victims Memorial** (韓国人原爆犠牲者慰霊碑). Many Koreans were shipped over to work as slave labourers during WWII, and Koreans accounted for more than one in 10 of those killed by the atomic bomb. Just north of this memorial is the **Atomic Bomb Memorial Mound** – the ashes of thousands of unclaimed or unidentified victims are interred in a vault below.

There are other monuments and statues throughout the park, and plenty of benches, including along the riverside looking across to the Atomic Bomb Dome, making this a pleasant area to take a break and reflect.

Hiroshima Peace Memorial Museum   Museum

(広島平和記念資料館; www.pcf.city.hiroshima.jp; 1-2 Nakajima-chō, Naka-ku; admission ¥50; ⏰8.30am-5pm, to 6pm Mar-Nov, to 7pm Aug; 🚇Genbaku-dōmu-mae or Chūden-mae) The main building of Hiroshima's premier museum houses a collection of items salvaged from the aftermath of the atomic bomb. The displays are confronting and personal – ragged clothes, a child's melted lunch box, a watch stopped at 8.15am – and there are some grim photographs. While upsetting, it's a must-see in Hiroshima. The east building presents a history of Hiroshima and the development and destructive power of nuclear weapons.

Hiroshima National Peace Memorial Hall for the Atomic Bomb Victims   Memorial

(国立広島原爆死没者追悼平和祈念館; www.hiro-tsuitokinenkan.go.jp; 1-6 Nakajima-chō, Naka-ku; ⏰8.30am-6pm Mar-Nov, to 5pm Dec-Feb, to 7pm Aug; 🚇Genbaku-dōmu-mae or Hon-dōri) FREE A softly lit internal walkway leads down into this cool, contemplative space, where the walls show a circular

Atomic Bomb Dome

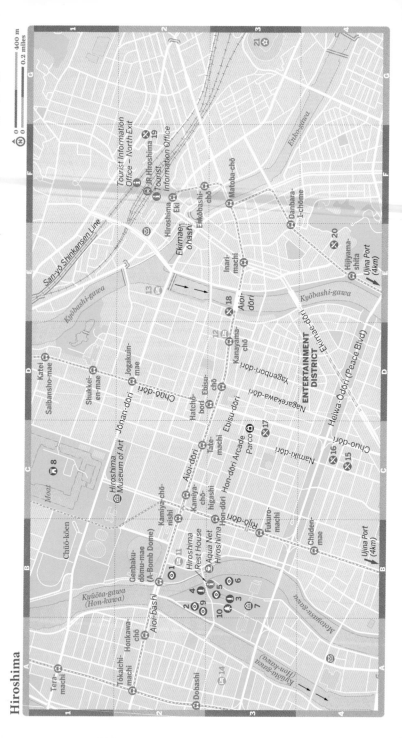

400 m
0.2 miles

San-yō Shinkansen Line

Tourist Information
Office – North Exit
JR Hiroshima 19
Tourist
Information Office

Hiroshima
Eki

Ekimae-
ōhashi

Enkōbashi-
chō

Matoba-chō

Danbara-
1-chōme

20
Hijiyama-
shita
Ujina Port (4km)

Inari-
machi

Enkō-gawa

Kyōbashi-gawa

Kyōbashi-gawa

13

18
Aioi-
dōri

12
Kanayama-
chō

Yagenbori-dōri

Nagarekawa-dōri

Ekimae-dōri

ENTERTAINMENT
DISTRICT

Heiwa-Ōdōri (Peace Blvd)

Katei
Saibansho-mae

Shukkei-
en-mae

Jogakuin-
mae

Chūo-dōri

Jōnan-dōri

Hiroshima
Museum of Art

Ebisu-
chō

Hatchō-
bori

Ebisu-dōri

Parco 17

Namiki-dōri

16
15

Chūo-dōri

Chūden-
mae

Ujina Port
(4km)

8

Chūō-kōen

Moat

Genbaku-
dōmu-mae
(A-Bomb Dome)

Kamiya-chō-
nishi

Kamiya-
chō-
higashi

Aioi-dōri

Tate-
machi

Hon-dōri Arcade

Rijō-dōri

Fukuro-
machi

Hon-dōri
Hiroshima
Hon-dōri

Kyū-ōta-gawa
(Hon-kawa)

Aioi-bashi

11
1
Hiroshima
Rest House
Aqua Net

4
9
2
10

5
6
7
3

Motoyasu-gawa

Tera-
machi

Tōkaichi-
machi

Honkawa-
chō

Dobashi

Kyū-ōta-gawa (Hon-kawa)

14

Hiroshima

panorama of Hiroshima and the names of its neighbourhoods at the time of the atomic bomb. The fountain at the centre represents the moment the bomb was dropped (8.15), while the water offers relief to the victims. An adjoining room shows the names and photographs of those who perished. Before leaving, it's well worth taking time to watch the evocative testimonies from survivors.

Hiroshima-jō Castle

(広島城, **Hiroshima Castle**; 21-1 Moto-machi; admission ¥370; ⏰9am-6pm, to 5pm Dec-Feb; 🚃Kamiya-chō) Also known as Carp Castle (Rijō; 鯉城), Hiroshima-jō was originally constructed in 1589, but much of it was dismantled following the Meiji Restoration. What remained was totally destroyed by the bomb and rebuilt in 1958. There's a small museum with historical items, but most impressive is the moat, and the surrounding park is a pleasant place for a stroll.

Mazda Zoom Zoom Stadium Stadium

(**Hiroshima Municipal Stadium**; 2-3-1 Minami-Kaniya) This stadium in Hiroshima is a good place to catch a baseball game and see the beloved local team, the Carp. It's a short walk southeast of the Hiroshima Station – follow the signs and the red-marked pathways. For schedule information in English, see www.japanball.com, or ask at the tourist office.

Sleeping

Hiroshima has numerous places to stay in every price bracket. Most accommodation options also have their own bikes for rent (around ¥500 per day).

Ikawa Ryokan Ryokan ¥

(いかわ旅館; 📞082-231-5058; www.ikawa ryokan.net; 5-11 Dobashi-chō; s/tw without bathroom ¥4860/8640, with bathroom ¥5940/9720; @ 🛜 🛗; 🚃Dobashi) On a quiet side street, this is a large family-run hotel-style ryokan with three connected wings. There are Japanese- and Western-style rooms, all very clean, and many have private bathrooms (though there's also a good common bath). Ikawa often caters to tour and school groups. Wi-fi is in the lobby.

Hotel Active Hiroshima Hotel ¥¥

(ホテルアクティブ広島; 📞082-212-0001; www.hotel-active.com/hiroshima; 15-3 Nobori-chō; s/d incl breakfast from ¥5380/7300; 🍴 ❄ @ 🛜; 🚃Kanayama-chō) With its satiny coverlets and backlit headboards, Hotel Active tries for a little more style than the average business hotel. It's right in the heart of things, and extras like free drink machines, a spa and an included buffet breakfast make this a good-value option.

Hotel Flex Hotel ¥¥

(ホテルフレックス; 📞082-223-1000; www.hotel-flex.co.jp; 7-1 Kaminobori-chō; s/d incl

breakfast from ¥7150/12,100;)
Curves and concrete are the features at this riverside hotel. Standard rooms are small but there is a more spacious maisonette and high-ceiling room option. All rooms are light with large windows; naturally, the ones facing the river have the views. There's a bright, breezy cafe downstairs where the included breakfast of a sandwich and drink is served.

Hiroshima Inn Aioi　Ryokan ¥¥¥
(広島の宿相生; ☎082-247-9331; www.galilei.ne.jp/aioi; 1-3-14 Ōtemachi; per person with meals from ¥19,900; ❄@; 🚃Genbaku-dōmu-mae) At this fine traditional inn, kick back in a *yukata* and enjoy city and park views from your tatami room, or while lazing in the large bath on the 7th floor. The meals are an elaborate traditional spread of dishes, and you can opt for breakfast or dinner only.

🍴 Eating

Hiroshima is famous for oysters and *okonomiyaki* (savoury pancakes; batter and cabbage, with vegetables and seafood or meat cooked on a griddle), served Hiroshima-style with individual layers and noodles. You'll come across plenty of places serving both.

Hassei　Okonomiyaki ¥
(八誠; 4-17 Fujimi-chō; dishes ¥600-1300; ⏱11.30am-2pm & 5-11pm Tue-Sun, dinner only Sun; 📖; 🚃Chūden-mae) The walls of this popular *okonomiyaki* specialist are covered with the signatures and messages of famous and not-so-famous satisfied customers. The tasty, generous servings are indeed satisfying – a half-order is probably more than enough for some at lunchtime.

Okonomi-mura　Okonomiyaki ¥
(お好み村; www.okonomimura.jp/foreign/english.html; 2nd-4th fl, 5-13 Shintenchi; dishes ¥800-1300; ⏱11am-2am; 📖; 🚃Ebisu-chō) This Hiroshima institution is a touristy but fun place to get acquainted with *okonomiyaki* and chat with the cooks over a hot griddle. Spead over three floors are 26 stalls, each serving up hearty variations of the local speciality. Pick a floor and find an empty stool at whichever counter takes your fancy.

Bakudanya　Noodles ¥
(ばくだん屋; www.bakudanya.net; 6-13 Fujimi-chō; noodles ¥700-1080; ⏱11.30am-midnight; 📖; 🚃Chūden-mae) Try the famous Hiroshima *tsukemen* at this simple street-corner eatery. *Tsukemen* is a *rāmen*-like dish in which noodles and soup come separately. This is the original outlet; the chain has spread across the country. Look for the green awning on the corner.

Tōshō　Tofu ¥¥
(豆匠; ☎082-506-1028; www.toufu-tosho.jp; 6-24 Hijiyama-chō; sets ¥1800-3000; ⏱11am-3pm & 5-10pm,

Hiroshima-style *okonomiyaki*
HANA/DATACRAFT/GETTY IMAGES ©

to 9pm Sun; 🔲; 🚋Danbara-1-chōme) In a traditional wooden building overlooking a large garden with a pond and waterfall, Tōshō specialises in homemade tofu, served in a variety of tasty and beautifully presented forms by kimono-clad staff. Even the sweets are tofu based. There is a range of set courses, with some pictures and basic English on the menu.

From the tram stop, continue walking in the direction of the tram and turn left uphill after Hijiyama shrine.

Oyster Conclave
Kaki-tei   Oysters ¥¥
(牡蠣亭; 🅙082-221-8990; www.kakitei.jp; 11 Hashimoto-chō; lunch/dinner from ¥1800/3800; 🕐11.30am-2.30pm & 5-10pm, closed Tue & 1st & 3rd Wed of month; 🔲; 🚋Kanayama-chō) Come to this intimate riverside bistro for local oysters prepared in a range of mouth-watering ways. Lunch is a set menu of oysters in various guises, served with salad and soup; an à la carte menu is available in the evenings.

Roopali   Indian ¥¥
(ルーパリ; 🅙082-264-1333; http://roopali. jp; 14-32 Wakusa-chō; lunch sets ¥720-1300, dinner sets from ¥1600; 🕐11am-3pm & 5-10pm; 🍽🍴🔲) Choose one of the generous set courses at this large restaurant dishing up filling authentic curries, or put together your own feast – individual dishes start from ¥850. The single naan orders are so big there ought to be a prize for finishing one. There's an English menu and English-speaking staff.

ℹ️ Information

Money
Higashi Post Office has ATMs that accept international cards and has currency-exchange services. ATMs in 7-Elevens also take international cards. Hiroshima Rest House tourist information centre has a list of banks and post offices that change money and travellers cheques.

Post
Higashi Post Office (広島東郵便局; 2-62 Matsubara-chō; 🕐9am-7pm Mon-Fri, to 5pm Sat, to 12.30pm Sun) Post office near the south exit

---

of Hiroshima Station. ATMs are accessible 24 hours except Sunday, when they close at 9pm.

Tourist Information
Tourist Information Office (観光案内所; 🅙082-261-1877; 🕐9am-5.30pm) Tourist office inside the station near the south exit, with English-speaking staff. There is another branch at the north (shinkansen) exit (🅙082-263-6822; 🕐9am-5.30pm).

Hiroshima Rest House (広島市平和記念公園レストハウス; 🅙082-247-6738; www.mk-kousan.co.jp/rest-house; 1-1 Nakajima-machi; 🕐8.30am-6pm, to 5pm Dec-Feb, to 7pm Aug; 🚋Genbaku-dōmu-mae) In Peace Memorial Park next to Motoyasu-bashi bridge, this tourist office has comprehensive information, English-speaking staff and a small shop selling souvenirs.

ℹ️ Getting There & Away

Air
Hiroshima Airport (www.hij.airport.jp) Hiroshima's airport is 40km east of the city, with limousine bus connections to/from Hiroshima Station (¥1340, 45 minutes).

Train
Hiroshima Station is on the JR San-yō line, which passes westwards to Shimonoseki. It's also a major stop on the Tokyo–Osaka–Hakata *shinkansen* line. Note that if you're travelling from

If You Like...
Historic Towns & Cities

If you like Hiroshima, we think you'll like these other less-visited but interesting towns and cities in western Honshū:

1 KURASHIKI
Not far from Okayama, this city has a fine historic district with canals lined with old *kura* (storehouses) converted into museums. It's 15 minutes from Okayama by train.

2 OKAYAMA
This western Honshū castle city is home to one of Japan's most famous gardens, Kōrakuen, and a nice collection of art museums. From Hiroshima it's 40 minutes by *shinkansen* (bullet train).

3 ONOMICHI
Between Okayama and Hiroshima, this port town on the Inland Sea has a temple walk with great views and is a gateway to the Shimanami-kaidō cycling route. It's one hour from Hiroshima by train.

Tokyo or Kyoto, you may need to change trains at Osaka or Okayama en route. Example *shinkansen* fares from Hiroshima:

Hakata ¥8420, 65 minutes

Osaka ¥9710, 1½ hours

Tokyo ¥18,040, four hours

ℹ Getting Around

Bus

The **Hiroshima Sightseeing Loop Bus** (the *meipurūpu*) has two overlapping routes – orange and green – taking in the main sights and museums of the city, including the Peace Memorial Park and Atomic Bomb Dome. Both routes begin and end on the *shinkansen* entrance (north) side of Hiroshima Station, running from about 9am to 6pm (the green route runs later during summer). Orange route buses run every half-hour; green route buses about every hour.

Passengers can get on and off the bus at any stop. A single ride costs ¥200; an all-day pass is ¥400 (you can buy this from the driver). Those with a JR Pass can ride for free. On the bus there are announcements in English, though the background info on the sights is all in Japanese.

Tram

Hiroshima has an extensive tram service that will get you almost anywhere you want to go for a flat fare of ¥160. You pay by dropping the fare into the machine by the driver as you get off the tram. If you have to change trams to get to your destination, you should ask for a *norikae-ken* (transfer ticket). Daily tram passes are also available and convenient if you're taking a few tram rides.

MIYAJIMA　　宮島
♪ 0829 / POP POP 1970

The small island of Miyajima is a Unesco World Heritage Site and one of Japan's most visited tourist destinations. Its star attraction is the much-photographed vermilion *torii* (shrine gate) of Itsukushima-jinja, which seems to float on the waves at high tide – a scene that has traditionally been ranked as one of the three best views in Japan. Besides this feted view, Miyajima has some good hikes, temples, and cheeky deer that rove the streets and will snatch anything out of the hands of unsuspecting tourists.

Turn right as you emerge from the ferry terminal and follow the waterfront for 10 minutes to get to the shrine. The shopping street, Omotesando, is packed with souvenir outlets and restaurants. This is also where you'll find the world's largest *shakushi* (rice scoop) – it is a block back from the waterfront.

◉ Sights

Allow a few hours to wander around the sights; more if you plan on hiking Misen (p324). Ideally, try to stay overnight on the island to experience it in the quiet of the evening, and for photos of the 'floating *torii*' at sunset.

Miyajima

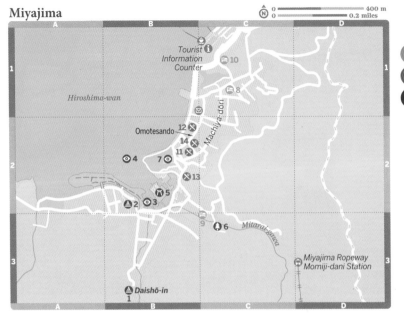

Itsukushima-jinja　　Shinto Shrine
(厳島神社; 1-1 Miyajima-chō; admission ¥300;
⏰6.30am-6pm Mar–mid-Oct, to 5.30pm mid-
Oct–Nov, Jan & Feb, to 5pm Dec) With origins
from as far back as the late 6th century,
Itsukushima-jinja gives Miyajima its real
name.

The shrine's pier-like construction
is a result of the island's sacred status:
commoners were not allowed to set foot
on the island and had to approach by boat
through the **torii** (大鳥居; shrine gate) in
the bay. Much of the time, though, the
shrine and *torii* are surrounded by mud:
to get the classic view of the 'floating'
torii, come at high tide.

The shrine's present form dates from
1168, when it was rebuilt under the
patronage of Taira no Kiyomori, head of
the doomed Heike clan. On one side of the
shrine is a **floating nō stage** (能舞
台), built by local lord Asano Tsunanaga in
1680 and still used for *nō* (stylised dance-
drama) performances every year from 16
to 18 April.

Senjō-kaku　　Pavilion
(1-1 Miyajima-chō; admission ¥100; ⏰8.30am-
4.30pm) Dominating the hill immediately
to the north of Itsukushima-jinja is this
huge pavilion that was built in 1587 by
Toyotomi Hideyoshi. The atmospheric

DELPIXEL/SHUTTERSTOCK ©

Don't Miss
Daishō-in

Just south of town at the foot of Misen, Daishō-in is a worthwhile stopping point on the way up or down the mountain. This Shingon temple is crowded with interesting things to look at: from Buddhist images and prayer wheels to sharp-beaked *tengu* (bird-like demons) and a cave containing images from each of the 88 Shikoku pilgrimage temples.

NEED TO KNOW

大聖院; 210 Miyajima-chō; ⊙8am-5pm

hall is constructed with massive pillars and beams, and the ceiling is hung with paintings. It looks out onto a colourful five-storey **pagoda** (五重塔) dating from 1407.

Daigan-ji   Buddhist Temple

(大願寺; 3 Miyajima-chō; ⊙9am-5pm) Miyajima has several important Buddhist temples, including the 1201 Daigan-ji, just south of Itsukushima-jinja, which dates back to the Heian period and is dedicated to Benzaiten, the Japanese name for Saraswati (the Hindu goddess of good fortune). The seated image of Yakushi

Nyorai here is said to have been carved by Kōbō Daishi.

Momiji-dani-kōen   Park

(紅葉谷公園; Momiji-dani Park) Momiji means 'maple', and their leaves come alive in autumn here in this pretty park along the river. It's at the foot of Misen, close to the ropeway station.

🏃 Activities

Misen & Ropeway   Hiking

(弥山; http://miyajima-ropeway.info; ropeway one-way/return ¥1000/1800; ⊙ropeway 9am-5pm) Covered with primeval forest, the sacred, peaceful Misen is Miyajima's highest mountain (530m), and its ascent is the island's finest walk. You can avoid most of the uphill climb by taking the two-stage **ropeway**, which leaves you with a 30-minute walk to the top, where there is an excellent observatory.

At the summit observatory, you can kick off your shoes and laze on wooden platforms while enjoying 360-degree views – on clear days you can see across to the mountain ranges of Shikoku.

Close to the summit is a temple where Kōbō Daishi meditated for 100 days following his return from China in the 9th century. Next to the main temple hall close to the summit is a flame that's been burning continually since Kōbō Daishi lit it 1200 years ago. From the temple, a path leads down the hillside to Daishō-in and Itsukushima-jinja. The descent takes a little over an hour, or you can take the ropeway down. While on the mountain you might see monkeys and deer around the ropeway station.

The ropeway station (Momiji-dani Station) to ascend Misen is about a 10-minute walk on from Momiji-dani-kōen, or a few minutes on the free shuttle bus, which runs every 20 minutes from a stop near Iwasō Ryokan. A four-hour hike of Misen is detailed in Lonely Planet's *Hiking in Japan*.

 Sleeping

It's well worth staying on the island as you'll be able to enjoy the evening quiet after the day trippers have left.

Guest House Kikugawa Ryokan ¥¥
(ゲストハウス菊がわ; ☏0829-44-0039; www.kikugawa.ne.jp; 796 Miyajima-chō; s/tw from ¥6500/11,600; ⊕❄@🛜) This charming good-value inn is built in traditional style with wooden interiors. There are both tatami rooms with futons and rooms with beds, all with attached bathrooms. The tatami rooms are slightly larger – the most spacious with a cosy mezzanine sleepng area. Dinners are available, as is a no-frills Western-style breakfast.

Yamaichi Bekkan Ryokan ¥¥
(山一別館; ☏0829-44-0700; http://yamaichibekkan.com; per person from ¥8500; P⊕❄) Just across from the ferry terminal, Yamaichi Bekkan offers simple, clean lodgings in one Western-style and three tatami rooms. Bathrooms are all private. The lady of the house couldn't be more welcoming and speaks some English.

Iwasō Ryokan Ryokan ¥¥¥
(岩惣; ☏0829-44-2233; www.iwaso.com; Momiji-dani Miyajima-chō; per person with 2 meals ¥20,100-42,150; @) The Iwasō, open since 1854, offers the grand ryokan experience in exquisite gardens. There are three wings: a stay in a lovely 'Hanare' cottage will set you back the most. Not all rooms have private bathrooms, but you can soak in the onsen in the main building. It's especially stunning in autumn when Momiji-dani (Maple Valley) explodes with colour.

 Eating & Drinking

There are plenty of places to eat along and around the main strip, where you can try the local oysters, as well as eel in various guises (on rice, or perhaps in a steamed bun). It's often very busy and at some places you may have to wait to get a seat. Just one street back from the main strip is the much quieter Machiya-dōri, with a few cafes and eateries. Most restaurants shut down after the crowds go home.

Baccano Ice Cream ¥
(バッカーノ; 435 Miyajima-chō; ice cream from ¥450; ⏰10am-6pm; 📱) Baccano gelateria dishes up refreshing swirls of handmade ice cream, from fruity standards to interesting local flavours like roasted green tea and black sesame.

Sarasvati Cafe ¥
(http://sarasvati.jp; 407 Miyajima-chō; coffees from ¥500, meals ¥990-1500; ⏰8.30am-8pm; 📱) The aroma of roasting coffee beans lures people into this cafe inside a former storehouse building from the early 1900s. Bare wooden floors and tables match a simple menu of traditional coffees

(espresso, latte, cappuccino), plus cakes, sandwich and pasta sets.

Yakigaki-no-hayashi   Oysters ¥¥

(焼がきのはやし; ☎0829-44-0335; www. yakigaki-no-hayashi.co.jp; 505-1 Miyajima-chō; dishes ¥900-1600; ⏰10.30am-5pm Thu-Tue; 📖) The oysters in the tank and on the barbecue outside are what everyone is eating here. Try a plate of *nama-gaki* (raw oysters) or *kaki-furai* (crumbed, fried oysters), or go for oysters on udon noodles. It's not all about the slimy shell-dwellers – there are other meals on the menu, such as curry and eel sets.

Mame-tanuki   Izakaya ¥¥

(まめたぬき; ☎0829-44-2131; 1113 Miyajima-chō; lunch sets ¥1400-2500, dishes ¥500-1500; ⏰11am-3.30pm & 5-11pm; 📖) By day at Mame-tanuki there are lunch sets, such as the tasty *anago meshi* (steamed conger eel with rice) and fried oysters, and at night it is one of the few places open late, serving drinks and *izakaya*-style small dishes. Look for the blue curtain; there's a menu signboard outside.

ℹ Information

Tourist Information Counter (宮島観光案内所; ☎0829-44-2011; http://visit-miyajima-japan.com; ⏰9am-5pm) Tourist info inside the ferry terminal.

ℹ Getting There & Away

Miyajima is accessed by ferry, and is an easy day trip from Hiroshima.

The mainland ferry terminal is a short walk from Miyajima-guchi Station on the JR San-yō line, halfway between Hiroshima (¥410, 26 minutes) and Iwakuni. The ferry terminal can also be reached by tram 2 from Hiroshima (¥260, 70 minutes), which runs from Hiroshima Station, passing the Atomic Bomb Dome on the way. Ferries operated by two companies shuttle regularly across to the island from Miyajima-guchi (¥180, 10 minutes). JR Pass holders can travel on the JR ferry for free.

Setonaikai Kisen (瀬戸内海汽船フェリー; ☎082-253-1212; www.setonaikaikisen.co.jp) operates high-speed ferries (¥1850, 30 minutes, six to eight daily) direct to Miyajima from Hiroshima's Ujina port. Another option is to take the **Aqua Net ferry** (☎082-240-5955; www.aqua-net-h.co.jp) directly from Peace Memorial Park in central Hiroshima (one way/return ¥2000/3600, 45 minutes, 10 to 15 daily). These boats cruise under the bridges of Kyūōta-gawa before coming out into the bay towards Miyajima. No reservation is required.

The Best of the Rest

Niseko (p328)
The roof of Hokkaidō offers some of the best hiking in Japan and plenty of onsen to soak in after your hikes.

Daisetsuzan National Park (p331)
Soaring mountains, active volcanoes, remote onsen, clear lakes and dense forest.

Iya Valley (p333)
Deep in the mountainous heart of Shikoku island, Iya Valley is a chance to step back in time to a simpler Japan and stay in a traditional rural house.

Nagasaki (p335)
Best known for its tragic fate in WWII, Nagasaki is a vibrant city that has played a major role in Japanese history for centuries.

Southwest Islands (p340)
The tropical south of Japan is pure cognitive dissonance: you'll often find yourself wondering, 'Is this Thailand or Japan?'

Top: Kazura-bashi, Iya Valley (p333); Left: Nagasaki Atomic Bomb Museum (p336)

Niseko

📱 0136 / POP 4650

HIGHLIGHTS

1 **Niseko United** Some of the most reliable lift-served powder skiing on earth.

2 **Hilton Niseko** Arguably the best accommodation in the area.

3 **Onsen** Nothing – and we mean nothing – beats a soak in a hot spring after a day on the slopes.

Hokkaidō is dotted with world-class ski resorts, but the reigning prince of powder is unquestionably Niseko (ニセコ). There are four interconnected resorts with more than 800 skiable hectares along the eastern side of the mountain Niseko Annupuri. Soft and light powdery snow and an annual average snowfall of more than 15m make Niseko extremely popular with international skiers.

 Activities

Niseko United   Skiing, Snowboarding (ニセコユナイテッド; www.niseko.ne.jp/en; 8hr/1-day pass ¥5600/6400; ⏱8.30am-8.30pm Nov-Apr) Niseko United is the umbrella name for four resorts, namely Niseko Annupuri, Niseko Village, Grand Hirafu and Hanazono. What makes Niseko United stand out from the competition is that you can ski or snowboard on all four slopes by purchasing a single all-mountain pass.

This electronic tag gives you access to 18 lifts and gondolas, 60 runs, as well as free rides on the inter-mountain shuttle bus. If you're planning on skiing for several days, a week or even the season, you can also buy discounted multiday passes.

Rental equipment is of very high quality, and can be picked up virtually everywhere at affordable prices. Rental shops also typically have a few foreign staff on hand to help English-speaking customers. A high percentage of visitors to Niseko are from abroad, with plenty of Australians and growing numbers from Europe and North America. English is everywhere you look and listen.

At the base, most of the après-ski action is in Hirafu; though luxury-seekers harbour in the Hilton at Niseko Village, and locals tend to stick to Annupuri.

Communal bathing in an onsen after a day on the slopes is a chance to jump into Japanese culture. Most hotels either have an onsen on the premises, or can point you in the direction of the nearest bathhouse.

Skiiers climb Niseko Annupuri

ONSEN

Niseko has a brochure with 25 onsen options in the area, be they for use in winter or summer. Prices are generally around ¥500 to ¥700 per person.

Winter visitors may like to opt for luxury at the Hilton Niseko Village (¥1000) or at the Niseko Grand Hotel (¥700), while those with their own wheels in summer will love Niimi Onsen (¥500) and Goshiki Onsen (¥600), both away in the mountains to the west of Niseko Annupuri and its ski fields.

Sleeping

Niseko proper is spread out along the base of the four slopes. The closer you get to the slopes themselves, the more options you'll have. Hirafu and Annupuri host the vast majority of accommodation, while Niseko Village is centred on the upmarket Hilton. Most places will provide pick-up and drop-off for the slopes in winter, or you can take buses and shuttles to move about. It's strongly recommended that you book well in advance in winter.

Hotel Niseko Alpen   Hotel ¥¥

(ホテルニセコアルペン; ☎0136-22-1105; www.grand-hirafu.jp/hotel_niseko-alpen/en; r from ¥12,000; P@🛜❄♨) Right next to the Welcome Centre and the lifts in Hirafu, this spacious place has it all. Plush western-style rooms, an indoor pool, onsen and buffet meals make staying here a real pleasure – and you're not far from the restaurants and bars of Hirafu. A very good option.

Hilton Niseko   Resort ¥¥¥

(ニセコヒルトンヴィレジ; ☎0136-44-1111; www.placeshilton.com/niseko-village; r from ¥20,000; P@🛜♨) The Hilton enjoys the best location of all – it is quite literally attached to the Niseko Gondola. Spacious Western-style rooms are complemented by a whole slew of amenities spread out across a self-contained village. Check the website before arriving as special deals are usually available, which combine discounted room rates with breakfast and dinner buffets.

Eating & Drinking

Many of the lodges and ryokan offer great meals cooked to order, and the slopes have plenty of snacks, pizza, *rāmen* and other goodies. After hours, things are tricky because lodging is spread out and buses are inconvenient, but there are plenty of watering holes in Hirafu.

A Niseko bar

Graubunden   Cafe ¥

(グラウビュンデン; ☎0136-23-3371; www.
graubunden.jp; ⏰8am-7pm Fri-Wed) Seriously good sandwiches, cakes, cookies
and drinks in Hirafu East Village. A local
favourite that has been open for decades,
Graubunden is the perfect spot to chill
out with good service, good food and a
relaxed atmosphere.

Jojo's Café & Restaurant   Cafe ¥

(ジョジョズカフェ; ☎0136-23-2220; www.
nac-web.com/niseko/cafe.html; mains from ¥750;
⏰11am-9pm; 📋) Excellent casual dining
to be had at the Niseko Adventure Centre
(NAC). We're talking burgers, salads,
pasta and tacos, and stupendous views
of Yōtei-zan from out on the terrace on a
good day.

ⓘ Information

At the base of the ski slopes lie several towns and
villages that compose Niseko's population centre.
Most of the restaurants and bars are clustered
together in Hirafu (ひらふ), while Annupuri
(アンヌプリ), Niseko Village (ニセコビレッ
ジ) and Hanazono (花園) are much quieter and
less developed. Further east are Kutchan (倶
知安) and Niseko (ニセコ) proper, which are
more permanent population centres that remain
decidedly Japanese.

Niseko Tourist Information (ニセコ観光案内
所; ☎0136-44-2468; www.nisekotourism.com;
⏰9am-6pm) Has offices at JR Niseko Station
and at the View Plaza Michi-no-Eki on Rte 66
heading into town. They have pamphlets, maps,
bus timetables and will help with bookings.

ⓘ Getting There & Away

Bus

During the ski season, both **Chūō Bus** (☎011-231-
0500; www.chuo-bus.co.jp) runs regular highway

buses from JR Sapporo Station and New Chitose
Airport to Niseko. The trip takes around three
hours depending on road conditions, costs ¥2300
(return ¥3850) and drops off at the welcome
centre in Hirafu before continuing on to the Hilton
and Annupuri. Reservations are necessary, and it's
recommended that you book well ahead of your
departure date. If you don't speak Japanese, ask
the staff at the tourist information centres or your
accommodation to make a reservation for you.

Car & Motorcycle

Scenic Rte 5 winds from Sapporo to Otaru around
the coast, and then cuts inland through the
mountains down to Niseko. Having a car will make
it easier to move between the various ski slopes,
though drive with extreme caution as fatalities
have tragically occurred here in the past. In the
summer (low season), public transport services
drop off, which provides more incentive to pick up
a car in Sapporo or at New Chitose Airport.

Train

While there is a JR Hirafu Station, it is far from the
town itself, and is not well serviced by local buses.
From JR Niseko and JR Kutchan Stations, you will
need to switch to local buses to access the villages
at the base of the ski slopes. For these reasons,
it's recommended that you travel to Niseko via
highway bus or car. If, however, the bus lines are
fully booked, trains run on the JR Hakodate line
between Sapporo and Niseko (¥2470, two hours)
via Kutchan (¥2150, 1¾ hours).

ⓘ Getting Around

There are twice-hourly local buses linking JR
Kutchan and JR Niseko Stations to Hirafu,
Niseko Village, Annupuri and Hanazono. Pick up
a schedule from the tourist information centres
so that you don't miss your connection. Also,
if you've purchased an all-mountain pass, you
can ride the free hourly shuttle bus between the
villages.

Known as 'Nutakukamushupe' in Ainu, Daisetsuzan (大雪山国立公園; Big Snow Mountain) is Japan's largest national park, designated in 1934 and covering more than 2300 sq km. A vast wilderness area of soaring mountains, active volcanoes, remote onsen, clear lakes and dense forests, Daisetsuzan is the kind of place that stressed-out workers in Tokyo and Osaka dream about during their daily commute.

Virtually untouched by human hands, the park has minimal tourism, with most visitors basing themselves in the hot-spring villages on the periphery. The three main access points into the park are **Asahidake Onsen** in the northwest, **Sōunkyō Onsen** in the northeast and **Tokachi-dake Onsen** in the southwest.

Daisetsuzan National Park

HIGHLIGHTS

1. **Hiking** Hike across the roof of Hokkaidō

2. **Asahidake Onsen** A great entry to the park and some fantastic hot springs.

3. **Asahidake Ropeway** Get up into the mountains without breaking a sweat.

Asahidake Onsen
旭岳温泉

☎ 0166

This forested hot-springs village, at 1100m above sea level, has a few small inns at the base of Asahi-dake, Hokkaidō's tallest peak. There are plenty of hiking options and healing onsen for afterwards.

Most onsen, even at the higher-end hotels, are open to the general public for day use. Prices range from ¥500 up to ¥1500.

Be prepared. There are no ATMs, shops or restaurants at Asahidake Onsen, so you'll need to have cash, and food sorted out if you are going camping or contemplating taking on the Grand Traverse. If you are staying, order meals at your accommodation house when you book.

🏃 Activities

Asahidake Ropeway   Ropeway
(旭岳 ロープウェイ; ☎ 0166-68-9111; http://wakasaresort.com/eng; one-way/return 1 Jun–20 Oct ¥1650/2900, 21 Oct–31 May ¥1100/1800; ⏰ 6am-5.30pm Jul–mid-Oct, 9am-4pm mid-Oct–Jun) This ropeway runs from Asahidake Onsen (1100m) up to Sugatami (姿見) at 1600m, making Asahi-dake (旭岳)

Hikers on Asahi-dake
GAVIN HELLIER/GETTY IMAGES ©

331

Hiking in Daisetsuzan National Park

There are a lot of options for hiking in the national park, ranging from half-day trips to the Daisetsuzan Grand Traverse, a hard-core five- to seven-day, 55km hike the length of the park.

Get a copy of Shōbunsha's *Yama-to-Kōgen Chizu Map 3: Daisetsuzan* (昭文社 山と高原地図３大雪山), be prepared, and check the weather forecast. Visitor-centre staff will be more than happy to update you on conditions.

The season for the Grand Traverse runs from early July to October. A tent and camping gear may be preferable to the extremely bare-bones huts. You'll need to carry in your own food and cooking supplies. This is also bear country, so be smart and tie a bell to your rucksack.

You could start at either Asahidake Onsen or Sōunkyō Onsen and you'll finish at Tokachi-dake Onsen. Pick up a copy of Lonely Planet's *Hiking in Japan*, do your homework before you go, and make the most of this adventure!

(2290m) a very feasible day hike. There are all sorts of hiking options and on a good day, the views are magnificent.

 ## Sleeping

Daisetsuzan Shirakaba-sō   Inn ¥

(大雪山白樺荘; ☎0166-97-2246; http://park19.wakwak.com/~shirakaba/english.html; incl 2 meals, dm from ¥6890, r per person ¥7940; P @) A cross between a youth hostel and a ryokan, this mountain lodge near the ropeway's lower terminal offers comfortable Japanese- and Western-style rooms and hot-spring baths. There is a large kitchen available if you're self-catering, but it's worth going for the meal plan. Lots of options, so check out the website. Non-guests can use the onsen for ¥500.

Lodge Nutapukaushipe   Lodge ¥¥

(ロッジ・ヌタプカウシペ; ☎0166-97-2150; r per person with 2 meals from ¥8000; P 🛜) 🛶 This log cabin–style place is an absolute joy, run by a real character who has hand-crafted most of the furniture and fittings

from local timber. The onsen is superb, as are the meals. You'll have to make a bit of an effort though as there isn't a website. Pick up the phone and speak slowly. You won't be disappointed.

ℹ Information

Hikers should pay a visit to the **Asahidake Visitors Centre** (旭岳ビジターセンター; ☎0166-97-2153; www.town.higashikawa.hokkaido.jp/vc; ⏲9am-5pm Jun-Oct, to 4pm Nov-May), which has excellent maps that the staff will mark with daily track conditions. If you're heading out on a long hike, inform them of your intentions. An onsen map is also available here, which lists the locations, prices and hours of the various baths.

ℹ Getting There & Away

There are three buses in both directions daily between bus stop 4 in front of JR Asahikawa Station and Asahidake Onsen (¥1320, 1½ hours). The first bus leaves Asahikawa at 9.25am, returning from Asahidake Onsen at 11am.

Iya Valley

The spectacular Iya Valley (祖谷渓) is a special place, its staggeringly steep gorges and thick mountain forests luring travellers to seek respite from the hectic 'mainland' lifestyle. Winding your way around narrow cliff-hanging roads as the icy blue water of the Yoshino-gawa shoots along the ancient valley floors is a blissful travel experience. The active soul can pick up some of the country's finest hiking trails around Tsurugi-san or try world-class white-water rafting in the Ōboke and Koboke Gorges.

Ōboke & Koboke
大歩危・小歩危

Ōboke and Koboke are two scenic gorges on the Yoshino-gawa, which fluctuates from languid green waters to Class IV rapids. Driving through these rural river valleys provides the first verdant glimpse into the magic of Iya.

Spectacular scenery abounds in the deep canyons along Old Rte 32. Infrequent public buses (¥880, 55 minutes, 7:15am, 10:15am and 12:15pm) ply this narrow route between Awa-Ikeda and the Iya Valley.

To orient yourself in this maze of valleys, stop by **Lapis Ōboke** (ラピス大歩危; ☎0883-84-1489; 1553-1 Kamimyo; admission ¥500; ☺9am-6pm Apr-Nov, to 5pm Dec-Mar) for basic tourist information. Its primary role is as a geology and local *yōkai* (ghost) museum – skip the rocks, but get acquainted with the folkloric apparitions, colourfully represented in a hall of delightful horrors (explained with some English signage).

Stop by the tourist complex **River Station West-West** (☎0887-84-1117; www.west-west.com) for river gear at the Mont Bell shop, road snacks and pit stops at the *conbini* (convenience store) and excellent *soba* at the restaurant **Momiji-tei** (もみじ亭; ☎0883-84-1117; meals ¥900-2000; ☺10am-5:30pm Thu-Tue) – try the *tempura soba* set (¥1450), either hot or cold.

HIGHLIGHTS

❶ Staying in a traditional Japanese house Sample the life of a rural Shikoku village.

❷ Iya Onsen (p334) Take a cable car down to this impossibly scenic onsen.

❸ Chiiori (p334) The original Chiiori Trust house is still the most spectacular.

Traditional millstone, Iya Valley

Activities

Happy Raft
Rafting

(ハッピーラフト; ☎0887-75-0500; www.hap-pyraft.com; 221-1 Ikadagi) South of Ikeda on Rte 32 between Koboke and Ōboke, about 20 companies run white-water rafting and kayaking trips from mid-March to mid-October. Happy Raft, steps from JR Tosa Iwahara Station, operates sensational rafting trips and canyoning adventures (¥9000) with English-speaking guides (half-day ¥5500 to ¥7500, full day ¥10,000 to ¥15,500).

Iya Onsen
Onsen

(祖谷温泉; ☎0883-75-2311; www.iyaonsen. co.jp; 367-2 Matsuo Matsumoto; ¥1500; ⊙7am-6pm for day-use guests) On Old Rte 32, this onsen is a great place to warm up after a chilling plunge through white-water. A cable car descends a steep cliff-face to some sulphurous, open-air baths on the riverside. The hotel is a fantastic place to slow down, enjoy spectacular views of the forested gorge and, of course, soak in the onsen.

Chiiori

High on a mountainside in the remote Iya Valley, looking out over forested hillsides and plunging gorges, is one of Japan's most unusual places to stay.

Chiiori (www.chiiori.org; s/d from ¥21,000/22,000 high season; lower rates for larger groups) – 'The Cottage of the Flute' – is a once-abandoned 18th-century thatched-roof farmhouse that has been painstakingly restored to its original brilliance. Unlike many such examples of cultural heritage in Japan, where concrete and plastic have wrecked the architectural aesthetic, here glistening red-pine floorboards surround open-floor hearths under soaring rafters. Set amid steep hillsides dotted by thatched houses and forests strewn with narrow mountain paths, Iya was for centuries an example of an untouched coexistence of humans and nature, albeit one that offered residents little hope of wealth and comfort.

In recent decades, however, the locals' traditional lifestyle and the balance with the environment have been rapidly upset; employment moved from agriculture to government-subsidised and frequently pointless construction, the effects of which – eg paved riverbeds – can be seen from almost any roadside. Part of the project's mission has been working with residents to promote sustainable, community-based tourism and realise the financial potential of traditional life, which until recently many locals saw as backward and valueless. It is a work in progress – many thatched roofs in the area are still hidden by corrugated tin sheets – but by adding to the growing number of tourists visiting the area, largely because of the work of those involved in Chiiori, staying here helps to encourage those conservation efforts.

The house was bought as a ruin by the author and aesthete Alex Kerr in the early 1970s, and he went on to romanticise the Iya Valley in his award-winning book *Lost Japan*. Chiiori remains a beautiful and authentic destination for sensitive travellers, with its *shōji* (movable screens), antique furnishings and *irori* (traditional hearths) – all complemented by a gleaming, fully-equipped modern kitchen and gorgeous bathroom, complete with *hinoki* (Japanese cypress) tub. Since the establishment of the nonprofit Chiiori Trust in 2005, the local government has approached the Trust to help restore several smaller traditional houses in the area. These houses have been renovated to a similarly high standard and aesthetic as Chiiori and are also available as accommodation. All are outfitted with modern kitchens and bathrooms, and even washing machines. Follow the Higashi-Iya Ochiai link on the Chiiori Trust website for information and rates on these smaller houses.

To stay in these extraordinary environs, you must reserve in advance through **Chiiori Trust** (☎0883-88-5290; www. chiiori.org; 209 Tsurui, Higashi-Iya; ⊙9am-6pm); payments must be made in cash.

Because of the remote locations of Chiiori and the other houses, the Chiiori Trust strongly recommends that guests bring private vehicles.

ℹ️ Getting There & Away

Access to the area is via Ōboke Station, reached by train from Takamatsu (¥2990) or Tokushima (¥3280) with a change at Awa-Ikeda, or from Kōchi (¥2460). From Honshū, Nanpū limited express trains depart hourly from Okayama (¥4020, 1¾ hours); Okayama is on the Sanyō Shinkansen line.

Getting around the valley itself involves some planning, because Iya's sights are widespread, and public transport is sporadic at the best of times. Four buses per day travel between Ōboke and Iya (¥660, 40 minutes). **Ikeda DK Taxi** (☎0883-76-0011) and **Ōboke Taxi** (☎0883-84-1225) are among several companies filling the gaps in the bus schedule.

The best way to explore the region is with your own wheels; you will thank the Daishi for the freedom and flexibility a car offers here. Rental cars are available in Shikoku's larger cities.

Nagasaki

📍095 / POP 440,000

HIGHLIGHTS

1 **Nagasaki Atomic Bomb Museum** (p336) and **Peace Park** (p336) These sobering memorials to man's inhumanity still manage to inspire hope for a more peaceful future.

2 **Dejima** (p336) This former Dutch trading outpost is a must for any fan of Japanese history.

3 **Glover Garden** (p337) Both historically significant and scenic, this is a must-see in Nagasaki.

Paper cranes at the Peace Park (p336)
MARTIN MOOS/GETTY IMAGES ©

How ironic it is that the name Nagasaki conjures up the tragic destruction of war, as for much of its history the city of Nagasaki was Japan's only link to the outside world; other parts of Nagasaki Prefecture (長崎県) served a similar role.

A visit to the scenes of atomic devastation is a must, but beyond them you'll find that this one-of-a-kind, embracing city boasts a colourful trading history, alluring churches, shrines, temples and an East-meets-West culinary scene, prettily set within hills around a gracious harbour.

Schedule a few days here to meet the people and get a sense of Nagasaki's spirit.

Sights

URAKAMI (NORTHERN NAGASAKI)

Urakami, the hypocentre of the atomic explosion, is today a prosperous, peaceful suburb. While nuclear ruin seems comfortably far away seven decades later, many sights here keep the memory alive.

Nagasaki Atomic Bomb Museum   Museum
(長崎原爆資料館; www.city.nagasaki.lg.jp/peace/english/abm; 7-8 Hirano-machi; admission ¥200, audio guide ¥150; ◷8.30am-6.30pm May-Aug, to 5.30pm Sep-Apr; 🚃Matsuyama-machi) An essential Nagasaki experience, this sombre place recounts the city's destruction and loss of life through photos and artefacts, including mangled rocks, trees, furniture, pottery and clothing, a clock stopped at 11.02 (the hour of the bombing), first-hand accounts from survivors and stories of heroic relief efforts.

Exhibits also include the postbombing struggle for nuclear disarmament, and conclude with a chilling illustration of which nations bear nuclear arms.

Nagasaki National Peace Memorial Hall for the Atomic Bomb Victims   Memorial
(国立長崎原爆死没者追悼平和祈念館; www.peace-nagasaki.go.jp; 7-8 Hirano-machi; ◷8.30am-6.30pm May-Aug, to 5.30pm Sep-Apr; 🚃Matsuyama-machi) FREE Adjacent to the Atomic Bomb Museum and completed in 2003, this minimalist memorial by Kuryū Akira is a profoundly moving place. It is best approached by quietly reading the carved inscriptions and walking around the sculpted water basin. In the hall below, 12 glass pillars, containing shelves of books of the names of the deceased, reach skyward.

Peace Park   Park
(平和公園; Heiwa-kōen; 🚃Ōhashi) FREE North of the hypocentre, the Peace Park is presided over by the 10-tonne bronze Nagasaki Peace Statue (平和祈念像), designed in 1955 by Kitamura Seibo. It also includes the dove-shaped Fountain of Peace (1969) and the Peace Symbol Zone, a sculpture garden with contributions on the theme of peace from around the world. On 9 August, a rowdy antinuclear protest is held within earshot of the more respectful official memorial ceremony for those lost to the bomb.

Atomic Bomb Hypocentre Park   Park
(長崎爆心地公園; 🚃Matsuyama-machi) FREE The park has a smooth, black stone column marking the point above which the bomb exploded. Nearby are bomb-blasted relics, including a section of the wall of the Urakami Cathedral.

CENTRAL NAGASAKI

Dejima   Historic Site
(出島; 🚃Dejima) In 1641, the Tokugawa shōgunate banished all foreigners from Japan, with one exception: Dejima, a fan-shaped, artificial island 560m in circumference (15,000 sq m) in Nagasaki harbour. From then until the 1850s, this tiny Dutch trading post was the sole sanctioned foreign presence in Japan. Today the city has filled in around the island

The Atomic Explosion

When United States Air Force B-29 bomber *Bockscar* set off from the Marianas on 9 August 1945 to drop a second atomic bomb on Japan, the target was Kokura on Kyūshū's northeastern coast. Due to poor visibility, the crew diverted to the secondary target, Nagasaki.

The B-29 arrived over Nagasaki at 10.58am amid heavy cloud. When a momentary gap appeared and the Mitsubishi Arms Factory was sighted, the 4.57-tonne 'Fat Man' bomb, with an explosive power equivalent to 21.3 kilotonnes of TNT (almost twice that of Hiroshima's 'Little Boy'), was released over Nagasaki.

The bomb missed the arms factory, its intended target, and exploded at 11.02am, at an altitude of 500m almost directly above the largest Catholic church in Asia (Urakami Cathedral). In an instant, it annihilated the suburb of Urakami and 74,000 of Nagasaki's 240,000 people. Ground temperatures at the hypocentre were estimated between 3000°C and 4000°C, and as high as 600°C 1.5km away. Everything within a 1km radius of the explosion was destroyed, and searing winds estimated at 1000km/h (typhoons generally top out at 150km/h) swept down the valley of the Urakami-gawa towards the city centre. With able-bodied men at work or at war, most victims were women, children and senior citizens, as well as 13,000 conscripted Korean labourers and 200 allied POWs. Another 75,000 people were horribly injured (and it is estimated that as many people died as a result of the after-effects). After the resulting fires burned out, a third of the city was gone.

Yet the damage might have been even worse had the targeted arms factory been hit. Unlike in the flatlands of Hiroshima or the Nagasaki port itself, the hills around the river valley protected outlying suburbs from greater damage.

and you might miss it. Don't. Seventeen buildings, walls and structures (plus a miniature Dejima) have been painstakingly reconstructed into the Dejima Museum (出島資料館; www.nagasakidejima.jp/en; 6-1 Dejima-machi; admission ¥510; ⊙8am-6pm, to 7pm mid-July to mid-Oct; 🚋Dejima).

Nagasaki Museum of History & Culture   Museum

(長崎歴史文化博物館; www.nmhc.jp; 1-1-1 Tateyama; admission ¥600; ⊙8.30am-7pm, closed 3rd Tue of month; 🚋Sakura-machi) This large museum with attractive displays opened in 2005 to focus on Nagasaki's proud history of international exchange. The main gallery is a fabulous reconstruction of a section of the Edo-period Nagasaki Magistrate's Office, which controlled trade and diplomacy. Detailed English-language explanations were in the works at the time of research.

SOUTHERN NAGASAKI

Glover Garden   Gardens

(グラバー園; ☎095-822-8223; www.glover-garden.jp; 8-1 Minami-yamate-machi; adult/student ¥610/300; ⊙8am-9.30pm 29 Apr–mid-Jul, to 6pm mid-Jul–28 Apr; 🚋Ōura Tenshudō-shita) Some former homes of the city's Meiji-period European residents have been reassembled in this hillside garden. Glover Garden is named after Thomas Glover (1838–1911), the Scottish merchant who built Japan's first railway, helped establish the shipbuilding industry and whose arms-importing operations influenced the course of the Meiji Restoration. It's a lovely spot to stroll around.

🛌 Sleeping

For ease of transport and access to restaurants and nightlife, we recommend staying near JR Nagasaki Station or Shianbashi.

Hotel Dormy Inn Nagasaki
Business Hotel ¥¥

(ドーミーイン長崎; ☎095-820-5489; www.hotespa.net/hotels/nagasaki; 7-24 Dōza-machi; s/d/tw from ¥6290/8290/13,900; 🚭@; 🚃Tsuki-machi) Adjacent to Chinatown, this hotel would be worth it just for the location. Rooms are crisp and neat as a pin, with quality mattresses. There are large gender-separated common baths and saunas in addition to in-room facilities. The breakfast buffet (¥1100) includes *sara-udon*, and there's free *soba* served from 9.30pm to 11pm. Prices vary widely based on season and online discounts.

ANA Crowne Plaza Nagasaki Gloverhill
Hotel ¥¥

(ANAクラウンプラザ長崎グラバーヒル; ☎095-818-6601; www.anacrowneplaza-nagasaki.jp; 1-18 Minami-yamate-machi; s/d/tw from ¥8700/13,400/16,440; 🅿🚭@🛜;

🚃Ōura-Tenshudō-shita) Near Glover Garden, Ōura Catholic Church and the Dutch Slopes, this hotel has three types of room: Standards that are relatively plain, then Superior and Deluxe, which are both quite stylish thanks to a recent renovation. About the only downside: no view to speak of.

Chisun Grand Nagasaki
Business Hotel ¥¥

(チサングランド長崎; ☎095-826-1211; www.solarehotels.com/english; 5-35 Goto-machi; s/d/tw ¥12,000/16,000/18,000; 🚭@🛜; 🚃Goto-machi) On the main drag, look for this hotel with 153 sleek rooms that come with dark wood panelling, separate shower, tub and vanity. Staff are used to foreign guests and there's a coin laundry. Discounted rates on the website.

Sakamoto-ya
Ryokan ¥¥¥

(料亭旅館坂本屋; ☎095-826-8211; www.sakamotoya.co.jp; 2-13 Kanaya-machi; r per person incl 2 meals from ¥15,575; 🅿@; 🚃Goto-machi) This magnificent old-school ryokan has been in business since 1894. Look for art-filled rooms, hallways lined with Arita-yaki pottery, postage-stamp-sized gardens off 1st-floor rooms, *kaiseki* meals (Japanese

Glover Garden (p337)

haute cuisine) and only 11 rooms for personal service, each with a *hinoki-buro* (cypress wood bath). From Goto-machi tram stop, walk past Chisun Grand Hotel and turn left. It's diagonally across from the TV broadcast tower.

Richmond Hotel Nagasaki Shianbashi
Hotel ¥¥¥

(リッチモンドホテル長崎思案橋; ☎ 095-832-2525; www.nagasaki.richmondhotel.jp; 6-38 Motoshikkui-machi; s/d/tw from ¥11,000/16,000/19,000; 🚭 @ 🛜; 🚃 Shianbashi) You can't be closer to the heart of Shianbashi than this travellers' favourite. Deluxe rooms are large by Japanese standards. There's cheerful, English-speaking staff and a terrific breakfast buffet (¥1000) including Nagasaki specialities.

 ## Eating

Nagasaki is a culinary crossroads and one of Japan's most interesting dining scenes. The **Mirai Nagasaki Cocowalk** (みらい長崎ココウォーク; ☎ 095-848-5509; www.cocowalk.jp; 1-55 Morimachi; ⏱ 10am-9pm; 🚃 Mori-machi, 🚉 JR Urakami) shopping mall features some 20 restaurants on its 4th and 5th floors. **Aletta** (アレッタ; ☎ 095-801-5245; lunch/dinner ¥1650/2070; ⏱ 11am-3.30pm & 5-11pm; 🚃 Mori-machi) is an airy buffet restaurant on the 4th floor, with a different national theme each month.

Organic Restaurant Tia
Japanese ¥

(ティア; ☎ 095-828-2984; www.tia-nagasaki.com; 6-24 Ginza-chō; breakfast buffet ¥1150, meals from ¥700; ⏱ 7-10am, 11:30am-3pm, 6-9pm; 🚃 Kankō-dōri) Mouth-watering homestyle Japanese cooking made with local, organic products. What's not to love? The breakfast buffet is fantastic. Below the Victoria Inn.

Hōuntei
Izakaya ¥

(宝雲亭; ☎ 095-821-9333; 1-8 Motoshikkui-machi; dishes ¥360-520; ⏱ 5-11pm; 🚃 Shianbashi) Patrons have been ordering the *hito-kuchi gyōza* (one-bite *gyōza*; ¥380 for 10) at this rustic hole-in-the-wall since the 1970s. Also try *butaniratoji* (pork and shallots cooked omelette style; ¥540). There's a picture menu. Look for the lantern and brown *noren* (door curtain) across from With Nagasaki.

Shippoku Hamakatsu
Kaiseki ¥¥

(卓袱浜勝; ☎ 095-826-8321; www.sippoku.jp; 6-50 Kajiya-machi; lunch/dinner from ¥1500/2940; ⏱ 11.30am-10pm; 📖; 🚃 Shianbashi) Come here if you would like to experience *shippoku ryōri* and still afford your airfare home. Course menus are filling and varied (the Otakusa Shippoku is served on a dramatic round tray). In addition, there is a choice of either Japanese- or Western-style seating.

Yosso
Japanese ¥¥

(吉宗; ☎ 095-821-0001; www.yossou.co.jp; 8-9 Hama-machi; set meals from ¥1350; ⏱ 11am-8pm; 🚃 Shianbashi) People have been coming to eat *chawanmushi* (Japanese egg custard) since 1866. Look for the traditional shopfront festooned with red lanterns. The Yosso *teishoku* (¥2376) adds fish, *soboro* (sweetened, ground chicken over rice), *kakuni* (stewed pork belly), dessert and more. There's no English menu, but a display case makes ordering easy.

ℹ️ Information

Tourist Information

In addition to tourist brochures available at locations below, look for the free English-language magazine *Nagazasshi*, published by local expats, containing events, sightseeing tips and features. A new multilingual call centre (☎ 095-825-5175) caters to English-speaking visitors.

Nagasaki City Tourist Information Centre (長崎市総合観光案内所; ☎ 095-823-3631; www.at-nagasaki.jp/foreign/english; 1st fl, JR Nagasaki Station; ⏱ 8am-8pm) Can assist with finding accommodation and has brochures and maps in English.

ⓘ Getting There & Away

Air

There are flights between Nagasaki and Tokyo, Osaka, Okinawa and Nagoya.

Train

JR lines from Nagasaki head for Sasebo (for Hirado; *kaisoku*; ¥1650, 1¾ hours) or Fukuoka (Hakata Station; *tokkyū*; ¥4500, two hours). Most other destinations require a change of train. Nagasaki is not currently served by *shinkansen*.

ⓘ Getting Around

To/From the Airport

Nagasaki's airport is located about 40km from the city. Airport buses (¥800, 35 minutes) operate from stand 4 of the Kenei bus terminal opposite JR Nagasaki Station and outside the Shinchi bus terminal. A taxi to the airport costs about ¥10,000.

Tram

The best way of getting around Nagasaki is by tram. There are four colour-coded routes numbered 1, 3, 4 and 5 (route 2 is for special events) and stops are signposted in English. It costs ¥120 to travel anywhere in town, but you can transfer for free at the Tsuki-machi (築町) stop only (ask for a *noritsugi*, or transfer pass), unless you have a ¥500 all-day pass for unlimited travel, available from tourist information centres and many hotels. Most trams stop running around 11.30pm.

Southwest Islands

HIGHLIGHTS

❶ **Hiking on Yakushima** From short strolls to an ascent of Miya-no-ura-dake, Yakushima offers some of Japan's best hiking.

❷ **Shuri-jō** (p345) It may be a modern reconstruction, but this castle still captures the magic of old Okinawa.

❸ **Kerama Islands** World-class beaches, whale-watching and great diving make the Keramas unmissable.

Yakushima Coast

Yakushima
屋久島

📞0997 / POP 13,700

Designated a Unesco World Heritage Site in 1993, Yakushima is one of the most rewarding islands in the Southwest Islands. The craggy mountain peaks of the island's interior are home to the world-famous *yakusugi* (屋久杉; *Cryptomeria japonica*), ancient cedar trees that are said to have been the inspiration for some of the scenes in Miyazaki Hayao's animation classic *Princess Mononoke*.

Hiking among the high peaks and mossy forests is the main activity on Yakushima, but the island is also home to some excellent coastal onsen (hot springs) and a few sandy beaches.

Keep in mind that Yakushima is a place of extremes: the mountains wring every last drop of moisture from the passing clouds and the interior of the island is one of the wettest places in Japan. In the winter the peaks may be covered in snow, while the coast is still relatively balmy. Whatever you do, come prepared and don't set off on a hike without a good map and the proper gear. An International Driving Permit will also vastly increase your enjoyment here, as buses are few and far between.

🎯 Sights

Yakushima's main port is Miyanoura (宮之浦), on the island's northeast coast. This is the most convenient place to be based, as most buses originate from here. From Miyanoura, a road runs around the perimeter of the island, passing through the secondary port of Anbō (安房) on the east coast, and then through the hot-springs town of Onoaida (尾の間) in the south. Heading north from Miyanoura, the road takes you to the town of Nagata (永田), which has a brilliant stretch of white-sand beach.

Nagata Inaka-hama   Beach
(永田いなか浜) On the island's northwest coast in the village of Nagata is a beautiful beach for sunsets, and it's where sea turtles lay their eggs from May to July. It's beside the Inaka-hama bus stop, served by Nagata-bound buses from Miyanoura.

Issō-kaisuiyokujō   Beach
(一湊海水浴場) A fine beach, located on the north coast of the island, about midway between Miyanoura and Nagata. It's a short walk from the Yahazu bus stop (served by any Nagata-bound bus from Miyanoura).

🏃 Activities

HIKING

Hiking is the best way to experience Yakushima's beauty. If you're planning anything more than a short stroll around Yakusugi Land, pick up a copy of the Japanese-language *Yama-to-Kougen-no-Chizu-Yakushima* (山と高原の地図屋久島; ¥1080), available at major bookshops in Japan.

ONSEN

Yakushima has several onsen (hot springs), from beautifully desolate seaside pools to upmarket hotel facilities. The seaside onsen listed here are *konyoku* onsen (mixed sex baths) where swimsuits are not allowed; women traditionally wrap themselves in a thin towel for modesty.

Hirauchi Kaichū Onsen   Onsen
(平内海中温泉; admission ¥100; ⏱24hr) Onsen lovers will be in heaven here. The outdoor baths are in the rocks by the sea and can only be entered at or close to low tide. You can walk to the baths from the Kaichū Onsen bus stop, but the next stop, Nishikaikon, is actually closer. From Nishikaikon, walk downhill towards the sea for about 200m and take a right at the bottom of the hill.

Yudomari Onsen   Onsen
(湯泊温泉; admission ¥100; ⏱24hr) This blissfully serene onsen can be entered at any tide. Get off at the Yudomari bus stop and take the road opposite the post office in the direction of the sea. Once you enter the

village, the way is marked. It's a 300m walk and you pass a great banyan tree en route.

🛌 Sleeping

The most convenient place to be based is Miyanoura. You'll also find lodgings in larger villages and several bare-bones *yama-goya* in the mountains. In July and August and the spring Golden Week holiday, it's best to try to reserve ahead, since places fill up early.

Sankara Hotel & Spa   Hotel ¥¥¥
(☎0997-47-3488, toll-free 0800-800-6007; www.sankarahotel-spa.com; 553 Haginoue, Mugio; r per person with breakfast from ¥35,000; P ✳ @ 🏊) ✿ Overlooking Yakushima's southeast coast, this stunning collection of luxury villas blends ocean views with Balinese design elements. It's also eco-friendly: all water used on the property is sourced from mountain runoff; and the restaurant utilises as much local and organic produce as possible, much of which is grown expressly for the hotel. Guests 15 years and older only.

MIYANOURA

Lodge Yaedake-sansō   Lodge ¥¥
(ロッジ八重岳山荘; ☎0997-42-1551; www17. ocn.ne.jp/~yakusima/lodge/index.html; Miyanoura; r per person with meals ¥8100; P) This secluded accommodation features Japanese- and Western-style rooms in rustic riverside cabins connected by wooden walkways. Soak up the beauty of your surroundings in the communal baths; children will enjoy splashing in the river. Meals served in the tatami dining room are balanced and exquisite. The lodge is located inland on the Miyanoura-gawa; staff can pick you up in Miyanoura.

NAGATA

Sōyōtei   Ryokan ¥¥
(送陽邸; ☎0997-45-2819; www.soyotei.com; per person incl meals ¥13,650; P ✳) On the northwest coast near Nagata Inaka-hama, this gorgeous, family-run guesthouse has a collection of semidetached units that boast private verandahs and ocean views. The traditional structures feature rooftops unique to Yakushima, with stones anchoring the roof tiles – you'll recog-

Cape Manza, Okinawa-hontō

nise the place immediately. There are several baths for private use, including an outdoor bath overlooking the crashing waves.

Eating

There are a few restaurants in each of the island's villages, with the best selection in Miyanoura. If you're staying anywhere but Miyanoura, ask for the set two-meal plan at your lodgings. If you're going hiking, you can ask your lodging to prepare a *bentō* (boxed meal) the night before you set out.

If you need to stock up on supplies for camping or hiking, you'll find **Yakuden** (ヤクデン; ⏰9am-10pm) supermarket on the main street in Miyanoura, just north of the entrance to the pier area.

Naa Yuu Cafe Cafe ¥
(なーゆーカフェ; ☎0997-49-3195; 349-109 Hirauchi; lunch sets ¥850-1250; ⏰11.30am-8pm Tue-Sun, closed 2nd & 4th Tue; 🏠) Down a dirt road and facing a field of wild reeds, this cute cafe feels vaguely Hawaiian. The menu, however, leans more toward Thailand. Lunch sets range from red curry to Kagoshima black pork–sausage pizza. Look for a green sign in English, about 3km west of Onoaida.

Shiosai Seafood ¥¥
(潮騒; ☎0997-42-2721; 305-3 Miyanoura; dishes ¥1200; ⏰11.30am-2pm & 5.30-9.30pm Fri-Wed) Find a full range of Japanese standards such as *sashimi teishoku* (sashimi set; ¥1700) or *ebi-furai teishoku* (fried shrimp set; ¥1400). Look for the blue and whitish building with automatic glass doors along the main road through Miyanoura.

ℹ Information

Tourist Information Centre (☎0997-42-1019; ⏰8.30am-5pm) Miyanoura's ferry terminal has a useful information centre in the round white building as you emerge from the ferry offices. It can help you find lodgings and answer all questions about the island.

ℹ Getting There & Away

Air

Japan Air Commuter has flights between Kagoshima and Yakushima (¥13,300, 35 minutes, five daily). Yakushima's airport is on the northeastern coast between Miyanoura and Anbō. Hourly buses stop at the airport, though you can usually phone your accommodation for a pick-up or take a taxi.

Boat

Hydrofoil services operate between Kagoshima and Yakushima, some of which stop at Tanegashima en route. Tane Yaku Jetfoil (☎in Kagoshima 099-226-0128, in Miyanoura 0997-42-2003) runs four Toppy and Rocket hydrofoils per day between Kagoshima (leaving from the high-speed ferry terminal just to the south of Minamifutō pier) and Miyanoura (¥9100, one hour 45 minutes for direct sailings, two hours 40 minutes with a stop in Tanegashima). There are also two hydrofoils per day between Kagoshima and Anbō Port (2½ hours) on Yakushima.

ℹ Getting Around

Local buses travel the coastal road part way around Yakushima roughly every hour or two, though only a few head up into the interior. Buses are expensive and you'll save a lot of money by purchasing a *Furii Jōsha Kippu*, which is good for unlimited travel on Yakushima Kotsu buses. One-/two-day passes cost ¥2000/3000 and are available at the Tane Yaku Jetfoil office in Miyanoura.

Hitching is also possible, but the best way to get around the island is to rent a car. Toyota Rent-a-Car (☎0997-42-2000; https://rent.toyota.co.jp; up to 12hr from ¥5250; ⏰8am-8pm) is located near the terminal in Miyanoura.

Okinawa-hontō
沖縄本島

☎098 / POP 1.39 MILLION

Okinawa-hontō is the largest island in the Southwest Islands, and the historical seat of power of the Ryūkyū dynasty. Although its cultural differences with mainland Japan were once evident in its architecture, almost all traces were completely obliterated in WWII. Fortunately, Allied bombing wasn't powerful enough to completely stamp out other remnants of Okinawan culture, and today the island is home to a unique culinary, artistic and musical tradition.

Prefectural capital Naha is a transport hub for the other islands. War memorials are clustered in the south of the island, while there are some good beaches and other attractions on the Motobu peninsula. The north is relatively undeveloped.

Naha 那覇

🎵098 / POP 315,000

Flattened during WWII, the prefectural capital of Naha is now a thriving urban centre. The city sports a convenient elevated monorail and a rapidly expanding skyline of modern high-rise apartments, as well as the inevitable traffic jams.

◎ Sights

Naha is fairly easy to navigate, especially since the main sights and attractions are located in the city centre. The main drag is Kokusai-dōri, while the Tsuboya pottery area is to the southeast via a series of covered arcades. The Shuri district is located about 3km to the east of the city centre.

Kokusai-dōri (国際通り) is a riot of neon, noise, souvenir shops, bustling restaurants and Japanese young things out strutting their stuff. It's a festival of tat and tackiness, but it's a good time if you're in the mood for it.

Many people prefer the atmosphere of the three shopping arcades that run south off Kokusai-dōri roughly opposite Mitsukoshi Department Store: **Ichibahon-dōri** (市場本道り), **Mutsumibashi-dōri** (むつみ橋通り) and **Heiwa-dōri** (平和通り).

Daichi Makishi
Kōsetsu Ichiba   Market

(第一牧志公設市場; 2-10-1 Matsuo; ☺10am-8pm) Our favourite stop in the arcade area is the covered food market just off Ichibahon-dōri, about 200m south of Kokusai-dōri. The colourful variety of fish

and produce on offer here is amazing, and don't miss the wonderful local restaurants upstairs.

Tsuboya
Pottery Street   Neighbourhood

(壺屋やちむん道り; Tsuboya Yachimun-dōri) One of the best parts of Naha is this neighbourhood, a centre of ceramic production from 1682, when Ryūkyū kilns were consolidated here by royal decree. Most of the shops along this atmospheric street sell all the popular Okinawan ceramics, including *shiisā* (lion-dog roof guardians) and containers for serving *awamori*, the local firewater. The lanes off the main street here contain some classic crumbling old Okinawan houses. To get here from Kokusai-dōri, walk south through the entirety of Heiwa-dōri arcade (about 350m).

Okinawa Prefectural
Museum & Art Museum   Museum

(沖縄県立博物館・美術館; 🎵098-941-8200; www.museums.pref.okinawa.jp; Omoromachi 3-1-1; admission prefectural/art museum ¥410/310; ☺9am-6pm Tue-Thu & Sun, to 8pm Fri & Sat) Opened in 2007, this museum of Okinawa's history, culture and natural history is easily one of the best museums in Japan. Displays are well laid out, attractively presented and easy to understand, with excellent bilingual interpretive signage. The art museum section holds interesting special exhibits (admission prices vary) with an emphasis on local artists. It's about 15 minutes' walk northwest of the Omoromachi monorail station.

Tsuboya Pottery Museum   Museum

(壺屋焼物博物館; 🎵098-862-3761; www.edu.city.naha.okinawa.jp/tsuboya; 1-9-32 Tsuboya; admission ¥315; ☺10am-6pm Tue-Sun) The excellent Tsuboya Pottery Museum houses some fine examples of traditional Okinawan pottery. Here you can also inspect potters' wheels and *arayachi* (unglazed) and *jōyachi* (glazed) pieces. There's even a cross-section of a *nobori-gama* (kiln built on a slope) set in its original location, where crushed pieces of pottery that date back to the 17th century lay suspended in earth.

SHURI DISTRICT 首里

The original capital of Okinawa, Shuri's temples, shrines, tombs and castle were all destroyed in WWII, but the castle and surrounding structures were rebuilt in 1992.

Shuri-jō
Castle

(首里城; ☎ 098-886-2020; http://oki-park. jp/shurijo/; 1-2 Kinjō-chō; admission ¥820, discounted to ¥660 with one-day monorail pass; ☺8.30am-7pm Apr-Jun, Oct & Nov, to 8pm Jul-Sep, to 6pm Dec-Mar, closed Wed & Thu in Jul) This reconstructed castle was originally built in the 14th century and served as the administrative centre and royal residence of the Ryūkyū kingdom until the 19th century. Enter through the Kankai-mon (歓会門) and go up to the Hōshin-mon (奉神門), which forms the entryway to the inner sanctum of the castle. Visitors can enter the impressive **Seiden** (正殿), which has exhibits on the castle and the Okinawan royals.

There is also a small collection of displays in the nearby **Hokuden** (北殿).

To reach the complex, which sits atop a hill overlooking Naha's urban sprawl, take the Yui-rail monorail to Shuri Station. Exit to the west, go down the steps, walk straight, cross one big street, then a smaller one and go right on the opposite side, then walk about 350m and look for the signs on the left.

Sleeping

Naha is the most convenient base for exploring Okinawa-hontō.

Hotel Sun Palace Kyūyōkan
Hotel ¥¥

(ホテルサンパレス球陽館; ☎ 098-863-4181; www.palace-okinawa.com/sunpalace; 2-5-1 Kumoji; s/d incl breakfast from ¥6500/9800; P ⊜ ✳ @) About three minutes' walk from Kokusai-dōri, the Sun Palace is a step up in warmth and quality from a standard business hotel. Staff are friendly, the fairly spacious rooms include small potted plants and a welcoming Okinawan feel, and there's even a rooftop terrace, a refreshing bit of outdoor space laced with greenery.

Kokusai-dōri, Naha

UNGCHEUNG/SHUTTERSTOCK ©

Hotel JAL City Naha   Hotel ¥¥¥

(ホテルJALシティ那覇; ☎098-866-2580; http://naha.jalcity.co.jp; 1-3-70 Makishi; s/d from ¥13,000/16,000; P🚗❄@🛜) In the middle of the action on Kokusai-dōri, JAL City has 304 swish, modern rooms, in which even the single beds are wide enough to serve as cosy doubles. Though staff here speak limited English, the service is excellent.

Eating & Drinking

Naha is the perfect spot to sample the full range of Okinawan cuisine.

Ashibiunā   Okinawan ¥

(あしびうなぁ; ☎098-884-0035; 2-13 Shuri-jō; lunch sets ¥800-1250; ⏰11.30am-3.30pm & 5.30pm-midnight; 📖) Perfect for lunch after touring Shuri-jō, Ashibiunā has a traditional ambience and picturesque garden. Set meals feature local specialities such as *gōyā champurū*, *okinawa-soba* (thick white noodles in a pork broth) and *ikasumi yakisoba* (stir-fried squid-ink noodles). On the road leading away from Shuri-jō, Ashibiunā is on the right, just before the intersection to the main road.

Yūnangi   Okinawan ¥¥

(ゆうなんぎい; ☎098-867-3765; 3-3-3 Kumoji; dishes ¥1200; ⏰noon-3pm & 5.30-10.30pm Mon-Sat; 📖) You'll be lucky to get a seat here, but if you do, you'll be treated to some of the best Okinawan food around, served in traditional but bustling surroundings. Try the *okinawa-soba* set (¥1400), or choose among the appealing options in the picture menu. On a sidestreet off Kokusai-dōri, look for the wooden sign with white lettering above the doorway.

Uchinā Chaya Buku Buku   Teahouse

(うちなー茶屋ぶくぶく; ☎098-861-2952; 1-28-3 Tsuboya; tea ¥800; ⏰10am-6pm) This incredibly atmospheric teahouse near the east end of the Tsuboya pottery area is worth a special trip. It takes its name from the traditional frothy Okinawan tea served here: *buku buku cha* (¥800), jasmine tea topped with toasty rice foam and crushed peanuts. It's up a small lane just north of Tsuboya-yachimun-dōri and overlooks an historic 160-year-old house.

Gahi-jima (p349)

TORORO REACTION/SHUTTERSTOCK ©

Information

Post offices are scattered around town, including the **Miebashi post office** (美栄橋郵便局); **1-1-1 Kumoji**; ⏰ ATM 7am-11pm Mon-Fri, 9am-9pm Sat, 9am-7pm Sun), on the ground floor of the Palette Kumoji building, the **Tomari-kō post office** (泊ふ頭郵便局; **3-25-5 Maejima**; ⏰ ATM 9am-7pm Mon-Fri, 9am-5pm Sat & Sun), in the Tomari port building, and the **Kokusai-dōri post office** (牧志郵便局; **3-13-19 Makishi**; ⏰ ATM 9am-11pm Mon-Fri, 9am-7pm Sat & Sun), around the corner from Makishi Station.

Tourist Information Counter (☎ 098-857-6884; 1F Arrivals Terminal, Naha International Airport; ⏰ 9am-9pm) At this helpful prefectural counter, we suggest picking up a copy of the *Naha Guide Map* before heading into town, and an *Okinawa Guide Map* if you plan to explore outside Naha.

Tourist Information Office (那覇市観光案内所; ☎ 098-868-4887; 3-2-10 Makishi; ⏰ 9am-8pm) The city office has internet access and luggage storage for a small fee, and free maps and information. It's in the Tenbus Building, which also houses the Naha Traditional Arts & Crafts Center.

Getting There & Away

Air

Naha International Airport (OKA) has connections with Seoul, Taipei, Hong Kong and Shanghai. Connections with mainland Japan include Fukuoka (¥33,200, 1¾ hours), Osaka (¥40,800, 2¼ hours), Nagoya (¥46,110, 2½ hours) and Tokyo (from ¥28,390, 2¾ hours); significant discounts (*tabiwari* on All Nippon Airways and *sakitoku* on JAL) can sometimes be had if you purchase tickets a month in advance. Note that this is only a partial list; most large Japanese cities have flights.

Boat

Naha has regular ferry connections with ports in Honshū (Tokyo and Osaka/Kōbe) and Kyūshū (Kagoshima).

Marix (マリックスライン; ☎ 0997-53-3112, in Kagoshima 099-225-1551; www.marix-line.co.jp) and **A Line** (☎ in Naha 098-861-1886, in Tokyo 03-5643-6170; www.aline-ferry.com) operate four to six ferries a month running to/from Tokyo (¥27,230, 47 hours) and Osaka/Kōbe (¥21,790, 42 hours), as well as daily ferries to/from Kagoshima

(¥15,870, 25 hours). Note that if you ask for a *norihōdai kippu* you can sail from Kagoshima to Naha and get on and off the ferries freely within seven days.

There are three ports in Naha, and this can be confusing: Kagoshima/Amami Islands ferries operate from Naha Port (Naha-kō); Tokyo/Osaka/Kōbe ferries operate from Naha Shin Port (Naha Shin-kō); and Kume-jima and Kerama Islands ferries operate from Tomari Port (Tomari-kō).

Getting Around

The Yui-rail monorail runs from Naha International Airport in the south to Shuri in the north. Prices range from ¥200 to ¥290; day passes cost ¥700. Kenchō-mae Station is at the western end of Kokusai-dōri, while Makishi Station is at its eastern end.

Naha Port is a 10-minute walk southwest from Asahibashi Station, while Tomari Port is a similar distance north from Miebashi Station. Bus 101 from Naha bus terminal (那覇バスターミナル) heads further north to Naha Shin Port (20 minutes, hourly).

When riding on local town buses, simply dump ¥200 into the slot next to the driver as you enter. For longer trips, take a ticket showing your starting point as you board and pay the appropriate fare as you disembark. Buses run from Naha to destinations all over the island.

A rental car makes everything easier when exploring Okinawa-hontō. The rental-car counter in the arrivals hall of Naha International Airport offers information on the dozen or so rental companies in Naha, allowing you to comparison shop.

Southern Okinawa-hontō
沖縄本島の南部

During the closing days of the Battle of Okinawa, the southern part of Okinawa-hontō served as one of the last hold outs of the Japanese military and an evacuation point for wounded Japanese soldiers. A visit to the area, a day or half-day trip from Naha, is highly recommended for those with an interest in wartime history.

Okinawa's most important war memorials are clustered in the **Memorial Peace Park** (平和祈念公園; ⏰ dawn-dusk), located in the city of Itoman on the southern coast of the island. The centrepiece of the park is the **Okinawa Prefectural Peace Memorial Museum** (沖縄県平和祈念資料館; ☎098-997-3844; www.peace-museum.pref.okinawa.jp; 614-1 Aza Mabuni, Itoman; admission ¥300; ⏰9am-5pm), which focuses on the suffering of the Okinawan people during the invasion of the island and under the subsequent American occupation. The main exhibits are on the 2nd floor. The museum strives to present a balanced picture of the Pacific War and the history that led to the invasion, but there is plenty here to stir debate. Outside the museum is the **Cornerstone of Peace** (⏰dawn-dusk), which is inscribed with the names of everyone who died in the Battle of Okinawa.

To reach the park, take bus 89 from Naha bus terminal to the Itoman bus terminal (¥560, one hour, every 20 minutes), then transfer to bus 82, and get off at Heiwa Kinen-dō Iriguchi (¥460, 30 minutes, hourly).

An interesting stop en route to the Peace Park is the **Himeyuri no Tō** (ひめゆり平和祈念資料館; ☎098-997-2100; www.himeyuri.or.jp; 671-1 Ihara, Itoman; admission ¥310; ⏰9am-5pm), located above a cave that served as an emergency field hospital during the closing days of the Battle of Okinawa. Here, 240 female high-school students were pressed into service as nurses for Japanese military wounded. As American forces closed in, the students were dismissed and the majority died. Bus 82 stops outside.

Directly south of Naha in Kaigungo-kōen is the **Former Japanese Navy Underground Headquarters** (旧海軍司令部壕; Kyūkaigun Shireibu-gō; ☎098-850-4055; 236 Tomishiro, Tomigusuku; admission ¥440; ⏰8:30am-5pm), where 4000 men committed suicide or were killed as the battle for Okinawa drew to its bloody conclusion. Only 250m of the tunnels are open, but you can wander through the maze of corridors, see the commander's final words on the wall of his room, and inspect the holes and scars in other walls from the grenade blasts that killed many of the men. To reach the site, take

bus 33 or 46 from Naha bus terminal to the Tomigusuku-kōen-mae stop (¥220, 20 minutes, hourly). From there it's a 10-minute walk – follow the English signs (the entrance is near the top of the hill).

Kerama Islands
慶良間諸島

The islands of the Kerama group are a world away from the hustle and bustle of Okinawa-hontō, though even these islands can get crowded during the summer holiday season. The three main islands here are Zamami-jima, Aka-jima and Tokashiki-jima. You can easily visit any of these as a day trip from Naha, but we recommend a few days in a *minshuku* (Japanese guesthouse) on one of the islands to really savour the experience.

AKA-JIMA   阿嘉島
☎098 / POP 279

A mere 2km in diameter, tiny Aka-jima makes up for in beauty what it lacks in size. With some of the best beaches in the Keramas and an extremely peaceful atmosphere, it's easy to get stuck here for several days. There's also some great snorkelling and diving nearby.

There are great beaches on every side of the island, but for sheer postcard-perfect beauty, it's hard to beat the 1km stretch of white sand on the northeast coast known as **Nishibama Beach** (西浜ビーチ). This beach can be crowded in summer; if you want privacy, there are quieter beaches on the other sides of the island.

Dive shop–hotel **Marine House Seasir** (マリンハウスシーサー; ☎0120-10-2743, in English 090-8668-6544; www.seasir.com; s/d with 3 meals from ¥9000/16,000; 🅿❄🛜), at the west end of the main village, has good, clean Western- and Japanese-style rooms. Most of the guests are divers. It offers whale-watching tours (¥4800) from January to March.

Kawai Diving (☎098-987-2219; http://oki-zamami.jp/~kawai/; 153 Aka; s/d incl meals from ¥7780/15,550; 🅿❄@🛜), located along Maehama Beach on the south coast, has simple rooms and a family atmosphere. English-speaking staff are happy to tell guests about the island and take them diving (one/two dives ¥6480/10,840, equipment rental ¥1260 per piece).

Zamami Sonei Ferry (☎098-868-4567) has two or three fast ferries a day (¥3140, one hour, 10 minutes) and one regular ferry (¥2120, 1½ hours) to/from Naha's Tomari Port. A motorboat also makes four trips a day between Aka-jima and Zamami-jima (¥300, 15 minutes).

ZAMAMI-JIMA 座間味島

☎098 / POP 586

A stone's throw from Aka-jima, Zamami-jima is *slightly* more developed, with its own lovely beaches. It's got some brilliant offshore islands and great diving and snorkelling in the surrounding waters. Pick up a map and excellent English-language information at the port's **Zamami Village Tourist Information Center** (☎098-987-2277; ⌚9am-5pm).

Furuzamami Beach (古座間味ビーチ), approximately 1km southeast from the port (over the hill), is a stunning 700m stretch of white sand that is fronted by clear, shallow water and a bit of coral. The beach is well developed for day trippers, with toilets, showers and food stalls. You can also rent snorkelling gear here (¥1000).

If you fancy a little solitude, you'll find picturesque empty beaches in several of the coves on the other sides of the island. The best beaches, however, are on **Gahi-jima** (嘉比島) and **Agenashiku-jima** (安慶名敷島), which are located about a kilometre south of the port. Ringed by delightful white-sand beaches, they are perfect for a half-day *Robinson Crusoe* experience. One boat operator who can take you to these islands and arrange snorkelling trips is **Zamami Tour Operation** (☎098-987-3586). The tourist information office can also help arrange boat tours (¥1500 per person round trip).

Stay overnight at **Joy Joy** (ジョイジョイ; ☎098-987-2445, 0120-10-2445; http://keramajoyjoy.com/index.html; 434-2 Zamami; r per person without bathroom incl breakfast from ¥5400; ❄📶), a pension in the northwest corner of the village with Western- and Japanese-style rooms that surround a small garden. It also runs a dive shop, with beach and sea dive tours (in Japanese only) from ¥4860.

A new option for accommodation is the convivial **Zamamia International Guesthouse** (☎098-987-3626; www.zamamia-guesthouse.com; dm/s/d ¥2000/5000/6000; ❄📶), run by a super-friendly Canadian expat who often organises barbecue dinners for guests. Dorm beds here are spacious and outfitted with privacy curtains; bathrooms are shared.

Zamami Sonei (☎098-868-4567) has two or three fast ferries a day (¥3140, 50 minutes) and one regular ferry (¥2120, two hours) to/from Naha's Tomari Port. The ferries usually stop at Aka-jima en route from Naha to Zamami. A motorboat also makes four trips a day between Aka-jima and Zamami-jima (¥300, 15 minutes).

Rental cars, scooters and bicycles are available near the pier.

Japan
In Focus

Umbrellas, Kyoto Handicraft Center (p254)
LONELY PLANET / GETTY IMAGES ©

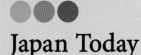

Japan Today

Yasaka-jinja (p220), Kyoto

The country is clawing its way out of economic stagnation and there is a sense of optimism in the air

belief systems
(% of population)

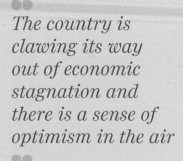

84 Shintoism
71 Buddhism
8 Other
2 Christianity

Note: total exceeds 100% as many people follow both Shinto and Buddhist belief systems.

if Japan were 100 people

64 would be 15-64 years old
23 would be over 65 years old
13 would be 0-14 years old

population per sq km

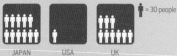

≈ 30 people

JAPAN   USA   UK

Japan is clawing its way out of three decades of economic stagnation and rebuilding from the disastrous earthquake and tsunami of 2011, and there is a sense of optimism in the air.

A Change of Course

Japan was hammered by the global financial crisis of 2008. The country faced previously unthinkable unemployment numbers and the old certainties of lifetime employment and age-based promotions started to look like mere pipe dreams. And to make matters worse, nations like China and South Korea were taking huge bites out of market sectors that Japan used to dominate. In the general election of 2012, the people of Japan made their dissatisfaction clear by choosing the Liberal Democratic Party (LDP) over the previously ruling Democratic Party of Japan. Headed by Abe Shinzō, the LDP wasted no time in bringing in changes.

VINCENT ST. THOMAS | SHUTTERSTOCK ©

Foreign travellers who had avoided the country in the aftermath of the 2011 earthquake and tsunami are now returning in record numbers. In October 2014, 1,272,000 foreign travellers visited Japan – a record for a single month. The largest growth has been in visitors from other Asian nations such as China, Taiwan, Thailand and Korea.

Healing Rifts

This surge of visitors from Asian countries couldn't have come at a better time for Japan. Despite the progressive economic policies of the LDP, the party is undeniably nationalist. And the statements and views of influential LDP politicians have inflamed passions in Asian countries that suffered Japanese aggression during WWII. Tensions between Japan and China focused on the ownership of a small group of islands known in Japan as the Senkaku Islands and in China as the Diaoyu Islands.

For a while, it looked as if tensions might escalate into a military conflict, but cooler heads have so far prevailed. In December 2014, Abe met President Xi Jinping of China and the two essentially agreed to disagree, acknowledging that the countries held different positions on the ownership of the islands.

Under the banner of 'Abenomics', the LDP pushed through a raft of policies that were decidedly radical in famously conservative Japan. One of the main aims of Abenomics was to weaken the yen, thereby making Japanese products cheaper overseas and (hopefully) increasing demand for Japanese exports. Japan enjoyed a 1.5% GDP growth in 2013 and the yen started to slide against other world currencies. The people of Japan re-elected Abe and the LDP by a landslide in 2014.

A Yen for Japan

In recent times, the yen has been trading against the US dollar at levels not seen since the late 1990s. For foreign travellers, this means one thing: Japan seems positively cheap (well, at least outside of Tokyo). Sure, there's been a little inflation, but Japan is now arguably one of the cheapest countries in the developed world.

The Olympics

For Japan, the best news of all in recent times was the September 2013 decision by the International Olympic Committee to award the 2020 Summer Olympics to Tokyo. The decision was a huge boon to the country and it's added a new urgency to a spate of infrastructure projects, including extended *shinkansen* (bullet train) lines, expanded international airports, and a drive to further develop facilities and services for tourists.

353

History

Japan's history is shaped by its distance from mainland Asia and the fact that China chose not to become an aggressive naval power. This allowed Japan to evolve into a truly unique culture. Japan's history can be divided into five main periods: prehistory, which comes to an end in about 400BC; preclassical, from 400BC until 710AD; classical, from 710 to 1185; medieval, from 1185 to 1600; and premodern to modern, from 1600 onward.

Prehistory

The origin of Japan's earliest inhabitants is obscure. There was certainly emigration via land bridges that once connected Japan with Siberia and Korea, but it is also thought that seafaring migrants from Polynesia may have landed on Kyūshū and Okinawa. It is likely that the Japanese people are a result of emigration from Siberia in the north, China and Korea to the west and, perhaps, Polynesian stock from the south.

c 10,000 BC
First evidence of the hunter-gatherer Jōmon people.

The first signs of civilisation in Japan are from the Neolithic period around 10,000 BC. This is called the Jōmon (Rope Mark) period after the discovery of pottery fragments with rope marks. The people at this time lived as fishers, hunters and food-gatherers.

This period was gradually superseded by the Yayoi era, which dates from around 300 BC and is named after the site near Tokyo where pottery fragments were found. The Yayoi people are considered to have had a strong connection with Korea and their most important developments were the wet cultivation of rice and the use of bronze and iron implements.

The period following the Yayoi era has been called the Kofun (Burial Mound) period by archaeologists who discovered thousands of grave mounds concentrated mostly in central and western Japan.

As more and more settlements banded together to defend their land, groups became larger until, by AD 300, the Yamato clan had loosely unified the nation through either conquest or alliance. With the ascendancy of the Yamato emperors, Japan for the first time became a true nation, stretching from the islands south of Kyūshū to the northern wilds of Honshū.

The Best...
Places for Japanese History

1 Nara (p287)

2 Kyoto (p197)

3 Hiroshima (p316)

4 Okinawa-hontō (p343)

Buddhism & Early Chinese Influence

In the mid-6th century, Buddhism was introduced from China via the Korean kingdom of Paekche. From the earliest days of the Yamato court, it was the custom to relocate the capital following the death of an emperor (presumably to free the capital from the taint of death). However, after the shift of the capital to Nara in 710, this long-held custom was altered as the capital remained there for the next 75 years.

Establishment of a Native Culture

By the end of the 8th century, the Buddhist clergy in Nara had become so politically meddlesome that Emperor Kammu decided to relocate the capital to insulate it against their growing influence. The site eventually chosen was Heian-kyō (modern-day Kyoto).

The Heian period (794–1185) saw a great flourishing in the arts and important developments in religious thinking as Chinese ideas and institutions were imported and adapted to the needs of the Japanese.

c 300 BC
The Yayoi people appear in southwest Japan (probably via Korea).

c 300
Suijin is the first verifiable emperor of Japan.

Mid-5th century
Writing, in the form of Chinese characters, is introduced into Japan.

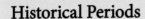

Historical Periods

Jōmon 10,000–300 BC

Yayoi 300 BC–AD 300

Kofun 300–710

Nara 710–94

Heian 794–1185

Kamakura 1185–1333

Muromachi 1333–1576

Momoyama 1576–1600

Edo 1600–1868

Meiji 1868–1912

Taishō 1912–26

Shōwa 1926–89

Heisei 1989 to the present

During the late Heian period, emperors began to devote more time to leisure and scholarly pursuit and less time to government. This created an opening for the Fujiwara, a noble family, to capture important court posts and become the chief power brokers, a role the clan was able to maintain for several centuries.

The Heian period is considered the apogee of Japanese courtly elegance, but out in the provinces a new power was on the rise, that of the samurai (warrior class), which built up its own armed forces and readily turned to arms to defend its autonomy. Samurai families soon moved into the capital, where they muscled in on the court.

The Fujiwara were eventually eclipsed by the Taira clan, who ruled briefly before being ousted by the Minamoto family (also known as the Genji) at the battle of Dannoura (modern-day Shimonoseki) in 1185.

Domination through Military Rule

The Kamakura period (1185–1333) followed on from the Heian period. In 1192 Minamoto Yoritomo conquered the inhabitants of what is now Aomori-ken, thereby extending his rule to the tip of northern Honshū. For the first time in its history, all of Japan proper was now under unified rule. After assuming the title of shōgun (military leader), Minamoto set up his headquarters in Kamakura, while the emperor remained the nominal ruler in Kyoto. It was the beginning of a long period of feudal rule by successive samurai families. In fact, this feudal system was to linger on, in one form or another, until imperial power was restored in 1868.

The Kamakura government emerged victorious in battles with the Mongols (who attacked twice in the 13th century), but it was unable to pay its soldiers and lost the support of the samurai class. In an attempt to take advantage of popular discontent, Emperor Go-Daigo led an unsuccessful rebellion against the government and was exiled to Oki-shotō, the islands near Matsue in western Honshū, where he waited a year before trying again. The second attempt successfully toppled the government.

712 & 720
Writing of the *Kojiki* (Record of Old Things; 712) and *Nihon Shoki* (Record of Japan; 720).

1156
Two major provincial families, the Taira and the Minamoto, engage in bitter warfare.

1185
The Taira are toppled by Minamoto Yoritomo, who becomes the most powerful man in the land.

Kofun Burial Mounds

The origins of the Japanese imperial line and the Japanese people in general are shrouded in mystery. Much of what we do know comes from large, earthen burial mounds scattered around the islands of Honshū, Kyūshū and Shikoku. These burial mounds, called *kofun*, served as tombs for members of Japan's early nobility. The practice of building these mounds started quite suddenly in the 3rd century and died out gradually by the end of the 7th century. It was during this period that the forerunners of the present imperial family, the Yamato clan, were consolidating their power as rulers of Japan.

Country at War

This heralded the start of the Muromachi period (1333–1576). Emperor Go-Daigo refused to reward his warriors, favouring the aristocracy and priesthood instead. This led to the revolt of Ashikaga Takauji, who had previously changed sides to support Emperor Go-Daigo. Ashikaga defeated Go-Daigo at Kyoto, then installed a new emperor and appointed himself shōgun; the Ashikaga family later settled at Muromachi, an area of Kyoto.

The Ashikaga ruled with gradually diminishing effectiveness in a land slipping steadily into civil war and chaos. The Ōnin War, which broke out in 1467, developed into a full-scale civil war and marked the rapid decline of the Ashikaga family. *Daimyō* (domain lords) and local leaders fought for power in bitter territorial disputes that were to last for a century. This period, from 1467 to around the start of the Momoyama period in 1576, is known as the Warring States period (Sengoku-jigai).

Return to Unity

In 1568 Oda Nobunaga, the son of a *daimyō*, seized power from the imperial court in Kyoto and used his military genius to initiate a process of pacification and unification in central Japan. Oda was succeeded by his most able commander, Toyotomi Hide-yoshi, who extended unification so that by 1590 the whole country was under his rule.

The Christian Century

In the mid-16th century, when the Europeans first made their appearance, foreign trade was little regulated by Japan's central government. The first Europeans to arrive were the Portuguese, who were shipwrecked off southern Kyūshū in 1543. The Portuguese found an appreciative reception for their skills in firearm manufacture, skills which were soon adopted by the Japanese. The Jesuit missionary Francis Xavier arrived in Kagoshima in

13th century
Zen Buddhism becomes established in Japan.
Monk meditating, Himeji

1400s & 1500s
Japan is in almost constant internal warfare, including the particularly fierce Ōnin War of 1467–77.

1549 and was followed by more missionaries, who quickly converted local lords keen to profit from foreign trade and assistance with military supplies. The new religion spread rapidly, gaining several hundred thousand converts, particularly in Nagasaki.

At first Oda Nobunaga saw the advantages of trading with Europeans and tolerated the arrival of Christianity as a counterbalance to Buddhism. Once Toyotomi Hideyoshi assumed power, however, this tolerance gradually gave way to a suspicion that an alien religion would subvert his rule. Edicts against Christianity were followed in 1597 by the crucifixion of 26 foreign priests and Japanese converts.

Peace & Seclusion

The supporters of Toyotomi Hideyoshi's young heir, Toyotomi Hideyori, were defeated in 1600 by Toyotomi's former ally, Tokugawa Ieyasu, at the Battle of Sekigahara. Tokugawa set up his field headquarters (*bakufu*) at Edo, now Tokyo, and assumed the title of shōgun. This marked the beginning of the Edo, or Tokugawa, period (1600–1868). The emperor and court continued to exercise purely nominal authority in Kyoto.

Under Tokugawa rule, Japan entered a period of *sakoku* (national seclusion). Japanese were forbidden on pain of death to travel abroad or engage in trade with foreign countries. Only the Dutch, Chinese and Koreans were allowed to remain in Japan, and they were placed under strict supervision. The Dutch were confined to the island of Dejima, near Nagasaki, and their contacts restricted to merchants and prostitutes.

By the turn of the 19th century, the Tokugawa government was falling into stagnation and corruption. Famines and poverty among the peasants and samurai further weakened the system. Foreign ships started to challenge Japan's isolation with increasing insistence, and the Japanese soon realised that their outmoded defences were ineffectual. Russian contacts in the north were followed by British and American visits. In 1853 Commodore Matthew Perry of the US Navy arrived with a squadron of Black Ships to demand the opening up of Japan to trade.

Samurai

The samurai were members of Japan's warrior class who were active in Japan from around the 12th century. The samurai's best-known weapon was the *katana* sword, though in earlier days the bow was also prominent. Arguably the world's finest swordsmen, samurai were formidable opponents in single combat. During modernisation in the late 19th century, the government, itself comprising samurai, realised that a conscript army was more efficient as a unified fighting force, and disestablished the samurai class. However, samurai ideals such as endurance and fighting to the death were revived through propaganda prior to WWII.

1543
The first Westerners, the Portuguese, arrive by chance, heralding the advent of firearms and Christianity.

1600
The warlord Tokugawa Ieyasu seizes power at the Battle of Sekigahara. Statue of Tokugawa Ieyasu at Tōshō-gū (p132), Nikkō

JUDY BELLAH / GETTY IMAGES ©

A Narrow Escape for the Old Capitals

Historians have suggested that both Kyoto and Nara were on a list of some 180 cities earmarked for air raids by the US during WWII. Kyoto, with a population of more than one million people, had been a prime target for atomic annihilation; however, it escaped because it was not home to a significant number of munitions factories (although others have suggested it was merely a vagary of the weather that saved the city). Nara, it has been suggested, escaped merely due to having a population under 60,000, which kept it far enough down the list not to be reached before the unconditional surrender of Japan in September 1945.

The arrival of foreigners proved to be the decisive blow to an already shaky Tokugawa regime. Upset by the shōgunate's handling of the foreign incursion, two large *daimyō* areas in western Japan, the Satsuma and the Chōshū, allied themselves with disenchanted samurai. They succeeded in capturing the emperor in 1868, declaring a restoration of imperial rule and an end to the power of the shōgun. The ruling shōgun, Tokugawa Yoshinobu, resigned, and Emperor Meiji assumed control of state affairs.

Emergence from Isolation

The initial stages of the Meiji Restoration (1868–1912) were resisted in a state of virtual civil war. The abolition of the shōgunate was followed by the surrender of the *daimyō*, whose lands were divided into the prefectures that exist today. Edo became Japan's new capital and was renamed Tokyo (Eastern Capital).

Under the slogan *fukoku kyōhei* (rich country; strong military), the economy underwent a crash course in Westernisation and industrialisation. An influx of Western experts was encouraged and Japanese students were sent abroad to acquire expertise in modern technologies.

Japan's growing confidence was demonstrated by the abolition of foreign treaty rights and by the ease with which it trounced China in the Sino-Japanese War (1894–95). The subsequent treaty recognised Korean independence and ceded Taiwan to Japan. Friction with Russia eventually led to the Russo-Japanese War (1904–05), in which the Japanese army attacked the Russians in Manchuria and Korea. The Japanese Navy stunned the Russians by inflicting a crushing defeat on its Baltic fleet at the battle of Tsu-shima.

1853–54
US Commodore Matthew Perry uses 'gunboat diplomacy' to force Japan to open up for trade.

1902
Japan signs the Anglo-Japanese Alliance, the first equal alliance between a Western and non-Western nation.

1941
Japan enters WWII by striking Pearl Harbor on 7 December.

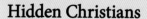

Hidden Christians

Japan's 'Christian Century' began in 1549 with the arrival of Portuguese missionaries on the island of Kyūshū. Within decades, hundreds of thousands of Japanese were converted.

The rapid rise of Christian belief, as well as its association with trade, new Western weaponry and control of Japanese territory, came to be viewed as a threat by the *bakufu* (military government) under Toyotomi Hideyoshi. The 1587 expulsion of missionaries began an era of suppression of Christians and thousands were estimated to have been executed during the next six decades. Many thousands of Christian peasants rebelled in the 1637–38 Shimabara Rebellion, after which Christianity was outlawed completely.

Other persecution took the form of *fumi-e*, where suspected Christians were forced to walk on images of Jesus. The Gregorian date on the front of the Dutch trading house on the island of Hirado was taken as proof of the Dutch traders' Christianity and used to justify their exile to Nagasaki's Dejima island, ushering in more than two centuries of *sakoku* (closure of the country).

Japanese Christians reacted by going under cover as *kakure Kirishitan* (hidden Christians). With no more priests, they worshiped in lay-led services in secret rooms inside private homes. On the surface, worship resembled other Japanese religions, including the use of Shintō *kamidana* altars and Buddhist *butsudan* ancestor worship chests in homes, and ceremonial rice and sake. The sounds of worship, too, mimicked Buddhist incantations. Scholars put the numbers of hidden Christians at about 150,000.

It was not until 1865, 12 years after the arrival of the Black Ships (the first European ships), that Japan had its first large-scale church again, Oura Cathedral in Nagasaki, and missionaries began to return to Japan with its reopening in 1868. The Meiji government officially declared freedom of religion in 1871. Today, estimates put the number of Japanese Christians at between one and two million (about one percent of the population).

Industrialisation & Asian Dominance

On his death in 1912, Emperor Meiji was succeeded by his son, Yoshihito. His period of rule was named the Taishō era (1912–26). When WWI broke out, Japan sided against Germany but did not become deeply involved in the conflict. While the Allies were occupied with war, Japan took the opportunity, through shipping and trade, to expand its economy at top speed. At the same time, Japan gained a strong foothold in China.

1945
On 6 August, Hiroshima becomes the first-ever victim of an atomic bombing.

1945–52
Japan experiences a US-led occupation.

1990s–early 2000s
After its 'bubble economy' bursts in the early 1990s, Japan enters a decade of recession.

Nationalism & the Pursuit of Empire

The Shōwa era (1926–89) commenced when Emperor Hirohito ascended the throne in 1926. He had toured extensively in Europe, mixed with European nobility and developed quite a liking for the British lifestyle.

A rising tide of nationalism was quickened by the world economic depression that began in 1930. Popular unrest was marked by plots to overthrow the government and political assassinations. This led to a strong increase in the power of the militarists who approved the invasion of Manchuria in 1931 and the installation there of a puppet regime controlled by the Japanese. In 1933 Japan withdrew from the League of Nations and in 1937 entered into full-scale hostilities against China.

As the leader of a new order for Asia, Japan signed a tripartite pact with Germany and Italy in 1940. The Japanese military leaders saw their main opponents to this new order for Asia, the so-called Greater East Asia Co-prosperity Sphere, in the United States.

IN FOCUS HISTORY

World War II

When diplomatic attempts to gain US neutrality failed, Japan launched itself into WWII with a surprise attack on Pearl Harbor on 7 December 1941.

At first, Japan scored rapid successes, pushing its battle fronts across to India, down to the fringes of Australia and out into the mid-Pacific. The Battle of Midway opened the US counterattack, puncturing Japanese naval superiority and turning the tide of the war against Japan. By 1945, exhausted by submarine blockades and aerial bombing, Japan had been driven back on all fronts. In August of the same year, the declaration of war by the Soviet Union and the atomic bombs dropped by the US on Hiroshima and Nagasaki proved to be the final straw: Emperor Hirohito announced unconditional surrender.

Postwar Reconstruction

At the end of the war, the Japanese economy was in ruins and inflation was rampant. A program of recovery provided loans, restricted imports and encouraged capital investment and personal saving.

By the late 1950s, trade was again flourishing, and the economy continued to expand rapidly. From textiles and the manufacture of labour-intensive goods, such as cameras, the Japanese 'economic miracle' spread into virtually every sector of economic activity. Economic recession and inflation surfaced in 1974 and again in 1980, mostly as a result of steep increases in the price of imported oil, on which Japan is dependent. But despite these setbacks, Japan became the world's most successful export economy, generating massive trade surpluses and dominating such fields as electronics, robotics, computer technology, car manufacturing and banking.

1995
On 17 January an earthquake with a magnitude of 7.2 hits Kōbe, killing more than 5000 people.

2011
Japan is hit by an earthquake and tsunami on 11 March that kills more than 15,000 people.

2013
The International Olympic Committee awards Tokyo the right to host the 2020 Summer Olympics.

The People of Japan

Sensō-ji (p86), Tokyo

CHRISTOPHER GROENHOUT / GETTY IMAGES ©

Japan is unusual among nations for the relative homogeneity of its population. This, combined with the distance of the Japanese islands from the Asian continent, has given rise to what some people – including some Japanese – refer to as 'Galápagos syndrome', namely, a truly peculiar culture. In point of fact, the Japanese are not as unique as outsiders and many Japanese like to believe. Rather, they exist within a continuum that contains Korean and Chinese cultures, with some notable differences.

Truly Unique?

The uniqueness and peculiarity of 'the Japanese' is a favourite topic of both Western observers and the Japanese themselves. It's worth starting any discussion of the people of Japan by noting that there is no such thing as 'the Japanese'. Rather, there are 127 million individuals in Japan with their own unique characters, interests and habits. And despite popular stereotypes to the contrary, the Japanese are as varied as any people on earth. Just as importantly, Japanese people have more in common with the rest of humanity than they have differences.

Why then the pervasive images of the Japanese as inscrutable or even bizarre? These stereotypes are largely rooted in language: few Japanese are able to speak English as well as, say, your average

Singaporean, Hong Kong Chinese or well-educated Indian, not to mention most Europeans. This difficulty with English is largely rooted in the country's appalling English education system, and is compounded by a natural shyness, a perfectionist streak and the nature of the Japanese language itself, which contains fewer sounds than any other major world language (making pronunciation of other languages difficult). Thus, what appears to the casual observer to be a maddening inscrutability is more likely just an inability to communicate effectively. Outsiders who become fluent in Japanese discover a people whose thoughts and feelings are surprisingly – almost boringly – similar to those of folks in other developed nations.

The Mongolian Spot

Almost all Japanese babies are born with a Mongolian spot, or *mōkohan*, on their bottoms or lower backs. This harmless bluish-grey birthmark is composed of melanin-containing cells. Mongolian spots are common in several Asian races including, as the name suggests, Mongolians, as well as in Native Americans. These birthmarks, which usually fade by the age of five, raise interesting questions about the origins of the Japanese people.

All this said, the Japanese do have certain characteristics that reflect its unique history and interaction with its environment. First, Japan is an island nation. Second, until WWII, Japan was never conquered by an outside power, nor was it heavily influenced by Christian missionaries. Third, until the beginning of last century, the majority of Japanese lived in close-knit rural farming communities. Fourth, most of Japan is covered in steep mountains, so the few flat areas of the country are quite crowded – people literally live on top of each other. Finally, for almost all of its history, Japan has been a strictly hierarchical place, with something approximating a caste system during the Edo period.

All of this has produced a people who highly value group identity and smooth social harmony – in a tightly packed city or small farming village, there simply isn't room for colourful individualism. One of the ways harmony is preserved is by forming consensus, and concealing personal opinions and true feelings. Thus, the free-flowing exchange of ideas, debates and even heated arguments that one expects in the West are far less common in Japan. This reticence about sharing innermost thoughts perhaps contributes to the Western image of the Japanese as mysterious.

Of course, there is a lot more to the typical Japanese character than just a tendency to prize social harmony. Any visitor to the country will soon discover a people who are remarkably conscientious, meticulous, industrious, honest and technically skilled. A touching shyness and sometimes almost painful self-consciousness are also undoubted features of many Japanese as well. These characteristics result in a society that is a joy for the traveller to experience.

And let us say that any visit to Japan is a good chance to explode the myths about Japan and the Japanese. While you may imagine a nation of suit-clad conformists or inscrutable automatons, a few rounds in a local *izakaya* (pub-eatery) will quickly put all of these notions to rest.

Population

Japan has a population of approximately 127 million people (the ninth-largest in the world) and, with 75% of it concentrated in urban centres, population density is extremely high. Areas such as the Tokyo–Kawasaki–Yokohama conurbation are so

densely populated that they have almost ceased to be separate cities, running into each other and forming a vast coalescence that, if considered as a whole, would constitute the world's largest city.

One notable feature of Japan's population is its relative ethnic and cultural homogeneity. This is particularly striking for visitors from the USA, Australia and other multicultural nations. The main reason for this ethnic homogeneity is Japan's strict immigration laws, which have ensured that only a small number of foreigners settle in the country.

The largest non-Japanese group in the country is made up of 650,000 *zai-nichi kankoku-jin* (resident Koreans). For most outsiders, Koreans are an invisible minority. Indeed, even the Japanese themselves have no way of knowing that someone is of Korean descent if he or she adopts a Japanese name. Nevertheless, Japanese-born Koreans, who in some cases speak no language other than Japanese, were only recently released from the obligation to carry ID cards with their fingerprints at all times, and some still face discrimination in the workplace and other aspects of their daily lives.

Aside from Koreans, most foreigners in Japan are temporary workers from China, Southeast Asia, South America and Western countries. Indigenous groups such as the Ainu have been reduced to very small numbers, due to intermarriage with non-Ainu and government attempts to hasten assimilation of Ainu into general Japanese society. At present, Ainu are concentrated mostly in Hokkaidō, the northernmost of Japan's main islands.

The most notable feature of Japan's population is the fact that it is shrinking. Japan's astonishingly low birth rate of 1.3 births per woman is among the lowest in the developed world and Japan is rapidly becoming a nation of elderly citizens. The population began declining in 2007, and will reach 100 million in 2050 and 67 million in 2100. Needless to say, such demographic change will have a major influence on the economy in coming decades.

Maiko (geisha in training), Kyoto
PAUL CHESLEY / GETTY IMAGES ©

Places to Meet the Locals

Izakaya The combination of sake and communal seating at these 'dining pubs' makes it easy to start chatting with your neighbours. More than likely, they'll break the ice by offering you a drink.

Sentō The Japanese are fond of pointing out that getting naked is a good way of removing barriers of class and profession. It's also a good way of removing the barrier of nationality. If you're okay with a 'full monty' approach to socialising, then a visit to the local *sentō* (public bath) is a good way to meet the locals.

Hiring a volunteer guide Volunteer guides are available in many sightseeing districts. Ask at the local tourist information centre.

In the mountains The Japanese are keen hikers and the ones you meet on the trail seem to be extra friendly. A good opener is *Ii tenki desu ne* (Nice weather, isn't it?).

Doing a home visit/homestay Many local tourist offices and community centres can arrange for you to visit a Japanese family for a meal or to stay the night.

Women in Japan

Traditional Japanese society restricted the woman's role to the home, where as housekeeper she wielded considerable power, overseeing all financial matters, monitoring the children's education and, in some ways, acting as the head of the household. Even in the early Meiji period (1868–1912), however, the ideal was rarely matched by reality: labour shortfalls often resulted in women taking on factory work, and even before that, women often worked side by side with men in the fields.

As might be expected, the contemporary situation is complex. There are, of course, those who stick to established roles. They tend to opt for shorter college courses, often at women's colleges, and see education as an asset in the marriage market. Once married, they leave the role of breadwinner to their husbands.

Increasingly, however, Japanese women are choosing to forgo or delay marriage in favour of pursuing their own career ambitions. Of course, changing aspirations do not necessarily translate into changing realities, and Japanese women are still significantly underrepresented in upper management and political positions, and there is a disproportionately high number of females employed as OLs (office ladies). This is, in part, due to the prevalence of gender discrimination in Japanese companies, as well as societal expectations. Japanese women are often forced to choose between having a career and having a family. Not only do many companies refuse to hire women for career-track positions, some Japanese men are not interested in having a career woman as a spouse.

Those women who do choose full-time work suffer from one of the worst gender wage gaps in the developed world: Japanese women earn only 66% of what Japanese men earn, compared to 76% in the USA, 83% in the UK and 85% in Australia (according to figures released by respective governments). In politics, the situation is even worse: Japanese women hold only 10% of seats in the Diet, the nation's governing body.

Food & Drink

Sushi at Tsukiji Market (p66), Tokyo

JAIME HOJJE LEE / GETTY IMAGES ©

Those familiar with Japanese cuisine know that eating is half the fun of travelling in Japan. Even if you've already tried some of Japan's better-known specialities in Japanese restaurants in your own country, you're likely to be surprised by how delicious the original is when served on its home turf. More importantly, the adventurous eater will be delighted to find that Japanese food is far more than just sushi, tempura or sukiyaki (sliced meat simmered with vegetables and sauce).

Eating in Japan

You may baulk at charging into a restaurant where both the language and the menu are likely to be incomprehensible. The best way to get over this fear is to familiarise yourself with the main types of Japanese restaurants so that you have some idea of what's on offer and how to order it. Those timid of heart should take solace in the fact that the Japanese will go to extraordinary lengths to understand what you want and will help you to order.

With the exception of *shokudō* (all-round restaurants) and *izakaya* (pub-style restaurants), most Japanese restaurants concentrate on a speciality cuisine. This naturally makes for delicious eating, but does limit your choice.

Restaurants: Here's the Drill

When you enter a restaurant in Japan, you'll be greeted with a hearty *irasshaimase!* (Welcome!). In all but the most casual places the waiter will next ask you *nan-mei sama* (How many people?). Answer with your fingers, which is what the Japanese do.

At this point you will be given an *oshibori* (a hot towel), a cup of tea and a menu. The *oshibori* is for wiping your hands and face. When you're done with it, just roll it up and leave it next to your place. Now comes the hard part: ordering. If you don't read Japanese, you can use the romanised translations to help you, or direct the waiter's attention to the Japanese script. If this doesn't work, there are two phrases that may help: *o-susume wa nan desu ka* (What do you recommend?) and *o-makase shimasu* (Please decide for me). If you're still having problems, you can try pointing at other diners' food or, if the restaurant has them, at the plastic food models in the window.

When you've finished eating, you can signal for the bill by crossing one index finger over the other to form the sign of an 'x'. This is the standard sign for 'bill please'. You can also say *o-kanjō kudasai*. Remember there is no tipping in Japan and tea is free of charge. Usually you will be given a bill to take to the cashier at the front of the restaurant. At more upmarket places, the host of the party will discreetly excuse themselves to pay before the group leaves. Unlike some places in the West, one doesn't usually leave cash on the table by way of payment. Only the bigger and more international places take credit cards, so cash is always the surer option.

When leaving, it is polite to say to the restaurant staff *gochisō-sama deshita* (it was a real feast).

The Best... Cities to Eat...

1 **Sushi** Tokyo (p99)

2 *Kaiseki* **(Japanese haute cuisine)** Kyoto (p243)

3 *Okonomiyaki* **(savoury Japanese pancakes)** Osaka (p277)

4 *Rāmen* **(egg noodles)** Nagasaki (p339)

Types of Restaurants & Sample Menus

Shokudō

A *shokudō* is the most common type of restaurant in Japan. Easily distinguished by the presence of plastic food displays in the window, these inexpensive places usually serve a variety of *washoku* (Japanese dishes) and *yōshoku* (Western dishes).

At lunch, and sometimes dinner, the easiest meal to order at a *shokudō* is a *teishoku* (set-course meal), which is sometimes also called *ranchi setto* (lunch set) or *kōsu*. This usually includes a main dish of meat or fish, a bowl of rice, miso soup, shredded cabbage and some *tsukemono* (Japanese pickles). In addition, most *shokudō* serve a fairly standard selection of *donburi-mono* (rice dishes) and *menrui* (noodle dishes). When you order noodles, you can choose between *soba* (buckwheat noodles) and *udon* (thick white wheat noodles), both of which are served with a variety of toppings. If you're at a loss as to what to order, simply say *kyō-no-ranchi* (today's lunch), and they'll do the rest. Expect to spend from ¥800 to ¥1000 for a meal at a *shokudō*.

Rice Dishes

katsu-don	かつ丼	rice topped with a fried pork cutlet
niku-don	牛丼	rice topped with thin slices of cooked beef
oyako-don	親子丼	rice topped with egg and chicken
ten-don	天丼	rice topped with tempura shrimp and vegetables

Noodle Dishes

soba	そば	buckwheat noodles
udon	うどん	thick, white wheat noodles
kake soba/udon	かけそば/うどん	*soba/udon* noodles in broth
kitsune soba/udon	きつねそば/うどん	*soba/udon* noodles with fried tofu
tempura soba/udon	天ぷらそば/うどん	*soba/udon* noodles with tempura shrimp
tsukimi soba/udon	月見そば/うどん	*soba/udon* noodles with raw egg on top

Izakaya

An *izakaya* is the Japanese equivalent of a pub. It's a good place to visit when you want a casual meal, a wide selection of food, a hearty atmosphere and, of course, plenty of beer and sake. When you enter an *izakaya,* you are given the choice of sitting around the counter, at a table or on a tatami floor. You usually order a bite at a time, choosing from a selection of typical Japanese foods such as *yakitori,* sashimi and grilled fish, as well as Japanese interpretations of Western foods such as French fries and beef stew.

agedashi-dōfu	揚げだし豆腐	deep-fried tofu in a *dashi* broth
jaga-batā	ジャガバター	baked potatoes with butter
niku-jaga	肉ジャガ	beef and potato stew
shio-yaki-zakana	塩焼魚	whole fish grilled with salt
yaki-onigiri	焼きおにぎり	triangle of grilled rice with *yakitori* sauce
poteto furai	ポテトフライ	French fries
chiizu-age	チーズ揚げ	deep-fried cheese
hiya-yakko	冷奴	cold block of tofu with soy sauce and spring onions
sashimi mori-awase	刺身盛り合わせ	selection of sliced sashimi

Soba & Udon

Soba and *udon* are Japan's answer to Chinese-style *rāmen* (egg noodles). *Soba* are thin, brown buckwheat noodles; *udon* are thick, white wheat noodles. Most Japanese noodle shops serve both *soba* and *udon* in a variety of ways. Noodles are usually served in a bowl containing a light, bonito-flavoured broth, but you can also order them served cold and piled on a bamboo screen with a cold broth for dipping.

Sushi & Sashimi

Like *yakitori*, sushi is considered an accompaniment for beer and sake. Nonetheless, both Japanese and foreigners often make a meal of it, and it's one of the healthiest meals around. All proper sushi restaurants serve their fish over rice, in which case it's called sushi, or without rice, in which case it's called sashimi or *tsukuri* (or, politely, *o-tsukuri*). There are two main types of sushi: *nigiri-zushi* (served on a small bed of rice – the most common variety) and *maki-zushi* (served in a seaweed roll).

ama-ebi	甘海老	sweet shrimp
ebi	海老	prawn or shrimp
hamachi	はまち	yellowtail
ika	いか	squid
ikura	イクラ	salmon roe
kani	かに	crab
katsuo	かつお	bonito
maguro	まぐろ	tuna
tai	鯛	sea bream
tamago	たまご	sweetened egg
toro	とろ	choicest cut of fatty tuna belly
unagi	うなぎ	eel with a sweet sauce
uni	うに	sea urchin roe

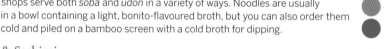

Vegetarians & Vegans

Travellers who eat fish should have almost no trouble dining in Japan: almost all *shokudō* (all-round restaurants), *izakaya* (pub-style restaurants) and other common restaurants offer a set meal with fish as the main dish. Vegans and vegetarians who don't eat fish will have to get their protein from tofu and other bean products. Note that most *misoshiru* (miso soup) is made with *dashi* broth that contains fish, so if you want to avoid fish, you'll also have to avoid *misoshiru*.

Most big cities in Japan have vegetarian or organic restaurants which naturally serve a variety of choices that appeal to vegetarians and vegans. (See the Eating sections of the destination chapters for specific recommendations. Reviews that include the 🖉 symbol throughout this guide indicate places with a good vegetarian selection.)

In the countryside, you'll have to do your best to find suitable items on the menu, or try to convey your dietary preferences to the restaurant staff. Note that many temples in Japan serve *shōjin-ryōri* (Buddhist vegetarian cuisine), which is made without meat, fish or dairy products. A good place to try this is Kōya-san in Kansai.

Yakitori

Yakitori (skewers of grilled chicken and vegetables) is a popular after-work meal. *Yakitori* is not so much a full meal as an accompaniment for beer and sake. At a *yakitori-ya* (*yakitori* restaurant) you sit around a counter with the other patrons and watch the chef grill your selections over charcoal. The best way to eat here is to order several varieties, then order seconds of the ones you really like. Ordering can be a little confusing since one serving often means two or three skewers (be careful – the price listed on the menu is usually that of a single skewer).

yakitori	焼き鳥	plain, grilled white meat
hasami/negima	はさみ/ねぎま	pieces of white meat alternating with leek
sasami	ささみ	skinless chicken-breast pieces
kawa	皮	chicken skin
tsukune	つくね	chicken meatballs
gyū-niku	牛肉	pieces of beef
tebasaki	手羽先	chicken wings
shiitake	しいたけ	Japanese mushrooms
piiman	ピーマン	small green peppers
tama-negi	玉ねぎ	round, white onions
yaki-onigiri	焼きおにぎり	triangle of rice grilled with *yakitori* sauce

Rāmen

The Japanese imported this dish from China and put their own spin on it to make what is one of the world's most delicious fast foods. *Rāmen* dishes are big bowls of noodles in a meat broth, served with a variety of toppings, such as sliced pork, bean sprouts and leeks. In some restaurants, particularly in Kansai, you may be asked if you'd prefer *kotteri* (thick) or *assari* (thin) soup. Other than this, ordering is simple: just sidle up to the counter and say *rāmen*, or ask for any of the other choices usually on offer.

rāmen	ラーメン	soup and noodles with a sprinkling of meat and vegetables
chāshū-men	チャーシュー麺	*rāmen* topped with slices of roasted pork
wantan-men	ワンタン麺	*rāmen* with meat dumplings
miso-rāmen	みそラーメン	*rāmen* with miso-flavoured broth

Eating Etiquette

Chopsticks in rice Do not stick your *hashi* (chopsticks) upright in a bowl of rice.

Polite expressions When eating with other people, especially when you're a guest, it is polite to say *itadakimasu* (literally, I will receive) before digging in. At the end of the meal, you should thank your host by saying *gochisō-sama deshita* (it was a real feast).

Kampai It is bad form to fill your own glass with beer or sake.

Slurp When you eat noodles in Japan, it's perfectly OK, even expected, to slurp.

Okonomiyaki

The name means 'cook what you like', and an *okonomiyaki* restaurant provides you with an inexpensive opportunity to do just that. Sometimes described as Japanese pizza or pancake, the resemblance is in form only. At an *okonomiyaki* restaurant you sit around a *teppan* (iron hotplate), armed with a spatula and chopsticks to cook your choice of meat, seafood and vegetables in a cabbage and vegetable batter.

mikkusu	ミックス お好み焼き	mixed fillings of seafood, *okonomiyaki* meat and vegetables
modan-yaki	モダン焼き	*okonomiyaki* with *yaki soba* and a fried egg

Tonkatsu

Tonkatsu is a deep-fried breaded pork cutlet that is served with a special sauce, usually as part of a set meal *(tonkatsu teishoku)*. *Tonkatsu* is served both at speciality restaurants and at *shokudō*. Naturally, the best *tonkatsu* is to be found at the speciality places, where a full set will cost ¥1500 to ¥2500. When ordering *tonkatsu*, you are able to choose between *rōsu* (a fatter cut of pork) and *hire* (a leaner cut).

hire katsu	ヒレかつ	*tonkatsu* fillet
tonkatsu teishoku	とんかつ定食	set meal of *tonkatsu*, rice, *misoshiru* (miso soup) and shredded cabbage

Sweets

Although most restaurants don't serve dessert (plates of sliced fruit are sometimes served at the end of a meal), there is no lack of sweets in Japan. Most Japanese sweets (known generically as *wagashi*) are sold in speciality stores for you to eat at home. Many of the more delicate-looking ones are made to balance the strong, bitter taste of the special *matcha* (powdered green tea) served during the tea ceremony.

Okonomiyaki

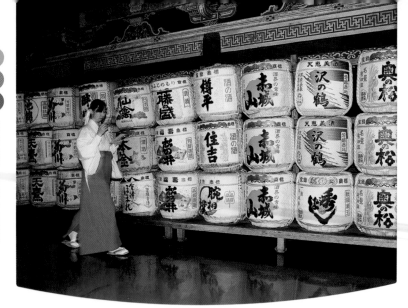

Some Westerners find Japanese sweets a little challenging, due to the liberal use of a sweet, red *azuki*-bean paste called *anko*. This unusual filling turns up in even the most innocuous looking pastries. The next main ingredient is often pounded sticky rice (*mochi*), which has a consistency that is unfamiliar to many Westerners.

With such a wide variety of sweets, it's impossible to list all the names. However, you'll probably find many variations on the *anko*-covered-by-*mochi* theme.

Okashi-ya (sweet shops) are easy to spot; they usually have open fronts with their wares laid out in wooden trays to entice passers-by. Buying sweets is simple – just point at what you want and indicate with your fingers how many you'd like.

Japanese Tea & Coffee

o-cha	お茶	green tea
sencha	煎茶	medium-grade green tea
matcha	抹茶	powdered green tea used in the tea ceremony
bancha	番茶	ordinary-grade green tea, has a brownish colour
mugicha	麦茶	roasted barley tea
kōcha	紅茶	black, British-style tea
kōhii	コーヒー	regular coffee
burendo kōhii	ブレンドコーヒー	blended coffee, fairly strong
amerikan kōhii	アメリカンコーヒー	weak coffee
kafe ore	カフェオレ	café au lait, hot or cold

Sake

Brewed from rice, sake has been enjoyed for centuries in Japan, and although it's been overtaken in terms of consumption by beer and *shōchū* (distilled grain liquor) in recent years, it is still regarded by most Japanese people as the national drink. Indeed, what we call 'sake' in the West is more commonly known as *nihonshu* in Japan: the drink of Japan. Sake has traditionally been associated with Shintō and other traditional ceremonies, and you will still see huge barrels of sake (known as *o-miki*) on display at almost every shrine you visit.

Not surprisingly, sake makes the perfect accompaniment to traditional Japanese food, and sake pubs (*izakaya*) generally also serve excellent seasonal fish and other foods to go with the booze. Sake is drunk chilled *(reishu)*, at room temperature *(jō-on)*, warmed *(nuru-kan)* or piping hot *(atsu-kan)*, according to the season and personal preference. The top-drawer stuff is normally served well chilled. Sake is traditionally served in a ceramic jug known as a *tokkuri*, and poured into tiny cups known as *o-choko* or *sakazuki*. A traditional measure of sake is one *gō* (一合), a little more than 180ml, or 6 fluid oz. In speciality bars, you'll have the option of ordering by the glass, which will often be filled to overflowing and brought to you in a wooden container to catch the overspill. If you're in company, the tradition is to pour for your neighbour first, and then be waited on by them in turn.

Sake is brewed during the winter in the cold months that follow the rice harvest in September. The main ingredients are rice and yeast, together with a benign mould known as *kōji* that helps to convert the starch in the rice into fermentable sugars. Sake is categorised by law into two main classes: *futsū-shu* (ordinary sake), which makes up the bulk of what's produced, and premium sake known as *tokutei-meishōshu*, further classified by the extent to which the rice is refined before fermentation to remove proteins and oils that interfere with the flavour of the final product. This is generally shown on the label as the *seimai buai*, expressed as the percentage of the original size to which the grain is reduced by polishing before the brewing process starts. As a general rule, the lower this number, the better, or at least, the more expensive the sake will be. Sake made from rice polished to 60% or less of its original size is known as *ginjō*; rice polished to 50% or less of its original size produces the finest sake of all, known as *dai-ginjō*. Sake made only with rice and *kōji* (without the use of added alcohol) is known as *junmai-shu*, or 'pure rice' sake.

Arts & Architecture

Wood-block prints, Kyoto Handicraft Center (p254)

FRANK CARTER / GETTY IMAGES ©

It's no secret that Japan has one of the world's richest artistic cultures. You can think of Japan as an oyster sitting at the end of the Silk Road: it absorbed all the artistic traditions of Asia and then polished them to produce the pearls you see before you today: sublime gardens, splendid decorative techniques, flamboyant textiles, ceramics to die for and the visual extravaganza known as kabuki, among many others.

Japanese Arts: Continental Roots with a Japanese Twist

Until the 19th century, the major influences on Japanese art came from China and Korea. While Japan was still living in the Stone Age, China had a well-developed technological culture. It's hardly surprising that when frequent contact was established Japan would be hungry for whatever skills and knowledge the Chinese had to give. In borrowing many aspects of Chinese culture, Japan also absorbed influences from distant cultures, such as Persia, Afghanistan and even ancient Rome, as China had maintained an active trade along the Silk Road. Perhaps the most important influence of all came from India, via China, in the form of Buddhism, which entered Japan in the 6th century.

Looking beyond these outside influences, the Japanese have always added something of their own to their arts. There is a fascination with the ephemeral, with the unadorned, with forms that echo the randomness of nature. A gift for caricature is also present, from early Zen ink paintings right up to the manga (comics) of contemporary Japan. There also exists a wildness and passion that is less evident in the arts of China. An interest in the grotesque or bizarre is also often visible, from Buddhist scrolls depicting the horrors of hell to the stylised depictions of body parts in the *ukiyo-e* (woodblock prints) of the Edo period.

Visual Art

Traditional Painting

From 794 to 1600, Japanese painting borrowed from Chinese and Western techniques and media, ultimately transforming them to its own aesthetic ends. By the beginning of the Edo period (Old Tokyo, 1600–1867), which was marked by the enthusiastic patronage of a wide range of painting styles, Japanese art had come completely into its own. The Kanō school, initiated more than a century before the beginning of the Edo era, continued to be in demand for its depiction of subjects connected with Confucianism, mythical Chinese creatures or scenes from nature. The Tosa school (1333–1576), which followed the *yamato-e* style of painting (considered the classical Japanese style, often used on scrolls during the Heian period, 794–1185), was also kept busy with commissions from the nobility, who were eager to see scenes re-created from classics of Japanese literature.

The Rimpa school (from 1600) not only absorbed the styles of painting that had preceded it, but progressed beyond well-worn conventions to produce a strikingly decorative and delicately shaded form of painting. The works of art produced by a trio of outstanding artists from this school – Tawaraya Sōtatsu, Hon'ami Kōetsu and Ogata Kōrin – rank among the finest of this period.

Ukiyo-e (Wood-Block Prints)

The term *ukiyo-e* means 'pictures of the floating world', and derives from a Buddhist metaphor for the transient world of fleeting pleasures. The subjects chosen by artists for these wood-block prints were characters and scenes from the tawdry, vivacious 'floating world' of the entertainment quarters in Edo, Kyoto and Osaka.

The floating world centred on pleasure districts such as Edo's Yoshiwara, and was a topsy-turvy kingdom, an inversion of the usual social hierarchies that were held in place by the power of the Tokugawa shōgunate. Here, money meant more than rank, actors and artists were the arbiters of style, and prostitutes elevated their art to such a level that their accomplishments matched the women of noble families.

The vivid colours, novel composition and flowing lines of *ukiyo-e* caused great excitement in the West, sparking a vogue that one French art critic dubbed Japonisme. *Ukiyo-e* became a key influence on Impressionists including Toulouse-Lautrec, Manet and Degas, and post-Impressionists. Among the Japanese the prints were hardly given more than passing consideration – millions were produced annually in Edo. They were often thrown away or used as wrapping paper for pottery. For many years, the Japanese continued to be perplexed by the keen interest foreigners took in this art form, which they considered of ephemeral value.

The Best...
Traditional
Architecture

1 Katsura Rikyū (p232)

2 Tōdai-ji (p292)

3 Chion-in (p220)

4 Nishi Hongan-ji (p207)

Ceramics

Ceramics are Japan's oldest art form: Jōmon-era (10,000–300 BC) pottery, with its distinctive cordlike decorative patterns, has been dated back some 15,000 years. When the Jōmon people were displaced by the Yayoi people around 300 BC, a more refined style of pottery appeared on the scene. While Jōmon pottery was an indigenous Japanese form, Yayoi pottery had clear Continental influences and techniques. Continental techniques and even artisans continued to dominate Japanese ceramic arts for the next millennium or more: around the 5th century AD, Sue ware pottery was introduced from Korea, and around the 7th century, Tang Chinese pottery became influential.

In the medieval period, Japan's great ceramic centre was Seto, in central Honshū. Here, starting in the 12th century, Japanese potters took Chinese forms and adapted them to Japanese tastes and needs to produce a truly distinctive pottery style known as Seto ware. One Japanese term for pottery and porcelain, *setomono* (literally 'things from Seto'), clearly derives from this still-thriving ceramics centre.

Today, there are more than 100 pottery centres in Japan, with scores of artisans producing everything from exclusive tea utensils to souvenir folklore creatures. Department stores regularly organise exhibitions of ceramics and offer the chance to see some of this fine work up close.

Shikki (Lacquerware)

The Japanese have been using lacquer to protect and enhance the beauty of wood since the Jōmon period. In the Meiji era (1868–1912), lacquerware became very popular abroad and it remains one of Japan's best-known products. Known in Japan as *shikki* or *nurimono*, lacquerware is made using the sap from the lacquer tree *(urushi)*, a close relative of poison oak. Raw lacquer is actually toxic and causes severe skin irritation in those who have not developed immunity. Once hardened, however, it becomes inert and extraordinarily durable.

Display of lacquerware

The most common colour of lacquer is an amber or brown colour, but additives have been used to produce black, violet, blue, yellow and even white lacquer. In the better pieces, multiple layers of lacquer are painstakingly applied and left to dry, and finally polished to a luxurious shine.

Traditional Theatre

Nō

Nō is a hypnotic dance-drama that reflects the minimalist aesthetics of Zen. The movement is glorious, the chorus and music sonorous, the expression subtle. A sparsely furnished cedar stage directs full attention to the performers, who include a chorus, drummers and a flautist. There are two principal characters: the *shite*, who is sometimes a living person but more often a demon or a ghost, whose soul cannot rest; and the *waki*, who leads the main character towards the play's climactic moment. Each nō school has its own repertoire, and the art form continues to evolve and develop.

Kabuki

The first performances of kabuki were staged early in the 17th century by an all-female troupe. The performances were highly erotic and attracted enthusiastic support from the merchant class. In true bureaucratic fashion, Tokugawa officials feared for the people's morality and banned women from the stage in 1629. Since that time, kabuki has been performed exclusively by men, giving rise to the institution of *onnagata* or *ōyama,* male actors who specialise in female roles.

Manga: Japanese Comics

The Japanese are insatiable readers of manga – a catch-all word covering cartoons, magazine and newspaper comic strips, and the ubiquitous comic book. Even high-art *ukiyo-e* (wood-block prints) were once a form of manga, evolving with the *kibyōshi* (yellow cover) wood blocks that were used to create adult story books. The great *ukiyo-e* artist Hokusai actually coined the word 'manga' by combining the characters for 'frivolous' and 'picture'.

The father of modern manga was Tezuka Osamu, who, in the late 1940s, began working cinematic effects based on European movies into his cartoons – pioneering multipanel movements, perspectives that brought the reader into the action, close-ups, curious angles and a host of movielike techniques. His adventurous stories quickly became movie-length comic strips – essentially films drawn on paper. What Tezuka started took off in a big way once weekly magazines realised that they could boost sales by including manga in their pages. As a result of Tezuka's innovations, Japanese comics are rarely slim affairs (weekly comics as thick as phone directories are not unusual).

You can find manga in any bookshop or convenience store in Japan, and these days, large bookshops in places such as Tokyo, Osaka and Kyoto will usually have a section devoted to English-language translations of popular manga. For real fans, we highly recommend a visit to the Kyoto International Manga Museum (p210).

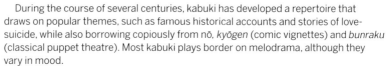

During the course of several centuries, kabuki has developed a repertoire that draws on popular themes, such as famous historical accounts and stories of love-suicide, while also borrowing copiously from nō, *kyōgen* (comic vignettes) and *bunraku* (classical puppet theatre). Most kabuki plays border on melodrama, although they vary in mood.

Formalised beauty and stylisation are the central aesthetic principles of kabuki; the acting is a combination of dancing and speaking in conventionalised intonation patterns, and each actor prepares for a role by studying and emulating the style perfected by his predecessors. Kabuki actors are born into the art form, and training begins in childhood. Today, they enjoy great social prestige and their activities on and off the stage attract as much interest as those of popular film and TV stars.

Traditional Architecture

Upon glimpsing the visual chaos of Japan's urban centres, it's hard to believe that once upon a time, the local architectural aesthetic was governed by a preference for understated, back-to-nature design. Long before the Japanese borrowed and bested Western design motifs, the island nation honed its craft and style during two centuries of self-inflicted isolation when Tokugawa Ieyasu defeated the last of his enemies and secured total control for the Tokugawa shōgunate.

Japan's flamboyant temples are undoubtedly the best examples of the nation's early architectural abilities. Important religious complexes were usually quite large and featured a great hall surrounded by smaller buildings such as pagodas – the ancient version of the skyscraper – and structures that served as quarters for devotees.

Equally as impressive were the country's collection of feudal castles, although most of the bastions we see today are concrete replicas of the original wooden structures destroyed by war, fire or decay. Initially, the first feudal castles were simple mountain forts that relied more on natural terrain than structural innovation when defending the keep from invaders. Castle construction boomed during the 16th and 17th centuries, each one more impressive than the next; however, most were later razed by Edo and Meiji governments.

Principally simple and refined, the typical house was also constructed using post-and-beam timber, with sliding panels of wood or rice paper (for warmer weather) making up the exterior walls. *Shōji* (movable screens) would divide the interior rooms. In more densely populated areas, traditional housing took the form of *machiya* (traditional Japanese townhouse) and were usually built by merchants. Although most of the neat, narrow rows of these structures have been replaced with flashier modern dwellings, one can still stumble across *machiya* in Kyoto. The reasoning behind the gossamer construction of domestic dwellings was twofold: light materials were favourable during broiling summer months, and heavier building products were inadvisable due to the abundance of earthquakes.

Onsen

A *rotemburo* (outdoor onsen) in Nagano

Japan is in hot water. Literally. The stuff percolates up out of the ground from one end of the country to the other. The Japanese word for a hot spring is onsen, and there are more than 3000 of them in the country. So if your idea of relaxation involves spending a few hours soaking your bones in a tub of bubbling hot water, then you've come to the right place.

Temples to Relaxation

Japanese onsen come in every size, shape and colour. And they are *everywhere*. There is an onsen on an artificial island in Tokyo Bay. There are onsen high up in the Japan Alps that you can only get to by walking for a full day over high mountain peaks. There are onsen bubbling up among the rocks on the coast that only exist when the tide is just right.

Over the millennia, the Japanese have turned the simple act of bathing in an onsen into something like a religion. Today, the ultimate way to experience an onsen is to visit an onsen ryokan, a traditional Japanese inn with its own private hot-spring bath on the premises. At an onsen ryokan you spend all day enjoying the bath, relaxing in your room and eating sumptuous Japanese food.

Etiquette

First: relax. That's what onsen are all about. You'll be relieved to hear that there really is nothing tricky about taking an onsen bath. If you remember just one basic point, you won't go too far wrong. This is the point: the water in the pools and tubs is for soaking in, not washing in, and it should only be entered after you've washed or rinsed your body.

This is the drill: pay your entry fee, if there is one. Rent a hand towel if you don't have one. Take off your shoes and put them in the lockers or shelves provided. Find the correct changing room/bath for your gender (man: 男; woman: 女). Grab a basket, strip down and put your clothes in the basket. Put the basket in a locker and bring the hand towel in with you.

Once in the bathing area, find a place around the wall (if there is one) to put down your toiletries (if you have them) and wash your body, or, at least, rinse your body. You'll note that some local men dispense with this step and just stride over to the tubs and grab a bucket (there are usually some around) and splash a few scoops over themselves.

Don't forget: the minerals in certain onsen can discolour jewellery, particularly anything made of silver. However, don't worry too much if you do forget to take off your silver wedding ring before jumping in the tub. After a few hours, the discoloration usually fades.

The Best...
Onsen

1 Kinosaki (p301)

2 The Kayōtei (p195)

3 Takaragawa Onsen (p136)

4 Hirauchi Kaichū Onsen (p341)

Tattoo Warning

If you have any tattoos, you may not be allowed to enter Japanese onsen (hot springs) or *sentō* (public baths). The reason for this is that Japanese *yakuza* (mafia) members almost always sport tattoos. Banning people with tattoos is an indirect way of banning gangsters. If your tattoo is small enough to cover with some Band-Aids, then cover it up and you'll have no problem. Otherwise, ask the people at the front desk if you can go in despite your tattoos. The phrase to use is: *'Irezumi wa daijōbu desu ka'* (Are tattoos okay?).

Ryokan

Hiiragiya Ryokan (p241), Kyoto

LONELY PLANET / GETTY IMAGES ©

Let's face it: a hotel is a hotel wherever you go. And while some of Japan's hotels are very nice indeed, you're probably searching for something unique to the culture. If this is what you're after, you'll be pleased to learn that Japan is one of the last places in Asia where you can find truly authentic traditional accommodation: ryokan.

The Ryokan Experience

Simply put, ryokan are traditional Japanese inns. They are Japanese-style accommodations with tatami mat rooms and futons instead of beds. Most serve Japanese-style breakfast and dinner as well.

The service is what sets ryokan apart from even the best hotels. At a good ryokan, you will be assigned a personal maid who sees to your every need. These ladies seem to have a sixth sense: as soon as you finish one course of your dinner, you hear a knock on the door and she brings the next course. Then, when you stroll down the hall to take a bath, she dashes into your room and lays out your futon.

Many ryokan in Japan pride themselves on serving *kaiseki ryōri* (Japanese haute cuisine) that rivals that served in the best restaurants. Staying at one of these so-called *ryōri ryokan* (cuisine ryokan) is like staying at a three-star residential restaurant, where you sleep in your own private dining room.

Another wonderful variety is the onsen ryokan: a ryokan with its own private hot-spring bath. Some of the top places have rooms with private en suite onsen baths, usually built overlooking gardens. When you stay at an onsen ryokan, your day involves a grueling cycle of bathe-nap-eat-repeat.

Of course, it would be irresponsible to suggest that all ryokan fit this description. A lot of places that call themselves ryokan are really just hotels with Japanese-style rooms. Some places may not even serve dinner. That isn't to say they aren't comfortable: simple ryokan are often very friendly and relaxing and they may cost less than hotels in some places.

Note that ryokan may not have en suite bath-tubs or showers and at some simple places, even the toilet facilities are shared. If this is an issue, be sure to enquire when you make a reservation.

The Best... Ryokan in Japan

1 Tawaraya (p241)

2 Hiiragiya (p241)

3 Beniya Mukayū (p195)

4 The Kayōtei (p195)

5 Nishimuraya Honkan (p303)

Architecture

A high-end ryokan is the last word in relaxation. The buildings themselves set the tone: they employ traditional Japanese architecture in which the whole structure is organic, made entirely of natural materials such as wood, earth, paper, grass, bamboo and stone. Indeed, a good ryokan is an extension of the natural world. And, nature comes into the ryokan in the form of the Japanese garden, which you can often see from the privacy of your room or even your bath-tub.

Ryokan Made Easy

Needless to say, staying in a ryokan (traditional Japanese inn) is not quite like staying at a hotel. Here are a few things to remember:

Shoes Remove your shoes in the entryway before stepping up onto the tatami mats or wooden flooring.

Bathing Rinse your body before getting in the bath-tub.

Luggage Should not be placed in the *tokonoma* (sacred alcove) in your room.

Yukata (light cotton robes) Can be worn in all areas of the ryokan and even outside (in places such as Kinosaki where people stroll to nearby onsen in *yukata*).

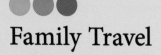

Family Travel

Kyoto Imperial Palace Park (p213)

FRANK CARTER/GETTY IMAGES ©

Japan is a great place to travel with kids. The usual worries that parents face when travelling with children – concerns about safety and food – are simply not concerns in ultra-safe and spotless Japan. Instead, your biggest challenge will probably be keeping your children entertained. The very things that many adults come to Japan to see – the temples, gardens and shrines – often bore kids silly. Luckily, there is no shortage of child-friendly attractions in Japan: you can't swing a cat without hitting an amusement park, game centre, zoo or kitschy shopping centre.

Older Children

If your children are older, get them out and about: go on a hike (Kyoto is perfect for this), rent a bicycle, or take a stroll through a youth-oriented shopping area such as Harajuku or Shibuya in Tokyo or Shinkyōgoku in Kyoto. If that fails, head to one of Japan's many amusement parks like Tokyo Disneyland or Universal Studios Japan.

Kids & Food

Food can be an issue in Japan if your child is a picky or unadventurous eater. Let's face it: even adults can be put off by some of the weird things found in Japanese cuisine – asking a kid to eat sea urchin or squid might simply be too much. Choose your restaurants carefully. If you're going to a *kaiseki* (Japanese haute cuisine) place, have your lodgings call ahead to see if they can make some kid-friendly dishes. Ditto if you'll be dining at your ryokan (traditional Japanese inn).

Need to Know

Breastfeeding Not usually done in public, but department stores have rooms for this.

Changing facilities In department stores, airports, large train stations and some public buildings.

Cots Available in many hotels (try to book in advance) but not usually ryokan (traditional Japanese inn).

Health Neither food-borne nor infectious diseases are a big problem in Japan. Do bring any medicine you'll need from home.

High chairs Available in many restaurants.

Kids' menus Usually only in so-called family restaurants.

Nappies (diapers) Widely available.

Strollers Available in Japan, but consider bringing your own.

Transport Comfortable and safe, but no child seats in taxis (but available for rental cars).

You'll find a lot of so-called family restaurants in Japan and these usually serve something that even finicky kids can stomach (pizza, fried chicken and French fries often feature on the menu). These places often serve special children's meals (sometimes called *o-ko-sama ranchii*).

Finally, if your child simply will not eat Japanese food, don't worry: the big cities are chock-a-block with international restaurants, while fast-food restaurants can be found even in smaller towns. In rural areas, however, you might find that Japanese food is the only thing available – you can always stock up on food your child likes at a supermarket before heading into the hinterland.

Most supermarkets stock a good selection of baby food. Organic baby food is hard to find, so if this is a concern, consider bringing a supply from home.

If your child has dietary restrictions or allergies, get them written down. If necessary, ask the proprietor of your first night's lodgings to write these for you in Japanese.

Getting Around

Most cities are fairly accessible to those with strollers. You'll find elevators in most train stations and many large buildings (departments stores etc). However, many attractions like temples and shrines do not have ramps, which makes it necessary to frequently pick up your stroller. One issue, particularly in Kyoto, is the relative lack of footpaths when you get away from the main streets – this can make walking with a stroller or a young child a little hair-raising. Luckily, Japanese tend to be safe drivers.

Child seats for taxis are generally not available, however, most rental-car agencies will provide a car seat if you request one in advance.

Finally, you will almost certainly find that Japanese love kids and will fawn over the young ones, declaring them to be *'kawaii'* (cute). Unfortunately, this love of children doesn't always extend to people giving up seats on trains or buses to those with children in tow. That said, most trains and buses do have *yūsen-zaseki* (priority seating for elderly, handicapped, pregnant women and those with young children). Standing near one and glaring at its able-bodied occupant is sometimes enough to free up a seat.

Survival
Guide

Shinjuku Station, Tokyo
WILL ROBB / GETTY IMAGES ©

A-Z

Directory

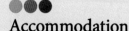

Accommodation

Japan offers a wide range of accommodation, from campsites to first-class hotels. In addition to the Western-style hotels, you'll also find distinctive Japanese-style places such as ryokan (traditional Japanese hotels) and *minshuku* (guesthouses). For more information about ryokan, see p381.

Reservations

It can be hard to find accommodation during high-season holiday periods (cherry-blossom season, autumn-foliage season, Golden Week holiday and the O-Bon holiday period). If you plan to be in Japan during these periods, you should make reservations as far in advance as possible.

Tourist information offices at main train stations can usually help with reservations, and are often open until about 6.30pm or later. Even if you are travelling by car, the train station is a good first stop in town for information, reservations and cheap car parking.

Making phone reservations in English is usually possible at larger hotels and foreigner-friendly ryokan. Providing you speak clearly and simply, there will usually be someone around who can get the gist of what you want.

Japanese Inn Group (☎ 06-6225-3611; www. japaneseinngroup.com) is a collection of foreigner-friendly ryokan and guesthouses. You can book member inns via its website or phone/fax. Pick up a copy of its excellent guide to member inns at major tourist information centres in Japan.

Hotels

You'll find a range of Western-style hotels in most Japanese cities and resort areas. So-called business hotels are efficient, utilitarian hotels that are geared to Japan's business travellers; while the rooms tend to be small, they are usually perfectly adequate for a night's stay. Luxury

hotels are what you'd find anywhere else in the world.

Customs Regulations

Customs allowances include the following:

Alcohol Up to three 760mL bottles.

Gifts/souvenirs Up to ¥200,000 in total value.

Perfume Up to 2oz.

Tobacco products Up to 100 cigars or 400 cigarettes or 500g.

You must be over the age of 20 to qualify for these allowances. Customs officers will confiscate any pornographic materials in which pubic hair is visible.

There are no limits on the importation of foreign or Japanese currency. The export of foreign currency is also unlimited, but there is a ¥5 million export limit for Japanese currency.

Visit Japan Customs (www.customs.go.jp) for more information on Japan's customs regulations.

Sleeping Price Ranges

The following price ranges refer to a double room for hotels, and per person without meals for ryokan. Unless otherwise stated, the national 8% consumption tax is included in the price, but note that some hotels quote exclusive of taxes.

¥ less than ¥6000 (less than ¥8000 in Tokyo)

¥¥ ¥6000–15,000 (¥8000–25,000 in Tokyo)

¥¥¥ more than ¥15,000 (more than ¥25,000 in Tokyo)

Electricity

Tokyo and eastern Japan are on 50Hz, and western Japan, including Nagoya, Kyoto and Osaka, is on 60Hz.

100V/50Hz/60Hz

Embassies & Consulates

Australian Embassy (☎ 03-5232-4111; www.australia.or.jp/en; 2-1-14 Mita, Minato-ku, Tokyo)

Australian Consulate (☎ 06-6941-9271; www.australia.or.jp/en/consular/osaka; 16th fl, Twin 21 MID Tower, 2-1-61 Shiromi, Chūō-ku, Osaka)

Canadian Consulate (☎ 052-972-0450; www.canadainternational.gc.ca/japan-japon; Nakatō Marunouchi Bldg, 6F, 3-17-6 Marunouchi, Naka-ku, Nagoya)

Canadian Embassy (カナダ大使館; ☎ 03-5412-6200; www.canadainternational.gc.ca/japan-japon/index.aspx?lang=eng; 7-3-38 Akasaka, Minato-ku, Tokyo; Ⓢ Ginza line to Aoyama-itchōme exit 4)

French Embassy (☎ 03-5798-6000; www.ambafrance-jp.org; 4-11-44 Minami Azabu, Minato-ku, Tokyo)

German Embassy (☎ 03-5791-7700; www.japan.diplo.de; 4-5-10 Minami Azabu, Minato-ku, Tokyo)

German Consulate (☎ 06-6440-5070; www.japan.diplo.de; 35th fl, Umeda Sky Bldg Tower East, 1-1-88-3501 Ōyodonaka, Kita-ku, Osaka)

Irish Embassy (☎ 03-3263-0695; www.irishembassy.jp; Ireland House, 2-10-7 Kōji-machi, Chiyoda-ku, Tokyo)

Netherlands Embassy (☎ 03-5776-5400; http://japan.nlembassy.org; 3-6-3 Shiba-kōen, Minato-ku, Tokyo)

Netherlands Consulate (☎ 06-6944-7272; http://japan.nlembassy.org; 33rd fl, Twin 21 MID Tower, 2-1-61 Shiromi, Chūō-ku, Osaka)

New Zealand Embassy (☎ 03-3467-2271; www.nzembassy.com/japan; 20-40 Kamiyama-chō, Shibuya-ku, Tokyo)

Russian Embassy (☎ 03-3583-4445; www.rusconsul.jp; 2-1-1, Azabudai, Minato-ku, Tokyo)

South Korean Embassy (☎ 03-3455-2601; http://jpn-tokyo.mofa.go.kr/worldlanguage/asia/jpn-tokyo/main; 1-7-32 Minami Azabu, Minato-ku, Tokyo)

South Korean Consulate (☎ 092-771-0461; http://jpn-fukuoka.mofa.go.kr/worldlanguage/asia/jpn-fukuoka/main/index.jsp; 1-1-3 Jigyōhama, Chūō-ku, Fukuoka)

UK Embassy (☎ 03-5211-1100; www.gov.uk/government/world/organisations/british-embassy-tokyo; 1 Ichiban-chō, Chiyoda-ku, Tokyo)

UK Consulate (☎ 06-6120-5600; www.gov.uk/government/world/organisations/british-embassy-tokyo/office/british-consulate-general-osaka.ja; 19th fl, Epson Osaka Bldg, 3-5-1 Bakurōmachi, Chūō-ku, Osaka)

USA Consulate (☎ 06-6315-5900; http://osaka.usconsulate.gov; 2-11-5 Nishitenma, Kita-ku, Osaka)

USA Embassy (米国大使館; ☎ 03-3224-5000; http://

Book Your Stay Online

For more accommodation reviews by Lonely Planet authors, check out http://hotels.lonelyplanet.com. You'll find independent reviews, as well as recommendations on the best places to stay. Best of all, you can book online.

Addresses in Japan

In Japan, finding a place from its address can be difficult, even for locals. The problem is twofold: first, the address is usually given by an area rather than a street; and second, the numbers are not necessarily consecutive, as prior to the mid-1950s numbers were assigned by date of construction.

To find an address, the usual process is to ask directions. Have your address handy. The numerous local police boxes are there largely for this purpose. Businesses often include a small map in their advertisements or on their business cards to show their location.

Most taxis and many rental cars now have satellite navigation systems, which make finding places a breeze, as long as you can program the address or phone number into the system. Needless to say, you'll have to be able to read Japanese to input the address, but phone numbers should be no problem.

japan.usembassy.gov; 1-10-5 Akasaka, Minato-ku, Tokyo; Ginza line to Tameike-sannō exits 9 12 13)

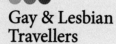

Food

For information on eating in Japan see the Food & Drink chapter (p366).

Gay & Lesbian Travellers

With the possible exception of Thailand, Japan is Asia's most enlightened nation with regard to the sexual preferences of foreigners. Shinjuku-nichōme in Tokyo is an established scene where English is spoken and meeting men is fairly straightforward.

In rural areas, there may be one drinking establishment where gay men meet. It would, however, often be difficult to locate such places without a local friend to guide the way.

The lesbian scene is growing but is still elusive for most non-Japanese-speaking foreigners. Outside Tokyo you may find it difficult to break into the local scene unless you spend considerable time in a

place or have local contacts who can show you around.

Staying in hotels is simple as most have twin rooms, but love hotels are less accessible; if you know someone Japanese and can overcome the language barrier, a stay in a love hotel may be possible, although some are not particularly foreigner friendly.

Utopia (www.utopia-asia.com) is the site most commonly frequented by English-speaking gays and lesbians.

There are no legal restraints to same-sex sexual activities of either gender. Public displays of affection are not really common, whether the couple be same-sex or heterosexual, but they are not usually a problem in cities. In the countryside, they may raise some eyebrows, but that's probably all.

Health

Japan is an advanced country with high standards of hygiene and few endemic diseases. There are no special immunisations needed to visit and, other than bringing prescription medications from home, no special preparations to make. Hospitals and clinics can be found all over the archipelago, and only the smallest outer islands lack medical facilities. That said, there are some things to keep in mind.

Medical Care in Japan

While the Japanese medical system is extensive and com-

Eating Price Ranges

Price ranges in this book refer to a standard main meal unless otherwise stated.

¥ less than ¥1000 (less than ¥2000 in Tokyo)

¥¥ ¥1000–4000 (¥2000–5000 in Tokyo)

¥¥¥ more than ¥4000 (more than ¥5000 in Tokyo)

prehensive, the level of care can be uneven. Here are some things to note if you need to seek medical attention:

o It is better to seek care at university hospitals or other large hospitals, rather than clinics.

o Japanese doctors and hospitals are sometimes reluctant to treat foreigners. It helps to carry proof of insurance and be willing to show it. If a doctor or hospital seems reticent about giving care, you should insist on it (even though Japan has no Hippocratic oath, doctors can be told that they have to treat patients in need of care).

o Most hospitals and clinics have regular hours (usually in the mornings) when they will see patients.

o Hotels and ryokan that cater to foreigners will usually know the best hospitals in a particular area and will also know hospitals with English-speaking doctors.

o Most doctors speak some English. However, it helps to bring along a Japanese speaker if possible to help you explain your condition and to navigate the hospital.

Insurance

A travel-insurance policy to cover theft, loss and medical problems is essential. Some policies will specifically exclude 'dangerous activities', which can include scuba diving, motorcycling and even trekking; if you plan to engage in such activities, you'll want a policy that covers them.

You may prefer a policy that pays doctors or hospitals directly rather than having you pay on the spot and claim later. If you have to claim later, make sure you keep all documentation. Some policies ask you to call (reverse charge) a centre in your home country where an immediate assessment of your problem is made. Check that the policy covers ambulances or an emergency flight home.

Bring your insurance card or other certificate of insurance to Japan; Japanese hospitals have been known to refuse treatment to foreign patients with no proof of medical insurance.

Worldwide travel insurance is available at www.lonelyplanet.com/travel-insurance. You can buy, extend and claim online anytime – even if you're already on the road.

Internet Access

You'll find internet cafes (with rates running from ¥200 to ¥700 per hour) and other access points in most major Japanese cities. As a rule, internet connections are fast and reliable.

In accommodation reviews, an internet symbol indicates that the accommodation

Climate

Hiroshima

°C/°F **Temp**
40/104 —
30/86 —
20/68 —
10/50 —
0/32 —
-10/14 —

Rainfall inches/mm
— 16/400
— 12/300
— 8/200
— 4/100
— 0

J F M A M J J A S O N D

Kyoto

°C/°F **Temp**
40/104 —
30/86 —
20/68 —
10/50 —
0/32 —
-10/14 —

Rainfall inches/mm
— 16/400
— 12/300
— 8/200
— 4/100
— 0

J F M A M J J A S O N D

Tokyo

°C/°F **Temp**
40/104 —
30/86 —
20/68 —
10/50 —
0/32 —
-10/14 —

Rainfall inches/mm
— 16/400
— 12/300
— 8/200
— 4/100
— 0

J F M A M J J A S O N D

Practicalities

o **Newspapers & Magazines** There are three main English-language daily newspapers in Japan: the *Japan Times, Daily Yomiuri* and *Asahi Shimbun/International Herald Tribune*. In the bigger cities, these are available at bookstores, convenience stores, train-station kiosks and some hotels. In the countryside you may not be able to find them anywhere. Foreign magazines are available in major bookshops in the bigger cities.

o **Radio** Recent years have seen an increase in the number of stations aimed specifically at Japan's foreign population. InterFM (76.1FM; www.interfm.co.jp) is a favourite of Tokyo's expat community, and the Kansai equivalent is FM Cocolo (76.5FM; www.cocolo.jp).

o **TV & DVDs** Japan uses the NTSC system.

o **Weights & Measures** Japan uses the international metric system.

option has at least one computer with internet for guest use and/or LAN cable internet access in guest rooms. We also note where wi-fi is available.

Most hotels and hostels offer free wi-fi for their guests, but some still charge for it and some places have no in-room wi-fi at all (this is particularly true of small older hotels in smaller cities and towns).

Note that some hotels have in-room LAN cable internet access instead of wi-fi. The hotels usually provide LAN cables, but you may want to bring your own to avoid having to ask for one everywhere you stay. These LAN connections usually work fine, but you may occasionally find it difficult to log on due to software or hardware compatibility issues or configuration problems – the front-desk staff *may* be able to help.

Wi-fi

Wi-fi is everywhere in some form, but is often only available to subscribers of various Japanese services, many of which are not easy for travellers to join (especially those who don't speak and read Japanese). There are a number of ways to get online, though, and Japan has been trying to improve the options for travellers.

Freespot Map (www.freespot.com/users/map_e.html) Has a list of internet hot spots. It's not exhaustive and the maps are in Japanese, but it's still quite useful.

Starbucks All Starbucks stores in Japan offer free wi-fi to customers. You must register online to use the service (go to http://starbucks.wi2.co.jp).

Iijmio Japan Travel SIM cards You can buy Iijmio Japan Travel SIM cards (https://t.iijmio.jp/en) from major electronics shops in Japan. Your device must be unlocked and you must be able to input the APN settings to use these. The cards are good for three months and offer 2GB of data. The company is tied in with Brastel and you can also make (but not receive) voice calls with these. Unlike some other SIM cards, no telephone call is required to activate these cards, making them a great choice for travellers.

B-Mobile SIM cards You can buy B-Mobile Visitor SIM cards from major electronics shops in Japan. You can also order them online (www.bmobile.ne.jp/english) and have them delivered to your first night's lodgings or even to the post office at your arrival airport. These data-only cards will usually allow internet use for a specific length of time (a month is common). Note that the amount of data you can download is limited and your device must be unlocked and you must be able to input the APN settings. A call is required to activate these cards (usually, but not always, someone at the shop can make the call).

Japan Connected Download this app (www.ntt-bp.net/jcfw) and register ahead of time for free wi-fi service, courtesy of the national telecom provider NTT. Connect at a variety of spots in Tokyo (including 7-Eleven convenience stores and Narita/Haneda airports) and a few other places across the country (primarily in

Hiroshima, Fukuoka, Osaka and Kanazawa); visit their Coverage Areas page for details.

Boingo Subscribers to Boingo's global plan (www. boingo.com) can use BB Mobilepoint wi-fi at McDonald's restaurants and some convenience stores and restaurants.

Portable internet connections You can rent data cards, USB dongles or pocket wi-fi devices from various phone-rental companies. The most user-friendly option with English service is provided by Rentafone Japan (p394), which offers two types of pocket wi-fi from ¥3900 per week with unlimited use.

Free city wi-fi Several cities in Japan, including Kyoto, Osaka and Hiroshima have launched free wi-fi services in train stations, tourist areas, and sometimes other areas. Check with local tourist offices or online for details.

Legal Matters

Japanese police have extraordinary powers. They can detain a suspect for up to three days without charging them; after this time a prosecutor can decide to extend this period for another 20 days. Police can also choose whether to allow a suspect to phone their embassy or lawyer, though if you find yourself in police custody you should insist that you will not cooperate in any way

until allowed to make such a call. Your embassy is the first place you should call if given the chance.

Police will speak almost no English; insist that a *tsūyakusha* (interpreter) be summoned. Police are legally bound to provide one before proceeding with any questioning. Even if you do speak Japanese, it's best to deny it and stay with your native language.

If you have a problem, call the **Japan Helpline** (📞 0570-000-911; www.jhelp. com/en/jhlp.html; 🕐 24hr), a nationwide emergency number that operates 24 hours a day, seven days a week.

Maps

If you'd like to buy a map of Japan before arriving, both Nelles and Periplus produce reasonable ones. If you want something more detailed, wait until you get to Tokyo or Kyoto, where you'll find lots of detailed maps in both English and Japanese.

The Japan National Tourism Organization's free *Tourist Map of Japan*, available at JNTO-operated tourist information centres inside the country and JNTO offices abroad, is a reasonable English-language map that is suitable for general route planning.

The *Japan Road Atlas* (Shobunsha) is a good choice for those planning to drive around the country; unfortunately, it's out of print (you might be able to find a copy online, but it won't be cheap). Those looking for something less bulky should

pick up a copy of the *Bilingual Atlas of Japan* (Kodansha). Of course, if you can read a little Japanese, you'll do much better with one of the excellent *Super Mapple* road atlases published by Shobunsha.

Money

The currency in Japan is the yen (¥). The Japanese pronounce yen as 'en', with no 'y' sound. The kanji for yen is 円.

Yen denominations:
¥1 coin; lightweight, silver colour
¥5 coin; bronze colour, hole in the middle, value in Chinese character only
¥10 coin; copper colour
¥50 coin; silver colour, hole in the middle
¥100 coin; silver colour
¥500 coin; large, silver colour
¥1000 banknote
¥2000 banknote (rare)
¥5000 banknote
¥10,000 banknote

ATMs

Automated teller machines are almost as common as vending machines in Japan. Unfortunately, most of these do not accept foreign-issued cards. Even if they display Visa and MasterCard logos, most accept only Japan-issued versions of these cards.

Fortunately, Japanese postal ATMs accept cards that belong to the following international networks: Visa, Plus, MasterCard, Maestro, Cirrus, American Express, Diners Club, Discover and China Unionpay cards. You'll find postal ATMs in almost all post offices, and you'll find post offices in even the smallest Japanese villages.

Note that postal ATMs work with bank or cash cards – you cannot use credit cards, even with a pin number. That is to say, you cannot use postal ATMs to perform a cash advance.

Most postal ATMs are open 9am to 5pm Monday to Friday, 9am to noon on Saturday, and are closed on Sunday and holidays. Some postal ATMs in very large central post offices are open longer hours; the central post offices in major cities are open *almost* 24 hours a day.

Postal ATMs are relatively easy to use. Here's the drill: press 'English Guide', select 'Withdrawal', then insert your card, press 'Visitor Withdrawal/Card Issued Overseas', hit 'Enter' (acknowledging that a commission will be charged), input your pin number, then hit the button marked 'Kakunin' (確認), then enter the amount, hit 'Yen' and 'Confirm' and the banknotes will be dispensed.

In addition, 7-Eleven convenience stores across Japan have linked their ATMs to international cash networks, and these often seem to accept cards that for one reason or other will not work with postal ATMs. These *are* open 24 hours. So, if you can't find an open post office or your card won't work with postal ATMs, don't give up: ask around for a 7-Eleven (pronounced like 'sebun erebun' in Japanese).

International cards also work in the ATMs at Citibank Japan (www.citibank.co.jp/en/banking/branch_atm). If you find that your card doesn't work in a postal or 7-Eleven ATM, this is a good last-ditch bet.

Credit Cards

Cash and carry is still very much the rule in Japan. If you do decide to bring a credit card, you'll find Visa the most useful, followed by Master-Card, Amex and Diners Club. Note also that Visa cards can be used for cash advances at Sumitomo Mitsui banks in Japan, but you might have

to go to a specific branch to do this.

International Transfers

To make an international transfer you'll have to find a Japanese bank associated with the bank transferring the money. Start by asking at the central branch of any major Japanese bank. If it doesn't have a relationship with your bank, it can usually refer you to a bank that does. Once you find a related bank, you'll have to give your home bank the exact details of where to send the money: the bank, branch and location, and the bank's SWIFT code. A credit-card cash advance is a worthwhile alternative.

Moneychangers

You can change cash or travellers cheques at most banks, major post offices, discount ticket shops, some travel agencies, some large hotels and most big department stores. Note that discount-ticket shops (known as *kakuyasu kippu uriba* in Japanese) often have the best rates. These can be found around major train stations. However, only US dollars and euros fetch decent exchange rates.

Tipping

There is little tipping in Japan. If you want to show your gratitude to someone, give them a gift rather than a tip. If you do choose to give someone a cash gift (your maid at a ryokan, for instance), place the money in an envelope first.

Japan is a Cash Society

Be warned that cold hard yen is the way to pay in Japan. While credit cards are becoming more common, cash is still much more widely used, and travellers cheques are rarely accepted. Never assume that you can pay for things with a credit card; always carry sufficient cash. The only places where you can count on paying by credit card are department stores, large hotels and at major JR ticket offices.

For those without credit cards, it would be a good idea to bring some travellers cheques as a back-up. As in most other countries, the US dollar is still the currency of choice in terms of exchanging cash and cashing travellers cheques.

Currency Warning

Exchange rates for the US dollar and euro are reasonable in Japan. All other currencies, including the Australian dollar and the currencies of nearby countries, fetch very poor exchange rates. If you want to bring cash to Japan, we suggest US dollars or euros. Or, if you must change other currencies into yen, we suggest doing so in your home country.

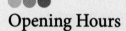

Opening Hours

Business hours in Japan are fairly standard. Almost all museums, many other sights and many businesses close over the New Year period (30 or 31 December to 3 or 4 January). Also, most museums in Japan are closed on Monday. Note that when a place is normally closed on a Monday, it will usually open on any national holiday Monday (in which case it will most likely be closed on the following Tuesday). Typical business hours:

Banks 9am to 3pm Monday to Friday.

Bars 6pm to midnight or later, closed one day a week.

Department stores 10am to 7pm, closed one or two days a month. Often open for all or part of the New Year's holidays.

Museums 9am or 10am to 5pm, Tuesday to Sunday.

Offices 9am to 5pm or 6pm Monday to Friday.

Post offices Local 9am to 5pm Monday to Friday; Central 9am to 7pm Monday to Friday and 9am to 3pm Saturday (larger city post offices may have an after-hours window open 24/7).

Restaurants 11am to 2pm and 6pm to 11pm, closed one day a week.

Smaller shops 9am to 5pm, may be closed Sunday.

Public Holidays

Japan has 16 national holidays. When a public holiday falls on a Sunday, the following Monday is taken as a holiday. If that Monday is already a holiday, the following day becomes a holiday as well. And if two weekdays (say, Tuesday and Thursday) are holidays, the day in between also becomes a holiday.

Ganjitsu (New Year's Day) 1 January

Seijin-no-hi (Coming-of-Age Day) Second Monday in January

Kenkoku Kinem-bi (National Foundation Day) 11 February

Shumbun-no-hi (spring equinox) 20 or 21 March

Shōwa-no-hi (Shōwa Emperor's Day) 29 April

Kempō Kinem-bi (Constitution Day) 3 May

Midori-no-hi (Green Day) 4 May

Kodomo-no-hi (Children's Day) 5 May

Umi-no-hi (Marine Day) Third Monday in July

Yama-no-hi (Mountain Day) 11 August (starting 2016)

Keirō-no-hi (Respect-for-the-Aged Day) Third Monday in September

Shūbun-no-hi (autumn equinox) 22 or 23 September

Taiiku-no-hi (Health-Sports Day) Second Monday in October

Bunka-no-hi (Culture Day) 3 November

Kinrō Kansha-no-hi (Labour Thanksgiving Day) 23 November

Tennō Tanjōbi (Emperor's Birthday) 23 December

You will find transport crowded and accommodation bookings hard to come by during the following high-season travel periods:

Shōgatsu (New Year) 31 December to 3 January

Golden Week 29 April to 5 May

O-Bon mid-August

Safe Travel

Japan has its share of natural disasters, including earthquakes, tsunami, volcanic eruptions, typhoons and landslides. Fortunately, there are robust public warning systems and evacuation procedures in place, should one of these things occur. Your lodgings will be a good source of information in the event of an emergency.

The Great East Japan Earthquake of March 2011 and the resulting tsunami caused a huge amount of destruction in northeast Japan. While most of the tsunami damage has been cleaned up and the local infrastructure largely restored, an exclusion zone with a radius of 20km is in effect around the Fukushima Dai-Ichi nuclear power plant, which was damaged by the tsunami. The plant is in Fukushima Prefecture in northeast Honshū.

●●● Telephone

Japanese telephone numbers consist of an area code plus the number. You do not dial the area code when making a call in that area. When dialling Japan from abroad, dial the country code 📞 81, followed by the area code (drop the '0') and the number. The most common toll-free prefixes are 0120, 0070, 0077, 0088 and 0800. Directory-assistance numbers:

Local directory assistance 📞 104 (¥60 to ¥150 per call)

Local directory assistance in English 📞 0120-36-4463 (9am to 5pm Monday to Friday)

International directory assistance 📞 0057

Local Calls

The Japanese public-telephone system is extremely reliable and efficient. Unfortunately, the number of pay phones is decreasing fast as more and more Japanese buy mobile phones. Local calls from pay phones cost ¥10 per minute; unused ¥10 coins are returned after the call is completed but no change is given on ¥100 coins.

In general it's much easier to buy a telephone card (*terefon kādo*) when you arrive rather than worry about always having coins on hand. Phone cards are sold in ¥500 and ¥1000 denominations (the latter earns you an extra ¥50 in calls) and can be used in most green or grey pay phones. Cards are available from vending machines (some of which can be found in public phone booths) and convenience stores. They come in myriad designs and are also a collectable item.

Mobile Phones

Japan's mobile-phone networks use 3G (third generation) mobile-phone technology on a variety of frequencies. Thus, non-3G mobile phones cannot be used in Japan and most foreign mobile phones will not work in Japan. Furthermore, SIM cards are not commonly available in Japan. For most people who want to use a mobile phone while in Japan, the only solution is to rent one.

Several telecommunications companies in Japan specialise in short-term mobile-phone rentals, including **Rentafone Japan** (📞 from overseas 81-75-212-0842, toll free within Japan 0120-746-487; www.rentafonejapan.com), which offers rentals starting at ¥3900 per week (domestic rates from ¥35 per minute and overseas calls from ¥45 per minute).

Prepaid International Phone Cards

Because of the lack of pay phones from which you can make international phone calls in Japan, the easiest way to make a call is to buy a prepaid international phone card. Most convenience stores carry at least one of the following types of phone cards: KDDI Superworld Card; NTT Communications World Card; or SoftBank Telecom Comica Card. These cards can be used with any regular pay phone in Japan.

Useful International Numbers

For international operator-assisted calls dial 0051 (KDDI; operators speak English).

There's very little difference in the rates of direct-dial international numbers. Dial one of

Important Numbers

Ambulance & fire 📞 119

Police 📞 110

Country code 📞 81

International access code 📞 001

International operator 📞 0051

the numbers, then the international country code, the local code and the number.

- KDDI 001-010
- NTT 0033-010
- SoftBank Telecom 0041-010

Time

All of Japan is in the same time zone: nine hours ahead of Greenwich Mean Time (GMT). Sydney and Wellington are ahead of Japan (by one and three hours respectively), and most of the world's other big cities are behind (New York by 14 hours, Los Angeles by 17 and London by nine). Japan does not have daylight-saving (summer) time.

Toilets

You will come across both Western-style toilets and Asian squat toilets in Japan. When you are compelled to squat, the correct position is facing the hood, away from the door.

Public toilets are free. The *katakana* for 'toilet' is トイレ, and the kanji is お手洗い. You'll often also see the kanji signs for female (女) and male (男).

Toilet paper isn't always provided, so it is always a good idea to carry tissues with you. You may also be given small packets of tissues on the street – a common form of advertising.

In many bathrooms, separate toilet slippers are provided – usually located just inside the toilet door. These are for use in the toilet only, so remember to change out of them when you leave.

It's quite common to see men urinating in public – the unspoken rule is that it's acceptable at night time if you happen to be drunk.

Tourist Information

You will find tourist information offices (*kankō annai-sho;* 観光案内所) in most cities and towns and even in some small villages. They are almost always located inside or in front of the main train station. Staff members may speak some English, but don't count on it. English-language materials are usually available. Naturally, places that get a lot of foreign visitors are more likely to have English-speaking staff and English-language materials. Nonetheless, with a little patience and a smile you will usually be able to get the information you need from even the smallest local tourist information office.

The Japan National Tourism Organization (www.jnto.go.jp) is Japan's main English-language information service for foreign travellers. JNTO produces a great deal of useful literature, which is available from its overseas offices as well as its Tourist Information Center in Tokyo. Most of its publications are available in English and, in some cases, other European and Asian languages. The organisation's website is a very useful tool when planning your journey to Japan.

JNTO has overseas offices in Australia, Canada, France, Germany, the UK and the USA (see the JNTO website for exact locations and contact details).

Travellers with Disabilities

Japan gets mixed marks in terms of ease of travel for those with disabilities. On the plus side, many new buildings have access ramps, traffic lights have speakers playing melodies when it is safe to cross, train platforms have raised dots and lines to provide guidance for the visually impaired, and some ticket machines in Tokyo have Braille. Some attractions also offer free entry for disabled persons and one companion. On the negative side, many of Japan's cities are still rather difficult for disabled persons to negotiate, often due to the relative lack of normal sidewalks on narrow streets.

Train cars on most lines have areas set aside for people in wheelchairs. Those with other physical disabilities can use the seats near the train exits, called *yūsen-zaseki*. You will also find these seats near the front of buses; usually they're a different colour from the regular seats.

The Accessible Japan website (www.tesco-premium.co.jp/aj/index.htm) is not updated regularly, but details the accessibility of hundreds of sites in Tokyo, including hotels, sights and department stores, as well as offering general information about getting around Japan. For good bilingual information on accommodation, activities, sights, shops etc, click the 'Accessible Tokyo' link on the Japanese Red Cross Language Service Volunteers website (www.tok-lanserv.jp/eng).

Visas

Generally, visitors who are not planning to engage in income-producing activities while in Japan are exempt from obtaining visas and will be issued a 90-day *tanki-taizai* (temporary-visitor) visa on arrival. Nationals of Australia, Canada, France, Ireland, Italy, the Netherlands, New Zealand, Spain, the UK and the USA are eligible for this visa.

Stays of up to six months are permitted for citizens of Austria, Germany, Ireland, Mexico, Switzerland and the UK. Citizens of these countries will almost always be given a 90-day temporary-visitor visa upon arrival, which can usually be extended for another 90 days at immigration bureaux inside Japan.

Japanese law requires that visitors entering on a temporary-visitor visa possess an ongoing air or sea ticket or evidence thereof. In practice, few travellers are asked to produce such documents, but it pays to be on the safe side.

For additional information on visas and regulations, contact your nearest Japanese embassy or consulate, or visit the website of the Ministry of Foreign Affairs of Japan (www.mofa.go.jp). Here you can find out about the different types of visas available, read about working-holiday visas and find details on the Japan Exchange & Teaching (JET) program, which sponsors native English speakers to teach in the Japanese public school system.

On entering Japan, all short-term foreign visitors are photographed and fingerprinted.

Women Travellers

Japan is a relatively safe country for women travellers, though perhaps not quite as safe as some might think. Crimes against women are generally believed to be widely under-reported, especially by Japanese women. Foreign women are occasionally subjected to some forms of verbal harassment or prying questions. Physical attacks are very rare, but have occurred.

The best advice is to avoid being lulled into a false sense of security by Japan's image as one of the world's safest countries and to take the normal precautions you would in your home country. If a neighbourhood or establishment looks unsafe, then treat it that way. As long as you use your common sense, you will most likely find that Japan is a pleasant and rewarding place to travel as a woman.

Several train companies have recently introduced women-only cars to protect female passengers from *chikan* (men who grope women and girls on packed trains). These cars are usually available during rush-hour periods on weekdays on busy urban lines. There are signs (usually in pink) on the platform indicating where you can board these cars, and the cars themselves are usually labelled in both Japanese and English (again, often in pink).

If you have a problem and you find the local police unhelpful, you can call the Japan Helpline (p391), a nationwide emergency number that operates 24 hours a day, seven days a week.

Transport

Getting There & Away

Flights, tours and rail tickets can be booked online at lonely planet.com/bookings.

Entering the Country

For most travellers, entering Japan is simple and straightforward. Visas are given on arrival for many nationalities. Foreigners are now fingerprinted and photographed on arrival.

Air

There are flights to Japan from all over the world, usually to Tokyo, but also to a number of other airports. Although Tokyo may seem the obvious arrival and departure point, for many visitors this may not be the case. For example, if you plan to explore western Japan or the Kansai region, it might be more convenient to fly into Kansai International Airport near Osaka.

Airports

There are international airports situated on the main island of Honshū (Nagoya, Niigata, Osaka/Kansai, Haneda and Tokyo Narita), as well as on Kyūshū (Fukuoka, Kagoshima, Kumamoto and Nagasaki), Okinawa (Naha) and Hokkaidō (Sapporo). Major airports include:

Tokyo The majority of international flights to/from Tokyo use Narita International Airport (www.narita-airport. jp), about an hour from Tokyo by express train, but some international flights now go via Tokyo International Airport (www.tokyo-airport-bldg.co.jp), better known as Haneda Airport, about 30 minutes from Tokyo by monorail.

Osaka Most of Osaka's international flights go via Kansai International Airport (www.kansai-airport.or.jp), which serves the key Kansai cities of Kyoto, Osaka, Nara and Kōbe.

Nagoya Central Japan International Airport (www.centrair.jp) has international connections with several countries.

Getting Around

Japan has one of the best public-transport systems in the world, which makes getting around the country an absolute breeze for travellers.

 Air

Air services in Japan are extensive, reliable and safe. In many cases, flying is much faster than even *shinkansen* (bullet trains) and not that much more expensive. Flying is also an efficient way to travel from the main islands to the many small islands, particularly the Southwest Islands (the southern islands of Kagoshima and Okinawa Prefectures).

Airlines in Japan

Japan Airlines (☎ 03-5460-0522, 0570-025-121; www.jal.

Domestic Airfares

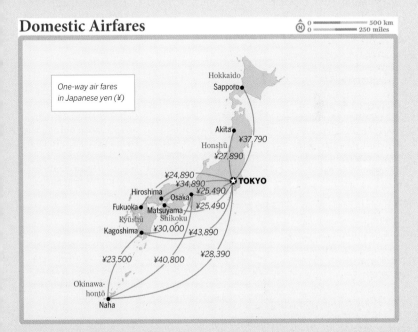

One-way air fares in Japanese yen (¥)

0 — 500 km
0 — 250 miles

Hokkaidō
Sapporo

Akita

Honshū ¥37,790
¥27,890

¥24,890
¥34,890 ★ TOKYO
Hiroshima ¥25,490
Osaka
Fukuoka Matsuyama ¥25,490
Kyūshū Shikoku
Kagoshima ¥30,000
¥43,890
¥23,500 ¥40,800 ¥28,390

Okinawa-hontō
Naha

Climate Change & Travel

Every form of transport that relies on carbon-based fuel generates CO_2, the main cause of human-induced climate change. Modern travel is dependent on aeroplanes, which might use less fuel per kilometre per person than most cars but travel much greater distances. The altitude at which aircraft emit gases (including CO_2) and particles also contributes to their climate change impact. Many websites offer 'carbon calculators' that allow people to estimate the carbon emissions generated by their journey and, for those who wish to do so, to offset the impact of the greenhouse gases emitted with contributions to portfolios of climate-friendly initiatives throughout the world. Lonely Planet offsets the carbon footprint of all staff and author travel.

co.jp/en) A major international carrier with an extensive domestic network.

All Nippon Airways
(☎ 0570-029-709, in Osaka 06-7637-6679, in Tokyo 03-6741-1120; www.ana.co.jp) A major Japanese domestic and international carrier.

Japan Trans Ocean Air
(☎ 03-5460-0522, 0570-025-071; www.jal.co.jp/jta) A smaller domestic carrier that mostly services routes in the Southwest Islands. Website in Japanese only.

Budget Airlines in Japan

Budget airlines often come and go, so we cannot guarantee that all of these will be flying when you're in Japan, but we recommend checking their fares online when making travel plans – you might save a bundle.

Skymark Airlines (www.skymark.co.jp)

Peach (www.flypeach.com)

Jetstar (www.jetstar.com)

Tickets & Discounts

For domestic flights, return fares are usually around 10% cheaper than buying two one-way tickets. You can also get advance-purchase reductions: both All Nippon Airways (ANA) and Japan Airlines (JAL) offer discounts of up to 50% if you purchase your ticket a month or more in advance, with smaller discounts for purchases made one to three weeks in advance.

Seniors over 65 also qualify for discounts on most Japanese airlines, but these are sometimes only available if you fly on weekdays.

ANA also offers the Star Alliance Japan Airpass for foreign travellers on ANA or Star Alliance network airlines. Provided you reside outside Japan, purchase your tickets outside Japan, and carry a valid international ticket on any airline, you can fly up to five times within 60 days on any ANA domestic route for only ¥10,000 per flight (a huge saving on some routes). Visit www.ana.co.jp/wws/th/e/wws_common/fare/special/airpass.html for more details.

Car & Motorcycle

Driving in Japan is quite feasible, even for just the mildly adventurous. The major roads are signposted in English; road rules are generally adhered to and driving is safer than in a lot of other Asian countries; and petrol, while expensive, is not prohibitively so. Indeed, in some areas of the country it can prove much more convenient than other forms of travel and, between a group of people, it can also prove quite economical.

In some parts of Japan (most notably Hokkaidō, the Noto Peninsula, some parts of Kyūshū and the Southwest Islands), driving is really the only efficient way to get around unless you have a good touring bicycle or fancy long waits for buses each time you need to make a move.

Crash helmets are compulsory for motorcyclists in Japan.

Automobile Associations

If you're a member of an automobile association in your home country, you're eligible for reciprocal rights with the **Japan Automobile Federation** (JAF; ☎ 0570-00-2811, 03-6833-9000; www.jaf.or.jp; 2-2-17 Shiba, Minato-ku, Tokyo 105-0014). Its office is near Onarimon Station on the Tōei Mita line.

Driving Licences

Travellers from most nations are able to drive (both cars and motorcycles) in Japan with an International Driving Permit backed up by their own regular licence. The

International Driving Permit is issued by your national automobile association. Make sure it is endorsed for cars and motorcycles if you're licensed for both.

Travellers from Switzerland, France and Germany (and others whose countries are not signatories to the Geneva Convention of 1949 concerning international driving licences) are not allowed to drive in Japan on a regular International Driving Permit. Rather, travellers from these countries must have their own licence backed by an authorised translation of the same licence. These translations can be made by their embassy or consulate in Japan or by the JAF. If you are unsure which category your country falls into, contact the nearest JNTO office for more information.

Foreign licences and International Driving Permits are only valid in Japan for six months. If you are staying longer, you will have to get a Japanese licence from the local department of motor vehicles.

Expressways

The expressway system is fast, efficient and growing all the time. Tolls cost about ¥24.6 per kilometre. Tokyo to Kyoto, for example, will cost ¥10,050 in tolls.

There are good rest stops and service centres at regular intervals. A prepaid highway card, available from tollbooths or at the service areas, saves you having to carry so much cash and gives you a 4% to 8% discount in the larger card denominations. You can also pay tolls with most major credit cards. Exits are usually fairly well signposted in English, but make sure you know the name of your exit as it may not necessarily be the same as the city you're heading towards.

Fuel

You'll find *gasoreen sutando* (petrol stations) in almost every town and in service stations along the express-ways. The cost of petrol per litre ranged from ¥135 to ¥144 for regular and ¥146 to ¥155 for high octane at the time of writing.

Hire

You'll usually find car-rental agencies clustered around train stations and ferry piers. Typical rates for a small car are ¥5000 to ¥7000 per day, with reductions for rentals of more than one day. On top of the rental charge, there's about a ¥1000-per-day insur-ance cost.

Communication can sometimes be a major problem when hiring a car. Some of the offices will have a rent-a-car phrasebook, with questions you might need to ask in English. Otherwise, just speak as slowly as possible

Driving in Japan

Unless you plan on driving in central Tokyo or Osaka or forget that the Japanese drive on the left, you should have no major problems driving in Japan. Still, there are a few peculiarities that are worth keeping in mind.

Turn signals Some Japanese drivers have the annoying habit of turning on their turn signals only after they stop at a light or enter an intersection. This seems to defeat the purpose of a signal (ie to tell people *in advance* what you plan to do). This doesn't cause too many problems, but be ready for it.

Petrol stations While self-serve petrol stations are becoming popular, full-service stations are still the rule. And in Japan, when they say 'full service', they really mean it. They'll empty your ashtray, take your garbage, wipe your windshield and wave you back into traffic. If you're wondering how to say 'fill 'er up' in Japanese, it's *mantan* (full tank). You might be asked how you intend to pay; the two possible answers are *genkin* (cash) or *kaado* (credit card).

Chains If you drive in mountain areas in winter, you might be required to put chains on your car. If you rent a car in these areas, it will probably come equipped. Petrol stations in mountain areas will usually put the chains on for a charge (¥1000 to ¥2000). There may be police stops in these areas to make sure that cars have chains.

and hope for the best. A good way to open the conversation is to say 'kokusai menkyō wo motteimasu' (I have an international licence).

Toyota Rent-a-Car (📞 in Japan 0800-7000-111, outside Japan 81-3-5954-8020; http://rent.toyota.co.jp) has the largest rental network. Its informative website allows reservations from overseas.

Hiring a motorcycle for long-distance touring is not as easy as hiring a car, although small scooters are available in many places for local sightseeing.

Parking

In most big cities, free curbside parking spots are almost nonexistent, while in rural areas you'll be able to park your car just about anywhere you want. In the cities you'll find that you usually have to pay ¥200 per hour for metered street parking, or anywhere from ¥300 to ¥600 per hour for a spot in a multistorey car park. You'll find car parks around most department stores and near some train stations. Fortunately, most hotels have free parking for guests, as do some restaurants and almost all department stores.

Road Rules

Driving is on the left. There are no unusual rules or interpretations of them and most signposts follow international conventions. JAF has a *Rules of the Road* book available in English and five other languages for ¥1000.

Maps & Navigation

If you can find a used copy of the out-of-print *Road Atlas Japan* (Shobunsha), grab it. It's all in English (romaji) with enough names in kanji to make navigation possible even off the major roads.

If you're really intent on making your way through the back blocks, a Japanese map will prove useful even if your knowledge of kanji is nil. The best Japanese road atlases by far are the *Super Mapple* series (Shobunsha), which are available in bookshops and some convenience stores.

There is a reasonable amount of signposting in romaji, so getting around isn't all that difficult, especially in developed areas. If you are attempting tricky navigation, use your maps imaginatively – watch out for the railway lines, the rivers, the landmarks. They're all useful ways of locating yourself when you can't read the signs. A compass will also come in handy when navigating.

These days, many rental cars come equipped with satellite navigation systems, making navigation a snap, provided you can figure out how to work the system; ask the person at the rental agency to explain it and be sure to take notes or, if you're just going from point A to point B, have them set it for you. With most of these systems, you can input the phone number of your destination, which is easy, or its address, which is just about impossible if you don't read Japanese. Even without programming in your destination, with the device on the default 'genzai-chi' (present location) setting, you will find it very useful.

Local Transport

All the major cities offer a wide variety of public transport. In many cities you can get day passes for unlimited travel on bus, tram or subway systems. Such passes are usually called an *ichi-nichi-jōsha-ken*. If you're staying for an extended period in one city, commuter passes are available for regular travel.

🚌 Bus

Almost every Japanese city has an extensive bus service, but it's usually the most difficult public-transport system for foreign travellers to use. Destinations and stops are often written only in Japanese.

Fares are usually paid when you get off. In Tokyo and some other cities, there's a flat fare regardless of distance. In the other cities, you take a ticket (known as a *seiri-ken*) as you board that indicates the zone number at your starting point. When you get off, an electric sign at the front of the bus indicates the fare charged at that point for each starting zone number. Just pay the driver the fare that matches your zone number (you put both the *seiri-ken* and the fare into the fare box). There is often a change machine near the front of the bus that can exchange ¥100 and ¥500 coins and ¥1000 notes.

🚕 Taxi

Taxis are convenient and can be found even in very small cities and on tiny islands; the train station is the best place to look. Fares are fairly uniform throughout the country. Flagfall (posted on the taxi windows) is ¥600 to ¥710 for the first 2km, after which it's around ¥100 for each 350m (approximately). There's also a time charge if the speed drops below 10km/h. A red light in the lower right corner of the windshield indicates if a taxi is available (it says 'vacant' in Japanese) – this can be difficult to spot during the day. At night, taxis usually have the light on their roof on when they're vacant and off when they're occupied, but there are regional variations.

Don't open the door to get into a taxi; the driver does that with a remote release. The driver will also shut the door when you leave the taxi.

Communication can be a problem with taxi drivers, but perhaps not as much as you fear. If you can't tell the driver where you want to go, it's useful to have the name written down in Japanese. At hotel front desks there will usually be business cards complete with name and location, which can be used for just this purpose.

Tipping is not necessary. A 20% surcharge is added after 11pm or for taxis summoned by radio. There may also be an added charge if you arrange the taxi by phone or reserve the taxi. Finally, taxis can usually take up to four adult passengers (one person can sit in the front). Drivers are sometimes willing to bend the rules for small children.

🚇 Metro & Subway

Several cities have mass-transit rail systems comprising a loop line around the city centre and radial lines into the central stations and the subway system. Subway systems operate in Fukuoka, Kōbe, Kyoto, Nagoya, Osaka, Sapporo, Tokyo and Yokohama. They are usually the fastest and most convenient way to get around the city.

For subways and local trains, you'll most likely have to buy your ticket from a machine. They're pretty easy to understand even if you can't read kanji as there is a diagram explaining the routes; from this you can find out what your fare should be. If you can't work the fare out, a solution is to buy a ticket for the lowest fare. When you finish your trip, go to the fare-adjustment machine (*seisan-ki*) or the staffed counter before you reach the exit gate and pay the difference.

JR train stations and most subway stations have posted above the platform not only their names in kanji and romaji but also the names of the preceding and following stations.

Many cities also have tram lines. Fares work on similar systems to bus travel and there are also unlimited-travel day tickets.

🚆 Train

Japanese rail services are among the best in the world: they are fast, frequent, clean and comfortable. The 'national' railway is Japan Railways, commonly known as 'JR', which is actually a number of separate private rail systems providing one linked service.

The JR system covers the country from one end to the other and also provides local services around major cities such as Tokyo and Osaka. JR also operates buses and ferries, and convenient

Train Reservations from Abroad

○ Keep in mind that you do not usually have to make reservations in advance for train travel in Japan. Do consider reserving in advance, though, for Golden Week, O-Bon (mid-August) and New Year travel.

○ It is not possible to make reservations for JR trains online in English. However, most travel agents who handle the Japan Rail Pass can also make train reservations and sell you tickets in advance (for a fairly hefty surcharge).

○ Note that if you have a Japan Rail Pass, you will not be able to reserve travel through a travel agent outside Japan, as you must activate the pass in Japan and show the pass when you make reservations.

○ It is always possible to walk into a JR office once in Japan and book all your train travel (you can reserve travel up to a month in advance). Because it is difficult and expensive to reserve train travel from abroad, many people reserve all their train travel for their trip soon after arriving in Japan at the nearest JR office.

ticketing can combine more than one form of transport.

In addition to JR services, there is a huge network of private railways. Each large city usually has at least one private train line that services that city and the surrounding area, or connects that city to nearby cities. These are often a bit cheaper than equivalent JR services.

Types of Trains

The slowest trains stopping at all stations are called *futsū* or *kaku-eki-teisha*. A step up from this is the *kyūkō* (ordinary express), which stops at only a limited number of stations. A variation on the *kyūkō* trains is the *kaisoku* (rapid) service (usually operating on JR lines). Finally, the fastest regular (non-*shinkansen*) trains are the *tokkyū* (limited-express) services, which are sometimes known as *shin-kaisoku* (again, usually operating on JR lines).

Shinkansen

The fastest and best-known services are JR's *shinkansen*, Japan's famed 'bullet trains'. *Shinkansen* lines operate on separate tracks from regular trains, and, in some places, the *shinkansen* station is a fair distance from the main JR station (as is the case in Osaka).

On most *shinkansen* routes, there are two or three types of service: faster express services stopping at a limited number of stations, and slower local services stopping at more stations. There is no difference in fare, except for the Green Car (1st-class) carriages, which cost slightly more.

Most *shinkansen* cars are nonsmoking, but there are also a limited number of smoking cars on each train. There are reserved and unreserved cars on all trains. If you're travelling outside peak travel periods, you can usually just show up and expect to get a seat in an unreserved car. If you're travelling during a peak period, it is a good idea to stop at a JR station to make a reservation a few days prior to your departure.

Classes

Most long-distance JR trains, including *shinkansen*, have regular and Green Car carriages. The seating is slightly more spacious in Green Car carriages (think of a typical business-class seat on an aircraft). The Green Car carriages also tend to be quieter and less crowded. However, all Green Car seats are reserved, so if you've got a Green Japan Rail Pass, you'll have to reserve every trip in advance (with a regular pass you just go through the turnstiles and get on the next available train).

Costs

JR fares are calculated on the basis of *futsū-unchin* (basic fare), *tokkyū-ryōkin* (an express surcharge levied only on express services) and *shinkansen-ryōkin* (a special charge for *shinkansen* services). Note that if you buy a return ticket for a trip that is more than 600km each way, you qualify for a 10% discountt on the return leg.

Surcharges

Fares for reserved seats are slightly higher during peak travel seasons (21 March to 5 April, 28 April to 6 May, 21 July to 31 August and 25 December to 10 January). The surcharge is usually ¥200 during these periods.

Further surcharges apply for overnight sleepers, and these vary with the berth type. Japan Rail Pass users

Train Terminology

PRONUNCIATION	SCRIPT	ENGLISH
futsū	普通	local
green-sha	グリーン車	1st-class car
jiyū-seki	自由席	unreserved seat
kaisoku	快速	JR rapid or express
kaku-eki-teisha	各駅停車	local
katamichi	片道	one way
kin'en-sha	禁煙車	nonsmoking car
kitsuen-sha	喫煙車	smoking car
kyūkō	急行	ordinary express
ōfuku	往復	round trip
shin-kaisoku	新快速	JR special rapid train
shinkansen	新幹線	bullet train
shitei-seki	指定席	reserved seat
tokkyū	特急	limited express

New Rail Passes

Note that the situation regarding rail passes in Japan is currently changing and new passes are being introduced at a furious pace. We strongly recommend that you check the latest offerings on the sites of JR East (www.jreast.co.jp), JR West (www.westjr.co.jp) and JR Kyūshū (www.jrkyushu.co.jp).

must still pay the sleeper surcharge.

Discount-Ticket Shops

Discount-ticket shops are known as *kakuyasu-kippu-uriba* (格安切符売り場) or *kinken shoppu* (金券ショップ) in Japanese. These shops deal in discounted tickets for trains, buses, domestic flights, ferries, and a host of other things such as cut-rate stamps and phone cards. You can typically save between 5% and 10% on *shinkansen* tickets. Discount-ticket agencies are found around train stations in medium and large cities – ask at your lodgings for the nearest one.

Schedules & Information

JNTO produces a handy English-language *Railway Timetable* booklet that explains a great deal about the services in Japan and gives timetables for the *shinkansen* services, JR *tokkyū* and major private lines.

Major train stations all have information counters, and you can usually get your point across in simplified English.

If you need to know anything about JR, such as schedules, fares, fastest routes, lost baggage, discounts on rail travel, hotels and car hire, call the **JR East Infoline** (📞 from inside Japan 050-2016-1603, from overseas 81-50-2016-1603; www.jreast.co.jp/e/customer_support/infoline.html; ⏱ 10am-6pm). Information is available in English, Korean and Chinese. The website Hyperdia (www.hyperdia.com) is also a useful online source for schedules and is probably the most user-friendly English-language site.

Tickets & Reservations

Tickets for most journeys can be bought from train-station vending machines, ticket counters and reservation offices. For reservations of complicated tickets, larger JR train stations have *midori-no-madoguchi*, which function as JR's inhouse travel agency. Major private travel agencies in Japan also sell reserved-seat tickets.

On *futsū* services, there are no reserved seats. On the faster *tokkyū* and *shinkansen* services you can choose to travel reserved or unreserved. However, if you travel unreserved, there's always the risk of not getting a seat and having to stand, possibly for the entire trip. This is a particular danger at weekends, peak travel seasons and on holidays. Reserved-seat tickets can be bought any time from a month in advance to the day of departure.

Information and tickets can be obtained from travel agencies, of which there are a great number in Japan. Nearly every train station of any size will have at least one travel agency in the station building to handle all sorts of bookings in addition to train services. Japan Travel Bureau (JTB) is the big daddy of Japanese travel agencies. However, for most train tickets and long-distance bus reservations, you don't need to go through a travel agency – just go to the ticket counters or *midori-no-madoguchi* of any major train station.

Sample train fares

The following are some typical fares from Tokyo or Ueno (prices given for *shinkansen* are the total price of the ticket):

DESTINATION	BASIC (¥)	SHINKANSEN (¥)
Hakata	13,820	21,810
Hiroshima	11,660	18,040
Kyoto	8210	13,080
Nagoya	6260	10,360
Niigata	5620	10,050
Okayama	10,480	16,300
Shin-Osaka	8750	13,620

Passes & Discount Tickets

JAPAN RAIL PASS

The Japan Rail Pass (www.japanrailpass.net) is a must for anyone planning to do extensive train travel within Japan. Not only will it save you a lot of money, it will save you from having to fish for change each time you board a train. The pass cannot be used for the super express Nozomi Shinkansen service but is OK for everything else (including other *shinkansen* services).

The Japan Rail Pass *must* be purchased outside Japan. It is available to foreign tourists and Japanese overseas residents (but not foreign residents of Japan).

Children between the ages of six and 11 qualify for child passes, while those aged under six ride for free. Anyone over 12 will need an adult pass.

DURATION	REGULAR (ADULT/CHILD)	GREEN (ADULT/ CHILD)
7 day	¥29,110/14,550	¥38,880/19,440
14 day	¥46,390/23,190	¥62,950/31,470
21 day	¥59,350/29,670	¥81,870/40,930

Since a one-way reserved-seat Tokyo–Kyoto *shinkansen* ticket costs ¥13,080, you only have to make one roundtrip between Tokyo and Kyoto on the *shinkansen* to make a seven-day pass come close to paying off (add a roundtrip between Narita and Tokyo and you're already saving money). Note that the pass is valid only on JR services; you will still have to pay for private-train services.

In order to get a pass, you must first purchase an 'exchange order' outside Japan at a JAL or ANA office or a major travel agency. Once you arrive in Japan, you must bring this order to a JR Travel Service Centre (in most major JR stations and at Narita and Kansai International Airports). When you validate your pass, you'll have to show your passport in addition to the exchange order.

When you validate the pass, you select the date on which you want the pass to become valid. You can choose to make it valid immediately or on a later date. So, if you plan to spend a few days in Kyoto or Tokyo before setting out to explore Japan by rail, set the validity date to the day you start your exploration outside the city. This can save you a lot of money (because the pass really pays for itself when taking long *shinkansen* trips – rather than a few local JR trips around a city).

For more information on the pass and purchase locations, visit the Japan Rail Pass website.

JR EAST RAIL PASSES

JR East (www.jreast.co.jp) operates rail lines in the north and eastern areas of Honshū, including the Tokyo area. They offer two passes that cover all or part of their service area.

JR East Pass The JR East Pass (www.jreast.co.jp/e/eastpass) is a great deal for those who only want to travel in eastern Japan. The passes are good on all JR lines in eastern Japan (including Tōhoku, Yamagata, Akita, Jōetsu and Nagano *shinkansen,* but not including the Tōkaidō Shinkansen). This includes the area around Tokyo and everything north of Tokyo to the tip of Honshū, but doesn't include Hokkaidō. The passes are good for travel on any five days of a 14-day period that starts with purchase or activation of the pass in Japan. The travel dates do not have to be declared in advance. The passes cost ¥22,000/11,000 per adult/child. The passes are only good for travel in ordinary cars (ie there are no Green Car passes). Unlike the Japan Rail Pass, the pass can be purchased inside Japan (by those holding tourist visas), as well as outside Japan. The passes can also be purchased online.

JR East Kantō Area Pass The JR East Kantō Area Pass (www.jreast.co.jp/e/kantoareapass) is a good option for those who want to explore only Tokyo and the surrounding area. It covers travel on all JR lines, including *shinkansen* in these areas (see the website for the exact lines covered).

The passes cost ¥8300/4200 per adult/child. The passes are only good for travel in ordinary cars (ie there are no Green Car passes).

JR WEST RAIL PASSES

JR West (www.westjr.co.jp) offers rail passes valid in the western parts of Honshū (Kansai, the Okayama area, the Hiroshima area and the Yamaguchi area). The pass can be purchased inside Japan at major stations in the areas covered by the respective passes (by those holding tourist visas), as well as outside Japan (at the same places where you can purchase Japan Rail Passes). The passes can also be purchased online. See the website for further details.

Kansai Area Pass A great deal for those who only want to explore the Kansai area, the Kansai Area Pass covers unlimited travel on JR lines between most major Kansai cities, such as Himeji, Kōbe, Osaka, Kyoto and Nara. It also covers JR trains to/from Kansai International Airport, but does not cover any *shinkansen* lines. The pass also entitles holders to reserved seats at no extra charge (you'll have to reserve each trip before boarding the train). Passes are only good on consecutive days. Passes cost a couple of hundred yen more if purchased within Japan.

DURATION	REGULAR (ADULT/CHILD)
1 day	¥2200/1100
2 day	¥4300/2150
3 day	¥5300/2650
4 day	¥6300/3150

Kansai Wide Area Pass This is similar to the Kansai Area Pass, but it also allows travel on the Sanyō Shinkansen between Osaka and Okayama as well as trains going as far as Kinosaki in the north and Shingū in the south, including a variety of *tokkyū* (limited express trains). The pass is valid for four days and costs ¥8500/4250 per adult/child when purchased outside Japan or online; ¥9000/4500 if purchased inside Japan.

Kansai-Hiroshima Area Pass This pass covers most JR trains, including express trains in Kansai, as well as the Sanyō Shinkansen between Osaka and Hiroshima, as well as other JR trains in the Hiroshima area. The pass is valid for five days and costs ¥13,000/6500 per adult/child when purchased outside Japan or online; ¥14,000/7000 per adult/child when purchased inside Japan.

Sanyo-San'in Area Pass This pass covers most JR trains, including express trains in central Kansai, and the Okayama, Hiroshima and far Western Honshū areas, as well as the Sanyō Shinkansen between Osaka and Hakata. The pass is valid for five days and costs ¥19,000/9500 per adult/child when purchased outside Japan or online; ¥20,000/10,000 per adult/child when purchased inside Japan.

KANSAI THRU PASS

This pass is a real bonus to travellers who plan to do a fair bit of exploration in the Kansai area. It enables you to ride on city subways, private railways and city buses in Kyoto, Nara, Osaka, Kōbe and Wakayama. It also entitles you to discounts at many attractions in the Kansai area. A two-day pass costs ¥4000 and a three-day pass costs ¥5200. It is available at the Kansai airport travel counter on the 1st floor of the International Arrivals Hall and at the main bus information centre in front of Kyoto Station. For more information, visit www.surutto.com.

Language

Japanese pronunciation is not difficult as most of its sounds are also found in English. You can read our pronunciation guides as if they were English and you'll be understood just fine. Just remember to pronounce every vowel individually, make those with a macron (ie a line above them) longer than those without, and pause slightly between double consonants.

To enhance your trip with a phrasebook, visit **lonelyplanet.com**. Lonely Planet iPhone phrasebooks are available through the Apple App store.

Basics

Hello.
こんにちは。　　　　　konnichiwa

How are you?
お元気ですか?　　　　o-genki des ka

I'm fine, thanks.
はい、元気です。　　　hai, genki des

Excuse me.
すみません。　　　　　sumimasen

Yes./No.
はい。/いいえ。　　　hai/ iie

Please. (when asking/offering)
ください。/どうぞ。　kudasai/dōzo

Thank you.
どうもありがとう。　　dōmo arigatō

You're welcome.
どういたしまして。　　dō itashimashite

Do you speak English?
英語が話せますか?　　eigo ga hanasemas ka

I don't understand.
わかりません。　　　　wakarimasen

How much is this?
いくらですか?　　　　ikura des ka

Goodbye.
さようなら。　　　　　sayōnara

Accommodation

I'd like to make a booking.
部屋の予約を　　　　heya no yoyaku o
お願いします。　　　onegai shimas

How much is it per night?
1泊いくらですか?　　ippaku ikura des ka

Eating & Drinking

I'd like ..., please.
…をください。　　　　... o kudasai

What do you recommend?
おすすめは何　　　　o-susume wa nan
ですか?　　　　　　des ka

That was delicious.
おいしかった。　　　oyshikatta

Bring the bill/check, please.
お勘定をお願い　　　o-kanjō o onegai
します。　　　　　　shimas

I don't eat ...
…は食べません。　　... wa tabemasen

chicken	鶏肉	tori-niku
fish	魚	sakana
meat	肉	niku
pork	豚肉	buta-niku

Emergencies

I'm ill.
気分が悪いです。　　kibun ga warui des

Help!
たすけて!　　　　　taskete

Call a doctor!
医者を呼んで!　　　isha o yonde

Call the police!
警察を呼んで!　　　keisatsu o yonde

Directions

I'm looking for (a/the) ...
…を探しています。　... o sagashite imas

bank
銀行　　　　　　　ginkō

... embassy
大使館　　　　　　taishikan

market
市場　　　　　　　ichiba

museum
美術館　　　　　　bijutsukan

restaurant
レストラン　　　　restoran

toilet
お手洗い/トイレ　　o-tearai/toire

tourist office
観光案内所　　　　kankō annaijo

Behind the Scenes

This Book

This 3rd edition of Lonely Planet's *Discover Japan* was coordinated by Chris Rowthorn, and researched and written by Chris Rowthorn, Ray Bartlett, Andrew Bender, Laura Crawford, Craig McLachlan, Rebecca Milner, Simon Richmond, Benedict Walker and Wendy Yanagihara. This guidebook was produced by the following:

Destination Editor Laura Crawford
Product Editor Luna Soo
Senior Cartographer Diana Von Holdt
Book Designers Jennifer Mullins, Mazzy Prinsep
Assisting Editor Ross Taylor
Assisting Cartographer Michael Garrett
Cover Researcher Naomi Parker
Thanks to Naoko Akamatsu, Imogen Bannister, Sasha Baskett, Daniel Corbett, Mark Griffiths, Marc Hanefeld, Kate Mathews, Jenna Myers, Wibowo Rusli, Ross Stockall, Damien van der Bijl, Lauren Wellicome, Tony Wheeler, Grace Yoxon

Author Thanks
Chris Rowthorn

I would like to thank my family for their patience and support during the writing of this guide. I would also like to thank Kitayama Jun, SK, KT, HK and IK for their assistance. Thanks are also due to the people of Kyoto, who help me every day in countless ways. Finally, I would like to thank all readers of Lonely Planet for their feedback and input. And if any readers see me in Kyoto, please don't hesitate to stop me and let me know what you think!

Acknowledgments

Climate map data adapted from Peel MC, Finlayson BL & McMahon TA (2007) 'Updated World Map of the Köppen-Geiger Climate Classification', *Hydrology and Earth System Sciences*, 11, 1633¬44.

Tokyo Subway Route Map, Bureau of Transportation, Tokyo Metropolitan Government, Tokyo Metro Co Ltd © 2014.6.

Illustrations p82-3 and p292-3 by Michael Weldon.

Cover photographs: Front: Himeji-jō, Himeji. John W Banagan/Getty; Back: Mt Fuji, Amanaimages/Corbis.

SEND US YOUR FEEDBACK

We love to hear from travellers – your comments keep us on our toes and help make our books better. Our well-travelled team reads every word on what you loved or loathed about this book. Although we cannot reply individually to postal submissions, we always guarantee that your feedback goes straight to the appropriate authors, in time for the next edition. Each person who sends us information is thanked in the next edition, the most useful submissions are rewarded with a selection of digital PDF chapters.

Visit **lonelyplanet.com/contact** to submit your updates and suggestions or to ask for help. Our award-winning website also features inspirational travel stories, news and discussions.

Note: We may edit, reproduce and incorporate your comments in Lonely Planet products such as guidebooks, websites and digital products, so let us know if you don't want your comments reproduced or your name acknowledged. For a copy of our privacy policy visit lonelyplanet.com/privacy.

Index

000 Map pages

000 Map pages

How to Use This Book

These symbols give you the vital information for each listing:

- ☑ Telephone Numbers
- ☺ Opening Hours
- ℗ Parking
- ☺ Nonsmoking
- ✳ Air-Conditioning
- @ Internet Access
- ☎ Wi-Fi Access
- ☒ Swimming Pool
- ☑ Vegetarian Selection
- ☑ English-Language Menu
- ☑ Family-Friendly
- ☑ Pet-Friendly
- ☑ Bus
- ☑ Ferry
- Ⓜ Metro
- Ⓢ Subway
- ⊖ London Tube
- ☑ Tram

Look out for these icons:

FREE No payment required

✐ A green or sustainable option

Our authors have nominated these places as demonstrating a strong commitment to sustainability – for example by supporting local communities and producers, operating in an environmentally friendly way, or supporting conservation projects.

All reviews are ordered in our authors' preference, starting with their most preferred option. Additionally:

Sights are arranged in the geographic order that we suggest you visit them, and within this order, by author preference.

Eating and Sleeping reviews are ordered by price range (budget, midrange, top end) and within these ranges, by author preference.

Map Legend

Note: Not all symbols displayed appear on the maps in this book

Sights
- Ⓑ Beach
- Ⓑ Bird Sanctuary
- Ⓑ Buddhist
- Ⓒ Castle/Palace
- Ⓒ Christian
- Ⓒ Confucian
- Ⓗ Hindu
- Ⓘ Islamic
- Ⓙ Jain
- Ⓙ Jewish
- Ⓜ Monument
- ⓜ Museum/Gallery/ Historic Building
- Ⓡ Ruin
- Ⓢ Shinto
- Ⓢ Sikh
- Ⓣ Taoist
- Ⓦ Winery/Vineyard
- Ⓩ Zoo/Wildlife Sanctuary
- Ⓞ Other Sight

Activities, Courses & Tours
- Ⓑ Bodysurfing
- Ⓓ Diving
- Ⓒ Canoeing/Kayaking
- ● Course/Tour
- Ⓢ Sento Hot Baths/Onsen
- Ⓢ Skiing
- Ⓢ Snorkelling
- Ⓢ Surfing
- Ⓢ Swimming/Pool
- Ⓦ Walking
- Ⓦ Windsurfing
- Ⓞ Other Activity

Sleeping
- ⊜ Sleeping
- ⊜ Camping

Eating
- ⊗ Eating

Drinking & Nightlife
- Ⓓ Drinking & Nightlife
- Ⓒ Cafe

Entertainment
- Ⓔ Entertainment

Shopping
- Ⓢ Shopping

Transport
- Ⓐ Airport
- ⊗ Border crossing
- Ⓑ Bus
- Cable car/Funicular
- Ⓒ Cycling
- Ferry
- Ⓜ Metro/MRT/MTR station
- Monorail
- Ⓟ Parking
- Ⓟ Petrol station
- Ⓢ Skytrain/Subway station
- Ⓣ Taxi
- Train station/Railway
- Ⓣ Tram
- Ⓤ Underground station
- ● Other Transport

Information
- Ⓢ Bank
- Ⓔ Embassy/Consulate
- ⊕ Hospital/Medical
- @ Internet
- Ⓟ Police
- Ⓟ Post Office
- Ⓣ Telephone
- Ⓣ Toilet
- Ⓘ Tourist Information
- ● Other Information

Geographic
- Ⓑ Beach
- Ⓛ Lighthouse
- Ⓛ Lookout
- ▲ Mountain/Volcano
- Ⓞ Oasis
- Ⓟ Park
-)(Pass
- Ⓟ Picnic Area
- Ⓦ Waterfall

Population
- Ⓒ Capital (National)
- Ⓞ Capital (State/Province)
- ● City/Large Town
- ● Town/Village

Boundaries
- International
- State/Province
- Disputed
- Regional/Suburb
- Marine Park
- Cliff; Wall

Routes
- Tollway
- Freeway
- Primary
- Secondary
- Tertiary
- Lane
- Unsealed road
- Plaza/Mall
- Steps
- Tunnel
- Pedestrian overpass
- Walking Tour
- Walking Tour detour
- Path/Walking Trail

Hydrography
- River, Creek
- Intermittent River
- Canal
- Water
- Dry/Salt Lake
- Reef

Areas
- Airport/Runway
- Beach/Desert
- Cemetery (Christian)
- Cemetery (Other)
- Glacier
- Mudflat
- Park/Forest
- Sight (Building)
- Sportsground
- Swamp

CRAIG MCLACHLAN

Best of the Rest Craig has walked the length of Japan (3200km in 99 days!), climbed Japan's 100 Famous Mountains, hiked the 88 Sacred Temples of Shikoku and scaled all of Japan's 3000m peaks. Books on his exploits have been published in English and Japanese and he has coauthored multiple editions of Lonely Planet's *Hiking in Japan* and *Japan* guidebooks. A 'freelance anything', Craig has an MBA and is also a pilot, karate instructor, tour leader, hiking guide, Japanese interpreter and budding novelist. See www.craigmclachlan.com.

Read more about Craig at:
https://auth.lonelyplanet.com/profiles/craigmclachlan

REBECCA MILNER

Tokyo Rebecca came to Tokyo for 'just one year' in 2002 and still hasn't been able to tear herself away. She's lived west of Shinjuku and east of the Sumida and now shares an apartment in Shibuya (the quiet part) with her husband and cat. Her writing has appeared in the *Guardian*, *Japan Times*, *CNN Travel* and *BBC Travel* and Lonely Planet guides to Japan.

SIMON RICHMOND

Mt Fuji & Around Tokyo Travel writer, photographer and videographer Simon Richmond won travel guidebook of the year for his first co-authored guidebook on Japan published in 1999. He's also written guides to Tokyo (where he lived and worked for several years as a journalist and editor in the early 1990s) and books on anime and manga. He's been an author with Lonely Planet since 1999, working on many titles for the company and features for its website. Read more about his travels at www.simonrichmond.com and on Twitter and Instagram @simonrichmond.

BENEDICT WALKER

Central Honshū Currently hanging by the beach near his mum, in hometown Newcastle, Ben's plan of 'livin' the dream', spending his days between his three great loves, Australia, North America and Japan, seems to be coming to fruition: it's not greedy – it's just sharing the love! Passionate about (almost) all things Japanese, Ben speaks the lingo pretty well: he's convinced he was a monk in a past life. Ben has also co-written Lonely Planet's *Canada*, *Florida* and *Australia* guidebooks, written and directed a play, toured Australia managing travel for rockstars and is an avid photographer toying with his original craft of film-making. He's an advocate of following your dreams – they can come true. For updates, see www.wordsandjourneys.com.

WENDY YANAGIHARA

Best of the Rest As the daughter of an Issei (first-generation Japanese-American) in California, Wendy grew up summering in Japan with her mother. But it wasn't until two years ago that she had the pleasure of exploring the 88-temple pilgrimage, the diversity of Ryukyuan dialects and an affinity for *jiimami-dōfu*. Previously, she has worked on several editions of the *Japan* and *Tokyo* guidebooks, among the 20+ guidebooks on which she has worked for Lonely Planet.

Our Story

A beat-up old car, a few dollars in the pocket and a sense of adventure. In 1972 that's all Tony and Maureen Wheeler needed for the trip of a lifetime – across Europe and Asia overland to Australia. It took several months, and at the end – broke but inspired – they sat at their kitchen table writing and stapling together their first travel guide, *Across Asia on the Cheap*. Within a week they'd sold 1500 copies. Lonely Planet was born.

Today, Lonely Planet has offices in Melbourne, London and Oakland, with more than 600 staff and writers. We share Tony's belief that 'a great guidebook should do three things: inform, educate and amuse'.

Our Writers

CHRIS ROWTHORN

Coordinating Author, Kyoto Chris Rowthorn has been based in Kyoto since 1992. He became a regional correspondent for *The Japan Times* in 1995 and joined Lonely Planet in 1996. He's worked on Lonely Planet's *Japan*, *Kyoto*, *Hiking in Japan* and *Tokyo* guidebooks. He speaks and reads Japanese fluently and has appeared on local TV to introduce secret temples in Kyoto. Chris's wife is from Kyoto's Arashiyama district and his two children are proudly multicultural. Chris runs Chris Rowthorn Tours (www.chrisrowthorn.com), which offers private tours and consulting about Kyoto and the rest of Japan. He also curates www.insidekyoto.com, his personal blog about the city of Kyoto.

RAY BARTLETT

Best of the Rest Ray arrived in Kagoshima in 1993 and in many ways never left: it's now a second home. While hailing from Japan's 'most southern mainland prefecture' he's proudly crisscrossed Kyūshū so many times he's lost count. His hobbies include onsen baths, surfing and hiking, all of which he enjoyed while researching this edition of *Discover Japan*. For more info or to contact Ray, visit www.Kaisora.com or check out his onsen suggestions at www.OnsenJapan.net. He divides his time between Japan, Mexico and the USA.

Read more about Ray at:
http://auth.lonelyplanet.com/profiles/kaisora

ANDREW BENDER

Kansai France was closed, so after college Andrew left his native New England for a job in Japan. It was a life-changing experience, as visits to Japan often are. He's since mastered chopsticks, the language, karaoke and shoe etiquette. Now based in Los Angeles, he writes about Japan for the *Los Angeles Times*, inflight magazines and about a dozen Lonely Planet titles, as well as the Seat 1A travel blog for Forbes. He also does cross-cultural consulting for Japanese businesses and escorts visitors around Japan. His website is www.wheres-andy-now.com.

LAURA CRAWFORD

Hiroshima & Western Honshū Laura first discovered Japan as an undergraduate studying Japanese in Kansai. She later travelled up and down the country, set up home in Osaka for two years, wrote a thesis on Japanese English, and eventually landed a job as an editor at Lonely Planet's Melbourne branch. She now works as a Destination Editor in London, but was kindly let out of the office to go on the road again in Japan. She tweets @crawfplanet.

Read more about Laura at:
http://auth.lonelyplanet.com/profiles/crawfplanet

 More Writers ....

Published by Lonely Planet Publications Pty Ltd
ABN 36 005 607 983
3rd edition – November 2015
ISBN 978 1 74220 567 0
© Lonely Planet 2015 Photographs © as indicated 2015
10 9 8 7 6 5 4 3 2 1
Printed in China